Rivers and Mountains

A Historical, Applied Anthropological
and Linguistical Study
of the Zaza People of Turkey
including an
Introduction to Applied Cultural Anthropology

Eberhard Werner

Bibliographic Information Published by the Deutsche Nationalbibliothek
The Deutsche Nationalbibliothek lists this publication in the Deutsche Nationalbibliografie; detailed bibliographic data are available in the Internet at http://dnb.d-nb.de.

ISBN 978-3-95776-065-4

© 2017 by Eberhard Werner

Cover photo: © CanTuncelili
https://commons.wikimedia.org/wiki/File:Tunceli.jpg

VTR Publications, Gogolstr. 33, 90475 Nürnberg, Germany
http://www.vtr-online.com

Table of Content

Tables 7
Table of Diagrams 8
Abbreviations 9
Preface 11
Introduction 15
1   Anthropology and Ethnography 17
1.1   Area of Research 17
  1.1.1   Cultural Anthropology vs. Social Sciences 20
  1.1.2   Ethnography 22
  1.1.3   Society - Culture, Language, Thought and Conscience 34
  1.1.4   Summary 49
1.2   Project-Description 50
  1.2.1   Sherefname and Seyahatname 51
  1.2.2   Linguistic and Anthropological Specifications 52
  1.2.3   Method of Research 52
1.3   Summary 54
2   The Zaza 56
2.1   The People 57
  2.1.1   Origin of the People Name 59
  2.1.2   Question of Identity - Kurds and / or Zaza or Zaza-Kurds 69
  2.1.3   Theories of Origin 85
  2.1.4   Settling Area - Homeland 102
2.2   The Language – Zazaki 115
  2.2.1   Zazaki – Part of the Indo-European Language Family 118
  2.2.2   A Northwestern Iranian Language within a Language Belt 120
  2.2.3   Zazaki – General Remarks 123
  2.2.4   Dialectical Disparity and the Zaza Ethnicity 133
  2.2.5   The Southern Group in Çermik – Investigations 135
  2.2.6   Reference resp. Standard Dialect - Renaming 136
  2.2.7   Çermik 138
  2.2.8   Illiteracy and Bilingualism 146

  2.2.9 Language Description and Specific Features 160
  2.2.10 Summary – Zazaki the Language 185
 2.3 **The Society** 186
  2.3.1 *Historical Background – Political Past and Present* 188
  2.3.2 *Fundamentals* 201
  2.3.3 *Religion* 214
  2.3.4 *Social Structure* 265
  2.3.5 *The Zaza – Traditionally Peasants* 301
 2.4 **Linguistic and Cultural Liaison - *Merdım*** 315
  2.4.1 *An exemplary Study - the Term "man" (merdım)* 315
  2.4.2 *Etymology of merdım* 316
  2.4.3 *Real versus Ideal Usage of merdım* 321
  2.4.4 *Summary* 328
 2.5 **The Perception of the World – "Zazaness"** 329
  2.5.1 *Cosmology and the Zaza-Pantheon* 329
  2.5.2 *Islam – Recent Foundation* 333
  2.5.3 *Feasts and Celebrations* 333
  2.5.4 *The Family – Centre of Society* 338
  2.5.5 *Envy* 341
  2.5.6 *Envy and the Concept of merdım* 342
  2.5.7 *Envy and Hospitality* 343
  2.5.8 *Culture Change in Zaza Community* 344
  2.5.9 *Summary* 345
 2.6 **Mother Tongue Issues - Projects** 347
  2.6.1 *The Mother Tongue Speaker* 348
  2.6.2 *Lingua Franca and National Language* 349
  2.6.3 *Mother Tongue – Entering a People's Heart* 350
  2.6.4 *Mother Tongue Education – A global Basic Right* 350
  2.6.5 *The Homogenous Unit Principle (HUP)* 352
  2.6.6 *Summary* 352
 2.7 **Summary** 353
3 **Turkey – A Socio-Historical Overview** 357
3.1 **Turkey and the Diverse Ethnicities** 358
  3.1.1 *Historical Sketch of the Turkish People* 360
  3.1.2 *Outside Turkey – Europe and the World* 378

Table of Content 5

    3.1.3   *Germany and Turkey* 381
    3.1.4   *The European Union and Turkey – A Rapprochement* 385
    3.1.5   *Summary* 387
3.2   **Inside Turkey – Linguistic Considerations** 389
    3.2.1   *Turkey (Asia)* 389
    3.2.2   *Turkey (Europe)* 391
3.3   **Anthropological-Linguistic Perspective** 392
3.4   **Christianity and Religious Orientation in Turkey** 393
    3.4.1   *Christians in Turkey* 394
    3.4.2   *Jewish Presence and Judaism* 407
    3.4.3   *The Crescent, the Star and the Coat of Arms* 411
    3.4.4   *Summary* 414
3.5   **Kurmanji Kurds, Zaza and the Turkish State** 415
    3.5.1   *History and Terminology – "Kurds", "Kurdish"* 415
    3.5.2   *Kurdish Population – Inside the Fertile Crescent* 417
    3.5.3   *Genetics, Space and Subjectivity* 418
    3.5.4   *Summary* 420
3.6   **Islam and Turkey** 421
    3.6.1   *Propagation Strategies* 422
    3.6.2   *The Islamic orders – Workforces of da'awa and jihad* 422
    3.6.3   *Principles of Invitation* 423
    3.6.4   *Anthropological Considerations* 424
    3.6.5   *Summary* 427
3.7   **Summary** 428
4   **Comprising Epilogue** 431
Appendices 440
Index 472
Bibliography 482
    Websites 524
    Personal Communication 527
    Exegetical Tools 528
    Material about the Zaza and Zazaki 529
    Linguistics 529
    Zazaki – Linguistics – Magazine 529

> *Linguistics* 529
> *Glossaries* 531
> *Language Learning and Literacy* 532
> *Culture and History* 532
> *Cultural Websites* 534
> *Magazines* 534

Final Summary 536

Detailed Table of Content 540

Tables

Table 1 Distinction of Cultural Anthropology vs. Social Sciences	21
Table 2 Estimated Zaza Population	58
Table 3 Differentiation of Zaza and Kurmanji Ethnicities	75
Table 4 Lack of Differentiation between both Ethnicities	77
Table 5 Overview - Struggle in Space and Subjectivities (Zaza focus)	80
Table 6 Self-Perception in relation to Descent and Environment	81
Table 7 Language Belt Theories based on the Daylam-Thesis	84
Table 8 Language Belt Theories based on other Theories	85
Table 9 Proponents of the Daylam-Thesis	90
Table 10 Critics of the Daylam-Thesis	92
Table 11 Dialectical Grouping	135
Table 12 Zazaki Alphabets vs. Turkish	139
Table 13 Lexical Borrowing from Armenian	155
Table 14 Loans in Nominalising Verb-Roots (Participle Imperfective)	157
Table 15 Code Switching and Language Use - Exemplary Study of Êxê	159
Table 16 Phrases of Emotive Language	168
Table 17 Dialect Varieties - Month Names	169
Table 18 Names of Cardinal Directions	170
Table 19 Standardization - Days	170
Table 20 Examples of various roots	184
Table 21 Popular Rebellions of the Zaza People	198
Table 22 Distinctive Split in Religion and Language	225
Table 23 Religious Influence	263
Table 24 Small Scale Societies of the Zaza and their Localisation	281
Table 25 List of Zaza Small Scale Societies	282
Table 26 Two Origins of Zaza Small Scale Societies	283
Table 27 Famous Zaza People	295
Table 28 The real usage of *merdım*	321
Table 29 Grammatical Functions of *merdım*	322
Table 30 Positive Features of *merdım*	324
Table 31 Negative Features of *merdım*	325
Table 32 Real - Concepts of *merdım*	326
Table 33 Ideal - Concepts of *merdım*	327
Table 34 Feasts and Celebrations	334
Table 35 Political Parties in Turkey	373
Table 36 Language Groups in Turkey - Asia	389
Table 37 Language Groups in Turkey - Europe	391
Table 38 Estimations of Kurds (overview)	417
Table 39 Overview – Struggle in Space and Subjectivity (Kurmanji focus)	419

Table of Diagrams

Diagram 1 Dyadic-dynamic Model 19
Diagram 2 Ethically Balanced Aspects of Anthropology 27
Diagram 3 Model of Human Memory (Fabbro 1999:94) 40
Diagram 4 Shannon & Weaver Code-Model 40
Diagram 5 Poles of Shame and Guilt Orientation (Müller 2009) 47
Diagram 6 Poles of Orientation in Conscience/LEIC 48
Diagram 7 Zazaki – Iranian Language Branch 121
Diagram 8 Influences on Zazaki by other Languages 149
Diagram 9 Model of Envy, Mana and Taboo 209
Diagram 10 Animistic Perception of the World by the Zaza 221
Diagram 11 Purity-Impurity Manipulation 234
Diagram 12 Religious Influence - History and Present 236
Diagram 13 Zaza Cult - Religious Life 255
Diagram 14 Structure of the Zaza Society 274
Diagram 15 Hierarchy of Zaza Society Leadership 276
Diagram 16 Social Small Scale Structures 278
Diagram 17 Standard Layout Plan of a House and Drawings 302
Diagram 18 Cosmology of the Zaza people 330
Diagram 19 Crescent and Star - Coat of Arms 413

Abbreviations

Token	Meaning
AD	Anno Domini
AH	Anno Hegirae / Hijra
Arab.	Arabian
b.	born
BC	Before Christ
BH	Before Hegirae / Hijra
C	Consonant
CE	Common Era
cit.	cited in
dir.	direct case
ed.	editor/edition/ edited
eds.	Editors
e.g.	for example
Engl.	English
etc.	et cetera
EW.	Eberhard Werner
EZ	Eastern Zaza
fem.	Feminine
FN	Footnote
Germ.	German
HB	Hebrew Bible
i.v.	intransitive verb
imper.	Imperative
ind.	Indicative
Qur.	Qur'an(ic)
Kur.	Kurmanji
Lat.	Latin
LEIC	Location of Emotions, Intellect and Character
masc.	masculine
MTS	Mother Tongue speaker
NE	North Eastern
NT	New Testament
NW	North West
NZ	Northern Zaza
obl.	oblique case
p.	page(s)
pers.	Person
Pers.	Persian
pl.	Plural
pres.	present
pret.	preterit
prohib.	prohibitive
resp.	respectively
rev.	revised
RL	Receiver-Language
RT	Receiver-Text
RT	Relevance-Theory
s.	see
s. a.	see also / see above
s. b.	see below
SEIC	Germ: Sitz der Emotionen, des Intellekts und des Charakters
sg.	singular
sic!	Lat. really so! (error in original)
SL	Source-Language
ST	Source-Text
s.th.	something
subj.	subjunctive

SW	South West	V	Vowel
TL	Target Language	Vol.	Volume
TT	Target-Text	vs.	versus
Tk./tk.	Turkish	w/o Date	without of Date
t.v.	transitive verb	w/o A.	without of author
uv.	uvular	Za.	Zaza/ Zazaki

Brockhaus	Brockhaus multimedial 2007 (CD-Rom)
DOM	Deutsche Orient Mission [German Orient Mission]
DTS	Descriptive Translation Studies
FOLTA	From one Language to Another (Waard & Nida 1986)
GNB	Good News Bible / Gute Nachricht Bibel
IRAL	International Review of Applied Linguistics
JOT	Journal of Translation
RGG	Religion in Geschichte und Gegenwart
SIL	SIL International (formerly Summer Institute of Linguistics)
SIM	Serving in Mission
TAPOT	The Theory and Practice of Translation (Nida & Taber 1969)
TASOT	Toward a Science of Translating (Nida 1964)
TBS	Turkish Bible Society
VTR	Verlag für Theologie und Religionswissenschaft
WJL	William James Lectures
UBS	United Bible Societies
UN/UNO	United Nations / United Nations Organization
UNESCO	United Nations Educational, Scientific and Cultural Organization

Preface

Ethnography is the driving force of *Cultural Anthropology* (in the francophone world known as *ethnology*; however *ethnology* relies to comparative studies as well). It is the study of foreign culture, language, perceptions of the world, religion, thought and conscience. Anthropologists participate within a foreign culture. As a result of their studies they unveil a previously little recognized people group to the public. This demands from them both responsibility and ethics summed up in loyalty to the object as well as to the audience of study.

The structure of this research is built on four chapters. Chapter 1 defines in an extensive way the complexity and context of ethnography from the standpoint of pragmatics. Applied anthropology, as it is introduced in Chapter 1, leads to the main content of this research, a specific people group in Eastern Anatolia. Chapters 2 and 3 are devoted to the practical outcome of anthropological, ethnographical and linguistical research on one of the various people groups in Eastern Anatolia with regard to their wider environment. Chapter 2 deals specifically with the people group around the Euphrates / Tigris headwater. Applied anthropology follows the modern pattern of "science in context" and the concepts of intersubjectivism (Germ. "Intersubjektivät") and deconstructuralism. For this reason Chapter 3 provides the reader with additional information on the surrounding people groups, their history, and their relation to each other and to the Zaza people in a more general sense (e.g. language, religious influence). Specifics about their relationship to the Zaza are covered in Chapter 2. Such "context" helps to understand recent developments and past struggles. The researcher thereby becomes part of his studies, because he participates proactively in the observation. In Chapter 4 the findings are summed up and comprehensively expressed.

Anatolia (Greek for *the land of sunrise*) is and was the native soil of a multitude of people groups. Today as part of the Republic of Turkey it has become a melting pot for 43 or more ethnic groups. One of these inhabits the ranges and strands of the River *Murat*, the main water source for the two Rivers called *Euphrates* (tk. *Fırad*) and *Tigris* (tk. *Dicle*), and the headwater area of these two large rivers. The term "river" (*ro*) displays the central symbol of life to one of these people groups. This is demonstrated by the fact that they refer to the Euphrates just by calling it *ro*, lacking a proper name. To find out more about this people group this ethnographical study gives an understanding about this people group to outsiders as well as insiders. Other influential rivers of the Zaza homeland are the smaller *Pulumuriye*, the *Munzur* and the *Peri* River.

The Zaza people number more than 3 million, which makes it even more astonishing that they are not much recognized. They are mainly ranked as a subgroup within the Kurds. This study will introduce these people and give more details of the ongoing linguistic and anthropological controversy as to whether they are a people group in their own right or a subgroup of the "Kurdish", mainly Kurmanji (Indo-European / NW Iranian) speaking community of Turkey. The most recent anthropological description of the Zaza people by Mehmed S. Kaya (2011) takes a stance on the latter. In contrast to my approach he takes the emic view as a Diaspora Zaza from the Eastern Group (see below; 2011:1-3). In contrast to him and others, I'll try to cover all three main dialect groups to give an impression of the diversity of this societal system. I am following a comparative model which understands a society as a dynamic part of its wider social environment.

From an anthropological-linguistic point of view the Zaza people of Turkey have a multitude of facets. Until recently they were an oral culture without any written tradition in their own language (only in Turkish). Hence they developed no written alphabet or any tradition that would archive the history of this group. Music, fairy tales, poems, and historical information were passed on orally by tradition. The Diaspora, a conglomeration of guest labourers or asylum seekers, noticed the ongoing assimilation of their people group in the homeland and in their hosting countries since the 1980's and they play a huge role in this study (see Appendix 1). Based in Germany, Sweden and France they tried hard to find solutions to archive the history and language of their people. They were confident that culture and language would enable a revitalization process. Hence *Zazaki* (tk. *Zazaca*), the name given to the language of the Zaza, became the main factor in fighting the loss of identity caused by assimilation or enculturation based on pressure from within and outside the people group.

Initiated by research from outside, in the 19th century, the Zaza started to receive publicity from 1980 onwards through magazines - thanks to *Abubekır Pamukçu* in Stockholm - and literature like *Kaleminden Sayfalar* by *Necmettin Büyükkay* (Büyükkaya 1992). The subject of "Zaza" and "Zazaki" was also promoted by the group called "Vatê" initiated by *Malmisanj* (since 1997). The latter group claims that small portions in Zazaki as a dialect of "Kurdish" (in the wider sense) had been published in Kurmanji magazines since 1860. The publication of poems and songs (*şır ve lawike*) since 1963 is proved by Nevzat Anuk (personal communication 2012 at the 2nd Symposium of the Zaza Language in Bingöl / Turkey). In the magazines *Roj Welat* (1963 – Istanbul) and *Rojname* (1977 / 1991 - Istanbul) poems written by Bedr Khan using the Kurdish alphabet were published. It was in the nineties that schooling of adults and children in the Diaspora had its beginning.

More than 20 years later the issue took a leap into Turkey itself. Nowadays there are modest beginnings of anthropological and linguistic study of the Zaza people and Zazaki in the homeland. Still most comes from those Zaza members living far away from their homeland. A lot more could be done. Healthcare information, children's education and oral material are still not available for the Zaza people. Obviously within this group the Diaspora plays an important role, thus it is hoped that the intertwined relationship of the Zaza people outside and within their homeland will be strengthened and the need for a revitalisation of the language will be grasped.

One of the advantages of this study compared to other emic (from inside) and etic (from outside) research into the Zaza people is that it takes the whole group into focus and tries to compare the three main microcultures within the Zaza people with each other. As far as I am aware this has not been done so far to this extent. Parts of this thesis are also found in German in my publication *Bibelübersetzung als Schnittstelle zwischen Kulturen* (2012) [Bible Translation as Interface between Cultures]. Nonetheless, I reworked and extended the research, so that with the additional information given here, members of the Zaza group and outsiders will gain from this comparative study since it unveils the complexity and diversity of this Eastern Anatolian society. The chronology of the East Anatolian area in appendix 4 is a translation of the German original in Kieser, Hans-Lukas 2000. *Der verpasste Frieden* [Engl.: The missed Peace.], 583-588. Zurich: Chronos. (by permission of author). I want to thank him here for his permission to publish this translation.

It is common knowledge that an ethnographic publication dealing with minority issues always risks departing from an objective and neutral attitude. This is more so as the author is of Christian and Western background, whereas the subject is from another religious - mainly Alevism and Islamic - and cultural environment. For cross-cultural and interlingual understanding of foreign cultures it becomes necessary to live with that bias. However every effort has been made to keep the balance between objective description and personal opinion. At least it seemed fair to identify the latter, where it seemed necessary to express it.

The author would like to thank everybody who made it possible to publish this study, including academic advice (Prof. Dr. Lothar Käser), the checking of the English (Judy Lakeman), as well as all the Zaza folk who helped him to manage the language and the anthropological insights that were offered to him. This was mainly done during personal meetings or by their participation in his empirical research with people of the Diaspora and the homeland. His gratitude is all the more, insofar as he experienced this good will from the Zaza people without them knowing what this "foreign guy" is up to with this information. For protection they are not listed by name, but by abbreviation or their pseudonyms.

May this work be a blessing to all the readers and the Zaza people.

IBO

„Her vaz kokdê xo roneno, her theyr zuwanê xo waneno!" (Gras has its own roots, birds their own chant) (to my Alevi Zaza friends)	„Vaj kokdê xo sero ruweno, dik slodê xo sero veyn dano!" "Kermê dari, dari miyan ra vıjyeno!" (Gras has its own roots, the cock sings his own chant. The woodworm lives within wood) (to my Sunni Zaza friends)

Introduction

Research in this study is based on 15 years of work with the *Zaza* people. Participating observation, close relationships, 4 fieldtrips to the homeland of the Zaza, as well as an extensive questionnaire with 50 questions about the perception of the world of the people group formed the foundation of this comparative cultural description. This questionnaire was produced in the years 2005/06 with the help of 15 Zaza, including
- male (10) and female (5),
- city-dwellers (8) and peasants (7),
- educated (12) and uneducated (3),
- religious (8) and non-religious (7),

participants. I will refer to this research by the abbreviation QN 2005 (questionnaire 2005).

Sources about the Zaza people can mainly be found in Iranistic studies, reports or scripts of Christian aid workers and political descriptions such as diplomatic or international letters from official representatives of the former colonial powers. Other sources are from the Armenian population and for some periods from the Russian powers that were stationed close to that area.

Any reference to the *Zaza* people is through the term "Zaza" either in singular or plural. The language is referenced as *Zazaki*. Any closer determination is given by the category that is addressed (e.g. *Zaza culture*, *Zaza location* etc.).

Zazaki words are marked either in italics or by simple quotation marks (e.g. 'ro' or *ro*). Mainly they are given in brackets and in italics when they refer to a name, concept or English phrases: e.g. ... like angels (*meleki*).

The citation in this work follows the Harvard System (Sauer 2004). Thus the author's name precedes the year of publication, followed by the page number (e.g. Werner 2011:12).

The *bibliography* is split into specific categories to demonstrate the work that is done for the Zaza people. An overview is given at the beginning of the bibliography.

Personal Communication includes discussions, e-mail or other communication forms and is listed under this category in the bibliography.

Internet sites are represented by author, title and year in brackets and quotes (e.g. Asatrian "Iranica" 2009). All Internet sites are found separately in the bibliography under "Internetsites".

Magazines run by Zaza are extensively listed and give an impression of the various attempts to publically represent the Zaza people.

Wordlists and dictionaries as far as they are known to the author are added under the same-titled rubric.

For this study Martin van Bruinessens *Agha, Sheikh and State - On the Social and Political Structures of Kurdistan* made a great contribution to the religious and political dynamics within the Republic of Turkey. I cited from the German version of 1989. The English version is taken into account but references are to the German version.

1 Anthropology and Ethnography

The description of a people group by a scientific tool like ethnography refers to the human phenomenon of society and culture. The whole process is embedded in the branch of cultural anthropology, which fits in the wider concept of anthropology. Anthropology spans the disciplines of social anthropology, biological or physical anthropology, archaeology, anthropological linguistics and cultural anthropology. Ethnography as the comparative study of culture forms the practical-oriented activity of anthropology and provides this discipline with data.

Following a deconstructuralist approach the main subjects of understanding are deconstructed and re-constructed as from the purpose of this study. Such terms include "ethnography", "culture", "thought", "conscience" and others.

The sheer complexity of the subject demands reference frames. These frames (e.g. shame vs. guilt orientation, Image of limited good etc.) represent details of the bigger picture (cosmology or perception of the world of a society). However every society, as part of humanity, has both a universal as well as a unique orientation. Thus one will be able to compile this picture out of the necessary pieces given in ethnographical descriptions and frame them into the scaffold of human societies and cultures. For this very reason the subject of anthropology and its associated area under discussion will be defined here.

How come the difference in using either the term *anthropology* or *ethnology*? In the English-speaking world the term "anthropology" became standard to describe the study of mankind. Recently, in the European language area both terms parallel each other (Kaschuba 2003:9-20). Historically the term "ethnology" replaced the subjects of folk life studies (Germ. "Volks- and Völkerkunde"). In the development of Europeanization the subject "European Ethnology" emerged, covering the francophone and European anglophone language area (:9-20, 21). Notable in this connection is the current trend in European science to replace the term *ethnology* by the term *anthropology*, that becomes most obvious in European Theology (e.g. Wolff 1984; Schnelle 1991; Müller 2003; Scheffcyk 2001:9-28 "Theological Anthropology"; s. a. Käser 1998:11-15).

1.1 Area of Research

Mankind diversified into more than 17,000 people groups ("Ethnopedia" 2010), covering more than 6.900 languages worldwide (Gordon 2005 Ethnologue 15th ed.). The resulting cultural diversity demands inter- and cross-cultural approaches within a globalized world. The fact that language shapes the main element of culture (see discussion about the Sapir-Whorf hypothesis or linguistic relativity hypothesis in Sapir 1961:13, 29; Whorf 1956:213-214; 1963:20; researched by Gipper 1972 and harshly critizised by Deutscher 2010; but generally approved by neurolinguistical studies)[1] requires linguistics and communication sciences to be the most important disciplines to bridge cultural gaps. But it is the description of societies that preserve and open them to other cultures. The cross-cultural encounter reciprocally widens the perception of the researcher's community. Hence both cultures experience at least a minimum of culture change as they profit from the knowledge about each other. This development has its assets and drawbacks, known to us as the "fruits of globalization" (e.g. Watson & Jones 2008 *The Fruits of Globalization*). The global open market and the opportunity to travel freely in most of the world's countries are only a few of the advantages that opened up, whereas global warming and terrorism indicate threats or bad fruits.

It is within this range that cultural encounter takes place. Cultural encounter takes place by a party that is intruding a foreign culture. Investigation ranges from pure interest (e.g. journalism) to extensive ethnographic studies sometimes lasting many years. The degree of immersion thus represents a spectrum from acquaintance to enculturation. The reactions to that immersion could be either a warm welcome or bitter antagonism. In both situations there is a dynamic and dyadic (two-part) process. The principles of the dyadic-dynamic encounter model are as follows. The term "enculturation" nowadays includes processes within a society or culture to integrate foreign concepts (e.g. religious symbols; Bosch 1991:447).

Diagram 1 illustrates the dyadic operations that elapse during cross-cultural encounter. In the beginning phase of approximation, the ethnographic researcher bringing along his cultural framework is foreign to the surveyed subject. Like a narrowing circle the parties come closer, exchanging and influencing each other. At the ideal level the participation of the researcher within the surveyed society leads to a maximum of understanding. At this point the researched society in-

---

[1] Deutscher, Guy 2010. *Through the Language Glass: How Words Colour Your World.* London: William Heinemann.
Gipper, Helmut 1972. *Gibt es ein sprachliches Relativitätsprinzip? Untersuchungen zur Sapir-Whorf-Hypothese.* Frankfurt: S. Fischer.

corporated as much from the researcher's culture as he tends to integrate on the surface level. After this stage the elements become enculturated, having a long term effect. The surveyed subject thereby diverges from the researcher's culture since it develops its own ways to contextualize the formerly foreign concepts. During the process of contextualization cultural elements become part of a culture (e.g. Cargo Cults in Melanesia; Nida 1990:129-130), so that sometimes the initial trigger could not be backtracked.

Diagram 1 Dyadic-dynamic Model

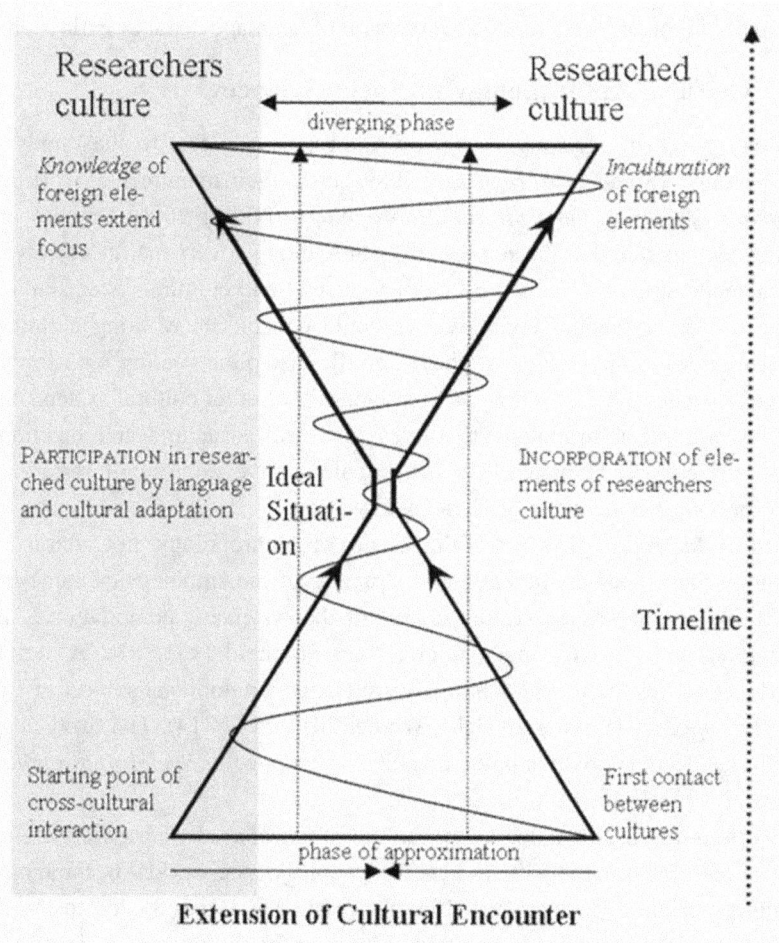

The researcher's culture diverges from the ideal situation, due to the fact that the ethnography is presented to the public and there becomes part of their mutual knowledge. On this level the surveyed culture becomes a point of reference for science, business and social activities.

The model obviously rejects any idea of a cultural crossing by men. This does not mean that individuals can't cross from one culture to another, or that one is not able to participate in more than one culture, but as a restriction to this study, the reference here is only to ethnography and the involved cultures.

Other matters of language and culture death or disbanding will also come into focus (see below). Parts of the Zaza people represent an illustrative example of an ethnicity in threat, close to the phenomenon of language death or extinction.

1.1.1 Cultural Anthropology vs. Social Sciences

Ethnology (German speaking world) or Anthropology refers to the "study of human beings" (Spradley & McCurdy 1989:1). By their monumental work *Encyclopedia of Social and Cultural Anthropology* ([1996] 2004) Barnard and Spencer demonstrate that the science of Anthropology covers many subjects related to social structure, human behaviour, societal and cultural systems and so forth. Since the subject is complex, one could conclude a working definition such as *cultural anthropology* is "that scientific discipline dealing with foreign cultures" (Fischer 2003:20). It is the "foreignness" of other cultural systems that generates cultural anthropology to survey historical, structural and functional processes in cultures (Eggan 1971:174). In comparative studies cultures are explored for common identities or obvious differences.

Cultural Anthropology is part of the science of Anthropology. In Cultural Anthropology the processes, function and structure of human societies come into focus. Ethnography or Observation represents the systematic compilation of the resulting research for wider publication (Evans-Pritchard 1971:187). In German speaking countries the term *Ethnology* parallels the Anglophone subject of *Cultural Anthropology* (Fischer 2003:17; Werner 2011:25 FN 14). The fuzzy edges of the terms become obvious in the branch of most popular *Social Anthropology* (see Eggan 1971:174).

The discussion in the 1930s about the future of *cultural anthropology*, as its object of research – namely the indigenous peoples of the world – become more and more moribund (Dozier 1955:193; Kroeber 1953:366-368), led to the determination of the relationship between cultural anthropology and social sciences (Müller 2001:45). Whereas some researchers asked for a unification of both sciences into one, others argued for their different methods and aspects within the same object of investigation, and a third group worked on the three main arguments of distinction as is shown and argued below (see Diagram 2). A functionalist approach in cultural anthropology revealed the *holistic* view on ethnical people groups as homogenous units (1.1.3.4; Eisenstadt 1961:202 cit. in Müller 2001:47).

Social sciences are concerned with society, civilization and community and not the individual (e.g. psychology; Bunge & Ardila 1990:42). Within this framework the disciplines of sociology, political sciences, education science, economic science, jurisprudence and the social branches of anthropology, history and psychology are ranked (Brockhaus 2009: Social science [CD-ROM] [my translation]). Besides human disciplines and natural science, they perform their own scientific course. The focus of research is on unique specifications within social units (*detail*-oriented). Hence the method is based on quantitative data.

Besides overlap in empirical research methods, such as qualitative or quantitative studies (e.g. questionnaires, interviews etc.), social sciences do look at the wider focus of societal processes. Cultural anthropology on the contrary is oriented around the description of foreign societies in comparison to the researcher's culture. Although both disciplines use similar methods the emphasis in cultural anthropology and German ethnology is on complex people groups as a whole, by producing qualitative statements about the function, structure and history of those groups. Likewise social sciences give emphasis to anonymously researched units within people groups to come to quantitative facts (Müller 2001:45, 47-48). Whereas the sociologist stays covered or anonymous to guarantee objective investigation, the ethnographer, using long-ranging investigation, aims for trust within the researched culture as a participant observer (:48).

Table 1 Distinction of Cultural Anthropology vs. Social Sciences

Object	*Cultural Anthropology*	*Social Sciences*
Focus	- on complex people group as a whole, mainly its history, daily life, language, structure, religion and perception of the world (*holistic-oriented*)	- on units within complex people groups (subgroups / microcultures) - focus is on unique social behaviour for comparative studies (*detail-oriented*)

Object	Cultural Anthropology	Social Sciences
Researcher	- long-ranging participation in the researched society, namely as participant observer - aims at gaining trust for a full spectrum of *qualitative* scrutiny	- anonymous and covered investigations to assure objectivity - stays behind as observer and represents *quantitative* facts
Method	- ethnographical research represented by regional monographs	- quantitative thesis for further comparative investigation

1.1.2 Ethnography

As part of empirical studies *ethnography* is built into the framework of humane, cultural, social and natural science. Within this framework ethnography is subject to the scientific branch of Cultural Anthropology (Carrithers 1992:22-23).

The single species of mankind exhibits such great variation in marriage pattern, the holding of values, believing in different gods, rearing children in different ways (Spradley 1979:10). Ethnography is possible due to global universals. Such universals can be found in the need for education, religion, living on the same world, dealing with the same physical forces like gravity, storms, weather etc. In other words besides great diversity mankind experiences on the other hand common features.

Thus all scientific applications that contribute to research in any way could theoretically contribute to ethnography as well. Nevertheless there are main strategies that are more helpful than others. Thus ethnography performed and tends to be a "surveying approach" culminating in the so called "participant observation". "Participant observation" is a recent way to describe the full participation of the researcher in his own study (Delamont 2004:217-220). Before this subject is explained, it is necessary to frame the wider concept of empirical research methods.

1.1.2.1 Empirical Research - Qualitative and Quantitative Methods

Empirical research performs quantitative and qualitative studies. On the surface the former deals with the outcome of physical science and asks for measurable results, as well as nomological or representative implications of facts and circumstances in the socio-cultural area. Methods are found in the standardized interview or observation, statistical analysis and calculation of content, sociometric analysis of social structures or relations, and in the schematic scaling of attitudes and motives (Hug 2001:22). By way of contrast qualitative study bring about results in human and cultural discipline. They focus on the survey of the known and familiar *realm of experience* (Germ. "Lebenswelt"). In this it specifies in social regulation and cultural orientation, a contextual and process-related representation of subjective positions and structures of meaning.

Qualitative research relies on symbolic orders in which individual methods and techniques are predominantly used for the development of hypotheses and theories and the improvement of their practice. The method spectrum reaches from a broad pallet of interview forms and group discussion methods to (non-)participatory observation variants and ethnographic processes way up to analytical methods of content and qualitative experiments for the uncovering and analysis of hidden structures. For both orientations the methods to be used prove to be the interview, observation, contents analysis and experiment (Hug 2001:23).

When it comes to practical terms the separation of both subjects is not as distinct as it seems to be. Thus a multiple choice questionnaire asks for both qualitative and quantitative findings, whereas an anthropological observation study on cultural behaviour in front of an elevator uses both qualitative as well as quantitative data (see Karan w/o year. *Simple Introduction*; Hug 2001; Krämer 2008:15-16).

1.1.2.2 Ethnography - Qualitative vs. Quantitative Research

As part of cultural anthropology, field work is the tool to gather information by participating with other cultures, asking questions in interviews and formulating the results in a monographic publication. As Spradley states "field work is the hallmark of cultural anthropology" and "ethnography is the work of describing a culture" (1979:3). In similar ways argues Delamont although she give modern alternatives (2004:217-229).

Ethnography is mainly built on social scientific and qualitative inquiry (Hug 2001:22; Kusch 2003:340-341; Krämer 2008:15; Mayring 1994:16; Sachs 1990:15-16). As mentioned before, because of the fuzzy edges of empirical research, ethnography also includes quantitative research, such as statistical data (e.g. cosmology, perception of the world), sociolinguistic survey and others (Trudgill 1983:32; Fasold 1984:246-247; Grimes 1995). Ethnography is the one systematic approach that reveals "what people think and shows us the cultural meanings they use daily" (Spradley 1980 vii: Preface). Spradley further assumes the aim of ethnography is "to understand another way of life from the native point". The approach to this disciplined study of what the world is like to others "means learning from people" (Spradley 1979:3). The ethnographer is asked to take part in the culture he is looking at. Ethnography thus is introducing separate realities that lie outside one's own encultured experience.

Assuming that ethnography makes use of both empirical research approaches, the next step will be the evaluation of its findings. Hence it comes to interpretation (Geertz 1993:14-15). Generally, in all interpretation the objective factor is missing. An interpretational science depends on the intuition and understanding of the researcher (see below; also :17). The outcome of any assumption is built on subjective research that follows the scientific paradigm introduced by Thomas Kuhn (1970:22). Research depends therefore on "*sudden* insights, leading to a breakthrough" (:122).

Bunge and Ardila implement the so called "indicator-hypothesis". They follow an operational understanding of theory. This means the researcher's approximation to the subject under investigation follows observable and non-observable processes (Bunge & Ardila 1990:194, 197). In the same way Weizsäcker speaks of the "cycle of understanding" that equals a "circular complementary" (1960:294). Kuhn's evolutionary paradigm of science emanates from primitive beginnings to complex correlations. In his view science follows constantly changing paradigms that are based on the "thesis-antithesis-synthesis" approach stemming from Greek philosophy (Kuhn cit. in Renner 1980:23-24; Bosch 1991:185). He is right when he therein verifies that the researcher represents a decisive factor (Clicqué 2001:224; Capra & Steindl-Rast 1994:56). Consequently an ethnographer forms the basic factor of ethnography (see below).

Sociolinguistics describes "language as a social and cultural phenomenon (Trudgill 1983:32)". Within sociolinguistics the matter of language-survey evaluates the number of speakers, language vitality, language distribution by dialects, geographical distribution and cultural factors, as well as the need for reading and studying material or education aid. But survey research is not only concerned with the observation of present or future need but in addition looks at the emergence of language branches (Fasold 1984:246-247).

1.1.2.3 Perspective of Ethnography

Ethnography has a humanitarian approach. Its goal is to bring foreign cultures close to one's own cultural background, thus taking away the fear of "foreignness" that goes within cross-cultural encounter (Müller 2001:59). In history this sometimes led to hubris of foreign cultures and denial of one's own cultural structures. Demonstrated by Margaret Mead's "portrayal of an idyllic, egalitarian Samoa", which was as shown by the anthropologist Derek Freeman to be "spectacularly wrong" (Pinker 1999:45-46; Mead 1937:493-500 und 1964; Freeman 1983 und 1998), the tendency in early ethnography was towards ethnocentric interpretation. Started by Boas, regarded "as the father of American anthropology" (Luzbetak 1993:36), Kroeber, Herskovits, Sapir, Lowie, Wissler, Hallowell, Radin, Benedict, Hoebel, and Mead contributed to the formation of the so called *Standard Social Science Model* (SSSM), which was also advertised by the American Anthropological Association and became a moral authority in science (Pinker 1999:44-45).

1.1.2.3.1 Definition of Ethnography

The term *ethnography* covers the *product*, the *process* (Sanjek 2004:193) and the *function* of ethnographic research.[2] The focus of the research is on *cultural behaviour* (what people do), *cultural knowledge* (what people know) and *cultural artefacts* (what people make and use; Spradley 1980:5).

Ethnography as a *product* (ethnographic writings) became a genre on its own. Starting with Louis Henry Morgans *The League of the Ho-de-no-sau-nee or Iroquois* (1851) this genre led to a literary art with multiple but characteristic tokens (Sanjek 2004:193).

The *process* of ethnography is closely bound to that of *contextualization* and *comparison*. Sanjek calls this the "operational system by which anthropologists acquire and use ethnographic data in writing ethnographies" (:193). This scientific spiral or circle follows the *hermeneutical circle* of Ricoeur (1988:88) and Gadamer (1972). Thus starting in wide circles the ethnographer targets his research by slowly getting closer to the core of his ethnography (assumption, conclusion, and thesis). Ethnography as a scientific *process* using the comparative method parallels this by developing new demands and rising standards (Sanjek 2004:193). Within the process of ethnography there is a distinction of *macro-*

---

[2] Here I follow Holmes who used the same tripartitae approach to describe "translation", as there are many similarities between both concepts (cit. in Toury 1995:9-12).

ethnography, leading often to *comprehensive* ethnographic studies and involving many ethnographers and *micro-ethnography* of a single social situation done by one ethnographer (Spradley 1980:30-31). Techniques used in both processes equal each other, unattached by the scope of a project.

The *function* of ethnography evolves from its history and its developing pattern. Ethnography as part of cultural anthropology belongs to "applied anthropology" as it provides anthropologists with observations from which they are able to conclude further research. This is done in an anthropological triangle of *ethnography*, *comparison* and *contextualization* that constitutes "the way in which socio-cultural anthropology works as a discipline to explain and interpret human cultures and social life" (Sanjek 2004:193). Results from this research cumulates in *hypothesis* about any cultural token used as a relation to further research and resulting in a new hypothesis (Spradley 1980:31; Kuhn 1970:22). Ethnography requires methods of processing the observed phenomena in such a way that the ethnographer can inductively construct a theory of how informants have organized the same phenomena. The construction of a theory for ethnography as part of anthropology is concerned with objectivity and an adequate approach to represent the data for future comparison or analyses. Goodenough summarises, "it is the theory, not the phenomena alone, which ethnographic description aims to present" (1957:168).

1.1.2.3.2 Poles and Points of View in Ethnography

Ethnography moves between the poles of ensuring objectivity and relative subjectivity. Whereas the former could never be reached from humans thus excluding transcendental or metaphysical information from outside of humanity the latter reveals ethnography's addiction to ethnocentrism and human ideologies. One could think of the religious claim of divine inspiration such as the direct revelation of the Qur'an or the historical - yet not concluded - canonisation of the Bible (also the divinization of the *Vedas* or the *Baghadvagitta*) or ideological divinization represented for example in the "The little Red Book" of Mao Tse Tung called "Mao's Bible" (Fenffe 2009 *The Mao Bible*).

Ethnography resides society-bound and dependent on the researcher's subjective interpretation, but within "participant observation" a high grade of self-perception of the researched culture is closely expressed to the audience (Spradley 1980:14-15). The suggested dyadic-dynamic approach and process (1.1; see Diagram 1) demonstrates that modern ethnography emphasizes the need to minimise the subjective influence of the researcher (1.1.2.5; Spradley 1980:21). The tenden-

1 Anthropology and Ethnography

cy towards objectivity and ethnical self description leads more and more towards indigenous and mother tongue ethnography, which subsequently gets presented to a wider audience by translation (e.g. Bible Translations in Sanneh 1990:16).

One alternative approach to ethnography, as well as anthropology in general comes from the Edmund Husserl's philosophical approach on the *phenomenology of Intersubjectivism* (1905-1935; Germ. "Intersubjektivität"). Intersubjectivism takes the stance of being woven into the observed or experienced events. There is a huge amount of critique given on that subject, yet later I will bring up a mediating point of view that the ethnographer could take up which includes considerable input from this approach. Some researchers see intersubjectivism as merely a state of a given perspective, others argue about its implementation. One of the basic arguments for intersubjectivity is to overcome foreignness or ethnocentrism. Although there is value in this, one has to be careful not to miss the aim of ethnography which is a presentation of a society in such a way that the audience addressed will understand it. The underlying ethnocentrism related to the hermeneutics of the observed is thus always included. I tried to make this clear in the dyadic-dynamic model (1.1; Diagram 1).

Diagram 2 Ethically Balanced Aspects of Anthropology

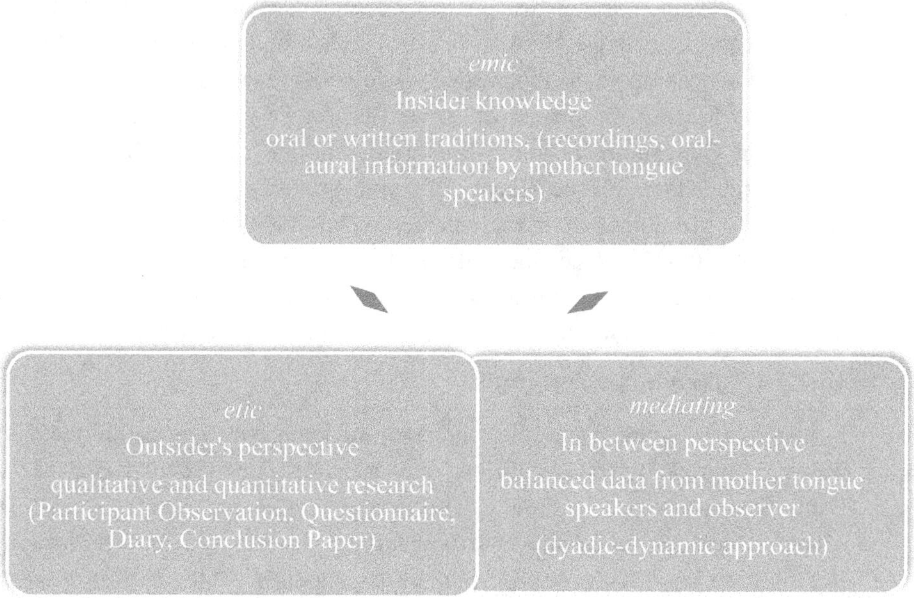

emic
Insider knowledge
oral or written traditions, (recordings, oral-aural information by mother tongue speakers)

etic
Outsider's perspective
qualitative and quantitative research
(Participant Observation, Questionnaire, Diary, Conclusion Paper)

mediating
In between perspective
balanced data from mother tongue speakers and observer
(dyadic-dynamic approach)

In general cultural anthropology distinguishes between an *emic* or internal point of view, an *etic view*, from the outside, and a *mediating* one which represents the effective balance between both (Andrews 2002:19; Gleason 1974:204).

1.1.2.3.3 Intuitive Enterprise

Ethnography, like the science of (Bible-) translation, forms intuitive enterprises. For that very reason these sciences do not fulfil the condition of "exact science" (Scorgie 2003:22; Barker 2003:51-52). Nevertheless it is possible to translate texts from one culture into another, as well as to describe a culture to other cultures. Although language thereby forms a restriction, since it is not possible to transfer all nuances of a culture in a monographic description, it likewise is the only tool to transmit such information.

The discipline of ethnography applies to empirical statistical methods (e.g. questionnaires, interview) or continuous records of observation (e.g. diary, situational card files etc.). By these tools research leads to conclusions about the mental representations forming the conception of the world or cosmology of the researched culture (Sperber 1982:28, 30). The next step will be "interpretive generalizations" that are spirit-of-times dependent (Germ. "Zeitgeist"), since the cultures of ethnographer and the researched group are changing continuously (:28). This becomes obvious when reading colonialist ethnography from the 19th century, e.g. "The Jungle Books" in which Indian culture is described from a western ethnocentric and colonialist perspective (Kipling [1894] 2000). Another example is found in the pamphlet "Does Germany Need Colonies?" from the head of the German organization "Rheinische Mission" [Rhenish Mission] Fabri, who argues that "for the security of Christian workers in Africa and for the political stabilization of Germany, colonies are absolutely required" (Fabri cit. in Bosch 1991:308-309). One would also add to these examples the translations of the Qur'an done by clerical leaders in the twelfth century for reasons of denunciation (e.g. B. Robert de Kenton 12th century; Chouraqui 1994:17).

1.1.2.3.4 Trends in Ethnography

In history ethnography presented the study of unknown "foreign cultures" by western anthropologists (see below; e.g. Morgans, Levi-Strauss, Boas etc.). Hence there was a large cultural gap between the researchers and the researched culture. During its expansion and progress the interdisciplinary ethnography (e.g. anthropology, social sciences, linguistics, missiology etc.) as part of cross-cultural studies was increasingly influenced by globalization and economic maturity. Hence the former approach of "studying people" moved to "learning from people" (Spradley 1980:3) with the recent tendency to "be with the people". Rather than coming from outside and being done by the educated and rich western researcher, nowadays most ethnography is done by "participant observation" in close and equally accepted relationship with the researched culture.

As mentioned above, contextualization leads towards mother tongue research which later becomes translated and hence presented to a wider audience. This is clearly recognisable in the area of Bible Translation. Nowadays the focus of training and education in the area of Bible Translation is mainly on Mother Tongue Speakers (MTS) as they bring with them all linguistical and cultural knowledge that a foreigner seldom is able to fully internalize (Ellingworth 2007:324). It is within that approach that so called comprehensive projects are started. Thereby one ethnographical subject is researched in different cultures by a group of MTS through a project manager. As an outcome the results are used for comparative studies in anthropology (e.g. Bollig 2006). The comprehensive project approach contributes to globalization with its interreligious and intercultural effects. The resulting comparative studies are increasingly needed for the growing market of cross-cultural encounter.

Another trend which is closely bound to the former developments comes from the insight that one's own culture is not recognized at all and needs to be researched to stand as a scientific subject for comparative studies. In other words researching "ethnocentrism", its causes, dangers and options is important to understand the dynamics of self-portraits and subjectivism in research. Moving thereby from sheer assumptions to empirical proved data brings ethnography close to social sciences. Thus the foundational facts about western societies and cultures being used in comparative studies have increased immensely.

As a result of the critique that nowadays Anthropology and ethnography – mainly participant observation – are considered to be the same, a school of thought tries to separate both. Obviously, as the short history of anthropology demonstrates, "participant observation" is a recent term used to replace observational description in anthropology (Forsey "Participant listening" 2010:558). A split of both areas of research would allow to describe ethnography on its own terms. One suggestion is to move from "participant observation" to "participant listening". Forsey argues that what an ethnographer really does is not "observing" but listening in to the society that is studied (:558-559). "Listening" here, addresses the many societies, which traditioning is based on orality. The "hearing cultures" are approached as listener, observation is just a side effect, although part of full participation (Veitmann 2004:1-4). Listening includes the "metaphysical nature of excistence" as Forsey cites Malinowski (2010:562). In terms of communication theory the meta-language, implication and symbolic language (gesture, mimic, rhetoric) are addressed with this term. We will leave it here and include participant listening in this study, as the Zaza culture belongs to the "hearing cultures" based on orality.

1.1.2.4 The Ethnographer and the Informant

As father of ethnography Claude Levi-Strauss introduced *structuralism*[3] to anthropology (Sperber 1982:64-65). Structuralism soon led to the implication made by Malinowski that utterances are bound to "context of situation", "context of culture" (Malinowski cit. in Blass 1990:29) and "social context" (Firth cit. in :29-30). These concepts are used by some linguists (e.g. Halliday 1984:8) till today (Blass 1990:29). This differentiation supports the ethnographer and hence he recognizes that it is very difficult to translate concepts of his own culture into another cultural background namely his audience. All three concepts are built on a cognitive approach in anthropology and linguistics.

As mentioned above the ethnographer launches his studies on empirical and intuitional bases. His conclusions drawn, during the start of language learning and increased mainly after being able to communicate within a cultural group, lead him to purposeful observations initiated by his intuition. He acts as the filter of all recordings from a culture that go public.

Field work is based on communication. Language is the tool to exchange information back and forth among the ethnographer and the informant. During the communicative act (speech act) both are either sender or receiver. As in all communication acts and human relationships there is an ideal way for the information transfer to works. Spradley assumes five factors that need to be considered in ethnography an informant or a language learning assistant to look out for,

- thorough enculturation,
- current involvement,
- an unfamiliar cultural scene,

---

[3] *Structuralism* is seen as "a method of analyzing phenomena, as in anthropology, linguistics, psychology, or literature, chiefly characterized by contrasting the elemental structures of the phenomena in a system of binary opposition" (The American Heritage Dictionary 2009: "Structuralism").

1 Anthropology and Ethnography 31

- adequate time management, and a
- non-analytic person (1979:46).

These guidelines will help to establish a productive ethnographer-informant relationship. This demands high ethics from the ethnographer. The next step will be to look at ethical questions on ethnography.

1.1.2.5 Ethics and Ethnography

First of all it seems obvious that ethics is not an important matter on the teaching and official level. Thus ethnographers are asked to handle ethical questions based on their own cultural and educational foundations (Tymoczko 2003:196). Some guidelines are given by the *American Anthropological Association* (AAA) to the ethnographer and anthropologist ([1971] 1986: "Statements of Ethics; 1998: "Code of Ethics"; 2004: "Statement on Ethnography"; Spradley 1980:15). Here the ethnographer and his product are restricted to western ethical norms and publication laws. These papers contain suggestions and represent recommendations. There is no overall statement on ethical expectations in ethnography on a global level, although the expectation and intention behind, has global validity. If one looks up ethical statements in linguistics one will find a similar shortcoming (about exceptions see Werner 2011:89-91; Kußmaul 2007:164-165; Chesterman 2001:147, 151-153 and 1997:184-186; Nord 2001:125 and 2004:141, 236).

Ethnography is the analysis of cultures not as "experimental science in search of law but an interpretive one in search of meaning" (Geertz 1993:5). Thus ethnography "in itself does not escape being culture-bound" (Spradley 1979:11 and 1980:14), the more so because not long ago all ethnography was focussed on small, non-Western cultures, which were not able to refuse research done by researchers from politically influential and often colonialist powers (Robinson 1997). Ethnography as interpretation is grounded in the ethnographer's intuition. Here one finds a close parallel with the translator's task (Werner 2011:88-90).

I want to add to the ethical foundation of anthropology and ethnography that the research is based on the principles of loyalty and faithfulness to the subject of research as well as the audience. Both terms evolve from functionalism as in translation theory, communication theory and linguistics. Mainly Nord was able to prove that a researcher has to be loyal to his object of study, his research and his audience (2001:125). In other disciplines the principle of loyalty is evaluated as the responsibility to rely on a mutually agreed understanding of the contecnt of research, even though one's own perspective is different (Chesterman 2001:140; Werner 2012:5). Anthropologists have to rely on the principle of loyalty to build trust and be taken serious.

The research done in this paper is based on a West-German perception of the world. Germany, as one of the European countries with a long-standing relationship with the Ottoman Empire and later the Republic of Turkey, has a long tradition of Turkish presence within its borders (see 3.1.3). One of Turkey's minority groups, which has partially settled in Germany as guest labourers since 1960, is part of this research (3.1.5).

1.1.2.6 Ethnography and Translation / Linguistics

Translation and Ethnography run together. The assumption is that the ethnographer understands the target language well. This means on a scale from 0-4 between the level 2 and 3. As such he is able to understand dialectical variations, can communicate, but still lacks the ability to write fluently, to understand written texts completely (level 4). This gap will be filled by his national mother tongue speaker who assists him. This language ability approach is not totally agreed upon in recent anthropology, the more so as linguistic anthropology, being a specified discipline within anthropology, is working specifically on language and linguistic issues (Werner 1996:79). Nonetheless translation is *the* task of the foreign ethnographer who is experiencing a cross-cultural and cross-linguistic transition (1.1; see Diagram 1; 1996:59). The ethnographer is translating the received information, either in written, observed, oral or aural form and translates and interprets it for his own research and later for his audience.

Werner notes the two extremes, between a Morpheme by Morpheme (word by word) translation and a Stimulus or Projective translation (communicative). Translation may use front-stage or background translation approaches (:61; Figure 1). He assumes that due to the intuition of the bilingual ethnographer all ethnographic translation is heading towards the Stimulus or Projective approach and tends to cover both front-stage and background translation (:61). The ethnographer is currently moving between the front-stage translation, which covers explicit or obvious information, and the background translation that represents the encyclopaedic or implicit communicational information.

Having in mind the given models or theories on translation the ethnographer / translator needs to find which model fits best with his expectations. He has the choice between

1 Anthropology and Ethnography

- the *dynamic-equivalent* resp. *functional-equivalent* (Nida 1964; Nida & Taber 1969; de Waard & Nida 1986),
- the *functional* or *Skopos* approach (Nord 2001 and 2003; Reiss & Vermeer 1991),
- the *mass communication* approach (Maletzke 1978; McQuail 2007),
- *cultural* approaches such as Katan (1999),
- the *relevance theoretical* approach (Gutt 1991 and 2000),
- *mixed* models that are based on reference frames such as Wendland (2003, 2006 a and b and 2008) or others.

Werner gives an overview of the strengths and weaknesses of those approaches (2011:359-378). The ethnographer communicates by means of translation to both, the researched culture and his own. Within the former he has to understand the implicit and explicit communication, given by the language and its contextual framework. Encyclopaedic, semiotic, semantic information forms the *metalanguage* which contains informational aspects that go with the spoken information. The same is true for the language into which an ethnographic description is translated.

1.1.2.7 Summary

Ethnography embodies the outgoing part of Anthropology. It is within ethnography that an anthropologist represents his research to a wider audience. This investigation is based on qualitative and quantitative research. Both scientific tools lead for example to questionnaires, interviews, survey and so on.

Ethnography covers the *process*, the *product* and the *function* of ethnographic research. The process reflects the ethnographer's or anthropologist's approach to studying a foreign group or microculture. The product is grounded in the findings of the research. Those findings are brought into format, and made ready to be presented to an audience. The product nowadays functions mainly as

- cultural descriptions to an audience to which such cultures or microcultures are unknown or
- as studies of comparison with other cultural phenomenon.

The latter serves also for the function of ethnography.

As an intuitive enterprise ethnography moves along the poles of subjectivity and objectivity. The ethnographer as an individual never occupies a neutral position. He follows instructions from his individual setting. His employer, the researching institution, the audience, his own culture, others and he himself reflect a perception of the world that is not neutral at all but egocentric. On the other hand he can work against his subjectivity by representing the researched culture's original "voice" in the form of citation in ethnography. Such would be noted in a diary that quotes his informants. By reflecting such balance, ethnographic studies give honour to both the researched and the researcher's culture.

In following the recent trend in science, the researcher increasingly needs to avoid any imperialistic or colonialist approach or impression. Yet "participant observation", under the cover of Intersubjectivism, is leading to contextualized ethnography. Ethnography in such an attempt is restricted to a recent and most time-limited representation of the culture or microculture in focus. It gives just a glimpse of a people group's history and tradition. By participating in daily life the anthropologist avoids assumptions that would not be characteristic of the cultural setting. Also high ethics are addressed towards the product, the value system of the scientist and the responsibility for the researched material.

The informant acts as the main partner in the anthropologist's study. Thus the relationship between the ethnographer and his informant is central for balanced information. An official global ethical declaration about cross-cultural examination is not give. The *American Anthropology Association* (AAA) and some other organizations, e.g. linguistic institutions, postponed ethical statements that are expected to take place in research. Those are general statements without any synallagmatic authority behind them.

1.1.3 Society - Culture, Language, Thought and Conscience

The subject of ethnography is "culture", but at the same time "culture" consists of social units, which are also objects of study. Whereas anthropology and ethnology uses ethnography to describe societies as cultures, social sciences are using ethnographical research methods to describe phenomena in social units. A clear differentiation between the understanding of culture and society helps the anthropologist in ethnographic research.

1.1.3.1 Culture – a Definition

The term "culture" is here introduced because many linguistic phenomenon, which play a role in this study are based on the concept (e.g. culture shock, culture change). However it has to be noted that in anthropology "society" and "culture" are nowadays very closely related terms, the more as Social Anthropology is on the increase. Culture is defined as "strategy for the mastery of existence" (Käser 1998:37) or as Kraft explicates, "culture is that in terms of which our life is organized" (1979:47). In cognitive anthropology, cultures are seen as "not material phenomena but cognitive organizations of material phenomena" (Waard 1991:745). Sperber puts it the same way when he says, that "cultures are the collective output of human mental abilities" (1982:3). Features like culture, language, tradition etc. are not universally shared. Coming back to cognitive properties, although psychology and anthropology differ in their methodological bias and their practical assumptions, both share the focus on the only common and shared ability by humans, that is their *mental* capacity. Cognition allows humans to develop a variety of languages, cultures, and social systems (:2), as such cognition comprises the deeper nature of humankind.

Culture instead forms the *mental software* which one uses to recognize his environment and his relation to it as is exemplified by Information Technology (Hofstede 1993:18). Values are in the core of one's culture. Up to the age of ten a child is enculturated in his culture. Values are in the core level of human behaviour, it is not possible to change or describe them from within a culture. The ethnographer acknowledges only the outcome of values and extrapolates them from the outcome (:23). We will take this very wide definition as a starter, being aware that society is also a dynamic and flexible understood subject (see below).

1.1.3.1.1 Culture Change

The most obvious feature of culture is *culture change*. However, this does not mean that culture is constantly changing, but that it is a dialectic process between internal models of the world and external reality (Katan 1999:21). Katan defines culture as made up of "culture traits" or "customs", "ideas" and "products" (:27-29). "Cultural customs" belong to one person, whereas cultural universals are part of the whole group. "Ideas" are shared concepts from which people carve up their beliefs and perceptions of the world. The outcome of these customs and ideas are the "products", as is seen in material artefact or tools. Customs, ideas and products of a culture are linked by "cultural configurations" (Hiebert 1976:30).

Culture change happens on the level of "cultural configurations", although the cognitive processes that lead to such change are on the core value level. The ethnographer or anthropologist goes back in history to find out about the formerly practiced or believed contents, and then he compares that to his recent findings and in some cases will be able to give predictions. One advantage of being an outsider (etic stance) as researcher is that the wider national, geographic, social and even global developments are taken into account. From an insider (emic stance) point of view such wider context is seldom taken into responsibility. Culture – and with it language – changes are the huge challenges to ethnicities under oppressed circumstances to survive in the ongoing globalization tendency. The threat to the Zaza ethnos is therefore taken specifically into account (2.2.7.2; 2.2.8.3; 2.3.4.5).

1.1.3.1.2   Culture and Society in Social Sciences

What then is the difference between culture and society? Hiebert states,

> Social organizations are learned patterns of thought and behaviour and, therefore, part of the culture transmitted from generation to generation. In short, culture is the creation of a group of people, and society is the group of people, itself. (1976:32).

Social groups are culturally constituted and necessary for human existence as are any of man's vital organs with whom they can be compared (Spiro 172:100). *Culture*, as a normative system, is a functional requirement of a human social order. (:104). The cultural dimension of human social systems is realized by the capacity for symbolization. Social units or social groups form microcultures (formerly called subcultures; Neuliep 2006:95-96). Their membership is defined by sex, race, ethnicity, or religion. People are born into those units, thus membership is not voluntary (:96). They are forced to marry and stay within the group (*endogamy* principle). Members are aware of their subordinate status as they experience segregation or discrimination in some way from the macrocultural unit (:96).

Another focus to look at society is presented by Max Weber. In his opus "*Economy and Society*" (Germ. "Wirtschaft und Gesellschaft") he defines the communitarisation of people groups in terms of

> similarities in their habitus or traditions or both of them, as well as the remembrance of colonialisation or migration reflected by a subjective belief in a common roots group. (1972:237).

In his definition blood relationship (*consanguinity*) is unimportant. He calls such societies *ethnical groups*. Their main factor is the "propagation of a communitarisation build on the subjective belief" (Auernheimer 1990:50). This view comes from people's history and defines societies from their common roots out of one group.

We will follow this approach and research the Zaza people group from this angle.

1.1.3.2 Language, Society and Thought – Cognitive Anthropology

Cognitive Anthropology is interested in the universal cognitive features of societies that concern their behaviour and its motivation (Kess 1993:250; Renner 1980:11, 25). It answers to the questions how different people organize and use their cultures. In other words how their material phenomena are significant for the people of some culture; and, how they organize these phenomena (McGee & Warms 2004:395-396). One way to research such issues, involves the relationship of language, thought and conscience in a people group and from there compares the results with others.

Language, society and thought reveal a triangular relationship. Neither one can be untwisted from the other. All of them are processed by innate procedures that lead to the forming of autonomous humans. The relationship of language, society and thought is so closely intertwined that even one of its binding constitutions, namely the conscience (Germ. "Gewissen") is difficult to describe or grasp (Müller 2009:14-18). As Johnson-Laird states, "nobody really knows what consciousness actually is, what it causes or which tasks it serves" (1983:448). Though consciousness is not the conscience per se, it does reflect the latter. All of these three given subjects are intuitive, global and higher- (e.g. meta-language; meta-conscience or Super-Ego) or deeper-levelled (e.g. cultural core values; philosophical thoughts) features of humanity.

Conscience and thought as inner tools of life-processing are only recognizable by their outwardly obvious impacts in language and cultural behaviour.

Elenctics as in the disciplines of philosophy and theology is part of apologetics and deals with the *conviction of people from other faith by dialogue*. Bavinck introduced the term *elenctics* in his *Introduction to Missiology* as the teaching about humankind's consciousness; as such it became popular in theological and missiological literature ([1953] 1960). Elenctics came out of the interdisciplinary need to understand the general orientation of conscience in cross-cultural encounter. The differentiation of a cultural orientation based on shame and honor or sin and guilt, as introduced by Ruth Fulton Benedict (1946) is nowadays questioned and mainly negated. A *"theory of face"* or *"theory of name"* in a symbolic way (Rynkiewich 2011:74) is sometimes used instead. However in the past, especially in Mediterranean Anthropology (Gilmore 1987), shame and guilt became the primary parameters to adjust, these contrasting with prestige and honour (Bavinck 1960:222, 226, 232; Liem 1997; Müller cit. in Roembke 2000:100; Stipek 1998; Wiher 2003:157). But still other conscience orientations are taken into account by researchers (2.3.4.4).

1.1.3.2.1 Language

The principal characteristic of culture is language. *Language* represents "the entirety of utterances, which can be produced in a language group" (Bloomfield 1976:38). It is a "system of ordering, in which terms are furnished with connotations" (Käser 1998:181). Renner in following Whorf puts it this way,

> the investigation of a cultures worldview is only possible within its language which alone mirrors its cognitive organization, beneath the disclosure of information she also defines a social situation. (1980:40).

This function of language becomes obvious, when under a variety of opportunities a decision which is appropriate to the situation is met by the speaker. Thus the culture and sociolinguistic environments are determinating this selection (Fasold 1993: ix).

Recent research on gender-related-language revealed that cognition and thought is determined by sex. Hence ones language is influenced in that direction too. Social competence and thought are relating to language. Authority is given by social competence and knowledge / intellect. Within culture authority is practiced. Foundational to authority and culture is the construction of a perception of the world by thought.

Women are linguistically more competent than men (Hines 2004:11; Bischof-Köhler 2004:234) since their interest in communication and interpersonal relationships dominate that of men (Maccoby 1999:46-50; Bischof-Köhler 2004:342-345). Hence social competence has a linguistical effect (Baron-Cohen 2004:12-13, 16; Bischof-Köhler 2004:348-351).

1.1.3.2.2 Thought and Language

Thought is also basic to the learning of a language and vice versa. Without language one cannot develop his thoughts. Thought and language are closely connected as is researched in the so called *Süssmilch'schen Paradoxon* [Paradox of Süssmilch]. The close relation between thought and language or thinking and speaking is expressed in principle in the *Süssmilch'sche Paradoxon*. John Peter Süssmilch claimed in 1756 that man without an operating system of thought would not be able to develop a language and that thinking is dependent on the

1 Anthropology and Ethnography

existence of a language on the other side (Süssmilch cit. in Liebi 2003:48). All other forms of informing expression, as in the animal kingdom, cannot be judged to be language, as there is no other foundation of reason to communicate than the instinct to survive (ibid.). Nonetheless the enormous capability to learn on top of the instinctive behaviour is best shown in guide-dogs with up to 50 trained processes. Another example is the intuitive and instinctive attitude e.g. from horses to protect children or handicapped people while they are in close proximity with each other.

In cognitive linguistics, mainly Relevance Theory dependent approaches are based on the assumption that thought is key to understand linguistics and translation (Sperber & Wilson [1986] 1995; Gutt [1991] 2000 and 1992). Thought is the capacity of humans to control conscious (brainstem [Truncus cerebri]; brain; mind) and unconscious (sympathetic and parasympathetic nervous system) processes. It is within the first sixteen years of life that half of all synaptic relays are completed. The process starts explosively during the first four months, when the Baby's brain grows. Afterwards the brain degrades until death. Neurons send out axons that form the chemical and electric synapses. During the first three years the general relays are built. Later, the main function of the brain is to connect different synaptic relays with each other (Buckingham & Clifton 2001:50). Thought opposed to conscience forms the intuitive physically measurable ability to store and access information in the dominant working- / short- and long-term memory and secondary storages (like encyclopaedic storage, implicit- or explicit-oriented memories) of the brain (Fabbro 1999:22-23, 74, 89, 94, 97; Callow 1998:90; Danks 1997; Kußmaul 2007:76-77; Pinker 1999:85). Whereas both procedures are not directly accessible (Wippich 1984:1) the hierarchy of storage and the time-dependent queries are measurable. The discussion about whether information is stored as engrams (Bunge & Ardila 1990:273), syllables (Myers-Scotton 2006:315) or otherwise is still ongoing and not solved yet. In this thesis the syllable-principle by language is favoured.

The *encyclopaedic knowledge* or *mental lexicon* plays an essential role as e.g. in Relevance Theory out of cognitive linguistics. Sperber explains it as a culture dependent concept that is at any time on demand from the memory (1975:91-94).

Nowadays this idea is rejected since this understanding proved to be far too short-sighted for the more complex and indirect recall system of knowledge (Holland & Quinn 1987:15-16).

Diagram 3 Model of Human Memory (Fabbro 1999:94)

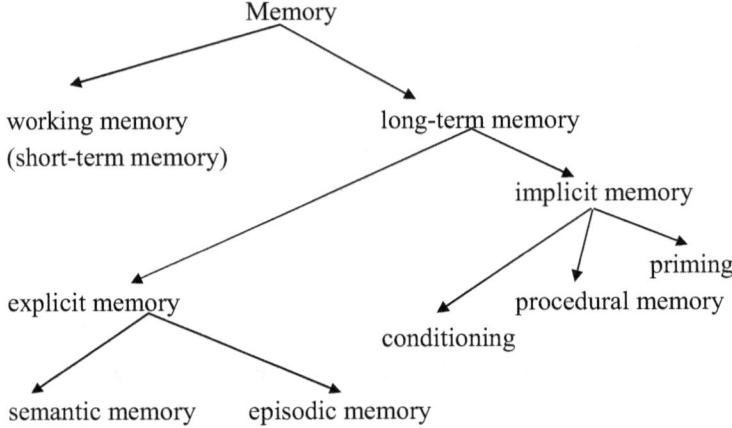

It is within neurolinguistics[4] that those operations are described and investigated. The model of the transmitting of information as signals, originated after WWII in the so called *code-model* of Information Technology (IT-branch). Shannon and Weaver described therein the process of information transfer. Their assumptions are based on experiences from coding procedures (black box principle; encrypted signalling) as used during the times of WWII (Shannon & Weather 1949; w/o. year *The Shannon-Weaver Model*). Information as substantial message is produced and encoded by a *sender* (S). Running through a *channel* (*conduit metaphor*) the information is decoded by a *receiver* (R). All influences (good or worse) such as frequential oscillation, receiving and coding problems etc. are sublimated in the so called filter or *noise* which is placed between *Sender* and *Receiver* (see Werner 2011:118).

Diagram 4 Shannon & Weaver Code-Model

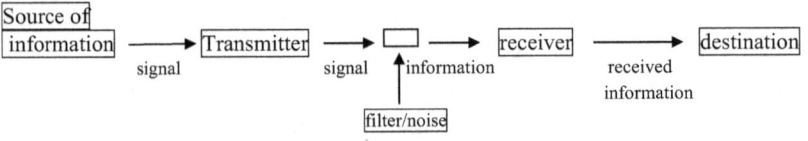

---

[4] *Neurolinguistics* adds cognition processes to *applied linguistics*, which deals with the four faculties of phonetics / phonology, morphology, syntax and semantics (Asher cit. in Fabbro 1999:1). *Phonetics* and *phonology* describe the physical constituents of language (Fabbro 1999:12), *syntax* describes the examination of the relation from language symbols between themselves, namely the rules of their hierarchy structure, their position and order in the complex sentence (1964:35). *Morphology* deals with the word forms, i.e. their outer design (Payne 1997:20).

Increasing research on the human brain, introduced by the French physician Paul Broca, brought forth the centres in the human brain, where language (left side) and thought is placed (Fabbro 1999:22; Steiner 2004:147). This was primarily stimulated by new medical research tools such as computer or MR tomography (Magnetic Resonance) and studies about cognitive and linguistic diseases (expressive aphasia, mutism, stammer etc.). Those diseases are caused by damage of cognitive functions but result in linguistic disorder (Bell 1991:243). But as critics made clear the "black box of memory is not opened until today" and the "sparse tradition and progress in neurolinguistics" is obvious (Bunge & Ardila cit. in Wilss 1992:149).

1.1.3.2.3 Sapir-Whorf-Hypothesis and Enculturation

In 1949 Edward Sapir (1884-1939) showed in his studies that on epistemological grounds "people do not simply live in the same world with *different* labels attached but in different worlds" [emphasis as in the original. EW.] (Hiebert 1976:33; s. a. Sapir 1961; Whorf 1963; Neuliep 2006:246-247; Clark & Clark 1978:227-228). Together with Benjamin Whorf (1897-1941) he formulated the hypothesis of linguistic relativity (Whorf 1956:213-214; 1963:20; Whorf cit. in Käser 1998:182). Whorf concluded that "people, who use languages with very different grammars, are led by these grammars to typically different observations and different evaluations with outward resemblance" (Whorf cit. Käser 1998:182). Language, as Whorf points out, does not only affect the mind, but rather also influences the thinking. While Sapir in 1921 stressed, how the culture will be achieved in the language (Sapir 1961:13), Whorf takes up this thesis and comes to the conclusion that language affects the perception of the world. A resolution of language and culture is not possible (Whorf 1963:19-21). As the "Sapir-Whorf hypothesis" this view won great acceptance in science. However, the "Sapir-Whorf hypothesis" was heavily criticized over the years. In 2010 Deutscher also criticized Whorfs assumptions about the Hopis (Indians living in Northeastern Arizona) language that he claimed has no concept of time. This was disproved by Malotki in 1983 (Deutscher 2010:142-144; see also Gipper 1972). Deutscher speaks against the "language prison-house" which would limit a human to his speech. He argues that every language is able to express all concepts (:148). We agree with such assumptions deeply.

Since the formulation of the *Sapir-Whorf-Hypothesis*, the discussion about whether language is culturally meaningful or part of the culture, finds echo even in the wide area of linguistics. It enforced the opinion that a society's language consists of whatever it is one has to know in order to communicate with its speakers as adequately as they do with each other and in a manner which they will accept as corresponding to their own. (Goodenough 1957:168).

This view implies *enculturation* in the mother tongue (Sapir 1961:13, 29). Such a dual role is also reflected in following descriptions of the functions of language. The process of *enculturation* is the natural procedure of learning a particular culture (Spradley 1979:47). *Enculturation* is based on the innate instinct to communicate and participate in a culture. It serves as a foundation to learn the mother tongue. Thus *enculturation* describes a "process of socialization", in which "every human learns certain rules of behaviour, following an internalized theory of his own culture and its morals". (Stolze 1999:204; Principe 1991:78).

Language has a binding constituent, by bringing people together as a communication network (*binding* principle). Equally it delivers a common history and identity of a language group as an ethnical unit. Thereby language functions by making a distinction between the personal and the people group's level (*identity* principle). At the mythical or religious level this becomes palpable. Traditions like myths or initiating rites of a culture are passed on secretly, as is exemplified by the language of the Sinte and Romani or other cants (Steiner 2004:85, 92, 101, 223; Fasold 1993:3-4, 26). Ostler sees the preserving of tradition as the most important function, since language has the opportunity to survive generations of speakers. "Every language has a chance of immortality, but this is not to say that it will survive forever" (Ostler 2006: xix, 7). Käser agrees with him as languages contain "complex structures in which culture is embedded by encoding, or better formulated in chart form" (Käser 1998:179; about language endangerment see 2.2.7.2; 2.3.4.5).

After a first great emphasis on the Sapir-Whorf-Hypothesis it was later criticised for negating the universalities of languages in the seventies and overemphasizing the function of culture in societies. Noam Chomsky criticised the theory from a linguistic viewpoint by saying that it does not display the universality of language, which could be found in a deeper transformational grammar level (Chomsky cit. in Pinker 2000:10). Against Whorf he said that similarities between languages are much greater than differences (Chomsky cit. in Hesselgrave 2002:152-154; Dil 1975:68). Bascom argues against a bias on culture to the disadvantage of language (Bascom 2003:82).

Looking critically at the extremes of the Sapir-Whorf-Hypothesis it would finally mean that communication between people who do not share the same mother tongue would be impossible, even if one had acquired this language

(Schogt 1992:194). The *hypothesis of linguistic relativity* moves between "extreme determinism and extreme relativism" (Hudson 1987:103; Gentzler proves this for the translation theory by Nida, Gentzler 2001:53). It is thereby integrated in the science for translation as its standard model.

Today the "pendulum of scholarly opinion seems to be swinging back to at least a moderate version of the Sapir-Whorf hypothesis" (Bascom 2003:82; Chomsky cit. in Pinker 2000:10).

Since Sapir's examinations about language, the close combination between culture and language or communication has been also covered and discussed repeatedly by others ([1949] 1961; Bascom 2003; Holland & Quinn 1987; Loewen 1975; Nida 1975 and 1990; Wendtland 1987; Wilt 2003).

1.1.3.2.4 Homogenous Unit Principle (HUP)

One approach to anthropological research can help to justify the focus of an ethnographer. The so called *Homogenous Unit Principle* or the "principle of the solid group" grew out of Christian development aid (Morea o. J. *The Homogeneous Unit Principle*, 1-2). Research in India revealed that decisions within social groups were made by referring to close social units. Those small scale social units are often called a microculture, tribe, clan or caste (Pickett 1953). Inferred from this observation any meaningful activity from development aid workers should focus on those units (McGavran 1973:4; s. a. Vicedom 2002:177). People are more open to communicational attempts if they share common culture, common customs and conceptions of faith" (McGavran 1955:38; s. a. Frost & Hirsch 2004:52; Kasdorf 1976:16-18). A disadvantage of this approach is its tendency to racism. As the researcher is always in the controversy to bring with him his own cultural view it is one effect that his ethnological descriptions imply a racist statement, the more so if he is not focusing on the wider and closer context of the researched culture (Bosch cit. in Frost & Hirsch 2004:52).

Despite this criticism there has not been another approach in Christian development aid that is more promising than the *Homogenous Unit Principle* (Frost & Hirsch 2004:51-52). I see good reason to link this approach to anthropology also, since it asks for target aimed research.

Out of ideological and social needs it was always the effort of man to organize himself in communities close to him (Spiro 1965). This presumption out of social sciences corresponds with what is demonstrated in religious groups, like Christianity (see the New Testament Acts 2.12; the conflict of Judaist against heathen Christian Acts 15).

1.1.3.3 Conscience – LEIC, Shame and Guilt - Orientation

There is not much research done concerning the relationship between language, thought and conscience. One reason for is the fact that conscience is not really comprehensible (see above). In describing conscience two problems occur; first; the conceptual description of the subject and second the empiric acquisition. The former asks for a definition by explication which is either done by postulation or by description of mental processes below the level of conscience (:353). The latter giving reliable indicators for (a) location(s) (Germ. "Sitz") of the / those social-ethical organ(s) and how the change of conscience is identified within a culture (Germ. "Volksgewissen"; Müller 2009:64, 90) or an individual (Bunge & Ardila 1990:353). One approach to the placement of the conscience due to a transcendental organ in our physical body could be found in the research of the so called "Location of Emotions, Intellect and Character" (Germ. "Sitz der Emotionen, des Intellekts und des Charakters"; Käser 2004:178, 181; referred to as LEIC / SEIC). This tool and model reflects all the parts that are referred to as shaping the conscience. In researching the conscience as a global phenomenon, anthropology offers many insights. Especially in comparative studies comparing cultures the LEIC will show the variety of presumptions where cultures will locate this transcendental organ. Currently the LEIC-model demonstrates the most developed tool to understand and locate conscience as the driving force of human behaviour (Werner 2011; 1.1.3.2).

The most recent and elaborate summary on conscience is found in Müller *Das Gewissen in Kultur und Religion: Scham- und Schuldorientierung als empirisches Phänomen des Über-Ich /Ich-Ideal* (2009) [Conscience in Culture and Religion: Shame- and Guilt Orientation as an empiric Phenomenon of the Super-Ego.]. The author gives an overview on the effects of conscience in humans. His interdisciplinary approach spans theology, cultural anthropology (Germ. "Ethnologie"), psychology, social sciences and medicine. An understandable limitation of Müller's work is his bias on religion and theology.

Conscience is an innate part of humans. Understanding conscience as a biological organ would parallel Bühler's view of language being an organ and therefore an essential and vital component of humans (Bühler 1965: xxi). This perception demonstrates conscience as enculturated, and such being the case it has to be understood as culturally coined. Following the Sapir-Whorf-Hypothesis, every culture would generate its own conscientious values, norms and ethics. As a working definition for conscience Müller states (2009:136 thesis 60 and 61):

> Conscience performs the intellectual-spiritual-physical organ of man within its culture, society and religion, that feels innate basic elements, is marked by the social environment, proceeding due to these elements and reacts through them on its environment reacts. The conscience is the organ for the culture, society and religion ability of man. The conscience is necessary for social control of man. .... The conscience of man is the instrument to ensure his dignity.

Whereas this definition is mainly built on anthropological grounds, the common religious and theological view that conscience is simply understood as an ethical organ that decides between Good and Evil is criticized by Käser. In his opinion "its functionality is extensively determined by the prerequisites that the culture provides in which an individual grows up" (1998:131). This cultural approach describes enculturation as the main factor in the development of conscience. In his approach of describing conscience as the "Location of Emotions, the Intellect and the Character" (LEIC; Germ. "Sitz der Emotionen, des Intellekts und des Charakters" = SEIC; 2.3.2.1; 2.3.2.2) he reverts back to the ancient (:179; Bunge & Ardila 1990:352), and in my opinion helpful concept, to consider *conscience* as a biological organ which is innate and developed during enculturation (:178-179, 181; see e.g. the Zaza people 2.3.1.1.2 and envy 2.3.1.1.4).

A main feature of conscience holds that although it works all the time within one's thought, language and culture it is recognized only if one falls out of the culturally given values, norms and ethics. The cultural insider moves within his behaviour between performance and inhibition. The latter performs the space of the culturally *taboo*[5] (Spiro [1965] 1975:399; 2.3.2.1.4; 2.3.3.2.5). Thus of conscience signals every transgression in either a satisfying ("good conscience") or concerning ("bad conscience") direction (:423). Besides the thoughts that this transgression determines, language is adapted to the generated emotion and perception. One would speak of emotive, emotional, timid or aggressive language. The way a culture expresses such emotions is different (see example of Zaza in 2.3.2.1).

---

[5] Hendry informs us that "Taboo is a word which was brought back by Captain Cook from his voyages in the South Seas. His sailors noticed that in Polynesia the use of this word designated a prohibition and they found it useful themselves when they wanted to keep visitors off the ship, or reserve a particular girl for themselves. It was also a word for which they had an existing category, though they may have found this new word more instantly expressive and appealing than previous ones like 'prohibited' or 'forbidden', just as their countrymen did when they returned to introduce it to the English language" (1999:35-36). Others fill in or refer taboo to the terms "unlawful", "sacred", "superlatively good", "profaned" or "polluted". For more information see Steiner, Franz 1956. *Taboo*. Harmondsworth: Penguin.

Coming from a western and Teutonic way of thinking and exploring (Galtung 1985:169; s. a. Oxbrow 2005:4-5) one could think of *conscience* as an "inner clock" or "pendulum" that signals every transgression. The functionality of the conscience could be described as

- shame- or guilt-oriented (initiated by Benedict 1946 and Mead 1937[6]; see excellent summary in Müller 2009:18-88; Hesselgrave 1983:461-483; Hofstede 1991, 1993:77; Spiro 1972, [1965] 1975:406, 409; Wiher 1998, 2003:6, 2007),
- honour- / prestige- and disgrace-orientation (Lomen 2003:21; Malina 1986, 2001) or
- envy- and honour-orientation (Hesselgrave 2002:211; Kehl-Bodrogi & Pfluger 1997; Malina 2001:109; Werner 2006:67-69).
- defilement- (Arabic *haram*) / clean-orientation (Arabic *helal*) as in Islamic influenced cultures and
- fear- / power-orientation as in tribal cultures (Muller 2001)
- honour- / justice-orientation (Wiher 2003:158).

Whereas *shame-orientation* levels the conscience between the poles of *shame* and *prestige / honour* (Müller 2009:137), *guilt-orientation* does so between the poles of *guilt* and *righteousness / justice* (ibid.). A person with a functioning and "normal" conscience levels his conscience somewhere in between both poles in conformity to his culture. Globally shame-orientation dominates as a cultural point of reference. In cross-cultural encounter contextualization is the main tool to adapt and overcome different cultural characteristics of conscience (Racey 1996:305-309).

As far as the author knows, the function of western conscience has not been researched from a non-western perspective so far. Having said this he is aware that perceptions of conscience in non-western literature could be totally different and not obvious at first sight. Asian research on expressions like Arabic *kismet* or Sanskrit *karma* which became fixed terms in today's English and German vocabulary, hint to global interest in understanding the general concept of conscience (see artistic research of the terms in Arts & Humanities Research Council 2010 *Between Kismet and Karma*). Considerations of conscience from and in foreign cultures became less popular but could be found e.g. in the Japanese subject of *amae* (Eymann 1996), or the Zaza term *ganê mı, zerrê mı* (see 2.4).

---

[6] Mead is criticized for her misunderstanding and misrepresentation of Samoan culture in her ethnographical studies (Freeman 1983 and 1998).

Diagram 5 Poles of Shame and Guilt Orientation (Müller 2009)

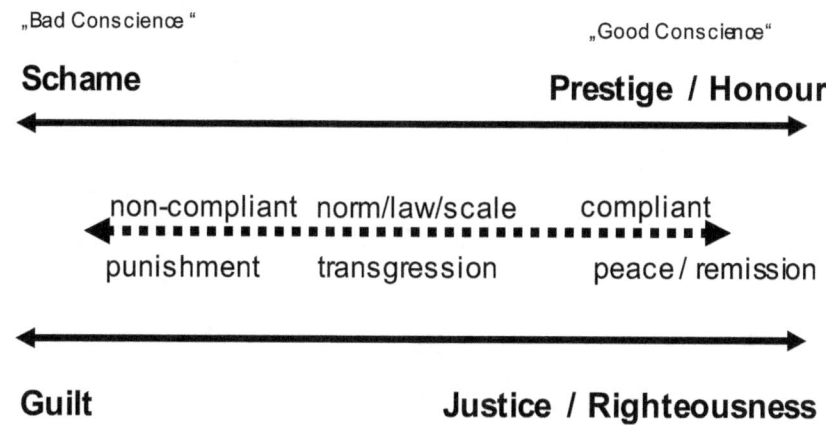

The shame- and guilt-oriented approach is critized for its subjectivity and its ignorance, because of the fact that it deals only with extremes, whereas the normal conscience-orientation does not (Schnelle 1991:114). Like Piers and Singer, Spiro rejects Benedict (1946) and Mead's (1937) distinction of guilt and shame cultures, particularly the idea that members of shame cultures don't show "conscience" in the Euro-American sense, because they have not internalised the cultural values (Wiher 2003:108). Hence conscience is embedded in a scale between justice- and honour-orientation (:153). One could question, either the demarcation of conscience by the suggested terms, or take his own poles on the scale. Either way the levelling of conscience somehow relates to these subjects or moves in between extreme poles (see pendulum-principle).

Religion as a main feature of culture affects in an extraordinary way the conscience of humans by a metaphysical or transcendental power. In (post-) modern philosophy and theology *conscience*, fate, kismet, nature, destiny or chance replaced "God" as *this* metaphysical or transcendent monotheistic being (Pöhlmann 1991:33-35; Diderot, Comte, Russell, Freud etc.).

Diagram 6 Poles of Orientation in Conscience/LEIC

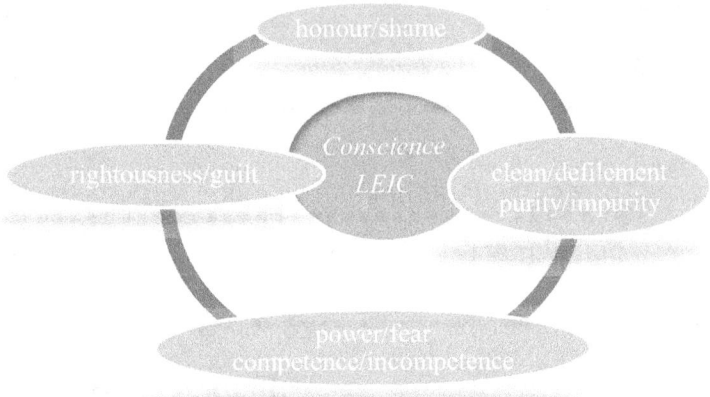

Transgression of cultural norms, values or ethics is punished vicariously for the outward power by the community. As in the case of monotheistic religions (Judaism; Christianity and Islam) the written revelation and its commentaries (Jewish *Midrash* and Islamic *Hadith*), offers all information on ruling daily life (e.g. circumcision; baptism and five pillars of Islam). Often the punishment of transgression is included in these revealed norms, values and ethics (e.g. lapidation; divorce in case of adultery; crucifixion). In situations of conversion the "tuning in" of converts to the new situation takes lifelong since the conscience needs to be newly wired up (Wiher 2003:157). Contextualization in conversion, namely the grade of adaption to the new religion is fluent, as nobody can see the heart or thought of a convert. His outward behaviour does not need to demonstrate the depth of his conversion (Corwin 2008:8-9; Bourne 2009:58-70). Conscience in the West is increasingly secularized, new norms, values and ethics mingle with the traditional Christian setting (Rommen 2003:15-16). The Bible itself reveals a mix of cultures. One can find stories, descriptions and reactions based on either shame- or guilt-orientation (Müller 2009:137; Wiher 2003:6, 157).

The conversion mechanisms in the area of the Zaza people and their surrounding neighbours are investigated below. Often conversion is used to adhere to changing religious or cultural settings. Every religious expansion, namely the Christian, the Judaist or the Islamic brought with it conversions of Middle Eastern people groups (2.1.2.6). The Zaza ethnicity, the Kurmanji speaking Kurds and other ethnicities follow his paradigm to ease either oppression or for reasons of identification.

1.1.3.4 Society and Religion – an Anthropological Stance

Geertz summed up the different approaches to religion in anthropology (Geertz 1966). In Structuralist and functional-Structuralist studies religion was considered on a social-structural basis. Foundational to anthropological assumptions on religion is an evolutionary approach. Only few anthropological studies are concerned about religion (e.g. Arens 2011:249-265; Käser 2004:223-234; 290-319; Rappaport 1999; Spiro 1966). Religion deals with the question of suffering, the evil and the good. Supernatural powers, metaphysical phenomena and concepts of a higher righteousness and judgement come into play. These fundamentmal human needs are addressed in questions of Theodicee, ritual and liturgy. Rappaport in his masterpiece *Ritual and Religion in the Making of Humanity* (1999) describes ritual as the fundamental task to generating acceptance. Ritual "is the basic social act" (Rappaport 1999:138). He suggests that, in rituals, encoding, formality, invariance, and performance go together. Ritual thus becomes communication (:50). One step further societies use these rituals to perform a litugy which is knitting a social fabric of a given community or institution. In performative or demonstrative acts rituals are embedded in "liturgical orders". Thes combine physical and verbal components and move into extremely invariant creedal statements. He calls these creeds "Ultimate Sacred Postulates" (:168). On the other hand Geertz assumes that the evil is just a reflection of ones postulates about higher divine powers (1966:21). The limitation to understand the reality of religious hypothesis is the inability to move beyond human existence. Something outside of the human experience can neither be approached nor denied. A revelation from outside, as far as it is transformed into human reality is always reflected in human terms and as such not approvable by humans. In Anthropology, thus, the description, function and process of rituals and liturgy become central to describe societies and their dealing with the social impact of the phenomena.

1.1.4 Summary

Anthropology, like translation and other human disciplines are is not an exact science. Their focus is on humanity and their methods are thereby restricted by human fallacy. Yet the demand of humanity is to compare one's culture, language and thought with others. By diachronic, synchronic and comparative studies such needs could be performed.

The area of research as in this study is the field of ethnography. The monographic description of the Zaza people from Eastern Anatolia belongs to the discipline of cultural anthropology. Social science deals with the anonymous and withholds description of unique and specific elements in a culture, whereas cultural anthropology presents a full picture of a culture to the audience of the ethnographer. Participant observation, as the momentarily modest technique of anthropological research, includes the learning of the researched culture's language, interviews about daily life, and the verbalization of the perception of the world with its deeper core values.

To gain an understanding of the researched culture the main factors to investigate are:
- Language and semantic content,
- Perception of thought and cognition,
- Relation of culture and language as represented in the Sapir-Whorf Hypothesis of linguistic relativity,
- Conscience and the orientation towards shame / guilt orientation or prestige / justice. This includes also the handling of envy, the Image of limited good,
- Restriction to one homogenous unit – a people group - only (HUP).

The ethnographer is responsible for the monographic representation of the researched culture in a way that is neither boastful nor downplays any observation or inference made. As ethnography, like translation, forms an intuitive and therefore non-reproducible discipline, his ethics are mainly responsible to other standards as in translation science. The subjectivity of his representation has to be clearly shown, so that the audience understands his conclusions and the restrictive character of his studies to his own culture.

1.2 Project-Description

The history of research about the Zaza people reaches far back to the 19th century. Linguists and Indo-European respectively Middle East researchers like Lerch (1857-1858) started with the area of people from the Kurdish small scale social units to do research. To historical travelogues, based on anthropological research it soon became clear that there are at least 4 main languages or dialects which refer to the same north-western branch of Iranian languages.

1.2.1 *Sherefname* and *Seyahatname*

Lerch's main source is the historical work of *Sheref Chan* (Sharaf Khan) from 1596 titled "Prince of Bitlis, Moush, Khinis, Akhlat the Dependencies thereof and of all the Lands and Strongholds inherited by him from his Forefathers" (Kreyenbroek & Sperl 2002:198). Written in Persian, as the name *Sherefname* (*Sharafname*) indicates (Bruinessen 2002:617), it represents the Kurdish chronicles in five books (see Francois-Bernard Charmoy cit. in Hadank 1930:1). *Evliya Çelebi* added in his work *Seyahatname* from his travels in the 17th century that Zaza is one of sixteen elsewhere fifteen Kurdish dialects (Leezenberg 1993a:11). Initiated by this trigger Kurdish literature, namely poetry and epic, started in this time, as is shown by "Melaye Cizn (1570-1640), Feqiye Teyran (1590-1660), and Amedi Xani (1650-1707), the author of the epic poem Mem û Zin" (Paul & Haig 2001:399). Lerch based his observations on the *Sherefname* and found the Kurdish branches of

- "Kurmandsch (Kurmanji). The term reveals wide variation and is also represented as *Kurmanc, Kırmanc, Kurmandshi, Kırmanji*.
- Lur (Luri)
- Kelhur
- Guran (Gorani/Hawrami)". (Lerch 1857-58:69 Vol 2 [Band 2]).

Lerch adds the branch of Zaza speakers who live at the upper Euphrates in the Palu area (Justi 2006: xxv). Blau delivered samples of speech showing that the dialect of the Duzhik Kurds follows Zaza. So that Duzhiki and Zaza speaking Kurds had to be added as a fifth branch to Kurdish and Kurdish related languages (: xxv),

- Duzhiki and Zaza (:69; see 2.2.1.1).

The early differentiation of the Zaza people as an own people group with a homeland area, as well as a distinctive language and culture reaches back to the middle of the 19th century modern interest started since 1980. Linguistic and anthropological research from different people and groups were mainly implemented from Europe (see SIL International; Ludwig Paul; Geoffrey Haig; McDowall). Beside the scientific purpose the research was in some cases combined with an attitude to evaluate help on literacy or sociolinguistic needs.

With the *Sherefname* the written history of the Kurds (here in a wider sense), as well as the surrounding people began. It became the main source for further investigations about the people groups of Eastern Anatolia (Charmoy 1868-1875; Bruinessen 2002:616-618; Hennerbichler 2004:130; Heper 2007:54; Izady

1992:74; Justi 2006: xxv; Leezenberg 1993:16). As it is closely connected to the very religious and mystical orders of the Zaza area it offers some details about this people group.

> The acculturation process in question, which has not ended up in voluntary assimilation (because the Kurds have retained their original ethnic identity, if they chose to) seems to have started as early as the sixteenth century. Şharaf Khan, the ruler of Bitlisi in the sixteenth century, wrote his Sharafnâma (an important source on the Kurdish history, penned in 1597) in Persian. In 1667, he had the Sharafnâma translated into Turkish, not into Kurdish. In 1861, Sharafnâma was again translated into Turkish, this time at the bebest of the Kurdish chieftains of Egil and Palu. (Heper 2007:54).

Only the Armenian Apostolic Church with their long written history offers more background information of this geographical area, since she is closely connected to Armenian politics as a National Church (Avetis 1911; Ter-Mikelian; 2.3.1.1; 3.2).

1.2.2 Linguistic and Anthropological Specifications

The Zaza people are split in an Alevi Northern group with at least three dialectical varieties (Varto, Mamekiye, Ovaçik), and a Sunni Central-/Eastern and Sothern group with also at least three main dialectical variations (Çermik/Siverek, Palu/Bingol, Hani/Dicle) as well as some enclavic language islands in the East (Mutki, Muş, Kulp). Interestingly the religious split goes with the linguistical division (Paul 2002:190-198). Therefore the Zaza people are a good example for a demonstration of how research done on language (linguistics) and culture oriented (cultural anthropology) foundation works hand in hand (Waard 1991:745-747; Werner 2011:30-31).

1.2.3 Method of Research

This investigation is based on personal communication, two survey trips to the East, analyse and excerption of literacy about the Zaza people, linguistic research (see revision of Todd's grammar), anthropological research (see introduction Hayıg 2008) and a manifold friendship within the people of the western part of Eastern Anatolia.

The method of research is based on the sociolinguistic approach of Fasold (1993), the ethnographic approach by participant observation of Spradley (1972, 1980; Spradley & McCurdy1989) and an applied linguistics approach as is promoted by Healey (1989), Barnwell (1992 and 1999) or Nida (1957, 1961, 1964 and with Taber 1969). The *scientific work techniques in cultural anthropology* follow Beer and Fischer's method with the same title (2003). Namely the way of transcribing the data that participating observation leads to and the excerption of the literacy is based on their instructions (2003:26-39, 65-82, 121-135).

As the mother tongue is key to the understanding of foreign cultures, the study of the Zaza language called Zazaki (*-ki* demonstrates the particle to mark languages) was essential to access the traditions, customs and specific features of the Zaza. Diagram 1 showed how the cross-cultural processes overlap during investigation (1.1). Both cultures – the researchers as well as the Zaza culture – profit from these means. Since the Zaza people are on their way to self perception they have a struggle of identity with politically active groups from out- and from inside (see 2.1.2). An important factor for objectivity forms the non-political endeavour that has been taken by the researcher. Hence the position of political motivated groups is left out or secondary in this research. For further investigation in this direction one should consult the Internet by using Kurdish platforms and researching Zaza there (e.g. Alis 2006 *The Kurdish Platform*).

Restriction to non-political groups of Zaza did not turn out to be an obstacle, since motivation in some groups is high to serve their people on linguistic and anthropological grounds. In the nineties of the last century the tendency within the non-political and culturally motivated group was mainly in finding orthography and defining a reference vs. standard dialect. Whereas the finding of the orthography made progress (2.2.1.1), the question of a reference dialect is still highly valued. Some argue that it should be set up by common agreement (Malmisanij, Vate-Group) although they are not really to discuss this with the representatives of the groups but go their own way. Others are denying any forced standardization at all and will let it up to the people (Paul 2002:190, 193; see 2.2.1.4). This latter argument lacks the peoples request to work on standardization and is at the end counterproductive. The same goes for the ones who call standardization colonialism / fascism or imperialisms.

Nowadays magazines, literacy on poetics and philosophy are published. Some works on history, few anthropological and grammatical studies are available, but the main problem is illiteracy in Zazaki and the problem of a working distribution network on Zazaki literature. Not everyone gets success to the works written in Zazaki, because the publishing houses are not organized well and the Zaza literature not spread widely in the East. It is sometimes laborious to get information or material from the publishing houses, even within the country.

For this very reason the in-country work on Zazaki is still in its early stage of development, even more as the official political line on Turkish minority languages changed only few years ago and led to more openness toward their use, distribution and research (e.g. Hürriyet Gazete Haberleri 2008 *DTP challenges PM in Kurdish*).

1.3 Summary

It is within the scope of applied cultural anthropology to use ethnography for comparative studies. Ethnography has global and mainly cross-cultural subjects of research in focus, whereas social sciences are more microculturally (or subculturally) oriented. Social sciences investigate and describe cultural phenomena within a cultural background.

The cross-cultural encounter of the ethnographer (in this study part of a central European culture) and the culture of the Zaza or any other culture is described in the dyadic-dynamic model (1.1; Diagram 1). Hereby both cultures start by approximating to each other during the research. The ethnographer joins the researched culture and tries to adapt by language learning and through cultural inquiry. This attracts the attention of the researched culture to learn about the ethnographer's culture and his motivation. Thus the participating cultures exchange cultural contents by communication, actions and interchange of ideas. At some later point the mother tongue speaking supporters of the ethnographer are trained by the ethnographer mainly through observation and reproduction. Thereafter both cultures start with the inculturation of the foreign knowledge (e.g. tribal systems, rituals etc.).

The whole process contributes to cross-cultural exchange, intercultural management and leads into globalized partnerships. The dyadic-dynamic model helps to recognize the needs of a minority and to support it throughout an ethnographic project. Both participating cultures gain publicity out of it. Hence globalization and ethnography are somehow intertwined. As an unknown people group becomes more public it gains profit by having a voice and representing itself thereby in an organizational form.

It is within this broad scope of cross-cultural relationship that the researcher – namely the anthropologist or ethnographer – is restricted to ethical norms and values, which are unenforceable but all the more essential to guarantee objectivity.

Ethnography describes traditions, myths and the cosmology and perception of the world of a people group. But as cultures are always changing it carves out the hidden foundations of a people group and works as a bedrock for following

1 Anthropology and Ethnography

comparative studies. In history ethnography was done by western researchers and lead to misconceptions or lopsided interpretations. Today increased mobility, worldwide markets and global communication lead to a multitude of ethnographic and social studies. |Research could seldom be done without focusing on a variety of cross-cultural encounter.

Thought, language, culture and conscience are closely connected to each other. This is demonstrated in the Sapir-Whorf-Hypothesis (language and culture) and the *Süssmilch'sche Paradoxon* (Language and thought) and a global shame- or guilt-orientation of the conscience. Their triangular dependency is foundational to humankind. Their global incidence in humanity and their intuitive characteristic indicates innate features that assist their development during growing up and the process of enculturation. Conscience and thought as inner tools of life-processing are only recognizable by their impacts, which are outwardly obvious in language and cultural behaviour.

Ethnography begins by looking at a people group or an object of examination as point of reference in comparative studies. A reason for focusing just on one people group or microculture is given by the *Homogenous Unity Principle* (HUP). Studies about coherence in societies and people groups revealed a high grade of harmony within those units. When the anthropologist or ethnographer limits himself to such subjects he finds it easier to learn the language and culture, than if his focus is far too widespread and on mixed examination objects.

The method of research for the Zaza people group follows the principles of Spradley, Beer and Fischer and Käser. Historically the book of *Sherefnamê* (16th century) represents the beginning of research on the Zaza people. The presentation of the results follows the outline of western ethnographical material.

2   The Zaza

This study is about the Rivers and Mountains that define the homeland of the Zaza ethnicity. The Zaza people relate to "their" Rivers (Euphrates, Tigris, Murat, Pulumuriye, Peri, and Munzur) and "their" Mountains (Duzgın Baba, Kerê Veyvikê, etc.) by religious and environmental adoration.

The people group that is brought into focus offers several names from within and outside their community (see below). To start with a term that became central to them, they are hereby referred to as *Zaza*. Despite the fact that *the Zaza* are not a homogenous and therefore heterogeneous unit, due to religious and linguistical diversity, and being aware that the term Zaza includes also negative connotations, it is expressing a distinction from the ethnically closely related Kurmanji speaking Kurdish people called "Kurds". Having said this the term "Kurds" and "Kurdish" covers a close and a wide spectrum of meanings. The close range refers to the inhabitants of the region of *Hakkari, Van, Mardin*, parts of *Diyarbakır, Kharamanmaraş, Sivas, Erzurum*, and along the borders to Armenia, Iran, Northern Iraq and East Syria. They all speak a more or less closely related dialect of Kurmanji. A wide definition would include all of the ethnically and linguistically related people groups in Eastern Anatolia, Armenia, West Iran, Northern Iraq and East Syria that speak an Indo-European, Iranian language related to Kurmanji. I do follow the closer definition in linguistical considerations and the wider definition when it comes to history or comparative studies. But in general I do not use the term "Zaza-Kurds" or "Zazaki a Kurdish dialect" since such connotations bear political significance and are in some circumstances (e.g. linguistics) not correct. The language of the Zaza, a conglomeration of at least three main dialects, is referred to as *Zazaki*, due to the suffix -*ki* that identifies languages (Todd 2002: FN d).

Looking at the history and origin of the Zaza people we face the problem that in historical descriptions the term "Zaza", "Kurds", Kurdish" or names of locations and practices are not consistently used in the way we understand those terms today. Terminology is ambiguous, inconsistent and differs either if it is from an emic (insider) or etic (outsider) perspective. Because of this, Kurdology, Zazaology and all sciences that deal with these issues have to start with vague hypotheses about the origin and history of these people groups. Especially when it comes to "Proto-Zaza" or "Proto-Kurdish" speculations, the nescience and lack of knowledge becomes obvious. Every attempt would lead to an assumption which could not be finally proved (s.a. Asatrian 2009:9). Nonetheless this is how science proceeds.

In introducing the Zaza society's complex structure and the variety of language variants (dialects) within this group it will be demonstrated why the terms Zaza and Zazaki are only auxiliary constructions to describe the phenomenon of a culture and its language.

2.1 The People

The Zaza people do not by any means consist of a small company that is living out there in the north-western part of Eastern Anatolia, but rather they embody a group that inhabits an area as huge as one of the provinces of Germany or the Netherlands (close to 40.000 square km). "Turkey has 81 provinces and the Zaza homeland stretches through 11 of these provinces" (Wilson 2010:1). Thus 5% of Turkish soil is inhabited mainly by this ethnicity (Appendices
Appendix 1 Homeland Area of the Zaza).

As history shows, before the Armenian ethnocide (Turk.: *soykırım*), the estimations about the Zaza people's population in their homeland region outnumbered the Christian and Kurdish population although the Armenian population was close in number (Olson 1989:18-19).

Estimation of the Zaza people reaches from one to four (Haig 2001:181; Çelker 1993:43) and up to six millions (Extra & Gorter 2001:336-340; Aygen 2010:1). A realistic scenario gives a figure of three to four million (Hennerbichler 2004:197), which makes them the second largest Turkish minority besides the Kurmanji speaking Kurds (Haig 2001:181; Andrews cit. in Höhlig 1997:115).[7]
Statistics given in Turkey before 2006 are questionable due to Turkish politics, all the more as data of minority populations from the Zaza homeland are not made public (last census in 1962) and the demographic changes are far too intense.[8]

---

[7] Such is true for other minorities too. Circassian people count more than one million (Höhlig 1997:115), whereas others suspect only 200-300.000 of them in Turkey (Boeschoten & Verhoeven 1991:4). In contrast to the Circassian people (Höhlig 1997:115), the Zaza see themselves as a sociological unit, owning a clear cut homeland area around the Eufrates-Tigris headwater.

[8] This discloses the lack of statistical material or its inaccuracy concerning minority matters in Turkey, where minorities are not protected by laws (Andrews cit. in Höhlig 1997:115), due to

Table 2 Estimated Zaza Population

Number	Source	Notice
1-2.5 Mill.	Çarkoğlu & Toprak cit. in Heper (2007:1)	1 Mill. in homeland area, 1.5 Mill. in West-Turkey or Diaspora
1,25 Mill.	Cuinet, Selenoy & Seydlitz (1896)	Historical Map of Dispersion (3.4.1.1.2)
1.5 Mill.	Andrews (2002:123)	Census 1965
1-4 Mill.	Haig (2001:181); Çelker (1993:43)	
3 Mill.	Andrews (2002:121)	Refers back to an International Relations census from 1977
4 Mill.	Paul (2009:545)	1.5-2 Mill. in homeland, the same amount in Diaspora
6 Mill.	Extra (2001:336-340) Aygen (2010:1-2)	Do not divide in Diaspora and homeland

Even recent raising figures (May 2006) contribute to more than 11 million Kurdish people in Turkey, whereas one third is constituted by the Zaza people. The estimation suspects 1.5 million Zaza people who are living in their homeland and more than another million in the West of Turkey (Çarkoğlu & Toprak cit. in Heper 2007:1; A). Besides that, close to 700.000 are guessed to live in the Diaspora out of a total of six million (Aygen 2010:1-2; 2.3.1.4; 2.3.4.6). It is therefore astonishing, how little they are recognized publically in the Turkey. One reason will be that they are pasted in the larger picture of the Kurdish population, with whom they have a common shared cultural background and a lively neighbourhood (Haig 2001:182; Leezenberg 1993a:12).

---

politically motivated nationalism based on language matters. Up until 2002 the Constitutional law outlines an obstacle or minority groups (Höhlig 1997:116, 120; Oehring 1983. *Die Verfassung der Republik Turkey vom 07. November 1982* [Engl. *The Constitution of the Republic of Turkey from 07th November 1982.*]). Since 2003 adjustment concerning these matters is apparent, also a clear cut since 2009 when a policy of freedom, at the official level, for minority languages took place.

2 The Zaza

The Turkish term for "minorities" is derived from the Ottoman subject *millet* (2.3.3.4; 3.1.1; 3.6; 0). The origin goes back to the Arabic word *mıllah* (ملة) and literally means "nation". Its initially religious connotation of non-Islamic "sect", transforms in modern Turkish to "nation", describing social units with a common language or culture (Seufert & Kubaseck 2004:69). Some consider the initial religious meaning of *millet*, was replaced by the term *ümmet* in Turkish (Ziya Gökalp cit. in Berkes 1959:77). The expression *millet* nowadays is used for all non-Turkish cultures or minorities (Löffler 2005:335; s. Jenkins 2006:40-41). The politicization of the phrase *millet*; since *Ziya Gökalp*, is stressed from many sides, and is caused by the founding of the Republic of Turkey as a multiethnic state (Heine 1988:116; Nestmann 2002:548; Fasold 1993:3; more on Turkey see 3.1-3.4). The head and leadership of a religious group in the Ottoman Empire was sometimes also called *millet*. They represented the religious group to the Sultanate and were given the position of an official (Yonan 1992:11). Unfortunately, only in the 19th century, acknowledged non-Islamic minorities or microcultures within the Ottoman Empire were given the status of a *millet*. Those 17 *millets* were represented by the Orthodox Christian churches, such as the Roman Catholics, Samaritans, Karaites, the Greek, Syrian, Aramaic, Armenian and Assyrian people groups as well as the Jewish people minority (a *millet* could be split into smaller ones). Not given any status of official recognition or millet were the Kurds, Zaza, Laz, Alevis, Circassian or other language or religion related clusters.

So when we speak of the Zaza people in Turkey we refer to an officially not recognized microculture that are not a millet and did and do not form an independent religious group or were represented by a leadership organization. This is the more startling as the Northern Group is part of the huge Islamic sect – although this is debatable - of Alevism which intermingles through Kurds, Zaza and Turks (Şener 1993).

2.1.1 Origin of the People Name

To understand the naming of this people it is necessary to recognize a linguistical and religious division in at least three main dialects and two Islamic sects. The main split consists of a differentiation in a Northern (NZ) and Southern / Central group (SZ). Regarding language issues, an additional separation of the central or Eastern Group (EZ) comes in focus. From a religious point of view the NZ are Alevis based on a mystical view of Islam, called in Turkish *alevilik*

(Alevism). The SZ are Sunni Muslims following the teaching of the Hanafi school, in contrast Kurds are mainly from the Shafi'i school (Nestmann 2002:548; 2.2.8.1; 2.3.3.2.5; 2.3.3.5; Table 22).

There are manifold theories about the origin of the term *Zaza*, as well as the *Zaza people* which are given below. Naming of people groups happens mostly from outside (exonym) and not from within the people (endonym), hence many factors count to this process (Payne 1997:13). A closer investigation on the variety of speculations asks for general objectives that need to be considered (ibid.).

In general it could be said that minority groups owe their designation often to *larger* people groups from outside that is an *exoterm* (Paul 2009:545). Those notations are forms of epithet or opprobrious names. This is originally also the case with the term *Zaza* that took a pejorative connotation (see below and :545), whereas nowadays the term shows more neutrality and is used for the whole group. The term *Dım(i)li* in contrast is an *endoterm* and mainly used from the Southern Group (:545; RH 2008).

2.1.1.1 Zaza and Zazaki

According to Selcan the name Zaza is reflected by a social unit (a tribe) called Zāzā which is mentioned in a "Genealogy of Kures" called *Secerê Kurês* from the year 1329/30 AD (Selcan 1998:119). 300 years later Evliyā Çelebi (1650 AD) again uses the name Zāzā for a social unit in the Bingöl area. N. Sakaoğlu refers to a small scale social unit with the same name in the Sivas region in 1744. J. G. Taylor, the British consul of Erzurum confirms this in 1866 (1868:304).

All these instances demonstrate the existence of a people group in the Euphrates (tk. *Fırad*) and Tigris (tk. *Dicle*) spring area who were known by the name Zaza, but reflect no proof that the group called itself Zaza or what they were called by other groups. It is even not clear if the modern Zaza people are the same as with the formerly likewise called tribes formerly called by that name. Yet the progression of a people name out of a tribal name occurs often (see extensive discussion about language issue 2 and the naming of the people group 2.1.3.2).

In contrary to those suggestions one will find obscure derivations. Just to mention one, the suggestion that the term *Zaza* displays a phonetical derivation of *Sasa* a descendant of Israel / Jacob who occurs in the Hebrew Bible (1Chronicles 2,33). Other more serious ideas are reflected below (2.1.3.1).

2.1.1.2 "Stammerer"

One suggestion about the name Zaza leads to the origin of "stammerer" in regard to ridiculing the numerous flectional particles on family and kinship terms (*za-*, *-za-*, *-za*), hence focussing on phonetical malapropism (RH 2008 *Zaza and Zazaki*; Hadank 1932:1; MacKenzie [1989] 2002:541-542).

Along with the argument that the term means "stammerer", goes the observation that the Zaza people are counted as hillbillies by other larger ethnicities in Diyarbakır (MT 2008 *Zazaki*; Hejaro 2007: *Kurdische Dialekte/Lehceyên Kurdî*). The reason for that reaches back to former times when they were popular for brigandage, aggression and plunder (Heper 2007:41). Besides the Kurds, who were known for similar undertakings but as nomads in these days, the Ottomans and later Turkish people took up this bad reputation surrounding the Zaza and refer to them in this way till today. (IS 2010 *Diyarbakır*).

The Zaza can follow the latter argument but do not see any connection to the former about using their flectional particle and the name Zaza, especially as they do not use these particles too often in daily language, as they refer to kinship and family designation only (personal communication).

2.1.1.3 *Zone Ma* and Geographical References

The Zaza ethnos from the Northern Group (NZ) refer to themselves by the term *zone ma* ("our language") in contrast to the Southern Group that used and seldom uses nowadays the naming *Dımıli* (2.1.1.4.1). The anthropological term for this phenomenon is called "self-referent or auto-denomination" (Payne 1997:13). *Zone ma* as a generalisation implies the meaning of "us", "people" or "human beings within the own ethnicity" (ibid.).

A self-designation like *zone ma* indicates that there was no need for the Zaza to describe themselves to outer organisations. Since this expression was of no use to identify themselves before the officials, it became obsolete as public administration grew. Within the people group the Zaza people used the names of their tribes (*aşiret*) or their priestly castes (*ocak*) to identify kin (Cengiz rec. in Neyzi 2002:95).

A look at the history of the Ottoman Empire and the Republic of Turkey shows that the *millet* (microcultures within the Turkish majority) were always separated and developed their own organizational and cultural structures. When there was movement from within the *millets* towards the official system, the individual referred to itself being a Turk. Mostly, *millets* stayed within their social unit (3.1.1; 3.6). From the time, when the bureaucratic political system in Turkey was established (1923), it became necessary to refer to a specific identification in contrast to the Kurds or other minority groups as well as to the Turks.

Another way to express one's background takes place by the suffix *–ij*, which is added to proper nouns and expresses geographical, familial or tribal descent (e.g. *Çermugij* "one from Çermug" or *Balabanıj* "one from the small scale social unit Balaban"). This way of referencing is validated by old oral traditions (Hayıg 2007).

2.1.1.4 Nuri Dersimi - Kırmancki

Another identity marking from within the Zaza people was introduced by *Mehmet Nuri Dersimi* who wrote during his Syrian exile *Kürdistan Tarıhınde Dersim* ([1952] 1988; Gündüzkanat 1997:43; 2.1.1.4). He called first the Northern Group *Kırmanc / Kırmancki* (Selcan 1998:121; Neyzi 2002:95). His derivation follows the term for *Kurmanc / Kurmanji* and he referred thereby to pro-Kurdish political activities (Gündüzkanat 1997:43; Leezenberg 1993a:8; Olson 1989:28, 35; see below). Down to the present day this undertaking precipitates controversial discussions about the origin of the Zaza people (see 1.1.3) or the relationship to the Kurmanji speaking Kurdish people. Besides political reasons it would also be plausible if *Dersimi* understood his distinction as a motivation to Zaza speaking people to separate themselves from the Kurdish majority.

His list of Kurmanji Kurdish and Zaza small scale social units as well as his realistic view about the separation of Alevi and Sunni Zaza and Kurds offer helpful insights into the conflicts in the past and the situation today (Andrews 2002c:123-125; Bumke 2002:514-516; Olson 1989:35).

2.1.1.5 Other Notations (Dımıli, Kızılbaş, Alevis, Nusayri or Dunbeli)

In literature one can also find the names *Dımıli/Dimili/Dimila/Dımili/Dımle* (Hadank 1932:1-6; Izady 1992:150; Kreyenbroek & Sperl 2002:70; Selcan 1998:121), *Kızılbaş/Qızılbash* ("red head"; Izady 1992:150; Baumann 2007:329; HT 2010), *Alevis/Alewis* (as a derivation from practised Alevis; Sweetnam/Jacobson 2004:225-226) or *Nusayri*. Other concepts about the origin of the term Zaza are linked to theories of their origin. Those will be discussed later (2.1.3).

2.1.1.5.1 Dımli / Dımıli and the Daylam-Thesis

The name *Dımli* / *Dımıli* and its derivations, is mainly used for SZ (Selcan 1998:121). One theory claims that the phrase *Dımli* / *Dımıli* evolved from the term *Daylam* or *Daila*. Alternatively this region is termed as *Dailäm*, *Dayläm* or *Dailâm*. Thus it is argued that the origin of the Zaza people lies in the province of *Dailam* or *Daylam* in ancient Persia and modern northern Iran, close to the South-eastern Caspian Sea (Hadank 1930:18; Olson 1989:95; detailed in 2.1.3.1.1). The idea behind this is that phonetical derivation and metathesis led to a rearrangement of the *l* and *m*. In Armenian the Zaza are "termed *delmik* / *dlmik*, and the like (Yuzbashian, 146-51), which must be derived from *dēlmīk Deylamite" (Asatrian 1995a und b *Dımlī*; Vahman & Asatrian 1990:267-275).

The Daylam-Thesis became the most favourite within the Zaza discussion about their origin. Historically the medieval *Daylamites* at the Caspian Sea established a number of kingdoms of which the *Buwayhids* resp. *Buyids* reigned during 932-1062 (Izady 1992:43). Names like that of the ruler *Sherzil* (983-990) indicate the ending *zil* which means in SZ "heart" (:44-45). Yet the phonetical proximity from the old Daylam to Zazaki is amazing. In addition Izady states that today's population of the Alburz mountain range in Daylam exists of Kurds who came there in the 16th century AD / 11th century AH including small pockets of Dımliki i.e. Zazaki speakers (:45). Some of the Kurds living in these region practice Alevism as part of the *Twelver Shi'ite* and *Ismâ'ili* influence in Iran (ibid.).

One can question why the language indicating suffix *–ki* like in Zaza*ki* is not given in the phrase *Dımli* / *Dımıli* as it is seldom mentioned *Dımliki* / *Dımılki*. This argument would support the Daylam-theory since it points to the derivation of a related proper name.

In the same way the word for Caspian Sea in Zaza is *Dengızê Hazari* (Engl. Thousand Sea), whereas the largest sea in the Zaza area is named in a similar way. As a loanword it is even in Turkish called *Hazar Gölü* (Engl. Thousand Sea). The phenomenon of taking over proper names from the homeland to the new settling area during mass migration processes is popular and reaches back to biblical times as for the naming of e.g. the *Euphrates* river or the mountain *Ararat* etc. that are mentioned in the creation story or the origin of mankind (Gen 2,14 and 8,4; RH 2010).

Another argument towards the Daylam-Theory is found in the linguistical closeness to Gorani / Hawrami (2.2.1.1) and the fact that their origin is as well suggested to be in that Persian region called *Daylam* (Mann cit. in Hadank 1930:17-18 and Hadank 1932; Izady 1992:43-44). The linguistical proximity of Zazaki, Hewrami and the dialects spoken in the modern province of Daylam is felt by the River People and scientists too (RH 2006 *Zaza and their neighbours* and 2008 *Zaza und Zazaki*; Temizbas 2003 *Dimli: Wir,* ...). But linguistical proximity is just an indicator. Research on this subject is listed below (2.1.3; 2.2.1.3.3).[9]

2.1.1.5.2 Kızılbaş / Qızılbaş or Alevis

In literature about the Zaza ethnos, the term *Qizilbaş* or *Kizilbaş* (Tk. Kızılbaş) often comes into focus. In Western literature on the *Qizilbaş* the form *Kizilbaş* prevails. I therefore use it here too. The Turkish term *Kızılbaş* is largely used by publications produced in Turkey. This phrase is primarily connected to Turkish, Kurdish, Arabian and Zaza Alevism (Tk. *Alevilik*).[10] Hence, within the Zaza people, it refers for the most part to the Northern Group (NZ; 2.3.3.2.2; 2.3.3.3). As the history of the expression demonstrates (see below), it was used from outside people groups, as an exonym, to designate

- a non-Muslim and non-Christian religious group in Eastern Anatolia (e.g. from the Armenian Patriarchate in Olson 1989:19; Heper 2007:36; Izady 1992:45),
- a religious but Muslim mystical group in Eastern Anatolia, without mentioning ethnical differences (Steinbach 1996:377),
- a variety of heterodox groups in Anatolia by adopting a strongly pejorative flavour (Bumke 2002:517 footnote 6),
- an ethnical distinction between Kurdish (Kurmanji, Sorani), Turkish and Zaza people, going along with the religious difference of Sunni and Shi'ite rites (Kehl-Bodrogi 2002:503-504), that is why *Kizilbaş* is sometimes used by non-Zaza to refer to the whole people group (NZ and SZ),
- non-Sunni groups that are in opposition to the political system in charge (Kehl-Bodrogi 2002:506-507).

---

[9] Linguistical affinity is not always a proof, but at least it gives hints on people's origin or history, as well as its development. The example of the *Kaingang* People of Brasilia and the assumed affinity to a Micronesian people group which lives isolated on an Island in the Pacific demonstrates this quite well (Pericliev 2009).

[10] Alevism as religion covers Turkish, Kurmanji, Zaza and Arabic speaking people groups (Kieser 2000:396-397; 2.3.3.3).

The term *Kızılbaş* / *Qızılbaş* refers back to medieval times. Nowadays it is used as an epithet from the Sunnis (also Zaza) in Eastern Anatolia for the Alevis. Under the influence of Gnosticism, Christianity and *Zoroastrianism* / *Parsiism* (used in India and Pakistan for devotees of Zarathustra) / *serduşt* (Zazaki), the underlying animistic Anatolian religion became a remnant, which migrated into a mixture of religions or better, a religious conglomerate (2.3.1.2.1). This conglomerate discharged into the mystical Islamic fraternity of the *Safavids* in Ardabil (North-western Iran) and later on by the end of the medieval times into the mystical Islamic school of the Shi'ites (15th century). Steinbach calls this the transition of "non-orthodox Islamic religious groups" into mysticism (1996:376-377). Sultan *Selim* in 1514 consolidated his regime over the heart land of today's Turkey. The *Kızılbaş* were in opposition to him and were declared apostates and outlaws (Allouche 1983:110-115). This new direction transformed the formerly hazy folk religion of the Anatolian population into a uniform community of faith.

But they feared the Sunni oppression so much that they started the attitude of *takiye*, in which they went underground with their belief system. Sometimes even their children didn't know what their religion was called. Every time repression increased, the rule of *takiye* became more popular. Even in the European Diaspora the principle of *takiye* was used, which is why you always get a "yes", if you ask a Northern Zaza either if he is a Turk, a Kurd or a Zaza (Sökefeld 2008a:20-22; 2.3.1.4; 2.3.4.6).

The underlying animistic and syncretistic religion of the Turkish population in Anatolia influenced the surrounding people groups significantly (2.3.1.2.4.). The Shabak and Gorani practice a faith is close to Alevism. Its rites include daily bowing to the rising sun and moon and the incantation of hymns for the occasion. This veneration is found in all of the Zaza religions, e.g. the ban to curse by the sun (2.3.3.2.2; Asatrian 2009). Izady sums up the forerunning ancient religions as "ancient Aryan cults". They led to modern *Alevism, Yârsânism* or *Yezidism* (1992:150-151; Kreyenbroek & Rashow 2005: xiv-xv Preface, 3). Those extreme Shi'a sects with a Sufi'istic background form the mystic orientation of Islam. Yet they are often claimed and considered as pagan or non-Islamic sects by Sunni Muslim.

After the dead of the Safavid ruler *Shah Ismail* in 1516 (Izady 1992:150-151), the mystical *Bektaşi* fraternity, founded by the charismatic *Haci Bektaş Veli*, became the religious centre of the *Kizilbaş*. *Haci Bektaş Veli* was from Khorasan in Northeastern Iran. He ministered and formed his religious order in the 13th century. Political and religious change caused by the proclamation of the *Twelver Shi'ite* and the *Ismâ'ili* in Persia and the resulting emergence of the Sunni school, under the Ottomans, marginalized the Safavid order to Folk Islam and a conservative use of the *Qur'anic* teaching and the *Hadith* (Islamic tradition; see Kehl-Bodrogi 2002:503-504).

It was within this process that the Ottoman rulers recognized the chiliastic and emotive bias of this movement that was expressed by

- an extreme adoration of Hz. Ali (Hz. Mohammed's cousin),
- the belief of the incarnation of divinity in humans, and
- the cult of saints.

The rebellions of those *Safavid* and other mystical orders against the Ottoman Empire in the 15th and 16th century were repulsed by Ottoman units from the second half of the 16th century onwards (Kehl-Bodrogi 2002:505-506). This military action brought forth the connotation of *Kizilbaş / Qızılbaş* as being in opposition to the Sunni Ottoman Empire (ibid.). Even today this connotation is used in political discussions (see below).

The Turkish expression *Kızılbaş / Qızılbaş* means "Redhead" and refers back to the traditional twelve-pieced red turban that was used in the Middle Ages by the mainly Turkmen members of the above mentioned religious conglomeration in Anatolia (Steinbach 1998:377).

With time, the phrase was narrowed down to mean those people groups who practise Alevism and was hence replaced by the term *Alevi / Alewi* (Ruciyar 2008 *Aleviten* ... [Alevis]; Bumke 2002:512; Kehl-Bodrogi 1989 und 2002:506; Kieser 2000:385-389).

But whereas the *Bektaşi* movement attracted followers of the Kızılbaş, because it stayed within the Sunni direction of Islam, the *Alevi*, from an orthodox Sunni viewpoint are considered and recognized as non-Muslim. The reason for that is found in the practice that they do not "take the Five Pillars seriously, pay only lip-services to Qur'ânic precepts and show no recognition whatsoever of their duties to God" (Bumke 2002:516; HT 2010; Izady 1992:43). Sunnis perceive them as "dirty" (Tk. *pis*) and express their contempt by stating that "killing one Kızılbaş, is worth more than killing 71 ordinary gâvur (unbelievers)" (Bumke 2002:517). This became obvious during WW I. and the preceding Armenian ethnocide when the Ottoman and Unionist movement tried to use the head of the *Bektaşi* order *Çelebi Ahmed Cemaleddin Efendi* to include the Der-

2 The Zaza

sim Zaza under his custody (Kieser 2000:396). In the same way in which *Çelebi* led the *Mevlevi Alayı* during WW I., the Alevis were asked to form an own army. They rejected this heavily and broke with *Çelebi* (:397). At least, since then the *Bektaşi* and the *Alevi* movement are institutionally split but practice few rituals in the same way, like the teaching of the "four gates" (Bumke 2002:512) or the day of remembrance on *Hacı Bektaş Veli* (Langer 2008:102-103).

The phrase *Kızılbaş / Qızılbaş* nowadays implies historical and pejorative connotations and is not used any more for Alevis at all.

2.1.1.5.3 Gini and Nusayri

A phrase that Selcan mentions but that until now was not discussed is *Gini*. He assumes that this name reflects the Kurdish naming of Zaza in the *Zara*, *Karabel* and *Sivas* area referring to a small scale social unit called *Ginian* (Selcan 1998:122).

Another term that sometimes intermingles with the Zaza people is *Nusayri*. It counts back to an expression that is either developed from the medieval Christian "Nazarenes" resp. "Nestorians" or a rebel active at that time called *Narseh*, who had to do with the people of the Zaza homeland (Izady 1992:150). This terminology could either be a mistaking of
- the Arabic term 'Alawi', who are also called *Nusairi*, in contrast to Alevi (Andrews 2002c:21) or
- a people group that is religiously closely related to Alevis, due to the fact that both are part of the *Cult of Angels*[11] (Izady 1992:150).

During the ethnographical research the term occurred only subliminally and mainly in reference to practices that are maintained within Alevism. It seems likely that there is a rudimentary knowledge of Christian practice and origin from which the term is derived and that is nowadays rejected (2.3.1.2.3; RH 2006; QN 2005 worldview).

2.1.1.5.4 Dunbeli, Dumbeli, Donbeli or Dombeli

Historical documents from the Ottoman Epoch around the 15th century present an ethnicity in Syria / Iraq. This small scale society named *Donbeli*, sometimes also called *Dumbeli*, *Dombeli* or *Dunbeli* moved to Diyarbakır and spread out to the North. There they settled; through a phonetic assimilation to Osmanlı Turk-

---

[11] The "Cult of Angels" as is practiced from Kurmanji, Zazaki and Arabic speaking groups involves the worshippers called 'Alawis, Alevis, Kizilbaş and Nusairi (Izady 1992:150).

ish, Farsi and Kurmanji, they were called and / or later called themselves *Dımıli* (Çağlayan 2011). Although the phonetic assimilation is proved, this theory has to stand some questions, which are similar to the request about the origin in Daylam (2.1.1.5.1 and 2.1.3.1.1). First, why is there absolutely no reference in oral traditions about any nomadic lifestyle or a larger move? Second, the *Dunbeli* are called a small scale society of a larger social unit. If, for instance the larger group were the Zaza, then this group would have turned to the recent motherland with their move and then, the argument would be a proof of the long ranging settlement in their recent homeland. The term Dunbeli appears in poems and songs of the Daylam area (Southern Caspian area). One popular poem about a lady is called *Xanımê Dunbeli* which speaks about a lady that emigrated in the 19th century to the region of Daylam. Some are suggesting that she was a Zaza lady (2nd Symposiyum of Zaza Language in Bingol).

The argument of some researchers is, that the *Dunbeli* called themselves "Kurds". So they would have settled on the western area of the main Kurmanji native soil. As a summary, the argument proves the existence of the Zaza in general in their recent homeland area a long time ago. It is very obvious, that this is only a hint and not a proof per se, since there is still little detailed information as to whether the *Dunbeli* and the *Dımıli* are the same and if they really moved back to their homeland or if they just resettled.

2.1.1.6 Summary

What could be said about the origin of the term *Zaza*? The naming comes from outside the group (exonym) and was used as a differentiation against other people groups. Within the Zaza, folk's terms like *Zone Ma* (Engl. our language)/ *Dımli / Dımili / Dumbeli*, the name of the small scale social unit (*aşiret*) or the priestly caste (*ocak*) were used to refer to someone's kin (endonym).

As was shown the derivation of the language name *Zazaki* from *Zaza* underwent wide spread acceptance. Scholars (Paul, Haig, Blau, etc.) as well as the people group themselves (RH, MT etc.) use it nowadays as a standard expression to describe the people group living in the Euphrates (tk. *Fırad*) and Tigris (tk. *Dicle*) headwater area, forming the main inhabitants. The term *Zaza* outweighed designations like *Zone Ma / Dımli / Dımili / Dumbeli* or other religiously or politically motivated connotations (*Kırmancki, Kizilbaş, Alevis* etc.). Also from the official side (SIL Ethnologue, UNESCO, EU etc.) this people group is now recognized as the *Zaza*. The origin of the term could be either a derivation from the kinship indicating particle *–za*, which was often heard by foreigners when Zaza spoke with each other. Therefore it was a malapropism and used as "stammerer" or someone who's language is not skilled. The terms used from within the Zaza people did not get wide acceptance as is often the case in non-dominant minority languages. Even the theory of a Daylam migration (2.1.3.1.1) did not prove to be influential for the naming of the Zaza people.

The small scale society called *Dunbeli* and its variations is suggested to have been moving to the Zaza homeland and passing on the naming *Dımılı* to the Southern and Eastern Group. This argument gives some proof to the long ranging settlement of the Zaza in their recent homeland.

2.1.2 Question of Identity - Kurds and / or Zaza or Zaza-Kurds

The terms "Kurd", "Kurdistan" and "Kurdish" are in general not defined. They cover a wide spectrum of people groups with different cultural and linguistic background. However the imaginary border is either geographically or linguistically given by intelligibility and ethnical separation (Asatrian 2009:1).

Before we discuss the question as to whether the Zaza people belong to the wider Kurdish ethnicities it is necessary to remember the e*mic* (from inside) and *etic* (from outside) point of view in ethnography. As such the researcher needs to take in account whether a source is from outside the people group like most Western linguists and ethnographers (*etic*) or from the ethnicity itself (*emic*). Also one has to be aware of the fact that the political situation before 1960 did not make it necessary to make any distinction as to whether the Zaza were part of the Kurds or not. With the uprising of Kurdish nationalism this changed and the situation called for their either being a separate group or participating as small group in the larger Kurdish movement.

The question of identity concerning the Zaza people has an inwardly and an outwardly directed perspective. Outwardly the differentiation to the Kurmanji, Sorani, Bahdeni or Kermanshah speaking ethnicities is challenging and reducing the energies of the Zaza populace oriented towards self-dependence. This is mainly due to the energy that is taken to strengthen the cohesive links within the Zaza community. Inwardly the three main dialect groups struggle on different levels with the assimilation effects that are initiated by the strong Turkish influence in the education and public sector. As such the Zaza dialect groups hold different stands towards each other as well as to the Kurdish movement or the Turkish assimilation attempts.

When studying the naming of the Zaza people, as is done above, one immediately enters the political sphere, especially the question whether the Zaza are Kurds or not (in detail discussed in Hennerbichler 2004:197-198). The discussion reaches far back to the rebellion of Sheikh Said (1925; 2.3.1.3.2) and went back and forth during history. It reached a new climax during the 1980s, when the Zaza people in Europe began their own publications and establishing of independent cultural (European *Dersim derneği* association) and religious clubs (*Alevi cemat* houses).

Preceding this development the *Kurdish nationalist movement* emphasized Kurdish nationalism based on the Kurmanji language issue. Obviously this was a simple takeover of Turkish nationalism based on the Turkish language proclamation (Turkish constitution sec. 3; Höhlig 1997:120; Oehring 1983:301-310). Hence this question needs to be discussed before going further. A summary of this discussion is given here, including a solution to solve this discussion and move further to deeper identity questions of the Zaza people.

The Zaza people are recently represented by
- a large group that assimilated into the "Turkish" culture, without claiming any loss of identity (~40 %), using Turkish at home and practising intermarriage,
- a large group that identifies with the "Kurds" in Turkey (~40 %), although only few understand and speak Kurmanji,
- a small but strongly promotional group of political motivated Zaza which proactively works linguistically and anthropologically towards the Kurds (~10 %; Vatê group),
- a small but growing group of Zaza working on political, linguistical and anthropological grounds towards autonomous perception from in- and outside the people group (~10 %).

As the numbers tell, the division is strong and leads to frustration among the Zaza people on the one side and extremist approaches on the other.

The "Struggle of Identity" (Germ. "Identitätskampf") which is effective, leads to confusion as to which group is really "political". Defamation, accusation of working with the Turkish secret service or promoting "separation" and mutual refusal of research results are ongoing endeavours on both sides. However one gets the impression that the pro-Kurdish party is more aggressive in defaming those Zaza that work towards self-esteem or self-dependence. This is the more astonishing as those are the lager group and would not lose anything due to their hold on to the larger Kurmanji speaking ethnicity. As such the power-flow goes from the larger to the smaller society.

2.1.2.1 Argument by Linguistics - Anthropological Considerations

The question as to whether the Zaza members are "Kurds" is answered differently. The close connection of culture and language in Zazaki started with research by Hadank. He first formulated the thesis that Zazaki outlines an individual language group. McKenzie followed that approach. Hence the discussion nowadays goes along scientifically proved linguistic lines (explicitly Hennerbichler 2004:132). Looking at this matter from a cultural perspective one could call it a gray zone. Researchers who adjust to the question anthropologically arrive at the conclusion that Zazaki consists of a dialect of Kurmanji. Others coming from a linguistical or political point of view call it a regional dialect of "Kurdish" (Germ. "Regiolekt" in Reiß & Vermeer 1991:22). In consequence they speak of the Zaza people being "Kurds" (Hennerbichler 2004:198).[12]

Haig proves, exemplified by Zülfü Selcan's grammar (1998), how the conflict is sometimes (un-) intentionally argued out (2001:182).[13] Recent research formulates the subject of politically motivated activity as follows,

> Like TRT, Med TV too is concerned to nurture 'Kurdish' folk dance, national costumes and music. Like TRT, it propagates a standardized Kurdish, as it teaches literacy to children whose first language may be Turkish, German or Swedish. News is presented first in Kurdish (Kurmanci) and then repeated in Turkish for those Kurds who speak a different dialect (for example Zazaki). (Houston 2001:128).

> ... Kurdish nationalism as a transnational practice is politicizing Kurdish subjects (in the context of the national policy of multiculturalism) in Sydney as much as those living in Istanbul or Frankfurt. The first Zazaki (a Kurdish dialect) radio programme in the World made its debut in Melbourne in 1997 on one of the multicultural / multilingual stations. (Houston 2001:129-130).

The argument using anthropological issues forces the closeness of religions (Sunnism, Alevism), celebrations (*Newroz*; *Kormışkan*, *Hewt Mala*; *Lent*) and

---

[12] An extensive discussion on the arguments from both sides is summarized in Hennerbichler (2004:198). My own summary will follow.
[13] Although *Selcan* offers the most detailed overview of literature dealing with the Zaza people, he misses works written by authors who are politically active and closely linked to Kurdish organisations. For example the Zaza author *Malmisanij* (Malmîsanij!) and the group called *vate* around him, publishing dictionaries and ethnological studies and the bi-monthly magazine "vate" (Haig 2001:182). This group was one of the first to publish and spread monolingual Zaza material in Turkey.

ethnomusicological considerations. One could easily find congruities in these areas but also differences (see below). Looking from this angle the Kurmanji speaking Kurds and the Zaza emphasize more their differences than their similarities.

2.1.2.2 Argument by Culture and Language

If one went as far as Hennerbichler, who stated that the term "Kurds" includes all "mountaineers of the Zagros massive and its extensions", then definitely the Zaza will be included, as they view themselves one of those people groups living within that range (2004:133-134). The shortcoming of his approach lies in the disregard of ethnical-linguistic factors (Fasold 1993:2-3). The homogeneity that is propagated by this statement is not reflected by the cultural diversity that is reflected within the so-called "Kurds". The expression "Kurds" embraces at least four distinct units, namely the *Sorani*, the *Bahdeni*, the *Kurmanji* and the Southern Kurdish dialect group. Other classifications are given by a grouping of *Northern Kurdish* (Kurmanji dialects), *Central Kurdish* (Sorani / Bahdeni) and *Southern Kurdish* (e.g. Kermanshah, Feyli etc.). For most people from Turkey (e.g. Turks, Kurds, Zaza, etc.) the term refers to the Kurmanji speaking people group.

Gündüzkanat cites three Turkish sources that researched the Zaza people in Turkey (1997:38): *Nazmi Sevgen* (1950) a Turkish officer, *İsmail Beşikci* (1960) a Turkish sociologist and *Hasan Resit Tankut* (1994). The former connected them to Turks, whereas the two latter stated very clearly that the Zaza people are an individual and distinctive people group with their own language in Turkey (2.1.2.3). Such rare emic research is notable due to the strict pro-Turkish language policy (see Turkish constitution) in Turkey.

Looking at it from a distance we face a problem between research results and the societal opinion of the two involved parties by some. Recent research including sociolinguistic survey reveals that there are no clear cut lines between the groups on dialectical and cultural grounds (following Grimes 1995). Also the Western Iranian languages of Southern Caspian influence:

- Gorani and Hewrami / Hawrami,
- Tāleshī (Talysh),
- Southern Tātī (Herzendī; Tati),
- Gilaki,
- Semnānī (Semnani),

2 The Zaza

- Laki,
- Bakhtiari,
- Luri,
- Sangsarī,
- Māzandarānī, and the
- Northern Iranian dialects of Shabak, Bajalan, Zengana and Kakai (Leezenberg 1993b:1-8),

are not clearly distinguished from the main Kurdish dialects or languages (2.2.1; 3.4.1.1.4). An area of closely related languages (language belt) reaching from the north-western area of the Zaza people down to the south-eastern part of West-Iran (Gorani) demonstrates obviously the close relationship of these languages and dialects (Leezenberg 1993a:10-12; Olson 1989:1-4; Paul & Gippert 2009; 2.2.1). Looking back in history, political developments and mass migration movements reveal the development of the recent language belt. Unfortunately, due to lack of written material, we do not know how this splitting or the movements were caused or how they were accomplished.

At the moment it is hard to distinguish how the Zaza will be placed in future. In reality there are two parties, one that distances the Kurds on cultural, linguistical and political grounds and another that counts itself as being part of the wider understood "Kurds".

2.1.2.3 Written Interior and Exterior Evidential

Apart from the rich oral traditions in the Zaza culture there is little written material about the history of this people group due to the late development of literacy in Zazaki. The existing evidence is closely connected with the history of the Kurds. Most sources therefore come from outside the people group and have to be looked at critically since they are motivated by religion or politics. Zülfü Selcan, in his work *Grammatik der Zaza-Sprache* (Engl. *Grammar of the Zaza-Language*) offers an extensive overview about the history and development of Zaza literature and its connection to Kurdish material (see also Hadank 1932:9-14). He lists the scientific research on the Zaza chronologically and whether there is

- none or less political background, meaning no differentiation of Zaza and Kurmanji, due to lack of recognition (mainly exterior sources; see p. 7-11),
- a pure linguistical interest on the Zaza language at all (p. 12-46), or

- sources with Kurdish background predominantly assuming Zazaki to be Kurdish (p. 64-94), or
- sources with Turkish background assuming that Zaza is either a Turkish language or a Kurdish dialect (p. 95-105).

His research demonstrates that early scientific interest started by mother tongue speakers due to religious and historical interest and endeavours to preserve the Zaza culture (16th – 17th century). This motivation lasts through the centuries and shows some of the sociological pressure that minorities in Eastern Anatolia experience. The next period is marked by Russian and European linguists and ethnographers (19th century). The 20th century started by politically motivated writers with the goal of demonstrating either Kurdish dependency or independency. The question of identity became central then and until today. Due to massive oppression and the instable political situation of Eastern Anatolia one can speak of a literarily *huge scientific silence* during the years 1906 to 1963 (Selcan 1998:105). The recent movement on literature started in 1980 with Zaza in the European Diaspora (2.3.1.4; 2.3.4.6). I will outline Selcan's findings in short.

Besides the Kurdish works on history like *Sherefname* (see below), the first written work on Zazaki is to be found in Arabic as a document of religious poems called *Mewlid Nebi* (Birthday Poem of the Prophet; Arab. *mawlid* Tk. *mevlid*) published in the province Diyarbakır. *The genre of mewlid* describes poetic rhymes, often they are about the birth of the prophet Hz. Mohammed (Appendix 5).[14] They, the *mewlids*, were written down and published by *Ahmed Xasê* (400 copies; 1898) and *Usman Effendi* (Osman Efendi) around 1903 respectively 1933. This was the most popular one in Zazaki (*Siverek*; 2.3.3.5.2). Even though he got official permission to publish in Zazaki, the intolerance of the authorities led him to exile on the Island of Rhodes.

Nuri Mehmet Dersimi 1893 was born in Axzonike / Dersim (Tunceli) and educated in *Hozat, Harput* (Elazığ) and *İstanbul*. As an eyewitness of Armenian massacres in Erzincan in the years 1914/1915 he became politically active. He worked as a consultant to *Seyit Rıza* during the *Koçgiri* rebellion in the Sivas area (1920 AD / 1338 AH; 2.1.1.4; 2.1.2.3; 2.3.1.1; 2.3.1.3.2) and afterward he moved back to Dersim. After the beginning of the Dersim rebellion in

---

[14] Appendix 1 is a copy of the original *mewlid* (Arabic). It was transcribed by RH in the recently used Zazaki alphabet that was introduced by Jacobson in *Zazaca Okuma-Yazma El Kitabı* (1997:124-125) and Werner in Todd *A Grammar of Dimili* (2002:157 Appendix G).

1937/1938 AD called *tertele* / *Tertelê Dêrsimi* (2.3.1.1; 2.3.1.3.2; 2.3.3.3) he flew into exile to Syria. As he was not able to get any asylum in an European country and because of fear that the French occupation power would send him back to Turkey he went on to Amman, but came back to Aleppo in Syria where he died in 1973. He is buried in Afrin (Kieser 1997). *Nuri Dersimi*, who was an eye-witness of the massacres of the Armenians, wrote in Turkish *Kurdistan Tarihinde Dersim* (Engl. *Dersim in the history of Kurdistan*) during his Syrian exile in Aleppo, an extensive historical treatise about the history of the Zaza ([1952] 1988; above 2.1.1.4). It became the ethnographic and geographical standard on the Zaza and their (inter-) relations to the "Kurds" especially the Kurmanji speakers (Gündüzkanat 1997:43). Occasional articles in Zazaki published by Zaza in the Diaspora in trilingual publications became popular from the mid 1970s onward (Diaspora language-Turkish-Zazaki). Starting with *Ronahi* in Zurich (1976), *Özgürlük Yolu* (1977) or *Roja Welat* (1978), the first Zazaki monolingual publication in Stockholm by *Ebubekir Pamukçu* called *Ayre* (1984-1986) made a breakthrough for Zazaki literature (see extensive list in Bibliography under magazines). Research on the Zaza culture focused primarily on the language and less on ethnographical studies. It started earlier and was mainly from outside (2.2).

Table 3 Differentiation of Zaza and Kurmanji Ethnicities

Author	Reasoning
Sherefname (1596)	Clear differentiation between Zazaki and Kurdish dialects, communication between both language groups is not possible but uses the term "subgroup of Kurdish" (Leezenberg 1993:11; Kreyenbroek & Sperl 2002:35).
Evliya Çelebi (1650)	Clear differentiation between Zazaki and Kurdish dialects, communication between both language groups is not possible but uses the term "subgroup of Kurdish" (Leezenberg 1993:11; Kreyenbroek & Sperl 2002:35).
Spiegel (1871) and Tomaschek (1887)	Call them dialects of New Persian but emphasizes the difference of both dialects such as being independent languages.

All of the following authors support the differentiation by the linguistic argument:

Adranik/ Antranig	(1880 and 1900:111-116)
Friedrich Carl Andreas	[1906] (1916) also in Hadank (1932:18)
Benedictsen / Christensen, Andreas	(1921)
Lentz	(1926:271, 281, 284)
Minorsky	(1928:193 / 1926:243 and 1965:189-194)
İsmail Beşikci (1960)	(cit. in Gündüzkanat 1997:38)
MacKenzie, David Neil	(1961-1962)
Lockwood	(1979:279)
Gernot L. Windfuhr	(1989)
Joyce Blau	(1989)
Ehsan Yarshater	(cit. in Vahman & Asatrian 1990:264-275)
MacKenzie, David Nei	([1989] 2002:541-542)
Olson	(1989:95)
Vahman & Asatrian	(1990:264-275)
Izady	(1992:44-45)
Paul	(1992:73)
Çelker	(1993:42-52)
Tankut (1994)	(cit. in Gündüzkanat 1997:38)
Asatrian, Garnik Serobi	(1995)
Gündüzkanat	(1997:16)
Paul & Haig	(2001:399)
Kreyenbroek & Sperl	(2002)
Hennerbichler	(2004:197)
Nasidze, Ivan et.al.	(2005)
RH *Zaza and Zazaki*	(2008)
Paul & Gippert	(2009)
Windfuhr	(2009)
White *Ethnic differentiation*	(no date)

Sherefname and *Evliya Çelebi* are taken into account by authors who suport the independence of Zazaki as well as those who lack such a differentiation. Reason for that is the term "subgroup" which lacks in itself a clear definition. But one finds the tendency of both authors is that they look at Zazaki as an independent language, when speaking of it.

2.1.2.4 Lack of Differentiation between both Ethnicities

Some authors do not differentiate at all between the Zaza people and the Kurmanji speaking Kurds. They describe Zaza history by calling and promoting it as "Kurdish" history or they consider Zaza leaders as "Kurds". In addition Zazaki is mainly addressed as a Kurdish dialect. Such happens when e.g. the Sheikh Said rebellion (1925 AD) is called a "Kurdish uprising" in the historical succession of others. As is often the case, lacks of knowledge or sometimes political reasons support such use. The following authors did not differentiate the Zaza people from the Kurds, who are then supposed to be Kurmanji speakers.[15]

The following table represents a profile of researchers and their opinion about the relationship between Kurds and Zaza.

Table 4 Lack of Differentiation between both Ethnicities

Author	Reasoning
Lerch (1857-1858)	Calls the Zaza a dialect of Kurdish (1857-1858:69).
Dunmore (1857)	Differs in Dersim-Mountain-Kızılbaş and Village-Kızılbaş. Is aware of their own language in contrast to Turkish (1857:220).
Müller (1864)	Counts Zaza to the Kurdish language branch (1864:228-234).
Geiger (1899)	Zaza is a Kurdish dialect (1899:388, 409, 411).
Justi ([1880] 2006)	Tracks back to fourteenth-century mystic *Jalaluddin bin Yusuf al-Kurani at-Tamliji al-Kurdi*, sixteenth-century Kurdish author *Sharaf Khan Bidlisi* (Sheref Chan) of the chronicles called *Sherefname* (1.2.1) and seventeenth-century Turkish traveller *Evliya Celebi*, who all assume the Zaza being a subgroup of the Kurds and Zazaki a Kurdish dialect (Justi 2006:2, 4).
Riggs (1911)	Calls the Alevi-Zaza Dersim Kurds and differentiates them on religious grounds from Kurmanji Kurds. Uses the term Kızılbaş (1911:741-742).
Sevgen (1950)	A Turkish officer who researched the Zaza but called them Turks (cit. in Gündüzkanat 1997:38).

---

[15] One has to keep in mind that some authors changed their opinion during their ongoing research.

Bruinessen (1989)	Calls the Zaza-led rebellions Kurdish uprisings (1989:29).
Tucker (1989)	Calls the Zaza-led rebellions Kurdish uprisings (1989: xviii).
Olson (1989)	Although he specializes Christian minorities and other groups he calls the Zaza led rebellions Kurdish uprisings (1989:1-4).
Leezenberg (1993a)	Recognizes the different category of Zaza as Northwestern Iranian language but still calls it a Kurdish dialect and the people Kurds (1993:1, 8). Knows about the Zaza uprisings and their cause (:12).
Mutlu (1996)	Recognizes the different category of Zaza as Northwestern Iranian language but still calls it a Kurdish dialect and the people Kurds, Zaza-Kurds or Zazaki speaking Kurds.
Steinbach (1996)	Calls the Zaza led rebellions Kurdish uprisings (1996:134-135).
Kieser (2000)	Differs in Christian and Muslim minorities, but calls the Zaza-led rebellions Kurdish uprisings (2000:18-19 etc.).
Haig (2001)	Argues that on linguistic grounds, like Selcan (1998), they could be called independent but mainly Zaza do call themselves Kurds (2001:182).
Andrews (2002)	Distinguishes Zaza from Kurds but points to MacKenzie and van Bruinessen in the same volume, who calls on the 'Kurdishness' of the Zaza people (2002:19-20, 122).
Bumke (2002)	Argues that mainly the Alevi Zaza call themselves Kurds and counts them as a Kurdish dialect (2002:511-512).
Kreyenbroek & Sperl (2002)	They are stating that Zaza consider themselves and are considered to be Kurds (2002:35).
Hennerbichler (2004)	Tracks also back to Kurdish history but describes in detail the discussion about Zaza and Kurds. The Zaza people do not speak Kurdish but would stick to the Kurds according to many Kurdologist (2004:130-134; 198).
Walter (2004b:1)	Refers to Zazaki as a dialect of Kurmanji.
Nasidze et.al. (2005)	Their genetical research showed close connection between these groups. They do understand the Zaza people as a subgroup of Kurds (2005:401-412).

Heper (2007)	Calls the descendant of Sheikh Said Kurds and the Zaza-led rebellions Kurdish uprisings (2007:3).
McCarus (2009)	Mentions the controversy about Zazaki being called a Kurdish dialect but addresses them as a linguistically distinct group being ethnically Kurds (2009:589).
Paul (1998; 2009)	Differentiates Zazaki to Kurmanji, but sees close anthropological connections. Wants to leave it to the people themselves to decide whether they feel independent or part of the Kurds. (2009:545).
Aygen (2010:1-2)	Refers to Zazaki as a dialect of Kurmanji.
Loizides (2010)	Refers to Zazaki as a less prominent dialect of the Kurds.
Kaya (2011:5)	Refers to Zazaki as a dialect of Kurmanji.

Another problem comes into play by the fact that the Eastern Group feels much more related to the Kurmanji group than the Northern or Southern Group. The reason is clear, it is their proximity to the larger Kurmanji speaking group. The Eastern Group also shares the same religious interests as some of them follow the Shafi'i school of Islam, which is predominant in the Kurmanji speaking ethnicity. The strong political influence of the Eastern Group also plays an important role. For instance an author like Mehmet S. Kaya (2011) who is looking from the Eastern angle comes to the conclusion that the Zaza are Kurds because his informants say so (2011:4). Authors from the Northern or Southern Group distinguish themselves more from the Kurmanji group since they are further away. In the Southern Group the tendency is mixed.

The same goes for researchers who work with a specific Zazaki dialect group as they often take over the view of their informants. As mentioned in the Introduction I want to cover all three perspectives (pro, contra, undecided).

No one can force somebody to accede to an opinion that is against his individual ideas. A differentiation in linguistic separation by unique features and ethnic conformity is helpful (see also Paul 2012:8, 17). With this publication the rich variety within the Zaza people and their homogeneity as a culture is demonstrated. Also the distinction from many Kurdish traditions is researched so that one can make up his mind about the identity question of the Zaza people.

2.1.2.5 Other Perspective – Space and Nationalism

Researchers from outside are mostly split when it comes to the discussion about identity, while the Zaza themselves found different ways to deal with the problematic nature of The Zaza identity. In social sciences the term "identity of ethnicities" corresponds to the "space and subjectivity" that an ethnicity takes up in a multiethnic surrounding (Bhabha 1994). Neyzi interviewed two musicians from the Northern Group and her research on space and identity in social unities revealed the foundation of *third spaces* within struggling ethnicities. Hence the struggle between "Kurdishness" versus "Turkishness" or "Kurdishness" versus "Zazaness" was by some Zaza solved by creating the space of "Dersimishness" realized by the term "Dersimlı" (Neyzi 2002:98). That does also solve the struggle of "Turkishness" versus "Alevism" or "Kurdishness" versus "Alevism" (:98). Such a Third Space within a people group reduces the ratio of possible members (3.5.3; 3.6).

Table 5 Overview - Struggle in Space and Subjectivities (Zaza focus)

	Zaza	Turks	Kurds	Alevis	Sunnis	Third Space
Southern Zaza	√	√	√		√	Zaza
Eastern/ Central Zaza	√	√	√		√	Zaza
Northern Zaza	√	√	√	√		Dersimlı, Kırmanc, Alevi

The table demonstrates that the gap between the Zaza people really reaches out into the question of identity. Even worse is the fact that the Sunnism following Zaza (SZ, CZ) view Alevis as an Islamic sect or a heathen culture, and NZ blame the Central and Southern Zaza for historical reasons, such as their active participation in the Armenian ethnocide and the close companionship with their Sunni Turkish brothers against Alevis (2.2.2.2; 2.3.1.2.1; 3.4).

It is within the Diaspora that such gaps are bridged by common interests in Zazaki language development and cultural preservation. Yet problems of standardization and a reference dialect come into focus here.

The main criticism by Zaza community members about the perspective that they are "Kurds" is that "Kurdish nationalism" asks the same from the minor Zaza as Turkish nationalism does for all the minorities in Turkey. This includes the denial of an independent history and tradition of the Zaza people. The problem here is that "Kurdish nationalism" is to some degree devoutly driven by Zaza people who lack an official "Zaza nationalism". The bewilderment that these intermingled nationalistic movements bring is enormous and hardly resolvable. Even the parties involved argue internally and are inconsistent about their identity or their politically goals for the Zaza people in relation to the Kurds. As in the past the driving political forces in the Kurdish nationalistic movement are coming out of the Zaza community (Tezcür 2009 *Kurdish Nationalism and Identity in Turkey*). They do not mirror the whole Zaza group's attitude but have a great influence on the nationalistic movements. The experiences of a Zaza nationalistic movement by *Sheikh Said* (1925) and *Seyit Rıza* (1937/38; 2.3.1.3.2) avert any independent nationalistic movement at the moment.

Another area of intersubjectivism and space orientation comes from the perception of a Zaza societal member as to how far he/she belongs to either ethnicity. The following table describes my experiences and observations how descent and environment affect the self-perception of a person:

Table 6 Self-Perception in relation to Descent and Environment

Parent	*Language*	*Environment*	*Child*	*Predominance*
Father	Kurmanji	Kurmanji	Both languages	Kurmanji
Mother	Zazaki			
Father	Zazaki	Kurmanji	Both languages	Kurmanji
Mother	Kurmanji			
Father	Kurmanji	Zazaki	Both languages	Kurmanji
Mother	Zazaki			
Father	Zazaki	Zazaki	Both languages	Zazaki
Mother	Kurmanji			
Father	Turkish	Turkish	Both languages	Turkish
Mother	Zazaki			
Father	Zazaki	Turkish	Both languages	Zazaki
Mother	Turkish			
Father	Turkish	Zazaki	Both languages	Turkish
Mother	Zazaki			
Father	Zazaki	Zazaki	Both languages	Zazaki
Mother	Turkish			

Predominant is the demand to belong to the stronger or larger ethnicity. Another main factor comes from the patriarchaic and paternalistic orientation of the Zaza people (2.3.4.2). Here the perception and division of the space of male and female comes into play. The male as bearer of the seed is the protector and outward-oriented part of society, whereas the female is the receiving, inward-oriented part. Descent is referred to the male as creator or generator. This makes him the image of the divine creator in the physical sphere. The metaphysical sphere is left to divinity or divinities. The space of the male is progressive from the household, to the tribal small scale society, to the nation, to the state to the world. The inner core – the house and home – is left to the female. In the first line the self-perception is thus related to the father-side and secondarily to the power dominance of the wider ethnicity that one can refer to.

2.1.2.6 Historical Perspective – Principle of Armenization

In East Anatolia, as a hot spot of different ethnicities, religions and ideologies the Zaza people – as well as other ethnical groups – face different influences. Besides the "Kurdish Question" stating that the Zaza are "Kurds" (Kurdishization) some argue that they are of Armenian origin. The argument goes that at least the Northern Group, which has an Alevism background (2.1.4.2; 2.3.3.3) was originally Armenian and converted by and then during epochs of persecution or political instability to Alevism and sometimes during epochs of (re-) Islamisation to Islam.

The common ground of such an argument is that the Zaza people lived and live in the area of the ancient Armenian Kingdom. Having a closer look at that argument one would expect a much larger Armenian influence on the Zaza people in traditions and remnants of cultic practice. Conversion in the Eastern Anatolian area goes back and forth. Sometimes due to the political state of affairs Armenians aline to Islam or Alevism and sometimes Alevis or Muslims aline to Christianity. In the same way Alevism turned into Islam and Moslems became Alevis (2.1.2.6; 2.3.3.7.2).

There is a close relation to the question of origin when it comes to the Armenian influence on the Zaza culture, because the question stays open who lived first and who was in charge in the recent Zaza homeland. For instance if one places the origin of the Zaza people to the Caspian Sea following the Daylam-Thesis (2.1.3.1.1) he will conclude that the Zaza people moved into the Armenian realm in the 11th century AD. But if the Zaza people lived in that area quite intermingled with the Armenians the question is unsolved how they developed into Alevism. The question is also related to the Armenian Christian history. Yet the foundation of the Armenian Apostolic Church is based on the Christian initiative of *Gregor the Illuminator* who founded the Church around 300 AD, which is why it is sometimes called the *Gregorian Church*. With Patriarch *Mesrop* the Church got its own written revelation based on an alphabet prepared by him. Their monophysitic or miaphysictic theology promotes the unity of the types / natures of Hz. Jesus from Nazareth. The pre-Alevism religions are still known by the Armenian people.

The supporters of the Armenian-background-theory point to the social and religious similarities of the Armenians and the Zaza people. Another argument for them is the close relationship between both ethnicities and their practices (intermingled marriage / godparenthood *kerwa*; 2.3.3.7.2; 2.1.4.4). The background or origin of the similarities can be traced back to pre-Christian times for both ethnicities.

Critics of such arguments address the political stance that such arguments contain. To argue for an Armenian origin leaves the impression that the Zaza people are obliged to support Armenian undertakings. Until today the "Eastern Anatolian Borders" and the realm of a wider Armenian nation, forms an open question, although it is slightly recognized worldwide (Papian 2010). Due to this underlying presumption of some Zaza groups, the mistrust about any support of Armenian activities within the Zaza people is high.

Recently there is a rapprochement at the scientific level to work closely on linguistics and anthropology. The State University of Yerevan sustains academic research about Zazaki and the Zaza society (Asatrian and Hykos conference in October 2011). The historically close neighbourhood in the area of the Zaza homeland contributes to the reconciliation of both ethnicities.

2.1.2.7 Summary

Closely related to the subject of the Zaza people's identity is the relationship to their more numerous neighbours the Kurmanji speaking Kurds. A separation on linguistic / cultural and political / ideological grounds is at least helpful to come to an approach which tends to leave open the decision to the Zaza people. As the pendulum towards cultural autonomy is moving back and forth one has to be cautious about any prediction.

Recently within an *emic* (inside) view of the Zaza people, they tend to hang on to the Kurds, whereas a smaller fraction asks for independence and sovereignty from the Kurmanji speaking Kurds. The *etic* (outside) view by the Kurds is inclusive by adding the Zaza to their wider nationalistic movement corpus. The *etic* view of the Turks is mixed but tends to include them in the larger group of the "Kurds". The *mediating* way will leave the identity question of the Zaza open for future developments.

On linguistic grounds Zazaki – as is demonstrated below – has its own characteristic which distinguishes it from any other Kurdish related dialect. These are the languages: *Kurmanji* (Northern Kurdish), *Sorani* (Northern Iraq), *Mukri* (Central Kurdish; Northern Iraq), *Kermanshahi* (Northern Iraq) and *Ardalani* (Northern Iraq; MacKenzie 1963; idem 1981; also Oranskij 1979:35-36), *Bahdeni* (Eastern Kurdish). Southern Caspian languages are even closer and give another hint to the so called Daylam-Thesis (2.1.3.1.1). Yet the group of languages including *Talysh* (Iran), *Southern Tati* (Iran), *Gorani*(Iran / Northern Iraq), *Semnani* (Iran), *Luri* (Iran), *Laki* (Iran), *Bakhtiari* (Iran), *Mazandarani* (Iran), *Sangsari* (Iran) or *Gilaki* (Iran) show some affinity. In general the Northern Kurdish dialects are called by the generic term *Kurmanji* and the Central ones by *Sorani*. However coming from a historical-linguistical point of view and referring to the Daylam-Thesis it is fair to speak of a wider 'Kurdish and related languages *language belt*' or '*Sprachbund*' (Germ.) in relation to the whole group of languages. Also in contrast to this, Zazaki can be referred to a close '*language belt*' or '*Sprachbund*' of the "Southern Caspian" languages and dialects.

Table 7 Language Belt Theories based on the Daylam-Thesis

Theory	Languages
Daylam-Thesis wider "language belt" (Germ. "Sprachbund") *Kurdish and related languages belt*	*Kurmanji* (Northern Kurdish), *Sorani* (Southern Kurdish; Northern Iraq), *Mukri* (Central Kurdish), *Kermanshahi, Ardalani, Bahdeni*
Daylam-Thesis close "language belt" *Southern Caspian language belt*	*Talysh* (Iran), *Southern Tati* (Iran), *Gorani*(Iran / Northern Iraq), *Semnani, Luri, Laki, Bakhtiari, Mazandarani, Sangsari,* or *Gilaki* (all Iran)

Table 8 Language Belt Theories based on other Theories

Other theories on general "language belt" Kurdish and related languages belt	*Kurmanji* (Northern Kurdish), *Sorani* (Southern Kurdish; Northern Iraq), *Mukri* (Central Kurdish), *Kermanshahi, Ardalani, Bahdeni, Talysh* (Iran), *Southern Tati* (Iran), *Gorani*(Iran / Northern Iraq), *Semnani, Luri, Laki, Bakhtiari* or *Gilaki* (Iran)

Referring to genealogical classification Zazaki is representing an individual language branch or '*language cluster*' together with Hewrami / Gorani (Gurani). I would go as far and call them 'Southern Caspian-Aturpatakan' 'language belt' or 'Sprachbund' although the hypothesis of the origin from the region of Daylam is in my opinion not proved yet (Asatrian 2009:11; 2.1.3.1.1). On anthropological and ethnical grounds, bringing together cultural and linguistical facts, the scientific world as well as the Zazaki and Kurmanji speaking people groups is split (see below; 2.1.3.1.1). A close historical and culturally anthropological identification among both people groups complicates the process of separation (if ever needed!) for outsiders.

Besides the frustration that is induced by such a division, the whole discussion resulted in a revival of research about the Zaza and Zazaki and the development of orthographic standards, as well as the establishment of monolingual publishing houses and an increasing number of authors and Zaza oriented researchers (see bibliography). Initiated by the Zaza people in the Diaspora, mainly in Germany and Sweden, the interest for cultural and linguistical development is growing (Paul 2009:546). That's why theories about the Turkish or Kurdish origin of Zazaki or the Zaza culture are increasingly questioned.

In the past the Kurmanji speaking Kurds and the Zaza people lived peacefully side by side, but every ethnicity had its own sphere of existence and realm of practising their core beliefs. Religious, existential or human resources were in general not shared. There is no common narrative of origin or historically shared traditions, yet due to their geographical location on the Silk Road and the realm of the past world dominations (Greek, Romans, Ottomans), parallels in the development of the perceptions of the world are obvious (2.5).

2.1.3 Theories of Origin

Theories of origin are essential to understand the descent of a people group. Central to the understanding of the people from Eastern Anatolia is the area of the Fertile Crescent (Eastern Anatolia, Western Iran, Iraq, Syria - the ancient area of Eastern Anatolia, Mesopotamia, West Persia in Hennerbichler 2002:134), as the cradle of mankind referring to the Hebrew Bible and ancient myths (e.g. *Gilgamesh Epic*, *Enuma Elish*). Beneath recent popular genetical research the descent of languages helps to reflect *mass migration* or *migration of the peoples* (Germ. "Völkerwanderung"). In between the Indo-European languages the Iranian languages form an Indo-Aryan and Iranian branch. The Western and North-western group of Iranian languages describe the Zaza / Gorani as well as the Kurdish language group (Appendix 2a).

In research, the origin of Kurdish people is closely connected to the origin of the Zaza people (e.g. McDowall 2004, Bruinessen 1992). Unfortunately this suggestion is not build on linguistic evidence. It seems more that the Zaza are somehow more related to the Parthians whereas the Kurds to the Medes and Persians (Gündüzkanat 1997:57-58; he refers to Lockwood 1979; 2.1.3.1.1).

One suggestion about a place of origin for the Zaza people group traces them back to the southern shores of the Caspian Sea. As Kreyenbroek and Sperl mention:

> It seems that the Kurdish tribe originally lived somewhat farther to the south than the Medes. At some stage, Kurdish tribes migrated to the north, and settled in Eastern Anatolia. It is possible that their migrations displaced another Iranian people, whose original home may have been near the Caspian. (2002:70)

A mass migration to the West for whatever reason led people from the southern shores of the Caspian Sea and Western parts of Persia / Iran into the Northern mountain ranges of the Tauros and Zagros Mountains. As a result of this mass movement a language belt (Germ. "Sprachbund") including all Kurdish languages and dialects as well as the Zazaki / Gorani branch reaches from the borderline of Iraq / Iran on the latitude of Suleymania (southern end) along the Tauros and Zagros ranges to the North up to the homeland of the Zaza who perform its North-western end (Leezenberg 1993a:1-5, 12; 2.1.2.2 and 2.2.1.1). The "Kurdish people" in a wider sense therefore inhabit the area of North Syria and Iraq, Western Iran and Eastern Anatolia (Tucker 1989: xv- xix). As Gippert supposes, the Caspian languages are closer to Zazaki and Gorani than Farsi / Persian, which is closer to Kurmanji and the other Kurdish languages (1996, 2005, 2007 and Paul in Paul & Gippert 2009).

Genetical research on *Y-chromosome Variation in Kurdish Groups* (Nasidze et. al. 2005:401-412) reveals that there is a close connection between "Zazaki and Kurmanji speakers from Turkey and Kurmanji speakers from Georgia" (:401). These three people groups are most similar genetically to other West Asian groups, and most distant from Central Asian groups, for both mtDNA and the Y-chromosome. However, Kurdish groups show a closer relationship with European groups than with Caucasian groups based on MtDNA, but the opposite based on the Y-chromosome, indicating some differences in their maternal and paternal histories. (ibid).

In the same study the authors refer to previous genetical studies starting in 1994 to 2004 (:402)[16]. As his study reveals (:409):

> The previous hypothesis of a close relationship of the Zaza people to populations from northern Iran (MacKenzie 1962) therefore does not gain genetic support, although the genetic evidence of course does not preclude a northern Iranian origin for the Zazaki language itself.

Looking at the origin of the Zaza people from linguistic and genetical evidence leads to the assumption that the modern homeland area of the Zaza group was long ago inhabited by a mix of people who are nowadays merged into the Zaza or Kurdish populace. The Zaza people, like the "Kurds", are closer related to European grassroots than to Central Asian people groups like the Turks, who inhabited the area of East Anatolia in the 11th century AD (Seljuk Empire).

The discussion about the origin of the name of the Zaza people is closely related to the question of their origin. I decided to split these two strings of argumentation to give as much information about the whole group as possible. The reader is asked to look at those arguments too (2.1.1). One has to be aware of other factors that contribute to the research of origin which need to be taken into account now.

---

[16] "Only a few genetic studies have been carried out on Kurdish groups. Previous genetic studies of classical markers (Cavalli-Sforza et al. 1994) indicated an overall genetic similarity of Kurds with other Middle Eastern populations. Comas et al. (2000) studied mtDNA HV1 sequence variability among Kurmanji-speaking Kurds living in Georgia (Caucasus), and found close European affinities for Kurdish mtDNA lineages. Richards et al. (2000) studied mtDNA HV1 sequence variability among 53 Kurds from Eastern Turkey and found that some mtDNA haplotypes found in Kurdish samples presumably originated in Europe, and were associated with back-migrations from Europe to the Near East. Wells et al. (2001) investigated Y chromosome SNP haplogroup distributions among Central Asian groups, including a group of Kurmanji-speaking Kurds living in Turkmenistan, but no specific conclusions were made regarding the history of the Kurdish group (see also Arnaiz-Villena et al.). Nebel et al. (2001) studied Y chromosome SNP and short tandem repeat (STR) loci among different groups from the Middle East, including a group of 95 Kurds from northern Iraq, and found close affinities for the Kurdish group to other Middle Eastern groups. Finally, Quintana-Murci et al. (2004) studied 20 Kurds from Western Iran and 32 Kurds from Turkmenistan, among other groups from Iran, Pakistan and Central Asia, but did not come to any specific conclusions concerning the Kurds."

2.1.3.1 Place and Culture of Origin

Since the 15th century BC mass migrations of Indo-European people groups that called themselves Aryan ("the noble") moved in waves from Central Asia to the South and West. Out of the Aryans the "Iranians" ruled since the 1st millennium the high plateaus of Eastern Anatolia. The name "Eran" as this area was called in ancient times derived from *Aryan* (Franz 1988b:41). From the beginning on they were farmers and their historical geographical setting was within the recent homeland area (Allen & Muratoff 1966: 14, 385). Such was the initial situation for a settlement of the Zaza people.

Besides some really obscure theories about the origin of the Zaza people which are shortly mentioned here, one will find a four-course hypothesis about the question of origin. They could be called *Daylam-thesis* (Parthian), *Anatolia-thesis* (Hurrians, Sumerian), and the *Sassanid-thesis* or *Medes-thesis*.

The *Daylam-thesis* gets the strongest support from outside as well as within the Zaza people therefore it will be extensively discussed. The other theories follow the series sorted by relevance and influence.

2.1.3.1.1 Daylam-Thesis (Parthian-Thesis)

As mentioned above one argument about the descent of the Zaza people from a province called *Daylam* on the southern shores of the Caspian Sea led to a phonetical derivation called *Dımli* or *Dımıli* (2.1.1.5.1). Those *Daylamites* (Greek: Δολομιται) are first mentioned in "classical sources in the late second century BCE" (Felix 1995). Windfuhr traces the Gorani and Zaza history back to this region on the southern part of the Caspian Sea (McKenzie cit. in Windfuhr 2009:30-31).

Other arguments are given below and a note about the origin of negation or support is necessary. Often the political and historical background of an argument reflects the promoters' point of view.

The *Parthian-Thesis* is closely related to the Daylam-Theory since Parthian was the language of the Parthian Province (in north-eastern Iran, south-east of the Caspian Sea; Bailey 2003:7)[17]. Some researchers and Zaza argue that they are descended from the Parthians. Like the *Sassanid-Thesis* the idea concerns a

---

[17] Samples of this language are found in the royal inscriptions dated in the third century B.C., found in Nisa (in today's Turkmenistan) and in literature of the Manichean religious community. There are also Parthian loan words found in texts from neighboring languages (Sundermann 1989: 138).

direct offspring from a people group. The following arguments shed light on these theories.

Referring to examinations of Christensen (1921), Minorski (1928) Hadank (1930) and many others (see below) it is assumed that in the course of large people movements they migrated. The assumption is that they moved along one of the main Silk Road ways in the direction of the West, coming from the region or province of *Daylam* by the Caspian Sea (Iran). These movements could either have taken place around the turn of the eras, as a consequence of Roman settlement politics or as a getaway caused by the first Mongol invasions of Europe in the 11th century AD[18] / 6th century AH (2.1.3.1.1). In either case it was part of wider mass migrations that involved the Fertile Crescent, the Balkans, East Europe and the Middle East by Slavic people, Jewish people, Celts, Southern Caspian ethnicities and others.

Before we look into detail about the pro and cons of the Daylam-thesis it is necessary to refer to a hypothesis by the well known Kurdish scholar *Mehrdad Izady* who claims there was a movement of the Zaza people from the West or their recent homeland area into the region of Daylam in today's Iran. Izady does not prove his arguments. However, for the record, it is noted here that this hypothesis was refused by White, due to unscientific and suspicious arguments (2003:22-23).

The so called *Daylam-Thesis* has many advocates and critics. Here is a small overview in chronological order of their date of publication by the researchers who dealt with this thesis.

---

[18] There were several Mongol invasions lasting from the 11th-14th century. That one of the Genghis Khan was the most well-known in the 13th century: "The Tartar invasion in the 13th century deviated from the usual scheme of looting and raid in close border areas. They were prepared by long hand and reached to the complete Eurasian area, to Silesia and into the Balkans." (multi-media 2007: *Genghis Khan*)

Table 9 Proponents of the Daylam-Thesis

Proponents	Argument
Lerch (1858:98-110)	Assumes *Dimli* to be a derivation from *Daylam*.
Adranik/ Antranig (1880 und 1900:111-116)	*Dimli* as derivation from *Daylam*.
Friedrich Carl Andreas [1906] (1916) also in Hadank (1930:18)	*Dimli* as a derivation from *Daylam*.
Soane (1912)	Refers to Andreas, but supports the idea because of the closeness to the history of the Gorani/Hawrami.
Benedictsen / Christensen, Andreas (1921)	Closeness to Gorani; understands *Dimli* as a derivation of *Daylam*.
Lentz (1926:271, 281, 284)	Closeness to Gorani; *Dimli* is a derivation of the term *Daylam*.
Minorsky (1928:193 / 1926:243 and 1965:189-194)	Closeness to Gorani; *Dimli* as derivation of *Daylam*.
Gernot L. Windfuhr (1989)	Understands *Dimli* as a derivation of *Daylam*.
Joyce Blau (1989)	*Dimli* is understood as a derivation of the term *Daylam*.
Ehsan Yarshater (cit. in Vahman & Asatrian 1990:264-275)	*Dimli* as derivation from *Daylam*.
MacKenzie, David Neil (1961-1962)	Zazaki, as distinct from Kurmanji, is close to Daylam dialects; en bloc mass migration from Daylam to the West is possible (see below critics).
Lockwood (1979:279)	Closeness to Gorani; the term *Dimli* as derivation from *Daylam*.
MacKenzie, David Neil ([1989] 2002:541-542)	Closeness to Gorani; *Dimli* as derivation from *Daylam*.
Olson (1989:95)	*Dimli* as derivation from *Daylam*.

Vahman & Asatrian (1990:264-275)	*Dimli* as derivation from *Daylam*.
Izady (1992:44-45)	*Dimli* as derivation from *Daylam*; Daylam a traditional kingdom since the 10th century.
Asatrian, Garnik Serobi (1995)	*Dimli* as derivation from *Daylam;* refers to the Alburz mountains.
Arakelova (2000:398)	Derives the term Dimli from Middle Iraninian **cleimik*, i.e. daylamit = dweller of Daylam. In Armenian Zaza-Kurder (see also Asatrian & Gevorgian 1988).
Paul & Haig (2001:399)	*Dimli* as derivation from *Daylam*.
Kreyenbroek & Sperl (2002)	Assumes an Armenian background of the term and references to MacKenzie.
Hennerbichler (2004:197)	Summary of proponents.
Nasidze, Ivan et.al. (2005)	Genetically there is close relation to Kurds but none to Northern Iranian people.
Paul (2007)	Hints towards the close relationship between Zazaki and Gorani and proposes a common originging (:293). Northern Gorani is closer to Zazaki than the southern Gorani dialects (:ebd.).
RH 2008 Zaza and Zazaki	Mother Tongue Speaker who understands the Daylam dialect with just little of adjustment.
Paul & Gippert (2009)	Closeness to Gorani; *Dimli* as derivation from *Daylam*.
Windfuhr (2009)	Cites Felix (1995) who researched the Daylamite / Deylamite dynasty. Windfuhr assumes that Zazaki and Gorani could be preserved languages due to the migration process (2009:30).
Kaya, Ali ([1999] 2010:25-27)	He refers back to others scholars and the mass exodus migrations from East to West.
Schulz-Golstein, Esther (2012)	Sozio-psychological study on the history of Dersim Zaza assuming their origin in Daylam and the language Dêlemî (2012:2,3
White (no date) Ethnic differentiation	Closeness to Gorani.

Table 10 Critics of the Daylam-Thesis

Critics	Argument
Carsten Niebuhr [1768] (1774-1778 and mainly Vol. 3 in 1837)	Was not able to distinguish Zazaki or other languages from Kurdish/Kurmanji.
Justi ([1880] 2006: xxv)	Gorani / Zaza are close to Kurdish and have their origins in Kurdish culture.
Le Cloq 1912, 1926 and 1928	Gorani / Zazaki are close to Kurdish and have their origins in Kurdish culture.
MacKenzie [1989] 2002	Is strictly against a mass migration, argues for initial settlement in their recent homeland.
Kreyenbroek & Sperl (2002:70)	Kurdish presence; Zaza are part of the Kurds.
Hennerbichler (2004:179)	Kurds were the first inhabitants in the Euphrates (tk. *Fırad*) and Tigris (tk. *Dicle*) spring area and there is no tradition of Zaza in this area. Late settlement thesis.
Nasidze et al. (2005:401-412)	No genetic affinity between Zaza and Daylamites population (:409).

As the tables clearly indicate, serious criticism on the Daylam-Thesis is rare. Nonetheless there is no evidence by written or oral traditional material that supports the thesis. That's why a summary of the arguments is given here for further discussion (additional to the ones above).

Looking back in history when research on this thesis started, the 15th century is shown to be a vital period. Muslim geographer, historian, and

> administrator Hamdullah Mustawfi, whose home town Qazvin was only a few miles from the borders of Alburz Daylamân, reckons the Daylamites as non-Muslims and polytheists. Taking their non Muslim religion as the pretext, the Gilâni Zaydi ruler, prince Kiyâ, embarked on a ruthless massacre of the remaining Alburz Daylamites in the 14th century. (Izady 1992:45).

Those events could have led to a migration of the Daylamites in either direction. There is no obvious reason why they should have fled into the west. The population of the Alburz mountain range (also called Aborz, Elborz, and Elburz) south of the Caspian Sea in Northern Iran which covers also the Iranian province of Daylam is still Kurdish (Ismaili.net *The Heritage Web Site* ...). A majority of these "Kurds follow the non-Muslim religions of Yârsânism and Alevism, albeit with some Twelver Shi'ite and Ismâ'ili influence" (:45). But as Izady mentions

> these Kurds are, however, late arrivals, dating only to the 16th century. They nevertheless fortify the notion that this area has long been the terminus for Kurdish migrations from the central and northern Zagros. (ibid).

He also notices a close relationship between the language of old Daylam spoken there and Zazaki (Dımıli).

Another central argument for the Daylam-Thesis is found in the close linguistical, anthropological and historical relationship to the people called Gorani / Gurani / Hewrami. Kreyenbroek and Sperl see a close connection to the Kurdish migration from "somewhat farther to the south than the Medes" to Eastern Anatolia where one branch moved more into the west becoming the Zaza and another to the south were they formed the Gorani people (2002:70). Thus the Northern dialects of Gorani called *Hawrami / Hewrami* are recently closer to Zazaki, than the Southern dialects, due to Persian influence (Paul 2007:293). Related to this issue is the fact that the Gorani people also represent a split in a Shi'ite school of the *Ahl-e Haqq* and a Sunni Hanafi and Shafi'i group. They are also under the influence and pressure of the larger *Sorani* speaking Kurdish group to call themselves "Kurds". History as well as similar political, social and cultural developments point to one origin that is the region of Daylam. The argument about heterogeneous division of "Kurdish and related ethnicities" in the Near East is observed all over. The background to this can be found in the manifold social, religious and ethnical influences in this region.

Obviously this theory of origin emanates from a close relationship of the Zaza ethnicity with the "Kurds" or even as part of these people groups. Leezenberg gives strong arguments against this view of origin, whereas he supports the close relationship of both ethnicities (1993a:16; 1993b). As historical evidence shows, the Gorani people nowadays are a mere shadow of their former influence (1993:16; Kreyenbroek & Sperl 2002:82; MacKenzie 1961:73; Paul 2007:285). Hence one should consider the realities existing in the Middle Ages and thereafter. A short overview about the powerful rule of Gorani people and the lively times of Zaza tribal systems reveals the following:

> There were ruling 'Goran princes with Kurdish tribes under their sovereignty' (Rich 2007:201). Hence the Goran were not primarily subjugated nontribal peasants under Kurdish rule (Justi [1880] 2006: xxv). They could be organized tribally and superior to non-Gorani tribes (Bruinessen 1992).

According to the *Sherefname* (1.2.1), the sovereigns of Erdelan are said to be derived from a member of the Merwanid dynasty of Diyarbakir (Hadank 1930:20). In the 17th and 18th century AD the dialect of Hewrami / Gurani was the court language of the rulers in Erdelan. The Ahl-i-Haqq used Gorani as a Koine (commercial language) in written mediums, such as epic and lyric poetry (Soane 1921; Minorsky 1920, 1921, 1928, 1943 and 1960). 'Towards the end of the eighteenth century, the Erdelan court was eclipsed by the nearby Baban court centered at Sulaimaniya' and the poets 'wrote in Sorani, which then rose considerably in status' (Leezenberg 1993a:7-8).

Groups within the Gorani (e.g. Kakai) originated from Luristan, according to findings on their religious practice (Edmonds 1957:1904).

In the same way this could be said for the Zaza people. They were never nomads like the Kurds, as is shown by their oral traditions (2.3; Mann cit. in Hadank 1930:18; interestingly this is also true for the Proto-Aryans Geiger 1882:87, 176-177, 192). Their tribal system is deeply rooted within the culture and shows distinctive features in relation to the surrounding societal systems (2.3.1.3). Those arguments support at least the independence of Zaza and Gorani people from *Kurmanji* and *Sorani* speaking Kurds. They show that there was less strategic and more economic interest in the relationship of the people groups living in Eastern Anatolia and the Tauros and Zagros ranges (Tucker 1989: xv).

Another argument has some political load in. Yet it has to be taken in account. It is about the Armenian claim that the Zaza people entered the realm of the Euphrates Tigris headwaters not before the 11th century AD. Since the Armenians settled in this area a long time ago, this argument has to be taken seriously. Unfortunately there is no written source about either a serious reference of the Zaza or the non-existence of such a people group but just suggestions. The lack of any debate about the existence of the Zaza people in Armenian sources is astonishing, however many files are not researched yet and a lot of writings got lost during the expulsion of the Armenians from East Anatolia in 1915-1923 (Asatrian & Gevorgian 1988:500-501). The political tendency of this argument has to do with some issues about the proclamation of Eastern Anatolia being occupied by the recent nation. Obviously history needs to be interpreted by such authors in a way that fits with this argument. The Zaza ethnicity is therefore put into the wider anti-Christian league of the "Kurds".

2.1.3.1.2 Medes-Thesis

The theory states that all of the Kurdish people, including Zaza and Gorani, are descendants from the ancient *Medes* (Justi [1880] 2006: v). The *Medes* theory was originally taken on by the Kurds as one of three theories of their origin and proves to be politically motivated (Heper 2007:35). The other theories of Kurdish origin state they are descendants of the Parthians or a distinct ethnical group (ibid). However parts of the Zaza ethnicity refer to this theory as their tradition of origin. The group promoting this is closely related to "Kurdish" nationalism.

Paul's comparison of Turkish with Kurdish Nationalism reveals that as the former assumed the origin of the Turks within the Hittite or Sumerian people (see e.g. the traditional *Eti* respectively *Sümer Bankasii* in Turkey) the Kurds origin is supposed to be placed in Mesopotamia, largely the Medes people (2002:197 and footnote 19). This argument is based on a geographical and linguistically understood closeness to the Medes (Hejaro 2007 *Kurdische Dialekte* [Kurdish Dialects]). It reaches far back to ancient times when indigenous people of the Fertile Crescent formed a multiethnic and multilingual population. Hennerbichler supposes that Old-Iranian populations like the Medes and Parths iranized those people groups by culture and language so that this North-western language branch formed its own New-Iranian dialects (Kurdish) and languages (Zazaki, Gorani; 2004:134). Izady's language maps assume the Medes-Theory (Appendix 2a; Izady 1992 *The Map collection of Geography* ...). Although Izady's research is criticised, his maps show at least the dispersion of the "Kurdish" and Iranian people groups in the Near East.

David Neil MacKenzie (b. 1926 - †2001), a guiding researcher on Iranian Studies, especially the Kurdish languages and dialects, disproves the Medes-theory for the Kurds and their languages (cit. in Hennerbichler 2004:132). His linguistic approach reveals instead influences of Middle-Persian (300 BC – 900 AD) to Kurdish dialects, whereas Zazaki and Gorani were influenced by *Parthian* (ibid; Gippert in Paul & Gippert 2009; Gippert 2012 *Iranian Language Tree*). The language of the *Medes*, although it is an Indo-European language, is not close to Kurmanji, hence the whole Medes-Theory is no more than a mere hypothesis (Bruinessen 2002:616; Paul 2002:197). In the same way but on other grounds Kreyenbroek and Sperl argue that the origin of the Kurds is "farther to the south than the Medes" indicating that both are different people groups (2002:70).

Interestingly the Armenian history, as directly influenced by the Medes and the Kurds, doesn't say much about the origin of the Kurds. The archives of the Orthodox Church are not extensively evaluated on the Kurdish and Zaza issue. One reason could be that the Armenians, Zaza and Kurds, as well as other minorities in Eastern Anatolia, always stayed between the Empires of the Fertile Crescent, either the Medes, later the Persian and then the Romans until the Byzantine or

Ottoman Empire (Hübschmann 1904 and 1962:9-16). Within recent Armenian research the Daylam-Thesis is preferred, whereas Kurmanji is linguistically also traced back to Parthian, which would counter Gippert's thesis of two Middle Iranian sources for Zazaki and Kurmanji (Asatrian 2009 vs. Gippert 2012 *Iranian Language Tree*; Asatrian & Gevorgian 1988). I would agree with the Daylam-Thesis but see also some difference in the historical background of the languages mentioned as e.g. the differences in family terminology demonstrate.

2.1.3.1.3 Sassanid- or Anatolia Thesis

The concept between these theories lies in the origin of the Zaza people on their own soil. As any mass migration is not proved yet and maybe never will be, some researchers started to argue that the place of origin is where the Zaza people live nowadays. Three pointers support the argument:

- As is generally accepted the nomadic Kurds moved from the south up to the Tauros-/ Zagros mountain ranges. In so doing they forced people groups forward to move northwest. The Zaza people as peasants found good pastures in the Euphrates (tk. *Fırad*) and Tigris (tk. *Dicle*) headwaters area where they settled down (MacKenzie 2002:542; Paul & Haig 2001:399). It is within this argument that Andrews infers a semi-nomadic history for the Dimili / Zaza people (2002b:121). This theory could not be validated since the practice of the Zaza shows a move to the summer pastures (*ware*) only for the herdsmen or specialists not for the community or extended family as a whole. In contrast some of the Kurdish (Kurmanji speaking) tribes such as the *Beritan* small scale society still follow until today a nomadic lifestyle.
- Historical evidence revealed that the Hittites (1750 BC) established a multiethnic state with many features that are again found in Zaza culture (sexual equality, differentiation of murder and second-degree murder etc.). Some specific features of the Zaza culture, as is shown later (0), display close connection to the ruling principles of the Hittites. Although one would not overwork this argument.
- The Armenians, who settled in the area since ancient times, do not directly mention the Zaza people, but their language and culture influenced the Zaza people (2.3.1.2.3). Also the close relationship between both people is rendered till today by oral traditions – even though the Armenian neighbours have been gone since 1915 (cf. Armenian ethnocide).

2 The Zaza

The *Sassanid* (like the *Parthian*; see above) ruled and inhabited at least partially the recent homeland area of the Zaza people. The Sassanid Empire also called second Persian Empire ruled from 224 AD to 636 AD, when the Arabian expansion armies vanquished *Yazdigird* III. at Qadisiya. It took 14 years until 651 AD before the whole Sassanid Empire vanished (Franz 1988b:41-42). The Armenians, standing between the Roman and Parthian and later between the Sassanid and Byzantine Empires, welcomed every new Kingdom afresh (Hübschmann 1962:10-11; Lockwood 1979:201-202; Schmitt 1981:26). If the Sassanid Empire had been a Zaza based kingdom there should be a tradition about the period of ruling in the Armenian history with cross-reference to the so called "Kurds" speaking the dialect of Zaza.

Obviously the Sassanid Empire, and therefore the Sassanid people could only have indirect influence on the Zaza people, as their metropolis was based in Iraq and not on the Euphrates (tk. *Fırad*) and Tigris (tk. *Dicle*) headwaters. One would also question the loss of any writing system and historical evidence (traditions) if the Zaza people are the descendants of the Sassanid people.

The main point in this argument is the settlement of Zaza people in their recent homeland - that is (Eastern) *Anatolia* - a long time ago. This argument is evidential, since there is good reason for an original settlement in the Euphrates and Tigris headwater area. All oral traditions of the Zaza people – as far as they are known to the people the ethnographer had contact with – fit absolutely to this assumption. These traditions supply the history; the ecological and political progress as well as the geographical and religious challenges (see Zazaki literature at the end of Bibliography). The tendency to assume such an original settlement is also displayed in the absence of any tradition on mass migration or settlements in the East (*Daylam-Thesis*). Also the fact that the dialects of Zazaki show diversity on religious grounds, which are also giving account to a division on close by geographical grounds in what is nowadays their homeland area (NZ as mountaineers / Alevites; SZ river people / Sunni; EZ both Sunni background).

2.1.3.1.4 Other Theories of the Zaza-Origin

It is within this fourth group of theories that non-scientific – one could say ideological assumptions – are presented. This does not say that not a scrap of truth is represented thereby. It becomes obvious that such theories are based either on the ideology of *Pan-Turanism*, also called *Pan-Turkism* (see 3.1.1.2.2) or could not be proved due to lack of evidence.

In 1960 officials in Turkey declared the origin of the Zaza people to be in Mongolia, referring to a mountain called *Zakzak*. The idea is that people from this area immigrated to (Eastern) Anatolia during the Mongol invasions in the thirteenth century AD / $5^{th} - 7^{th}$ century AH (2.1.3.1.1; 2.1.3.1.5; 2.3.1.1; 2.3.3.4; 3.1.1; 3.3; 0). The name has been shortened phonetically to "Zaza" (other arguments out of Pan-Turkish constraints in 3.1.1.4.5).

On other grounds, the thesis that the term *Dumbeli* would correspond to a leading small scale social unit, cannot be traced back further. It is argumented that this small scale society was specifically responsible for the politically and economically strengthening of the later Zaza people and therefore contributed fundamentally to their origin. Hence, only the derivation of the name *Dimli* from the term *Dumbeli* stands out in this approach.

A further assumption about the origin of the Zaza people states that *Gerger (Alduş)* was a cultural centre in former times. Gerger is a town on the foot of the mountain Nemrut where the touristic attraction of the excavation site from the Seleucid *Antiochus* I. *Theos* can be found. This site, so the idea goes, represents an archaic demonstration of the primal Zaza, who are descendants from those Seleucids. The concept of historical authority behind this implication is clear but lacks any scientific and historical evidence. Yet the Seleucid emperors are descended from the Greek *Alexander the Great*, so a relationship to the Indo-European-Iranian language group is far from being realistic (2.1.4.1).

Another curious derivation motivated by Kurmanji speaking people is found in the expression *dı milli* (2 peoples). Here it is claimed that the name *Dimili / Dimli / Dımli* originates from the composition of *dı* (2) and *milli* (plural for people = two people) and delimits the Zaza from the Kurds (RH 2008 Zaza and Zazaki). The concept then has assimilated itself in the use to *Dimili* (RH holds the written documentation / schoolbooks). This argument goes along with the political statement that "all Kurds are Turks". Such was e.g. stated by the pro-Turkish Alevi small scale social unit *Xormek* during the criticism of the Sheikh Said / Seid rebellion. The main agent of this hair-raising argument was *Firat*. However since its appearance it was broadly rejected and more or less not taken seriously (Bruinessen 2002:381-382). Also Gökalp emphasized the descent of the "Kurds" from the Turks (Berkes 1959:43-44; see above; 3.1.1.2.3).

In the historical writings of the *Achaimenides*, the king *Dareios* or *Darius the Persian of Babylon* (his title) mentions during one of his raids along the Euphrates a place called *Zazana* (Schmitt 2009:50). This king is well documented in the

Bible, namely in the book of Ezra (10 times; e.g. Ezr 4,5), Daniel (8 times; e.g. 6,1), Haggai (3 times, e.g. 1,1), Zecharjah (3 times; e.g. 1,1) and Nehemiah (1 time; e.g. 12,22). This is a hint about the existence of a place or area which reflects the name of a group called "the Zaza". There is no other information given. Also the statement *as I didn't reach Babylon yet* (Germ. Original: "als ich Babylon noch nicht erreicht hatte", :ebd.) indicates the closeness to Babylon and points rather to a place that is closer to the Gorani area in Western Iran.

2.1.3.1.5 A Framework of the Origin of the Zaza People

Leaving the scenario of ideologically motivated speculation, it will be possible to fix at least some key-events in the history of the Zaza people's origin. What follows will be an attempt to gather those historical facts and presenting a framework of the origin of the Zaza people. For this the main source will be the Zaza and their oral traditions as well as results extracted from the historical lore of surrounding people groups. As is often the case a mixture of the above given theories proves to be the main string in the history of the Zaza people.

If one likes to start out from a movement of the Zaza people at all, than recently no reliable information is available around the time before 1000 AD / 390 AH. There is good reason to assume that the Zaza people originally lived at the Euphrates / Tigris headwaters, maybe a little further East of what is nowadays their homeland. Certainly during the Middle Ages nomadically living Kurdish emigrants from South Iraq were drawn to Anatolia. Due to their spread, they dispersed the sedentary peasant Zaza and other people groups (Armenians etc.) to the West where they settled in the triangle of Diyarbakır, Sivas and Erzurum (Kreyenbroek & Sperl 2002:70; Paul & Haig 2001:399).[19] Some of these people groups (were) intermingled with the Kurds but others like Zaza, Gorani and Armenian people seem to be resistant to assimilation (Izady 1992:96). Reasons for that could be found in their foundation of bigger settlements and towns as they can be found on the map today (appendix 1) or the far distance from any Kurdish influence as is obvious in the linguistic belt that reaches down to the Gorani area on the Iran / Iraq border (2.2.1.1). These researchers also follow the idea of

---

[19] Andrews presents another picture as "of semi-nomadic Dimili of the lower-lying areas, living in the hills between Karacadağ in Urfa and Derik in Mardin, apparently extending northward to Çüngüş and Cermik in Diyarbakır" (2002b:121). In my research I did not find any hint on nomadic traditions in the history of the Zaza people. I assume that Andrews infers from Kurdish lifestyle that the Zaza people were also nomads in the past. Such conclusion is not based on real facts.

an earlier mass migration from the Caspian Sea to the West (ibid.; 2.1.1.5.1). Another hint for this argument is found on linguistic grounds due to the derivation of Zazaki from Parthian, since it is of importance that this language was used "as a living language from the 3rd till presumable the 6th century in Parthia" (Sundermann 1989:114). The Parthians, located in Middle-Asia (:114; Iran / Persia) influenced Zazaki during this period. Thus there is strong evidence that this influence took place in the area of Daylam (see Daylam-Theory) before a mass migration movement.

But one has to go further by looking at other historical facts about the recent homeland area. Some researchers emphasize a settlement in Eastern Anatolian (Euphrates-Tigris headwaters) long ahead of any Kurdish presence there (MacKenzie 2002:542). This would already be before the turn of the eras since the settlement of the Kurds could be pointed to this early time (Hennerbichler 2004:179; Kreyenbroek & Sperl 2002:70). As there is no (oral) tradition of any migration during the Mongol invasions (11th – 13th century AD / 5th – 7th century AH; Franz 1988b:33; (2.1.3.1.1; 2.1.3.1.4; 2.3.1.1; 2.3.3.4; 3.1.1; 3.3; 0) but a tradition that points to the recognition of those Mongol storms during the inhabitation of the Euphrates (tk. *Fırad*) and Tigris (tk. *Dicle*) headwater. This leads to the assumption of an early stage of Zaza dispersal before 1000 AD out there (RH 2008 and 2010). Such is demonstrated by tradition about the person of *Genghis Khan* (Jenghiz Khan), who is closely connected to the Arab invasions. Lack of tradition about the Islamisation period of the Arabian conquests (7th-8th century AD/ 1st–2nd century AD) merged the Mongol invasions with times of Arabic influence. As an outcome the term "Ereb" (Arab) is filled with a variety of negative connotations like mistrusted, ruthless etc. (Hayıg 2007:6, 7, 12 etc.).

The Zaza people recognize in their long history, passed through oral traditions, the Aramaean and Armenian Christian people (Aramaic and Armenian) as their neighbours (2nd-4th century AD / 4th–2nd century BH). Also they are acquainted with at least some Turkish social units or a small group of Turkish speaking settlers. The latter being called *Gok / Gök Turks* (English *Heavenly Turks*; primal Turkish small scale social units), already popular in Anatolia since the 5th century (Laut 1996:25; RH 2006, 2008 and 2010 e.g. *Zaza and Zazaki*). During and after the settlement of the Seljuk in the course of the 11th century AD / 6th century AH Turkish-speaking people invaded Anatolia in the 13th and 14th century following behind the Mongol invasions. Within this period the well known dynasty of Osman started its story of success by the Ottoman Empire. It was the Mongol Emperor Genghis Khan who became popular with his invasion throughout Asia and Eastern Europe. The Turkish-speaking people settled down in Anatolia and mixed themselves with the people living around (Franz 1988b:33).

Hence the Zaza people know about the Mongol invasions in relation to their homeland and there is strong evidence of a long-lasting and native settling.

The Proto-Indo-European language theory concludes that in the area of the Balkans or Turkey this language evolved around 2500 BC. It was affected by migration movements from the Celts along the Danube river. Those mixed with each other and later dispersed into Anatolia and Eastern Anatolia. Such a people group also settled in the area of the Zaza homeland. Nonetheless we do not know which one and how their culture and language developed.

2.1.3.2 Summary

The discussion about the place of origin of the Zaza people demonstrates the close connection to the political questions a propos a "Kurdish" or "Turkish" background of the Zaza people. Lacks of written and longstanding oral traditions hamper the reconstruction of any serious theory about the history of the Zaza. Due to that very reason any hypothesis about a "Turkish" (*Zazak-* or *Sun-language* theory) or "Kurdish" descent, like the Medes- or *dı milli* (2 peoples) theory, seems not to be realistic.

Besides this preferred theory of an original settlement in the recent homeland area of the Euphrates / Tigris headwater region (*Anatolia Thesis*), the so called *Daylam-Theory* has alternatively been taken into consideration. The latter starts from the premise that a mass migration from the province of Daylam south of the Caspian Sea - in the former Fertile Crescent nowadays a north-western province in Iran - led the Zaza people to the West into their recent homeland. These migration movements could either be around the turn of the eras, due to political and ecological reasons or during the Mongol invasions in the 11th - 13th century AD / 5th – 7th century AH (2.1.3.1.1; 2.1.3.1.4; 2.1.3.1.5; 2.3.1.1; 2.3.3.4; 3.1.1; 3.3; 0). Strong support holds this premise by the fact that the dialect spoken in the *Daylam* area nowadays is closely comprehensible to Zazaki and Gorani.

The theory of an originated settlement in the Euphrates / Tigris headwater area before the turn of eras achieves support by some facts. First in the historical Zaza traditions the settlement or presence of Christians (Aramaic and Armenian people; 3rd-4th century AD), Arabs and Gok / Gök Turks (Engl. *Heavenly Turks*;

primal Turkish small scale social units; 5th-7th century) as well as the Mongol invasions (11th - 13th century AD / 5th – 7th century AH) is anchored. Also the ancient written histories of the Armenians assume the presence of other people groups – not mentioned as "Kurds" or Zaza – in the area of the contemporary Zaza homeland (2.1.4.4 and 3.2).

2.1.4 Settling Area - Homeland

A *people group* is a territorial, linguistical and sociological unity, made up of several subunities (e.g. tribes, clans, dialect groups; Fasold 1993:2-4; Franz 1988:35). In this paragraph we want to discuss how the Zaza people apply to this definition.

"Anatolia", the "Land of the rising sun", is a derivation from the Greek verb ἀνατολή *anatolā*, meaning "rise" or "a rising / East", and pointing to the sunrise in the East. The term dates back to Greek settlement since BC 1000. It was taken over in Turkish as *anadolu*. Panturkic linguists derived it from the Turkish term *anne* and the verb *dolmak*, the term then meaning "stuffed mother / fertile land". "Anatolia" stands for the whole Asiatic part of modern Turkey. The demarcation line from Kayseri to Sivas splits West Anatolia from Eastern Anatolia (Brockhaus multimedial 2007: entry *Anatolien* [Anatolia]). There is also a religious division within West and Eastern Anatolia, whereas the West is split by the "belt of Alevism" apart from the Sunni South and East (Nestmann 2002:552). The Zaza people are mainly settled in the western areas of Eastern Anatolia (West Eastern Anatolia). Paul designates the homeland of the Zaza between the triangle of the cities *Siverek, Erzincan* and *Varto*, as well as some exclavic structures near Mutki (:2009:545). They inhabit the Euphrates / Tigris headwaters and their upper reaches (see Fig. 1; linguistic classification in McDowall 2004: XVI, Fig. 4; Nestmann 2002:548). This is the north-western peripheral area of the so called *Kurdish areas* (Izady 1992:150; s. below), which became popular in the treaty of Sèvres (1920), but which was revoked by the Turks in the treaty of Lausanne (1923). The river Euphrates (tk. *Fırat*) forms the centre of the Northern and Southern Group, whereas the river Tigris (tk. *Dicle*) does so for the Eastern Group. This becomes indeed obvious by the fact that the people, pointing to their homeland, use the term *ro* (Engl. river) for the Euphrates without stating its geographical name (RH 2006 *Zaza and their neighbours*).

In sum the Zaza people live side by side with other ethnicities and thereby they inhabit 5% of Turkish soil and stretch out over 11 of the 81 provinces of

Turkey (see section under point 2; Wilson 2010:1; Appendix 1 Homeland Area of the Zaza).

Historically the area of Dersim with the centres of *Hozat, Mazgerd, Pertek*, the Munzur River headwater and *Duzgın Baba*, also the cities of *Gerger, Palu, Heni* and *Muş* played a significant role. They formed cultural, ideological and religious centres. For instance *Gerger* is until today considered to have a pagan and Christian background, and *Palu, Muş* and *Hani* had religious centres such as *madrassa* of different Islamic schools (3.6.4.2).

Cultural language centres are the areas of *Gerger, Çermik , Siverek* (Southern Group; 2.1.3.1.4), *Dersim, Varto* (Northern Group), *Bingöl, Palu* and *Mutki / Muş* (Eastern / Central Group). Spreads or exclave settlements in *Northern Iraq* point to linguistically and culturally closely related ethnic groups. Personal statements by Zaza, who were working in these areas and who could communicate easily, point to unexplored splinter groups of linguistically and culturally closely related people. Such groups would be found around *Irbil* (Arbil), south of *Mosul*, south of *Urmia* and in eastern Syria close to Iraq (Izady 1992:171, Map 39: *Linguistic Composition of Kurdistan*). Besides the *Shabak*, the *Gorani* people are also felt to be closely related to the culture and language of the Zaza (RH 2007 *Zaza tribe names*). So far reasons for the spread and dispersion of those splinter groups are not known due to a lack of oral tradition. The whole spread of Zazaki related languages points to a "language belt" (see 2.2.1.1), including the East of Northern Iraq and smaller parts of western *Iran*.

2.1.4.1 Southern Group (SZ)

The area of the Southern Group (SZ) includes the cities of *Çüngüş, Germıg* (Tur. *Çermik*), *Sowreg* (Tur. Siverek), *Adıyaman, Ergani* and *Elazığ* (similar Kaya 2011:6). This area enfolds

- the former Armenian capital *Harput* (close to *Elazığ*) with its rare and unique wooden houses and the tomb of Arap Baba,
- *Nemrut Dağ* (Engl. Mountain of Nemrut; close to *Adıyaman* and *Gerger*(Alduş); see below; 2.1.3.1.4; 2.3.4.4.2),
- the hot spring of *Germuk* (Tur. *Çermik*) with its *hamam* (public bath), ruins of a castle, a karawansaray and the historical *pirdê Haburmani* (stone bridge of Haburman),
- *Hazar Gölü* (Engl. Thousand Sea) a main Turkish tourist centre in the East,

- *Keban* and *Karakaya Baraj* (Engl. Keban and Karakaya dam) as part of the *Güneydoğu Anadolu Projesi* (GAP; Engl. Southeastern Anatolia Project)[20],
- *Çüngüş* with its ruins of a huge Armenian school, hospital and church.

Gerger lies at the foot of the historically meaningful Nemrut Dağ (Tk. *mountain of the Nemrut*). This mountain in the Tauros ranges is close to the city of *Adıyaman* (86 km north-eastern). It is one of the few historically rich areas in the East which is open to the public. On its top the monument of King *Antioch I. Theos the Seleucid* (69-36 BC) attracts lots of tourists. Excavations of the mountain since 1881 (introduced by Karl Sester) and international recognition led in 1987 to the approval of the monument as a World Cultural Heritage Site by the UNESCO.

As shown above some Zaza conclude that this site hints at their ancestors, wrongly assuming that the monument is from the Medes, Persian or Seleucids. Hence Nemrut becomes a king of the Zaza who ruled a huge empire. Hereby the Zaza follow the Kurds on their *Medes-theory* (3.1.3.1.2). On historical, linguistical and cultural grounds such inference proves to be wishful thinking (2.1.3.1.2). However *Gerger* is considered a historical centre and had great importance to the Zaza people (RH 2007 *Names of Zaza Tribes*). There is still research necessary to claim the impact of the *Gerger* area for the Zaza.

The area attracts little tourism due to lack of economical development and bad conditions of public transport, streets and facilities. The main connections with the outside are visits by relatives from Europe. Apart from that, the main migration movement is away from the homeland area to the large cities and tourism centres of *Diyarbakır, Adana, Antalya, Izmir* and *İstanbul*.

The two main cities of *Diyarbakır* and *Elazığ* lie within this territory. One third of their population is Zaza. These cities are centres of commerce for the Zaza people and not a few made their way into economy, politics, military and

---

[20] GAP is Turkey's greatest developmental project with "22 dams and 19 hydroelectric plants on the Euphrates [Tk. *Fırat Nehri*. EW.] and Tigris river ... include an irrigation network for 1.7 million hectares of land, covering eight provinces corresponding to approximately 10% of Turkey's total population and surface area" (Serap 1995 *The GAP Project*). Its centerpiece is represented by the rocks and earth filled *Atatürk Dam* which forms the sixth largest dam in the world.

science through them. Both cities have a university and have a strong military presence.

The characteristic landscape of this area consists of huge plains and deep valleys formed by huge rivers. Due to deforestation the hills are rocky and sandy. Woods, forests and bushes are only found in the valleys or at the foot of the mountains. Sometimes deep holes and surface cracks occur without warning. All together the area looks very dry in summer. The continental climate represents a mix of cold and dry winters and hot, humid summers. In winter the snow can be up to 2 meter, whereas in summer temperatures of 40°C and in winter of -25°C are normal. Summer lasts from June to September while winter starts in November until March. Hence spring and autumn are very short and bring with them intense ecological change.

The rough climate has its economical influence on the people groups of the area. Heating in winter as well as cooling in summer for humans and livestock play important issues for housing, farming and trade. The market place is often central in a city and covered shops surround it, so that the market can also go on when the weather is bad. Here is a difference from the Mediterranean ethnicities which live by the sea. The mild weather there allows for uncovered and unlimited open trade markets.

Since 2011 the local university of Bingoel started public advertisement of Zazaki and the Zaza. For two years this symposium existed. The universities of Tunceli and Mardin, as well as others, also started language research and courses on Zazaki giving the opportunity to academic enterprise.

2.1.4.2 Northern Group (NZ)

High mountains and mountain ranges, up to 3400m like the *Mercan Dağları* and deep valleys are characteristics of the region of the Northern Group (NZ). The whole area is mountainous with small forests or bushes, but lot of water springs and larger or smaller creeks. The northern border is marked by the headwater of the Euphrates River. *Pülümür Creek* (Tk. Pülümür Çayı) and others flow into the many ribbons of the Euphrates. The *Keban Baraj* with its huge dammed up water reservoirs nowadays forms the southern border of the Northern Groups homeland. Main cities are *Dersim / Tunceli, Mazgirt, Çemişgezek, Ovacık, Pulemoriye* (Pülümür), *Nazimiye, Hozat, Pertek, Kığı* and *Varto*. Objects of interest are

- *Munzur Mountains* in the northern part of *Tunceli*,
- the spring issuing from the *Munzur River*, today called Gözeler in the district of *Ovacık* (national park area),
- *Munzur Valley*, *Mercan Valley* and *Mercan National Park*,
- the *Gelin Spring* or *Gelin Waterfall* located 63 km away from *Nizamiye*, with its stalactites and stalagmites,
- *Pertek* Township which is near *Keban Dam* with orchards and shades of green,
- *Bağin* Thermal Springs in *Mazgirt* Township.

The continental climate brings cold winters and short summers to the Northern Groups area. In winter, temperatures can be down to -30°C, whereas summer temperatures do not climb above 28°C. There is always a fresh breath of air around.

The Northern Group fell under a resettlement degree in 1938 AD, after a time of upheaval against the national forces, and in 1994 AD after the so called "emergency rule" (*Olağan üstü Hal*). In both periods many villages were emptied and burnt down by the national forces. In between, after 1948 AD when the ban on settlement was lifted, many Zaza people went back to their homeland area and rebuilt their villages.

Since the establishment of the annual Munzur festival in *Tunceli* in 2006, a regional movement about environmental questions, the identity of Alevis in Turkish society and the question of nationality for the Zaza people were made public. A newly established university in Tunceli offers Zaza courses.

2.1.4.3 Central / Eastern Group (EZ)

The Eastern / Central Group (EZ) of the Zaza people lives at or close to the banks of the *Murat* River that outlines its northern edge and which flows into the *Euphrates*. The southern margin is represented by the river *Tigris* (Tk. *Dicle Nehri*). Main cities are *Palo* (Palu), *Heni* (Hani), *Çabaxçur* / *Çewlig* (Bingöl; Engl. thousand lakes), *Lice*, *Piran* (Dicle), *Genç*, *Muş* and *Kulp*. Points of interest are:

- *Çapaxçur*/ *Cewlig* (Bingöl) with its many lakes and the so called *wandering islands* and its *Hamam* (Tk. Yüzen Adalar),
- the castle of *Palu* over the banks of river *Murat* and an archaeological site with a stele from the Urartaic king *Menua* from the 8th century BC,
- the *madrassa* of *Heni* (religious school in Hani),

- *Muş* with its long lasting history was a kingdom (Urartraen, Assyrians, Greek, Romans, Parthians) and a place of massacres (*Sheikh Said* rebellion, Armenian ethnocide),
- all over the Zaza homeland one will find ruins of churches (Syrani, Nestorian and mainly Armenian), in the larger settlements and cities added by synagogues and school buildings from the *Great Experiment* (Blincoe 1998; Kieser 2000; 2.1.4.5; 2.6.2).

The geographical landscape as well as the climate is similar to the Southern Group (3.1.4.1). One of the Silk Roads from the West to the East and back followed the course of the river *Murat*. Yet so called *karawansaray's* (guest- and storehouses) for trade caravans along the caravan track were spread along the river (2.2.2.2).

The intermingling of the Eastern Groups homeland with the Kurmanji speaking "Kurds" is strong. Yet the discussion about Zaza autonomy from Kurdish influence is much greater among this group. Such is obvious on the naming of some cities which even in Zazaki take up "Kurdish" names (e.g. *Piran*). History proves the close relationship to Kurmanji Kurdish as was demonstrated by the *Hamidiye* troops of the Ottoman Empire at the end of the 19th century (3.1.1.2; called after the founder Sultan *Abdul Hamid* II.). The *Hamidiye* in general did *not* allow for any non-Kurmanji speaking Kurd and hold a strong inner- or cross-tribal (only tribes with good relation) network (2.1.4.4; 2.3.1.3.1; 3.5; HC 2011). Whereas the Northern Group was due to their Alevitic religion treated as an enemy, the Sunni Zaza sometimes even worked closely with this organization. Now stories about rivalries of Sunni Zaza and the Ottoman *Hamidiye* troops are known too, but they tend to be not as severe as what the non-Islam groups experienced. Theories about the origin of the Zaza are likewise close to Kurdish theories and somehow traditions show much more affinity to Kurmanji speaking Kurds than in the Northern or Southern Group. Political activities were and are numerous in the *Çapaxçur* (Bingöl; Petrov [1863] 1998:148-159) area. It is this area that reflected the main autonomous and separatist activities during the foundation of the Republic of Turkey (3.1).

2.1.4.4 Neighbouring peoples - Turks, Armenian and Kurmanji Kurds

A short introduction about the relationship of the Zaza to neighbouring people does not replace a main historical outline of those communities as is presented in chapter 3. To understand the history, tradition and cultural settings of the Zaza their closely interlocked background with those other people groups is important. In this paragraph the recent practices in relation to the surrounding cultures are displayed. Mainly the Turks, the Armenians and the Kurmanji speaking Kurds influenced the Zaza people as much as they influenced those cultures more or less.

During their relative independence under Ottoman Empire, due to its practice of *millet* sovereignty (2.1), only a small number of Turkish inhabitants lived with the Zaza in their homeland. Information or traditions about intercultural connections during the Ottoman period were not handed down, either by Turks or by the Zaza. Neighbourhoods between Zaza and Turks developed firstly by the specific settlement policy of Turkish authorities concerning moving administration and armed forces to settle in the east of the republic. Language and cultural barriers and different Islamic opinions, based on the respective schools (either Hanafi or Shafi'i; 2.2.8.1; 2.3.3.2.5; 2.3.3.5; Table 22) represent the main factors of disturbance. Also the Zaza were seen as "Agents of Iran" to vilify their reputation and find reasons to oppress them (Küçük 1990:65). Nowadays intercultural marriages are possible and not socially ostracized by both sides. In general the Zaza community avoids any influence from the national powers. Judicial authority (e.g. judges, attorneys) and protection by local and national executive authorities (e.g. police, military) are not addressed, due to high distrust build on the experience of decades-long oppression and despotism. The ongoing increasing disbandment of self-ruling institutions like the *sheikhdom*, the religious and political leadership and its hierarchy, with its loss of authority and responsibility, opens up a huge vacuum in the areas of group leadership and the relation to the nation state. In some cases the mullaharchy takes over those responsibilities with the negative effect of Islamic totalitarianism.

Prior to 1915 the Zaza lived in neighbourly community with the Christian Armenians. A historical but partially conflictual interaction of conversion and cultural integration between Armenians, Kurmanji speaking Kurds and the Zaza ethnicity is verifiable (Izady 1992:96; Seufert & Kubaseck 2004:78). Armenians and Jewish neighbours, who usually appeared as skilled craftsmen or in a leadership role, were regarded as educated and wealthy by the Zaza (Justi 2006: xix). Religious difference or orientation did not disturb the relationship. Remains of synagogues and churches in the east of Turkey validate this religious acquaintance as was observed during different journeys to the East of Turkey in 2002, 2005 and 2011. Christian Armenians worked predominantly as dealers

2 The Zaza

and craftsman (Baumann 2007a:81; Zürcher 2004:196, 227), Kurmanji speaking Kurds rather as cattle nomads and carpet weavers, while the Zaza chiefly appear as farmers (Nestmann [1989] 2002:574; Mann cit. in Hadank 1930:18; differently Kaya 2011:6 who compares the Zaza with the nomadic *Beritan Kurds*). Ahead of the (Re-) Islamisation of the Zaza people during the 16th century AD contact between Christian Armenians and Zaza, as well as Jewish citizens was so intensive that public life was shared totally (e.g. schools, hospitals, trade). Even after the Islamisation there was no detection of larger armed conflicts, although due to the Islamic influence Christian and Jewish groups became second class citizens (*dhimmis*). Until the end of the 19th and the beginning of the 20th century such changes did not end in direct violence against the local people (RH 2006 *Zaza and neighbouring peoples*).

The extinction of the *Armenians* during the - from Turkish side – controversially considered 'ethnocide' (Arm. *Mets Eghern*, Մեծ եղեռն, Mec Yeġeṙn; Turk.: *soykırım*) led to a vacuum in the Zaza area, which was filled by Kurds and Turks who took over the Armenian property (Seufert & Kubaseck 2004:78; Zürcher 2004:196, 227).[21]

At that time an inglorious episode of Zaza history took place. Colonial claims of England and France in the Middle East led to the militarization Kurmanji speaking Kurds including parts of Zaza. Since 1894 the *Hamidiye* (called after Sultan *Abdul Hamid* II.) fighting troop of Kurmanji speaking Kurds and parts of the Southern and Eastern Zaza enforced the expropriation and expulsion of Armenians and their property (2.1.4.3; 2.3.1.3.1; 3.1.1.2; 3.5; HC 2011). The evidence of the deportation centres which were located largely in the Zaza homeland area is overwhelming. Besides others, there were such headquarters and rallying points in *Elazığ*, *Malatya*, *Çunguş* (Çüngüş), *Diarbakır* (Diyarbakır), *Ergani* and *Muş*. The abolishment of feudalism and nomadism at the turn towards the 20th century worked as a foundation to the Ottoman Empire to implement such politics (Seufert & Kubaseck 2004:78). A specific settlement policy of Turks in the east started during different epochs of the Turkish Republic. As

---

[21] On the discussion about the genocide / ethnocide see Dadrian 1997a:182-183; Diedrich cit. in Baumann 2007a:407; Hofmann cit. in Baumann 2007a:117; Lepsius 1986 cit. in Baumann 2007a:117; Lepsius 1986; Richter around 1930, s. 2006:76-77; Schäfer 1932:122; in detail Zürcher 2004:114-115; Steinvorth & Elger 2008:36; Keyser 2008:3; Pikkert 2008:162. In sum a German proactive initiation or participation is refuted, but indirect support with weapons and military training etc. proved by observation (3.1.3).

early as the 19th century attempts to introduce the fight against the overdue feudalism in the east came into being (Zürcher 2004:30-50). During the repression phases that followed the years of 1948, 1961 and 1982, in which military coups took place, state offices were promoted particularly by Turkish officials in the east (Höhlig 1997:122-123). Throughout these periods the isolation of the Turkish minorities became one aim among others, due to the need for security, regarding the unsound political situation (Kreyenbroek & Sperl 2002:73).

To escape reprisals of the Kurmanji Kurdish and the Southern and Eastern Zaza populace most of the Armenians that stayed, remained converted to Alevism in the North and to Sunnism in the South (Kreyenbroek & Sperl 2002:38; 2.3.1.3.2; 2.1.4.4; 3.1.3; 3.4 3.4; 3.4.1.1). The Kemalist assimilation policy (1935) which is practised to this day introduced a new approach. This policy was a consequence of attempts during Ottoman times to settle Turks from Western Turkey among the cities and villages of the Zaza ethnicity and the Kurmanji speaking Kurds. Nowadays only a few villages are left without Turkish population, nonetheless the Zaza still form the majority in many villages of its native soil.

Another group of people lived within the Zaza homeland area. Their Jewish background did not exclusively state where they are from. It seems likely that they moved out of Western Turkey and settled in the Zaza inhabited region. Another argument refers back to the Assyrian time (8th century BC) when the Jewish tribes were resettled from Israel to the homeland of the Zaza. In the larger Zaza cities people remember places of old and ancient synagogues. With the resettlement and distinction of the Armenians and other Christian denominations the trace of Jewish life got lost too. During this time the movement to the British occupied area (1920-1948) called Palestine started. This area was always claimed by the Jewish people as their native soil named Israel, which reflects their close tie to that area due to their sacred and holy scriptures called *Tanach* (hebr. תנ״ך; Torah, Prophets, Writings also called Hebrew Bible).

The *"Kurds"* in a wider sense are valued at 20-30 million worldwide. It is the biggest people group of the world without a country of its own. They populate areas in Northern Iraq, North-western Iran, Western Armenia, North-eastern Syria, Russia and Eastern Turkey (Paul & Haig 2001:398-399). The term "Kurd" emerges in Arabian descriptions since the 7th century AD/ 1st century AH (:399). The history of the Zaza is narrowly coupled to the development of the Kurds. Being minorities with a similar religious and cultural structure both

2 The Zaza

are exposed to the same political, social and economic influences in Turkey (3.1 and 3.4; EUbusiness 2006: *Turkey* Kurds yearn...). "Kurdish" is a term which is not conclusively substantiated in science (Asatrian 2009:1). To the contrary it is an expression of brisance since it describes a 'Kurdish and related languages" *'language belt'* or *'Sprachbund'* (Diagram 7; 2.1.3.1.1). Having said this, 'Kurdish' in a closer sense as wider 'language belt' is part of the Iranian family of languages and consists of four or five main dialects (Skjærvø 2009:625; 2.1.3.1.1; Table 7 and Table 8):

- *Central Kurdish* (North-eastern Iraq particularly *Sorani*; Mukri),
- *Eastern Kurdish* (West Syria and North-eastern Iraq especially Bahdeni),
- *Iranian Kurdish* (Kordi, Bakhtiari)
- *Southern Kurdish* (Kermanshahi, Ardalani, Laki and Luri in Iran),
- *Northern Kurdish* (Kurmanji Kurdish in Turkey, from Armenia to Kasachstan),
- some languages or dialects are discussed controversly as being part of an own group or considered to be "Kurdish": Laki, Gilaki and Luri.

In contrary Paul and Haig assume two main dialects namely a *Northern Kurdish* (Kurmanjî) and *Southern Kurdish* (Sorani; 2001:398). Others classify Kurdish in *Sorani, Bahdeni, Luri, Feyli, Dimli/Dimıli* and *Kurmanji* (Hejaro 2007: *The Kurdish Dialects)*. In general the Northern Kurdish dialects are addressed by the generic term *Kurmanji* and the Central dialects by *Sorani*.

While in the larger cities Armenians, Kurds and Zaza lived closely together, the villages formed monolingual and independent entities (RH 2006 *Zaza and their neighbours*). For economic reasons the main parts of the population in the cities was trilingual in Kurmanji-Kurdish, Armenian and Zazaki (2.1.2; 2.2.2; 3.4).

2.1.4.5 The "Great Experiment"

The Zaza were directly affected by a development in Eastern Anatolia that occurred during the period of 1830 to 1915 among their traditionally Christian neighbours. Foreign Christian development aid workers were largely supporting the Armenian population by setting up schools, hospitals and social centres. Although their social engagement was among the Christian neighbours, the non-Christian ethnicities (e.g. the Zaza, the Kurmanji speakers, Laz etc.) were also welcomed to their institutions. It is well documented that within the Zaza area churches, orphanages and hospitals were visited and used as cultural centres by

Zaza and the other non-Christian ethnicities (Schäfer 1932:16-20; Richter 2006:14). Education, medical care and to a lesser extent interreligious relationship were on the agenda of those organizations that were doing their work out there in Eastern Anatolia during the times of the Ottoman Empire. Blincoe offers a glimpse into the beginnings, when he writes "protestant assignment in Kurdistan began with a journey. In 1830 Eli Smith and Harrison Gray Otis Dwight of the ABCFM left Smyrna (now Izmir) to explore the interior of Turkey ..." (1998:31; 2.3.3.7.1).

The boresight of Christian activity then consisted in a "direct" that is a straight orientation towards the traditionally Christian churches such as the Armenians, the Syriac Churches and the Nestorians and an "indirect" that is long-ranging orientation towards their neighbours. The latter including the

> revitalization of the old ethnical people's churches (Nestorians, Armenians Antes 1988:51) with a view that those would automatically reach out with the Christian message to their neighbouring people such as the Kurds, Zaza, Arabs etc. (Livingstone 1993:39-40; Feldtkeller 1997:188; Richter 2006:14-15).

This Christian approach of foreign development aid appeared in literature as the "Great Experiment" as part of Christian development aid in the 19th century. This whole methodology is today described as a failure (*Peter Pikkert on The Great Experiment* 2008; Pikkert 2008:24-27; Vander Werff cit. in Pikkert 2008:41; Kieser 2000: 44-45; Löffler 2005:335; Blincoe 1998; Kieser 2000; 2.3.3.7.1; 2.6.2). The political powers, mainly Northern America, of the 19th century greatly supported "Christian minorities, whose Creed accorded to their native one" (Löffler 2005:337; s. a. Seufert & Kubaseck 2004:78). Such combinations of clerical and political interests arouse hatred and anti-colonialist associations and did not help oriental Christians like the Armenians. Quite to the contrary it culminated in deportations and ethnocidal abuses in the years 1880, 1896 and 1915-1923, when the Christian population in Eastern Anatolia was reduced to a small heap of misery. The system and practice of deportation, used against the Armenians and other non-Islamic ethnicities, was established by Sultan *Abbas the Great* (1620) who was responsible for the resettlement of 50,000 Armenians, of which 25,000 arrived in Isfahan (Renz 1985:94). At the beginning of the 20th century the supportive establishment of the *German Orient Mission* developed out of the 'Great Experiment' approach (Germ. "Deutsche Orient Mission"; DOM: Baumann 2007; Feldtkeller 1997; Lepsius 1925 und 1986; Richter 2006).

It is mainly through the notes and records of such foreign organisations that the period from 1830 to 1920 and all of its developments can be reconstructed nowadays. The American reactions to those events are with dismay, as the Turkish actions violated the founding principles of the the United States (Wheatcroft 2005:323.324). Henry Morgenthau, U.S. ambassador at Istanbul from 1913 to 1916, told the engineer of atrocity Mehmed Talaat Pasha that the people of the United States will never forget the massacres, and will always look upon it as like murder (ibid.). Armenian sources from these days are rare since the comprehensive anti-Christian undertakings by the Ottoman Empire and the interim of the revolutionary Young Turks left no space for inner-Armenian records. The rapid actions impeded any saving of notes or previous documents. Comparable to the effect of the *Shoa* under the Jewish people initiated by the German national-socialist movement the goal of obliterating the memory of a people group had extensive effects (3.4.1.1). In consequence the effect of such enterprises is not just the obliteration of people groups but also their historical and traditional knowledge and existence.

2.1.4.6 A Religious and Cultural Turkish Minority

As indicated already, the relationships to the Turkish "neighbours" are charged by the "minority" status. While such a minority status in the case of the Southern Group (SZ) is concentrated on the cultural-language level *and* the differences of affiliation to Islamic schools of jurisprudence, the Northern Group (NZ) suffers additional discrimination due to Alevism. In this context the latter form a "minority" within a minority, separated by a deep ditch from each other (2.1.1.5.1; 2.1.1.5.2; 2.1.4.1 and 2.1.4.2).

Both groups suffer from repressive politics, but fortunately abuse from the Sunni side on Alevism became sanctioned by the Turkish state. The last example of cruelty in 1993, the massacre of Sivas left deep traces in the Turkish society, resulting in 37 dead who were burned by a Mob during an Alevi literature festival (Durak 2006:13; Zürcher 2004:290). The propaganda around the incident led to more repressions and streams of refugees out of their native country. Alevism in general, paired with the minority question of the Northern Group, was to the Sunni Turkish leadership a thorn in the flesh. Until today Alevism provided a target for ongoing repressions (3.3; Steinbach 1996:379-383). The consequence is a noticeable double discrimination due to religion and language to this day.

Nationalistic movements, minority questions and Alevism form the unsolved problems of the Turkish republic to this day (Steinbach 1996:385; 3.1). Since Alevis amount to almost 20% of the population, the Turkish republic has to deal with finding a solution for the numerically second biggest religion on its soil (:375). Their incorporation into Sunni customs such as celebrating Ramadan and visiting the mosque, the official refusal to allow religious education in Alevism at state schools and subsidies, as well as the total denial of an Alevi problem, all failed to contribute to a solution yet did not lead to the fragmentation of Alevism (:379-383). That this programme used to be a purposeful politically strategy became obvious in its culmination by the destruction of Zaza and Kurmanji Kurdish villages in the 1990s (*Forced Evictions and Destruction of Villages in Turkish Kurdistan*: 8-9; *The destruction of Kurdish Villages* w/o year). Similarly others speak about the Turkish education policy in terms of:

> The existing schools, in which only Turkish is spoken, are accepted badly by the Kurds because they are not responsive to the people and because the children do not understand the foreign teachers and therefore learn too little. If one would allow the introduction of a mediating lesson within the first two years, with the approval also of Kurdish and Arabic and with a focus on literature for such foreign-language requirements, Turkish language and education could be conveyed much faster. One could alternatively introduce Turkish by the direct method under the use of only the Turkish language. However, the teachers then should, be specially educated for such a lesson and in an intercultural pedagogic. Also in this case one needs specially prepared teaching material for the minority areas. (Nestmann 2002:551; Höhlig 1997:120-121).

The concept introduced here has been promoted by UNESCO and UNICEF since 2007 as *Multi-Lingual Mother Tongue Education* (MLE). The idea is to introduce children to school education in their mother–tongue during the first year and transfer to the national language in the second year. An introduction to other religions would be promoted in such an approach too, but would not be central to the idea.

2.1.4.7 Summary

The Zaza people inherit the area of the Euphrates and Tigris headwaters. They live in the triangle of the cities *Erzincan*, *Siverek* and *Varto*. *Diyarbakır* and *Elazığ* are the main cities within this area. One third of their population is represented by the Zaza people. The Southern Group (SZ) lives in huge plains and valleys with continental climate influence. The Euphrates is central for them, which is why they just call it *ro* (Engl. River). The Northern Group inhabits a mountain range with peaks up to 3400 m and deep valleys. Many rivers and

steep slopes are characteristics of their homeland. The Central / Eastern Group (EZ) lives on the banks of the Murat river which serves as a source for the Euphrates (tk. *Fırad*) and Tigris (tk. *Dicle*) rivers, although it finally runs into the Euphrates close to Malatya. The Tigris is also central for the Eastern Group. Some exclavic centres can be found in Mutki (Appendices
Appendix 1 Homeland Area of the Zaza). The Euphrates holds a unique status for the whole Zaza ethnicity.

The neighbouring Armenians, Nestorians, and Jewish people had linguistical and anthropological influence on the Zaza people. The Kurmanji Kurdish influence is still there. Whereas the Zaza people are dominant in their many monocultural villages, the cities (up to 5000 citizens) became intercultural centres between Turkish, Kurmanji Kurdish and Zazaki speakers. The increasing Christian development aid in the 19th and beginning of the 20th century revealed close interaction and relationship between all of these groups as is provable by the many ruins of churches, synagogues and places of worship all over the Zaza area. The so called "Great Experiment" failed in reaching out to all the Eastern inhabitants. It worked just for the Christian *millet* (2.1; 3.1.1; 3.6). Due to the Armenian and Christian / Jewish ethnocide with its climax in 1915 the Muslim population remains. Nowadays the cities in the Zaza area are mixed by one third Turks, one third Kurds and one third Zaza.

Dominance and repression by the Turkish republic left the Zaza and the Kurds as economically and educationally isolated minorities. The formerly rich and civilized Eastern Anatolia became the poorhouse of the Republic of Turkey. Even the great modern efforts from the Turkish side to bring wealth and civilization back to the East have not helped so far to solve the minority problem caused by the cultural and linguistic division.

2.2 The Language – Zazaki

A *genealogical-historical* description of languages has its roots in the idea of dispersed primal languages as a source of many evolved branches (Gabelentz [1891] 1972:12; Sapir 1961:143). Another approach lies in the *morphological* or *structural* classification of languages in branches (Liebi 2003:89). A *comparative* method of linguistics uses such classifications to contrast languages within a language group or across such groups (Nichols 1992:2, 4, 14). The *genealogical-historical* approach demonstrates the opportunity to add geographical specifications of languages which make it easier to identify linguistic dependencies. Such an approach is used in the *Ethnologue*, a global interactive description of the world languages, which serves as a foundation here (Gordon 2005: *Ethnologue*; Werner 2006:88; Grimes & Grimes 2000; Appendices 2a and 2b).

Modern linguistics of the genealogical kind refers language families back to a "Proto" language stem. For the Indo-European language family the Proto-Indo-European root has recently been identified as two coordinate languages, *Avesta* and *Sanskrit* (Mallory & Adams 2009:6-7). Avesta is considered to be related to modern Persian (ibid.). It is therefore not astonishing that many Zazaki and Kurmanji speakers refer back to Avesta as the source of their language (Çar 1997).

The Indo-European language family (Thomas Young in 1813) started as Indo-Germanic by Conrad Malte-Brun in 1810. It extended from India in the east to Europe with its western-most language (Mallory & Adams 2009:6). The many independent language branches at the beginning grew into nine major language groups which ended with Armenian being added in 1875. However the huge supergroup of the *Indo-Iranian* and *Germanic* language groups took longer for identification (:6-9).

In short Zazaki is part of the Indo-European language family, which traces down to the Iranian language group and becomes therein an individual branch as North-western Iranian language together with Gorani (Gurani, Hewrami; Iran/Iraq). A second language branch within the North-western Iranian language group forms the "*Kurdish*" languages and dialects with

- *Bahdeni* (also found a little in Syria), *Sorani*, *Surchi* as Central Kurdish and small Southern Kurdish dialects (e.g. *Kermansha*: all in Iraq),
- *Herki* (Iraq/Iran/Turkey),
- *Shikaki* (Iran/Turkey) and
- *Kurmanji* as Northern Kurdish (Turkey; all references see Ethnologue 15th ed.; Appendix 2a).

Sorani is sometimes used as a collective for the Central Kurdish dialects including all the Kurdish languages of Northern Iraq and cross-border Iran, sometimes even including Southern Kurdish. Referring to Paul *Kurmanji* and *Zazaki* came out of a *Proto-Westiranian* language and seemed to split two thousand years ago (2002:192). While Zazaki refers more immediately back to *Old Persian* (Indo-European / Old Persian) and has some tendency to *Parthian / Arsacid Pahlavi* and *Pahlavanik* (Indo-European / NW Iranian), the Kurdish languages trace straight back to *Middle Persian* and are much more closely related to *Persian / Farsi* (Gnoli 2007:109, 111, 116; 2.2.1; 3.2.1). Through Middle Persian they go back to *Old Persian*, and also, but to a lesser extent, *Parthian* and *Median* (3.5).

The Zaza people hand down their culture orally. Hence we could speak of a culture using oral tradition as a way of conserving their history. Only a few documents were written before 1980, when a writing movement started in the European Diaspora (Paul 2009:546; Selcan 1998:17-123; 2.3.1.4; 2.3.4.6). For thirty years now an increasing interest is perceptible in monolingual written research, material and literature. Such interest involves not more than 10% of the Zaza. The rest of the Zaza community do not read or write their language. The reason for that is the education in Turkish and a lack of interest in developing Zazaki as a language of wider communication. Although such education did not work well until the 1960s, almost all Zaza society members know at least Turkish for daily survival. Zaza who were educated in Turkish before 1960 did mainly learn the basics in Turkish. After 1960 until the beginning of the nineties, a repressive educational style pressed children to either deal with intense learning of Turkish or to skip the school system after 5 years of learning. Such pupils were not well prepared to find a place within the economic system of Turkey. This is why the big cities around the Zaza homeland, like *Diyarbakır, Elazığ* and *Adana* became shelters for such poorly educated Zaza. Since the nineties Turkish policy towards their minority education focused on preschool and Kindergarten. As the Zaza people have little self esteem about their culture they increasingly adapt to the Turkish system, by speaking Turkish with their children or by intermarriage with a Turkish partner. Assimilation processes in the diaspora led to the development of an active scholarly linguistic community working on Zazaki. Besides grammars, wordlists and lexicons an extensive language learning handbook of the Northern Zazaki dialect for German audience was published in 2012 (Keskin 2012, *Zonê Ma Zanena?*). A monolingual childrens teaching book in Zazaki is planned to be published in Turkey for a Turkish audience in the year 2013 (ZazaDer together with Tıj Yayinları).

An idea of the people, the culture and the language as well as its development regarding the aforementioned small linguistic and cultural awakening, will be in the foreground of this description.[22] To understand the differences in description

---

[22] About the historical development of the written tradition primarily in the North Dialect see Selcan (1998a and 1998b:7-103) and Werner (2006:16-27, 34-54).

one has to be aware of the distinction of nation (*nationality*) and people (*nation*) mentioned by Fishman (1972:3). The Zaza people are a nation with Turkish as nationality. As an adjectival derivation of Zaza the term *"Zazaic"* could be suggested, but in literature this term has not been used so far.

Essential to this chapter is the fundamental question of the identification of the language as part of an ethnos (see above). A language is an expression of culture or vice versa, so the basic question of identity is again central to understand dynamics within the Zaza culture (see discussion 1.1.3.2; 2.1.2.7). Hence the issue of the Zaza mother tongue[23] called *Zazaki*[24] being a *"Kurdish"* dialect or an independent language in a linguistic-ethnological sense needs to be examined. With that goes the question as to whether the assimilation of the last decades has resulted either in a dissolution of the culture or only in a customization by preserving their own cultural components. It will become apparent that primarily because of the political reasons of other parties, much bewilderment is raised, and that the linguistic research of recent time regarding Zazaki also contributed to raising questions that need to be answered. Whether or not and how far such questions already existed before 1950 or 1960, as dates of targeted Turkish repression, within the Zaza people group, is not part of this examination. Verbal statements of older informants (60 years and older) do not reveal any ethnic or linguistical unease (*Questionnaire about the World View of the Zaza*, Werner 2006).

Zazaki belongs to one of the three dominant language families in the Middle East, namely the Semitic, the Turkic and the Indo-European language family. It is the latter that will be referred to here (Franz 1988b:29; see also Appendices

Appendix 1 Homeland Area of the Zaza; Appendix 2a Branch of Indo-European Languages).

2.2.1 Zazaki – Part of the Indo-European Language Family

The origin or homeland of Proto-Indo-European is still a mystery. Some argue that Proto-Indo-European attracted other people groups by religion, military expansion or trade and thus became a *lingua franca* in the area of today's Balkans,

---

[23] Mother tongue is understood as a "not-standardized language of an ethnic group" (Fasold 1993:62). Regarding Zazaki one could speak of a language used "primarily for communication within a particular speech community, identifying it as a specific sociocultural group in the country". Fasold calls this characteristic the "group function" of language (:63).

[24] The particle *-ki* in the term Zaza*ki* denotes languages (e.g. English is called İngiliz*ki*, German is named Alman*ki*, French is described as Frans*ki*, Persian is called Fars*ki* etc.).

Turkey and Greece which is considered to be the homeland. In 7.000 BC evidence is given that a farming population established a new language in southeastern and central Europe (Neolithic model; Mallory & Adams 2009:460). Since 4.000 BC, mass migration from around Ukraine and Southern Russia to the West led also to settlement in the Anatolian area where these cultures developed very fast (ibid.)

The Indo-European language family was previously every now and then called the Indo-Aryan (Aryan = Noble; Franz 1988b:41) or Indo-Germanic language family. Nowadays the term Indo-European has become the generic term for the language family, whereas Indo-Aryan as well as German were declared language branches (see Appendix 2a).

The qualification for languages to be in the *Indo-European language family* goes with the hypothesis of prototypes of all language branches in this group (see above; Sapir 1961:143). One method to track the Indo-European language group back to *one* Proto-Aryan language is called *monophyletic*. This hypothesis levels each subgroup down from a Proto-Aryan origin. Each subgroup is also supposed to track back to its own prototype. Hence for instance the Iranian group traces back to a *Proto-Iranian* language (Sanskrit in Ostler 2006:174, 176, 178; Wolf 1975:21), Zazaki and Kurmanji to a *Proto-Westiranian* language, the Germanic group to a *Proto-Germanic* etc. Obviously such an approach, although it could be outlined by historical phonological processes (morphological, structural), opens up a lot of questions. These questions are when, why and how a language develops out of its prototype and form its own phonemic and grammatical rules, or at which point could it be called a prototype of a subgroup or a language. The questions are so far not answered, while some scientists use different approaches. But for the categorization here, as part of a comparative method, the historical-genealogical approach clearly shows the differences and similarities with the wider and closer "Kurdish" languages.

Proto-Indo-European is marked by universalities that are found in the branches of this language family. "Proto-Indo-European grammar is primarily characterized by extensive inflection in nominal and verbal elements, OV or left-branching word-order patterns, and nominative syntax" (Bauer 2000:336). Grammar, as for example in the Indo-Germanic language family, can be traced back to a Proto Indo-Germanic language (Sapir 1961:143).

Another approach that is just mentioned here tracks back to more than *one* Proto-language. Thus one could also assume that there are similar prototypes of languages which form a language family. Such an approach is called *polyphyletic* (Liebi 2003:77).

Eight Indo-European languages were spoken in Eastern Anatolia during the first and second millennium before Christ (Seufert & Kubaseck 2004:47). As mentioned above Zazaki and Kurmanji-Kurdish refer back to a "Proto-Westiranian" language. But as long as 2000 years ago – due to historical changes in phonology – a split between the two languages became apparent (Paul 2002:190-192). Kurmanji developed closer to Farsi, whereas Zazaki tended towards *Parthian / Arsacid Pahlavi / Pahlavanik* (Indo-European / NW Iranian), yet Zazaki developed its own branch and Kurmanji split later from Middle Persian (Indo-European / West Iranian). Kurmanji is much more closely related to Farsi than Zazaki. Nonetheless Persian still had an impact on Zazaki due to its geographical closeness (Table 14).

2.2.2 A Northwestern Iranian Language within a Language Belt

The *Iranian languages* form a supergroup within the Indo-European language family. They are sometimes compared to a language group called *Anatolian* (Mallory & Adams 2009:74). *Anatolian* is not yet accepted as a former language group by all linguists. The Iranian languages are distinguished as Old and New Iranian languages. The language groups that are of interest here belong to the *New Iranian language* family (Windfuhr 2009:12). Zazaki and Kurmanji belong to the *Northwestern Iranian* language group. Together with Gorani (Gurani, Hewrami) it forms its own language branch based on linguistic historic-genetical evidence. *Kurmanji* and its related languages, such as *Sorani, Bahdeni, Herki, Shikaki, and Surchi* are derived from Middle Persian (Hadank 1930:1-6, 17-19, 65-66; Bailey 2003:10; Kreyenbroek & Sperl 2002:70; s. Appendix 2b; 3.2.1).

The Indo-European resp. Indo-Aryan and the Iranian family of languages as a part of it, especially shows, in comparison with other families of languages, a common feature is the category of "inflecting language" like most languages of this group (Liebi 2003: 90). The assumption that Zazaki and Kurmanji could be in the same group of languages due to their similarity is therefore understandable but questionable (geographical representation of the Iranian languages in Schmitt 2000. *The Iranian languages*. Map in the appendix; s. a. Werner 2006:88 there genetic structure, appendix 1 and 3.1.2.1). Blau compares Gorani with Zazaki and comes to the conclusion that both are independent languages and clearly distinguished from Kurmanji and Sorani (1989:336-340).

2 The Zaza

Hadank compares the living style of both peoples and provides as the most conspicuous similarity a missing tradition about nomadism and with that a settledness of both people. I disagree with him about this, because the Kurds, or sections of them, practice nomadism until today and the Zaza ethnicity never did. For instance some of the Kurdish (Kurmanji speaking) tribes such as the *Beritan* small scale society still follow a nomadic lifestyle. Also Hadank notes the preference for mountains as residential areas as well as the cultivation of fruits and vegetables in preference to corn (1930:18). Yet on an anthropological-sociological level one would count Zazaki a language of one of the Kurdish people (Appendix 2a Branch of Indo-European Languages and Appendix 2b Branch of Iranian Languages).

Diagram 7 Zazaki – Iranian Language Branch

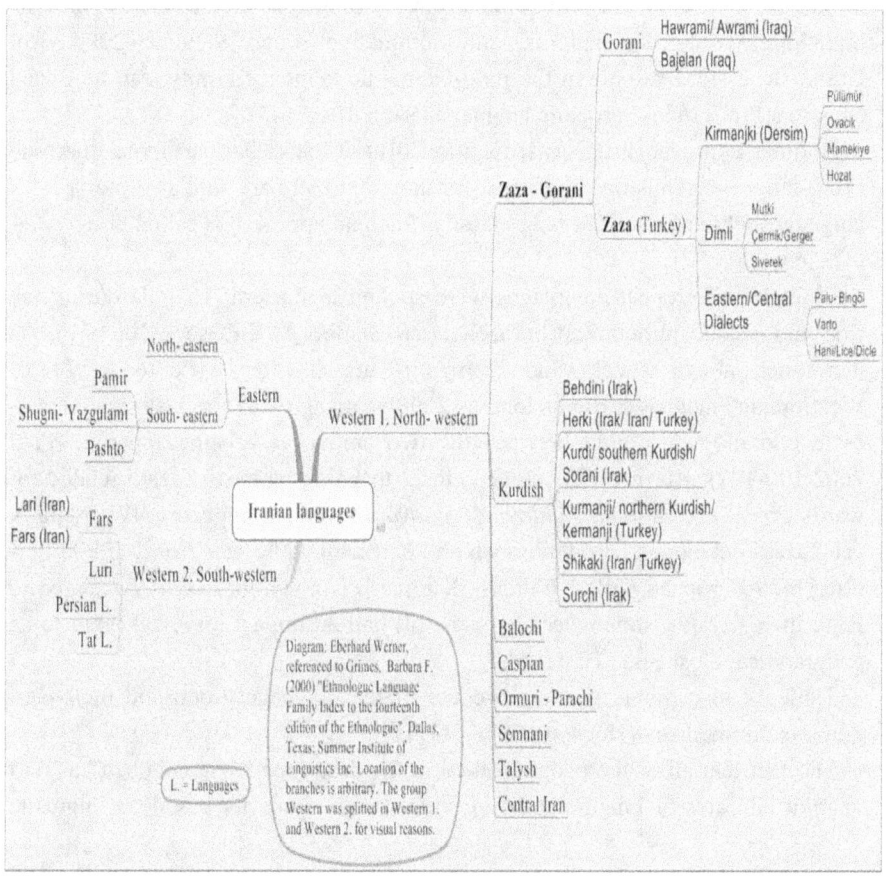

The whole spread of Zazaki and Kurdish related languages points to a "language belt" (see 2.1.2.2), reaching from the Euphrates (tk. *Fırad*) and Tigris (tk. *Dicle*) headwaters down to the East of Northern Iraq (McCarus 2009:587). It follows a south-eastern line and thus includes parts of the western Iranian border within the provinces of Khordestan, Ilam and Kermansha. Hence a lot of so called "Kurdish" languages are revealing close affinity to Zazaki and Gorani (see below). Beside the affinity one could speak of a rich "interference with language shift (traditionally better known as substratum) and borrowing with language maintenance" (Leezenberg 1993a:35; s. a. Windfuhr 2009:26-27, 30-31). The influence of Kurmanji on Zazaki and that of Sorani on Gorani is essential.

Proto-Indo-European is marked by universalities that are found in the branches of this language family. "Proto-Indo-European grammar is primarily characterized by extensive inflection in nominal and verbal elements, OV or left-branching word-order patterns, and nominative syntax" (Bauer 2000:336). Grammar, as for example in the Indo-Germanic language family, can be traced back to a Proto Indo-Germanic language (Sapir 1961:143).

Another approach that is just mentioned here tracks back to more than *one* Proto-language. Thus one could also assume that there are similar prototypes of languages which form a language family. Such an approach is called *polyphyletic* (Liebi 2003:77).

Eight Indo-European languages were spoken in Eastern Anatolia during the first and second millennium before Christ (Seufert & Kubaseck 2004:47). As mentioned above Zazaki and Kurmanji-Kurdish refer back to a "Proto-Westiranian" language. But as long as 2000 years ago – due to historical changes in phonology – a split between the two languages became apparent (Paul 2002:190-192). Kurmanji developed closer to Farsi, whereas Zazaki tended towards *Parthian / Arsacid Pahlavi / Pahlavanik* (Indo-European / NW Iranian), yet Zazaki developed its own branch and Kurmanji split later from Middle Persian (Indo-European / West Iranian). Kurmanji is much more closely related to Farsi than Zazaki. Nonetheless Persian still had an impact on Zazaki due to its geographical closeness (Table 14).

Table 14 also points to the closeness of the language group and their geographical immediacy (Hudson 1987:35-37).

The fact that all of the people settled in the described "language belt" as part of joint emirates or kingdoms demonstrates their similarity based on linguistic and cultural proximity (e.g. Sheik and Agha as leadership for larger groups in Olson 1989:3-4).

Until recently most of the language groups within the language belt were not researched, concerning the need of their own orthographic systems. In the same way their language vitality versus their bilingualism is also an unknown to us. Appendix 2 gives a short impression of the relationship of these languages and their need of research.

2.2.3 Zazaki – General Remarks

The following features describe Zazaki within the setting of non-Turkic and thus *minority languages* in Turkey. Zazaki as a *minority language* belongs to those languages which are spoken as a *mother tongue* of more than 100.000 people and that are [theoretically. EW.] taught in school from the age of six. Primers and textbooks have to be available (Fasold 1993:62). Since 1996 language learning material for the whole Zazaki group have been available from Jacobson (1999 and 2001). In official politics minority language education in school is not recommended, and the reading and writing of such language material cannot be used in school. Lack of language trainers and the missing perspective to use the skill of writing in Zazaki brings forth a deficiency in learning either reading and / or writing the language. As a result there is little development of any trigger in the education of Zazaki.

Zazaki does not belong to the "historical languages" as its speakers did not develop their own identity or a cultural horizon for their language in the past. Also there are recently no educational applications available either for public schools or in public life (theatre, film etc.), although the language is actively used in the families and in everyday life.

Another aspect of Zazaki is that its function that goes beyond a "language of special use" (1996:62) since it covers all aspects of daily life. Furthermore Zazaki has to be understood as a *standard language*[25] given that it unites different dialectical variants and a variety of idiolects (Coseriu 2007:24, 142-143). This aggravates the process of standardization of the dialects (Paul & Gippert 2009; Paul 2009:546; Keskin 2008:51).

---

[25] The concepts of *Special-* and *Standard* language are until today not defined finally (Fluck cit. in Stolze 1999:21; s. a. definition of North 1974: xvi on *Standard* language). Nevertheless *Special*-languages overlay the *Standard* language (:21-22) or reconcile different dialects with each other (Coseriu 2007:142-143).

2.2.3.1 Language versus ("Kurdish") Dialect - Definitions

The disparity between *language* and *dialect* is not defined finally by linguistic or communication science. Language is a subsystem or device (organ) acquired by enculturation which by means of an immanent quality of inherent delimitation has a *culture- and identity-giving denotation*. Language displays itself through time- and life-forming, and it

- is perceptible in an *acoustic-symbolic* way, i.e. by means of double articulation and linking of physical expressions (gesture, mimic, body language) with linguistic utterances,
- is a *partial strategy of the mastering of existence* that forms a cognitive ordering system which is established in the brain. There, invisible, and by means of stacking and query (memory structure) it associates information with other information and functions as a mediator of the same (Werner 2011:74).

Wolf suggests a "norm" which allows the language community - taken as a corpus - to accept or refuse actualizations of their communication system (Wolf 1975:4-5). Any *diasystem* outside of such a "norm" is considered a *dialect*. Hence a *dialect* is part of regiolects (geographically bound), sociolects or idiolects (very small units) that are either *diachronic*, meaning linguistically homogenous units, or *synchronic* such as social units that share common tasks (Fuchs 1984:97; Reiss & Vermeer 1991:22).

2.2.3.2 Language vs. ("Kurdish") Dialect – Discussion (Vate Group)

Having such definitions in mind, the question mentioned in this paragraph will be approached by starting with a historical outline about the debate on Zazaki. As mentioned above (1.2.1) early research or documentation on languages in Eastern Anatolia started with the *Sherefname* of *Sheref Chan* (16th century) and the *Seyahatname* of *Evliya Çelebi* (17th century). Sixteen Kurdish *dialects* (or languages!) are mentioned therein, and Zazaki occurs as one of them. Zazaki and Gorani are since then described as "Kurdish" *dialects* (Leezenberg 1993a:11-12; Paul 1994).

On the Internet the discussion is backtracked to the first research about Zazaki and Gorani which gives an overview of recent opinions (*Kurdische Sprachen* [Kurdish Languages] 2010):

> What a language and what a dialect is, depends on a whole number of factors...
> Northern Kurdish (Kurmandshi) and Southern Kurdish (Sorani) are considered as im-

portant language forms [of Kurdish. EW.]. Besides these two language forms there are still other important ones, but their speakers are rather restricted, however Zazaki (Dimili) and Gorani are part of it. The relation of Zazaki (Dimili) to Kurdish is controversial. The German Iranist Oskar Mann (in cooperation with Karl Hadank), described Zazaki (Dimli) as an independent language just like the institute for linguistics at the TU in Berlin and many others. (Mann 1932: Preface).

The first written discussions about Zazaki date from 1932. In their linguistic description Hadank and Mann report about two expeditions into the area of the Zaza from 1901-1903 and 1906-1907. Their research was the most groundbreaking work on the Zaza people and their language. An excellent overview about research and the designation of the Zaza is found in Selcan (1998:7-122) as Haig states, "Selcan has compiled the most comprehensive survey of the literature on Zazaki available, which will remain an invaluable source for future reference" (2001:182; see also "dialectology" in Keskin 2008).

The deceased English linguist and researcher David Neil MacKenzie (1926-2001) was

one of the first recorded as saying that dialects like Gorani or Hawrami are non-Kurdish. Since then other western linguists say that Zaza/Dimili also has to be judged as non-Kurdish, independent languages. This is intensely opposed and refused by Kurdish authors. For them Gorani/Hawrami and Zaza/Dimili also belong to Kurdish. (Hennerbichler 2004:132).

Research reveals substantial differences between Zazaki and Kurmanji in vocabulary and grammar, so that Zazaki is put in order with the latter almost unanimously by linguists. A small list of researchers in relation to the publishing date of their results reveals this very clearly (Table 3). Obviously this to some degree parallels the study of the origin of the Zaza people, since their cultural cradle goes closely with their linguistical roots (see Table 4) and there is lack of differentiation due to linguistical disparity but ethnical closeness (2.1.2.4).

Recent research takes the linguistical disparity of Zazaki and Kurmanji as a standard to describe the people group and asks for more openness to ethnical affinity between Kurmanji speaking "Kurds" and the Zaza ethnicity (Leezenberg, Paul, Gippert, Windfuhr, etc.). The reason for that lies in the people groups themselves. Mainly political interests drive "Kurds" to gather Zaza under their wings in order to increase their influence and power. Yet Zaza people tend to gather with Kurmanji "Kurds" due to their ethnical proximity and against the overwhelming power of the Turks. On linguistical grounds the political group of interested Zaza uses the Kurdish alphabet as introduced by *Bedr Khan* and tries to establish an artificial language with many Kurmanji loanwords and borrowings as well as grammatical constructions.

For instance Hadank reports:

> On November 28th in 1932 the emir told me ... from time to time, Kurdish herdsmen from Damascus got by ... now two Zaza shepherds from Paul arrived here ... I expressed the desire to get to know more Zaza rehearsals, he turned off; apparently he only prevails here with doubled regard, primarily on the political sight - the emir classes the Zaza as Kurds and would like to see them all Kurdisized. (cit. in Selcan 1998:83).

This trend prevails in political "Kurdish" circles to this day. A group around the pseudonym "Malmisanij (Malmîsanij)" from Stockholm (Sweden) operates in such ways. Since 1997 they have published an excellently researched three-monthly monolingual magazine named *Vate* (36 editions; Zilan 2011). The so called "Vate Çalışma Grubu" (*Grûba Xebate ya Vateyî* GXV) claims the standardization of Zazaki by using the alphabet of the Kurd *Jeladet Ali Bedr Khan* (1893-1951). This was invented in the 1930s for Kurmanji, the Northern Kurdish dialect spoken in Turkey. (Khan & Lescot 1986:3-6; Honeyboon 1995; 3.4). Their attempt towards standardization is following the rules of majority usage. If a word or a grammatical rule is used in the same way in all regions that is the preferred use in the common written language. The following rules describe their method or strategy of choice in vocabulary:

- "If a word or a grammatical rule has not a common usage, the following procedure is suggested:
  - etymological research about the word
  - pronunciation of other forms of Kurdish dialects is taken into account as part of etymological research
- If the word originated from other languages, one which is close to the original language's form is preferable.
- Borrowed words are not rejected if they are convenient to use in Kirmanchki.
- If there is no agreement, the majority decision of people who attended the GXV meeting will be accepted." (Zilan 2011).

The *Vate group* holds a strict pro-Kurdish / pro-Kurmanji stance. The idea is to unify and combine all "Kurdish" related people groups out of fear of separation. The driving force is the dread that the political and societal power which the entire "Kurdish" group carry will be weakened. On a higher level such politics provide the main reason for performing links of cohesion, whereas on the ground level the Zaza people really feel divided.

The work of GXV (*Grûba Xebate ya Vateyî*) is enormous and every attempt towards standardization has to be taken seriously. The following questions arise with such an approach:
- the final say lies within the core of the group that are pro-Kurmanji, so how will the GXV decide on non-Kurmanji, but originally Zaza, words, if they are not agreed on a common spelling of this word?
- why does this group not allow for someone who states that he is a "Zaza speaking Zazaki" but just for one stating he is a "Zaza Kurd speaking Zaza Kurdish"?

Isn't the nationalistic and undemocratic stance counterproductive towards the development of independence or self-esteem of a specific linguistic and cultural movement with its educational material? A democratic way would be that Kurmanji and Zazaki speakers develop their own identity and watch out for working partnerships to form larger units. These should be in the fields of mother tongue education, care of children, medical care and social welfare in the community.

To follow up the discussion about Zazaki being an independent language vs. a "Kurdish" dialect, a focussed look at the linguistical relationship to related languages such as Gorani seems helpful.

2.2.3.3 Language versus ("Kurdish") Dialect - Gorani

Gorani, also called Gurani or Hewrami / Hawrami, is spoken by the Euphrates east of Baghdad. The basic group of speakers lives on both sides of the border formed by the Euphrates on either Iranian or Northern Iraqi soil. Pockets of Gorani resp. Hewrami are spread out to the north as far as close to Diyarbakır (Paul 2007:285-293; 2.1.3.1.1). These northern groups are better known as *Shabak* or *Bajalan* and have a relationship to the Zaza population.

Gorani is historically a closely related language to Zazaki and together they form a branch of the New Iranian languages and within it the *Northwestern Iranian* language group (Gordon 2005 Ethnologue15[th] ed.; Windfuhr 2009). The Goran and their language have not been investigated much (Hadank 1930:1-15, 17-18, 55-65; Ruciyar 2003 *Hewramî-Gorani*; current research project of Hamburg university by Ludwig Paul). The whole group is recently estimated at

20.000 or more speakers who are fluently bilingual in their national languages (Leezenberg 1993a:6; MacKenzie 2003:402).

In 1880 modern research on Gorani started (Justi 1880:2, 4). The researched linguistical factors pointed to many commonalities with Zazaki and a few with Kurmanji-Kurdish (Bailey 2003:17-18; Hadank 1930:65-66; Kreyenbroek & Sperl 2002:70). Back then this was astonishing, the more so as the habitat of those people groups was almost 500 km apart, and they lived under different ruling powers. Also Gorani showed more affinity to Southern Kurdish resp. Sorani.

Since 1912 Gorani was treated as an independent language (Hadank 1930:1-43, 57)[26]. Research based on ideological grounds states that Gorani - like Zazaki – is a "Kurdish" language or dialect by referring to the people group itself and their identification with the "Kurds" (e.g. Loizides 2010; Leezenberg 1993; Kreyenbroek & Sperl 2002:35, 70). The *Daylam-Thesis* (2.1.3.2.1.1) is also applied for the Gorani speakers (MacKenzie 2003:401-402; Hadank 1930:18). Some linguists and researchers studying Iran trace the origin of this people group back to the Caspian languages area south-east of the Caspian Sea (Hennerbichler 2004:197). So far no definite proof is given for this thesis but it is scrutinized e.g. by Leezenberg who takes into account that the Empire of Erdelan has its origin in Diyarbakır (Leezenberg 1993a:7, 16). Following the arguments about the Daylam-Thesis the process shows much commonality about the religious and economic background of the Gorani and the Zaza people (see below; 2.1.3.1.1). Having said this, the critique against the Daylam-thesis also has to be considered; however the "Kurdish" movement has the same effects on the Gorani as on the Zazaki speakers.

If, as I argued in 2.1.2.3, the Zaza and Gorani (Gurani) settled in their current homelands a long time ago, the main Kurmanji speaking Kurdish penetration by nomads occurred around the 6th century AD as the Targumic translations of Scripture prove. Before the 6th century the region of the Ararat was called the heartland of Armenia, whereas afterwards it became referred to as "Kurdistan" and the "Kurds" (Targums of Genesis 8:4, Isaiah 37:38, and Jeremiah in Izady 1992:96; Paul & Haig 2001:399). There is some evidence that Kurdish speaking groups again overran the influential and powerful Gorani Empire that used Go-

---

[26] Interestingly the Iranian gouverment used such western statements to differentiate the Gorani people from "the Kurds" (Hassanpour cit. in Leezenberg 1993a:8 footnote 19).

2 The Zaza

rani as a "court language at the Kurdish principality of Erdelan, which flourished in the 17th and especially the 18th century" (:ibid; also Kreyenbroek & Sperl 2002:70). Thus the languages merged. This becomes obvious by the evidence of an "archaic" Kurmanji area in the north and a Gorani influenced Sorani area in the south, close to the homeland of the Gorani (Windfuhr 2009:30). Gorani makes up the southern tip of this researched closer "language belt" and thus its influence on neighbouring groups like Sorani is evident (ibid.). Recently Gorani is on the edge of extinction through Farsi (Iran), Sorani or Arabian (both Northern Iraq) influence.

The Zaza and Gorani ethnicities have in common, that both:
- do not link with any nomadic tradition or recent habitation (Justi 2006: xxv Preface; Hadank 1930:17-18, Leezenberg 1993:11),
- are named from outside (exonym) and refer to themselves (endonym) with different terminology (Zaza: *Dımıli, Zone Ma*; Gorani: *Haramani, Hawrami*),
- were involved historically in upheavals and rebellions against the national ruling systems and experienced huge waves of discrimination, deportations and massacres (2.1.4.6, 2.3.1.3 and 3.5). An important point here is the upheaval of the Gorani-speaking populations from their traditional locations because of the *Anfal* campaign and the deportation into the concentration camps in the late 1980s,
- refer to themselves as "Kurds", although they distinguish themselves from the "Kurds" on historical and linguistic-ethnical grounds,
- are split into a Sunni and a Shi'ite tradition, the latter being *Alevism* for Zazaki and for the Goran the *Ahl-i Heqq* (Ahl-ê Haqq) tradition (Bruinessen 1992: 139-151; Paul 2007:285). Both groups thus follow the Twelver Shi'ite tradition originally from Persia (Izady 1992:44-45).

Bailey gives a summary of language groups surveyed by Leezenberg and other research on Gorani and related languages (2010; Leezenberg 1993a:5 and 1993b; alphabetical order):
- *Bajalan (Gorani)*: an ethnic group living near Khanaqin and north of Mossul in the Khosar Valley.
- *Kakai (Gorani)*: also called *Ahl-ê Haqq, Ali-Illahi* or *Yaresan* (in Iran), according to religious background (near Topzawa, and Khanaqin). The dialect is sometimes called *Macho*. Some Kakai speak other languages (Turcoman, Sorani, Arabic).

- *Roshkakai* (*Gorani*): spoken in the same area near Khanaqin, considered a dialect by one of Leezenberg's contacts.
- *Sarlî* or *Sarlû* (*Gorani*): actually Kakai, and the name Sarlî is used by others for this group; it is apparently perceived as negative by the members of the group. This dialect is perhaps in-between *Shabak* and *Macho* (i.e., Kakai in Sfêye village, near Eski Kalak; Leezenberg 1993b: nr. 2).
- *Shabak* (Gorani): also living near Mosul. Some scholars treat Bajalan and Shabak as names for one group, but others consider them distinct (e.g. Leezenberg): Bajalan are *Sunni* (though heterodox) and their social organization is tribal-based. Shabak are *Shi'ite* heterodox and their social organization is not based on a small scale social unit. Some assume that there are three 'sects' of Shabak, which are the Shabak proper, the Zengana, and the Bajalan.
- Zengana (*Gorani*): refers to a tribal confederation located southeast of Kirkuk, also near Khanaqin. Zengana speakers were located throughout the entire area of Germian until the late 1800s (later deported to that area in the 3rd Anfal operation s. Leezenberg 1993b).
- Rojbeyani (*Gorani*): a Gorani dialect (Leezenberg 1993b: nr. 1.1).

2.2.3.4 Zazaki - Independent but Ethnically close to the "Kurds"

To evaluate the Zaza people's feelings, respecting their ethnical disposition and the linguistical evidence, many researchers nowadays come to the following conclusion. They assume that linguistically Zazaki, together with Gorani, represents an independent language group, belonging to the North-western branch of the Iranian language family. At the same time, the ethnical proximity to "Kurdish" culture and tradition makes them part of the wider "Kurdish society or societies". Hennerbichler quotes Blau who speaks of a "national Kurdish unity" that Zaza and Kurds share (2004:198). In the same way Paul, coming from the actual terminology of unity and identity within a nation, suggests also differentiating between linguistical and cultural factors. Yet the identity question should be answered by the Zaza themselves, whereas linguistically they are independent but culturally they identify *with* and *as* Kurds (2002:198; Paul & Gippert 2009). For Haig self-identification based on linguistical, religious and anthropological grounds is also essential as he states that every people group should decide for themselves (2001:182). The decision includes, either

2 The Zaza

- to belong to a wider environment with similar anthropological features (e.g. worldview, envy-concept, evil-eye concept, etc.),
- to participate in a wider alliance of languages or dialects (e.g. Kurdish and related language belt),

or

- to separate totally from socially and anthropologically close cultural units.

2.2.3.5 Main Dialects of Zazaki - Classification

Following the given definition and limitation of the term "dialect" (2.2.3.1) the geographical and linguistical structure of those dialects comes into focus. In literature one will find a split in

- a Northern Dialect called Northern Zazaki (NZ),
- a Southern Dialect referred to as Southern Zazaki (SZ) and
- an Eastern Dialect nominated as Eastern Zaza (EZ) vs. Central Dialect or Central Zaza (CZ).

Hence, recently the grouping by at least *three main dialects* became standard.

Dialectology on Zazaki started with Hadank (1932:14-17). Paul offers the first and most extensive research on dialectical variations of Zazaki (1998) following the tripartite division. He differentiates between the southern *Çermik /-Siverek* dialects (CSD), the eastern *Palu / Bingöl* dialects (PBD) and the northern Alevi dialects (AD). He counts the less researched south-eastern *Kulp / Mutki* dialect as one of the PBD's, though with an affinity to CSD's (Eğil; Paul 1998: xxi, map 2, 205-207). Paul speaks of a *dialect continuum* (2002:191).

Zazaki as with many minority languages (e.g. Kurdish) lacks a *standard* or *reference* dialect such as is represented in High-German or Oxford English. Hence one should "not speak of Zazaki but Zazaki dialects to be correct" (:190). As will be shown below the recent writers' activities led to a standardization of the dialects (Jacobson 1993, 1999 and 2001). Selcan and others in the same way use this tripartite division of the Zazaki dialects following linguistical, religious and geographical lines (1998:7-120).

Other divisions are focusing on a two part division only, such as a Western and Eastern Group (Hadank 1932:14) or a Southern and Northern Group (Kausen 2006; Temizbaş 2003; Temizbaş w/o Date. *Dimli: Wir, unsere Heimat und unsere Sprache*. [Engl. We, our native country and our language]). In this way, those scientists divide primarily in linguistical and secondarily in religious categories.

Newer research by Keskin (2008) follows a tripartite classification but indicates historical development by assuming that the Eastern dialects are the most archaic, yet most original forms of Zazaki. He calls them Central Zazaki (CZ; 2008). As Keskin summarizes, looking at the research results of Selcan and Paul, he comes to the conclusion that a historical approach could be of help for dialectical classification (2008:21-26). As noted above the main problem is that a dialectical standardization is not yet in sight.

Zazaki dialects vary in vocalization and pronunciation. Grammatical differences are carved out by Paul (1998). In Zazaki it is of secondary importance to divide in dialect groups whereas the socio-cultural differences in religion and cultural practices verify at first place (2.3).

Following the rules of comparative linguistics "the oldest language levels are significantly complex in the morphology compared to the younger ones" (Liebi 2003b:212). Compared with the northern dialect variations, the southern dialect variations show overweighing syntactical (compound) forms in contrast to the analytical ones. Referring to comparative linguistics this would mean that SZ represents the older dialectical form compared to the NZ (:206). Looking at a tripartite division, the Eastern dialects reveal phonetically shorter and less analytical forms compared to SZ. Nevertheless as will be shown below anthropological studies on culture and religion are an obstacle for that (2.3 and 2.5).

2.2.3.6 Summary of the Zazaki – Discussion on "Kurdish"

Based on linguistical grounds, whether the three main dialects that are representing Zazaki as a *dialectical continuum*; are part of a wider "Kurdish" language group can be denied. The Southern dialect variations (SZ), the Northern dialect variations (NZ) and the Eastern (EZ) resp. Central dialect variations (CZ) are so far *not* standardized. Other two partite divisions are contradicted by recent research. All together each geographical dialect group splits itself into a minimum of three more subdialects. The NZ divide into the dialects of *Mamekiye* (Dersim / Tunceli), *Pulumoriye* and *Ovaçık*, SZ into the dialects of *Çermik*, *Siverek* and *Gerger*, CD or ED into the dialects of *Palu*, *Bingöl* and *Varto*.

Like other minority groups, e.g. the "Kurds", the lack of standardization leads to a wide variation of orthographical representations. Kurmanji orthography was triggered by *Bedr Khan* and Zazaki orthography by *Jacobson* (1993, 1999 and 2001). Both of their alphabets are chiefly used by the language groups nowadays.

Zazaki represents a *dialectic continuum*. On linguistical and anthropological grounds the whole group signifies an independent people group and Zazaki an independent language. Looking at the proponents who agree with the independency and the critics who state that Zazaki is a Kurdish dialect, it becomes obvious that political or economic reasons cause such statements. Yet on anthropological or ethnical grounds one is not free to judge the Zaza people. The cultural proximity to the "Kurds" overweighs the linguistical gap between Zazaki and Kurmanji, the more as a large group of the Zaza society tend to refer to a "Kurdish nationality" and take part in the "Kurdish nationalism movement". Often for them their language then becomes a "Kurdish dialect", which is a problem of definition of "Kurdish languages". The whole uncertainty of the future for a "Kurdish province" or self ruling district within Turkey means that at the moment it is an open question as to how the region will develop. However one has to be aware of a growing national self esteem based on language and cultural identification within the Zaza and the Kurmanji speakers. Hence Zazaki literature, language and dialect development as well as the badly needed standardization are on the edge of a breakthrough. In contrast to the Kurmanji speaking group, monolingual education and language development in the Zaza community are behind. The result is a tension between both ethnicities, with the tendency that the former and larger ethnos oppresses the smaller Zaza cluster. The power flows from the larger to the smaller group.

2.2.4 Dialectical Disparity and the Zaza Ethnicity

Besides the tripartite linguistical split into a Northern, Southern and Eastern faction, there exists a historical-religious partition into a Northern and Southern cluster. The causes and effects of the separation can be summarized as follows:

> The social and political ratio of the Alevi Kurds from the mountainous area to their Sunni neighbours of the lowlands and between state and region is burdened historically. The clashes between the Alevi tribes of the mountains and the Sunni beg's of the Murad plain, the military expeditions [of the Turks. EW.] of the 19th century, with the purpose to subdue the region, to gather recruited and collect taxes, as well as unrest until the thirties, leading to persecution and resettlement of the mountaineers to Anatolia, has an effect on consciousness, attitude and political behaviour until today. (Nestmann 2002:555).

This possible temporal specification about the cultural and religious separation of the Zaza people cluster points to the disparity of Zazaki within the 16th century (2.1.3.1.1; 2.2.1.7.2). At this point a reference is necessary to a different naming and assignation of the Zaza. Contrary to my observations the controversial research by Izady describes the Northern Group as *Dimila* and the Southern Group as *Zaza*. Thereby the *Dimila* appear as Alevis and the *Zaza* as Sunni (Izady 1992:15-151). It is not clear where he got his information from. In contrast to Izady, but in accordance with the most scientists, I start out from the general division by which the phrase *Zaza* describes the complete group, and at least partially the Southern Group as *Dımli* (2.2.1.31).

Following the Ethnologue 15th ed. a differentiation is made between *zzz* for *Zaza* covering the Northern group (NZ) and *diq* for the *Southern Group* (Gordon 2005. *Diq)*. Out of the Zaza this has been questioned recently as self esteem increases. The 16th edition still follows this division. For the next (17th) edition of the Ethnologue a main entry is requested with *zzz* for Zaza, the whole set, and *kiu* for Alevi Northern subgroup, as well as *diq* for the Southern Group.

Religious and historical reasons argue for a separation in a religiously and geographically split Northern, Southern and Eastern Group. This division performs the frame of the ethnographic description as herein the most significant differences come into action. In other words and summed up above, a linguistical separation is just one reason to divide the Zaza into three *main* dialects. In going one level deeper one will also find a relevant anthropological *tripartite disparity* within the Northern, Southern and Eastern Group based on a common perception of the world but split in different lifestyles (see 2.3.1.1; 2.3.3.1).

Table 11 follows the classification of Paul. He summarizes and divides into the language of
- the Northern Group as the *Alevi Dialects* (AD; 1998:183-193),
- the Eastern Dialects as the *Palu/Bingöl Dialects* (PBD; 1998:194-203) and
- the *Çermik/Siverek Dialects* (CSD), to which the historically important Gerger Dialect is counted to (Paul 1998:173-182).

Marked in italics are the best investigated (reference-) dialects that could emerge to be *Standard Dialects* in the future. As a point of reference the *Çermik* dialect of Zazaki is here used for further comparison. The Eastern resp. Central Dialects lack deeper investigation concerning sociolinguist data.

Table 11 Dialectical Grouping

Northern Group (Alevi Dialects)	Southern Group (Sunni Hanafi)	Eastern Group (mixed)
Mamekiye/Pülümür-Dialect	*Çermik/Siverek-Dialect*	*Palu/Bingöl-Dialect*
Varto-Dialect	Lice/Dicle-Dialect	Hani-Dialect
Ovaçık-Dialect	Mutki/Kulp-Dialect	Hazro-Genç-Dialect
Hozat-Dialect	Gerger-Dialect	Muş-Dialect

Looking at these dialects, the Northern Group is the most active in writing and translating material. Jacobson worked out the alphabet that is widely used recently, in close cooperation with the Zaza in the Diaspora, (1993, 1997 in Turkish). This process leads to the incipient standardization of the Southern and Northern dialects. Such standardization became foundational to newer language-related projects as is obvious in publications from Paul, Windfuhr and Internet appearance. Besides the linguistic work from Jacobson there is a rich load of grammatical works on Zazaki. Just to mention here the foundational grammar of the Southern dialect in English (Todd [1985] 2002), the dialectical differentiating grammar on the whole group (Paul 1998), the grammar of the Northern dialect both in German (Selcan 1998), a discourse grammar for the Mamekiye dialect presented as unpublished master thesis in English (Crandall 2002) and smaller drafts (s. Hayıg 2007:205-209).

2.2.5 The Southern Group in Çermik – Investigations

The Southern Group lacks literary activity. An alphabet that was developed by Jacobson together with mother tongue speakers increasingly also finds distribution within the *Çermik/Siverek* dialect (s. a.). For SZ, an English *grammar* which was revised meanwhile is available (see above Todd 1985 and 2002). Following Todd a grammar and dialectology about the whole dialect continuum of Zazaki came into being by Paul written in German (1998). An unpublished dialectology by Keskin covers also all dialects of Zazaki (2008).

Wordlists and dictionaries are aids of language learning as well as language development and they serve as a base for common and technical dictionaries. It is therefore recommended to collect such studies early and open them up to the public (Stolze 1999:58). Umpteen public so called "dictionaries" in Zazaki (Malmisanıj; Canbolat; Turgut etc.) outline in reality wordlists (s. bibliography; Bartholomew & Schoenhals 1983:17). There are single works on linguistics and cultural idiosyncrasies about the Zaza and the Zazaki that are mentioned in the bibliography. In progress are extensive dictionaries and word studies as well as translations of single Bible parts. On the Internet one will find numerous cultural descriptions and lists of formerly mentioned available language material for the SZ dialect (e.g. Todd 2002; particularly www.zazaki.de). However Northern Zaza is better researched so far and the least investigated dialect is Eastern Zaza.

2.2.6 Reference resp. Standard Dialect - Renaming

As far as I know, less research has been done on a *reference dialect* in Zazaki. The few existing works represent statistical work papers that compare the Northern with the Southern dialects based on vocabulary, as well as questionnaires on language activity and worldview (SIL 1999; SIL 2001; SIL 2005 gathered by author). A look in history will reveal some details.

A workshop in 1999 started the discussion about a planned dictionary project. Basically a *reference dialect* is necessary to decide on main entries in a dictionary, whereas other dialects or derivations need to be marked (Gutt 1999). A standardization of the dialects or a reference dialect would in general relieve the work on translations, dictionaries and magazines. Yet at the moment the available works in progress function so far as a trigger but do not lead into a reference dialect. This corresponds to experiences from other projects in which it became clear that it takes a long time before a standard crystallizes out or in the worst case sometimes does not even develop at all (Bartholomew & Schoenhals 1983:3-4). *Standardization* changes the previous hierarchy, which is why a hesitant attitude is understandable. Nida warns of the expectation that standardization could rescind language change or a produce a violent standardization as happened in Turkey with Turkish (1975:210-212). Standardization in Europe (Germany, England and Italy) had the isolation of the spoken word as a consequence. The stress of the written word plays a special role in standardization (Ong 2002:95, 105). All told, one has to be cautious with any prediction about developments in languages; hence the trends represented here are rough directions towards understanding disparity within the Zazaki dialects and their progress.

In NZ the dialect from *Mamekiye* becomes prevalent against the dialects from *Varto* or *Pulumoriye* (Tk. Pülümür). *Mamekiye* lies in the centre of the *Dersim* region nowadays called Tunceli province (Hirschler 2001:146). In the Southern Group the *Çermik-Siverek* dialect gained high acceptance in competition to the

Bingöl or *Palu* dialect. There are grave attempts to fix the *Varto* dialect as the *standard* and *reference* dialect for the whole group of Zazaki. The argument therefore is that it represents geographically the largely central dialect and that it shows the most archaic morphological forms (Werner 2009; discussion after dictionary workshop).

To look at the wider context, in 2002 a process started in which many applications were made to change geographical and children names into the mother tongues of the various people groups in Turkey. Before, this was opposed by the Turkish officials and children were given Turkish names. However the flood of application procedures led to a new law in 2005 which allowed for the renaming of places and regions that were implemented during the process of Turkization in the 1930s and 40s (e.g. Dersim => Tunceli 1935; IHD 2002 *Türkischer Innenminister gründet* ... [Turkish Minister of Interior establishes ...]). In the *Dersim* region the last resistance movement from *Seyd Rıza* in 1938 proceeded against the central Turkish government based in Ankara (2.3.1.4; Kieser 2000:390). For that reason it was especially affected by the Turkish establishment activities after the foundation of the Republic. Here standardized practices were used by the officials to keep to one representation and to refuse variations.

For this research it is helpful to have a "standard dialect" that is a point of reference as foundation for comparative studies. As the most researched one, the *Çermik-Siverek* dialect is perfectly proper. Two arguments are to be mentioned. First the rich linguistic material that is available, namely the grammars (Todd 2002; Pamukçu 2001; Paul 1998), word lists (Turgut 2001; Malmisanıj 1992; Paul 1998 appendix) and cultural material (Malmisanıj 2000; Hayıg 2007 and 2012). Yet the dialect became popular and enhanced prestige and self-esteem. Second the *Çermik-Siverek* dialect has a sort of mediating role for the Southern dialects. For a long time both cities have been central market places for the surrounding villages and have tight reciprocal economic relations. The reason for that is the closeness of both dialects demonstrating a high comprehensibility. Although this dialect is not an official reference dialect it is used as such in a dictionary project, in comparative studies and elsewhere.

A group of investigators worked from 2010 on standardization in Zazaki. One approach is to go back to etymological roots of either Pahlavi or Avesta and look up which dialect uses the closest form nowadays in which way. This word functions as a recommendation. If there are dialectical variants they go in brackets together with this word. The authors slowly build up a reference dictionary with all entries and look up those variants and the main entry (2.2.9.1.12; Table 17; Table 18; Table 19). Approaches like this are pushed all over the globe and in some cases they worked out well, in others not (Fasold 1993:70; Bauer, Holmes & Warren 2006: 22-23). The recent experiences do not allow for further predictions.

2.2.7 Çermik

Geographically Çermik lies in the triangle of Siverek-Elazığ-Diyarbakır. Çermik has a population of close to 30.000 people. The whole hinterland covers a lot of villages and small farmsteads. The town had in the past a central importance for stock turn. Residents of the surrounding villages came there to trade (economic centre; s.a.), for cultural exchange, as ruins of churches and a synagogue demonstrate, or went to it as a spa. *Çermik* (tk.) is derived from the Zaza term *Germıg / Germug* which literally means a "hot little place". Yet to the subject *germ* for "hot" was pinned the diminutive suffix *-ik*. The "hot sources" (spa) also served as a centre of attraction for surrounding city dwellers from *Urfa* and *Diyarbakır*. *Çermik* was a local seat of state authorities like armed forces or government due to its location on one of the arterial roads (Silk Road) from South to North as from Syria to Georgia or the Black Sea in the past. These functions stressed the location from an ethnological-linguistic point of view.

A small sociolinguistical survey of Zazaki is given by Jacobson in which he emphasized the fact that as the Mamekiye dialect is for the Northern, so the Çermik / Siverek-dialect is central to the Southern Group (1993 and 1997).[27] Further approaches are planned by SIL International, specifically a rapid appraisal survey on the dialectical variants of Zazaki (Wilson 2010).

---

[27] *Sociolinguistics* and its tool *survey research* leads to the so-called language-survey examination or survey map (Fasold 1984:246-247). Thus the number of speakers, language vitality, language distribution of the dialects, their geographical distribution and cultural disparateness determines whether it is a dialect or a language and whether need exists for reading, learning material or education aid. *Survey* research not only occupies someone with the observation of temporary or future need but furthermore with looking at the emergence of language branches. For example there is a European dialectology about a retrospective *sociolinguistic* study on the origin of the *European standard languages* (e.g. High German, Oxford English, Parisian French; Wolf 1975).

2.2.7.1 Orthographic Alphabet Proposal

Jacobson presented a proposal of an alphabet for the Northern (1997:64-65) and the Southern dialects (:124-125).

Both have gained high acceptance in modern literature and turn up in scientific works (Selcan 1998; Todd 2002:243). Another hint is given by the use or orientation of these alphabets in Modern Zazaki magazines.[28] The alphabet follows the Turkish standard alphabet. The Turkish standard in the following Table 12 is represented and described by e.g. Hengirmen (1997:34), the North Dialect by Jacobson (1997:64) and the South Dialect by Todd (2002:219-220; Walter 2004a:3).

Table 12 Zazaki Alphabets vs. Turkish

Tk.	North Dialect	South Dialect	Feature	IPA[29]	German Diaspora	Zazaki Dimili	English	Türkçe
			ʾ [30]	pharyngeal	[ʕ]		'ereba	car	araba
Aa	Aa	Aa		[ɑ]	Aa Ää	aw	water	su
Bb	Bb	Bb		[b]	Bb Cc	bız	goat	keçi
Cc	Cc	Cc		[dʒʰ]	dsch	cıtêr	farmer	çiftçi
Çç	Çç	Çç		[tʃʰ]	tsch	çit	kerchief	başörtü sü

---

[28] A final listing of all magazines related or published by Zaza is found in Hayig under the column of *magazine* (2007:209, s. bibliography under *magazines of the Zaza*). Up till now there is only *Miraz* which appears monolingual in Zazaki. The majority of the contributions in the magazines are in Turkish. About 30% of the articles are in Zazaki. Monolingual presentation is still often accompanied by a discussion in the language group due to dialectical differences.

[29] The realization of the phonemes is taken from the *International Phonetic Alphabet* (IPA) and represents the pronunciation of Zazaki only. Turkish and German phonemes are realized differently in Hengirmen (1996) and Langenscheidt (1995). It should be taken into account that the pronunciation of the vowels moves within the dialectical variants. The representation listed here relates to the Çermik dialect.

[30] The pharyngeal (ayin) happens to occur rarely and only in loan words from Arabian. At present one could be aware of the tendency for the written form of the pharyngeal to be realized corresponding to the pronunciation of the vowel as a, e or ı with and without a sign of pharyngealisation (e.g. = araba 'car'; 'erd/'ard/erd/ard = 'ground'; 'estor/'ıstor/estor/ıstor = 'horse/stallion'). This is justified with the environmental variants that are responsible for the customization of the sound.

	Çh çh[31]		unaspirated	[tʃ]		**çhem**	river	nehir
Dd	Dd	Dd		[d]	Dd	**dest**	hand	el
Ee	Ee	Ee		[ɛ][ə]	Ee	**engur**	grape	üzüm
	Êê[32]	Êê		[e]		**êl-kane**	boar	erkek domuz
Ff	Ff	Ff		[f]	Ff	**fek**	mouth	ağız
Gg	Gg	Gg		[g]	Gg	**ga**	ox	öküz
Ğğ	Ğğ	Ğğ		[ʁ]		**ğele**	wheat	buğday
Hh	Hh	Hh		[h]	Hh	**her**	donkey	eşek
		'H 'h	pharyngeal	[ħ]		**'heme**	all	hepsi
İi	İi	İi		[ɨ]	Ii	**i'sot**	pepper	biber
Iı	Iı	Iı		[i]		**ışkıj**	raisin	kuru üzüm
				[j]	Jj			
Jj	Jj	Jj		[ʒ]		**jew**	one	bir
Kk	Kk	Kk		[kʰ]	Kk	**ko**	mountain	dağ
		Kh kh	Unaspirated	[k]		**khoçike**	spoon	kaşık
Ll	Ll	Ll		[l]	Ll	**lıng**	foot	ayak
		-ll[33]	velarized	[ł]		**'leym**	mud	kir
Mm	Mm	Mm		[m]	Mm	**manga**	cow	inek
Nn	Nn	Nn		[n]	Nn	**nan**	bread	ekmek

---

[31] The Northern Dialect common unaspirated phonems çh (çhem = 'river'); kh (khoçıke = 'spoon'), ph (phıt = 'baby') and th (thomur = 'Saz') are also found in an attenuated form in the northern Eastern dialects.
[32] Realized as [ʲe] in the Northern Dialect.
[33] Velarized „Ll/ll" occurs also in loanwords from Arabic (e.g. word beginning 'Leym/'leym = 'dirt'; word internal and –ending boll = 'herd'; 2.2.1.8.1 and 2.2.1.8.2).

2 The Zaza

Oo	Oo	Oo		[o][ɔ]	Oo	**omıd**	hope	ümit
Öö				[œ]	Öö		extract	özel
Pp	Pp	Pp		[pʰ]	Pp	**pûçık**	sock	çorap
	Ph ph		unaspirated	[p]		**phonç**	five	beş
				[ᵏv]	Qq			
	Qq	Qq	soundless. uvular plosive	[qʰ]		**qatır**	mule	katır
Rr	Rr	Rr	flapped vibrant	[r]	Rr	**rı**	face	yüz
-rr	-rr		thrilled vibrant	[ɾ]		**her**	donkey	eşek
Ss	Ss	Ss		[s]	Ss	**sa**	apple	elma
Şş	Şş	Şş		[ʃ]	Sch	**şêr**	lion	aslan
		'S 's ('si)	pharyngalized[34]	[sˤ]		**'si**	stone	taş
Tt	Tt	Tt		[t]	Tt	**tira nani**	rolling-pin	oklava
	Th th		unaspirated	[tˤ]		**thomur**	saz	saz
		'T 't	pharyngalized			**'teyr**	eagle	kuş (genel)

---

[34] Some assume that the modification for 's and 't is either pharyngealization (Todd 2002:7) or velarization (Paul 1998:4). As research showed, the variation within this range changes from village to village.

Uu	Uu	Uu	back / rounded	[ʊ] [u]	Uu	kutık nûncık	dog fist	köpek yumruk
Üü	ü			[y]	Üü	lüye	fox	tilki
Vv	Vv	Vv		[v]	Vv	verg	wolf	kurt
	Ww[35]	Ww		[w]	Ww	werway	barefoot	yalınay ak
			syllable final	[u]		dew	village	köy
	Xx	Xx	voiceless uvular guttural	[x]		xağ	raw	çiğ
Yy	Yy	Yy		[j] [ts]	Yy Zz	yağır	rain	yağmur
Zz	Zz	Zz		[z]		zerej	partridge	keklik
29	37	39			29			

The Eastern dialects follow the Southern dialects. Yet they tend to use additionally „Üü" [y; Y] as a vowel (*lü* = "fox"). In those dialects standardization is advanced the least of all.

2.2.7.2 Distribution of the Speakers – Danger of Language Death

Nowadays speakers of Zazaki are placed in the metropolises of Turkey as well as in exile or the Diaspora in the Federal Republic of Germany[36] (2.3.1.4;

---

[35] In a Turkish declaration the official use of the letter „Ww" was restricted and to be replaced by the letter „Vv" (e.g. *wa* => *va* = "sister"). As in the given example the word *va* means "wind", yet such language policy is troubling the use of the language in written and spoken form. Authors using „Ww" (e.g. *ware* = "pasture") are thereby demonstrating their opposition.

[36] It is estimated that 150.000-200.000 Zaza live in the Federal Republic of Germany (similar estimates are found in Kausen 2006. *Zaza*, 1-6 also at Wikipedia 2009. *Zaza;* s. a. Selcan 1998:7-103). Kausen presents a brief overview in his presentation of the research history about the Zaza.

2.3.4.6), in France, the Netherlands, the USA and Australia (approx. 10.000 emigrants). It is assumed[37] by internal estimations of Zaza people, based on families and villages in the East, that less than half of all speakers (~1 Mio.) are still settled in their home territory. Estimates start out from a total of 3 – 5 million speakers worldwide (Asatrian cit. in Hennerbichler 2004:197; Haig 2001:181; Aygen 2010:1-2). The four censuses taken from 1945 to 1965 had questions on language issues but not about ethnicity (Türkdoğan cit. in Houston 2001:101; Höhlig 1997:120). Their data is long outlived, but fortunately modern research about ethnic minorities started in the 1970s and 80s represented by Andrews ([1989] 2002a; namely W. Arnold, R. Benninghaus, E. Karakuş, H. Temel, and J. den Exter). He argues that the grounds of his research are to be found in the governmental *Imar ve Iskan* (later *Köy İşleri*) *Bakanlığı* – under the department *Toprak ve Iskan Genel Müdürlüğü* (Dr. Nejat Berkmen) led census called *Köy Envanter Etüdleri (KEE:* Nestmann 2002:544). Also his research includes six regional surveys (Andrews 2002a:11). However at present no reliable and concrete numbers are available due to lack of statistical research and an official policy of underestimating minority populations (Höhlig 1997:115; Andrews 2002:167; Seufert & Kubaseck 2004:152). Yet smaller research on language activity started in 2008 and is available (*Türkei Information 2008* [Turkey Information]). Interestingly a German based research project affected studies in Turkey, as such a compilation was written by S. Aydın called *The ethnic and religious mosaic in Turkey and its reflection in Germany*. Unfortunately it is not available any more as far as the author knows. Yet the Diaspora once more refers back to the homeland and vice versa.

The streams of exiles from Turkey to Germany could be traced back to three batches. All of them refer back to the political situation in the native country. As a result of the economic boom after WWII. workers from the East of Turkey were recruited to Europe in the 1960s. The Turkish government was in a crisis at

---

[37] A 140-paged booklet of the Turkish government lists "current" populations for the district of "Çermik". The numbers are based on a census of people carried out in the eighties. For political reasons concrete numbers are renounced by minorities (*Çermik* 2007). That Turkey, practised politically motivated "understatement on data about minorieties" (Andrew cit. in Höhlig 1997:11) is denounced in literature. It has its origin in the disillusionment which originated in the "regional disparities and the special position of the Eastern provinces within the nation" and which came to a climax in the 1960s performed by the *Köy Envanter Etüdleri* (KEE). This and the census carried out later in Turkey brought forth explosive data about the East of Turkey which is why the results were closed for public acquisition (Nestmann 2002:544; Höhlig 1997:120).

that time and the economy was weak (Zürcher 2004:5). In 1960, 1980 and 1992 to 1994, because of political disturbances, separatist groups, mainly the "workers' party of Kurdistan" (*Partiya Karkerên Kurdistan* = PKK) used the weak economy of the East as a reason to pursue their goals. In 1977 the PKK was found by *Abdullah Öcalan* to establish an independent province of Kurdistan, based on Marxist ideology and close hierarchical structures (Andrews 2002a:21-23; Hirschler 2001:146; 2.3.1.3.1; 3.5). The response of the armed Turkish forces created such unrest in the east that the formerly called batches led to streams of asylum seekers towards Europe with a main emphasis on Germany (:5 and Höhlig 1997:116, 120).

Due to the persistent movement of the Zaza, primarily into the western Turkish cities, some from within and outside of the people group claim that the language could die out (Dias; 2.3.1.4; 2.3.4.6). It also was recently classified as "unsafe" in the context of international observations (Selcan 1997:25-27 *Die Entwicklung der Zaza Sprache* [The development of the Zaza language]; UNESCO 2009 *Interactive atlas)*.[38] Following the scale of Reyhner about language vitality, Zazaki is placed on the fifth level. Severe endangering, as in level one, cannot be taken into consideration due to the use of the language which is recently still verbally handed down in the homeland. Reyhner recommends propagating the language publicly and promoting their establishment in the educational public school system (Reyhner 1999: vi-vii; s. a. Höhlig 1997:121). A side effect of the Zazaki language threat is represented by the motivation of modern artists to spread and promote the language as widely as possible by music (e.g. Estare, Aslan, Berz, Zaza Vaj, Şervan), literacy (e.g. Dewran, Çelker, Çengiz, Malmîsanij) and politics (e.g. Büyükkaya, Group Serbest).[39] This is real-

---

[38] The field of research about "language threat and language dead" increasingly comes into public focus (Tsunoda 2006:30) . Höhlig emphasizes the threat of language dead, since the politically motivated "replacement of the mother tongue", appears to demonstrate "a particularly successful way to the assimilation" (1997:120). Following the "law of communication preservation" (Liebi 2003a:205) one will find a loss of morphological contents in Zazaki, whereas a stable adjustment could be observed at the level of syntax, lexis and semantics (2.2.1.9).

[39] Höhlig also recommends the education of the children in the mother tongue. She justifies this by her criticism of the Turkish language assimilation politics (1997:120-121). The "medical and economic linking" to the west of Turkey would be an important element "to offer minorities prosperity" (Nestmann 2002:550-551; Steinbach 1996:161). An actual example within the Kurdish language group is represented by the program *Kurdistan Save The Children* in Iraq. In especially accomplished centres, mother tongue education in Kurdish (Sorani) and other activities are given. Secondary schools offer the transition from the mother tongue into English, what is described as great success (Kurdistan Save The Children 2009. *What We Do).*

2 The Zaza

ized by the foundation of publishing houses, folk festivals, music festivals and political activities on the local, European and global level. Particularly to be thrown into relief are:

- the annual "Munzur festival" since 2000 in the *Dersim* area, mainly in Tunceli, with more than 10.000 visitors (see dersiminfo.com/turkish/munzur-festivali-29-temmuzda/ [accessed 2010-10-09]);
- a publishing house in France (e.g. APEC), Sweden (e.g. İremet Förlaget, vate), Turkey (e.g. Tij Yayınları, vate) and Germany (cooperation with Tij Yayınları);
- various globally available magazines (Hayıg 2007:193; see list of the Zaza magazines in the bibliography);
- the recognition of the Zaza by UNESCO (UNESCO 2007: *UNESCO register of Good Practices in Language Preservation*; UNESCO Bangkok 2007: *Promoting Mother Tongue based Education*).

The Dersim or Northern Zaza are more active in propagating their culture and language to the public than the Southern or Eastern Group. Yet looking back in history the Southern Group initiated the promotion of their people group in Europe by wordlists and magazines. *Necmettin Büyükkaya* with a wordlist and *Ebubekir Pamukçu* by the magazine *Ayre*, started both in Sweden, to write in Zazaki by using the Turkish alphabet (Büyükkaya 1992; Pamukçu 1984-1986).

2.2.7.3 Summary on "Çermik"

The *Çermik-Siverek* dialect (CSD or SZ) covers the southern area of the Zaza homeland. It is the linguistically best researched dialect of the Zaza people, although the research material is not easy to come by (Jacobson 1999; Pamukçu 2001; Paul 1998; Todd 2002; Pamukçu 2001; Hayıg 2008 and 2011).

Çermik, a small town of 30.000 citizens has a close relationship to *Gerger* and *Siverek*. Both are old centres of Zaza life. *Gerger* was the place of origin for many ethnicities (small scale social units) or microcultures within the Southern Zaza group. Still today *Siverek* holds a position of authority from the state, as it did under the Ottoman Empire, due to a strong feudalistic tribal system led by the *Bucax*. The main source of linguistic activity – although there is less in the Southern Group – arrives out of the *Çermik-Siverek* area.

2.2.8 Illiteracy and Bilingualism

Looking back into the educational system of Eastern Turkey, it becomes apparent that foreign Christian developmental aid functioned as a trigger. Since the 18th century the former Ottoman and the modern Turkish education system in Western Turkey was based on European standards. The Eastern provinces obtained public education through the initiative of Christian organizations that focused on the Christian minorities from 1840 AD until 1915. The most well known organization was the *American Board of Christian and Foreign Mission* which was active in the Middle East in the 19th century (see Kieser 2000 for more details). Besides the education of Nestorian, Armenian, Greek and Syriani Christians, mainly Kurmanji and Zazaki speaking men were given the opportunity to join the Christian diaconate represented by medical and educational institutions (ibid; Kaya 2011:8; see 3.1 and 3.2).

Since the 1930s there have been several approaches to counteract the illiteracy rate. This was primarily by laymen who were educated in a six-month writing and reading introductory training, secondly by primary teachers from the villages and then from 1948 by means of a state pedagogical education system in villages and cities (Zürich 2004:194-195).

Not until the consistent penetration of compulsory school attendance for all in the 1970s was a higher education quota triggered. This approach was mainly ideologized by the idea of "Turkisation" derived from Pan-Turkism (Höhlig 1997:120-121). The Turkish constitution based any minority policy on language issues, and as a result literacy attempts within the Zaza people were actively suppressed up until now. Even though the freedom to use minority languages is guaranteed by law since 1992, the long lasting oppression is still in the people's and the officials' minds. In 2002 the Turkish-only concept was limited in the constitution and opened the way for the development of other languages in Turkey.

Zazaki is classified as a "non-standardized literate language". As such it is represented on the fourth layer of the scale for the standardization of languages (scale in Kloss 1968:78). Illiteracy within the Zaza has its main emphasis within the group of women that are over 50 year old. These women are usually monolingual since only men were trained in the public Turkish school system until the 1970s. As a result of lack of money and the predominance of men in society, women could not take part in school education. Other factors that caused illiteracy are the position of women,

2 The Zaza

- as full-time labourers in peasant-cultures,
- as mothers and educators of the small children within the family,
- within Islam as subordinated to men.

Since 1992 and anew with constitutional change in 2002 the use of all minority languages in public, including Zazaki and Kurmanji, is allowed (e.g. academic sessions). Yet the social pressure multiplies for the Zaza populace to send their children to no-cost Turkish language based nursery schools or day-nurseries. Such politics will reveal its long-term effect only within some years but promises a high grade of language loss (3.1 and 3.2).

An obvious consequence of this long-lasting minority politics based on the language issue is a bilingualism that economically brings along a positive grant primarily for the Zaza in Europe.[40] On the other side multilingualism constitutes a big challenge to them due to the language drift that causes deep religious and cultural changes (Fasold 1993:240). The Zaza perceive such language drift as a huge threat either in the Diaspora or in the homeland. Yet many activities nowadays are justified by that very reason. Discussions about the language Zazaki (2009 Berlin) or the culture (2010 Mannheim), the foundation of cultural oriented associations (2010 Istanbul) or the publication of magazines (1990-) are justified by the preservation of culture and language.

Nonetheless, multilingualism of the Zaza in the Diaspora (Turkish, Zazaki and the language of their emigration country) becomes an essential sustainer for Turkey as one of the most important trading partners of the EU (Steinbach 1996; 2.3.1.4; 2.3.4.6). For example Germany with its high share of Turkish-speaking foreigners (recently 1.7 millions in Burghardt 2006 *Foreigner after their nationality 2006*) has a special need with regard to services in the areas of translation and trade.

---

[40] Myers-Cotton understands by bilingualism both bi- as well as multilingualism including pluri- or multilingualismus (2006:2), others interpret it only as multilinguism (Payne 1997:18). *Bilingualism* describes the ability "to use two or more languages, by being able to lead a reasonable conversation". Thereby linguistic proficiency or knowledge are playing subordinate roles (Myers-Scotton 2006:44; also Kielhöfer & Jonekeit 1998:11). It means the use of two or more languages or dialects in daily life by an individual (Fabbro 1999: xi). Bilinguality and Bilingualism are traded synonymous in literature. Bilingual speakers, also the Zaza, are subjected under special neuro-linguistical processes which cause specific problems (Fabbro 1999:107).

2.2.8.1 Linguistical Influences – The Mother Tongue Lexicon

Multilingualism of the Zaza in their native country mainly exists through the knowledge of Kurmanji and Turkish due to the geographical and political situation of the people (Paul 1998: xix; Werner 2006:37; Malottke 2006:4). By means of literature evaluation social dependences of Turks, Kurds, Armenians and Zaza were examined together (Walter 2004a:97). As a result, a membership structure diagram based on ethnic-linguistical feelings was prepared (Werner 2006:37). It turned out that hardly any loans are made from Armenian or Aramaic/Hebrew, although, as described above, the Zaza lived in close contact to the Christian Armenians and the Jewish ethnic group. One reason for that could be the usually inferior position of such groups in Islam. That is why their languages took second place after the higher social prestige of Kurmanji Kurdish, Farsi and Arabic or they were even "disdained" (Justi 2006: xix; few examples are given by Hadank 1932:32-34). Having said this, further investigation will reveal more facts about any further linguistic influence, but Zaza and Kurmanji speakers do not feel much influence from these two other groups in their language (Paul 1998: xix).

As shown above the history of the Zaza people points back to ancient times (2.1.3). That's why the longest influence on Zazaki comes from Armenian and Kurmanji as these people groups also settled in the Zaza homeland. In the 11th to the 13th century Arabic speaking people groups and the Seljuk Turks inhabited Anatolia. The conglomeration of races set the foundation of the Ottoman period. Osman the founder of the Ottoman Empire started with his campaigns in 1293. *Ottoman Turkish* became widespread and had a great impact on Kurmanji and Zazaki (Walter 2004a:97 Figure 1).

High Arabic was penetrated first by the Pan-Islamic policies of the Ottoman rulers. Their aim was to guarantee the loyalty of its citizens. Again a re-islamisation movement within the Zaza and Kurds by Islamic Wahhabite missionaries started in the 16th century (Benninghaus 1989:483-484). Their fundamentalist approach was initiated by Islamic powers centred *in* and *out of* Mecca. The wave of Islamic *da'ahwa* (invitation) that began with the Wahhabite movement led to an (Re-) Islamisation of the Southern Zaza Group and turned them towards the Hanafi school of Islam, whereas the Kurmanji speaking Kurds took part of the Shafi'i school (RH 2007 *Zaza tribes*; 2.3.3.2.5; 2.3.3.5; Table 11). These changes led to a huge linguistic influence of Arabic (Walter 2006:98).

Diagram 8 Influences on Zazaki by other Languages

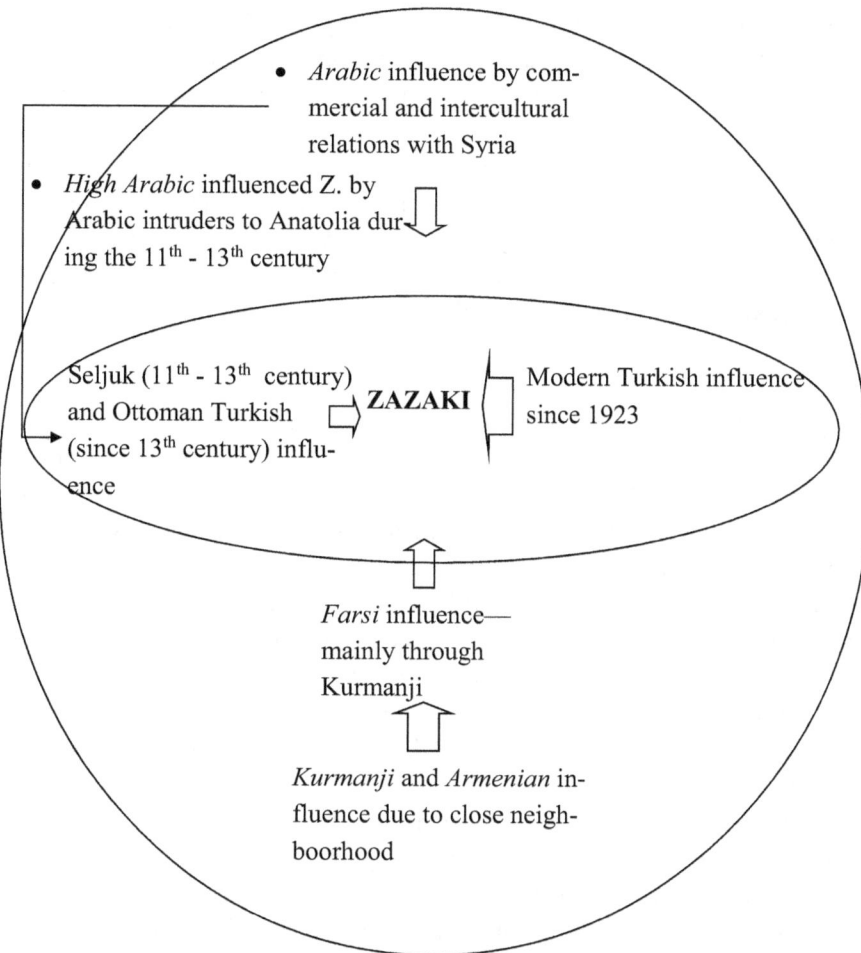

Zazaki shows, in contrast to religious (Islam) and military language, an accumulation of Iranian loanwords. These are found primarily in the field of "key-terms" in connection with relationship terminology or the religious life (Zoroastrianism / Parsiism / *serduşt* in Zazaki and Animism). These are phonetically adapted to the respective Zazaki dialect (Werner 2006:61-66). Iranian loanwords are also found in Turkish by way of back coupling by dint of Zazaki or Kurmanji (Bläsing 1995).

"Keyterms" are key concepts that are subject to special theological-exegetical and translation-technical control. They are translated by the translator from their word origin, depending on his ideology (theological cultural opinion) into the target culture (Barnwell 1992 and 1999). For Zazaki this could be illustrated by the example of the concept "man" (*merdim*). The research pointed to its real and idealistic usage, as well as to its etymological development, clarifying that it is a loan from Iranian (Werner 2006:59-69; 2.4.3). Thereby the pronunciation varies in the three main dialects as well as in the local idiolects of population groups as demonstrated by Paul (1998). Keyterms have long been of interest in the science of translation. Eugene A. Nida was one of the first emphasizing their importance in translation (e.g. concept for God either *Allah 'Elay* or *Hoda, Xoda*; 1969 and 1986).

To this day, no proof of the Kurmanji influence on Zazaki by a scientific scale is given (Paul 1998: xix). A comparison of Kurmanji and Zazaki dictionaries reveals a minimum of ten to fifteen per cent (10-15%) lexical conformity of both languages (Aydar 2003; Can 1997; Çem 1994; Erdem 1997; see Bibliography Zazaki: Glossaries). Most obvious is the different orthographic vowel system. Yet phonetically these phonemes are not that far from each other.

Authors who prove a greater influence from Kurmanji on Zazaki (see Diagram 8) mostly want to give the impression of *one* language, that's why they come up with lexeme accompliance of 80 – 90% (e.g. Gündüz 2006). For that very reason only such authors who are in general neutral in regard to this are here compared. Since one hardly knows how deeply authors agree with a political idea the presentation given here is only an indication. As for example looking at the dictionary of *Verroj* in which he provides Kurmanji, Zazaki and Turkish besides each other one will find an accordance of 20 - 30% (2003). In the same way *Malmisanij* (Malmîsanij), who ideologically comes close to the Kurds, has approx. 20 - 30% consensus (1992). Likewise *Turgut*, representing the eastern Bingöl dialect (Petrov [1863] 1998:148-159), comes up with a conformity of approx. 15 per cent (2001).

As bi- and multilingualism is high under the Zaza people, it also affects the necessary application and vitality of Zazaki as mother tongue (see discussion 2.2.1.7.2). Hence the argument demands further consideration in research. Language development programmes must evaluate which effects would revitalize the use of Zazaki at home and in public. Programmes like *Mother Tongue based Multilingual Education* (MLE) offered by UNESCO are known to the Turkish government as they take part in the global movement against illiteracy (UNESCO / SIL International 2007 *Promoting* ...).

The lexicons of Zazaki (Turgut, Malmisanıj, etc.) show various degrees of foreign language influence but one would not go as far as Walter by saying that "at least half the vocabulary is foreign" (2004:98). It seems that her research does not provide a representative picture of the Zazaki lexicon. Her assumption which looks mostly on the orthographical output of a lexeme by connecting it to a foreign language is questionable. It takes a cognitive standpoint concerning the brain's linguistic memory. Malottke criticises Walter for the fact that she does not relate to the etymological processes of so called loanwords (Malottke 2006:21). That's why the lexical borrowing of Zazaki has to be split in different hierarchies (Itô & Mester cit. in Malottke 2006:16). Following Itô and Mester in their hierarchy of lexical borrowing, the closest lexicon (Lex 1) to the Mother Tongue lexicon (Lex 0) is formed by *indigenous* loan words. Going one step further the lexicon with *assimilated* loan words (Lex 2) is used to memorize information. *Non-assimilated* loan words (Lex 3) are indirectly connected to the Lex 2. This structure demonstrates why the lexicon 1 of indigenized loan words is hardly defined as separated from the mother tongue lexicon. The information stored at this level is closely connected (Malottke 2006:16).

At which point does a foreign concept become indigenous, especially when it changes its semantical content? Interestingly mother tongue speakers of Zazaki are aware of foreign influences, while they have fewer struggles with identifying foreign concepts than with keeping alive the original terminology (RH 2008).

2.2.8.2 Ottoman-Turkish Influence

Turkish[41] influenced Zazaki in two intervals.[42] Before the foundation of the Republic of Turkey (1923 AD) during the Ottoman age (16th – 20th century), administration titles and religious concepts from Arabic have entered Zazaki.

---

[41] *Turkish* is part of the southwestern branch of the Turkic Languages within the Altai family of languages. Modern Turkey Turkish is based on the dialect of Istanbul from the 1930's, has approx. 45 m. speakers, and splits up into seven dialect variants (Underhill 2001:766; Werner [2013] „Turkish").

[42] Ziya Gökalp, who himself was a Zaza, points out in his linguistic examinations that Kurdish and its related dialects (including Zaza) are an altered form of Turkish. He draws on Turkish loanwords for the proof of his thesis (Berkes 1959:43-44). His approach refers back to panturkic tendencies that were introduced by Sultan Abdul Hamid II. and reinvented by Ziya Gökalp. The main problem with his argument lies in the relatively high share of Arabic loanwords in Ottoman Turkish that he uses to support his thesis.

These concepts moved into the Turkish-Kurdish settlement area through the Arabic speaking ethnicities. They performed a tribal segmentation. The subsequent conglomeration of races occurred in the Eastern Provinces of Anatolia from the 11th until the 15th century AD (Izady 1992:95). Up until now there was no investigation, into which form a direct Arabian influence on Zazaki took place. The closeness of the Syrian Arabic border to the Zaza home territory suggests an influence from Syrian Arabic on Zazaki and vice versa, the more as commercial relationship is handed down orally by tradition (RH 2007 *Zaza tribes*). The pharyngeal phoneme ' and the velarization of *l* (*ll*), *s* (*'s*) and *t* (*'t*) intimates Arabic loanwords (Diagram 12). A list of such lexemes is represented and included in the dictionary of Hayıg (2012). Nevertheless further research is necessary.

During the second phase the Turkish republic has primarily reached men due to its oppressive policy on education (Kenstowicz 2004:102; Höhlig 1997:120). As a result a strong bilingualism has been developed among men of Kurdish, Zaza and other minority ethnicities since the 1920s. Anyhow there has only been a restricted increase in Turkish in the home territory. But Turkish education policy causes bilingualism from the fifth year of life. Since this influence takes place after the *enculturation*, the mother tongue remains untouched. Regardless of this, the Turkish language becomes the main factor for language borrowing (Kenstowicz 2004:102; see also 3.4 and examples below 2.2.1.8.3).

Ottoman Turkish has influenced Zazaki on the military level by its terminology. The Silk Roads went through the Southern Groups homeland from west to east and north to south. The caravansaries (Tk. *karawansaray*) along the Silk Roads were centres of commerce, tax, informational exchange and on these grounds linguistic plurality. During Ottoman times the axis from the Eastern parts of the empire to the centre of power - Istanbul - went right along the river Euphrates, Murat and Tigris that is the area of the Southern Zaza. In contrast the Northern Zaza were more isolated by their high mountains. Their Alevi religion opened the whole language group to new concepts, since it reveals a very nature- and environmental-oriented and liberal form of Islam or Animism. The close relationship to the Armenians, Nestorians, Syrians and Jewish people is also reflected by loanwords. But research is still necessary, since the ethnocide, starting in 1895 by Sultan *Abdul Hamid* II. and 1915 by the Young Turks and the Unionists, stopped the linguistic impact of these people groups on Zazaki (Kieser 2000:140-142; 201; 394; 2.1.4.3; 2.2.8.2; 2.3.1.3.1; 3.1.1.2; 3.5; HC 2011; Turk.: *soykırım*).[43]

---

[43] Kieser points out that the "Alevi Dersim-Kurds" gave shelter twice, in 1895 and 1915, to

2 The Zaza

Politically active groups within the Zaza people have themselves been integrated into the Turkish education system due to the continuous language politics. They achieved complete bilingualism. The majority of the Zaza used Turkish in the form of a *lingua franca* that is a language of trade and economics, up to the 1980s.

Something has changed in language politics since then with which the Zaza have come to terms. In the Northern Group one can therefore speak about a language change, relegating the mother tongue purely to the inner domestic area. Publicly, for reasons of municipal interest, Zazaki plays no role in today's daily life. In the Southern Group Zazaki is used publicly; however Turkish gained higher acceptance in trade or commerce with other ethnic groups or foreigners.

This leads to the situation that should people within the Zaza meet, who have not met yet, they start a taster conversation about the town of origin, family or region to sort out each others status. Sometimes conversations with foreigners are conducted only for short periods in Zazaki and then change to the dominant Turkish again. Despite the long lasting language policy to the disadvantage of minority languages the hoped-for language assimilation did not come into action in the case of the Kurmanji-Kurds and the Zaza to this day (Izady 1992:108). Turkish is the language of wider communication that offers a safe haven for Zazaki mother tongue speakers with middle or low linguistic self esteem.

2.2.8.3 Language Prestige

The main question behind the status of Zazaki among its surrounding languages lies in the perception of prestige. Asked about the value of their mother tongue, in the context of Kurmanji and Turkish, the Zaza people refer to low prestige. The lack of prospects about the future of the people group and their language originates in

- the oppressive language policy of Turkey,
- bi- and multilingualism of the Zaza people,
- the dominance of the Kurdish population and their penetrating integration efforts,

---

Armenians persecuted by the Turks. Despite this, they were took some part in their looting, but not their slaughter. In contrast the Sunni Southern Zaza actively took part in the slaughter and annihilation of the Christian minorities in their homeland area (2000:430-431 "slaughter house at Göljük sea" [Hazar Gölü. EW.]).

- as well as the emigration to the big cities either in the West of Turkey and Europe or far away.

A revitalization of the language started in the Diaspora, it is recently demonstrated by the increase of monolingual websites on the Internet, the production of magazines, the attempt to start their own television channels or radio programmes and the participation in the publicly run channel TRT6.

More recently Zazaki has been building up prestige in translation services at institutions of the EU and in the civic administration of the Diaspora. Also the public discussion about the historical developments of the Eastern parts of Turkey, concerning the Armenian ethnocide (1915) or the Dersim massacre (1938) give the impression that the Zaza people and their language increasingly gain public attention.

2.2.8.4 Lexical Borrowing

So called *lexical borrowing* refers to the integration of words from one language into another (Myers-Scotton 2006:211). In general, during the process of integrating new concepts, languages tend to grasp back on "available" vocabulary. Word-construction out of nowhere is not known (Liebi 2003:239). Payne emphasizes that one can only talk of lexical borrowing if foreign components were integrated into the lexical basic vocabulary of the mother tongue (1997:18). He sees the necessity of *lexical borrowing* and *code switching* occurring from the fact that corresponding conceptualities do not exist in a language (:18).

The borrowing of Zazaki from the *Armenian lexicon* has not yet been researched in depth (Kahn 1976). However there is a lot of evidence that as Turkish and Kurmanji took loanwords from Armenia, so did Zazaki (ibid.; Leezenberg 1993). The long historical existence of both language groups side by side leaves its trace e.g. the suffix *-ox /-oğ* is forming *nomina agentis* with the past stems of verbs and is certainly the Armenian formant *-oy* (Classical Arm. –awł), which has the same function in literary Armenian and dialects (see Schmitt 1981:85). At a linguistic Zaza language conference held in Yerevan, Mesut Keskin proposed the following possible loanwords based on lexical borrowing (2011, PowerPoint Presentation, with permission of the author). One has to keep in mind that some terms can also be loans of other words into Armenian. Interestingly the Armenian audience did not question the terms, although further investigation is under way (Warm = West Armenian; EArm = East Armenian).

Table 13 Lexical Borrowing from Armenian

andêr ~ ondêr "damned"	WArm. *ander*, EArm. *anter* անտեր "ownerless, masterless"
çok ~ çhok "knee", Zaz. *zani*	EArm. *cownk* ծունկ, PIE *ǵónu
Gağan(d) "December ; Kaland festival"	WArm. *gayand(kʻ)* "Silvester", EArm. *kayandk* կաղանդ-ք a.a. < Lat. *calendarium*
gocage, gocege "knob"	WArm. *gojag*, EArm. *kočak* կոճակ
kırı ~ kırē "sunday"	EArm. *kiraki* կիրակի < Gr. Κυριακή
mısêle biyaene "to freeze"	WArm. *msel* մսել, EArm. *mrsel* մրսել "to be cold, freeze"
mozık "1 year old steer/cow"	Arm. *mozi, mozik* մոզիկ
-oğ participle present or nomen agentis suffix, e.g. *werdoğ* "eating, eater"	Arm. *-oy* –ող
sung "mushroom"	Arm. *sowng* սունգ < (?) Grg. *soko* სოკო.
şêmuge ~ şêmıge "door sill"	Arm. *šem* շեմ + WArm. *–ug* -ուկ
xaşıle "haşıl yemeği, kuymak" (cooked wheat and flour poured over with hot oil)	Arm. *xaşil* խաշիլ "flour soup". *xarş* խարշ, *xaşel* խաշել "to cook".
xêğ "crazy"	Arm. *xey* խեղ
xoz "pig"	Arm. *xoz* խոզ < (?)

Additional Asatrian supposes other borrowings from Armenian (2009:41):
jil (ik), cil (ik) "bough, branch, scion"   Arm. *cil, jil* "reed; vine; sinew"

Following the "principle of prestige" within bilingualism, Zazaki borrows words from Turkish which is recognized as the more prestigious language (Myers-Scotton 2006:211). Thus foreign nouns are mostly combined with auxiliary verbs of Zazaki. This principle is well demonstrated by the verb "write". The original Zazaki verb *nustış* was replaced by the Turkish-Zazaki construction *yazi kerdış* [44] in which the Turkish verb covers the meanings of

> *yazmak,* 1. write, write down 2. type in, register, 3. compose, draw up 4. make-up, decorate, 5. bring, distribute, 6. work as a writer for etc. (Steuerwald 1974:1017).

Derivations of such a construction contain the meaning

> yazi 1. letter, written work, paper work, 2. letter quality, calligraphy, headline letter, film, 3. Graphical fixation, letters, characters, types, 4. document, written material, film title, label, 5. article, essay treatise written, thesis, work paper etc. (:1016).

Zazaki integrates the nominalised derivation *yazi*, by using the auxiliary verb *kerdış* (Engl. make, work) to express the concept "write" (compound verbal phrase; light verb construction Csirmaz & Ceplová 2004:11-12). This goes so far that the original word *nustış* is nowadays explained by a footnote or does not appear any more in articles (see Zaza newspapers: *Miraz*; *Cime, Dersim*; s.a. 3.1.2).

Turkish nouns are assimilated into Zazaki in their orthographic Turkish form. By the processes of phonetic customization and the addition of the corresponding grammatical ending these words enter Zazaki. Often the semantic function of such loans changes in the Zazaki lexicon into one specific direction (Malottke 2006:16). So e.g. the Turkish noun *sarhoşluk*, which means "1. being drunken, high; 2. drunkenness, delirium, exhilaration (Steuerwald 1974:799) becomes *serxoşey* in Zazaki (Hayıg 2012:243), and the corresponding language-specific Turkish nominalizer *–luk* changes into the ending *-ey* in Zazaki. Yet in the Zazaki lexicon it is specifically related to alcohol consumption and excludes other functions (ibid.).

Language loans can be distinguished in *cultural* and *core* resp. *basic borrowing*. Thus *cultural* loan words are filling out missing concepts and *core* resp. *basic* loans are representing an additional verbal image to the existing one (Myers-Scotton 2006:215). Both are found in Zazaki.

2.2.8.5 Examples of Lexical Borrowing

The above mentioned example of Turkish "drunkenness" (*sarhoşluk*) fills out a continuum that either never existed or got lost and found entrance in the Zazaki lexicon via the noun *serxosey*. Yet we speak of "cultural language borrowing".

---

[44] The Turkish verb *yaz* covers both the activity of "writing" and a reference to the verb to "tell", if it refers to written documents or letters/signs (Jaeckel & Erciyes 1992:444-445).

2 The Zaza

A synonym does not exist in Zazaki; therefore the new concept was adapted by reference to the misuse of alcohol.

Compared to this, the verb *yazı kerdış* (s. o.) illustrates an additional and therefore more common verbal image, which is why we can speak of a "core resp. basis language loan". In the religious word pool the majority of loan words were taken from Osmanlı Turkish. Turkish in turn, took its loans from the religious wording of the Arabians. Consequently Arabian concepts find themselves through this path again in Zazaki. The result of such a transmission of language loans is realized and exemplified by the Arabian concepts of *'elah* (Tk./Arab. *allah* „God"; Steuerwald 1974:33-35), *cin/cinek* (Tk./Arab. *cin* „demon"; :159), *İsa* (Tk./Arab. *İsa* „Hz. Jesus"; :442), *gunah* (Tk./Arab. *günah/gınah* "sin"; :348) and many others. One will also find grammatical loans from Turkish in Zazaki, particularly discourse markers (Werner 2007:8-9).

Another range of examples is given by the following suffixes that are all derived from verbs and used as nominalizers (note the first three Verbs as close to Farsi):

Table 14 Loans in Nominalising Verb-Roots (Participle Imperfective)

-dar	*zordar* 'tyran'
	zor 'power, might' + *dar* (from *daştan* (Far.) 'possess')
-kar	*gunakar* 'sinner'
	guna 'sin' + *kar* (from *kardan* (Far.) 'do' (see - *ker*); Turk.: *günahkar* 'sinner"
-wan	*ardwan* 'miller'
	ardi 'flowr' + *wan* (Variant from *–ban* (Far.) 'guarding'; Horn 1988:41)
-ber	*asnawber* 'swimmer'
	asnaw 'swimming' + *ber* (from *bar-* 'bear' 'carry' Talysh: *bārde* Schulze 2000:14; Old Persian *bar-* (ibid.); Avesta: *ber-*, Pahlavi: *burten* / *ber-* (Akkoç et al 2010:34)
-dar	*fotrafdar* 'photographer'
	fotraf 'photograph' + *dar* (*dayış*'dan 'give'; Talysh: *doe* Schulze 2000:80; Old Persian: *dā* (ibid.); Avesta: *dā*, Pahlavi: *dāten* (Akkoç et al 2010:39)
-ger	*asınger* 'smith'
	asın 'iron' + *ger* (Variant from *–kar* /–*ker* 'doing' (see *–ker*; Horn 1988:197, 199)

-gêr	*gangêr* 'death angel'
	gan 'soul' + *gêr* (from *gırotış* 'take'; Talysh *gate* Schulze 2000:82); Kurmanji *girtin* Khan & Lescot 1986:109
-ker	*botanker* 'slanderer'
	botan 'slander' + *ker* (from *kerdış* 'do'; Talysh *kārde* Schulze 2000:23; Old Persian *kar*- (ibid.); Kurmanji *kirin* Khan & Lescot 1986:25); Avesta: *ker*-, Pahlavi: *kerten* (Akkoç et al 2010:49)
-veş	*pizeveş* 'devoured by love'
	pize 'stomach' + *veş* (from *veşayış* 'burn'); Kurmanji *şewitîn* Khan & Lescot 1986:111
-vin	*tengvin* 'narrowminded'
	teng 'narrow' + *vin* (from *vinayış/diyayış* 'see'; Talysh *vinde* Schulze 2000:87; Old Persian *vaināhiy*- (ibid.); Kurmanji *dîtin* Khan & Lescot 1986:142; Avesta: *dāi / veēn*-, Pahlavi: *dīten / vēn*- (Akkoç et al 2010:41)
-wer	*merdımwer* 'canibal'
	merdım 'human being' + *wer* (from *werdış* 'eat'); Kurmanji *xwarin* Khan & Lescot 1986:108
-zan	*neyzan* 'reed floote player'
	ney 'reed flute' + *zan* (from *zanayış* 'know')[45]; Talysh *zəne* Schulze 2000:88; Old Persian *dān*- (ibid.); Kurmanji *zanîn* Khan & Lescot 1986:118; Avesta: *zānā*, Pahlavi: *dānisten*- (Akkoç et al 2010:71)

The influence of Farsi is obvious, although other Southern Caspian languages (e.g. Talysh) and Kurmanji could also be responsible for such loans. Farsi as the strongest language cluster seems to be the most appropriate source.

2.2.8.6 Code switching

A further phenomenon of the influence of the Turkish language on Zazaki forms the so-called *code switching* (:10). The person affected changes unconsciously during a sentence or over several sentences from one language into another (Haugen cit. in Myers-Scotton 2006:256). The cognitive performances and the causes of these speech acts take place unconsciously. One assumes that bilingual

---

[45] Nowadays *–zan* is seldom used, instead the participle *–zanayox* 'knower' is used for compounds. For example *zıwanzanayox* Turk.: 'dilbilimci' (Engl.: linguist).

speakers perform two separate memories for the particular language dictionary and the necessary semantical system, both of which they are able to access at the same time (Fabbro 1999:94; Myers-Scotton 2006:291-299). The educated Zaza people under the age of 40, perform from at minimum bi- or mainly trilingual storage, due to the fact that they must actively process two or three different cognitive conceptions. There is the mother tongue perception expressed in the lexicon by Zaza world knowledge and lexicon and the same goes for their Turkish insight. In Zazaki this applies not only to some words and whole phrases, but is reflected e.g. in the salutation clause, where the original *xêr amey* (Engl. "mercy comes / hello" Hayıg 2008) changed to *maraca* (Tk. /Arab. "Hello"; Steuerwald 1974:627). It is important to emphasize that the whole cognitive setting, including perception of the world, during the language call up is processed in different languages. *Nazmi Çiçek* researched such bi- and multilingual effects for his home village *Êxê*, in the disctrict of *Elazığ*. He investigated in his research under 40 members out of 1500 inhabitants the following language distribution (2001 Yerevan, Power Point):

Table 15 Code Switching and Language Use - Exemplary Study of Êxê

	Zaz.	Turk.	Kur. Zaz.	Kur. Turk.	Zaz. Turk	Kur. Zazaki Turkish	Total
5-15	0	2	0	0	5	3	10
16-35	0	0	0	1	0	9	10
36-55	0	0	0	0	0	10	10
56 and over	1	0	4	0	0	5	10
Total	2	2	4	1	5	27	40

Although the village of *Êxê* is only representative of the Eastern or Central dialect, Table 15 shows which linguistic cognitive processes drive the call up of *Zazaki*, *Kurmanjki* and *Tirkki* (Zaza, Kurmanji, Turkish; 2.3.4.5).

These observations on bilingualism of Zazaki speakers demonstrate how cross-cultural and multilingual these people have become. Unusual features of Zazaki and a general description of the grammatical structure are shown below.

2.2.8.7 Summary

The Zaza people experience illiteracy as a result of linguistic oppression. The national language was promoted as a result of children having no chance to read and write their mother tongue. As a result bi- or multilingualism developed. Negatively as only the national language was written, the Kurmanji and Zazaki literacy was not able to develop.

Zazaki possesses loanwords and borrowed from all of their surrounding ethnicities. Following this sequence, Turkish, Persian, Kurmanji, Armenian and Russian influence have been affecting Zazaki.

Bilingualism in Turkish-Zazaki, Kurmanji-Zazaki, or multilingualism in Turkish-Zazaki-Kurmanji developed in geographical and social areas of contact such as trade centres (larger towns), Silk Road caravansaries (*karawansaray*), the military, etc. In the Diaspora the freedom of research led to an academic interest in the language and culture of the Zaza. Bi- or Multilingualism opened the path to broad economic activities between Europe and the homeland.

2.2.9 Language Description and Specific Features

Payne recommends starting with ethnographic studies in his instruction for the description of morphosyntactic language studies (1997:13). He advocates this to offer the interested parties a general impression of the described culture. Here I will not give a general impression, but I assume that this whole work will instead function as such. However I follow Payne's advice to demonstrate the close relatedness of language and culture by describing Zazaki within its cultural setting (:13; see Sapir-Whorf hypothesis under 1.1.3.3.3). Comprehensive grammars, such as Paul (1998), Selcan (1998), Pamukçu (2001), Todd (2002), Aygen (2010) and Turgut (w/o Date) give an overview of Zazaki and the interested scientist is asked to look them up. In this description specific features are highlighted. Such features are mostly interesting for those who are looking at cultural distinctiveness or who are looking at translations of Zazaki in other languages or who want to translate into Zazaki.

Western linguistics refers mainly to grammatical concepts represented by the Latin based sciences (Teutonic research style). Yet Indo European languages fit best into such categories (Payne 1997:73-74). Such an effect of "Eurocentrism", named after Payne and others, refers back to Greenberg's influence on typology and language universals (:73-74; Dil 1975:64; Greenberg 1963, 1968 und 1978; Gass & Ard 1987:53, 61; Roberts 1997:15-16, 18).). He suggests an alternative model. In this the relational structures and connections of the components of a sentence, on the sentence and discourse level, are taken into account. Such relationships and their function could then be expressed individually for every language (Payne 1997:75).

Having said this, the author realizes that other approaches such as describing a language by native approaches or looking at grammar from a holistic view, e.g. following a Nipponese research style, would add beneficial information to the research of Zazaki. A short introduction in Zazaki based on the verbal aspects of a predicate or the impact of a sentence is given by Werner in Hayıg (2012:421-421). As Paul mentions in his introduction, "all in all this description moves along the traditional grammar outlines and their terminology" (1998: xviii). The author of this work is also aware that his ethnocentric and subjective focus is just one attempt to approach the manifold facets of Zazaki.

2.2.9.1 General Description

Zazaki sentence word order follows: *subject, object, verb* and *goal*, such is the general pattern, and represents the unmarked sentence form S-O-V-G (Crandall 2002:64; Werner & Werner 2007:11)[46]. In contrast to the unmarked the marked form is emphatic and stressed (Roberts 2003:13). Referring back to Greenberg's typology and Payne's observations it is one of the three most frequent worldwide word orders that covers about 85% of the known languages (Comrie 1989:87; Payne 1997:75). Within "Iranian languages", this is the general but not at all a "typical" SOV word order (Comrie cit. in Bailey 2003:11).[47] As a proof Bailey presents common concomitants from SOV languages, namely the existence of pre- and postpositions, the position of modified sentence parts (relative clauses) etc. She shows that within the "Iranian family of languages" this does not take place regularly. Zazaki for example stands out because the adjective follows the noun (Werner & Werner 2007:11-12). Every change of word order mentioned above is characterized as a "stressed structure" or *marked word order* (Croft 1990:65, 71; Werner & Werner 2007:11). The *natural information flow* in Za-

---

[46] *Sentence* is hereby understood as the global smallest and mostly used communicational information-unit, which transmits coherent issues in a complex way (Armstrong 1993:114; Payne 1997:71; Sapir 1961:40).
[47] By comparing Iranian languages with Turkish it becomes obvious that both languages are contradistinctive. Such approaches that are based on the suffixation and the language type, whereas Turkish is polysynthetical and Zazaki rather isolating (Comrie 1989:91).

zaki is indicated by means of *points of departure, sentence articulation, fore- and backgrounding* und *highlighting* (Werner & Werner 2007:18-26). These technical terms come from the research on text discourse. All of them are paraphrasing text immanent signals which are pointing out certain contents to these. In the comparative discourse study of Werner and Werner those text discourse features are shown for Zazaki in comparison with Farsi (2007).

Zazaki represents a rather isolating language, since morphemes are mainly split, and not linked up (Payne 1997:27-28). It tends to build up independent and separated morphemes, as is well demonstrated in the relatively short word roots (e.g. *ma* "mother", *roj* "day", *ray* "way" etc.).

2.2.9.1.1 Syllable Pattern

The typical syllable pattern is realized by the C-V-C, C-V-C-V and C-V-C-C-V clusters. Yet in the onset not more than one consonant (C) and in the coda two following consonants are possible (Malottke 2006:8). Research on loan adaptation processes in Zazaki revealed that any rupture of the syllable pattern is filled by vowel harmony. Yet such an epenthesis follows the concepts of Persian / Farsi as a related language, in which vowels (V) are copied. In contrast to Persian only /u/ and not /o/ and /i/ can be copied in Zazaki (ibid.).

There is no rule about which vowel has to be implemented. As e.g. demonstrating the common syllable patterns *çok* "knee" (C-V-C), *deme* "time" (C-V-C-V), *derbe* "hit" (C-V-C-C-V; Hayıg 2008). Including a foreign concept such as the German name "Berlin" goes without any phonetical changes. But words like English "brown" become "bırowın".

So much is now said about the general characteristics of Zazaki, for we will now take a look into grammatical characteristics.

2.2.9.1.2 Grammatical Characteristics

In the following we will look at some outstanding grammatical features. Such are found in the forming of,
- the ergative,
- the two case systems,
- the ezafe constructions (Arab. *Izafe* „binding particle/addition") and
- the complex verbal system.

2.2.9.1.3 Ergative

Many syntax models show discrepancies and inconsistency in the classification of the ergative case (Carnie 2002:236). The ergative system contrasts to languages which follow the nominative case system by marking the "subject" of transitive verbs *and* the corresponding marking of "direct objects" and "subjects" of intransitive verbs (Bauer 2000:11; s.a Haig 2004:15-25). Thus transitive verbs go with the unmarked nominative case, whereas in the case of intransitive verbs the subject and object turn their tables (Kenstowicz 2002:13-14). Payne emphasizes that the ergative case is "patient-oriented", which contrasts with the nominative/accusative system that can be thought of as "agent-oriented" (1997:159). Languages containing an absolute ergative are called *"deep ergative languages* [emphasis as in original. EW.]" (Givón 1990:166). Givón also observes in the ergative a syntactic challenge about understanding the relationship of subject and object in sentences (1990:166; called "canonical""in Haig 2004:80-81). The ergative is partly traced back to the linguistic universal of *head noun marking* (Nichols 1992:113).

Zazaki represents a *split-ergative paradigm* (Kenstowicz 2004:13; Payne 1997:135,149). In general some explain the ergative as a former passive construction. In Zazaki one will not find any leftovers of such a pre-passive construction, also the passive is expressed by a marker (verb-root-*y*-personal-ending; Kenstowicz 2002:15; 2.2.9.1.9; 2.2.1.10.5). The object is not marked, but the subject is marked and represents the *casus regens* (see below). In the future form the marker system is exactly the other way around. In Zazaki the ergative is part of the past tense structure (Kenstowicz 2004:29) and is called an *ergative absolutive system* (Comrie 1987:21-22; Crandall 2002:28). Such Zazaki follows the linguistic universal of the *ergative absolutive system in the past tense* (DeLancey cit. in Payne 1997:158, 162). The function of the ergative is emphasized in some languages in contrast to an accusative-orientation (Comrie 1987:22). In the given framework Zazaki demonstrates an unambiguous tendency by the use of the ergative in this contrast. Summing this paragraph up, we can definitely say that Zazaki functions absolutely regular within the ergative languages (2.2.9.2.7).

2.2.9.1.4 Case System

Zazaki owns an unmarked *casus regens* (standard format; complies with the English and German nominative case) as the direct case (Todd 2002:33-34) and a marked *casus rectus* (complies with the genitive / dative / accusative function in English and German). The syntactic relationships of declinable words in a sentence are labelled by these two cases. In Zazaki the *vocative* or *allative* are seldom used, or in the case of the vocative led to fixed expressions that follow the nominative (e.g. terms of relationship). Todd describes the allative as locative (2002:34-35). The locative particle *–dı* functions differentially and points to a place / location. The directional goal thus described has to be understood as an allative (Werner 2008b).

Locative -ı is referred to as *remnant of a third case* (Todd 2002:34). It only occurs on feminine nouns as goal of direction in case of a known reference (:34-35; e.g. *Dı Zazay şınê Sewregı* "Two Zaza are going to Siverek"). In two terms of kinship the vocative shapes its own varieties which are closely related to Kurmanji-Kurdish dialects: e.g. *pi* "father" becomes *keko* or *baw* (Lk 15,12; Werner 2003b and Appendix 3; Todd 2002:35).

Vocative or calling forms have taken specific functions in Zazaki. Thus the respectful salutation of older men is represented by the term *kalo* a derivation from *kal* "ancients" (Todd translates it sometimes as "grey beard"). Based on this, elderly women are addressed respectfully as *xalê mına* "my aunt". The male counterpart *dedo* "uncle" points to the respectful salutation of foreigners. Equally ranking or same aged male friends or close relatives are called *keko* "elder brother" (partially in Todd 2002:35; Werner 2008). In the same way female persons in those relationships are addressed as *waya* "sister" (Werner 2003b and Appendix 3).

2.2.9.1.5 Ezafe-Structures

Zazaki borrowed the *ezafe*-structure (*ezafe* means "connecting link") which functions to form nominal phrases *and* to differentiate in gender, attributive forms and direct vs. indirect position of the object (Jacobson 2001:106-116; Todd 2002:40-41, 119). The ezafe-structure follows four different functions, the *descriptive, genitive, subordinated* (Todd 2002:40) and *absolute* ezafe (Paul 1998:46). In Zazaki nouns ending with a vowel attract the linking semi vowel -**y**- that moves between the stem and the ezafe (:40). The *descriptive* ezafe represents the general case of such linking endings (e.g. *bıra-yo gırd* "big brother"; noun/pronoun - adjective). The *genitive* ezafe links two parts of a sentence to each other (e.g. *ma-ya mı* "my mother"; noun/pronoun - noun/pronoun). In contrast the *subordinated* ezafe connects multiple parts of a sentence, if those are represented by the allative or are following prepositions (e.g. *kewno ray-da xo* "he hits the road"; noun – noun - adjective; Werner 2008a:2). Relating to the descriptive ezafe this structure is realized by the insertion of an additional -d- (Todd 2002:40; Werner 2008b). Paul adds the *absolute* ezafe to the ezafe structure of Zazaki. This particle can either stand on its own while it shows property as in a genitive function, or it functions like an adjective if the antecedent is introduced and known (e.g. *ê toyê* "those are yours"; pronoun - noun/adjective; Paul 1998:46 and Werner 2008b). The absolute ezafe is referred to as the *genitive* ezafe by others (Todd 2002:40; Werner 2008b).

2.2.9.1.6 System of Personal Suffixes

The southern dialects display a *feminine* personal suffix system in the paradigms of the verb, the ezafe and the copula, like Semitic languages. Such is not found in Kurmanji and Gorani. But in one of the dialects of Gorani, named *Kändûläî* Hadank found gender specific differentiations in the verbal paradigms; the other - so far researched - Gorani dialects do not represent such a pattern of gender declination (Hadank 1930:63-64).

2.2.9.1.7 Reflexive and Impersonal Pronouns

Zazaki possesses a reflexive pronoun *xo* and an impersonal personal pronoun *cı*. In a reference-identical environment, including the agent, the reflexive form *xo* is used, if it does not function as an agent. In reference-identical surrounding with a patient the personal pronoun *cı* is used (Paul 1998:68; Todd 2002:70; Werner 2003a).

Examples:
Ey ez keydê xo ra esta tever.   "He threw me out of his house." (agens).
Mı çinay xo cı ra gırot.   "I took my dress from her." (patiens).

2.2.9.1.8 Verbal System

Linguistics divides the grammatical description of a language into a *traditional* and a *functional* approach. Zazaki is well researched and described by the traditional approach. So far only Werner in Hayıg used the functional approach (2012:421-441; see Givón 1990). The following grammatical overview follows the traditional description.

The *verb* is the category that includes "lexemes which express the least time-stable" concepts (Payne 1997:47). Contrary to languages of other language families Zazaki displays no difficulty in categorizing the verbs, as they are classified precisely.

Following the traditional linguistic approach, the verbal system in Zazaki is built on a *present stem*, a *perfect stem* and a *subjunctive stem* (Crandall 2002:31; Jacobson 2001:130-205; Todd 2002:72-73). It thus follows the Old-Iranian language, which counts as its origin (Windfuhr 1989). Zazaki possesses a *historical present*. In the Southern Dialects a future tense is demonstrated by the particle *do* that is replaced in the Northern Dialects by the present tense thus the context becomes important (Todd 2002:100; Crandall 2002:31).[48]

By switching their pre- or suffixes verbs are aligned to temporal demands (Todd 2002:72).

Zazaki displays "comparatively few verbal roots". Hadank estimates "80, whereas complex roots that contain prefixes or foregoing verbal parts are counted in. This research consists of 150" verb roots (Hadank cit. in Todd 2002:72). In the course of this, the partition in *complex* and *compound* verbs has to be emphasized (Todd 2002:79-80). The former attach a prefix to their verbal stem and thereby modify their semantics, the latter express their semantics, the latter are expressing their verbal function by the construction of an auxiliary verb together with a noun / adjective / adverb (Comrie 1989:91; Gass & Ard 1987:40-41; Payne 1997:84). The verbs *kerdış* ("to do") and *dayış* ("to give") could be used for a great variety of meanings in their linkage to a noun, an adjective or an adverb (Todd 2002:79-80).

The *aspect* of a verb in Zazaki is expressed either as *imperfective* (uncompleted process) or *perfective* (closed or completed process; Payne 1997:239). The imperfect in the present is signalled by the marker *–ê* and in the perfect by an adjusted form of the verb "to be" (*–vı*; Todd 2002:72).

Zazaki features a *linear* concept of time. Thus the present outlines the point of reference, out of which the perfect and the future are considered.

The marker *-en-* indicates the present, followed by the personal ending (s. b.).

2.2.9.1.9 Passive and Causative

Zazaki possesses a passive marker that is considered to be a *morphological passive* (Payne 1997:205). Payne introduces the verbal modifications "passive" and "causative" in relation to the valence of a verb. Markings of the verb lead to changes in valence (:171-206). The marking on the verb takes place by the infix *-y-* (see above ergative; 2.2.9.1.3):

---

[48] The *temporal system* of a language "mirrors also its worldview" (Payne 1997:236; 3.1.5).

Example

vıraz-en-o "he builts" => *vıraz-y-en-o* "it is built" (Todd 2002:73).

Also there exists the causative marker *-n-* which also functions as an infix on verbs:

Example

veş-en-o "it burns" => *veş-n-en-o* "he burns it" (:75).

2.2.9.1.10 Copula

Zazaki displays a *copula* . The copula is part of the *predicate nominal construction* (Payne 1997:114) and links two nominal elements together (:117). In Zazaki the copula generally takes over the function of a verb and is derived from the verb *biyayiş* ("to be / to exist"; :115). In the present and subjunctive the paradigm is consistent (Todd 2002:54, 63), not so in the perfect, related to the existential verb *biyayiş* (:60).

Some of the previously mentioned specifications are also to be found, in different manifestations in the "Kurdish" languages of *Sorani, Kurmanji* and *Bahdeni*.

2.2.9.1.11 Emotive Language in Zazaki

In this segment we want to look at emotive language in Zazaki. This belongs closely with the "Location of the Emotions, the Intellect and the Character" (LEIC / SEIC; 1.1.2.3; 2.3.2.2; 2.4.1). Language reveals the underlying core values and as such hints at the placement of the non-biological organ of the LEIC (see 2.3.2.2). The phrases are explained in relation to the concept of LEIC.

Table 16 Phrases of Emotive Language

Zazaki	Translation (literally)	Explanation and relation to LEIC
Çima serr.	You're welcome! (on your eyes)	Blessings are referred to the eyes, as they are leading ones path.
teşqelê kerdış	making fun	-
zewt dayış	insult and curse someone	The religious motivation of hurting someone.
qufr kerdış / lengi cenene	offend someone	Loanword from Arabic which refers back to non-believers in Islam.
Kuceyra bımanê.	Stay away. (on street stay)	Street as a symbol of impurity and place to avoid.
Şari bımanê.	Dto. (people stay)	Here the reference is given to people on the street, not relatives. (Clear distinction.)
Qeç 'Elay dayo.	Child was born. (child God gave)	The religious view of birth and transcendency is revealed in this phrase.

2.2.9.1.12 Example of Dialectical Variations – Months and Days

In this paragraph I will show the dialectical variations of the Northern, Eastern and Southern dialects. The examples are taken from basic words that are relating to the description of yearly periods. A group of Zaza people is working towards standardization and some suggestions are from their research (2.2.6). It is suggested that in very early days a sun calendar replaced the recent Western calendar.[49]

---

[49] ND = Northern Dialects (*Zazakiyê Zımey*); ED = Eastern Dialects (*Zazakiyê Merkezi Palu-Çewlig*); SD Southern Dialects (*Zazakiyê Veroci* = *Çêrmug-Sêwrege-Aldûş*).

2 The Zaza

Table 17 Dialect Varieties - Month Names

Month	ND	ED	SD Sêwrege / Siverek	SD Çêrmuge/ Çermik	Wikipedia Proposal[50]
January	Çele, Zemperiye	Kanuno Peyin	Çıle, Kanûna dımayêne	Çıle	Çele
February	Gucige	Sıbat	Sebat, Sıbat	Sıbat, Heftan	Şıbate
March	Mart	Edar	Adare, Rişiki	Mart	Adar
April	Nisan	Nisan	Nisane, Lisane, Avrile	Lisan	Nisane
May	Gulane	Gulan	Gulane	Gulan	Gulane
June	Amnania Verêne	Heziran	'Hezirane	Amnano Verên	Heziran
July	Amnania Wertêne	Temuz	Tirmehane, Timahane, Tirmehe, Vaşterini	Amnano Werteyên	Temuz
August	Amnania Peyêne	Tebax	Tebaxe	Amnano Dımayên	Tebaxe
September	Paizia Verêne	Keşkelun	İlone, Çirina sıftekêne	Paizo verên	Keşkelun
October	Paizia Wertêne	Tişrino Verin	Cotane, Çirina dımayêne	Paizo Werteyên	Tışrino Verên
November	Paizia Peyêne	Tişrino Peyin	Teştine, serisnag	Paizo Dımayên	Tışrino Peyên
December	Gağand (Gağan)	Kanuno Verin	Berçıle, Berçıke, Kanûna Sıfteyêne, İsnag	Çıleyo Verên	Kanun

Below another agreement exemplifies the options that are possible if the Zazaki speakers decide to work together on a written standard. Obviously it would be necessary to refer to the variations that are given in the other dialects. After some experience with such a system authors should be able to manage the chosen standard.

---

[50] See http://de.wikipedia.org/wiki/Zaza-Sprache [accessed 2017-04-05]. [Engl.: Zaza Language].

Table 18 Names of Cardinal Directions

Cardinal Direction	ND	ED	SD
North (*Kuzey*)	zıme	Zıme	zıme
West (*Batı*)	mığrıb, ğerb	Rocawan	rocawan
East (*Doğu*)	mışrıq, şerq	Rocvetış	rocakewtene
South (*Güney*)	veroc	Veroc	veroc

Interestingly in the case of naming the days of a week, Zazaki dialects do not show a lot of variants.

Table 19 Standardization - Days

Days	Name of Days (Common Agreement)
Saturday	şeme/ peyê yeney / badê yeni
Sunday	bazar / kırê / bırarek
Monday	Dışeme
Tuesday	Sêşeme
Wednesday	Çarşeme
Thursday	Paşeme
Friday	Yene

2.2.9.2 Summary - A Grammatical Scetch

This sketch sums up the findings of almost 10 years linguistic fieldwork on the dialects of *Dersim* and *Çermuk / Siverek*. In this the latter serves as a point of reference. The given description is just a summary that adds to the extensive works of *Selcan* (1998, Dersim dialects), *Paul* (1998; all dialects), *Todd* (1986/2002; Çermuk dialect) and *Pamukcu* (2001; Çermuk dialect). As such this summary will show the main grammatical features and some additional findings. All example sentences are taken from the following folktales, published in "*Mahmesha – Zaza Folktales then and now*", by *Rosan Hayıg* (2007), ed. by Eberhard und Brigitte Werner.

The examples are identified by number of story, paragraph number (roman numbers) and sentence number. For example 3,V,15 means, story number 3, paragraph V, the fifteenth sentence in this paragraph. The order and numbers of the stories are:

1. *'Elicanek u Warda Xoya*
2. *Gorma'hmed*
3. *'Heşo Çı'harçım (Musıko 'Etar)*
4. *Keçel Ahmed*
5. *Lazê Axay*
6. *Mesela Lu u Ardwaniya*
7. *Ma'hmeşa*
8. *Na Xalxuma - hewna Keremata Gırda dıma*
9. *Qolo Poto*
10. *Şêx Biyayena Gawandê Çermugızi*
11. *Mêrdeko Tersanok - Camêrdo Zuray*
12. *Lazeko Zerez*
13. *Axa beno, nêbeno?*
14. *Kırtleme niyo, Zırtlemeyo*

2.2.9.2.1 Nouns

Nouns follow masculine or feminine gender. They are inflected for case, number and specificity.[51]

The unmarked noun is primarily understood as *definite*. The indefiniteness is made explicit whether by a suffix *–ê(n)*, or the use of the cardinal number *one* "ju, jew".

The suffix *-ên* and the *d*-ezafe is always used when the noun is linked to a modifier.

Example for definiteness:

keynek	zi	boll xasek	bena.
girl	also	many.much beautiful	be-IMPFV-3SF

'[...] the girl was also very pretty.' (1, V, 2)

Examples for indefiniteness:

ban-ê	'A house ; one house.'
jew ban	'One house (not two houses).'

Wext-ê dı,	**zew** gawanê	dew-**ên**-da Çermugı dı	beno.
time-IDF in	one cow.herder-IDF-OM	village-IDF-ZF2 C. in	be-IMPFV-3SM

'Once upon a time, there was a shepherd in one of the villages in the Cermık area.' (10, 1)

Roz-ê,	rêze	yeno	ney.
day-IDF	row.line.ADV	come-IMPFV-3SM	3omn

'One day it was his turn.' (11, III, 3)

---

[51] Paul (1998, p. 17) He adds animacy and definiteness.

zû pir bena, zû torına cı bena.
one old.lady be-IMPFV-3SF one grandchild-ZF 3osp be-IMPFV-3SF
'[...] there was an old woman and her grandchild.' (3, 1)

Noun with modifier:
maya mın û wa-r-**ên**-da mına,
mother-ZF 1o and sister-OF-IDF-ZF2 1o-ACC
'[he took away] my mother and one of my sisters,' (7, VII, 11)

Noun with modifier, but both, marker and number, are used:
jew mêrdek-**ên**-do çımvete xoya
one man-IDF- eye bring.out-PAST- rflx-
ZMD2 NOM ACC

ardo diyar.
bring-PAST-PART-3SM upward
'[...] [he] was carrying with him a man whose eyes had been ripped out.'
(7, V, 8)

2.2.9.2.2 Case Endings

The morphologically unmarked case is called ***direct***. The morphologically marked case is called ***oblique***. Nouns do not take oblique case markers when the reference is indefinite or non-specific.
For kinship terms, a latent –*r* becomes overt in oblique case.
The ***Vocative case*** can be unmarked for non-kinship terms.

	MASCULINE	FEMININE	PLURAL
DIRECT	ø	Ø	-i
OBLIQUE	-i	-er	-a(n)
KINSHIP OBL.	-r	-r	-ra(n)
VOCATIVE	-o (ø)	-ê~i (ø)	-êno

Examples Direct Case:
Ez 'hend dew-**i**, 'hend duwêl-**i**,
1d how.much village-DP how.much country-DP

… 2 The Zaza

'hend tıxtor-**i**   geyraya.
how.much doctor-DP wander-PAST-1S
"I have searched so many villages, countries and doctors [to find a medicine]." (3, VII, 11)

Oblique Case:
   No   na   keyn-**er**   gırêdano   kendır-**i**-ya.
   3dmn this.f   daughter-OF   bind-IMPFV-3SM   cord-OM-INSTR
   'He binds this girl to the cord.' (4, I, 21)

   Ceniyeka   cı   kêver-**i**   akena
   woman-ZF   *osp*   door-OM   open.T-IMPFV-3SF
   'His wife opens the door.' (13, 3)

   ew nê   keyn-**an**-ê   na dêw-**er**   gênê
   now*thus 3dpn   daughter-OP-ZP   this.f giant-OF   take.hold-IMPFV-PL
   '[...] then they take the daughters of the female giant [...].' (3, IV, end)

Kinship Oblique Case:
   Nê   bırar-**ran**   ra   zew ji   namey cı   'Hes beno.
   these   brother-KOP   from   one also   name-ZMG   Hes be-IMPFV-3SM
   One of these brother's name is Hesen. (3, II, 8)

Vocative Case:
   Keyn-ê,   tiya   tiya dı   çıçi   geyrena?
   daughter-VOC.S   2d-2SF.COP   here in   what   wander -IMPFV-2SF
   "Girl, what are you here looking for?" (3, IV, 4)

2.2.9.2.3 Ezafe Morphemes

The "ezafe" refers to a linking morpheme that links a head noun to a following modifier. The subordinated ezafe, also called *d-ezafe* is an oblique-case ezafe.

DESCRIPTIVE	GENITIVE	SUBORDINATED
(adjective linked to noun/ pronoun)	(noun or pronoun linked to noun/pronoun)	(if preposition follows, or this nominal phrase is oblique)

MASCULINE				
cons. stem	-o	-ê	-dê / - do	
vowel stem	-yo	-y	-dê / - do	
FEMININE				
cons. stem	-a	-a	-da	
vowel stem	-ya	**-y(a)**	-da	
PLURAL				
cons. stem	-ê	-ê	-dê	
vowel stem	-y	-y	-dê	

e.g.

Gorma'hmed bıraran-dê xo nêveyndano.[52] (obl. masc. pl. subord.)
Gormahmed doesn't wake up his brothers. (verbally: ... calls them not.)

2.2.9.2.4 Pronouns

Personal pronouns

The pronouns distinguish *person, number, case* as well as *near* and *far* deixis by marking. Near deixis is demonstrated by adding the prefix-letter *n-*, far deixis is unmarked and serves also as a neutral pronoun, without pointing to any distant participant.

	SINGULAR		PLURAL	
			plurals do not distinguish gender	
	DIRECT	OBLIQUE	DIRECT	OBLIQUE
1st pers.	**ez** (I)	**mın** (my, me)	**ma** (we, our)	
2nd pers.	**tı** (you)	**to** (your)		**şıma** (you pl., your pl.)
3rd pers.				
masc.	**o** (he)	**ey** (his, him)	**ê** (they)	**ina(n)** (their)
fem.	**a** (she)	**ay** (her)		

---

[52] Gormahmed (*Gorma'hmed* 2007: 8-14).

Demonstrative pronouns paradigm

		SINGULAR		PLURAL	
				plural distinguishes no gender	
		DIRECT	OBLIQUE	DIRECT	OBLIQUE
masc.	near	**no** (this)	ney	**nê** (these)	nina(n)
	far	**o** (that)	ey	**ê** (those)	ina(n)
fem.	near	**na** (this)	nay		
	far	**a** (that)	ay		

No zi nê dêwi kışeno. (Kecel Ahmed in Hayıg 2007:21-25)

Personal pronoun *cı*

The anaphoric pronoun *cı* is a generic. It refers to a party (patiens / object) whose identity is already established.

e.g. *Ceni zi bêro se, eza çay biyara cı ver.*
  'If a woman comes too, I'll bring her tea.'

  Mı cıra perey gıroti.
  'I got money from him.'

Reflexive Pronoun *xo*

The reflexive pronoun (*xo~xu*) not only reflects the reflexive meaning '*self*', but it also functions as a pronoun with reference to a subject or the agent.

e.g. *Oyo lajdê xorê vajo.*
  'He will tell his son.'

Relative Pronoun *kı*

The relative pronoun *kı* is not inflected. It is used as a real relative pronoun, referring to an already mentioned person ('which, who'). Secondarily it serves as a complementizer 'that', and could be omitted in the sentence without loss of meaning.

e.g. *Na keyneka kı yena, xalkeyna mına.* (functions as relative pronoun)
  This girl, who is coming, is my cousin (my mother's sister's daughter).

O vano kı wuni niyo. (O vano, wuni niyo.) (functions as complementizer)
'He says *that* it is not like that.'

2.2.9.2.5 Adjectives

Adjectives are inflected for *number* and *gender*. They can follow the head (noun) being linked by a descriptive ezafe, stand alone or serve as predicate.

Inflections:

singular	masc.	Ø	*Vergê gırd kerga weno.*
			'... great wolf ...'
	fem.	-ı[53]	*Del verga gırd-ı ame nezdı.*
			'... great female wolf ....'
all plurals		-i	*Vergê gırd-i kerga wenê.*
			'... great wolves ....'

Demonstrative Adjectives

They point to a nounphrase and can't replace a noun like the pronouns. But morphologically there are very few distinctions to pronouns.

		NEAR	FAR
MASCULINE	Direct	**no** (this)	**o** (that)
	Oblique	**nê** (this)	**ê** (that)[54]
FEMININE	Dir. & obl.	**na** (this)	**a** (that)
PLURAL	Dir. & obl.	**nê ~ ni** (these)	**ê ~ i** (these)

Examples

Na keyner çay ardı.
'This girl brought the tea.'

Lazê mı, şo, ê mêrdeki rê vaz: Wa bêro tiya!
'My son, go and tell that man, he should come here.' [55]
Nê merdıman pirtoki herinay.
'These people bought books.'

---

[53] Some speakers and writers drop this morpheme, because it is unstressed and hardly heard.
[54] The singular oblique inflections are the only lexically difference to the Demonstrative Pronouns.
[55] Four eyed Hesen (*Heso Çı'harçım*; Hayıg 2007:15-20).

2.2.9.2.6 Numbers

1	jew, jû	11	jandes, des û jew
2	dıdı, dı	12	dûwês, des û dıdı
3	hirê	13	hirês, des û hirê
4	çe'har	14	çarrês, des û çe'har
5	panj	15	pancês, des û panj
6	şeş	16	şiyês, des û şeş
7	'hewt	17	'hewtês, des û 'hewt
8	'heşt	18	'heştês, des û'heşt
9	new	19	newês, des û new

10	des	0	çıniyo
20	vist	100	se
30	hirıs	1000	'hazar
40	çewres	1,000,000	mılyon
50	pancas	21	vist û jew
60	şeşti	25	vist û panj
70	'hewtay	129	se û vist û new
80	'heştay	200	dı sey
90	neway	210	dı sey û des
		2000	dı 'hazari
		2010	dı 'hazar û des

Noteworthy is the pluralization of the numbers 100 *se* and 1.000 *'hazar* when more than a single hundred or thousand is designated.

2.2.9.2.7 Verbs

Verbs are inflected for *person*, *number* and *gender*. Zaza has two categories, *intransitive* and *transitive* verbs. Transitive verbs follow the *ergative* marking system[56] in past tense (2.2.9.1.3).

---

[56] The *ergative* case demonstrates the shift of cases from transitive verbs in perfect tense. The agent (agens) is marked as oblique in perfect tense (as normally the object in present) and the patiens (object) is marked by direct case. *Mı tı di.* = I saw you. (verbally: Me you saw.).

Present tense:
Keyneka çay ana.
'The girl is bringing tea.'

Past Tense:
Keyneker çay ardı.
'The girl (obl.) brought tea.'

Stem System

In Zaza there are three stems for any given verb.[57] All the inflectional forms of a verb are based on one or the other of these three stems. The stems will be referred to here as the *present* stem, the *subjunctive* stem and the *past* stem.

TENSE	STEM	Example
Present Tense	PRESENT	**A şin-a.** = 'She goes.'
Present progressive	PRESENT	**Aya şin-a.** = 'She is going.' (copula follows pronoun)
Subjunctive	SUBJUNCTIVE	**A şır-o.** = 'She wanted to go.'
Future	SUBJUNCTIVE	**Ado şır-o.** = 'She'll go.'[58]
Imperative	SUBJUNCTIVE	**Şo!** = 'go!'
Prohibitive	SUBJUNCTIVE	**Meşo!** = 'Don't go!'
Preterite (Simple Past)	PAST	**A şi.** = 'She went.' (**O şı.** = 'He went.')
Past Imperfect	PAST	**A şi-yê.** = 'She went (long time ago).'[59]
Past Perfect	PAST	**A şi bi.** = 'She had gone.'
Present Perfect	PAST	**A şi-ya.** = 'She has gone.' (copula follows the past stem)
Subjunctive Perfect	PAST	**A bı şiya-yê.** = 'She should have gone.'
Gerund	PAST	**şiya-yış** = to go/ going

---

[57] There are other grammatical approaches that analyze Zazaki and especially its verbal system in other categories (Hayıg 2012 there especially the grammatical overview by Werner). As for now the given differentiation represents the tense system well.
[58] **do** becomes **dê** in **3rd Pl**. Particle *do* follows subject and is handled by some writers as suffix, but only after pronouns, in other cases it is written separately. **Ado şır-o.** vs. **A do şır-o.**
[59] Imperfect ending – *ê* (- *yê*) is the same for all persons.

2 The Zaza

Endings

	Pres.ind.	Subj.	Imperative	Preterite
1 sg.	-a[60]	-a		-a
2.sg.m.	-ê			-ê
		-ê	Ø	
f.	-a			-a
3.sg.m.	-o			-Ø
		-o		
f.	-a			-ı
1. pl.	-m(ı)~-ê	(-ım)		
all pl.	-ê	-ê	-ê	-i

Ending chart: expl. şiyayış= go (unregular);kerdış=do (regular)

Present stem: şın- / ken-
Subjunctive stem: şır- / ker-
Past sem: şi- / kerd-

Paradigm of Stem System şiyayiş

	pres.ind.	subj.	imperative	preterite
1 sg.	şın-a[61]	şır-a		şiy-a
	ken-a	ker-a		kerd-a
2.sg.m.	şın-ê			şiy-ê
	ken-ê			kerd-ê
		şır-ê	şo	
		ker-ê	bık(ı)	
f.	şın-a			şiy-a
	ken-a			kerd-a
3.sg.m	şın-o			şı

---

[60] Archaic root for all 1. sg: - *an*.
[61] Archaic root for all 1. sg: - *an*.

	ken-**o**			kerd
		şır-**o**		
		ker-**o**		
f.	şın-**a**			şi
	ken-**a**			kerd-**ı**
1. pl.	şı-m(ı)~şın-ê	şer-ım~şır-ê		
	ke-m(ı)~ken-ê	ker-**ım**~ ker-ê		
all pl.	şın-ê	şır -ê	şır-ê	ş-**i**
	ken-ê	ker-ê	bıker-ê	kerd-**i**

Verb of Existence

The verb of existence occurs only in present tense[62]. It is most frequently used to express possession.

			negated
3rd pers.	masc.	est-o	çıni-yo[63]
	fem.	est-a	çıni-ya
all plurals		est-ê	çıni-yê

e.g. *Cayê dı areyê esto.*[64]   *Çewrês bıray mı estê.*[65]
      'Some place there is a mill.'   'I have 40 brethren.'

Qeçekê ma çıniyê.
'We don't have children.'

Passive Morpheme

The passive morpheme is represented by *-y-*.

-**y**-   e.g. *vıraz-y-eno*   'it is built' (but: *vırazeno* = 'he builds')
                                 Zuwan qısana vırazyeno.
                                 'Language is built upon words.'

---

[62] For past tense the verb 'to be' is used. e.g. *Qeçê ma zi bi.* 'We had children, too.'
[63] The shortend form *çınyo* is sometimes used by writers.
[64] Fox and miller (*Lu u ardwaniya*; 2007:33-36; 28).
[65] Mahmesha (*Ma'hmeşa*; 2007:37-44, 31).

Causative Morpheme

The causative morpheme is expressed by -*n*- (2.2.1.9.10).

-**n**- e.g. veş-**n**-eno 'he burns (s.th.)' (but: *veşeno* = 'it burns')
  Banê xo veşneno.
  'He burns his house.'

The Copula

The verb 'to be' is manifested as an unstressed *copula* that is usually suffixed to the adjective or noun phrase. The chart below shows the present tense copula forms.

1st pers.		-a
2nd pers.	masc.	-ê
	fem.	-a
3rd pers.	masc.	-o
	fem.	-a
all plurals		-i~ê

Paradigm of Copula

		copula pres.	copula pret.
1st pers.		derg-**a**	derg viya~biya
2nd pers.	masc.	derg-**a**	derg vi~bi
	fem.	derg-**ê**	derg viya~biya
3rd pers.	masc.	derg-**a**	derg vı~bı
	fem.	derg-**o**	derg vi~bi
all plurals		derg-i~-ê	derg vi~bi

When negated, the copula is attached to a stressed negative stem **niy-**. In past tense the copula is identical with the verb "to be".

e.g. *Nan germ-o.*
'The bread is warm.'

Ez Tırk niy-a.
'I'm not a Turk.'

Nan germ bı.
'The bread was warm (at that time).'

Ez Tırk nêbiya.
'I wasn't a Turk (at that time).'

Complex Verbs (with verbal affix)

ro-	+	*nıştış* 'mount'	→	*ronıştış* 'to sit, dwell'
a-	+	*nıştış* 'mount'	→	*anıştış* 'to land' (plane, bird)
cı-	+	*kerdış* 'do, make'	→	*cıkerdış* 'to cut off'
çe-	+	*kerdış* 'do, make'	→	*çekerdış* 'to throw'
ro-	+	*nayış* 'set, place'	→	*ronayış* 'to put, place, plant'
ver-	+	*dayış* 'give'	→	*verdayış* 'to grow' (a beard, hair)
vera-	+	*dayış* 'give'	→	*veradayış* 'to release, let go'

Compound Verbs (two-part verbs)

Paul calls them *Zusammengesetzte Verben* (Engl. Compound Verbs), implying that they are combined phrases of a noun or adjective with an auxiliary (1998:100).

yazı 'writing'	+	*kerdış* 'do, make'	→	*yazı kerdış* 'to write'

pay	+	*dayış*	→ *pay dayış*
'foot'		'give'	'to kick'
pak	+	*kerdış*	→ *pak kerdış*
'clean'		'do, make'	'to clean'(t.v.)

Samples of negated complex verb roots.

Past tense:
Ay   mase   pak nêkerd.
she   table   clean not-made
'She did not clear off the table.'

Imperative:
Pay   medı   pıro.
foot   don't-give him-on
'Don't kick him!'

Prohibitive:
Mektûv yazı mekı.
letter   write don't do.
'Don't write the letter!'

Subjunctive:
O nêwazeno mektûv yazı kero.
he not-wants letter   write
'He doesn't want to write the letter.'

Table 20 Examples of various roots

pres.ind.	subj.	imper.	prohib.	pl.imper	pl.prohib.	past stem	gerund

'to open' (t.v.) (includes preverbal **a-**)

akeno	akero	akı	Makı	akerê	makerê	akerd	akerdış

'to bring' (t.v.)

ano	biyaro	biya	mêya	biyarê	mêyarê	ard	ardış

'to be; become' (i.v.)

Beno	bo	bı	Mebı	bê	mebê	bi / bı (m.)	biyayış

'to carry' (t.v.)

beno	biyero	bi	mey	biyerê	meyerê	berd	berdış

'to throw' (t.v.) (incl. preverbal **çe**)

çekeno	çekero	çek	meçek	çekerê	meçekerê	çekerd	çekerdış

'to give' (t.v.)

dano	bıdo	bıdı	Medı	bıdê ~ bıderê	mederê	da	dayış

'to get, buy' (t.v.)

geno~ gêno	bıgero~[66] bıgêro	bıgi	Megi	bıgerê~ bıgêrê	megerê~ megêrê	gırot	gırotış

'to do'

keno	bıkero	bık(ı)	mek	bıkerê	mekerê	kerd	kerdış

'to fall' (i.v.)

kewno	(bı)kewo	kew(ı)	Mekew	bıkewê	mekewê	kewt	kewtış

'to go' (i.v.)

şıno	şıro	şo	meşo	şırê	meşırê	şi / şı (m.)	şiyayış

---

[66] Dialect variant: **biy-** (instead of **bıg-**) for all subjunctive inflections.

'to say' (t.v.)

| vano | vajo[67] | vaj(ı) | mevaj(ı) | vajê | mevajê | va | vatış |

'to stop, stand' (i.v.)

| vındeno | vındero | vındı | mevındı | vınderê | mevınderê | vınderd | vınderdış |

'to want, wish' (t.v.)

| wazeno | buwazo | buwazo | mewazı | buwazê | mewazê | Waşt | waştış |

'to eat' (t.v.)

| weno | buro | bur | mewı | burê | mewırê | werd | werdış |

'to get up' (i.v.)

| werzeno | werzo | werz(ı) | me-werzı | wferzê | mewerzê | werışt | werıştış |

'to come' (i.v.)

| yeno | bêro ~ biro | bê | mê | bêrê ~ birê | mêrê | ame | amayış |

2.2.10 Summary – Zazaki the Language

In this section it was demonstrated that Zazaki as part of the North-western branch of Iranian languages within the Indo-European language family is closely related to Gorani/Hewrami. Kurmanji has Middle Persian as a predecessor. A common origin of Zazaki and Kurmanji would date back to Proto-Iranian which would be spoken about 2.000 years ago.

Although linguistically Zazaki and Kurmanji are two languages, they share some common features (tense structure, ezafe system, ergative case). Also both ethnicities have common anthropological practices (2.2.3.4). Both areas are not easy to differentiate as they influence each other.

Zazaki has *three main dialect clusters*, the southern, the eastern or central and the northern dialects. Recently the discussion is about a *reference* or *standard dialect* which will support approaches to official mother tongue education. The Çermik dialect was specifically taken into account in this linguistic description to perform a foundation for comparing studies (comparative linguistics).

---

[67] Dialect variant: **vaz-** for all subjunctive inflections.

Bi- and multilingualism is one of the great advantages of the Zaza people. Not only in the Diaspora but also for the Turkish economy this supports relationships to other markets of economy (2.3.1.4; 2.3.4.6). A sketch on Zazaki topped this description off.

The specific features of Zazaki are a complex verbal system with a lot of combination possibilities with pre- and suf-fixes. Those suffixes are *directional*, *temporal* or *modal*. Only around 150 verbal roots form the base for such combinations and follow a *subjunctive*, *present tense* and *past tense* TAM (tense-aspect-mood) classification. A split-ergative system in the past, a gender based ezafe system and a far / near oriented pronoun system are specific characteristics of Zazaki.

2.3 The Society

Cultural and social descriptions of the Zaza people are manifold (Temizbas 2007; Koymaz 2005; Selcan 1998; Werner 2011; Gündüzkanat 1997; Kaya 2011). Most if not all scratch mainly on the surface and do not go into depth on specific ethnographic issues, such as *worldview*, *LEIC*, *envy* or *ethnomusicology* (2.3.5.3). The Zaza society is not a homogenous culture which can be defined in one way only. Quite the opposite, the very recent and exhaustive social description of the Zaza society of the *Solhan* area (close to Bingoel) by *Kaya* (2011) gives a good impression of the manifold cultural variations that we face. For this reason we can differentiate the observations as overall observations and specific ones, the latter referring to a subunit of the larger ethnicity. Unlike a social description this ethnography is focusing on the wider phenomenon of society that drives it (1.1.1). However a comparative study will always make use of social findings.

Another preliminary remark seems to be necessary in relation to the rapid transformation that the Zaza culture goes through. The big challenge for the Zaza group within the transformation from a peasant feudalistic structure into an industrial capitalistic society consists of the divergence of pace in which the diverse groups follow. The Northern Group, due to assimilation is the forerunner in this process, whereas the Eastern Group is the farthest back. Looking at Kaya's description one recognizes that the old structures still work out there. For modern Zaza his description sounds outdated, since they went through these stages before the 1960s. The Southern Group is recently more in the midst of

2 The Zaza

this transformation. Having said this, an anthropological description or ethnography will never cover the status of every group in every stage. However the study passes on historical facts and puts them in relation to recent observations and developments.

For sure the Zaza people are not distinctive from any other people in that area group by their race. All historical and recent descriptions of the Zaza do not mention any racist uniqueness on which critics or racist could build their ideology (Lerch 1857-1858: xvii–xviv).

The Zaza people are a culture that hands down tradition orally. They pass on their culture and language orally and not in written form. As such narration and the oral-aural factor become important issues. The background for such oral aural passing on of traditions could be found in the fact that their social system is split up into many small scale social units with an average of 250 to 300 members that are ruled by a feudalistic leadership that forms its own social class (Gündüzkanat 1997:73-75). As such the institution of ritual and chanted tradition is basic to this ethnos. The professional function of "passing on traditions" through the social institutions of the Alevi *tikme* (student) by the *rayber / rehber* and the *pir* (pirdom: , *rayber*, *mürşid*, seldom by Turkish influence called *dede*), the Sunni *sheikh* (sheikhdom / mullaharchy) and the political *agha* (aghadom) is or was part of the Zaza society and guaranteed the continued existence of the Zaza people (MT 2012. Personal Communication at 2nd Symposium of the Zaza Language in Bingol / Turkey; Hiebert & Hiebert 1995:111; 2.3.4.3). As recently as the migration movements, the long going oppression of the mother tongue use and the collapse of the feudal system the institution got lost and the need for "written traditions" arose. At the end of the twentieth century "written traditions" in the Zaza ethnicity occurred and started to preserve the culture and the language. Because of political reasons and an increase of self-esteem this happened first in the Diaspora.

Since the year 1980, literarily publications point out increasingly the traditional and modern life of the Zaza. Music, newspapers and novels are the main genres of writing (extensive list of newspapers in Hayıg 2007:191; s. a. Bibliography: *Newspapers of the Zaza*).

For that very reason the focus in the following description is on a short general account and a detailed picture of some outstanding particularities.

2.3.1 Historical Background – Political Past and Present

The Zaza people underwent a turbulent political history. The geographically caused partition in a Northern and Southern Group / Eastern Group led to a religious and linguistic subdivision. The location of the Silk Roads, reaching from the Black Sea to the Mediterranean and from the East to the West, brought them in close contact to ancient ideologies and religious sects (2.3.3.4). The passing peoples, like Greeks, Christian monks, traders etc. influenced the peasant small scale society that was structured in smaller tribal units. The foundation of the Republic of Turkey in 1923 led to a minority status that caused a lot of repression within the newly established nation state (2.3.3.4; 3.5). This was also the first time that the Zaza people lost their political independence as a whole group to a stronger force for what is now almost one century.

Reports about the Zaza ethnicity from the 19th century show a poor and simple-living society. The three class system is ruled by the upper *Agha*, *Sheikh* and *Mılah* class (Petrov 1998:148-150). After this picture we will now look into more details of the religious and social division of the Zaza people.

2.3.1.1 Northern- and Southern / Eastern Group

A possible division of the Zaza language group into an Alevism practicing Northern Group and an Islamic-Sunni Southern / Eastern Group is thought to date back to the 16th century AD / 10th century AH. One reason seems to be the strengthening of a fundamental-Islamic activity to spread Islam in the Middle East. An Islamic school of law took its invitation to Islam (Arab. *da'awah*; *dau'wah*) forward very aggressively. The goal was the re-islamisation of the Islamic people groups within the Ottoman Empire, based on a strong sending and eschatological attitude (Benninghaus [1989] 2002:483-484).

The Zaza of the Northern dialect that is the Northern Group, live in a mountainous and difficult to access region. This region belongs to the Tarsus / Zagros mountain range that belong to the global Alpine belt – with mountains high up to 4.000 m or 13.123 feet. The latter reaches from Europe to Asia. The Southern Group in contrast inhabits the valleys of the headwaters of the big rivers the Tigris, Euphrates and Murat. The Northern Group dwells around mountain creeks and streams. The Northern area is comparable to Switzerland or Austria in Europe.

The area of the Zaza was part of different mesopotamic dominion territories. Following their historical time line it started with the ruling period of the,

2 The Zaza

- Hittites,
- Assyrian,
- Hurritian,
- Babylonian,
- Medes,
- Persian,
- Arab,
- Seljuk,
- Ottoman and
- recent Turkish Government

as the most popular people groups of the ancient and the Middle Ages.

According to the Daylam-Thesis argument (2.1.3.1) the emigration from Daylam to the recent settlement area could be an aftermath of the Mongolian Storms ($11^{th} - 13^{th}$ century AD / $5^{th} - 7^{th}$ century AH) during the ruling period of the *Seljuk* emperors (Encyclopaedia Iranica: entry *Dimple*; 2.1.3.1.1; 2.1.3.1.4; 2.1.3.1.5; 2.3.1.1; 2.3.3.4; 3.1.1; 3.3; 0). Nonetheless, most Zaza argue that they are the indigenous people of their recent settlement area; or at least that they have inhabited this area for more than two thousand years. Most of the Zaza that were interviewed in 2005 argued that they derive from the *Hittites* and that the larger than life-size stone sculptures on top of *Nemrut Dağ* are proof of that (Questionnaire / Fragebogen 2005 in Werner 2006). This historically wrong assumption is still in force, although it is archaeologically proved that the sculptures show the Seleucidian *Antiochos I. Theos* (69–36 BC).

The Zaza of the Southern dialect dwell in the flat and wide open plains towards *Syria*. This location – contrary to the closed mountain area of the Northern Group – meant that their homeland became "until the 19th century a staging area" (Nestmann 2002:551). "Neither the Turkish, nor the Armenian and Iranian powers and culture were able to carry themselves through, such the regional culture could be obtained" (:551) and the Southern Group ruled themselves relatively autonomous until the foundation of the Republic of Turkey in 1923.

The Zaza people were successful in revoking the influence of the *tanzimat*-reforms (Seufert & Kubaseck 2004:71; 3.1.1.5) or the nationalization movements of the Turks (Berkes 1959:27-29; 1905-1923 AD). Yet individual advocates were open to such influences (s. o.; Izady 1992:110).

2.3.1.2 Silk Road – Influence by Ruling Powers

One of the Silk Roads runs from East to West right through the settling area of the Southern Group (2.1.4.1). International contacts from Europe to India were known by the Zaza ethnos throughout the centuries, but interestingly it seems that the influence on the Zaza people was minimal (linguistical influence see 2.3.3.4; 3.6). In consequence the people groups passing through had little influence and if they did, then only on linguistic and religious grounds (2.2.8.4; 2.3.3.4). Besides that the division of labour between Armenians, Kurds and Zaza led to economic associations (2.3.3.7.1). Guest houses on the Silk Road in the Zaza-area called *karawansaray* were run by the ruling powers such as the Seljuks, the Ottomans or the Turks. The Zaza as vassals were responsible for the maintenance of those guest houses but just by providing the necessary utilities. The basis of this reciprocal relationship between the ruling powers and the leadership of the Zaza communities was based on a political independence and autonomy that lasted until the foundation of the Republic of Turkey.

Since the 19th century the new archaeological research has taken different main routes of the Silk Roads into account. The intercultural / cross-cultural aspects of the Silk Roads is well demonstrated in the communicative character of the guest houses (*karawansaray*) in which oral-aural traditions were passed through, trading going on and cultures from all nations met and affected each other (Brockhaus multimedial 2007. *Seidenstraße* [Silk Road]).

2.3.1.3 Foundation of the Republic and Status as Minority

The foundation of the Republic of Turkey on the 29th of October 1923 was the beginning of a minority status for microcultures in this Nation State. Those linguistically and religiously diverse groups that neither speak Turkish nor follow Sunni Islam became minorities within the nation. In other words *non-Turks / non-Turkish speaking* or *non-Muslims* became separated social units within the Nation State. Thus their struggle for freedom and acceptance in one or the other way started (Höhlig 1997:115-116, 120-123). In the very beginning the Turkish Republic paid attention to autonomy and independence, or at least gave some freedom to those groups. During the initial years, when the governmental structures were established, this attitude changed (:116; Steinbach 1988:158-161; 3.1.1.5). The Zaza people were not able to mobilize their own people in a larger framework. Their only help was to look for allies within the Nation State and from outside.

2.3.1.3.1 Zaza and / or Kurdish Initiatives

The religious and Islamic attitude of the Zaza led them towards the Kurmanji speaking Kurds as well as the wider "Kurdish movement" (2.2.3.6). This became obvious when the Christian and Jewish people were annihilated in those days by the exclusively "Kurdish" *Hamidiye* (initiated and derived from Sultan *Abdul Hamid* II.) troops but also with the support of the Southern and Eastern Zaza (2.1.4.3; 2.1.4.4; 2.1.4.3; 2.2.8.2; 2.2.8.2; 3.1.1.2; 3.5; HC 2011). At this point it is interesting that the only uprising in the 19th century was led by the Kurmanji speaking Kurd *Ubeydallah* who came from *Nehri* in the *Hakkari* area. His interest was to proclaim a Kurdish state in the politically unstable border area of Persia and the weakened Ottoman Empire. He asked the British and Russian troops for help (Bruinessen 1989b:111). Besides this triggering rebellion the main "Kurdish" uprisings of the 20th century were lead by Zaza (*Sheikh Said* and *Seyit Rıza*; s. b.; Kieser 2000:19-20).

In 1978 the reciprocal relationship of the neighbours found its climax in the foundation of the *Partiya Karkerên Kurdistan* or *PKK* ("Workers Party of Kurdistan") in *Ziyaret* close to the city *Lice* (2.2.7.2). So far no research has been done as to how much the Zaza were and are involved in the activities and politics of the PKK. It would be interesting which positions they took up and if they started moving towards their own independence within this organisation. The PKK as an organization included men and women, Zaza and other minority people. The promoted and intended goal is still an independent province or state of "Kurdistan" in Eastern Anatolia. An open question is whether within such a political structure the Zaza would gain a district, a province or even a self-governing political structure. Since some Zaza are taking part in leading the movement, the expectation would be to have a huge say within any upcoming structure. The alliance or even their "leading of" the PKK led to a political division and a crisis of identification within the Zaza ethnicity (Kehl-Bodrogi 1998:11-135; 3.1.3.2). The recent leader of the *Barış ve Demokrasi Partisi* (Peace and Democracy Party; BDP), a successor of the pro-PKK HADEP, is *Selahattin Demirtaş* from Palu (parents from *Elazığ*). He is a Zaza claiming to be a "Kurd". He is part of the parliament for the *Diyarbakır* district with the former *Democratic Society Party* (DTP), which re-formed as the BDP. There are many examples of Zaza being in leading positions within the Kurdish nationalist movement, which has to do with the fact that many consider themselves being as ethnically "Kurds" (2.2.3.2; 3.5).

Recently, since 2005, the independence of "Kurdistan" in Northern Iraq and the Arabic uprisings in Syria empowered the Kurdish nationalist movement. Although the former leader of the PKK is in prison, his successor *Murat Karayılan*, born 1954 in *Birecik* (district of *Şanlıurfa*, Turkey), as the acting leader of the PKK (member since 1979) continues proceedings actively. The growing impact of this development is also visible in Germany where an increase in pro-PKK activities is discernible (e.g. public speeches of *Demirtaş* in Frankfurt 2012-01-21 etc.; MA 2012 *personal communication*; Cultural festival in Mannheim with 40.000 visitors from all over Europe on 2012-09-08; 2.3.4.6.6; 3.1.1.5).

2.3.1.3.2 Sheikh Said and Seyit Rıza - Rebellions

The Ottoman / Turkish nationalist propaganda picked up the colonialist and imperialistic power play between the British and Russian troops during the Ubeydallah uprising (1879-1882). They blamed these powers for the struggles of independence that followed (Tunçay 1989b:67-68). These powers promoted and taught the use of military tactics and weapons to support the uprising that was motivated by a mix of nationalistic and religious orientation run mainly by the Kurmanji speakers and less by the Zaza ethnicity (Bruinessen 1989b:162; Tezcür 2009 *Kurdish Nationalism and Identity in Turkey*).

The rebellion of *Sheikh Ubeydallah* from *Nehri* in Hakkari (1879) functioned as an example for the uprisings of *Sheikh Said* (1925), the *Koçuşagı* rebellion (1926) and the one of *Said / Seyit Rıza* called *tertele / Tertelê Dêrsimi* (1937/1938; 2.3.1.1; 2.3.1.3.2; 2.3.3.3).

The religious background of Sheikh Said is important to understand his motivation for the uprising. Sheikh Said was following and part of the Naqşebendi / *Naqshebendi tarikat* (2.3.4.4.3). His grandfather was indoctrinated in the Islamic order by the *Khalid Halif Ahmed of Erbil* (Bruinessen 1989b:148). The order followed the rules of sobriety and a fundamental practice of the Islamic law, the *Sharia* (Turk.: *şeriat*). The issue of sobriety can be traced back to the founder *Abu Bakr*, one of the adepts of *Baha ad-Din Naqshband* (died 1389), who himself is traced back by his devotees in direct line to the prophet Hz. *Mohammed* (Algar 1989:167-168). After the establishment of the Naqşebendi / Naqshebendi tarikat in Istanbul and the Ottoman Empire by Molla / Mulla / Mıllah *Abdullah Ilahi of Simav* (died 1490). *Maulana Khalid Bagdhadid* (died 1826) reformed the order. He gave it a *Rabita* that is the heart relationship between the *murid* (student/adept) and the teacher. His instructions are the only point of theological

2 The Zaza

reflection, they remain valid even after his death (:70-71). Following this background, *Sheikh Said* was part of this important and widely spread Sunni order that followed the Shariah strictly. On top of that he became politically prominent through his marriage into the dominant Kurmanji-Kurdish small scale society called *Cibran* (Bruinessen 1989b:151; 2.3.4.3.1; 2.3.4.4.3).

The origin of such a revolt traces back to the descent and disbanding of the Ottoman Empire. The very religiously oriented Sunni Zaza discredited the liberal tendencies of the newly found Turkish Republic and fought against it. The motivation was to support the Sultanate and Caliphate as a God-given institution (Gündüzkanat 1997:122). As reason for his uprising Sheikh Said claimed in his trial after he and his leadership were captured:

> The madrassa'are closed, the ministry for religious matters and religious foundations is disestablished and the religious schools have been brought under control of the ministry for national education. A gang of unbelieving authors in their newspapers has the courage, swearing at the religion and soiling the name of the prophet. As far as it concerns me, I am ready for the protection of the religion, if necessary today and fight (Cemal cit. in Gündüzkanat 1997:122).

Related to the question of the Zaza people group being part of the wider "Kurds", the historical descriptions of the uprisings in Eastern Anatolia in general are missing a clear cut differentiation of the participants. Steinbach who was influenced by Bruinessen (1989a:29 and 1989b:109) is wrong when he describes the Zaza unrest during those days by referring them back to "Kurdish" origins, without even differentiating between the participants:

> The Kurds ... represented the only larger minority that had remained in the new Republic of Turkey after destruction, expulsion and resettlement of the Armenians and Greek. They revolted under Sheikh Said of Palu. ... A mixture of feudal tribal interests, Kurdish-national emotions and a religious reaction started the rebellion in Dersim (Tunceli) in February 1925 and threatened the cities of Elazig and Diyarbakir. ... The fight against the Kurdish uprising developed into a real campaign (Steinbach 1996:134-135).

Sheikh Said (also called Sayid / Sayıd / Seyid e.g. Bruinessen 1992:379 or *Ware* 12/1989) was a Zazaki-speaking and not a Kurmanji speaking Kurd (Zürcher 2004:170). One has to keep in mind that in those days the division of Zaza and Kurds was not really an issue on political but on cultural terms (see below). He was from *Piran* in the region of *Dicle*, but active in the *Palu* area. Yet the whole uprising was based on a Zaza initiative and not a wider Kurdish revolt, with this in mind it is obvious that a wider "Kurdish" initiative would have mobilized much more resistance. The "Sheikh Said uprising" as it is called in Turkish history, caused a caesurae in the history of the Zaza people and the domestic politics of the newly found Republic of Turkey led by Mustafa Kemal Paşa Atatürk. As an immediate cause the Zaza, Kurmanji-Kurdish and other minorities were totally neglected and forced to integrate into the Turkish Nation State by using *Turkish* only (Seufert & Kubaseck 2004:150; Zürcher 2004:172; explicitly 3.6).

Arfa describes another course for the Sheikh Said rebellion. The upheaval started in *Çüngüş*, *Palu*, *Piran*, that is the area of the Southern Group, and spread quickly to the north in the direction of *Dersim* and to the east in the direction of *Diyarbakır* (1966:37-39; s. a. Zürcher 2004:169-173).

As mentioned above my strongest argument is that a revolt from within the Kurmanji speaking Kurdish group would have mobilized more powers of resistance. This also proves the fact that, for a long time, the "Kurds" had an eye on Mustafa Kemal Paşa Atatürk who promised them relative independence. In contrast to this Sheikh Said mobilized only moderate Zaza and Kurdish forces, "the participants were almost exclusively Sunni Zaza, both tribesmen and urban poor" (Kreyenbroek & Sperl 2002:52). It does not seem that it came to a strong Zaza-Kurdish confederation. Sheikh Said's revolt is a further reference to the cultural distance between the Zaza and the Kurmanji speaking Kurds.

27.000 Zaza were killed, 200 villages destroyed and 9.000 houses burned. The newly established Turkish air force was a main factor in this fight. It was installed with German help during the preparation to WWI. against the Russians. It was also very disastrously used during the ethnocide of the Christians in the east as was proved by Dadrian (1997a; 2.1.4.4; 3.1.3). Intellectuals and members of the *Naqshebendi* order were sent into exile to the west of the Republic. The idea was to destroy its structure, so for example was *Said Nursi* exiled to Isparta (Mardin 1989:206).

This revolt was preceded by another uprising in the region of *Dersim*, today's renamed province of Tunceli. In 1920 / 1921 the Alevi small scale social units of the Northern Group revolted in the so called *Koçkiri / Koçgiri rebellion* (Tk. Koçkiri; an estimated militia of 25.000). They were not heard by the newly grouping military forces of the new Republic at the Treaty of Sivas (1919) and the colonial masters such as France, Italy, Greece, Russia and the United Kingdom (Zürcher 2004:170).

The Sheikh Said uprising started by the Sunni Southern Zaza and was mainly for political reasons and as a reaction of the *Koçkiri Rebellion* without any contribution from the Alevi Northern Zaza Group. Not only did the Northern Group ignore the uprising, but some of the Alevi social units were opposed to it, because they feared that the Turks and the Zaza would ally against them as both follow Sunni Islam. As a reaction to this rejection and opposition the Sunni Southern Zaza ignored the cry for help from the Northern Group in the "Turmoil of Dersim" in 1937/38 (*Tertelê Dêrsimî*) which caused a deep emotional division of both groups until today (Kreyenbroek & Sperl 2002:52). *Seyit Rıza* (also Said Rıza, Seyt Rıza or Seyit Reza, 1862-1937) was the main actor in this uprising. It was directed against the construction of Turkish schools and public constitutions as well as the overwhelming Turkish presence in the preceding years (Arfa 1966:43). *Seyit Rıza* was involved in the *Koçkiri* Rebellion, although he was not able to help his allies due to seasonal winter storms. He also was one of the opponents of Sheikh Said's revolt in 1925 because of the religious rejection of Sunni Islam, fearing a Zaza-Turkish Sunni alliance against the Northern Zaza group.

The *Sheikh Said* revolt in the year 1925 led to dramatic changes in the political situation in the Eastern provinces of Turkey inhabited by Kurmanji speaking Kurds, Zaza and other minorities. This revolt could be labelled the beginning of the "Kurdish National Movement". The Zaza were and are until today the main protagonists in this movement (Bruinessen 1992:379; Zürcher 2004:171).

Sheikh Said offered resistance to Mustafa Kemal Paşa Atatürk's assimilation endeavours. The Turkish leaders aim was to destroy the feudal system of the small scale society units within the Zaza ethnicity and the Kurmanji-Kurds. Mainly because he didn't trust Mustafa Kemal Paşa Atatürk's promises of giving them independent provinces and, as is proved by history, his lack of trust was justified. Those promises made in the 1920s guaranteed the Zaza and the Kurmanji speaking Kurds their own provinces if they fought for Mustafa Kemal Paşa Atatürk (Zürcher 2004:170; 3.1.1.5). Sheikh Said's mistrust was built on the rejection of Mustafa Kemal Paşa Atatürks laicist reforms concerning an absolute division of religion and politics. Such was not compatible with the Sunni teaching of the "House of Islam" (*dar al-Islam*) in which politics and religion go hand in hand (Schirrmacher 2008a:108-109). As an influential leader of the congregation of the Islamic *Naqshebendi* fraternity *Sheikh Said* was able to mobilize a huge faction of supporters both within and outside nationalistic circles (Seufert & Kubaseck 2004:88; Zürcher 2004:12, 170; (2.3.1.3.2; 2.3.4.4.3; 2.3.4.3.1). Bruinessen and Arfa regard the uprising as mainly religiously caused reactions against the laicist direction of the newly established government and the dismissal of the Sultanate. They argue that this is the reason why he - as the first in history - wanted to establish a religious and autonomous "Kurdish nation" (Kurdistan), whereas preceding revolts (e.g. 1880 AD) never had such ambitions (Bruinessen 1992:379; Arfa 1966:37-39). The argument supports *Seyit Rızas* request for military help. Another factor could be found in following statement:

> The background of the Sheikh-Said rebellion was obviously neither clearly religious nor clearly nationalistic nature. Apart from elements of the two directions a traditionalistic resistance to any intervention of the Turkish government came into effect (Gündüzkanat 1997:122).

In contrary to the argument that the whole uprising was only possible because of *Sheikh Said's* leading position within the *Naqshebendi* congregation goes the observation that he was only mobilizing religiously motivated powers and not political-nationalistic oriented groups. In support of this goes the zealot fighting spirit of his supporters (Bruinessen 1992:274; Seufert & Kubaseck 2004:88). As is often the case, both religion and nationalism intermingled and led to the beginning of the uprising and the Kurdish nationalistic movement. Until today the region of the *Sheikh Said* Revolt represents the heartland of the Kurdish military and political movement for autonomy and independence (Zürcher 2004:169-172).

Interestingly the revolt started in the mountainous area of the Northern Group, but quickly moved south into the region of the Southern Group. In 1926 the Turkish military started a reprisal action in connection with the small scale societal group called *Koçuşagı*, which invaded Çemisgezek to free it from military oppression. The brutal assault on the members of this societal group was well planned and conducted as an action with a deterrent effect. The whole military proceeding demonstrates that the main goal was to weaken the Dersim region once and for all (Gündüzkanat 1997:123).

In contrast the Northern Group that lives in a naturally heavy-to-enter area was able to sustain resistance any approaches of repression for longer. With the growing military force of the Turkish troops the boot was on the other foot, by the end of the 1930s, when, before the close of Mustafa Kemal Paşa Atatürk's life, massive discrimination started. In 1937-1938 the climax was reached, when the political situation led to the so called "Turmoil of Dersim" (*Tertelê Dêrsimi*; Kreyenbroek & Sperl 2002:73; Zürcher 2004:176). This, the worst period historically of the Zaza-Turkish relationship, was during the leadership of *Seyit Rıza*. The term *seyit* evolved from the Arabic term *seyyid*. The so titled leaders of Islamic orders or fraternities had a status like a *Sheikh* and can be compared to the abbot of Christian orders. Mainly he is an insider and is either chosen or inherits his position as religious leader. As such the term gives high prestige and addresses influential people.

To come back to the *Tertelê Dêrsimi*, this incident takes up a lot of investigations and writings in the recently occurring authorial period of the Northern Zaza Group. An extensive summary of eye-witness reports by *Çağlayan* (2003) and the questioning of relatives from *Seyit Rıza* by *Mergarıji* (1997) give witness to such efforts. The politically unstable time before WWII and the inner conflicts in the Republic of Turkey, caused by the illness and subsequent death of the Turkish hero Mustafa Kemal Paşa Atatürk (10. Nov. 1938) supported the mainly religious and political unrest and uprisings in the Eastern parts during this later period.

In consequence of the Sheikh-Said uprising the Southern Group came into focus for further Turkish repressive sanctions. In succeeding cycles up to the climax of the "Dersim Turmoil" (*Tertelê Dêrsimi*; s. b.) in 1937-1938, the Northern Group alternated with the Southern Group as far as Turkish military interventions were concerned. The situation boiled up to a civil war which happened in the homeland of the Northern Group. The Turkish officials set an example to future revolutionists and the Eastern provinces in general, by demonstrating that they were not willing to accept any uprising any more. The Tukrish name *tedip harekâtı* "extermination campaign", suggests that the Turks considered the *Tertelê Dêrsimi* less a rebellion. It can well be that the Turkish military was planning in a military operation to discipline or "break" the rebel spirit of Dersim. The naming as a a rebellion is maybe a Zaza or Kurdish attempt to prove the coherent line of resistance against Turkish oppression (Bruinessen 1994). If as mentioned in some comments about the *Tertelê Dêrsimi* chemical weapons (toxic gas) was used is not proved yet. The Anfal attac of Saddam Hussein against Iraqi Kurds (1988) generates such assumptions.

Authors from that time recorded the emotions and actions of those days, beginning in 1920, moving on to 1925 with the documentation of the Sheikh Said uprising and ending in 1938 when pressure from Turkish side prohibited any records. In 1928 Sureya Bedr Khan declares:

> The Turks' policy toward non-Turks - Greek, Armenian, Kurd, Arab and others - from the beginning ... In reality, the root of all these abnormal manifestations has been and are the desire of the Turks to strengthen and sustain his race - by... (Khan cit. in Honeyboon 1995:11).

The military intervention led to the status of the Zaza people being colonialisation. In this way the closely organized pressure and observation from the officials is well structured and leaves no room for independence (Gündüzkanat 1997:53).

Table 21 Popular Rebellions of the Zaza People

Name	Time	Place	General Information
Sheikh Ubeydallah from Nehri in Hakkari – Kurmanji speaking Kurd	1879	Sunni Groups; Eastern Anatolia to modern Iran	Islamic and mystic *Naqshebendi* Order; could not form broad alliances with other Sheikhs
Koçkiri rebellion (Tk. Koçkiri); Zaza	1920 / 1921	Alevi Groups; *Northern* Group and Dersim region	Small scale upheaval
Sheikh Said; Zaza	1925	Sunni Groups; Euphrates / Tigris headwater area	Islamic and mystic *Naqshebendi* Order; claimed as Kurdish revolt but mainly Southern and Eastern Zaza
Koçuşagı rebellion; Zaza	1926	Alevi Groups; Northern Group and Dersim region	Led to massive oppression; Turkish focus on Zaza
Ararat rebellion (Serewedarıtışê Ağırıye); Kurmanji speaking Kurds	1927-1931	Region around Mount Ararat (province Ağrı); Kurmanji speaking Jibran Tribe	Little participation by small Zaza tribes; the declaration of the "Republic of Ararat" provoked harsh resentments by Turkish forces
Seyit Rıza; Zaza	1937 / 1938	Alevi Groups; Northern Group and Dersim region	"*Tertelê Dêrsimi*"largest uprising led to repressive measure and resettlement politics until 1948

2.3.1.4 Developments in the Homeland and Diaspora

Beginning with the economic boom in the 1960s, European companies in the automobile, construction and electronic sector started to recruit unskilled manpower from the East of Turkey. It was easy to mobilize huge amounts of people from the underdeveloped Eastern provinces (Schirrmacher 2008b:7). The subsequent emigration from the homeland and migration to Europe - mainly Germany - formed the first planned and organized mass migration movement based on economics in history. The process led to the settlement of those labourers in the economic centres of e.g. Germany.

The enrolment of labourers from Turkey in the sixties was not mainly focused on minorities, but affected them the most. Besides the Kurds and the Zaza, other people groups reacted also, such as the Circassian and Adyghe minority (Höhlig 1997:115-116). It is not totally clear why the Republic of Turkey allowed such economic movements, but the military coup in 1960 and the subsequent political situation contributed largely to such a situation.

Another migration movement started in the 1980s. The waves of labourers, combined with refugees in the eighties triggered a slowly increasing Islamisation process in Europe, to be seen in the phenomenon of Euro-Islam (Troeger 2005; Triebel 2007:353-358) and the recent debate on foreigners integration due to religious issues. A ghettoization in Berlin / Kreuzberg (called "Small Istanbul"), Colon (company: Ford), Augsburg (company: Audi), Munich (company: BMW), Stuttgart (company: Mercedes Benz), Wetzlar / Giessen (company: Buderus) took place and is an ongoing process, criticized by the German public (Caglar 1998:17). This happened and continues to happen even though e.g. in Germany the department of integration has a policy to distribute foreigners all over the country. The consequences of this migration movement and the ghettoization in the big cities still causes keen debate about the best policy of integration for the second and third generation (see Migration-approach Sinus A23 in Icken 2010:45-46).

The recent rise of Islamic "fundamentalism" led to an increase in missionary efforts and activities (*da'hwa*) by Islamic groups. Paralled by these missionary endeavours, the global increase in terrorist activities based on Islamic perceptions of the world has recently created an explosive mixture in Europe. Thus after fifty years the situation has changed totally; whereas the first guest labourers were given a friendly welcome, nowadays Europeans are cautious about the outcomes and trends caused by the mass movement from Turkey to European countries (3.1.3).

The background of the political-economic relationships between Germany and the Ottoman Empire reaches back to the imperial time of the German Empire (Germ. "Deutsches Reich"). Back then the Emperor *Kaiser Wilhelm* II. and King of Prussia contemplated to the formation of an anti-Russian alliance with the Golden Horn at the Bosporus. Prussian military personnel structured and formed the military apparatus of the Ottoman Empire from 1860 to 1918. As the latter date demonstrates the close alliance between the Prussians and the Ottomans extended to the end of WWI when both war parties thought that they could fight the Russians and the European powers (Zürcher 2004:41, 44, 82, 113 and 121; 3.1.3).

Since the year 2002 the oppressive approach of Turkish politics has changed, due to the efforts toward candidacy for the *European Union* (EU). The relationship with the EU, formerly *European Economic Community* (Germ. "Europäische Wirtschafts Gemeinschaft") reaches back to the 1960s when the huge amount of guest labourers made it necessary to work out visa, tax and social security issues between the European countries of residence and Turkey. The enrolment status since 2004 led to an application status that discomforted the Turkish government from the beginning.

As an essential outcome of the EU enrolment the minority matter became more central and recent Turkish politics support finding a solution to the "Kurdish Issue". This is being done by making the minority languages more public and giving them the opportunity for development, training, and use in public schools. The change of direction by the Turkish government is promoted by the official slogan "The Kurdish Initiative". Such mother tongue initiatives were requested a long time ago, as is shown by the *United Nations Educational, Scientific and Cultural Organization* (UNESCO) and others (Höhlig 1997:120-121). To increase social justice the centralistic, Ankara oriented system, needs to develop federalist structures in the east. The Eastern region especially, with its huge Kurdish and Zaza population, needs to be heard politically. Minority issues on the regional administrative organization level could be also be managed by federalist local institutions. In this way smaller minorities would also get the right to have a say (3.1.1.5).

2.3.1.5 Summary

The Zaza ethnicity was defined by its history, and its political, religious and geographical environment. They split into a Northern and Southern / Eastern Group, due to religious and linguistic differences (2.1.1.5.2; 2.1.42.2.3.5; 2.2.4; 2.2.4). The history of both groups is therefore partially different because their concerns about and their relation to the officials or ruling powers was caused by religious and political factors.

The Northern Group follows the Shi'ite school of *Alevism*, the teachings of *Hacı Bektaş Veli* (buried in the sanctuary in *Hacıbektaş*) and a dualism of Good and Evil from *Zoroastrianism*, called *Parsiism* in India and Asian countries and *serduşt* in Zazaki and Kurmanji. On the contrary the Southern and Eastern Group follows the Sunni tradition. Although there are some differences in their school of Islamic law (Hanafi versus Shafi'i *madrassa*), the latter supported the Seljuk and Ottoman rulers, whereas the Northern Group was persecuted due to their religious confession (2.3.3.2).

Politically this people group managed to stay independent and autonomous under all the previous kingdoms, realms and empires that ruled the homeland area before the foundation of the Republic of Turkey in 1923. The Hittite, Assyrian, Babylonian, Persian, Medes, Greek, Roman, Armenian, Byzantine, Seljuk or Ottoman empires seemed to oppress the Zaza neither as a minority nor as a political part of their empire. These empires only expected taxes, military and economic support by manpower and loyalty to the ruling regime. Thus the year 1923 was a turning point. As an outcome, the uprisings of 1925 (Sheikh Said), 1926 and 1937-1938 (Seyit Rıza) all led by Zaza leadership, caused the oppression of the Zaza ethnicity and their use of their language in public. The Kurmanji speaking ethnos was also oppressed.

Since 1980 a cultural and linguistic revival, acknowledging their traditions, started in the Diaspora and is affecting the homeland (2.3.1.4; 2.3.4.6). Thus the numbers of authors, publications, public discussions about the Zaza people group and activities on an international level are increasing.

2.3.2 Fundamentals

Essentially cultures follow either a shame or a guilt orientation as every culture tends to deal with either the status of prestige or of guilt (Hesselgrave 2002:206; Spiro 1965:406, 409; Neuliep 2006:271; Lingenfelter & Mayers 1991:84-85; Melina 2001:109; Müller 2009:137; 1.1.3.2; 1.1.3.3).

2.3.2.1 Shame-orientation, Collectivism and Envy

The Zaza people follow shame-orientation. This becomes obvious when their dealing with envy and honour is observed. In both fields the Zaza exhibit the features of shame oriented societies. Spiro researched such tendencies in the educational outcomes of children in Israeli social institutions, namely the Kibbutz. In guilt oriented situations the children developed their conscience by trespassing norms and rules, which could even be felt without other participants (1965:406, 409; 1975). This is not true to the Zaza people as they follow a "collectivistic" shape (Werner 2006:56-57; s. a. Hofstede 1993:77), in contrast to "individualistic cultures" (Stolze 1999:204). Having said this, a pure or extreme appearance of either social orientation is rare and mixed forms with the tendency towards one performance are the rule.

As Malina demonstrates the Mediterranean cultures that can be traced back to the "ancient world" reveal similar attributes, as demonstrated in the New Testament. Shame orientation and collectivistic shape parallel each other (2001:93, 109-110, 122). Shame orientation is based on a group related regulation system in which the individual is subordinated to the group; as such the collectivistic shape is central to such societies. Differences refer to the

- personal profile,
- moral values,
- the Location of the Emotions, the Intellect and the Character (LEIC/ SEIC; 1.1.3.3; 2.3.2.1.4; 2.3.5.3),
- the strategy to reduce or prevent uncertainty and
- the gender relationship.

2.3.2.1.1 Collectivism

The phenomenon of *collectivism* concerns the group-oriented behaviour of humans. Societies that follow the collectivistic paradigm do not reveal an interest in individualistic tendencies.

> This is the group-embedded, group-oriented, collectivistic personality, one who needs another simply to know who he or she is. Since collectivistic personality derives its information from outside of the self and, in turn, serves as source of outside information to others, anything unique that goes on inside of a person is filtered out of attention. Individual psychology, individual uniqueness, and individual self-consciousness are simply dismissed as uninteresting and unimportant. (Malina 2001:75).

The opposite to collectivistic societies is represented by an *individualistic* structure. Hofstede lists nations that tend toward individualism (cit. in Stolze 1999:204). All western, especially European cultures and the North American culture are ranked here. Mediterranean and Asian cultures in contrast tend towards *collectivism*". Additionally, Malina substantiates those Mediterranean cultures following the collectivistic paradigm in contrast to the individualistic characteristics of the Scandinavian or Northern European people groups. This becomes specifically obvious in dealing with suicide. In a collectivist society the public is not avenged by the whistle-blower but the denounced person will punish others. This will be done by honour killing or blood feud, substitutionally for the whole society in which he was losing face (Malina 2001:110, 139, 141). The Holy Books of such cultures, as expressed in the Hebrew Bible and the Qur'an reflect those attitudes by forbidding them due to the sacrifice of salvation. In Islam and the Qur'an following hints are given:

- Parshal (1994:137; Sura 7:450-51; 71.56.670).
- Reuter, generally suicide is sin against Allah but he describes the glorification of suicide attacks against unbelievers as a religious act of obedience (2003:20-21).
- Schmidt-Salomon (2005:80; see the foregoing argument by Reuter).
- Schirrmacher (2008.14-15; Sura 4:29, 4:74, 3:195, 47:4-6, 3:157) shows the Islamic concept of sin for murder and the fight against unbelievers in which murder is permissable.

In Judaism and the Hebrew Bible the following ethics are given:

- Kraus, Altner & Schwarz (1999:23) claim that in Jewish ethics, based on the TaNaCH (Torah, Prophets and Writings) the body is a gift from God. Nobody created his or the other's body, in consequence something whose existence I am not responsible for I am also not allowed to destroy. Exceptions are possible in the case of illness or a threat to one's life with no way out. In such cases suicide is understood as "free death" (Germ. "Freitod").

In the collectivistic Zaza culture one becomes a member "from his birth on by the integration to strong, closed We-groups, that protect him life-long by demanding unconditional loyalty" (Hofstede 1993:67; 2.3.4.12.3.4.4.1). The social system which is based on an extended family-oriented small scale society structure exemplifies this by the fact that every relationship to one's relatives bears its own title. Those titles replace the name of the relatives and are also used to honour older non-relatives or to label foreigners respectfully (Werner 2003b; Appendix 3). The Zaza society is built on the *core family*, which is embedded in close relations to the *extended family* relations which are then embedded in *small scale societies* that form a loose alliance build on specific religious or political needs and linguistic and cultural proximity or "Zazaness". Thus the collectivistic alignment of the Zaza follows the small scale society paradigm (2.3.4; 2.3.4.4.3).

2.3.2.1.2 Uncertainty Reduction Theory

The so called *Uncertainty Reduction Theory* (*URT*) was introduced by Neuliep for the communication theory. Its goal is to research the strategic ways in communication and behaviour that are used by relational partners to reduce social uncertainty (Gudykunst cit. in Neuliep 2006:343). The phrase was coined in American sociology-organizations and designates the "resistance of a culture to avoid ambiguous situations" (Cyert & March cit. in Hofstede 1993:130). The grade of power distance and power-flow is also measurable by fundamental climatic, population and wealth-oriented features (Thomas 1996:40).

As an authoritarian based culture the Zaza disclose a low score of uncertainty reduction. Because of their distinctive collectivistic society structure, the need to prevent uncertain situation is weak and they can live with a high grade of ambiguities in daily life situations (Hofstede 1993:135-136).

The authoritarian society structure, the geographical location close to the Mediterranean, their low population and the balanced wealth system all point to a high grade of power distance (:53). In other words, the high grade of power distance provides an indication of their authoritarian structure. Such societal rules are not judged by justice or law, but follow the rule of "power goes ahead of law" (ibid.). Structures of power are offering the society's members security and protection to gain or guard societal positions. As will be shown later *envy* is one of the driving forces to regulate this balance in shame oriented societies as well as in the Zaza culture (2.3.2.1.3).

2.3.2.1.3 Envy, Religion, LEIC and Conscience

The focus in ethnography and general research in cultural anthropology is not yet too much on the issue of *envy* (2.5.6). There is a lot to do in catching-up with this topic (Hesselgrave 2002:211). Two main factors contribute to the matter of *envy*:
- the religious background of cultures and their individuals, and
- the orientation of the conscience towards shame or guilt.

It is clear that the religious setting has a deep influence on the conscience of culture members. But as there is a metaphysical or transcendent factor in religion that is not predictable and that can change over times, this transcendental influence performs its own category of authority on conscience. Most Middle East cultures had an animistic background and some of them developed into High Cultures (Greek, Hittites; Assyrians, Babylonians, Persians, Medes), which reflect their religiosity in developing a world of gods and goddesses. Thus the animistic background was seldom overcome but often mixed with the new religious orientation (see "evil eye" 2.3.2.1.4). Envy is placed in the "Location of Emotions, the Intellect and the Character" (LEIC). It has in the Zaza ethnicity a foundation and placement in the mix of animistic and more recent religious sphere.

Concerning the latter factor, in shame oriented societies, which constitute the global majority; envy embraces the deep core values of the cultural setting. The Zaza people reveal central features to demonstrate such background (2.5.5).

In general the concept of *envy* in the Middle East and Asian cultures traces back to metaphysical forces or is projected on such. In contrast to the West where the Enlightenment set humanity and its perception in the centre of the world, many of the Eastern cultures rely on an unseen world as a secondary reality. Within this concept the realities of the visible and invisible worlds are intermingled relating to the supernatural powers, but closed to any passing of animated beings from the visible to the invisible world. In contrast to such a perception of the world, the West declares the human intellect or mind as the centre of all emotions, feelings and decision making and declares this the one and only reality. Supernatural powers are reflected by the human mind and the invisible world is a fiction or product of it. We deal with two concepts here:

- *transcendence* as part of human-thought-reality (West) *and,*
- a parallelism of humanity and transcendence in two overlapping realities (East). The two concepts of reality awareness are important to distinguish in ethnography.

Käser introduced, for Asian and Animistic ethnicities, the principle of the "spiritual counterpart" (Germ. "spirituelles Doppel"; 2004:110-11, 130-131; extensively 1977:119-127). The visible reality is reproduced in another invisible world or worlds. Every living creature as well as the inanimate environment possesses a *spiritual counterpart* which is influenced by forces that are stronger than humans. The behaviour and dealings with animated and inanimate beings and things in this world influences the other. At the same time the supernatural forces bridge the gap from the invisible world into the human world to influence it. The forces can be good or evil; and as such they guard or hurt in the visible world. The animated beings cannot trespass the gap between both realities (Käser 1977:229-232). The only way for animated beings to get in contact with the transcendental world is by professionals, such as a mediator (shaman, sorcerer etc.), prayer / appeal or trance.

Powers like demons (*dew*) or even angels (*melek*) are responsible for guarding or hurting the soul or the conscience of an individual. If those powers are not held in balance the result will be envy, caused by imbalance of the honour-shame stability. All in all envy works on the level of power balance within the society.

Envy works towards the balance of shame and prestige / honour in a shame-oriented society. Its function is either *preventive* or *deeply regulating*, that is
- to hinder the appearance of any envy (preventive),
- to keep the power balance within society *and* the visible and invisible reality or world (2.3.2.1.2).

The preventive function leads to a societal system of control by explicit and implicit rules and regulations. Envy is seen as a force that could harm people through metaphysical forces. The society has a mandate to behave in such a way that those powers are not provoked. The whole mechanisms are encultured and build on the need to secure the weak mainly women and children in a society.

Another function of envy can be traced back to *social power balancing* or *power-flow* processes. Thus if someone tries to bridge social gaps he will cause envy. As shown in the story *Şêx Biyayena Gawandê Çermugızı* ("How it Came to Pass that a Shepherd from Cermug became a Sheikh"; Hayıg 2007:54-58, 117-120, 171-174) the society protects the social levels. Only through miracles and egocentric behaviour could one go beyond social regularities. Envy opens up the social process of *mistrust* and *investigation* towards any infringement and the breach of social rules. During the process the honour and prestige of the suspect are questioned. Losing face, which can eventually lead to murder or suicide, will be the most extreme outcome of envy. The Zaza people therefore have the institution of *honour suicide, blood feud* or *relative killing* (2.3.2.1). The term used, when one enters the area of trespassing or envy is called *eyb* (Turk. "ayıp"; Engl. disgrace). In a closer sense the expression is said to express grudge or rejection. In a wider and more religious sense its meaning ranges from "shame", "without honour" to "disgust". The concept of *eyb* describes social rejection, lack of *namuz* (Engl. honour" and "prestige) and it results in losing face (1.1.3.3).

Envy is an impact of the LEIC which also contains the conscience as an encultured organ. In the Zaza ethnicity the main location for the LEIC is in the gastrointestinal body area called *zerri* (inner parts). Out of that placement the decision will be made whether or not the boundaries of honour or prestige are trespassed. This has nothing to do with anger or fear that in western thinking will cause rash decisions and could also be placed in the gastrointestinal body area. No, the whole setting of envy-related decisions emanates from a transcendent organ that is based in the area of the stomach and the intestines. This contradicts western thinking where such a decision would be made with the head out of controlled or uncontrolled rationality (intent, conditional intent, and negligence).

Envy is addressed below as an essential driving human force in relation to the concept of *merdım* and the perception of the world of the Zaza people (2.5.6). Envy is an interreligious and social phenomenon but as we are dealing here with Muslim groups the Islamic perspective of envy comes in focus. The former Muslima *Nonie Darwish* said in an interview that envy is deeply felt as a curse. It is seen as the reason for a general mistrust in societies based on Islam. To distract from this deeply held religious core value political and religious leaders use the instrument of "hate sermon" mainly addressed against the West or Israel and never self-critical or critical about inner-Islamic relations (Gilbert 2008:30).

This demonstrates that behaviour is just on the surface of the inner-human relations but that envy is the force that drives such behaviour. In shame-oriented Islamic cultures envy is not just an inner-relational issue (inner authority by conscience) but also a force steered by an external authority (outwardly directed folk conscience).

2.3.2.1.4 Envy and the "Evil Eye" in the Mediterranean Area

As an example of the importance of research on *envy* in ethnography we will have a look at the so called *cimê xırav / nazar* "evil eye" (Tk. *nazar*; Arab. *'ayn al-ḥasūd* عين الحسود; Kurman. *çavê xirab*). It reveals the underlying potential to fight curses (Malina 2001:120-123; Werner 2006:31, footnote 31; s. a. "evil mouth", "evil hand" or "hamza"). The widely spread institution of the "evil eye" in the Middle East and in the Zaza culture prevents for example a child and his family from losing face (Sweetnam 2004:183). This happens when somebody is praising the appearance of a child in public, as this behaviour provokes the envy of demons which will hurt the child. The whole sanction provokes envy, which averts a public compliment about the look of somebody. Because of this, expression about someone's appearance is never used to gain of honour in shame oriented societies (Brandes 2008:45). In Islamic cultures such an envy-structure is widely observed (Gilbert 2008:30). This traces back to the Jewish culture of the New Testament (Malina 2001:123-124) and the modern Jewish culture of Israel

(Brandes 2008:45) as well as the Hebrew Bible (Malina 2001:122; 3.4.2; 3.4.3). Also the prophet Hz. Mohammed referred to this concept, "the influence of an evil eye is a fact..." in his traditionally passed on sayings [Sahih Muslim, Book 26, Number 5427].

Interestingly the New Testament reflects the practice of the "evil eye". Hz. Jesus the Christ notices the presence of such a cultural issue when he warns the people around him that this practice pollutes their thoughts and their hearts (Mark 7,1-23; also Bascom 2003:110). Equally Paul, the apostle, warns the Galatians against the "evil eye" when he combines witchcraft with the viewing of the crucified Christ (Gal 3:1; 2.3.3.2.4; 2.3.3.7.1; 3.4.2). In the Mediterranean, mainly in the context of Islam, but unfortunately also in the traditional Churches, the Jewish groups and other religious sects, the „evil eye" goes side by side with the *Chamsa* or *hand of Fatima*. There it is ubiquitous and symbolized by a hand with either five or four fingers of which two are thumb-like fingers on the right and left. An eye in the centre of the hand symbolizes the evil look (Brandes 2008:45).

The Qur'an builds on the Jewish and Christian revelation. Therefore it reflects the idea of God's protection against harmful forces like the "evil eye" from those who are envious (113:5), curses that bind people through occult practices (113:4), and harmful spirits (114:4). The perception of the world of the Qur'anic author(s) refers back to an animistic understanding of transcendent worlds in which animate and inanimate persons and things are represented.

Envy is viewed as the enemy that one has to struggle with in daily life, in the Islamic tradition called *Hadith,* as well as in traditional Islam or Folk Islam (Germ. "Volksislam"). Thus to prevent envy in others, women should when receiving or giving hospitality not wear expensive, luxurious clothes that may encourage wasteful or envious desires (Houston 2001:44; (2.3.2.1.4; 2.4.3.2; 2.5.4.3; 3.6.4; 3.6.5; 0). On the other hand, for celebrations or on special occasions it is expected to show jewellery and demonstrate the wealth of the family.

Diagram 9 Model of Envy, Mana and Taboo

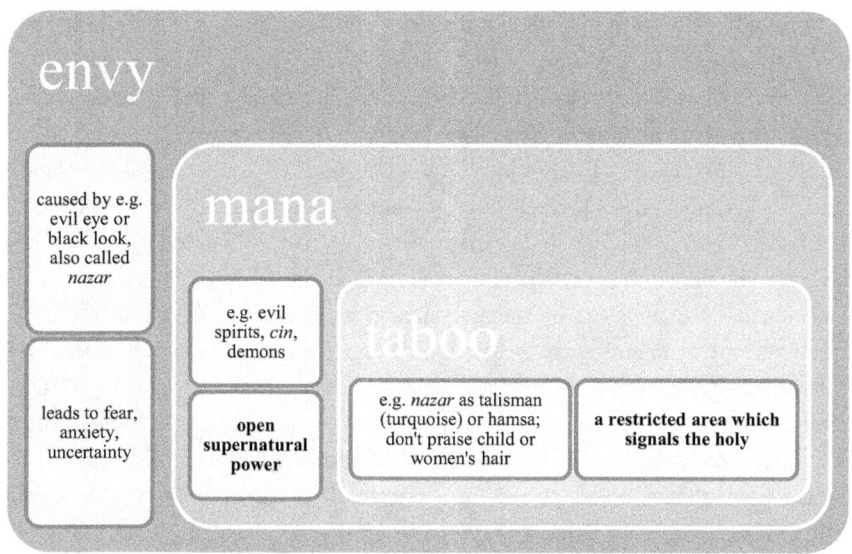

Another reason for envy could be full hair. If a woman with full hair loses her hair she contributes this to envy of her by others (Sweetnam 2004:90-91). The concept behind this is that metaphysical forces are mobilized. This idea is not just a general religious one, but also expressed in the Qur'an. The regulations set down in the Qur'an, Hadith and traditional Islam are part of the Zaza perception of the world (2.5.5).

Another example is given by the essential practice of reciprocity in Zaza society. Zaza proverbs say that "only the despots think of themselves" and that "one who gives, will also find" (personal communication). It is expected that relatives, neighbours and friends share things in common with each other. For instance when one is building a house the young men of the village are expected to help. The patriarchs send their sons. Or if someone slaughters a lamb or calf he follows the traditions by sharing the meat with his relatives and neighbours. Not everybody will get the same share, but everybody has to be considered. He will be accused in the gatherings if he does not. He loses face; to avoid a loss of prestige he will prevent such allegations. In the worst case he will be cursed since he broke a taboo and raised envy.

2.3.2.2 "Location of Emotions, Intellect and Character" (LEIC)

Cultures offer different ideas about the location of thoughts, mind, feelings, soul or consciousness in the body (Käser 2004:178-179, 181 and Badenberg 2007; Nida 1990:45, 138-139; Kassühlke 1978:23). The phrase that is used here to classify the place of moral values and thinking refers back to Käser who coined the term "Location of Emotions, Intellect and Character" (LEIC; Germ. "SEIC"; 1.1.2.3.1; 2.4.1). Until now not much investigation has been done on this issue (Käser 2004:178, 181; exception see Werner 2006 and 2011b; 1.1.3.3).

Käser showed that most societies assume that the LEIC, as a vehicle of the conscience, is a physical or metaphysical organ. This implies that the LEIC functions not as a biological *organ* which is responsible to preserve vital life functions but as an organ of psychological processes. The history of the Hebrew Bible and the New Testament offers insights in the perception of such an organ in ancient times. Both religious revelations anchor the LEIC in the region of the human body that is called "heart" or "intestinal" (Werner 2006:28-29, 33 and 2011b; Kassühlke 1978:23; Nida 1990:138-139). The former is described by the phrase,

- וַיָּפָג לִבּוֹ "Jacob's heart fainted" (Gen 45:26) is translated in the Greek versions of the Hebrew Bible as ἐξέστη ἡ διάνοια. Due to the different concepts of Judaism and Greek philosophy the emotion placed by the Jewish people in the heart was transferred by the Greeks to the mind (e.g. Larson 1984:3).
- ἐπλήρωσεν ὁ Σατανᾶς τὴν καρδίαν σου "Satan filled thine heart" (Act 5:3). The heart as the centre of emotions and thoughts (Schnelle 1991:122).
- Σπλαγχνίζομα "Hz. Jesus had compassion" (Mat 20:34 KJV: Mar 8:2), the phrase is etymologically derived from "intestinal".

These examples demonstrate where the LEIC was placed in the past. In contrast Europeans think with their "head" and rejoice with the "heart". Many Africans think with their "head", but they rejoice with the "liver", whereas the Hebrews rejoiced with their "kidneys". Europeans and North Americans express their compassion out of the "heart", the New Testament authors placed compassion to the "intestinal".

Malina divides the individual person in an *eye-heart*, *mouth-ears*, and *hands-feet* sphere. The first region is defined as the location of the *emotion-fused thought* and covers eyes, heart, eyelid and pupil the second is called the zone of *self-expressive speech* and deals with mouth, ears, tongue, lips, throat, teeth and jaws, while the thirds is the zone of *purposeful action*: hands, feet, arms and fingers (2001:69). Following this classification the ancient culture during the time of the New Testament falls into the second and third zone. It acknowledges this and forms an active culture (s. Werner 2006:28-29, 33 and 2011:188). Western cultures tend towards the first area and exhibit an emotionally fused behaviour (Malina 2001:69). We want to look now at the Zaza people and how this three-zone model fits the culture. Therefore the written and oral traditions as well as a worldview questionnaire from 2005 are researched and taken into account.

The Zaza people express themselves mainly by *purposeful action*. The hand, feet and arm function is omnipresent. Activities process the whole social, economic, religious and political life of this people group. The main focus is about the organization of daily life and to put the needs of the family in order. One strong motive is related to peasantry and climate conditions, thus summer activities are concentrated on surviving the extreme winter seasons. Agriculture, house construction and repair, and economic procedures (trade) are all oriented towards the seasonal conditions.

Emotions are expressed in Zazaki by figures of speech that refer to the area of the gastrointestinal body region (Werner 2006:59-61; 2011:188-190). Temper is allocated to the face area (*ri*) as well as to the name (*name*) of a person. A name represents one's honour and prestige. Cursing, insulting or dragging one's name through the mire is equivalent to losing face and accordingly punished by social measures. The intellect is located both in the head (*serre*) as well as the heart (*zerri*) area. The heart (*zerri*) also functions as the placement of the emotions and describes the inner part of the gastrointestinal body region. Blessing is set "upon the eyes" (*çımê to serr*), because the eyes are responsible for the leading the way physically *and* spiritually. Pleasure and fear are positioned in the stomach (*zerri*). A common expression says:

Xewf kewt pizê   mı.
fear   sits stomach mine
I fear.

The multiple meanings and functions of *zerri*, as heart, inner parts of the body or the centre of the body causes foreigners a lot of headache during language learning (RH 2007 *Zaza Tribes* and MT 2008 *Zazaki*). This reflection of the LEIC / SEIC in the centre of the body closely parallels the New Testament (Werner 2006:60; 2011:188-190; Käser 2004:179; from an exegetical viewpoint s.

Kassühlke 1978:23). This perception points to a centre-oriented and holistic perception of the world of the Zaza (2.5).

Defiance of LEIC leads to misunderstandings. Especially in a cross-cultural setting miscommunication and wrongdoing will be caused thereby. Käser gives some examples (2004:177). His main point is to search from the beginning onwards, specifically during the language learning phase, the underlying cores that exemplify the LEIC. He highlights that in areas like cross-cultural counselling or pedagogical programmes within a culture there needs to be an awareness of the LEIC, especially to start a holistic counselling programme (:229). A few examples in the Zaza culture will demonstrate some traps as to how one will miscommunicate or misbehave if one does not know of the LEIC. For example, if in a religious ceremony one blesses a Zaza by holding or touching slightly his head, but doesn't close the eyelids, one has not performed the appropriate action for blessing a Zaza. Likewise if one congratulates someone on his academic studies one will refer to the *zerri,* which is the inner part of the body, and not to the head, as in western countries.

2.3.2.3 Centralistic and Holistic Perception

We conclude that *zerri* (the inner parts, heart) represents the location of the conscience and the sentiments. It is a metaphysical organ, placed above the stomach and the intestines. In consequence this leads to a centralistic perception of the world. The centralistic view embraces the four extremities as they are all the same distance from the centre. The centralist perception of the sphere around an individual is recognized as same-distanced because of the similar distance of the four extremities. Going one level higher, universe and space are measured as held in harmony and balanced.

Daily life activities like travelling, running and working with the hands are considered to come out of the inner centre where the "motivation" as vital energy is seated. The inner composure becomes a high value and has to be balanced. Crafts, eating, social gathering etc. are often performed in a sitting position due to this centralistic perception of the world. Life - and with it life-time in general - is perceived as a circular course of events. However "time" does also follow other perceptions.

Time becomes a life-circle during which the individual is participating in annual feast and celebrations, as well as activities like harvest, planting, winter preparations and summer activities. The individual becomes part of the cycle by following the society. This general time perception does not exclude the opportunity for the individual or smaller groups to perform their own schedule. Those iterative or wave-like individual schedules will have the wider circular time frame in mind. For instance in the case of riot, resistance or ongoing inner reorganizations the Zaza society is flexible to admit those.

In sum, the time-conception of the Zaza ethnicity as a whole is following a circular emphasis. The individual is performing daily life on iterative or wave-like time notions. The circular time-perception of the Zaza is based on peasantry and its dependence from seasonal climate conditions.

2.3.2.4 Prototype Theory – Connecting Language and Thought

The *prototype theory*, introduced by Rosch, advocates the influence of a perception of the world by language (1973 and 1978). She found out, with the help of psychological tools, that the human system of thought is oriented towards central terms by using natural categories represented in symbols or pictures. Those keyterms and symbols organize our thinking. For example if in the western cultures one thinks of a "little bird", he has the picture of a "sparrow" in mind, thinking of "big birds" a German will picture a "buzzard" and an American an "eagle". Those terms, and the pictures or symbols behind, replace the concept of "little bird" or "big bird".

This model detaches the old Greek model in which "categories" are "fuzzy pictures" when used in thinking, so reflect reality only vaguely. In contrast, Rosch's model states that human thinking has a "focal centre and fuzzy edges" (Vannerem & Snell-Hornby 1986:187). In other words her approach replaced the concept of additioning components and clear boundaries of conceptualities that followed Aristotle (Goerling 2007:185). Prototype theory claims the "best representative of one category" (Bußmann 2002:543). Through linguistics this model entered anthropology (Holland & Quinn 1987:23).

The Zaza culture uses, for example the picture of the *billbill* (nightingale) or *mırçık / mırıçık* (sparrow) for "small birds" and for "big birds" the *zerrej / zerej* (pheasant / partridge). The story of *Lazeko Zerej* (Partridge Boy) demonstrates the important variable of the "partridge" (big birds) in the perception of the world of the Zaza (Hayıg 2007:63-64, 125-126, 179-180). Other prototype implementations are demonstrated by the use of figurative speech relating to the LEIC (1.1.3.3; 2.3.2.2).

2.3.2.5 Summary

In this paragraph we investigated the fundamental features of the Zaza culture. The Zaza ethnicity performs as a collective people group. Decisions are built on competence which is processed in the realm of collectivism. The individual is part of the collective; it can only implement new ideas if these are collectively processed. In collectivistic cultures uncertainty reduction (see Uncertainty Reduction Theory) shapes a feature dealing with fear and anger. In the Zaza culture a strong and complex small scale societal system is built on the structure of the *aşıret* (tribe), the *ezbet* (tribe and tribal subgroup), the *kuflet / mesra* (extended family) and the *key* (family / house). *Envy*, is an essential driving vital energy as part of daily life. It reaches out into the spiritual and thus religious reality. The *evil eye* plays an important role to fight uncertainty, fear and evil spiritual influence. The Zaza people express their "Location of the Emotions, Intellect and Character" (LEIC) in the middle of their body. Hence their awareness of reality, illness and spirituality is directed to this centre. The perception of time and the afterlife are based on a centered circular and eternal view of life. The *Prototype Theory* (Rosch) supports the discernment of the Zaza people with language and thought. Semiotics signals the semantic context in the understanding of Zazaki. The language thus becomes much more understandable to the Western researcher as the semantical environment is revealed. Through this investigation one can track back to cultural specifics in the Zaza culture. Symbols and pictures that represent the linguistic concepts of keyterms are basic to understand the cognitive link between the verbal production of words and the thought system or perception of the world of the Zaza people.

2.3.3 Religion

Religion is one of the globally observed driving forces for societies. It has a psychological, social and ideological component which can be described in anthropology. Nonetheless, it is also that area which carries forth the largest criticism about ethnocentrism of the researcher. Religion belongs to the area of world perception. Religion contains core values and norms which are not reflected, because one is not aware of its widespread effects on one's thoughts, conscience and behaviour. Whereas in the past decades anthropologists and sociologists wanted to get rid of religious study, putting it aside into the box of theology or philosophy, it found its way back in the last two decades (see Banton 1966 compared to Hiebert & Hiebert 1995; Morris 1987:92-93, 148-149).

2 The Zaza

From an anthropological point of view religion is "an institution consisting of culturally patterned interaction with culturally postulated superhuman beings" (Spiro 1966:96). An *institution* is a shared practice which can be traced back to a common enculturation process of a people group. Religion shares the same ontological status as those of other cultural systems because its beliefs "are normative, its rituals collective, its values prescriptive" (ibid.). Members with the same ontological perspective interact with each other on the foundation that their activities are carried out, embodied, or are consistent with the will or desire of superhuman beings or powers (transcendental power). The individual also believes that his activities will somehow influence the superhuman beings to satisfy the needs of the actors (human satisfaction).

The whole conception of religious commotion, which is obviously driving the Zaza people (2.3.1.3.2, is built on the assumption that those activities reflect the putative value system of superhuman beings, which constitutes partially also the actor's value system. Thus metaphysics or the transcendence meets humanity. Superhuman beings are believed to possess greater power than man, they work on good or evil and they relate to man by a relationship built on the above mentioned transcendental interactions or activities. Geertz adds to Spiro's definition of religion a sense of symbolism. It functions to formulate conceptions of a general order of existence in such a way that its moods and motivations seem realistic (1966:4). This symbolism is performed in rituals, traditions and deeds (see activity above).

As Hiebert and Hiebert point out, the social structure of a society has an enormous effect on their perception of the world about the supernatural. They emphasize that small scale societies, following a tribal segmentation, tend toward a holistic perception of reality (1995:113, 117). Religion in such settings becomes the foundation of culture and not just a segment. The perception of reality covers both the seen and the unseen world consolidated in one reality. For people *witchcraft*, which is refused or irrelevant to Western societies, becomes a force to conform members of a society to the social norms and deters deviance by the group. In non-Western societies the insider-outsider perspective that performs witchcraft raises the social pressure on the individual to follow the collective group orientation (Evans-Pritchard 1937). The Zaza ethnicity performs witchcraft on the level of Folk Islam or in very closed social areas, either geographically or internally. Yet witchcraft is not openly practiced and accessible to everyone, though in some regional areas and within a social setting it is more practiced than in others. Rural areas are more affected by witches and sorcerers.

In a religious sense the Zaza ethnicity does not represent a homogenous group. Animism, Iranian religions (Zoroastrianism), Judaism, Christianity and Islam leave their marks on the Zaza people. Following the above mentioned definitions and the social structure of this people group, then its collectivistic character as a small scale society displays a holistic system of at least three main directions of the main religion Islam. These are Alevism out of a Shi'a school (Shi'ite) and Sunnism in the school of Hanafi and Shafi'i.

2.3.3.1 Religions of the Zaza People

The Zaza people nowadays practice *Sunnism* in the Southern and Eastern Group and *Alevism* in the Northern Group. The underlying beliefs are built on a mixture of an animistic and Zoroastrian perception of the world. Although, within the same ethnicities a split in religion is not that unusual, especially in the Fertile Crescent area, we find an astonishing analogous parallel in the sociolinguistically closely related Gorani / Hawrami group. Here one group follows the *Ahl-i-Haqq* sect, the other the *Shi'ite* school and Sunnism (Bumke 2002:511-512). Thinking of the Kurmanji speaking group in Turkey, they are also split into an Alevi, a large Yezidi, a small Christian and a mainly Sunni Shafi'i group.

The origin of the people is closely related to the origin of people and their split in smaller groups. The missing evidence about a clear cut history of the Zaza people makes it difficult to trace back their religious foundation. At least the debris of a close relation to nature and the devotion of the four basic natural elements water, earth, fire and air, as described by the Greek philosophers, as well as rocks, springs, trees and mountains demonstrate a foundation of deep animism and Old-Iranian religions. This goes for the whole group. As in all follow-up religions the overlying practices from that deeper belief system intermingles with the religions introduced later. In the case of the Zaza this is modern Alevism, Christianity and Islam. In Germany and German for example the Teutonic theotechny of the German cults is still reflected in the use of daily language, as is seen in the word *Freitag* (Friday) coming from the goddess *Freya* which stood for love and honour, or *Donnerstag* (Thursday) derived from *Donar* the god of the thunder.

2.3.3.2 Origins of the Zaza Religions

In his historical, although controversial, review Izady links the origin of the Zaza to the *Daylam-Theory*. He also mentions that the religion of Daylam in Iran up until today bears polytheistic and non-Islamic traits. He concludes that if the

2 The Zaza

Zaza are descendants from polytheism following forefathers their culture and religion should reveal rudimentary features of those polytheistic religions (Izady 1992:44).

The Northern Group relate to the Iranic cults. Two sectarian approaches demonstrate this. The "Cult of Angels" that is practiced by the Yezidi people and the "Custom of the Seven". The latter describes a divinity that juts out like a sword from the ground and which forms the centre of devotion (Izady 1992:151). This tradition parallels the King Arthur myth (:151). During my research both cults seemed to be known by the Northern Group yet they were not practiced but had just a status of folktales. Angels and Demons, respectively the antagonism between Good and Evil, play a central role in Alevism and derive from *Zoroastrianism*, called *Parsiism* in the Asian area and *serduşt* in Zazaki and Kurmanji (2.1.1.5.2). Rites concerning the dualism between good and evil powers in a Kurdish environment including the Zaza people were reported since 1908 (Mark Sykes cit. in Izady 1992:152). The principle of the seven is also described in the Avestan concept of sacredness and immorality *amərəta* (> *aməša*; amereta) 'immortal'. The title *aməša-spənta* (amesa-spenta) describes a group of seven divinities. These preside over the material and moral life of man. Although they bear abstract names, they were each - at an early date - incarnated and materialized in a basic element: water, earth, plants, metals, etc. Each of them is both the symbol of a virtue and the guardian deity of an element of the world and serves the Supreme Being *Ahura Mazda* (Benveniste 1973:446; Shaked 2007:15; 2.4.2.1). Zoroastrinistic dualism balances power between two spirits that are subordinate to Ahura Mazda. They represent life and non-life and only secondary creation and counter-creation, but in general good and evil. Also they are accompanied by *Fravashis*, spirits that support the well being of mothers (Shaked 2007:15; Skjærvø 2007:68).

Zoroastrianism (Parsiism) represents the religious foundation for the majority of Iranians who are Muslims nowadays. Zoroastrianism plays an important role in understanding the Zaza people and why Shi'ism is spread all over Iran. This lies in the mystical perception of the world that accompanies it. Zoroastrianism originated in the region of today's Iran and influenced Christendom deeply by the *Gnostic* movement and *Manichaeism* (Winter 2008:4; Latourette 1953:22-23; Gen 11). Manichaeism influenced the Turkish religion and had an effect on the mixture of ethnic groups in the Ottoman Empire (Laut 1996:26). The folktale *Gorma'hmed* (Gormahmed; Hayıg 2007:8-14) indicates traits of Manichaeism and refers to the well known story of the "Prince and the three Demons" that became popular in this religious approach (Laut 1996:26, 28). It influenced parts of the religion and culture of the Zaza (s. b.) as well as characterizes its importance as a moral institution through the mentioned story / folktale as a part of the oral passing on of traditions and their aural reception.

2.3.3.2.1 Animism

The term *Animism* has its origin from Sir Edward Burnett Taylor's research on belief systems that represent spirits and the spiritual world in the supernatural sphere (1874). He emphasized this from an evolutionary point of view and calls Animism the "Proto-religion" (Kohl 1993:112). For identification of animistic practices in religions that own a written revelation one has to approach the mindset and the perception of the world of animistic cultures (detailed Käser 2004:65).

It has to be stressed out that I do not follow an evolutionary view of religion by stating that all religion started with Animism and developed into monotheistic religions (Eliade 1991). Instead it became obvious in the last twenty years of religious study that religion is a central part of culture and that the origin of some religions cannot be plausibly explained by the human mind. To declare animism basic to all religious ideas seems far too easy, the more so as Animism in itself is a heterogeneous and often controversial concept. Some religious revelations like the Babylonian *Gilgamesh* or the *Enuma Elish* Epic are considered to be astrologic reflections (Papke 1999 *The Sign of the Messiah*). Others like the Hebrew Bible or the New Testament are amazingly stringent and coherent in their narration and this over more than a thousand years. The whole conception of the Jewish and Christian revelation is knotted by a view of salvation that begins in the first chapter and ends in the last one (Werner 2011:303-304). The revelations and concepts of Hinduism and Buddhism are not linear but cyclic and thus the centre of salvation lies in the arms of the humans. All religious practices could be integrated in such a system, yet Animism is fully adaptable and performs only one part of this belief system. The Qur'an, as the revelation of Islam, arose in a very short time period and therefore reflects the common view of this time. Its strong doctrine about unbelievers, who practice idolatry and Animism, forced Animists to adapt to the Islamic practices. Yet, like it is well demonstrated by the Zaza, a superficial Folk Islam is sometimes the result (see below).

The term Animism is derived from Latin *anima* or *animus* and means "soul, spirit". Therefore Animism is called "belief in spirits" (Käser 2004:22, 65). Lack of definition asks for the demarcation of Animism against other belief systems. The outstanding basic element of Animism is exemplified in the "ensoulment of nature". In this worldview the real beings and physical things have a counterpart in a spiritual world, where they are represented by spiritual beings or things. Both worlds form the complex reality of Animists and interact with each other. The spiritual world is given more power play but in the real world the so called *mana* also represents a power display (:65). Moving between the spheres is possible only by a *medium* or for everyone in *trance, dreams and visions* or by *death*.

An animistic perception of the world or its remnants is reflected for instance by the Zaza people in symbols or traditions that,

- represent the struggle between Good and Evil,
  - like the *nazar* or *chamzah*, as a protection against the "evil eye" (2.3.2.1.4). The palm of Fatima, represented in the chamzah - a four-fingered hand – stands for the symbol of the (five) main characters in Shi'ism, the prophet Muhammad, 'Ali, Fatima, (Hasan) and Husayn. It is an essential element of the talismans and amulets that offer protection from evil spirits and demons (Asatrian & Arakelova 2004:248). In Alevism the tradition is to have a representation of the chamzah or "The palm of Fatima", "alongside a portrait of 'Ali, whose image has also accumulated certain characteristics of Old Iranian mythical personages - from Verethragna to Rustam", as a sign of a god-fearing Shi'a house (ibid.),
  - like the *da'hri* that is an iron hook which is laid for forty days under the pillow of a woman after she gave birth. Due to the custom of impurity this time period is called *cewresê / cerisê* (the forty). The term *cerise* refers both to the days of defilement after birth, as well as the (period of) mourning after the loss of close family members. The hook protects the mother against evil forces (2.3.3.7.2). Unlike the Yezidi belief no divine protecting power like *Pirā-Fāt* or *Xatūnā-farxā* is protecting the infant against evil powers, at least such is not known any more (:250, e. g. *Al* in Asatrian 2001:150),
  - Comerd tells about a practice of the peasants to mention the protecting powers *Sarikō-šuān* and *Mamō-gāvān* ("Lord of the Herds-

men", "Memed of the working animals") at the same time defaming *Wāyirō xirāv* ("Lord of the Evil"; 1996). In some way the perception of the world behind the divine powers mentioned leaves space for a pre-Islamic Zaza pantheon that dealt with many gods, which had and still have an effect (e.g. in Folk Islamic traditions) from the supernatural into the physical realm (2.3.3.3; 2.5.1; close to the Yezidi pantheon in Kreyenbroek & Rashow 2005),

o like the prayer to the prophets and Allah for protection from *x-ray*, or evil, which are demons and/or evil influences (see *Mewlid Nebo* Appendix 5)

- are describing both intermingled worlds, like the devotion of holy springs or trees (2.1.2.2; 2.3.3.3).

In either way the deeper rooted animistic beliefs are integrated as part of Folk Islam or Alevism. This is possible because all the Holy Books are built on a perception of the world that parallels and reflects the angle on Good – Evil. Demons, angels, faith, truth and good deeds are *interreligious* concepts and adapt easily to indoctrinated or newly incorporated concepts.

The Zaza ethnicity and their Kurdish neighbours view the spiritual world with mainly negative reference (Sweet am 2004:165). The main challenge is to avoid any evil attempt from evil powers, for instance demons, and protect yourself and your environment against the envy which they cause. They generate envy through accidents, illness, and spawn emotions like hate, fear or other distress that harm human relationships and destroy social structures. Thus the protection of the latter is one of the main motives to balance envy against social harmony.

I assume that while some animistic cultures try to harmonize life between their physical and the spiritual world to get a balanced reality, the situation with the Zaza people is imbalanced due to Islamic belief. The balance moved towards the spiritual world through the Qur'an and its spiritual implications. Yet the struggle is to balance things in this physical world while the spiritual world is overwhelmingly powerful. Looking at the Zaza folktales and their practices in Folk Islam, implications are given about the ongoing pressure that a member of society has to deal with.

Diagram 10 Animistic Perception of the World by the Zaza

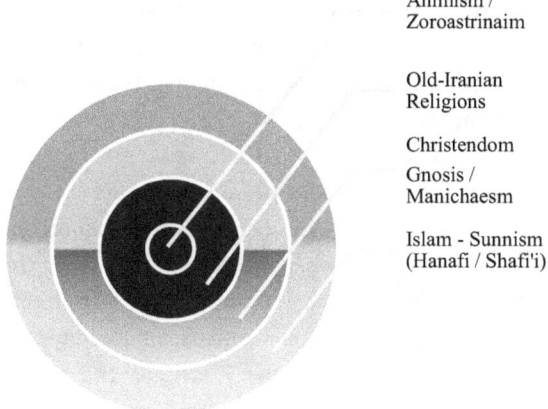

Animism /
Zoroastrinaim

Old-Iranian
Religions

Christendom
Gnosis /
Manichaesm

Islam - Sunnism
(Hanafi / Shafi'i)

This is mainly true for Sunnism following the schools of Hanafi and Shafi'i as it is practiced by the Southern and Eastern Group (2.2.8.1; 2.3.3.2.5; 2.3.3.5; Table 22). Zoroastrianism as is shown below has integrated and adapted to animistic beliefs much better, and Alevism performs a self regulating religious belief. The whole Zaza ethnicity deals with Animism on the level of Folk Islamic practices and beliefs.

2.3.3.2.2   Zoroastrianism / Mazdaism and Alevism

The founder of *Zoroastrianism* is called *Avesta* resp. *Zoroaster* lived during the 6th century BC in Persia. This religion is called *Parsiism* in the Asian / Indian area and *serduşt* in Zazaki and Kurmanji. Whether it is a legend or a real person has not been solved up to now. His ideology was based on the principle of dualism derived from nature. Hence the reciprocal and complementary interaction between day-night, light-darkness, fire-ice and heat-cold were in his focus. Humanity, which is in subjection to these life-giving energies has constantly to appease them (Brockhaus multimedial 2007: *Zoroastrianism*; 2.1.4.2; 2.3.2.1.1;- 2.3.3.3; 2.3.3.7.3). His teaching is established on the Greek philosophical theories of Socrates, Plato and Aristotle (3rd century BC). Hence the basic elements of nature like fire, water, earth and air cut a figure (Gignoux 2001:31, 34). In the 8th century AD the Uyghurs introduced *Zoroastrianism* (*serduşt* in Zazaki) in the syncretistic religion of Manichaeism, through which it became widespread in (Eastern) Christianity, Parsiism and Buddhism (Laut 1996:26).

Zoroaster's teachings reject polytheism, accepting only *one* supreme God called *Ahura Mazda* (light and wisdom). The worship of the Supreme Being led to the naming *Mazdaism*, concerning the movement and *Mazdaist* for his disciples. In early Zoroastrianism, the struggle between good and evil was seen as an eternal rivalry between Ahura Mazda's twin sons, *Spenta Mainyu* (good) and *Angra Mainyu* (evil). After a climax and widespread acceptance as an official religion it remained until the 7th century AD. The spread of Islam reduced it to a small group called *Gabar* in Iran and *Parsis* in India (w/o A. 2011 *Zoroastrianism and Parsiism*). The teachings of Zoroaster are written down in the language *Avesta*, called after the founder that was spoken and used those days.

For the duration of the Greek Invasion in the 3rd century BC, also during the times of the Roman Empire which ruled from the turn of eras until the 4th century AD, as well as during the rise of Christianity, Zoroastrianism earned the status of a primitive religion, due to its dualistic perception of the world and its practice of fire worship. However, Zoroastrianism was vibrant and practiced as a foundation of belief, on all social levels. All of these Empires followed the politics of ruling by implementing their own government above the national structures. Thus, the national structures remained and the religion could be relative freely practiced under the new rulers. During the Persian reign Zoroastrianism became very strong and rejected the growth of Christianity (Hoyland 1997:17, 23-24). This changed with Islam, as idolatry was the worst sin called *shirk* (bring partnership to Allah). Yet the followers of Zoroastrianism were fiercely persecuted and annihilated.

The *Gnosticism* of the 1st to the 4th century AD was also built on a dualistic principle and transformed it as a religious system (Bumke 2002:511). Philo, Marcion, Irenaeus, Hermes Trismegistus and other Gnostics "demythologized" the Hebrew Bible. They interpreted the Christian dogmas on the grounds of *Manichaeism* and a metaphysical dualism between the spiritual and material world, the soul and body or the light and darkness (Latourette 1953:30, 31, 46; Nida 1990:50; Sanneh 1992:17). Therein the Evil and the Good were considered as theistic powers which have to be kept in balance by devotion. This concept obviously traces back to Zoroastrianism and the struggle between *Ahura Mazda* and the enemy, exemplified in the contrasting pair water and fire (Gignoux 2001:31, 51-52). Christianity's first doctrinal challenge in the 1st and 2nd century

AD came up with a lot of Christians adapting to Gnosticism as a hermeneutical way to interpret their faith. The emanation of God into the world is widespread and well reflected in Alevism (Steinbach 1996:376). Even the Old Persian root *şahr* (kingdom), which generated the Armenian term *aşahr* and Zazaki *şar* is expressing Gnostic thinking via Manichaeism (Gnoli 2007:110-112).

The influence of Zoroastrianism and mystical sects is observed all over the area. This geographic allocation is in general considered to be inhabited by ethnically 'Kurdish and related' people groups. Included are the main Kurdish ethnicities such as the Kurmanji-, Sorani-, Bahdeni- and Kermanshah-speakers, as well as the Goran, Zaza, Lur, Gilak, Bakhtiar, Kor and Lak. Zoroastrianism was the main "Pre-Islamic religion" that drove those ethnicities in ethnical provenance. In combination with the central worship of fire, the stars and the devil a Zoroastrian-Yezidi nexus could be assumed. Unfortunately nowadays the Sunni and Alevi Kurds and the Zaza do not show any affinity to the Yezidi, on the contrary all of them more or less reject any similarity with the Yezidi. In the case of the Zaza people we do not even find any Yezidi devotees. Such lack makes it hard to prove such a nexus and the hypothesis has to be taken cautiously (Asatrian 2009:6-7).

One finds a lot of traditions, hints and remnants from *Zoroastrianism* (in India *Parsiism* and in Zazaki *serduşt*) in the Zaza culture (see above the "evil eye" and the "*dahri*"; 2.3.2.1.4). The "feast of the bull" which is common to Yezidis and some other Old-Iranian / Persian cults is not known to the Zaza Alevis (Asatrian 2009:9). Some narratives derive from the sayings of Zoroaster. The supreme being Ahura Mazda has fire as his son. Thus the basic element of fire influenced the concept of the world in Zaza cosmology also (Skjærvø 2007:64).

The language *Avesta* that was used in the times of Zoroaster is sometimes brought in close relation to Zazaki (Çar 1997:5-7). This has some reason in the cultural setting of the Parthians which ruled the area of the followers of Zoroaster, as well as the region of Daylam (2.1.3.1.1) and the later homeland of the Zaza. Thus at least an influence of Avesta on the later cultures and Zazaki is obvious. This can be based on regional and linguistic evidence, but it is not justified to say that Zazaki is directly derived from Avesta since this would go far beyond the evidence.

Later on, Alevism was mainly influenced by *Haci Bektaş Veli* (1209-1271 CE). He was a

> Muslim mystic and founder of a Sufi brotherhood which saw Hz. Ali, the Prophet Hz. Mohammed's nephew and later son-in-law, as the rightful successor to the Prophet.

The tomb of Haci Bektaş Veli is in the Bektaşi brotherhood lodge in Hacibektaş, a town north of Nevşehir, Turkey. In the sixteenth century, the Bektaşi order adopted the beliefs of Twelver Shi'a Islam. At some point during that century, there was some contact between the Bektaşi and the Ahl-e Haqq sect, or 'People of the Truth', of Iran. These people are primarily speakers of Gurani, a language closely related to Zaza, and the two groups apparently share a number of similar beliefs. Historically the Bektaşi brotherhoods' dervishes were responsible for converting many ethnic Christian peasants of Anatolia and the Balkans to Islam. The brotherhoods were associated with the elite army unit of the Ottoman Empire called the Janissary Corps. (Sweetnam 2004:225-226).

The *Bektaşi* movement was always perceived as Islamic. In contrast, Alevism or the *Kızılbaş* were recognized as non-Islamic. The close relation between the followers of *Bektaş* and the *Ahl-e Haqq* sect parallels the linguistic proximity between Zazaki and Gorani / Hewrami (2.2.2; 2.2.3.3; Bruinessen 1989a:139-150; Paul 2007:285). Also the division of both groups in two different dialect variations and two religious groups is very interesting, although it is not uncommon in the religiously heterogeneous world of the Fertile Crescent. The Kurmanji speaking group offers a tripartite split of its Islamic members. They follow Alevism, Sunnism, and Yezidism (2.3.3.3; 2.3.3.3) beside small non-Islamic groups. One can say for sure that the Turkish and Kurmanji speaking Alevis do have a much stronger propensity to the *Bektaş tekke* and *seyyids* than the Zaza Alevis. In this they equal the Yezidis (Kreyenbroek & Rashow 2005:6-7; e.g. Adawiyya-Order). The reason for that could be found in a general tendency of the Northern Zaza to mistrust any organized religious institution. The seclusive and exclusory nature of the Northern Group led to an isolated and independent variation of the Alevitic perception of the world.

2 The Zaza

Table 22 Distinctive Split in Religion and Language

Group	Islamic Sect	Sunnism	Yezidism	Zoroastrianism
Northern Zaza	Alevism (nominal elements of Bektaş)	-	-	Zoroastrianism, Dualism
Southern Zaza	-	Hanafi	-	Some remnants
Eastern Zaza	-	Shafi'i / Hanafi	-	Some remnants
Gorani (Southern Group)	Ahl-e Haqq; some are Shi'ites	-	-	influence
Hewrami (Northern Group)	-	Sunnism	-	-
Kurmanji Group	Alevism (Mevlana; Dervish; Bektaş)	Shafi'i	Armenia; Russia	The Alevism following group

2.3.3.2.3 Jewish Influence - Judaism

According to the old Greek and Roman historians Jewish people settled all over the Roman Empire. This movement started with the destruction and replacement of the ten Northern tribes of Israel by the Assyrians in the 9th and 8th centuries BC as it is written in the Hebrew Bible (2Ki 17-18; 2Chr. 32-33). Later on in the 7th century BC the two tribes of Benjamin and Judah were also led into captivity by the Babylonians (e.g. 2Chr 28-30; Jer 29 etc.). After the destruction of Israel in 70 AD and the second Jewish uprising under Bar Kochba in 132 AD, the country Israel was erased from maps and the regional term *Palestine* incrementally replaced the term *Israel*. The Jewish population spread out again into the Diaspora which became the normal state of life until 1948 when the state Israel was declared. In the Diaspora Jewish populations also settled in the Zaza homeland area. All the larger cities own a synagogue. The Jewish population mainly traded or worked in the financial sector.

Unfortunately the Jewish Diaspora doesn't offer much information, due to the persecution and oppression that they faced. A historical reconstruction of the close relationship to the Zaza is therefore very difficult. Christianity comes out of the grassroots of Jewish belief, and developed into the non-Jewish people groups of the Old World. However the derivation of recent practices to one of the Abrahamitic religions is a difficult task (2.1.4.4; 2.3.3.7.1). Jewish people settled in the Zaza homeland area and specialised in trade and business. Other public areas were not open to them. As far as my informants knew, they recognized themselves as the first generation after the exodus or deportation of Jewish people from Eastern Anatolia. Having said this, they do not remember having personal relations with Jewish people, but do know from their parents about their interactions with the Jewish population in the Zaza homeland. The Jewish people formed their own community which was self serving. They were mainly engaged in trade, craft and arts. The public market was the place of mutual communication and business was restricted to that realm. This is why the market place becomes the main social institution of the pre-Industrialized epoch. The Jewish citizens settled close to the market place, due to their business. Such a central geographical position also brought them into the centre of social tension. Encroachments and discrimination from the Islamic side had an ongoing effect on their social life. This field of research would need further investigation (3.4.2; 3.4.3).

Speaking about the influences of the Jewish religion, called Judaism, on the Zaza people different issues have to be taken in account:
- the general religious influences that are widespread all of over the Mediterranean (Animism, sects etc.),
- the closeness of the Abrahamitic religions - Judaism, Christianity, Islam -, and
- the non-homogenous performance of the society's strata.

In the Ottoman Empire the sphere of the *millets'* was clearly defined. Yet interreligious dialogue or mutual interchange was not on the agenda. Influence happened through hearsay and exchange of traditions. Circumcision of boys and girls for instance can be traced back to Egyptian manuscripts as far as 163 BC. Nowadays the circumcision of girls (*Female Genital Mutilation*, FGM) is practiced mainly in Africa (with Yemen as an exception). The religiously motivated circumcision of boys can be traced back to the covenant with Abraham (Gen 17:11). This covenant was taken over by the Mosaic laws (Lev 12:3) and as such became a commandment for the Jewish people. Christianity for instance refused to introduce circumcision as part of an initiation ritual but the issue was highly controversial and today parts of Christianity practice circumcision (Apostolic Council Acts 15 and 21:21; Galatians 2 and 5; 3.4.2; e.g. the Sundanese Church of Indonesia, African Churches). Islam took over the Pre-Islamic tradition of circumcision for boys as a rite of initiation to manhood. The Qur'an does not recommend circumcision but the Hadith which encompasses commentaries of the Qur'an does. The Hadith are considered to be the flesh for the bone (Qur'an); as such they give life to the Qur'an and are mandatory.

A little bit off the track is the recognition of the circumcision of girls called *Female Genital* Mutilation (FGM). This phenomenon not only occurs in Islamic circles, but is also attributed to animistic practices. The general secrecy about FMG in the Islamic countries and the fact that it is mainly restricted to the area of Africa and Yemen does not allow for assumptions for the Zaza people or their Kurmanji speaking Kurdish neighbours. From some hints from Zaza informants I inferred that such a practice is at least known. It seems that this practice was sometimes used to take non-Zaza girls into the society who had been abducted or who lost their family. Obviously the tendency was to do this with members of non-Islamic background. But yet there is no authentic evidence to my knowledge.

2.3.3.2.4 Christianity

During the early stages of the proliferation of the Church, the Jewish Diaspora became the centre of attraction for the Jewish apostles. The message of the Messiah was culturally, and by the revelational string of the Salvation Plan (Germ. "Heilsgeschichte"), nested into the Jewish environment. The apostles Peter (Acts 9), but mainly Paul bridged the gap with the non-Jewish audience.

During his second, out of three journeys to spread the news of the Messiah, Paul came close to the Zaza homeland. His hometown Tarsus was right in the middle between Jerusalem and the area of the Zaza. Christianity in Anatolia has its roots back to the 1st century AD. During that time the Apostle Paul actively travelled through today's area of Turkey then called Asia Minor. Referring to the Biblical "Letter to the Galatians" (Gal1:21; 2.1.1; 2.3.2.1.4; 2.3.3.2.4; 2.3.3.7.1) some historians argue that the Apostle Paul travelled to the North of Galatia which would be the Zaza homeland area. This "Northern Galatian Theory" causes some problems in the reconstruction of the time frame for the Apostle's travelling. Hence most of the presentations given on the travels of the Apostle Paul refer to the "Southern Galatian Theory". Following this theory, he was mainly around his hometown area of Tarsus and Antiochene and would only go as far as Urfa, today's Şanlıurfa. Either way, soon after its introduction the spread of Christianity reached the homeland area of the Zaza (Longenecker 2002: lxvi in Introduction; Bligh 1969).

Due to its geographical location north of the Mediterranean and the lack of economic centres, the Zaza area was not the centre of attraction for the Church founders. Its placement at the North-South Silk Road, which leads to the Black Sea, gives good reason to assume that the Zaza people came in contact with Jewish people and Christians (2.3.3.7.1). This would be either from the beginning, or when they settled in the 11th century AD.

The power struggle between Zoroastrianism and the Jewish religion (Judaism) is not described in the oral traditions of the Zaza people. My investigations of the Zaza culture show a tendency for the Jewish influence was to be intermingled with the Christian, but the latter was more recent and therefore better reflected and obvious to the outside ethnographer (etic stance).

Christianity in the homeland area of the Zaza soon was represented by the first national church of Armenia (3.4.1.1). The Armenian Apostolic Church became the oldest national church in history and proved to be very vital and capable of surviving in even hostile environments. During the 1st century AD the first contact of the Armenian people with Christianity was started by the apostles Thaddeus and Bartholomew. Mesrop translated the Bible by introducing a very effective alphabet. This combination was the initial moment of the Armenian nation and church and lasts until today as a centre of identification. Even within modern Armenia the Armenian Apostolic Church is part of politics referring to the constitution Article 8. Armenian scholars claim today that due to the Daylam Theory the Zaza people came as intruders into their realm (2.1.3.1.1). The lack of an Armenian intrusion in Zaza history and tradition would confirm this argument, the more so as the Armenian history is well documented due to their writing system since the 4th century AD.

The other churches like the Assyrian Church of the East were located more to the South of the Zaza area but never formed their own nation state. The traditional seat was in *Konak* (Qodchanis, Qudshanes, Qudshanis, Kochanes or Koçanis) a city in the province *Hakkari* close to the Iranian border. After the genocide in 1915 the village structure was destroyed. Another Christian movement by the Nestorians was more oriented to the East and never formed a state. Yet the teachings of those denominations influenced the neighbouring Zaza people (see 2.3.3.7.2). During the whole phase the Byzantine Empire (Greek: Βασιλεία Ῥωμαίων, Basileia Rhōmaiōn) was in decline, but still in power. The Armenian Apostolic Church, the Syriac churches (431 and 451 AD) including the Maronites, the Orthodox and Catholic branches as well as the Assyrian and the Chaldean church together with the Byzantines formed a Christian block within and against the Islamic Seljuk (3.4).

A unique phenomenon can be found in the existence of five villages around Gerger (*Alduş*) which are considered to be of Christian origin, although today many inhabitants of these villages practice Islam. Looking back in the history of the Zaza homeland, the to and fro of conversion and belonging to influential institutions led to a variety of strange situations. The above mentioned Christian villages claim their origin in the Assyrian / Syrian Church, but one would presume that they were in the past Armenians who converted a long time ago. The assumption comes from the fact that the Armenian Apostolic Church dominated the area and the Syrian Churches come in later. It could be that the Syrian rite was not enforced so harshly during the religious and ethical cleansings of the past. Until today these villages are recognized as *Hristian* (Christians) for their Christian background and history.

Today some practices are traced back to Christian origins but are fixed constituents of the cultural heritage. The language is reflects the close vicinity to the Armenians and the proximity between Christians and Muslims. The Armenian sources show very clearly that Christians had to suffer as *dimmis* in their status of the so called *dhimmitude* under the *dar al-Islam* or *dar as-Salam* (Ellul 2009:18; 2.3.1.3; 2.3.3.2.3). This second class citizenship within the "House of Islam" guaranteed the Christian or Jewish groups' protection against any penetration, and self-administration in religious and judicial matters. The "price" they had to pay was specific extra taxes, the restriction, until today, of any proselytising among Muslims, and no entrance to some of the political important institutions like police, military or Special Forces. The attitude towards the *millet*'s changed referring to the Sultan. The Armenian *Avestis* informs us about the situation in the 19th century (1911). His descriptions show the repression of the Armenians from Zaza, Kurds and the Ottoman Forces. Besides rape, kidnapping of girls, and brutal enforcement or displacement of families he shows that none of the political forces of those days, be it the Ottoman troops, the colonial forces or even the Zazaki or the Kurmanji speaking neighbours came to help if an incident happened against the Armenians (3.4.1.1).

To sum this up we could speak of a close but unequal power play in neighbourhood between the Zaza and their Christian neighbours mainly the Armenians. This parallels the situation of the Christian with the Jewish population (3.4.2).

The 19th century brought with it a Western Christian developmental aid movement which started in the West of Anatolia and moved slowly to the East of Anatolia. The movement worked towards the Christian minorities or *millet* that lived all over Anatolia. The gain for the Zaza people was that the hospitals, the educational system and the counselling of developmental aid workers were open to most people in the Anatolia area. In 1902 a Bible translation in Zazaki was published with 25 copies. They were spread out in the Zaza homeland area (personal communication with Mardin Artuluk University 2011). During these days many Zaza were aware of some Christian traditions they knew about. They also practiced traditions that were derived from Christianity (2.3.3.7.2).

The Alevi group adapted much more easily to the Turkish school and economic system than the Sunni Zaza, paying with the loss of their cultural and religious identity by strong assimilation. The Southern and Eastern dialectical groups belonged to Sunni Islam and therefore were less oppressed. They developed a stronger self esteem for the price of economical weakness. The repressive Turkish school system that forced children from their sixth year of life on to change totally to a new linguistic and cultural setting cut off the cognitive abilities of these children.

Oppression which leads to less educated people leads to high economical costs and political instability because of illiteracy. As a result of these negative effects, many governments around the globe restructured their educational principles and systems. To produce in education full cognitive effects for all pupils, these countries worked towards a superior bilingual education. In a two year programme the child is first educated in his mother-tongue and slowly moves towards the language of wider communication. The programme called *Mother tongue-based Multilingual Education* (MLE) represents the experiences of minorities and governments in the Philippines, in Africa and in some Asian states (UNESCO / SIL International 2007 DVD on *MLE*). Two aims are perceivable,

- basic mother tongue based education with a fast transition into the language of wider communication (two-year approach)
- mother tongue based education leading into its own educational system but on a higher level (full-education approach).

The first approach fits with most of the recent settings in the Near and Middle East as most of those countries have a school system in a language of wider communication. The latter approach would work in countries were two or more languages have the same prestige but are not yet equally treated in education.

The Zaza people experience the same negative cognitive effects of their forced education in Turkish. They are limited by their restricted knowledge of the Turkish language and culture. The children often experience a feeling of inferiority which aggravates the tendency for pupils to drop out of school. The result will be poor education as well as a rejection of the national governmental system.

The Zaza people want to be part of the Turkish higher education system, because it works fine and it helps to get well paid jobs. So the vision is to pass on their cultural and linguistic heritage to their children and at the same time to be part of the language and culture of higher education. A smooth transition from reading and writing the mother tongue into the language of wider education needs to take place. Bilingual well educated citizens are a great resource for a nation. They can trade on a much wider base and they will earn more money thus guaranteeing a broader and stable Middle Class in a country.

2.3.3.2.5 History of (Sunni) Islam – Purity / Impurity Manipulation

The wider historical and religious background of Islam in the Ottoman Empire will be demonstrated later (2.3.3.4; 3.6). Some historical remarks will follow here.

After the death of the prophet Hz. Mohammed (born ca. 570 AD / 74 BH; Mecca) in Medina (632 AD) the Arabian disciples spread out forcefully over the Near East. Christianity and the two ruling empires of Rome and Byzantine were so weak that there was no resistance at all. Although the disciples had no experience in how to set up an Islamic state or commonwealth, they introduced the "house of Islam" or "house of peace" (*dar al-Islam* or *dar as-Salam*) against the "house of war" (*dar al-harb*). This division made it obvious to the conquered people groups and nations that from now on they are part of an Islamic Commonwealth. This common practice led to religious and ethnical minorities, which were called *dhimmi*. Christian and Jewish groups were handled as second class citizens. They could either convert or live under the Islamic law (Sharia; Turk.: *şeriat*) with restrictions in daily life. Special taxes and a ban on entering the security forces, as well as assigned locations for living became standard practice. During the Ottoman Empire the Roman Catholics, Samaritans, Karaeites, the Greek, Syrian, Arabic Orthodox Churches, the Armenians, the Protestants (only for a short time in the 19th century) and the Jewish population all had the status of *millet* (nation; 2.1; 3.1; 3.6).

Islam as the most recent religious movement affected the Zaza people during the foray of the Seljuk around the 11th and 12th century. This movement as part of the later Mongol invasions (11th – 13th century AD / 5th – 7th century AH) changed the scenery of Eastern and Middle Anatolia totally (2.1.3.1.1; 2.1.3.1.4; 2.1.3.1.5; 2.3.1.1; 2.3.3.4; 3.1.1; 3.3; 0). The Christian populations became minorities and second class citizens. Since the Zaza people followed either Christianity, Alevism (Northern Group), Sunnism (Southern and Eastern Group) or some forms of Animism, mixed with Zoroastrianism, their culture was changed or at least challenged to adapt.

A second penetration started with the expansion of the Ottoman Empire in the 16th century. Juristical Schools of Islam concurred during this epoch. In the 17th century a re-islamisation process started which was based on the Islamic *Arabian Wahhabism* movement agitating with missionary zeal (2.3.3.4). Against this it has to be said that most of the Sunni Zaza follow the school of Hanafi, and less the Islamic school of Shafi'i (Paul 2002:193; 2.2.8.1;2.3.3.2.5; 2.3.3.5; Table 22). Paul's argument goes that affiliation to the Shafi'i school brings the Zaza close to the Kurds which is also the main line of thought there. Although it is possible that this connection exists at least for a part of the Zaza people, I did not hear one statement agreeing with this argument. Quite the opposite the Zaza would not go in the same mosque or hold close ties with Kurmanji speaking Muslims, hence my research leads me to the conclusion that even the religious segregation of both ethnicities goes very deep. What they share is a strong and conservative practice of Islam (Zürcher 2004:247; Pikkert 2008:90).

Analogous to the past (2.3.1.3.2) today areas like Palu, Bingöl (Çewlig / Çabaxçur), Hani (Heni) and *Siverek* (Sowreg) are strongholds of Islamic schools. Izady mentions bigotry as one of the key features of Kurds and Zaza (1992:57; 2.3.3.4; 3.6). Nowadays the Islamic schools *madrassa* are gone, which were the places of education, development and discussion of Islamic rites. The remnants are the practices of Ramadan, Şeker-Bayram, purity-impurity manipulation regulations, the daily duties of *namas* (five times) and the *zakat* (pittance; Arab. "being pure") as a duty of pity for the poor. Until now no social institution replaced the former madrassa system. Religious education is included in the public school system.

2.3.3.2.6 The Purity – Impurity Manipulation – *haram* and *helal*

The contrasting religious principles of *halal* / *helal* حلال 'allowed, pure' and *haram* حرام 'illicit, pollute, taboo, holy' describe the area of taboo, as well as the profane and sacred (2.4.2.1). The contrasting pair describes the framework of religious behaviour in which a society member has to stay. The area of *haram* is describing the zone of the *taboo*. One is not even allowed to come close to this area on geographical, spiritual or physical terms. For specific tasks some of the given restrictions can be trespassed if the conditions allow it. Thus e.g. a cleric is allowed to enter restricted geographical districts that are not open to others (approaching a corpse, cemetery etc.). In the same way the gender segregation can be breached by doctors or clerics. The principle of *haram* in food restrictions is left more or less to the individual and his conscience; however the society recognizes any violation soon, as is well demonstrated on the month of Ramadan in Islam. The public sphere is penetrated by the ideal of fasting during day times and fast-breaking. During Ramadan the pressure on the individual by the group conscience is so strong that people fall into depression and sleep long during daytime to forget about the fasting (own observation).

From an anthropological point of view the *purity-impurity manipulation* in the Zaza society shows some interesting points. Its proclamation and control is performed by the local religious leader the *mıllah* (Arabic *mullah*).The ideal state of purity is proclaimed by *Qur'an* (Sura 2:152, 174, 222 etc.), *Hadith* (Islamic Traditions), *Sira* and Islamic Commentaries (Islamic Exegetical Works). The believer is asked to stay in purity. Hence the state of Impurity is accepted short term. A long-term impurity would cause penalty from the *umma*.

In Zaza society washing of feet and hands before the *namas* (prayer), ritual cleaning with perfumes and the sexual segregation from the other gender either in public, during menstruation or after giving birth (*cewresê* = the forty) pervade daily life. Defilement is accepted for short periods. Long-term impurity is seen as *taboo* (1.1.3.3; 2.3.2.1.4; 2.3.2.1.4; 2.3.3.2.5). The power behind is called *mana*[68] (Allah). The executive powers are either "good" angels or good, neutral or evil *cin* (demons). The individual has to stay in the purity sphere. His duty is to be balanced in daily life, not to trespass across the small line of defilement for a longer period, hence falling in the state of impurity. One regulation system is the proximity to the sacred, which stands for the holy and ideal sphere. As the individual stays in the profane (real state), his longing is towards the sphere of the holy (ideal vs. real management). He therefore refers to the mentioned pow-

---

[68] *Mana* is an open principle (Käser 1998:213-214). It describes the power or principle behind taboo or areas of sacredness. Demons, cins or other powers protect the sacred against the profane.

ers. He blames or praises those powers for imbalance, caused by illness, accidents, misfortune and fortune but still sees the overlaying power - *Allah* - behind it. Regulations of impurity in the Zaza culture are,

Diagram 11 Purity-Impurity Manipulation

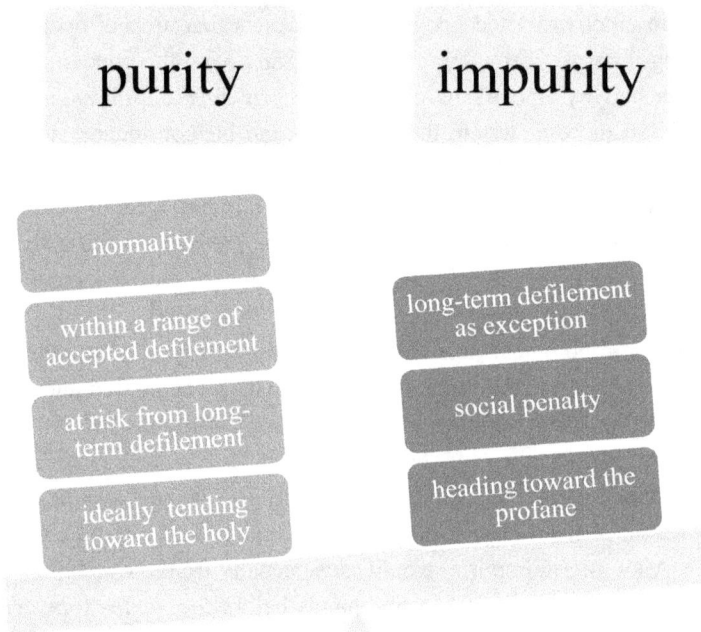

- Repudiation in the case of causing shame on the family. This applies to sons (e.g. murder; blaming father) and daughters (sexual offense; adultery, etc.), honour killings, suicide.
- Blood feud in the case of serious matters such as sexual defilement (rape, adultery), murder etc.
- Social restrictions, such as judgements of less social or cultural adjustment, etc.

The observations made here, refer to the Southern and Eastern Sunni Group of the Zaza people. Only some few elements are observable in the Northern Group and will be mentioned below (2.3.3.3).

2.3.3.2.7 Religious Influences - An Historical Attempt

The main religions in the Fertile Crescent Area were spread out through the Silk Roads. Pre-Christian Judaism, Parsiism, Zoroastrianism, Christianity and Old-Iranian mystic cults left their marks in the Zaza religion. Islamic influences thus can be followed up by the migration from the Zaza region to the West. For instance parts of the Eastern Zaza Group follow the Islamic school of Shafi'i like their predominant Kurmanji speaking neighbours. The Southern Zaza Group follows the Hanafi school like their predominant Turkish neighbours. The Northern Group follows Alevism and have influenced pockets of the Turkish and Kurmanji speaking population in the East. A move from the East to the West in direction to *Sivas* on the height of *Kayseri* left its marks on the Turkish and Kurmanji speaking population (HD 2011 *personal communication*).

A remaining question will be who influenced whom? From an evolutionary anthropological point of view the larger groups (the Turks and Kurmanji speakers) would have left their marks in the Zaza community. Contrary to this point of view the strong cohesion of the Zaza small scale societies in times of need would also hint at the thesis that this could also be the other way around (2.3.1.3.2). We will look now into the latter hypothesis in detail.

Historically the Alevism of the Northern Zaza people group can be traced back to a religious movement in Iran as Shi'a offshoot. In general, extremist Shi'a groups (*ghulat*) appeared at the early stages of the outspread of Islam. They were particularly active in Iran, where Shi'ism was always popular. The absence of the centralized state and the official religious doctrine in the 10th-15th century gave fertile ground for the expansion and increase of extremist Shi'a groups as well as of Sufi'i *tarikats* (Amoretti 1993). Both of them, especially the first, embraced a lot of local pagan and Christian elements, which became a part of their doctrine. The remainders of Gnosticism and Manichaeism influenced those groups as well. One interesting fact is that the Turkish, Turkmen and some Kurmanji speaking Alevis do have a general affiliation with the *Bektaşi tekke* whereas the Zaza Alevis and their *seyyids* only reflect them nominally or have no affiliation to them (2.3.3.3).

The following Diagram attempts to demonstrate the religious influences on the Zaza people group in the past and their recent religious setting.

In the Zaza ethnicity the mountains possess divine qualities (Comerd 1997:90). Comerd mentions *Xızır* / *Xıdır* and *Baba Duzgın* as the main protective powers of the Zaza belief(1997: 15-31; 1998:83-100). The best example in the North is *Baba Duzgın* (Dedekurban 1994: 12, 15).

Diagram 12 Religious Influence - History and Present

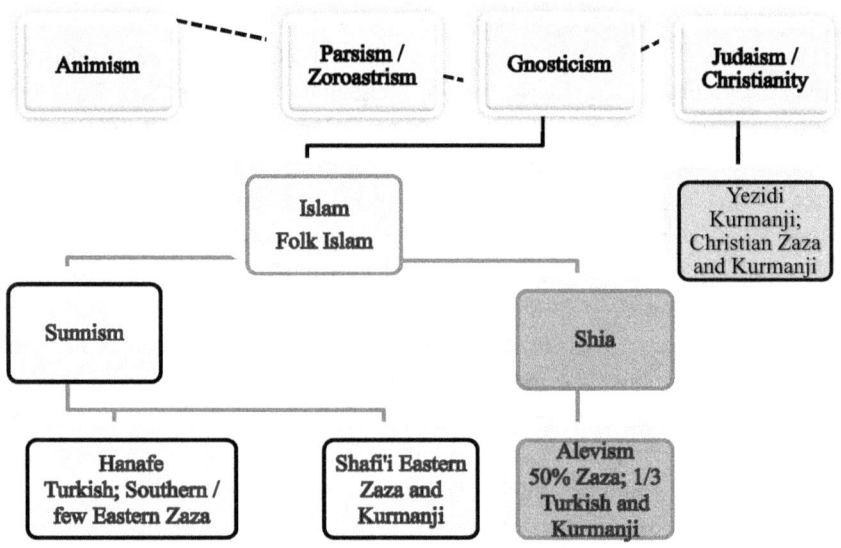

In the South, especially in Çermik it is the "mountain of wedding" – a mountain range that looks like a wedding procession and surrounds the city, referred to as a guarding force. Also in the East, one finds local references to the surrounding mountains by allocating supernatural powers to them. The same is true for rivers, wells and pools. Behind those, spiritual powers are expected, either good or evil. The individual relates to these powers by obligation or keeping his distance (see parallel in Yezidism in Asatrian and Arakelova 2004:231-279).

2.3.3.2.8 Summary

The religions of the Zaza people reflect influence from the East (Iran), from the South (Arabia, Israel) as well as from the West (Greece). All major religions penetrated the Zaza society due to immediate proximity of the Silk Roads that passed their homeland. Zoroastrianism or *serduşt* (Zazaki) originated from Persia / Iran (6th century BC). *Parsiism* as it is also called in Asia mixed with or was based on *Animistic* elements. It had some influence on the whole Zaza society, but mainly on the Northern group. Today's Alevism practice and spread reflects those influences well. Christianity started in Israel but soon spread out over the whole homeland area of the Zaza called Asia Minor. The Armenians became the first people converting to Christianity and starting a National Church called the Armenian apostolic Church (4th century AD) which is still alive today. This kingdom was completely in the homeland area of the Zaza people. If the Zaza settled there before the foundation of that Church, then the influence of *Christianity* on them would be from early on. The so called "Northern Galatian theory" mentions that the Apostle Paul was going to the North of Galatia which would be the homeland area of the Zaza. If he did so Christian influence would be from the 1st century AD on. If on the contrary he stayed in the southern part of today's Turkey, the Zaza people would only have contact with Christianity by hearsay. Remnants of Christian practices are documented but do not allow for proof.

Islam had at least two breakthroughs. It entered the area and sphere of the Zaza people, either during the main spread in the 7th and 8th century or by the Seljuk expansion (11th to 12th century AD / 5th – 6th century AH). It is not known if the conversion was as usually forced. The status of the Zaza during the time Sunni Muslims ruled the Ottoman Empire gives the impression of relative independence, although the Alevism practicing Northern Group was subject to discrimination. In the 17th century Islamic *Wahhabism* missionary zeal led to a programme of re-islamisation which started out of Arabia. The current split in an Alevism following Northern Group and a Sunni Southern and Eastern / Central Group can be traced back at least to this movement. Islam is currently the whole-hearted religion. The Sunni Zaza people are well known as a Sunnism practicing group in alignment with bigotry.

2.3.3.3 Alevism – Animism in Northern Group

In their study about the "Yezidi Pantheon" Asatrian and Arakelova show a lot of common features within Alevism and other Shi'a extreme sects (2.3.3.2.1; 2.5.1). Their historical view is expanded by my findings (2004:231-279). Parallels are found especially in the concept of a Holy Triad (:231; Ali-Xızır-Cemaat), the devotion of mountains and natural formations (:238-242; e.g. the mountain *Duzgın Baba* in Dedekurban 1994: 12, 15; rocks in Molyneux-Seel 1914: 58), the formation of a sacred clergy (:232-233; *pir*, *seyyid*, *baba*, *sheikh*, *mursid*), the scarification of the seven not closer defined spiritual powers (in Yezidism seven avatars of Malak-Tāwūs; :232),

Asatrian and Arakelova mention the Yezidi Thunder-God Māma-řašān and his epithet "lion" (Šēr Mahmadē řašān, or Šēr Mahmad řašān; :234). As in the Yezidi Pantheon the lion plays an important role in the Zaza religion too. The heroic folktale *Ma'hmeşa* (Hayıg 2007:37) describes the lion as a protecting power also performing supernatural activities. Many Zaza idioms refer to the lion as a gods-like spiritual force.

Asatrian and Arakelova mention the assimilation of the elements of the cult of Surb Sargis (St. Sergius), the popular Armenian Christian saint in charge of the natural elements by "Māma-řašān and Dūzgin, as well as Khidir-nabi (among the Yezidis, see below), and Khizir" (*Baba Duzgın* and *Xızır / Xıdır* by the Zazas) in (2004:241, 270). It is, in my opinion, not quite clear if such similarities go back to a common Zoroastrian belief or if the Armenian culture had such an influence on the people groups of East Anatolia.

The Zaza people, the Gorani speakers and the Kurmanji people underwent a unique historical development by experiencing a religious and linguistical split (Table 22; 2.3.3.2.2). Nowadays the Northern Group follows Alevism whereas the Southern and Eastern Groups are part of the wider Sunni Islamic movement (see above). During the centuries of isolation in a mountainous area, the Northern Group was perceived as a non-Islamic and heathen group of animists or polytheists. Since the foundation of the Republic of Turkey in 1923, both the Zaza Alevis by themselves and the surrounding Sunni Muslims started to recognize this group as an Islamic sect. Nonetheless the Alevis in the Diaspora developed their own identity by stating that they are a non-Islamic group (Sökefeld 2008b:204). It is therefore interesting to see what the Alevi Zaza people nowadays make out of their religion as part of their perception of the world.

2.3.3.3.1 Alevism in Turkey - Revival

Estimations of Alevis range from 10 to 25% of the Turkish population (Neyzi 2002:92). After a short claim to the Republican party (CHP) and her move to Sunni Islam the Alevis became socialist leftists (:92-93). With this move persecution of Alevism started again, the main event being the uprising led by *Seyit Rıza* which led to the genocide of 1937/38 called *Tertelê Dêrsimi* (2.3.1.1; 2.3.1.3.2). Since the 1980's Alevism in general but mainly in the Northern Group is experiencing a revival and comeback as a way of life within the Northern Group (Seufert 1997:172). Nowadays the Alevis in Turkey face a political struggle between extreme Anti-Islam and pre-Islam Turkishness which splits the group politically (Houston 2001:105). Still the Turkish officials prosecute Alevism either directly or indirectly by impeding the opening of cem / cemat houses, by defamation, or by ignoring the existence of this group (Sökerfeld 2008:15-16). Out of this developed the internal principle of *takiye* which made Alevism invisible and inaccessible to outsiders (2.1.1.5.2).

2.3.3.3.2 Origin and Practices

Alevism is based on Animistic, Gnostic, Jewish, Christian, Zoroastrian, and Sufi'i / Shi'a foundations (2.3.3.2.1). As Jacobson makes it clear Alevism represents a form of "Shi'a Islam, *Bektaşi* Sufi'ism, Zoroastrianism, and Judeo-Christianity, as well as elements of natural religion" (cit. in Sweetnam 2004:224; s. a. Steinbach 1996:375-376; Neyzi 2002:94). Asatrian and Arakelova compare Alevism to Yezidism, since both are Shi'a extreme sects, geographically close to each other (2004:231, 237). The *Chishtiyya*, the *Bektashis*, and the *Ahl-i Haqq* can be counted as part of the same religious mystical orientation (:237). The *endogamous* Alevitic Zaza group represents a homogenous unit in contrast to Turkish or Kurmanji speaking Alevis, although intermingling with Armenians was practiced in the past (Neyzi 2002:94-95). Such, exogamy within this endogamic ethnicity was practiced to some extend (2.3.4.2.1). Paul suggests a litmus test by proving that Alevis would never marry a Sunni Muslim, either from Turkish, Zaza or Kurmanji origin (:193). There is a clear distinction and segregation to other Alevism practicing groups (Taşçı 2008:146-147). This is why in history they were often recognized as *Kızılbaş / Qızılbaş / Kızılbaş* (red-headed; Kieser 2000:69-71). Especially the Turkish, Turkmen and some Kurmanji speaking Alevis and their religious leaders the *seyyids* follow the *tekke* (rite) of the *Bektaşi* who are only nominally affiliated to the Zaza Alevis (2.3.3.2.7). In the 19th century the Christian aid worker Trowbridge reported that the Alevi Kurmanji speaking population of Antep (Gaziantep near Malatya), whom he knew well, considered the Ahl-e-Haqq *seyyids* of *Tutshami* (near Kirind, west of Kermanshah) to be their highest religious authorities (Bruinessen w/d *The debate* ...).

Due to the mingling of Zoroastrian and Alevitic customs, it is difficult to find anything about the animistic elements in the Zaza culture. Folk Islam forms a combination of all[69] and as a very complex belief system makes it difficult to

---

[69] *Folk Islam* demonstrates the "conglomeration between animism and Islam" (Reifler 2005:32). In consequence it leads to an "undogmatic understanding of Islam" (Eberhard 1970:27). Such popular piety is "strongly mingled with the Islamic high religion and has its

trace back the religious practices to its origin (Wiher 2007:224; Hiebert & Hiebert 1995:255; Jabbour 2008:55; Nida 1975:151). Conceptions of the afterlife as well as practices of healing shape the remnants of animistic beliefs and reflect the deeper perception of the world of people (2.5; 2.5.1). For example, the *snake* has a special meaning in peasant cultures as protector and enemy (2.3.5.5). Prayers, amulets or charms reach out into the transcendental or spiritual world. Their protective function is to defend one against evil influences by demons (*cin*) or curses (2.3.2.1.4; Werner 2006 *Questionnaire on Zaza worldview*). Some shamanistic elements, such as the transformation of humans into birds of the other world, are expressed in Alevism through the treasury of songs and dances (Markoff 1995:3; Kehl-Bodrogi 1989; 2.3.5.3; 3.3). These elements are not considered to be animistic at all.

Before the *Tertelê Dêrsimi* many mausoleums were known. It was common practice to give popular leaders like the *pir*, *rayber* or *baba*, which were said to possess mystical powers, a final resting place in the form of a mausoleum (2.3.3.3.5). These places soon became the destination of pilgrimages and the source for legends and traditions. Alongside healings, miracles and unique visions they functioned as a space for community and prayer. Due to their popularity they became the target of devastation after the rebellions of 1920/1921 and 1937/1938. Only two mausoleums still exist in their original design, those of *Sari Saltik ocağı* in *Hozat*, and the one of the *Aguiçen ocağı* in *Pertek*.

2.3.3.3.3 Recent Peculiarity of Alevism

Today's Alevism of the Zaza is recognized as a philosophy or way of life and not a religion. Due to the lack of traditions that are not passed on any more and against all the recent attempts to describe Alevism as a system of beliefs, Alevism can only be described by some of its very vague outcomes. It performs a perception of the world that is passed on by education and which defines itself quite contrary to the surrounding religions especially Sunni Islam (Neyzi 2002:92).

---

roots back to the pre-Islamic period" (Brockhaus 2008 *Volksislam*). Reifler distinguishes six representations of Islam, namely the secular, conservative, fundamental, radical, sufistic and Folk Islam (2005:33). "Folk Islam" is not unambiguously defined yet (Schirrmacher 1994b:95), although I would subsume all practices of Muslims that are based on dogmatically non-Islamic perceptions under it.

Alevism provides attraction to Christian and Humanistic thinking, well demonstrated in the 19th century by Christian aid workers in Eastern Anatolia. The holistic and humanity-based ideology of Alevism fits well into postmodern thinking (Kieser 2000:385-387; Sökefeld 2008a:17). Compared with the strict division between Mankind and God in orthodox Islam and Christianity, Alevism emphasizes the unity between God and Creation and the mystical unity between all Beings. The main motto behind Alevism was formulated by *Hacı Bektaş Veli* which reads in Turkish: *Eline diline beline sahip ol!* which means "be on guard about your hands, your tongue and your loins!" (Sökefeld 2008a:17). This rule of life sounds like a summary of the Biblical Ten Commandments (*tewrat*; Exodus 20). It describes the social ethics of controlling the self in a way to avoid conflict with others. Self-control and conflict prevention relates to inner-human relationships, to the unseen world and to nature. The principle of a balanced life leads the devotee to "Harmony" with these three realities (the self, other humans, nature as physical and transcendental world).

2.3.3.3.4 Content and Implication

The following description only reflects some observations which, as the author is well aware, can be interpreted differently and are not dogmatic. One can find the following areas of focus in the Northern Zaza group (Steinbach 1996:375-376; Neyzi 2002:94):

1. The foundation of Alevism is presented as a humanistic ideal in which all creation is in line with each other. All parts sum up to a harmonious whole. This mystical belief, also based on being in close touch with nature, is expressed in songs and dances (*semah*; Markoff 1995:3). Yet the treasury of songs contains the mystical love (*deyi*), mystical experiences (*nefes*), adoration of the twelve Imams since Hz. Ali (*düvaz/düvâzdeh imâm*), the dirges about the martyrdom of Hüseyin at Kerbela (*mersiye*) and the ascencion of the Prophet Hz. Mohammed (*miraclama*). The following dances are known: Dance of the crane (*Turnalar Semah*) and dance of the forty (*Kırklar Semah*). In the former, the shamanistic tradition of a transformation into birds and in the latter the realization of God in Hz. Ali through Hz. Mohammed after his ascension is expressed (Markoff 1995:3).

2. Alevis accept the five pillars of Islam only partially and interpret the motivation behind them as "God being outside of Mankind" (thesis of transcendentalism) whereas they follow the principle of "God being in

every human and the creation" (Sökefeld 2008a:17-19). Thus the deistic component of orthodox Islam gets lost (Kehl-Bodrogi 1989:229).

3. Hz. Ali, a cousin of the prophet Hz. Mohammed, functions as a model. This applies for most Shi'ite rites which like Alevis align their ethics to the traditions about Hz. Ali (s. a. Gibran 2003). Even the term Alevism is a derivation of the name *Ali*vism.

4. The *cem* or *cemat* / *cemat* (assembly) displays the religious and social-political centre of the Alevitic society (Shindeldecker 2001; Kaplan 2005. *Grundlagen des alevitischen Glaubens* [Foundations of the Alevitic Religion). In the cem, Alevis practice and pass on their traditions and enculturated perception of the world. The cem represents the strengthening institution of reciprocal solidarity (Sökefeld 2008a:19). In the cem behaviour is developed by penalty and reward. This gender mainstreaming institution covers and rules over the political, social, juristic and ethical aspects and questions of the Zaza society (Markoff 1995:3). According to Langer, elements of cem are (2008:97-98),

- *sohbet* of rayber or pir (seldom by Turkish influence called dede) addressed to the cem (sermon);
- restitution of *râzîlik* (reciprocal agreement), in case this does not exist the time is taken for *barıştırma* (establishment of peace);
- request for adherence to *edeb erkâna dâvet* (the rules of the community);
- *salavât* and *selâmlama* (prayers and greeting of the "prophets family" resp. the "twelve Imams");
- the *zâkir* sings the song of the "twelve responsible servants" which at the same time form a half circle before the pôst (the coat for the rayber's or pir's, seldom dede's, seat);
- the rayber or pir practices *tezekkâr* (washing of hands) while praying with the cem / cemat;
- ministry of the "inflaming of the light" in which three candles are kindled under the invocation and in honour to Allah, the prophet Hz. Mohammed and the prophet Hz. Ali;
- service of the "sweeping" (*süpürgeci*), three times sweeping motion with a hand brush;
- *gözcü*, duty of the guardian;

- *tövbe/tevbe* which contains the collective appeal for forgiveness in the expression "tövbe günâhlarımıza estâğfirullâ estâgfirullâh";
- *secde duâsi, gülbâng* the rayber / pir prays while the assembly stays in *secde* (prostration);
- the singing of the *mirâclama*-Hymn by the *zâkir*. The Hymn refers to the ascension and the meeting of the prophet Hz. Mohammed with the "assembly of the forty" (Tk. kırklar meclisi), in which the first primordial *semâh* was danced;
- the rite of the "water splashing" in remembrance of the Kerbela desert;
- *mersiyye*, the dirge about the events in Kerbela;
- service of the *kurbânci*, symbolized in the person of the *lokma*-distributor or –sacrifice. He hands out the kurbân (sacrifice) which is blessed by the rayber or pir.
- *namas* (prayer) of the rayber or pir and common meal.

5. *Feasts*: One feast of mourning and fasting is twelve days long. It ends on the tenth day in a remembrance of the murder of Hüseyin, which is dated to the "tenth" day (Âşûrâ) of the month Muharrem in the Hijra-year 61 (680 AD). Another shorter - mainly five day - fast happens in February and parallels the *Hızır orucu* (Hızır-fasting). *Hıdırellez* is a spring-feast from the 5th to the 6th of May. An Iranian celebration is found in *Sultân Nevrûz* which is the outset of spring on the 20th or 21st of March. The Alevis often transfer Newroz / Nevrûz into *Hazret-i Ali Doğum Günü* that is the birthday of Hz. Ali. In parallel they celebrate *Hewt Mal(a)*, a 4 / 7-day celebration of the spring season.

6. In the Alevi community the *pir* or his assistant the *rayber* (*ray berdış* = leader of the Path / scout) hold a leading function. In Turkish Alevism this function is covered by the *dede* (2.3.5.3). The student *tikme* is lead by the *rayber*, who is trained by a *pir* (MT 2012. Personal Communication at the 2nd Symposium of the Zaza Language. Bingol / Turkey). The *pir* functions as a protector of tradition, a judge, a teacher, an educator or trainer and a religious manager (Kehl-Bodrogi 1989:167-179; s. a. Pkt. 3.1.4.6.3). His discipleship is called *müşit*. Normally students have to pay the *pir* for training or education. *Pir* is the vocative for "father" and phrases a close relationship (2.3.5.3). The overall ideological or religious institution – Alevis don't like the term religion for their way of life – is

given by the *mürşıd / murşıd / mürşid*. He also represents the last religious and social institution in cases of struggle or civil rights.

7. Incarnation and metempsychosis are known. They are not handled as dogmatic statements but as esoteric doctrines. Even Hz. Ali, the central figure of the Alevis, is not understood to be a godly incarnation, although he is sometimes referred to as God himself. Generally speaking it is obvious that "conceptions of the afterlife in the belief system of Alevis play only a subordinated role" (Kehl-Bodrogi 1989:144).

8. In the centre of the Alevitic religious philosophy stands the human, but besides that, *Xızır / Xıdır* represents a manifestation of *Haq* (truth; righteousness, God; Barihas 2003; Asatrian & Arakelova 2004:2421, 270). *Xızır* portrays a metaphysical and transcendental power which functions like a manifestation of God. *Xızır* is omnipotent and omnipresent. Due to the humanistic approach of Alevism, *Xızır* can live within humans and give them self esteem and dignity. *Xızır* and *Baba Duzgın* are considered to be the main divinities in the Zaza belief (Comerd 1997 and 1998).

2.3.3.3.5 Leadership in Alevism - Then and Now

Leadership in Alevism is represented by the *pir*, who is replaced in Turkish as *dede*. They trace themselves back to the twelve holy and sacred Alevis lineages called *ocaks*. The *dedes* are to be distinguished in *baba, rayber, mürşid* and *pir*. According to the *dedes* eight out of these twelve *ocaks* are located in Dersim: Ağuiçenler, Sari Saltiklar, Derviş Cemallar, Baba Mansurlar, Kureyşanlar, Celal Abbaslar, Seyit Sabunlar, and Pilvenkliler (Törne 2011).

Since Western societal formations always build on a top-down structure it is confusing to compare the hierarchy of the Alevitic Leadership from an *etic* point of view. As such, although the *mürşid* is considered to be the most respected position in Alevism, it is not a title one takes over. For this reason the title of a *pir* is given the most attention, but one has to keep in mind that the *rayber / rayver* or *mürşid* represent higher social prestige and hold more influence. Equality as the main principle of the *cem / cemat* leads to an ongoing confirmation of the leadership holders. But to take this argument not too far, an influential family will often hold the position of the pir-institution and thus the authority that goes with it. In Alevism the position of a *pir* can also be appointed by a *pir* who is in a directive position.

In the past the leadership was able to overcome distrust by the strong structure of the small scale society's tribal orientation. The *agha* and the subleaders covered the decisions and deeds of their mystical *pir*. After the foregoing upheavals (1920/1921; 2.1.2.3; 2.1.2.5), the foundation of the republic and the *Tertelê Dêrsimi* (1937/1938) mistrust in the ethnicity arose that the religious leaders were collaborating with the government. The role and power of the *pir* decreasingly got lost after a socialistic move of the leaders in the 1970s and early 1980s of last century. Their hope that socialism would lead to more liberty was not fulfilled. At the same time feudalistic tribal structures dispersed due to migration and industrialization. Recently the remainders of the leadership are changing into industrial collectivistic and leading positions. This development parallels the roles of the *sheikh* and *agha* in the Southern and Eastern Group and their move from a tribal peasantry collective small scale society to an industrial capitalistic society. Wealth formed by leadership, includes ground, houses, prestige and man power, thus the transformation from one economic system into another is performed. In politics the formation of support groups by leadership follows the same principles. A leader is expected to take up such a leadership role and he gets support in so far as his prestige, and as long as his party is not totally against the interests of the subordinated small scale society (2.3.3.3.2).

2.3.3.3.6 Summary

The outstanding feature in Alevism is represented by the religious and political gender mainstreaming, the close contact with nature, the religious adoration of holy men and the superficial practice of Sunni Islam in a mainly orthodox Islamic environment. As for the whole group the Alevis act according to basic values which are still spread over the whole Zaza group but which are on a deeper level or rudimentary in the Sunni Southern and Eastern Group. For an evaluation of the whole group's perception of the world the Alevitic elements are essential to understand the practices and outcomes of religious rituals.

2.3.3.4 Islamisation Process

Although we do not know too much about the process of Islamisation within the Zaza people, one can find hints in Church and Islam history. For start it is necessary to assume that the recent homeland of the Zaza was their living area for the last 2000 years. I will give other suggestions of Islamisation later, but at this point we will stay with this presumption. Also we will assume that the Kurdish Kurmanji speaking neighbours entered the area before their Islamisation process.

The Islamic expansion started right after the death of the prophet Hz. Mohammed in 632 AD in Medina. Within two generations in the 7th century AD the Arab tribes conquered the former Byzantine Southern provinces of Egypt, Syria and Persia. The Byzantine churches, the remaining Roman Empire, as well as the traditional Zoroastrianism (Mazdaism), Buddhism, Hinduism and Shamanism following people groups of Persia, the Maghreb and the Near and Middle East were split into small chiefdoms, princedoms or kingdoms (2.3.3.2.2; 2.3.3.3; 2.3.5.3; 3.3). Most of them were unable or unwilling to form confederations. Regular wars, struggles and ambushes led to mistrust and a lack of an anticipation of the great challenges caused by the expansion of Islam.

During the initial periods of this expansion the Arab tribes, following the principles of *jihad*, either subordinated the conquered people as *dhimmis* or annihilated them (2.3.3.4; 3.4.1.3.4; 3.6.1; 3.6.5; 0). In further cases mainly Christians and Jewish people become second class citizen owning restricted rights and financially dependent on the new rulers. The latter were asked to convert before they were plundered and their booty divided under the Muslims (Ye'or 2009). It is within this first wave of Islamic expansion that "Kurds" were participating in the oppression of their Christian neighbours as early as the 8th century AD/ 2nd century AH. The term "Kurds" in the manuscripts refers to the wider sense and includes all the Zazaki and Kurmanji related languages speaking people groups (2.2.3.1). "Turks", "Arabs" and "Kurds" became a fixed expression during the second wave of Islam from the 11th - 13th century / 5th – 7th century AH (:92-115). The Mongol invasions of Europe and the Near and Middle East which fell in this period are today's best known Islamic expansion movement (2.1.3.1.12.1.3.1.4; 2.1.3.1.5; 2.3.1.1; 2.3.3.4; 3.1.1; 3.3; 0). A third Islamic missions-oriented wave led by the Wahhabites in the 17th century was mainly focusing on Eastern Anatolia and the nations around Arabia.

Regular conditions during the two main expansions were *Arabization*, *Islamisation* and *Nationalisation*. During the initial period of *Arabization* (7th – 8th century AD / 1st – 2nd century AH) Islamic expansion was built on the subordination of people to the *dar al-Islam* or *dar as-Salam* (House of Islam / House of Peace). Financial and logistical support was taken from the conquered people groups' wealth. The prospect of power, wealth and prestige in the upcoming Islamic Commonwealth encouraged people to join the movement. Often the conquerors made use of the intelligentsia elite. Thus in the long run the conquered people became deliverers of Islamic success, due to their status as *dhimmis*. As *dhimmis* they were either taken as slaves, or were relocated, had to pay high taxes and had to support the Islamic troops with food and logistics. Such status warranted the Islamic conquerors loyalty to the captured people as they were under their ongoing oppression.[70] Later on during the phase of *Islamisation* (11th – 13th century AD / 5th- 7th century AH) the principle of women and children abduction from *dhimmis* was converted into a levy called *devshirme* (:113-115, 132-133). *Sultan Orkhan* (1326-1359) introduced it officially during his reign. A fifth of the Christian children had to be given to the palace. They were educated to become fanatics and then were an important power factor for the Ottoman Empire as they often were the cruellest weapons against their own people. This practice combined with the pillage and confiscation of non-Islamic people groups produced another time of wealth and dispersal for Islam.

The "Kurds" in a wider sense participated in all of these expansions. As such the community between Jewish people, Armenians and other Christian groups was never based on equality but on oppression and subordination to the Kurdish prince- and chiefdoms. A little bit different was the situation for the Jewish and Christian group in the neighbourhood of the Northern Alevis. Here to some extent the people groups lived together and even participated on the same level with each other. Unfortunately the given records started in the 19th century AD / 14th century AH when the Ottoman Nationalistic movement of *Pan-Islamism* and *Pan-Turkism* was introduced. The *Tanzimat* reforms reorganized the administrative apparatus of the sultanate and drifted towards the oppression and annihilation of the Jewish and Christian *millet* (2.1). The Alevitic Zaza were forced to stay neutral or cooperate with the stronger (Sunni) regime to avoid oppression.

The mission-oriented Wahhabism based re-islamisation programme in the 17th century produced a strong and orthodox religious orientation within the Southern and Eastern Group as well as the Kurmanji speaking population in Eastern Anatolia. During the 17th to the 20th century the Zaza as well as the Kurmanji speaking Kurds were widely known as a bigoted and brutal people group (see Karl May 1951; 2.3.3.2.5; 3.6).

---

[70] Documentations show that in some Islamic countries during the Middle Ages until the 20th century Christians and Jews could only ride donkeys, had to bow down before a Muslim and were not allowed to look a Muslim in the face (Niebuhr 1778:81-83).

2.3.3.5 Sunnism (Southern and Eastern Group)

Sunnism is a derivation from the term *Sunnah* (Arabic سنة), which refers to the sayings and actions of Hz. Mohammed that are recorded in *Hadiths* (collections of narrations regarding Hz. Mohammed). The Hadith is nowadays the central guidance for the spiritual and practical life of a Sunni. The Islamic clergy speaks of the *Hadith* as the flesh on the bone, the latter being the *Qur'an*.

The above mentioned Sunni re-islamisation movement in the 17th century was mainly focusing on the Southern and Eastern Group due to their location on one of the Silk Roads (Laut 1996:31; 2.1; 2.3.1.2). Although we should assume a split before this period between the Shi'ism following Alevitic Northern Group and the Sunni Southern / Eastern Group the gap widened. There was never again a time of coming closer between the two groups which were split based on religious mistrust. This changed during the 20th century when the upheavals that led to the foundation of the Republic of Turkey challenged the Northern and the Southern Group. The Northern Group was confronted by government led religious persecution and the Southern Group by the downfall of the Sunni Caliphate which functioned as a support for orthodox Islam (2.3.1.3.2; 2.3.3.5; 3.6).

The recent Zaza movement shows some signals of approximation based on the need for a linguistic standardization and the distinction to Kurdish nationalism (2.2.3.6). The Sunnis claimed Alevis were either non-believing heathen or sectarians of Islam; in consequence they were allocated as *taboo* (1.1.3.3; 2.3.2.1.4; 2.3.2.1.4; 2.3.3.2.5). In reverse, Alevis blame Sunnis of being the nemesis of Shi'ism especially Alevism. Hence Alevis grew a sense of superiority and absolute refusal of Sunnism (Kehl-Bodrogi 1989:228-230).

2.3.3.5.1 Four Schools of Sunnism - Hanafi

Sunnism represents the official belief system in the Republic of Turkey and is therefore closely linked to the national consciousness which supports a more or less underlying Pan-Islamism and Pan-Turkism. The Hanafi movement finds its origins in the pre-Islamic epoch (2.2.8.1; 2.3.3.2.5; 2.3.3.5; Table 22) and started as inner-Islamic school in the 8th century AD / 2nd AH. It describes people in the area of today's Saudi Arabia who followed a monotheistic concept of God and who were called "deists" or "Followers of God". Their belief in a creator and their devotion to Arabic as a language of cult marked them out from Jewish and Christian fellows. The Biblical Abraham formed their role model as he was a non-Jewish and non-Christian "Proto-believer, who believed in a Creator"

(Troeger 2007:236-237). The prophet Hz. Mohammed was very much influenced by their doctrine, as he claimed later on the association with any divinities beside the original Creator God a sin (:236-237; *shirk*). In Islam this movement is continued and led to the formation of an independent *madrassa* (School of Islamic Law). The four School of Laws are *Hanafi*, *Shafi'i*, *Maliki* and *Hanbali* (Schirrmacher 1994a:283ff). While the Kurmanji speaking "Kurds" are mainly of the Shafi'i school, the Southern Zaza are from the Hanafi *madrassa* (Berkes 1959:44 cit. in Gökalp around 1900 AD; RH 2008 *Zaza and Zazaki*; Nestmann 2002:548, 552).

2.3.3.5.2 Mewlid – A Poem representing a Religious Stance

One interesting religious document which proclaims the miracle of the birth of the prophet in the Islamic world is called *Mewlid Nebi / Mevlid* (Appendix 5). Its translation is one of the oldest written testimonies of Zazaki from around 1900. The Arabic term *Mevlit* means "birth place", "birthday", "coming to life". It became a genre on its own, following the form of *mesnevi* (*masnavi*, a Persian poem by *Jalal al-Din Muhammad Rumi* 13th century AD / 6th century AH; Aksoy 2004:482-484; Ateş 1979:127-133).

Traditionally it follows the principle: Problem/Theme – Complication – Resolution. During its existence the Mewlid became a sort of prayer for Muslims. It is mainly recited or sung during

- the celebration of the prophet's birthday, the night of *Qadr* (Lailatul Qadr' Arabic: ليلة القدر the night of the revelation of the first verses of the Qur'an) which is in the Islamic calendar the most spiritual night,
- circumcision parties,
- wedding celebrations,
- funeral ceremonies, mourning and
- lamentation periods (*cewresê* the forty days).

The tradition of celebrating the prophet's birthday started officially during the Fatimid dynasty in Egypt (969-1171 AD /3rd century AH). The *Mevlit* traditions were not restricted to the Prophet Hz. Mohammed's birthday but also to birthday parties in honour of Hz. Ali, Fatima and the ruling caliph's. Some few Islamic scholars regarded Mevlit as a form of *bi'dat* (bad innovation) and urged its prohibition. The first recorded Mevlit among the Sunni Muslims was composed by *Ebu Said Muzaffereddin Gökbörü* governor of Iraq's *Erbil* province and *Saladin Ayubi's* close relative, in 1207. It follows a list of different versions of the

Mewlid arranged by their authors and their biographic data as well as an example of their dialects and spellings:
- *Ehmedê Xasi* (1867-1951), was born in the village of *Hazan*, in the district of Lice. This Mewlid was published in 1899 (Xasî 1899). Published also in the *Hawar* Journal in 1933 and transcribed by Malmisanîj in the magazine *Hevi* Nr. 4 (1985). This is the most researched Mewlid (Merdımin 2005). An evaluation is made by Lezgin 2011: Internet). Title: *Mewliduén-Nebiyyiél-Úureyşiyyi*. (Mewlid of the Prophet).
  - *Ez bı bismıllahi ibtida kena* (I was praised in the name of the highest).
  - *Razıqê 'aman û xasan piya kena* (Praise and honour go together?)
- *Osman Efendi Babıj* was born in *Siverek* district of Şanlıurfa province (1852-1929).
  - *Ame Nuh menga çehari beguman* (It came Noah the forth month)
  - *Va kı: 'Pizey to yo wahirê Quran'*. (He said: Your inner parts are watching over the Qur'an).
- *Mela M. Eli Hunij* was born in 1930 in the village of the *Hun / Hûnis* in the district of *Palu*. Title: *Mela Hunij and Mevlidî Peyxemberî*
  - "Medina sukey peyxembêr, islami heyna biy sey vêr Xelifeti resay 'Umêr, (Medina town of the prophet, Islam spread from there to the Caliphate of Umer)
  - dinya ra şi peyxembêr ma". (the world went to our prophet)
- *Mela Puexi Kamıl* was born in Puex / Poxi, both a precinct and a tribal name, in the province of Bingöl (Aşağıköy), in 1938. Title: *Mela Kamilê Puexê And Mewlıdê Nebi*
  - "Nur to ruaşn da pêro dinya, (The light shone over the whole earth)
  - Hemını Riy erdûn d' tari nêverda derûn dı". (The whole face of the earth and hell was not given to all)
- *Mela Mehemedê Murada* lived in the village of *Murada* (Muradun) in the district of *Hani*. Title: *Mela Mehemedê Muradan And Mewlıdi Zazaki*
  - "Hukmi yi qaim o ta Weqti qiyam. (Right and wisdom was time)
  - Pe yi cehdey xwi şinasnen xas û 'am". (Behind him went man and people).

The *Mewlid Nebi*, presented in Appendix 5, is from *Osman Efendi Babıj* (2.1.2.3). My informant presented it in the Arabic script. After transferring it into Latin script we translated it in German and English. The *Haci Hiob* – Osman was born in 1853 in the city Siverek. His father was *Haci Hiob*, his mother *Emina*. The father *Haci Hiob* was a judge in the town *Suleymaniye* and he died there. The gentleman Osman studied in Bagdad at the University, and when he finished here he came back to Siverek. He stayed there some time, after that he went to Egypt. There he studied at the faculty in *Ezheriye*, finished, and again came back to Siverek, to work there as Mufti and he became a member of the city council and chairman at the court. Osman became popular and he was warmly welcomed in the area of *Siverek*. About his reputation, it is said: He was gentle, humble and a friend to the people. He never hurt anyone and his door was always open to guests. People came to him to learn about religion and questions of the Islamic Law. In these days our people knew less Turkish and they asked the Mufti, "we don't know Arabic and Turkish, we ask you to preach and teach in Zazaki, and recite us the poem of the Prophet's birthday (*Mewlid*) in Zazaki, so that we understand the things about him." *Osman* took their request serious and supported them in understanding things better, by preaching and teaching in Zazaki. In the year 1886 he published the poem of the Prophet's birthday in Zazaki and read it. The village that *Osman* was from is called Bab that is why he is also called *Osman the Baban*. *Osman* died on the 24th March 1929. Bab is a village in Siverek as well as the name of a tribe, Chirab, Keloschk, Boxcik and Kufri are closely linked to Bab. A few say that some extended families from Bab came from the city Gerger and the village Gudhayıg. They call it Alıkan. Bab derives from Arabic and means in Zazaki "door" or "gate". When they from Gudhayıg came to Bab, the Arabs left the village. This birthday poem was sent in 1906 to Diyarbakır, but nobody was able to read it. Following the Osmanic Law (1908) of the town regent from Piturge (province Malatya) *Faiz Bedırxan* took it to İstanbul but there also nobody was interested in reading it, which was a shame. The poem of the birthday of *Osman Efendi* was transcribed from Arabic in 1933 (copy of the original is with the author) by *Celadet Ali Bedirxan Scham* (sources: taken from my informant MP 2012; Berz 1995b: 33-35; Hêvi, Nr. 2. Mai, 77-85. Paris; Appendix 5)

Every genre follows different styles and performances. The main literary arrangement of Mewlid is performed by five main parts:
- "*münacat*" or plea to God,
- "*viladet*" the birth of the prophet Hz. Mohammed,
- "*risalet*" or being of the final prophet,
- "*mirac*" or the prophet Hz. Mohammed's ascent to heaven,
- "*rıhlet*" or the demise of the prophet and "dua" or prayer.

The rhyme of the Mewlid follows the general verse form of A A' B B' C C' ... Every paragraph takes the same shape. A common refrain (chorus) finishes a paragraph and signals the end of one section (see also 2.3.5.3).

The importance of the Mewlid, in the religious setting of the Zaza people, becomes obvious when following the mourning ceremony after someone's death. Almost all members of the community know parts of the poem by heart and can recite it in the form of a prayer. This practice builds up the common identity of the society. As an outsider one is not expected to share this practice. The liturgical practice parallels the Christian "Our father" (Matthew 6:9) or Psalm 23 as well as the Jewish credo *Shma Israel* in 5Mose 6:4. It is not only the liturgical, but also the textual aspect of the Mewlid which parallels the Jewish and Christian revelation (Hebrew Bible, New Testament). As approved by textual criticism these revelations are preceding the Qur'an, the Hadith (Islamic tradition) and thus function as a template to the Mewlid. Now the references and connections between these written sources are about historical persons. Noah, Iob, Maria, Hz. Jesus of Nazareth and other protagonists of the Jewish peoples, the Christian and the Islamic history are linked to the Prophet Hz. Mohammed. The Mewlid connects these persons not to their deeds, described in the revelations, but to their importance for the Islamic umma (community of faith). As a poetic document it is used to convey comfort about the Islamic religion or to strengthen faith. It does not, above all, as other divine revelations, claim to be historically relevant.

2.3.3.5.3 Leadership – Islamic Clergy

Sunnism adopts from its beginning a strong hierarchical structure. The concept of *Imams* (Zazaki: *imam*) led into a system of Islamic clergy who were represented by theologians called *mullah* (ملاه; Zazaki *mıllah*). This term means in general a religiously educated teacher and is also found in e.g. in Sephardic Jewish communities, which use Arabic or the closely related Semitic language of Hebrew. Due to Islamic belief a *mullah* can never be a woman. There is a domain of man controlling the paternalistic system of *mullaharchy*. The *sheikhdom* and the *mullaharchy* are closely related. Whereas the *sheikhdom* is built on descent and represents a religious and political stance for a kindred ethnic group, the mullaharchy is locally oriented and builds on theological knowledge and training of the devotees, though is sometimes inherited by descent. The *madrassa* is the centre of theological discussion and training. The mullaharchy often plays together with the *sheikhdom* to gain and increase its political influence on the people group within which it is functioning In history the Ottoman Empire with its Caliphate represented a very huge mullaharchy. Its local leaders derived their position by the Sultan's degree. A mullaharchy in general represents the Islamic clergy like the Western Churches do with their system of Cardinals, Bishops, Pastors or Elders. The hierarchical structure of *clergy* is known throughout the antique cults and religions, the world religions and social structures in general (Eliade 1991).

In the Zaza community of the Southern and Eastern Group the *sheikhdom* plays an important role. This is mainly because the stratification of the religious and political leadership is performed by the *sheikh* and his kindred as well as the *agha* and his kinship (2.3.4.3). Yet another party comes into play represented by the *mıllah*. The conception of *mullaharchy* in the Zaza society is a mix of descent and occasionally educational institution. It is in general expected that a family which holds the position of a *mıllah* in a village will be concerned about its kindred. Thus a son or other closely related kindred male is sent for theological education. The theological centres within the Zaza area were Çermik , Palu, Muş, Hani / Heni. Outside of the Zaza homeland if affordable, people were sent to Syria (*Xet*), Bagdad (*Bağdad*), Mekka (*Mek*) or İstanbul (*Estemol*) for their theological education. They often came back with a wide knowledge that gained them superficial appreciation which extended for a couple of generations. Every mosque (*camii*) had his *mıllah*. Sometimes the position of *mıllah* was passed on by descent if the relative was theologically educated; in other cases the *cemat / cem* appointed the *mıllah* to his role. The *mıllah* in the Zaza homeland was always a Zaza using *Arabic*, which was used as the language of religious wisdom for cultic practices. Zazaki was used for the informal training of the devotees. In some cases, e.g. in larger cities with Turkish population, Turkish replaced Zazaki. There was sometimes the attempt from the Turkish nation to install Turkish speaking *hocas* (Tk. for *mıllah / mullah*) as religious leaders in the Zaza homeland area. This was never accepted and did not work out in the long run. On the other hand *Arabic* never made it as a language of wider communication. It found its niche as a religious cult language while in more recent times Turkish often replaced *Zazaki* as the language of theological education.

2.3.3.6 Different World Conception – Alevism and Sunnism (2 Ex.)

	Alevism	**Sunnism**
Death (world and afterworld)	- Transition process from the "here" to the "there" - Both worlds are interrelated, a person can move from hither to yon - Eschatology as Reincarnation (eternal life cycle) and metempsychosis (soul transfer)	- No return or crossing from the physical into the metaphysical or spiritual sphere - Eschatology as intransigent Last Judgement (Paradise or Hell) - Dead is perceived as dreadful
Purity / Impurity Manipulation	- Humanism asks for reciprocal respect, gender and social equality, forgiveness, - The sphere of purity is to be in harmony with nature and people - The sphere of impurity is bordered by hurting others or nature: a. Disrespect against elders, family or tribal leaders, b. exploitation of nature, c. infringement of community law (e.g. insulting women or children)	- The *umma* (religious community) is to be held in high esteem. - Spiritual life overlaps with physical needs. - The sphere of Purity is balanced by playing for safety, not to cross borders. In consequence an ongoing struggle of staying pure limits personal freedom of movement. - The sphere of Impurity is marked by a. exploitation of the Islamic Law (*şeriat*; e.g. *şırk*) b. Disrespect for elders, family, religious or tribal leaders, and c. losing face by luring envy, evil spirits, and wrath of Allah.
	-	-

2.3.3.7 Modern Religious Life

Many of the concepts mentioned above are lost concerning their historical background but still reflected by practices in the Zaza cult (Çağlayan 1998:178). It is good to understand the basic principles that drive the modern religious life of the Zaza people.

Diagram 13 Zaza Cult - Religious Life

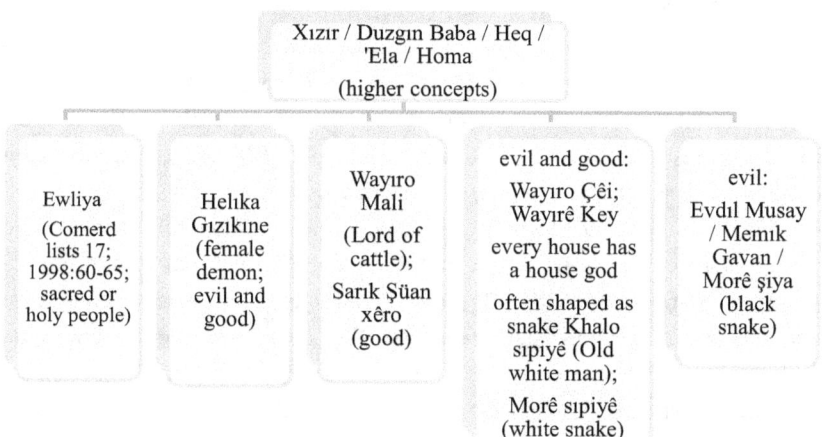

One note about *Helıka Gızıkıne* (Comerd 1997:32.37). This female divine force is considered to be evil and good. She acts like a wild kid and rides a horse, drives people mad, but also cares for children. The sacred concept of *cewresê* (the forty) is related to her. Meaning she has forty children that she takes and deals with (:36-37).

Obviously the divine forces that are mentioned above could not be seen as only good or mainly evil. The religious concepts of the Zaza allow for divinities, gods and goddesses that are either good or evil or both. The Western concept of angels, demons and evil spirits only covers such concepts partially. It would be better to speak of a pantheon which reflects the physical world in a way that unforeseeable or supernatural events are taken as activities from a non-physical realm that have an effect on the material world (2.5.1).

Nowadays the religious daily life of the Zaza people shows some specifics that are of interest here. Religiously one finds a clear cut split between the Alevitic Northern Group and the Sunni Southern and Eastern Group (2.3.1.1; 2.3.3.5). Alevism as it is practised today reflects elements from Zoroastrianism which have not been researched in depth so far (Shindeldecker 2001; also Kehl-Bodrogi 1989).

2.3.3.7.1 Christian-Islamic Influence on the Religious Identity

The religious development of the Zaza is accompanied by Jewish, Christian and Islamic Influence (2.3.3.2.3; 2.3.3.2.4; 2.3.3.2.5). The Diaspora of the Jewish people until the 6th century BC, the expansion of Christianity starting from the 1st century AD / 5th century BH and the spread of Islam until the 7th century AD / 1st century AH all started off close to the Zaza homeland. The latter two religions had a strong impact, because they are expansive by a commission of sending. The closeness to the former Edessa and Diyarbakır influenced the Zaza people enormously. Edessa, today's Şanlıurfa / Urfa (Zazaki *Rı'ha*, Kurmanji *Riha*, Aramaic *Urhoy*) was a centre of Eastern Christianity (Byzanz) and a well known Christian theological centre. The same applies to Diyarbakır (Zazaki and Kurmanji *Diyarbekir / Amed*; Aramaic *Amid / Amed / Amida*) as part of the patriarchate of Antioch. In 638 AD (year 17 AH) Islamic invaders conquered Edessa and Diyarbakır and Islam called out the *dar al-Islam* or *dar as-Salam* (House of Islam / Peace in contrast to *dar al-harb* House of War). Both centres represented Christianity, namely the West Syriac Church in the form of the Aramaeans and later the Armenians. Both centres were close to the Zaza and Kurmanji speaking population of Eastern Anatolia (3.4.1.1). The so called Great Experiment in the 19th century AD / 12th century AH was meant to strengthen Christian Churches through Western Christian development workers. It found its abrupt end in the genocide of the targeted people groups in 1915 and WWI (Blincoe 1998; Kieser 2000; 2.1.4.5; 2.6.2). When looking at the deeper influence of Christianity on the Zaza culture one has to go back to the times of the Apostle Paul and his journeys. The hometown area of Paul is not that far from the Zaza area and referring to the letter to the Galatians it is possible that he visited the area of the Zaza people (Apg 13,14; 14,6; 16,1-6; Siebenthal 2002 on Acts 16:6: CD-ROM; Rienecker & Maier 2002 on "Galatien" [Galatia]: CD-ROM; Seufert & Kubaseck 2004:56; 2.3.3.2.4; 2.3.3.7.1; 3.4.2). The foundation of the West Syriac and the Armenian Apostolic Church would well fit with the Northern Galatian Theory (Neill 1974:30). But so far there is no documentation concerning that period and the influence on the Zaza people.

The prohibition of rabbit and pork goes back to Islamic influence. The rabbit restriction reaches even back to Pre-Islamic times when the rabbit, as a menstruating animal, was emphasized as *haram*, or unclean (2.3.2.1). Parallel to the rabbit defilement the bathroom is a restricted area into which no food, clothing or object used for daily life will be brought (Jakobson 2009 and cit. in 2004:109-114).

2.3.3.7.2 Christian Influence and Practices

The Zaza people express the knowledge of a Christian history in their traditions as well as in their practices. This information is only reluctantly passed on in form and guise, since the Zaza people do not clearly trace back their origin. That's why today we have no unequivocal evidence of a Christian past by sung or orally transmitted traditions. But one finds a variety of hints as exemplified in the following (Questionnaire Werner 2005). The wide extension of the Christian Development Aid in relation to the Zaza people presented in this presentation refers to the long history of interests of European Powers in the region of Eastern Anatolia.

Christian influence was also harmful to the Zaza. During the 8th and 9th centuries the Byzantine Rulers tried to deport and resettle the tribal and feudal people groups of Eastern Anatolia (Izady 1992:163). At the same time they experienced in the 11th century AD / 4th AH threats by the advancing Islamic Seljuks. The surrounding Kurds and the Ottoman Empire were suppressing the Zaza people politically during the whole age (serfdom and financial stifling by taxes; Izady 1992:96, 163-164). If the Zaza people settled in their homeland long ago, then the Byzantine Emperors did no better than the following empires. For some people groups in Eastern Anatolia the Islamic expansion was received as a relief (3.1.1.1).

The Christian influences can be traced back to the close vicinity of the Zaza ethnicity to the Armenian Apostolic Church. The Armenians formed one of the oldest National Churches - the other being the kingdom of *Orshoene* in the North of Mesopotamia (Neill 1990:27) - from the 3rd century AD. Since then their kingdoms were based in the area of the Zaza people and further East (Latourette 1953:23, 105). The Christians provided the technical knowledge for irrigation systems, pottery, the textiles sector and craft. Later on they developed military features to guard the Armenian kingdoms against enemies from outside. The Armenian relationship between Zaza and Kurmanji speakers caused conversions to Christianity as mentioned by Izady. One has to expect that it happened vice versa after the phase of Arabization and (7th – 9th century AD / 1st – 2nd century AH) Islamisation (11th to 13th century AD / 4th to 7th century AH; Ye'or 2009:58-60). Christians also converted to Islam, either forcefully or to avoid being the subject to discrimination. For the Northern Alevitic Group we have no report that Christians converted to the very attractive belief system of Alevism, but the practice of godparenthood (*kerwa*) and intermarriage points to such assumptions (2.3.3.2.2; 2.3.3.3).

Some of the Zaza people of the Bingöl area take an oath by the term "*Kelun Kadın / Kadım*" and refer thereby to the Old Testamen. Also they use the name *Mıshef* (Qur'an) an *Tarat / Torat* (Old Testament) using an Armenian pronounciation (MP 2012 Personal Communication at 2nd Bingöl Symposium TC Bingöl University from 04-06th May 2012). In the Dersim, Hani and Genc area - close to Varto - some traditions that have been handed down talk about many Armenians that entered Alevism. In the same way an Islamisation movement pressed Armenians to convert in the 17th century AD to Islam, whereby their Manichaeistic influence swept over as syncretism of their new religion. The Bingol province and the Varto area which is still today split into a Northern Alevi and Southern Shafi'i Group holds a rich pool of "dönme"-traditions (conversion stories).

Before the persecution of the Armenian Apostolic Church in 1892, 1895/1896 and the ethnocide in 1915/1916 (Baumann 2007:41, 81), Armenians were legally second class citizens (*dhimmi*) from an Islamic point of view with equal respect in public under the Islamic leaders of the Zaza (Izady 1992:164; RH 2007 *Zaza Stämme* [Zaza Tribes]; 2.1.4.4; 3.4). In the 15th century AD conversions by Muslims to Christianity from Zaza and Kurds are also described in Nikitine (cit. in Izady 1992:164). Even today e.g. the villagers of *Cimnazköy* close to *Hani* are considered to be "impure and pagan" (*gayri*) and were officially called "Gayri". The Muslim community looked at them as being Christians or Animists (RH 2006 *Zaza und Nachbarvölker*). Christian Development aid was focusing on the Zaza community, mainly the Northern Group, in the 19th century (Kieser 2000). The experiences then, be they good or bad, are part of the reflection on the recent relationship between Christianity and the Zaza people (s. Map of Christian Developmental Aid from the 19th century by Grundemann 1867:39-44). The German theologian and Christian development worker *Johannes Lepsius* (Baumann 2007a) together with the Danish Christian Developmental worker *Karen Jeppe* championed the support for the Armenians (Sick 1932; Löffler 2005:272-277; Reifler 2005:221-222). Both provided medical and political support to the Armenians out of Europe. Whereas Lepsius travelled back and forth to promote the issue of the Armenians in German politics, mainly before the German Kaiser

2 The Zaza

Wilhelm II, Karen Jeppe lived in Eastern Anatolia with the people group. Lepsius' organisation called "Deutsche Orient Mission" (*German Orient Mission*; DOM) became the example of subsequent Christian interventions in the Islamic world (Löffler 2005:337; Schäfer 1932). Jeppe concentrated her energy on her work as a teacher in one of the Lepsian Armenian orphanage's. Later, she earned the title "voice of the Armenians" as she protested before the Ottoman rulers as well as the European powers against the emergency situation of the Armenians (Reifler 2005:222; Baumann 2007a).

RH told me that in the late 1890s and early 1900s his grandfather was receiving education from American Christian Developmental Aid workers at a school in the larger Armenian city of *Çüngüş* within 20 miles of his city *Çermik*. Not only educational training but also medical help was provided in a hospital there. The schools as well as the hospitals were always considered to be foreign (American) run Christian stations. The surrounding Zaza welcomed this help and their local tribal leaders supported their running, although the main focus of the Christian development workers was on the Armenians. RH's grandfather was so well educated during his childhood that he achieved the religious career of a *Hoca* or *mullah* (Muslim religious teacher; both positions were not differentiated in the villages). The Developmental workers also offered Biblical Studies and the promotion of Christian values and generated an inter-religious debate in the East which developed into a political issue (see notes from the meeting by the author).

Schäfer informs us about the whole spread of medical care from DOM in Eastern Anatolia since 1897 when it was started officially (1932:16). Johannes Lepsius focused from the beginning "on the Christian work under Hz. Mohammedans" (Lepsius 1925 cit. in Baumann 2007a:41). He was overwhelmed by the negative experiences of the "Fabersche Christian Development Agency" (Drescher 1998:29; Lepsius 1897 cit. in Baumann 301) and the persecution of the Armenians in the years 1895/96 und 1915/16. As a result and because of the tense political situation on the Armenians the DOM concentrated on this Christian *millet* (Schäfer cit. in Baumann 2007a:42, 81). Feldtkeller describes different approaches of Christian Development Aid in these days and differentiates between "direct" and "indirect" strategy in the 19th century. American presbyterian-anglican Churches were involved in the "direct" approach, what means that as foreigners Muslims were openly presented with the Christian message. Political and economical reasons caused the "indirect" approach, in that the existing

Churches were strengthened in this way to mobilize them for outreach to the surrounding Muslim populations (Feldtkeller 1997:86-91; *Great Experiment*; 2.1.4.5).

Rudimentary Christian practices are nowadays not any more perceived to be Christian. In the last three centuries the dispute of the Zaza people with other religions, mainly Christianity started out to confront the culture. This dispute started in the Diaspora but reached the homeland via the returnee or the close interaction between the Zaza in the Diaspora and the homeland. The emigration situation caused the Zaza people to think about practices that could have a Christian background and either to reject them out of fear of losing their Islamic identity or to use them to find common ground with their host culture.

Links to original Christian practice include the painting of a cross on the forehead as well as the laying-on of hands in cases of illness, or to protect someone against deterioration and to express convalescence. A practice that is well known in the Mediterranean is the placing of a metal hook (*da'hri*) under the pillow of a mother who has recently given birth during her forty days of impurity (*cewresê* meaning "the 40"). Also as a practice of protection against evil, as well as a blessing, a cross is painted on the *meşk*, a pouch made out of the skin of a goat and used to prepare yoghurt. The whole procedure corresponds with the request that the blessing will also apply to the food that is prepared in that *meşk* (RH 2005 *Questionnaire on the Zaza Worldview*). Another practice is to light a candle on Friday for a close relative who died recently. This reminds us of the sanctuary lamp of the Roman Catholic Churches (2.4.2.2).

In the Alevitic Northern Group a holiday called *Khalê Gağani* is celebrated. *Khalo Sıpe*, as it is called also, reflects the main character and resembles the biography of *Nicolaus from Myra* (4th century AD) well known as "Santa Claus" or "Nicolaus" in the West and celebrated within the holiday of "Christmas" without the weight of Christian reference as expressed in the New Testament (Dewran 2007). Another practice in the Northern Group is represented by the ritual of immersing a baby three times for naming. The phrase "I name you …" accompanies the symbolic procedure (Jacobson 2009 *Anthropological Insights*; Jacobson cit. in Bailey 2004:110; against it Asatrian & Gevorgian 1988:500). This practice resembles the ritual of infant baptism in the Old Byzantine Church (Müller 2001:680). It has to be added that baptism has its origin in many religions as a ritual cleansing. But combining it with the naming of an infant and the blessing of God became popular in the early Church.

2.3.3.7.3 Zoroastrianism Influence and Practices

Another religious influence on the Zaza was introduced by *Zoroastrianism* (Zazaki: *serduşt*; 2.3.3.2.2). This had an enduring affect to this day and led into a cult that adores nature and leads the devotee into close touch with it. In the whole group this becomes vivid in sanctuaries and places of adoration on mountains, oddly formed trees, shelter groves (Kehl-Bodrogi 1989:145-150), springs, caves which are protected by non-human creatures living therein (s. Hayıg 2007; e.g. snake-man). One step further goes the Alevitic worldview of the Northern Group by an equalisation of humans *in* and *with* nature. As an outcome they develop a socialistic tendency towards Marxism. This is politically forced by lack of alternatives and drives the younger generation towards a realization of the principles of Alevism. Their expectations of "harmony" and "peace" are grounded on an implementation of Alevism within the existing socialistic political structure (Steinbach 1996:379).

The *sun*, *moon* as well as *fire* hold unique positions in the tradition of the Zaza people and are objects of veneration. As such it is indecent to urinate in the direction of the sun or fire (2.1.1.5.2). To emphasize the importance of the sun, an oath (*sond*) can be taken on the sun, but it is forbidden and emphasized as a taboo to swear or curse by either the sun or the moon. The half moon is considered an ideal of beauty, e.g. ... *na 'hendık xaseka zey asmida pancêsiya* ("her beauty was as the moon in his 15th (day)" Hayıg 2007:16). The powers behind shelter groves, trees, springs or mountains are accused of throwing lightning and causing thunder during Thunderstorms (s. a. 2.3.2.1.4). Trespassing of this religious-cultural threshold is morally reprehensible and therefore a *tabooed* (1.1.3.3; 2.3.2.1.4; 2.3.2.1.4; 2.3.3.2.5). Punishment was given from the larger unit like the *ezbet* that is the conglomeration of extended families as well as from the nuclear family (RH 2008 *Zaza and Zazaki*). The sphere of taboo was eagerly protected and any person who did not respect it was ostracized (2.3.5.5).

The worship of the sun, the moon and the stars was reported by the American traveller Melville Chater who witnessed it during a stay at night in a village in Dersim (Chater 1928). An adoration of the sun, the moon and the stars is obvious, but it is not quite obvious how deep such worship goes. Recently the Zaza people are living on remembrance of these traditions and they adhere to a general respect of the nature and its environment.

One other area of Zoroastrian influence can be found in the pilgrimage to holy places called *jiare*. These are trees, high mountains e.g. *Baba Duzgın* (Dedekurban 1994: 12, 15) or locations of unique natural phenomenon. Here the headwater of the *Munzur River* with its rich history in oral tradition plays an important role (Jacobson cit. in Sweetnam 2004:228-229). The village *Ziyaret* is close to the source spring and it is said that the goddess *Anahit* is worshipped there. As a sacred place even enemies make peace there with each other so that a positive influence is expected from the headwater area (Halajyan 1973). Recently a sign in Turkish and English at the headwater spring of the Munzur River explains how father Munzur while travelling lost some milk on the ground and thereby planted new summer pastures. The imminent building of a dam as part of the GAP project (South Eastern Anatolia project / Great Anatolia Project) is destroying the villages of the Munzur River and the construction is accompanied by many protests (Seufert & Kubaseck 2004:20). The goddess *Anahit* can be traced back to pagan Armenia. Her temple was in the region of Dersim the former Armenian districts of *Mananaghi* and *Yekeghyac*.

The practiced form of Folk Islam reveals some linking *to* and *with* Animism, Zoroastrianism, and Christianity (Wiher 2007:224). Predominantly, in Near and Middle East cultures that either practice or which are historically influenced by Zoroastrianism such mixing is observable (Winter 2008:4). From a historico-religious viewpoint this process refers to syncretism (Reifler 2005:32).

In its specifically mystic orientation the Dervish congregations acquired vogue within the Zaza (2.3.1.3.1; 2.3.1.3.2; 2.3.3.2; Richter 2006:6). Mysticism describes the spiritual sphere in which a human experiences the transcendental, by passing the border between the physical and metaphysical reality. As in the Islamic Dervish orders the goal is mainly to reach oneness between the *ego* and the higher spiritual being called *God* (Lepsius cit. in Baumann 2007a:89). In ecstatic dances which lead to a trance-like state the divine unification is at the centre. Out of this setting a mix of religions is quite possible because they are playing a secondary role. The so called "travelling Dervishes" and the foundation of order-monasteries can be traced back to Buddhism. (Laut 1996:31-32).

The above mentioned prohibition to eat rabbit can also be traced back to Zoroastrianism. In the same way whistling is perceived as *xırav*, or evil since it is emphasized as calling the devil or as prostitution (Jacobson 2009 and cit. in Bailey 2004).

Another observation from Armenian traveller *Andranik*, who travelled through the Dersim area in the beginning of 20th century who reports an unusual perspective concerning a man or woman that is a sleepwalker or lunatic in a delirium. If people are considered to be in that state they are said to be blessed and archangels have brought him / her to the sky, to meet the Lord and he / she would see the wonders of heaven and the horrors of hell. When he or she wakes up, they can disclose information about the place of each person in hell or heaven. Such superstitious knowledge attracts people from all around to visit the "clairvoyant", with the expectation of being informed of what is prepared for him or her after death. This practice can be traced back to the Zoroastrian legend of *Arda Virap*. The main hero drinks *haoma*, falls into ecstasy and travels to hell to learn the divine truth, which reveals dualism as the basic principle of life.

Another practice is found in the prohibition of throwing away cut hair or nails. This practice is found in *Khorazan* and has its roots back to Zoroastrianism and the Zoroastrian creed. Here the pollution of e.g. water is strictly forbidden. Throwing away parts of the body can cause damage because spirits or other human can take it and use it for cursing. Such beliefs are also found in Animism.

2.3.3.8 Summary

At this point a summary of the inter-religious influence on the Zaza culture and their belief system is shown in the following table:

Table 23 Religious Influence

Influence	Impact	Practice
Animism (basic)	- in touch with nature - adoration of striking characteristics in nature (tree or rock formations, springs, caves, mountain tops, shelter groves) - spiritual powers surround striking specifics of nature	- localities of worship are put under *taboo* - the Zaza people are living closely with those powers as they are invocated for protection or help (*namaz* = prayer)
Zoroastrianism / Parsiism / serduşt (Zazaki: since the 5th century BC)	- Conceptualization of Dualism in relation to Good-Evil, Light-Darkness and the interpersonal relationship (e.g. Hate-Love; Peace-War) - the basic elements of nature are regarded as balanced (fire, light, earth, water) - imbalance or disturbance is	- the sun and fire must not be made impure or defiled by improper behaviour (e.g. urinating in their direction) - an oath on the Sun affirms it - fire reveals its very own powers - disturbances between peo-

Influence	Impact	Practice
	treated as imbalance that asks for balancing	ple and people and nature must be solved to keep the balance of the dualistic powers
Christianity	- Jewish and Christians are counted as second class citizens (*jihad*, tax obligation system, job restrictions) but respected (Armenians; Christian minorities) - A theological-religious rejection of persons of another religion goes without concrete persecution	- *da'hri*: an iron hook underneath the pillow of a mother who has given birth and remaining throughout the time of defilement, that is *cewresê* (the forty) to protect her and the child against witches, demons and evil forces - the symbol of a cross on the forehead in case of illness and the laying on of hands to protect against more evil - the symbol of the cross on the *meşk* as a sign of blessing (*berka ano*), this blesses the yoghurt that is prepared in this preparation vessel
Islam (since the 16th century AD)	- Folk Islam connects all religious tendencies - the *evil eye* superimposes Islamic values (five pillars) and then relates to evil influence - Islam is perceived as the highest stage of the religious development which replaces the deficient Animistic, Zoroastrian, Jewish and Christian forerunner - Sunnism is based on the	- Excerpts of Qur'an are used as charms (*nustış*) - defence of negative / evil powers - mosque attendance not obligatory - emphasis of inner values of Islam like brotherhood, peace, prayer of the heart - the plenary assembly of the village community fulfils the religious require-

Influence	Impact	Practice
	Hanafi school of Islamic law (Southern Group) and a mix with the Shafi'i *madrassa* (Eastern Group) - Shi'ism of Alevitic orientation (Northern Group)	ments of Islam (*cemat*) since there all religious and political issues are regulated

After this overview of the Zaza religion we will now focus on the social structure of the Zaza people in former times and how it developed to modern-time organization.

2.3.4 Social Structure

When speaking of the Zaza society the differences of an *emic* and *etic* view as well as the background of the informants comes rigorously into play (see Preface). Mehmed S. Kaya looks at the Zaza people from an emic point of view as Zaza although he is living in the Diaspora. His view of the Zaza society reflects the situation of the Eastern Group (Solhan; 2011:4). He emphasizes peasantry and the feudalistic background of the Zaza as ruled by landowners and paying tribute as destitute employees. As mentioned above this description does not cover all of the Zaza people and also not the different historical developments within this people group.

The Zaza society underwent huge changes. Persecution and mass migration by virtue of economical improvement towards the West of Turkey and Europe since 1960 led to new concepts in the order of the Zaza people's society. However to understand the overlaying and more recent settings we need to look into history and the structure then. In a second stage recent developments will be considered.

The Zaza society formed a homogenous *Three-Class-system*. Thus its collectivistic orientation is built on descent and kinship. This principle has to be emphasized since it is a deep social structure which performs all of the social stratification within the community. The individual is determined by its descent and its kinship. In contrast to the West, all that a person represents is not built on his achievement or knowledge but on his family background. The individual is born into one of these classes from which normally there is no way out. Thus interclass transmission is not possible. Once again kinship by descent represents the basic institutional setting. A person is classified not according to his job or deeds but to his kinship relation within the wider community (Kaya 2011:18).

Class Societies in general do not offer disparate access to economic resources or power, but dissimilar access to prestige (Ember & Ember 1993:142). Shaw and Van Engen present an overview of cultural types and their subordinating systems that I use to describe the social structure of the Zaza people (2003:139). The reference to the New Testament makes sense because the Jewish society of the New Testament offers similar structures, the more so as the widespread Jewish Diaspora, reaching far beyond the Zaza homeland area is well reflected in the book of Acts and the New Testament letters (2.3.3.2.3).

> In collectivistic societies, people stay in the status in which they were born. Social standing is determined by birth, one's ethnic group in general, and one's status within that ethnic group. There is little, if any, social mobility, upward or downward. Even when the elite are dispossessed and defamed by their elite peers, they remain elite at the lowest levels of elite status. (Malina 2001:109).

Having this in mind, the Zaza culture offers the members within every class the same entry to economic and social resources. A member cannot gain or lose prestige in a way that his class profile will change (:109). Thus the smaller units he refers to are the nuclear family (*ma u piyê ey*), the extended family (*kuflet*), the small scale society or microculture (*ezbet, aşiret*) and their subordinated segments.

2.3.4.1 Structure of the Zaza Society

The structural prerequisites given above reveal the following societal bottom-up system:

- An *under* or *low class* which included the tribeless or people from other tribes, such as foreigners, e.g. Romanes speaking people, Kurds and Arabs.
- A *middle class* consisting of the workers and farmers.
- An *upper class* that is represented by the religious (*mıllah, şeik* and village president) and feudal elite (*axa / agah / aga; paşa*).

The *under class* is represented by members of those neighbouring people groups who practise close economical and social activities (e.g. trade, protection association etc.). Caused by growing mobility and international contacts, the integration of host countries spouses or the influx of (mainly Russian) foreigners confronts the Zaza society with a number of questions. Foreign spouses are so far not a huge problem as generally no family wants to return back to the Zaza homeland. That means the only contact with the Zaza homeland. Such the only contact to the Zaza homeland is via short holiday trips or reciprocal visits. The question of religious identity is mainly solved by an alignment of the children to Islam based on Islam practices stated in the *Sharia* (Muslim law; Turk.: *şeriat*) which satisfies the Muslim Zaza. The integration of Russians has so far not caused huge social problems, they are treated in a friendly way, their help is welcomed and they mainly return home.

Although the society is divided into three classes, there is high value of being an entirety in which the individual functions as a fixed part of the culture. Such gives proof towards the homogenous self-conception of the people group. As a *homogenous group* the Zaza people demonstrate a hierarchy in which the foreigner is not totally included, and in some cases is even refused (e.g. family conflict, etc.). In a homogenous society all or most members of the society participate in the activities of daily life. Although such societies sometimes show different profiles in leadership structures or the diversification of authority the society by itself forms an integrated whole which share the same system of ethical values. Yet it performs not just a collective of microcultures, which function on different levels but demonstrates unity as a whole (Nida 1990:159).

Besides these factors, poor medical care led to a lifespan of not more than 50 years. Child mortality was extremely high, mosquito plagues brought in malaria or other diseases. As a result of these problems, the Zaza people always kept to themselves and acculturation and initiation were the vehicles to prepare a child for full responsibility for daily life as well as for the task of holding the society together (collectivism). The latter function of social cohesion is encultured by a strong focus on honour and prestige in relation to the honour of the core and extended family.

2.3.4.2 Descent and Family Structures

In anthropology a discussion about kinship and kindred relationship started in the 1970s and led to a rejection of any kinship proclamation until the middle of the 1990s. The argument was mainly built on the fact that any perception of kinship from an *etic* point of view would either miss parts or take a subjective stance and thus lead to misinterpretation (Parkin 1997: ix-x Preface, 3). The reservations brought forward have recently been overcome by the need to describe kinship and descent from the ethnicities themselves and the more flexible terminology and diagramming that is used today. Nonetheless it is necessary to explain a kinship diagram well, in so doing to use a consistent and understandable kinship terminology, to mark the centre of focus (who is the central figure) and to give the reason for the representation (:13).

In the Zaza society descent is a factor, if not *the* important factor. As Kaya mentions, an individual is nothing without his kindred. His "name" that is his reputation relates to his status in his kinship structure. As a paternalistic society the father's side holds a higher levelled prestige orientation than the relatives on the mother's side. The responsibilities that a father passes on to his son are manifold and oriented outward, they do mainly relate to societal duties, whereas the daughter is instructed towards inward that is family oriented responsibilities. Kaya lists 15 responsibilities; he calls them rights, obligations and opportunities, which can be summed up by total *loyalty* and surrender to the clan (2011:21). I list them here to give an impression of what this loyalty contains.

- The right to membership in the group that confers belonging.
- The right to settle at the same place with the group members.
- The right to cultivate land. (This right is incorporated patrilineally.)
- The opportunity to contract marriage with group members. (This type of right can be perceived as a priority right with respect to people external to the group. It is not an automatic right but as a group member one is favoured to some extent.)
- The right to protection by group members.
- The right to convey one's views through decision-making processes within the group.
- The right to demand solidarity, for instance, during economic difficulties.
- Access to confidential information within the group.
- Possibilities for extended kinship through circumcision of boys.
- Opportunities for close friendships.
- Opportunities for external support.
- Strict demands of loyalty.
- Strict demands of family commitment.
- Tight emotional attachments.
- Looser emotional attachments. (Kaya 2011:21).

Solidarity, loyalty, family planning, relationship and the decision making process stick out in this list. Although most of these responsibilities do not reflect unique obligations in Zaza society the whole bundle gives an impression as to which one count as core values (2.5.4).

2.3.4.2.1 Nuclear and Extended Family

The nuclear, elementary or conjugal family is represented by the parents and their children. It is recognized as the central part of Zaza culture, although the extended family represents the household and is thus the normative standard (:28). An incest taboo in the nuclear family is performed (Parkin 1997:37). Although this applies also to the ascending family structures it is only implemented casually on the extended family level. Hence marriages between 1st grade cousins are common. Marriage is pre-arranged and prescriptive. Marriages are pre-arranged because the stability and consistency of the lineage and tribal hierarchy is guaranteed by the consistent flow of authority. Marriages are prescriptive since the patriarchaic system allows for self-reliant alliances based on economic or social benefit for the authoritarian leaders. A study by Dicle University from 2002 reveals that in the wider area of Kurmanji speaking Kurds and the Zaza people prescriptive marriages are up to 45 percent. The figure is valid mainly for the rural remote villages.

The Zaza live in unilineal extended families which represents the default societal unit (Werner 2006:89 there Appendix 2). An *extended family* is a conglomeration of relatives out of three to four generations in which newlywed are integrated to be part of the whole fixed family unit (Ember & Ember 1993:183-184). Extended families are normative to Zaza culture which is why the naming of kinship is very complex compared to Western cultures. Zaza extended families all live in one household. The daughter-in-law is incorporated into the household and the family clan of the sons which follows a patrifocal or virilocal pattern (Todd cit. in Geert 1993:87). Extended families in the Zaza culture follow a general pattern (Parkin 1997:28) and include:

- Nuclear family (parents and children; Ember & Ember 1993:183),
- Grandparents and Great-grandparents, although the latter are rare as the life expectancy is not high,
- Unmarried relatives, widowed aunts and uncles, orphaned cousins as well as disabled kinship.

Often other closely related nuclear families (uncle, aunt, etc.) are mainly living close by and form a *hamlet* (Seufert & Kubaseck 2004:29). A *village* consists of three to four or even more of such hamlets. The next larger unit is a small scale society which is often organized following a tribal structure (Werner 2006:50-54).

The basic attitude toward disabled society members is principally positive. Partly they are recognized as a good luck charm, partly as a carrier of blessing. In contrast to this, Islam in general offers very little and a more fatalistic stance in which the disabled are treated badly or are left alone. The positive mindset may have its background in Zoroastrian thinking combined with Christian charity and welfare.

2.3.4.2.2 Descent and Kindred

Social Anthropology developed an antagonism towards the definitional and formal presentation of descent and kinship. The idea was that based on the assumption that kinship is not a biological or genealogical concept but based on a dynamic social conception it cannot be described at all. The many different conceptions of culture led to a denial of the term "culture" which was replaced by the practice of speaking further of "society" (Parkin 1997:129).

I will refer here to a so called "cultural" approach, which hints at either closeness or distance to the ego. This "egocentric" view lacks an objective and generalized approach but on the other hand represents the given terms in daily use. Comparative studies and linguistic research profit from this approach (1.1.2.5).

Descent in the Zaza culture is built on blood relationship that is relations of *consanguinity*, a term that implies "of the same blood" (s. Parkin 1997:139). The conception of "ideal" versus "actual" relatives is based on the patrifocal assumption that the ideal and the more prestigious kin is from the same blood. This covers a biological point of view and follows a unilineal string. On the contrary the actual or real social oriented outcome includes outsiders:

- like *musayiv*, or God-parenthood, that is a friend of same sex who is lifelong, unrestricted included into the family by a ritual (Jacobson in Bailey 2004:110),
- like a *kêwra*, or godfather, for the child who can be from another people group, with even Christian or Jewish background (:110).

Until their 13th year the children perform *matrifilitation*, which is a close tie to the mother in education, religion and enculturation. For the sons the father takes over and starts the *initiation* process up from that point. Hence an orientation towards *patrifiliation* starts. The basic enculturation falls under the authority of the mother, who is closely connected to her husband as the head of family. Thus patrilineal blood relationship is overlapped, but on the other hand strong endogamy is demanded to preserve blood relationship. This combination leads to a strong parent-child relationship that forms the basis for the extended family. We observe in the Zaza culture a split enculturation process for sons, and a unilineal matrifilitation by the mother. The mother-son relation in Near and Middle Eastern societies represents strong ties which are obvious in a respect close to adoration for the mother. The mother due to her position as the organizer *of* and her restriction *to* the household is strongly interested in educating the sons to strengthen her sphere of authority into the male and outer sphere (2.3.2.1.2; 2.5.4).

The Zaza people follow a strong kinship-by-descent principle which is mixed with paternalism. In consequence the families and religious responsibilities concerning honour, prestige and shame are managed by men from the father's side. Kaya gives an example of those concerns when an uncle from the father's side was responsible for joining his brother's daughter to visit a distant medical centre for treatment (2011:18). Even in the Diaspora such acculturated core values become obvious when the big brother or nephew from the father's side is responsible to join his little sister / cousin during public visits (doctor, hospital, etc.) instead of the older sister.

2.3.4.3 Gentry – Sheikhdom, Aghadom and Mullaharchy

Although the modern Zaza society no longer mainly relies on small scale societies the function and understanding of this feudalistic nobility system is important. Zazaki and Zaza culture will not be understood without these social tasks. The *sheikh* (Arab. *shaikh* or *sheikh*; Za. *şeik*) is superior to the *agha* concerning his twofold roles. The Zaza Sheikhdom and Pirdom concept equal equal the Yezidis (Kreyenbroek & Rashow 2005:6-7; e.g. Adawiyya-Order).

2.3.4.3.1 The Sheikh - Sheikhdom

The term *Sheikh* refers etymologically back to Arabic 'Elder/Patriarch'. Originally this duty belonged to the head of a small scale society. Since the 13th century AD the term has been used for the clerical and secular Supreme Head of a religious brotherhood. Later on the term became an honorary title for an Islamic clergy or individuals with theological education. Arab village elders and heads of Islamic dominion are also given this title as part of their name (Brockhaus multimedial 2007: *Scheich* [Sheikh]). The sheikhdom of the Zaza people does not relate to the Arabic understanding. It is built on myth and does not reach back too far. One myth claims that *Sheikh Ali* from Palu gained his enthronement by direct divine order. In the beginning of the 18th century AD he passed on his superficial powers to the *sheiks* of the *Naqshebendi* order that he sent out to form a network of political and religious influence. Most of the sheikhs in the Sunni Zaza area claim their enthronement by *Sheikh Ali* (2.3.1.3.2; 2.3.4.4.3). Palu became an important centre. The Sheikh conceptions of Indonesia also reveal a spiritual and divine charisma of the sheikh. He bears *barakat* and even being close to him or being touched by him heals or liberates one from wrong ideologies (e. g. non-Islamic beliefs) as shown by Lukens-Bull (2005:2-5).

The hero in the story *Şêx Biyayena Gawandê Çermugızi* [How it Came to Pass that a Shepherd from Cermug became a Sheikh] shows impressively extraordinary ways which lead to such a social function. Also it reveals the religious and political understanding of the duty of a Sheikh in Zaza society (Hayıg 2007:117-120). Sunnism, following its lawful Islamic nature, by enforcing the observance of the five pillars, demands for an emotional argument in mysticism. The spiritual and mystical elements are complemented in the leadership,

> commonly called sheikhs. Highly esteemed in their villages, they are the ones who know how to make mystical contact with Allah. Mystics assume that the Sheikhs are friends of Allah who intercede with him on their behalf. Sheikhs reveal the path to blessing and bestow Allah's blessings. (Peters 1989:366).

Sheikhs are partially comparable to messianic figures (:366). The manifold societal functions that a Sheikh can fulfil are best described from Bruinessen (British Vice-consul Van Bertram Dickson cit. in Bruinessen 1992:272-273),

> ... the sheikh should be considered that religious function, which often functions political ... this is mainly because they are sometimes subject to an adoration which reminds of devoutness. Yet they could take over the positions of prophets, Mahdi and (in an extreme case) that of God, insofar their devotees did not even force them to this position. "Some of them [the Sheikhs. E.W.] are hardly anything good (sic!) as street robbers but their power about the small Aghas is great and usually can force them to submit to their will."

The concentration of power in the state of the *sheikh* is based on the religious awe of the people, which refers to his divine authority (RH 2007 *Zaza Stämme* [Zaza tribes]).

In terms of the context of the Kurmanji speaking Kurds and the Zaza the function of the sheikh is perceived as that "... religious position ... which most often acts as a political institution" (Bruinessen 1992:272). This double function goes contrary to the original line-up as a religious institution (Zürcher 2004:170). For that very reason interviewee only refer to the religious function of a *sheikh* and are not aware of the immense political influence that this position holds. Thus far it is clear that the sheikh possesses a religious task with a political function,

the latter in addition paralleling the position of the *agha* (see below). There are different ways of achieving the position of a sheikh,
- charismatic leadership skills, including the ability to consolidate larger societal units under one umbrella,
- qualities of leaders in relation to religion, which often goes together with the foundation or the takeover of religious orders e.g. Sufi'ism (Peters 1989:366),
- militant contentions, by which a chief emerges as head and secures the title as well as the function of a sheikh for himself,
- thaumaturgy and group manipulation.

Looking at the quotation from Vice-consul Van Bertram Dickson above, the *sheikhs* sometimes travelled as "journeymen" or "bards" before they gained glory, sometimes also afterwards. Through their travels they became well known, gathered information from other small scale societies and they knew best about national politics. The function and role of *sheikh* was also passed on by heredity.[71] Often those families recruited their own royal household and thereby formed feudalistic structures which became fixed institutions in the Zaza culture.

2.3.4.3.2 The Millah / Mullah - Mullaharchy

The position that a *sheikh* holds in religion is overlaps with the institution of the *mıllah / melah / mullah*. He is responsible for the religious education of the children and the community members. He often lacks charismatic or mystical abilities. In the region of the Eastern Group the *mullahdom* or *mullaharchy* developed into an influential body of society. *Hani* owned a huge *madrassa* with popular Islamic theologians. The mullaharchy was interwoven into the societal structure of the Zaza people based on the kinship by descent system. Since 1925

---

[71] The term "sheikh" became well known by the publication of Karl May called *Durchs wilde Kurdistan* [Engl. Through wild Kurdistan]. Here May, based on travel reports by others, demonstrated that the small scale societies of the Zazaki and Kurmanji speaking group are often refered to as aggressiv and rapacious (May 1951). The sheikh and the agha are institutionst that are accepted by the community based on their perseverance, any rules of recognizance are not known (Hennerbichler 2004:86). Bruinessen instead states that the tribal system declares the roles and functions belong to families by heredity and are determined long ago. We can assume that class societies appoint institutions and pass them on by heredity. Only in very few cases is an exception possible.

the politically motivated fight against the feudalistic structures of the Zaza people caused the disbanding of such centres of education (2.3.3.5.3).

2.3.4.3.3 The Aghadom – Landownership and Political Leader

The social role of an *agha* represents a village administrator which holds a political-social position in the Zaza community. He manages daily life activities, larger events, and the representation of the village to the outside in the interest of the villagers, e.g. before the Turkish officials. The *aghadom* represents a central administrative position with a lot of authority. Traditions, narratives and anecdotes tell a lot about the *agha* and his role in the Zaza community (Hayıg 2007). As an outcome of their authority they hold a strong regional influence. For this very reason they were welcomed as partners to the ruling parties on the national level. Mainly the military and the administrative officials of the Ottoman Empire and later the Turkish republican emissaries dealt with them (Kreyenbroek & Sperl 2002:44).

Diagram 14 Structure of the Zaza Society

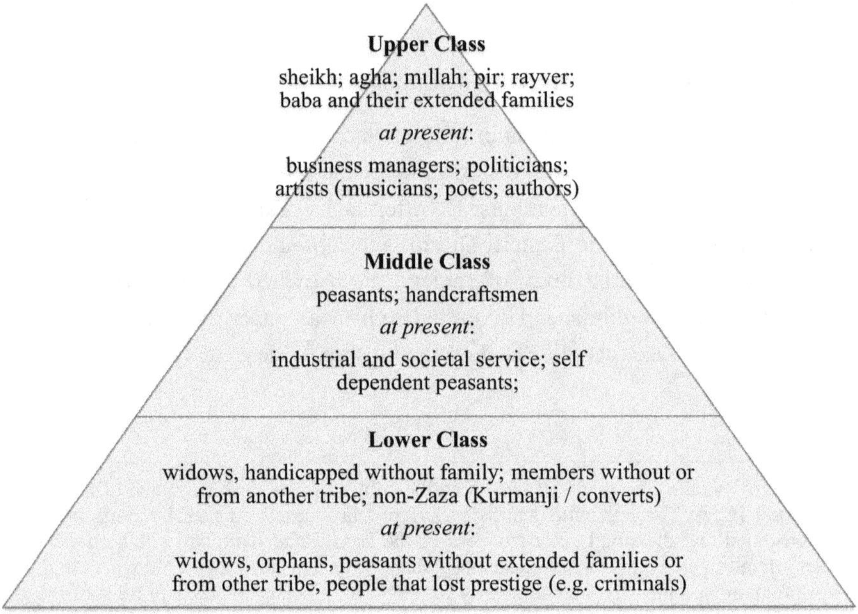

Upper Class
sheikh; agha; mıllah; pir; rayver; baba and their extended families
at present:
business managers; politicians; artists (musicians; poets; authors)

Middle Class
peasants; handcraftsmen
at present:
industrial and societal service; self dependent peasants;

Lower Class
widows, handicapped without family; members without or from another tribe; non-Zaza (Kurmanji / converts)
at present:
widows, orphans, peasants without extended families or from other tribe, people that lost prestige (e.g. criminals)

In the new Republic of Turkey the conflict that was caused by the struggle to fight feudalism led at the same time to a decrease in ongoing communication with the Zaza people, due to those feudalistic structures, represented by the Aghas and their families. Since the 19th century AD methods of expropriation, disempowerment and expulsion were used to get rid of any feudalistic structure. The attempt was made to replace the vacancies with stewards loyal to the national institution (Zürcher 2004:30-50). Unfortunately this didn't work out in all cases. The formerly feudalistic structures moved into a social-capitalistic system. Thereby the *agha* and *sheikh* moved together with the reformation of a peasantryand animal husbandry practising society into an industrializing people group in which those institutions became business and management roles. With industrialization the flow of money also changed and the positive trust of former times, based on the individual giving protection and offering help, moved to the general attitude of negative mistrust against those social institutions. The new question would be, how well everybody was pleased by the leadership if all resources were shared equally. Looking at the diagram below the change becomes obvious. The capital and influence of the formerly feudalistic leadership gave them new ruling positions with different responsibilities. In Yezidism the spiritual *Sheikh*dom and the *Pir*dom are secularized by a *Mir*dom, which is performed by a princedom (Kreyenbroek & Rashow 2005:6-7, 9). In the Yezidi society the secular and spiritual authority is taken by the Shemsani, Adani and Qatani clans, whereas the Mirdom is in the hands of the Qatani Sheikhs southwest of Lalish (ibid.). This interesting parallel shows the affinity of the people groups in the Eastern Anatolian area.

It would not be fair to describe the recent structure only in negative ways. The possibility that the new capitalistic oriented *three class system* offers is that the leading persons can implement mother tongue education together with other non-Turkish ethnicities (e.g. the Kurmanji or Laz speaking societies). Also they can provide work for their small scale societies and help to develop gender equality, raise living standards and put into service new creative businesses.

2.3.4.3.4 Summary

The flow of authority in the Zaza community is built on religious and political institutions. Some of these institutions can also be found in the larger Kurmanji speaking ethnicity, which performs other connotations of its leadership due to different historical setting. The system of Kurdish Princes based on the principality of the *Mir* is structured differently from what we find in the Zaza community.

The political and religious institution of the *sheikhdom* within the Zaza society is mainly built around the restructuring of the *Naqshebendi* order in the 18th century by *Sheikh Ali* from *Palu*. He filled the existing vacuum that *Sultan Mahmud II.* in his fight against *feudalism* under the Kurmanji speaking ethnicity created. A political, economic, religious and social network of Islamic clergy evolved, which was based on mysticism and apocalyptic prophesies (eschatological perspective). During this process the Ottoman Empire forced replacement of the *Haçi Bektaş* tekke by the *Naqshebendi* order. This led to a deep distrust of all non-Islamic people. Until today this institution is feared or at least mistrusted (2.3.1.3.2; 2.3.4.4.3; 2.3.4.3.1).

The religious institution of the *mullaharchy* works closely with the *sheikhdom* and operates on a local level. It represents the religious conscience of the collective and performs sanctions to guarantee the social balance.

The political institution of the *agha* represents a form of landownership, working closely with the *sheikhdom* and the *mullaharchy*. It protects the inner peace of the society as well as the outwardly oriented security of ethical and physical borders (e.g. honour killing, rape, abduction, and border violation).

Diagram 15 Hierarchy of Zaza Society Leadership

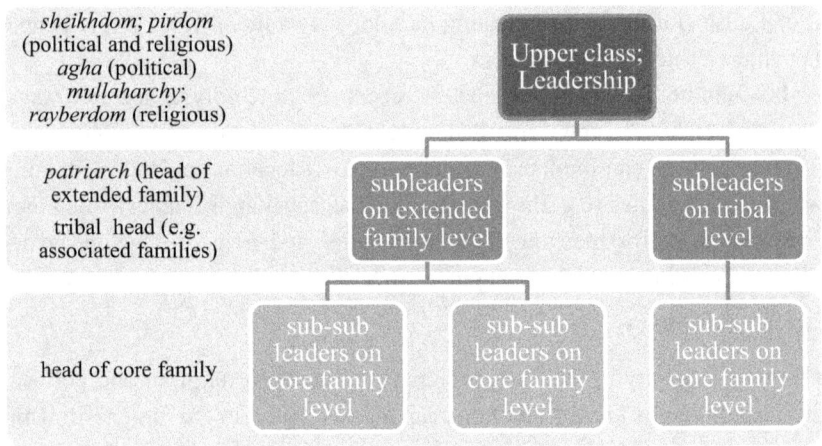

All of these institutions are expected to guarantee the well being of the people group. Therefore judicial and executive power is given to them by the people group. They make decisions and rule conflicts. They trade and organize undertakings for the community.

2.3.4.4 Small Scale Society – Tribal and Clan System

The feudalist hierarchy of small scale societies building on tribal structure, contrasts with Western individualistic configurations. The Zaza society follows the feudalistic structure until today. Needless to say the Zaza structures are developing into an increasing individualistic system following the influence of the West. Here we will take the time to introduce the concepts that contrast to Western cultures.

Social units are defined differently in Anthropology. A social network needs to be guaranteed in a small scale society based on tribal structures (Hiebert & Hiebert 1995:25). The necessity of these tribal structures reaches back to humanity's given universal biological need for social proximity as e.g. family, mother-child relation. Another reason is presented by the global feature of social organisation (:22). The tribal small scale society presents the higher level of kinship organisation. Their structure is based on bloodline and leads to reciprocal marriage. Endogamy in this setting covers overall tribal marriage. A restriction in choice is given to those social units that have a good reputation and are considered to be trustful (Werner 2003b; Appendix 3).

2.3.4.4.1 Structures of Small Scale Societies – The Patriarchate

As mentioned before the Zaza people clan system follows a patrilineal *and* segmentary pattern (see Parkin 1997:18). Lower segments such as small scale societies called tribes or clans are of lower prestige than larger ones. This is exemplified in history by the *Sheikh Said* uprising in which less prestigious small scale societies participated but were led by the one of Sheikh Said. Recently the very strong societal unit of the *Bıçax* in *Siverek* still rules the area, whereas smaller units are mainly powerless. One cannot make this argument too strongly but it gives an implication.

Zaza clans perform an endogamous and patrilineal structure in which nowadays marriages from outside are allowed but don't represent the default. Yet a deviation from the former intermarriage with non-Islamic people groups is observable but still sanctioned with underlying accusations from peers (see above; Hiebert & Hiebert 1995:28).

Etymologically the Arabic term *aşiret*, or tribe, slipped into Zazaki through Ottoman Turkish, called Osmanlı. Another term *ezbet* is used to describe those and segmental units.

The widely used terms for "tribe" in the Near and Middle East are on the one hand performed by the designations stemming out of Arabic qabila and 'ashira (Tk: aşiret) as well as the on the other hand out of the Mongolian Turkish terms il (Tk.: il) and oymak/aymak. Within the formations described as "tribe"in the area one will find different patterns of organisation. They all show a common and extensively political autonomy in their inner affairs. (Franz 1988a:514).

In Zazaki the Turkish expression *aşiret* persisted. Zazaki also uses the name *eşir* which is derived from the *lingua franca*, as well as *ber*, which describes a subgroup of the clan system. The phrase *ezbet* describes branches of the tribe and family which are not directly related to the small scale society. Those expressions will be found in traditions. Sometimes they are used out of context due to overlap. I will here refer only to those tendencies that a mother tongue speaker explained to me (MT 2008 *Zazaki*).

In Zazaki a small scale society following a tribal structure forms a monoethnical unit. Following the literature and my own research, such a unit is based on a joint culture, language and territory (Hiebert & Hiebert 1995:31, 87 diagram there). All three features are represented in the Zaza culture by an emphasis of unity, marked by Zazaki the common language, in the homeland area around the headwaters of the rivers Euphrates and Tigris.

Diagram 16 Social Small Scale Structures

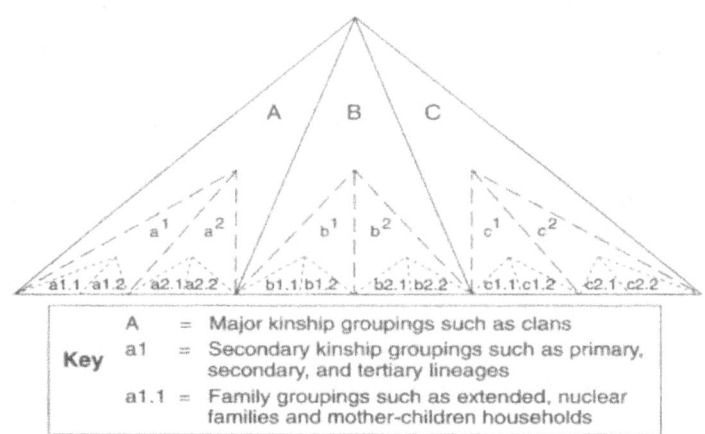

Key	A	=	Major kinship groupings such as clans
	a1	=	Secondary kinship groupings such as primary, secondary, and tertiary lineages
	a1.1	=	Family groupings such as extended, nuclear families and mother-children households

Offence against the values and norms of the structural settings will be punished by expulsion and impoverishment due to social isolation. Both social processes are triggered by the principle of shame orientation (elenctics; 1.1.3.2; 1.1.3.3).[72] The punishment practice gives another hint towards the underlying and historical Animistic background of the Zaza people (Wiher 2003:295-311). In such societal units a person is designated to be a non-person, by losing face and therefore honour and prestige.

The result of such a state leads to impoverishment and isolation by exclusion from social institutions. In most cases the reappearance of a person is not possible. The hurdle that needs to be taken is set so high that in folktales the hero has to do miracles to get back his status. Thus the average society member is implicitly taught and warned by the folktales not to be assigned to such a state. A gradual movement which would allow a transfer into a lower status class is not possible due to strong class affiliation (2.3.4.1).

A specific feature of "segmentary Sunni groups", like the Kurmanji speaking Kurds and the Zaza, is given by the centre of the people group. This centre contains the religious leaders that bridge the factional rivalries between the small scale units in the overall structure (Tapper 1983:51-52). The institution of the "Sheikh" includes this circle of persons in the Zaza people group. Before the foundation of the Republic of Turkey (1923) these smaller units, including their leaders or "Sheikh's", functioned in the social structure of the Ottoman Empire as an autonomous and self ruling political constituent. Due to the option for *encapsulation* they formed principalities (:51-52). The only request from the national power concerned taxes and administrative reporting. Hence the balance of power between nation and small scale unit was ruled out. After the foundation of the Republic of Turkey those units were driven into interdependence from the state via provincial government and the set up of a central led nation-wide Turkish education and school system. The driving force was mainly the Turks, although few people out of the small scale units helped and supported the Turkish direction actively.

A member of a tribe is asked to acknowledge at least seven male forefathers to prove he belongs to his small scale society. The tribal leaders express their lineage with the forefather of their tribe by sharing the same blood or a common substance with them. Often a lineage can be traced back up to 13th ancestors

---

[72] Hayıg describes in his folktales namely "The Son of the Agha" (*Lajê Axay*), "Mahmesha" (*Ma'hmeşa*), "Gormahmed" (*Gorma'hmed*) and "Qolo Poto" (*Qolo Poto*) how the loss of honour leads into isolation and repudiation (2007).

(Kaya 2011:31). This practice is not actually working, since the disbandment of the tribal system made the affiliation secondary.

The hierarchy and flow of authority within a tribe goes from the *agha* or patriarch to subleaders of larger extended families who by themselves lead subordinated leaders on the level of (extended or core) families. This top-down principle is found all over in the Zaza area, as well as in the Kurmanji speaking Kurdish areas. The system asks for strong trust in authority, which forms one of the core values and norms in the Zaza society. Within this structure conflicts, common undertakings and social development are discussed and determined. The principles that drive a tribe are based on honour and prestige. The "name" of a tribe carries its reputation against other small scale societies and outside powers. In collectivistic societies an individual is what his tribe represents, the individual is not self-reliant in a sense that he stands outside of the community.

Female descent is not of relevance in the Zaza societal structure. The patriarchate is expressed in a way which is not easy to understand from a Western point of view. The basic assumption by an individual from a patriarchal standpoint is his belief in the inviolability of his authority given by experience, his age and the Holy Scriptures. He expects to be honoured and accepted by his kindred and subordinated subjects. In return he undertakes the responsibility to guard the subjects, the traditions and the property of his people group. Male subjects get great attention and are favoured by responsibility for social needs (e.g. trade, maintenance, military, construction, agriculture etc.). Female members get less direct attention but are expected to take over the responsibility for horticulture, well-being and education of children and the care and provision of their families. In the case of the female members the patriarch is only active in cases of conflict. Higher education and the delegation of authority follow the rules of legacy. The oldest son as main heir is not sent to higher education since he is trained by the passing on of the patriarch's experience and knowledge. The second and third sons are expected to receive higher education to provide for the extended family. The ethical and moral purity and the protection and gain of high prestige and honour of his people group are obligations for the patriarch and his oldest son.

2.3.4.4.2 Designation of Small Scale Societies

The small scale societies named *Qırwi* (or *Pırwi*) and *Mıqri* are considered to be the Proto-tribal societal units of the Zaza from which all the other microcultures

2 The Zaza

derive. Their area of settlement can be traced back to the regions of *Gerger* (Alduş), *Çermik* and *Siverek* (2.1.3.1.4; 2.1.4.1; 2.2.3.2;2.2.7).

Designations of small scale Zaza societies are either derived from geographical and local conditions as well as from leading figures or family notations (e.g. *Balaban*). Those designations are en passant describing spiritual contents (e.g. *Melekan* and *Axşan*; RH 2007 *Zaza small scale societies*).

The constitution of the Zaza tribal society follows the general schemata on hierarchical structures in such societal units (Hiebert & Hiebert 1999:87; 2.3.4.4.1).

Izady offers an extended register of all Kurdish rural people groups. He bunches all small scale societies of one people group in organizations, which are loosely linked to each other (1992:78-85). Remarkably he notes only *one* Zaza tribe (*Buçax* from Siverek). The most detailed and recent research about the social structure of the Northern Group is from *Fırat* (1997:227-247 und 248-250). The following small scale societal units including their localisations (in brackets) are known. These tribal segments of the Zaza society are the best known out of tradition and present.

Table 24 Small Scale Societies of the Zaza and their Localisation

Northern Group	Southern Group	Eastern Group
Balaban (Dersim/Pülümür)	Bıçax/Buçax (Siverek)	Solaxan (Solhan)
Qerewan (Dersim)	Bab (Siverek)	Umeran (Solhan)
Demenan (Dersim)	Qer'han[73] (Siverek)	Tavzi (Solhan)
Lolan (Varto/Muş)	'Hesran (Çermik)	Bilikon
Hormekan (Varto/Muş)	Qırwar (Çermik /Siverek)	Chomergij
Sheikh Hesen (Hozat/Ovaçık)	Karağan (Çermik /Siverek)	Xelbij
Ağuiçenler	Kalendêr (Çermik /Siverek)	Guevij
Sari Saltiklar	Alkan (Siverek/Çermik /Gerger)	Zikti
Derviş Cemallar	Azu (Bingöl)	Begler
Baba Mansurlar	Nexşan (Bingöl)	Ki mele Kal

---

[73] *Qer'han* and *Qerewan* are derivations of the terms "road/travel route" (Tk. *karawan, kara*) and "house" (Tk. *xan*). Both terms relate to the travel routes and the harbourages (Pers. *xan/'han*), which are along the Silk Roads. The main routes went through the Zaza homeland from East to West (2.3.1.2). The term *Alkan* points towards such *karawansaray*-institutions and describes a derivation of *Ali-Han* meaning "House of Ali" (RH 2007 *Zaza-Stammesnamen* [Zaza-Tribenames]).

Kureyşanlar	Melekan (Hani)	Ki mele Azin
Celal Abbaslar		Hezarshayij
Sultan Munzur		Shexon (Xirbizun)
Pilvenkliler		Bilikon
Sheik Hasan		Hushajion
Seyit Sabunlar (Kirmanj)		Xezon (Keshkon)

A more detailed list for the Northern Group is given by *Fırat* (1997:227-247 and 248-250) and a very extensive list of 126 tribes of the Dersim area in *Kaya* (2010:108-131). Kaya also refers to the language that these tribes use. Interestingly 26 (20,64%) small scale societies are bilingual in Kurmanji and Zazaki, whereas 16 (12,7%) are monolingual in Kurmanji and yet count as Zaza. For the Eastern Group a list if presented by *Kaya* (2011:30).

The list given below, is to demonstrate the wide range of popular small scale societies of just one out of the three main dialect groups. From this, one can assume that more research will bring forth a lot more of historically important tribal units of the Zaza society.

Table 25 List of Zaza Small Scale Societies

01 Alu*	08 Baxliyu	15 Bomosuru
02 Alxanu	09 Bexteru	16 Bozu
03 Arezu	10 Bextiyaru	17 Chareku
04 Armenier	11 Bezgöru	18 Circassian
05 Avasu	12 Birumu	19 Civan
06 Axucan	13 Bolchuku	20 Dedanin
07 Balavanu	14 Bolu	
21 Demenu	31 Karsanu	41 Maskanu
22 Dewres	32 Kemu	42 Milu
23 Dewres-Gewher	33 Kirdasu	43 Mistu
24 Dewres-Gewru	34 Kirgu	44 Mosku
25 Feratu	35 Kismerchuku	45 Pilvanchuku
26 Gewu	36 Kosu	46 Pilvenku
27 Guresu	37 Kurmeku	47 Pir Sultanu
28 Heyderu	38 Kurmesu	48 Pirechuku
29 Hizol	39 Lacinu	49 Qerebalu
30 Horneku	40 Lolu	50 Qeymachuku

2 The Zaza

51 Qozu	63 Seyit Sawugu	75 Suranu
52 Rutu	64 Shadi	76 Suru
53 Sari Saltik	65 Shix Hesenu	77 Susank
54 Sawalu	66 Shix Mamedanu	78 Tetu
55 Seviku	67 Shix Memedu	79 Veliku
56 Semu	68 Shixu	80 Welguzu
57 Semuku	69 Silemanu	81 Xiran
58 Seneku	70 Sisu	82 Yusuvu
59 Seterchuku	71 Sowaru	83 Zeruku
60 Seydalu	72 Sozu	84 Zeval.
61 Seyiku	73 sunni. Kurds	
62 Seyit Savunu	74 sunni. Turks	

Gündüzkanat (Northern Group) refers to the oral tradition of Dersim. Therein it is stated that two small scale societal groups formed the *origin* of all other small scale groups (1997:75-76).

Table 26 Two Origins of Zaza Small Scale Societies

Seyh Hasanlı	Dersimli
Keçeluşağı	Haydaranlı
Baluşağı	Ariel
Abbasanuşağı	Demenanlı
Gâvuşağı:	Lolanlı
Beytiuşağı, Alanuşağı, Maksutuşağı Koucuşağı, Birmanliuşağı, Asuranliuşağı, Demanliuşağı, Bezgevruşağı, Gulabiuşağı, Seyyit Kemaliuşağı, Lacinuşağı, Ferhatuşağı	Savanlanlı, Alanlı, Haydaranlı, Kureysanlı, Yusufanlı, Rotanlı, Baytiyaruşağı, Balaban, Sisanlı, Sadillı, Cariklı, Karasanlı, Seyh Mehmedanlı, Kemanlı, Kirganlı (they claim also to be Sey Hasanlı), Hormeklı, Komsonlu, Maskanlı, Caferlı

The most *important* small scale societal groups stand alone. Note that Gündüzkanat refers to the tribes named *Kemali* (1992) and *Kocadağ* as those that display the origin of the Zaza ethnicity (1992). Unfortunately the Eastern tribes are not researched as well as the Northern and Southern ones.

2.3.4.4.3 Hierarchical Structure – The Naqshebendi

Amongst traditional descriptions from the Ottoman Empire's past and its political administration, one will find a far reaching freedom for the smaller units such as the extended families. In cultural descriptions and overviews about the hierarchical structure of the Zaza people it becomes apparent that on the one side the collective societal alignment restricts the individual to its class and extended family, on the other side it offers the extended families a large independence from higher organizational levels (2.3.2.1.1).

Intertribal Zaza formations or alliances on religious or political grounds were only taken into account in case of outer threats. Their goal was either military defence against political or religious upheavals or the defeat of religious and political movements which were recognized as a threat to their own belief system or societal structure (Bruinessen 1992; 3.5).

> Members of tribal segments of the Zaza society owned land and practiced animal husbandry. Such a structure made them vulnerable against nomadic and other travelling peoples. They developed a defence strategy by making it easy to mobilize and make quick strikes against those threats which were based on armed groups within the tribes. Leaders of tribal units had „absolutely no economical power over the people; they were also not richer", but they were well known to be "above all devout, even fanatical" (Mela Hesen a member of the tribe Zirqan cit. in Bruinessen 1992:424).

Because of this religious tendency Kreyenbroek and Sperl conjecture a link to mystic monk orders of those days. Many of the leading elite, including the *Sheikh* and the *agha*, participated and participate up until today in such very active and influential groups (2002:36). The *Naqshebendi* order stands out especially (2.3.1.3.2; 2.3.4.4.3; 2.3.4.3.1). The linking of conservative Islamic religion with politics through this order reaches out through the centuries. Also today's governance in the Near and Middle East, specifically in Turkey, takes part in this mystical order. This applied to the former Prime Minister *Erbakan* and the recent one *Erdoğan* (Fröhlich 2008:23).

The mystical orders, especially the *Naqshebendi* order, started in the 14th century as spiritual institutions. Increasing influence on the population due to their attractive life standards and their support of the poor and often oppressed peasant population changed their attitude towards politics. In 1811 AD *Mewlana Khâlid* (Kurd) made this order popular and brought it to its height. The Kurdish feudal princes called *Mir* formed a system, which was formerly supported by the Ottoman Empire with militia. This system was attacked and dismantled by Sultan *Mahmud II.* (1808-1839). The resulting vacuum was recognized by the

Naqshebendi order and led to its formation as a spearhead of the Islamic monk movement. It was *Mewlana Khâlid* who sent out *sheikhs* everywhere and established a close network which increasingly gained religious and political influence. The main so called "Kurdish uprisings" were lead by leaders of these orders (2.3.1.3.2). All of their families hold high prestige until today, namely the descendant of *Sheikh Ubeydullah* of Nehri, *Sheikh Said* of *Palu* and *Mullah Mustafa* of *Barzan*. This parallels the development of the Christian monk orders in the Middle Ages such as the Franciscans or Dominicans which started as religious institutions and soon developed into influential political organisations and remain so today (Schirrmacher 1992:22-23).

During these times links and connections to the Arabic *madrassa* of Bagdad, Egypt (Cairo) and Damascus were frequent. In the 19th century sacred instruction by these centres of theological education was normal and welcomed (Levtzion 1997:150-151). These centres proactively invited people and after education send them out to form so called *Khalwatiyya* branches all over the area of East Anatolia. Sheikh *Kâlid*, developed a strong dependence on what he called a centralistic *Khâlidi-Naqshabandiya* organization (:ibd.).

At this point it has to be said that the *Naqshebendi* order was not always welcomed as a positive institution. Sheikh Said for instance called it "a gangster band in Kurdistan" (Bruinessen 1992:312; 2.3.1.3.2; 2.3.4.3.1). The predominantly Kurdish influence in this order mixed with an increasing Turkish dominance. Nowadays the structures are active and dominant people come from different ethnical background. In the case of the *Naqshebendi* order the devout bias of the *Sheikh* as a social institution moved towards a political duty. Based on the socially motivated power play in tribal societies a leading position was required to balance the religious and political needs and challenges from within and from outside of the small societal units. Nowadays the remnants of this power play is reflected in the following functions of a Sheikh, as described by Yalcin (2002:26), as

> ... political patron saints and mediators for the relationships of gouverment and small scale society. In most cases tribes without leaders ask for auspices of other leaders of tribes, to get to services and goods. Within a dominant network inner tribal linkings can replace kinship ties, when in direct kinship no influential person is in reach.

The small scale society *Bıçax/Buçax* from Siverek demonstrates this well, as it even embodies military functions in this area. This tribe stands for a political power factor. In consequence there is less Turkish presence in this area, since Turkish officials count on the loyalty, although limited, and collaboration of this tribe. In return a far reaching political freedom on the local level is offered. The political task is connected up by this tribe with a religious sentiment. The complete veiling of women in blue velvet in public is one of the obvious outcomes of such attitudes as was observed in 2002 and 2005 during trips into this region.

Inner tribal cohesion is built vertically on solidarity, loyalty to the authorities and horizontally on brotherhood formed by the descent and kinship structure, the Three-Class system and the core values reflected in the perception of the world of the Zaza people.

The Naqshebendi order reaches out through the whole Islamic geographical sphere. The Qadiri-Naqshebendi of Muslim Java are well known for their social engagement in so called *pesantren*. These Islamic schools focus on students of secular science by accompanying their education with religious input. The students can live their religious life beside their study programmes (Lukens-Bull 2007). The sheikhs that run such *pesantren* are linked through either the Naqhebendi or other Islamic orders.

Another connection between the *Naqshebendi* and other Islamic fraternity orders, mainly those following Sufi'ism, has to be mentioned, although the Sunni *Naqshebendi* Order is not fully integrated in this history. *Freemasonry* in the Ottoman Empire reaches back to French influence (Levantine / Latin Christians). In 1721 they started their activities but it was 1856 (Macedonia) before a Turkish *Grand Loge* evolved. In 1909 the Grand Lodge in İstanbul became a permanent part of society although it was closed from time to time (1922; 1935) and suspiciously considered as Western (see Al Qaeda attack in 2004). A split in 1966 caused by Süleyman Demirel's denial that he was a Freemason, led to two different Lodges namely the *Grand Lodge of* Istanbul and the *Liberal Freemasons of Turkey*. A list of active politicians and managers shows that Freemasonry has an influence in Turkey: *Murat V.* (the 33rd Sultan and brother of *Abdul Hamid II.*), *Mustafa Kemal Paşa Atatürk*, *Talât Pascha* (first Master Mason), *Cemal Pascha* (Young Turks), *Süleyman Demirel* (President of Turkey), *Ziya Gökalp* (3.1.1.2.3), *Haluk Tezonar* (sculptor), *İbrahim Edhem Pascha*, *Namık Kemal* (poet, author), *Emmanuel Carasso*, *İbrahim Hakkı Pascha*, *Kâzım Özalp*, *Mehmed Fuad Pascha* (politician), *Mehmed Emin Ali Pascha*, *Midhat Pascha*, *Teodor Kasap*, *Reşat Nuri Güntekin* (w./o. A. *Sufis - Die Freimaurer des Ostens*? [Engl. Sufis - The Freemasons of the East?]. Some of the *Naqshebendi* leaders were and are also Freemasons. The mystic orientation of the fraternity opens it up to humanity in a way that original Sunnism doesn't.

2.3.4.4.4 Signs of Disintegration

Modern tendencies like "internationalisation" and "globalisation" bring about the decay of small scale societal structures. They are conducive to an "increasing mobility, rising migration movements, the implementation of widespread economical markets, sprawling urbanization and incremental compressing medial interconnection networks" (Stolze 1999:202). As part of feudalistic formations tribal structures are recently becoming less important. Since the foundation of the Republic of Turkey the destruction of feudalistic societal organizations due to the perception of backward oriented systems became part of the constitution and politics. In consequence a mixture of Islamic and socialistic ideas penetrated the tribal structures of the Zaza society. The former structures lost their meaning and became more and more obsolete, due to those developments, the more so as they joined with a restrictive education policy implemented by institutions of the language of wider communication (Höhlig 1997:120). Increase of mobility, decimation caused by fleeing from a bad economic situation or persecution into the large Western Turkish cities and the Diaspora led to a disbandment of most of the tribes (2.3.1.4; 2.3.4.6). The main reasons for the disintegration are,

- oppressive national politics based on a monolingual education system (education in Turkish is established in the constitution). This leads to,
    - loss of self esteem, prestige and identity of the Zaza people,
    - devaluation of the mother tongue as the language of education, wider communication or higher education,
    - overemphasis of the language of wider communication – Turkish – and its cultural background as language and culture go hand in hand.
- higher education needs and the hunger for better living conditions. Education at the universities and jobs in politics, huge companies and afar.
- demographic changes due to migration movements into the big cities and the Diaspora.

The former Three-Class structure including a majority of small farmers (peasantry) and landless tenants moved into a huge population that has become landless in the last 30 years (40 per cent). The landless live either as tenant farmers or as seasonal workers in the Southern and Western cities.

De facto the leadership with its institutions of *sheikhdom*, *aghadom* and *mullaharchy* (2.3.4.3) which in the past fell under a *taboo*, if they were questioned face increasing criticism because of growing education and distrust of authorities. Declining authority structures generate new social structures which fill out the vacuum of power play. The decline in the authority and power of the *sheikh*, the *agha* and the *mıllah* affects the Zaza society enormously in view of the fact that their slavish following of authority was central to their perception of the world and societal structure. The whole concept of mystical and superficial (Folk) Islam operated through such values based on unquestioning obedience. As mentioned above the replacement of peasantry structures by industrial ones is an ongoing but mainly tow down process initiated by the recent leadership.

2.3.4.4.5 Summary

Small scale societies built on peasantry and animal husbandry reveal a tribal character when no national or overruling system developed. The Zaza people follow a blood lined descendant structure. As such one stays within his class, extended family or clan due to relational coherence. Endogamy generates bridewealth, pre-arranged or prescriptive marriage and the patrilocal settlement of the bride. As a consequence paternalism drives the authority structures of the Zaza society.

Political rulers are the *Agha* or *Pir*, as well as the *Sheikh*. The three class structured community allows not for class transition. Religious leaders are the *Sheikh* (SZ / EZ) or the *Pir* (NZ). Modern migration movements led to damage of the feudal system. New developing structures follow the national tendency to political and economic elites as an outcome of democratization and capitalism.

2.3.4.5 Language Endangerment and Identity Loss

Language endangerment goes hand in hand with culture change and loss. It is impossible to divide both developments or to reason the one against the other (Fasold 1993:213, 215, 239). Although a culture and language in itself often changes or shift and does not die (exceptions would be ethnocide or genocide), it can be in danger. Often bilingualism either stable or just temporarily accompanies endangerment. The following steps can be marked out in the development of Zazaki as a language of endangerment and the Zaza society losing self esteem and identity.[74]

---

[74] In an article about recent research on language endangerment in Turkey from UNESCO it becomes clear that at least 15 languages – including Zazaki – are considered to be in danger of extinction within the next decade (w/o A. 2009. 15 languages endangered. Online im Inter-

- First there was strong self esteem based on monolingualism and less penetration from surrounding cultures or languages such as Armenian, Arabic, Osmanlı Turkish or Kurmanji (until the end of the 19th century).
- Then the persecution, displacement and extinction of the surrounding Christian neighbours by Turks, Kurds and Zaza lead to a religious vacuum without a non-Islamic enemy. Thus the Islamic structures were shaken and newly ordered politically. Now the Zaza people together with the Kurmanji speaking Kurds came to the attention of the new regime. Zazaki, Kurmanji and all other minority languages were banned from the public. Zazaki became a language restricted to be spoken and not used at all for writing, education or wider communication (1915 – 1980). Turkish becomes the language of wider communication and (higher) education. Stable bilingualism develops and goes hand in hand with loss of cultural identity.
- Triggered by the Diaspora the Zaza society started writing and using their language for translations and a few publications. Unfortunately until now the movement finds little response in the homeland (1980 - present). Due to intermarriage and decreasing self esteem children are more and more educated in Turkish only. This trend is countered by a small group of authors and culturally active groups that offer mother tongue education in kindergarten or special language courses.
- Although there were High Cultures around the Zaza people they never developed their own writings. Education was part of acculturation and initiation rites. The modern school system was able to reach the Zaza people only for the last thirty years. Kaya offers a very negative picture when he speaks of "more than half of the population" which "have either never had schooling or is functionally illiterate" (2011:8). The regular education level comprises five years of schooling, which is reached by about 40 per cent of the Zaza population. Unfortunately the oppression of the mother tongue issue hinders children from developing their full cognitive abilities. A bilingual school system would be of great support. In the recent setting the Zaza people were forced to make social arrangements based on their own experiences without relying on the Turkish education system.

---

net: URL: http://www.hurriyet.com.tr/english/opinion/11068922.asp?yazarid=294&gid=260 [accessed 2017-06-27].

- Recently a trend towards educating the children only in Turkish and at the same time a revival of Zazaki is observable. The outcome of these contrary trends is not predictable. How far the cultural revival triggered by the Diaspora has an influence on the homeland is also not foreseeable.

In the Diaspora the tribal societal system found no revival. Even the controversies with political Kurdish groups (PKK, Kurdish tribes) did not lead to Zaza formations to counteract Kurdish aggression. In the homeland the decimation of the many tribal small scale societies to very few but still strong and active units led to a local power concentration. Larger formations or alliances of such units are not known recently to have overcome threats from outward, be they from the Turks or the Kurmanji speaking Kurds. Summarizing the development of the small scale society structure of the Zaza community, it can be said that the former foundational structure is more and more being replaced by a Western lifestyle which goes hand in hand with the modern Turkish way of life implemented by the laicist system of Mustafa Kemal Paşa Atatürk (3.6).

I will add to this discussion some very recent and meaningful research on language shift from *Nazmi Çiçek* with reference to 40 persons of all ages (2011). He found out that in his home village *Êxê* in between *Elazığ* and *Bingöl* (Çewlık; Petrov [1863] 1998:148-159) most people are trilingual in Kurmanji, Zazaki and Turkish. They use the language of a common cognition, especially the same lexicon and perception of the world in relation to the communication partner. For instance a Zaza would use Turkish to communicate with a Turk (20 of those under 36 years uses Turkish in meetings with friends), Kurmanji for a Kurmanji speaker (5 use Zazaki to 27 Kurmanji; 15 less than 30 years use Turkish) and Zazaki for his people group (32 use Zazaki to 2 Kurmanji; 14 less than 30 years use Turkish). Nonetheless the generation under 20 (0 per cent) is not trained in Zazaki at all at home and does not hear it any more. This case is not representative for the whole group but shows clearly the trend. Turkish is replacing the language in the public and private sphere.

2.3.4.6 Emigration and Immigration – Diaspora and Bilingualism

Before we go into the specifics of the Zaza society as emigrants in a diasporic situation and the reflections about the immigrant status in foreign countries we consider some concepts of migration. Migration movements are nowadays manifold and migrants form so called "microcultures", "milieus" or "social backgrounds" within a national setting.

2.3.4.6.1 A Microculture in the European Union

A microculture *reflects* its milieu and at the same time *displays a milieu* to its environment (Icken 2010:39-46). A migrant is part of a migration movement, but his development as a migrant is always an individualistic one. Yet every migrant has his own migration milieu, which is part of a larger migration process. In this study we will research the migration of the Alevi and the Muslim Zaza to the Christian Western countries, mainly to Germany and Scandinavia (Sweden). We will see that their milieu is reflected by religious, cultural-linguistic and economic differentiation to their host countries.

Icken describes a tool to investigate migration societies in relation to aspects of equality and discrimination. This tool was developed by a German company called SINUS. Significantly the tool is also called the SINUS scale. The lifestyle of migrants is measured based on outer conditions *and* inner values (2010:40). "Social milieus" or "microcultures" are groups of individuals with similar aims in life or lifestyles with a common mentality and disposition. The SINUS scale differentiates between traditional, mainstream and hedonistic milieus. Thereby in those societal units *core values*, *lifestyle* and *conditions of life* are alike.

The Zaza society fits in the *traditional* setting under the SINUS A23 scale, namely the traditional guest labourer milieu. Cultures that are called traditional in the scale are those that hand down tradition orally and avoid including or adapting to new concepts. Their core values are based on time-proven traditions and practices. These core values are enculturated from generation to generation. Any deviation is refused or sanctioned by the community. The SINUS scale refers to traditional lifestyle as living up to one's principles. The Zaza ethnicity sticks to their tradition in *lifestyle*. Any damage to this lifestyle is punished by social measures. For instance fornication or marriage without the permission of the patriarch is avenged by the male family members with honour killing. Other punishment procedures are given in 2.3.2.1.1. And lastly the *conditions of life* refer to an environment that expects stable processes of daily life (e.g. men as producers and sellers), like a traditional trade system (e.g. currency system, bargaining) or a fixed market place. The Zaza community adheres to these traditional principles, which is why they fall under the category traditional.

2.3.4.6.2 Bi-, Multi- and Polylingualism

Another important aspect of migration is found in bi- or poly-/multilingualism. Bilingualism is mainly the "capacity to coordinate two or more languages in accordance with the grammatical constraints of both or all languages" (Wei 2007:15). The advantage of bi- or multilinguals is that they own two or more worlds of experience and that they develop or have a unique linguistic and psychological profile. Often bi- or polylinguals show a wider cognitive conception of the world, including faster and more flexible communication. This leads to better and more economic advantages given by a wider portfolio of jobs available (:15, 20; see below). Bi- and Multilingualism is one of the main advantages that the Zaza people experience by their history and as a small people group within a pluri-cultural environment.

2.3.4.6.3 Multilingual Mother Tongue Education

The advantage of *Multilingual Mother Tongue Education* (MLE; Turkish: *Çok Dilli Eğitim / Çift Dilli Eğitim* ÇDE) comes into play. Ideally Zazaki as a mother tongue[75] would be taught as a transfer language into Turkish as the language of wider community. Such Zazaki could be learned for one to two years in school or preschool before the pupils were integrated to the regular Turkish curriculum. The smooth move from the mother to the national language in education is nowadays globally recommended (UNESCO; EU; SIL International). At the moment mother tongue education for children is not addressed in public and any approach towards it is built on private initiatives. Those are started throughout the Diaspora and the homeland area. Material for children's mother tongue education is slowly developing and training is available in some locations. Parallel to this training for adults in the language and the culture is also done in the Western cities of Turkey and the Diaspora. Let us now turn into the specifics of the Zaza culture especially in view of the (representative) situation in Germany.

2.3.4.6.4 Germany – A representative Stance

From an emic and etic European point of view (1.1.2.3.2) the modern societal structure of the Zaza people is best described on the basis of the huge amount of migrants and their influence on their culture and the cultures of their host countries. Out of the 7,255,949 foreigner (8,8% of Germanys population), 1,738,831 are from Turkey. Close to 300,000 of them are Zaza, a total of close to 20 % (Statistik-Portal 2006 *Gebiet und Bevölkerung*; Orientdienst w/o year *Muslime verstehen* [Engl. Statistics-Portal 2006 *Area and Population*; Orientdienst w/o

---

[75] About the sacredness of the mother tongue and MLE programmes see Todd & Werner 2012.

year *Understanding Muslims*]). Besides the integration efforts, an increasing interest in political and cultural work to preserve the Zaza culture developed from within the Zaza ethnicity and with the support of the European countries. Sweden and Germany became the preferred countries of action, followed by the Netherlands and France. The politics on integration and assimilation in these countries encouraged foreigners to promote their origin (e.g. the right to get a translator in every language before judges or officials; every city installed the position of a "commissioner for foreigners" etc.).

Integration processes in migration movements always cause a generation gap with the second generation (Hiebert & Hiebert 1995:285). The second generation develops different social processes towards the host and the country of their parents. This leads to,

- either a schizophrenic way of life in two cultures, by rejecting the old culture and implementing the new one, or
- the rejection of the new culture and the overemphasizing of the parent's culture, or
- a constant and unwavering move between both worlds (:285-286).

The advantages of all of these three ways of life are obvious. A full integration is mainly possible with the third generation, although there is no guarantee or automatic given in social development. Sometimes it is the third generation that develops an extreme refusal of the host country, but mainly people adapt to the host culture.

Emigrants are passing on financial and material support to their family members in the homeland. In the last decade the trend was to buy estates in Turkey for renting. The migrated family members send money which is invested in estate projects. The rent goes to the extended family and parts of it are transferred back to the migrants in Europe to appreciate their investment and support of the wider family. The support from European migrants also includes household appliances and household resources. In return the family members in Turkey support the migrated family members with Turkish or traditional household utensils (e.g. wedding or circumcision endowment or decorations etc.).

Although a booming tourism industry has arisen in the West and Southwest of Turkey, the historically and culturally valuable East has not been discovered yet. Even archaeological traditions in this region have not been developed. As mentioned above a lot of historical discovery is not yet excavated. Before the foundation of the Republic of Turkey an archaeological and anthropological spirit of optimism went through the homeland area of the Zaza. This was related to the findings of historical data about the East of Turkey and the history of the Fertile Crescent. The collapse of the Ottoman Empire and the following unrests, caused by the foundation of the new Republic, brought an end to those explorations. In general the East of Turkey was troubled by the Russian-Turkic wars (1710/ 1711; 1774; 1792; 1828/1829; 1853-1856; 1877-1878; 1917/1918) and the colonialist interventions around the turn of the 20th century. The East became a war and conflict zone of instability and uncertainty hampering all long-term explorations and daunting its population.

Within the migration movement a keen interest in the historical maturity of their homeland area began. Western and Eastern scientific research flows together here as Islamic, Arabic and Ottoman literature contain many unpublished facts. More recently Boğazıcı University in İstanbul, Mardin Artuluk Unversity and Alparslan University in Muş have been investigating these old sources on a scientific level. The main focus of such research is on written evidence of traditions in Zazaki, religious developments of the *madrassa* (Islamic theologian education centres) and the historical relationship of the Zaza people to their neighbouring people groups mainly the Kurmanji speaking ethnicity. The European sources are more or less evaluated by Western researchers.

2.3.4.6.5 The EU and Turkey – Partners of Trade

Today the Zaza migrants are active in trade with Europe and America in the marble, agricultural, carpet and arts business. To give just one example, in the year 2006 the import of German goods to Turkey was around 12,8 billion Euro whereas Turkey exported goods of 8,3 billion Euro to Germany despite the huge difference in their total trade volume (dpa-Grafics in Gießener Anzeiger 27. May 2006:7).

Besides those businesses Zaza migrants are mainly involved in service industries in their host countries, such as the catering industry by so called "Döner / Doner Kebab" or "Kebap / Kebab" houses. Also work in garden maintenance or in construction attracts many Zaza. One reason for that is the low level of education due to language and cultural differences in the host country. Zaza people are also involved as translators for the officials and law courts. Legal regulations in the European Union compel those institutions to offer every applicant a mother tongue based agent for asylum application, family reunion, work and residence permission. Also a few work as lawyers or doctors to address the needs of their people in the Diaspora.

2.3.4.6.6 Integration and Education – Famous Zaza People

The above mentioned integration attitude plays an essential role in how well one adapts to the host culture. In general there are no restrictions to entering every level of education or study programme in the European Union, but language issues and the understanding of the taught material is essential to finish a study programme. This is a global requirement and should not be used as a political weapon against the host countries as some associations do, when they claim this as racism (e.g. the Turkish Islamic Foundation). Fortunately the Northern European countries also offer linguistical help for foreign students. The number of Zaza students with university degrees show that it is possible, although not easy, to study in Europe.

2.3.4.6.7 Famous Zaza People of the Past and Present

In history and present some famous Zaza people stick out. They often do not refer to their "Zazaness" but mainly to "Kurdishness" (2.2.3.2; 2.1.2.7):

Table 27 Famous Zaza People

Person	*Nationality*	*Prominence*	*General*
Bucak, Faik (Zazaki: Faîk Bûcak; 1919 - 1966; born in Hedro / Siverek); son Sertaç Bucak (1951; Berz 1995b:22-33; 2.3.3.5.2; see Appendix 5 Mewlid)	Parents: Zaza; Ottoman, Turkish, Kurdish	Advocate, lawyer	Proclaimed Kurdish nationalism; strong tribal leader of *Bıcax* tribe; leader of Türkiye Kürdistan and Kurdistan Democratic Party (KDP)
Büyukkaya; Necmettin (Zazaki: Necmettîn Buyukkaya; 1943 – 1984; born in Qerexan / Siverek)	Parents: Zaza; Turkish, Kurdish, Zaza	Political journalist	Died of torture in Diyarbakır prison; relations to PKK; first to write some material in Zaza;

Demirtaş, Selahattin (1973-; born in Palu; parents from Elazığ; 2.3.1.3.1; 3.1.1.5)	Parents: Zaza; Turkish, Kurdish	Advocate, Lawyer, politician	Active leader of Barış ve Demokrasi Partisi (BDP) with seat in parliament; claims Kurdish nationalism
Efendi, M. Eli Awni (Zazaki: M. Eli Awni Efendi; 1897-1952; born in Siverek; Berz 1995b:36-38)	Parents: Zaza Ottoman, Turkish; Kurdish	Studied Islamic theology in Egypt and	Interest in Islamic teaching and active in Kurdish nationalism
Efendi, Osman Babıj (Zazaki: Heci Eyyub Efendizade Osman Efendi; 1853-1929; born in Siverek; Berz 1995b: 33-35; 2.3.3.5.2; see Appendix 5 Mewlid)	Parents: Zaza Ottoman, Turkish; Kurdish	Studied Islamic Law and theology at Universities in Baghdad and Egypt	Influential as *mufti*, judge and *mıllah*. Brought much of Arabic Islamic teaching to the Zaza people.
Ehmedê Sofi Heseni (Zazaki: Mıla Ehmedê Xasi, Seydayê Xasi û Xoceyo Xasi; 1867-1951; born in Licê Hezan)	Parents: Zaza Ottoman, Turkish, Zaza, Kurdish	Studied Islamic theology, worked at Diyarbakır medrese; author	Wrote *Mewlidê Kırdi* and *Kıtab-ut Tesdid Bi Şerhi Muxteser-it Tewhid* Studied at Kurdish Diyarbakır Medrese and got angry because they denounced the Zaza people
Elçi, Sait (Zazaki: Mehmet Konuk; 1925-1971; born in Zeynep / Bingöl)	Parents: Zaza Turkish, Kurdish	Accountant; Politician	Founded with Faik Bucak (see above) the KDP in 1965;
Ensarioğlu, Mehmet Salim (1955- ; born in Dicle / Diyarbakır)	Parents: Zaza Turkish; Kurdish	Politician with AKP	Active in Kurdish movement but stands as Zaza

2 The Zaza

Gökalp, Ziya – Mehmed Ziya (1875 / 1876 – 1924; born in Çermik; 3.1.1.2.3)	Parents: Zaza Turkish; Zaza	sociologist, writer, poet, and political activist	Called himself "Turk", referred to Pan Turkism; nationalist
Güney, Yılmaz – Yılmaz Pütün (1937 – 1984; born in Yenice / Adana)	Father: Zaza (Siverek) Mother: Kurmanji (Varto) Turkish; Kurdish	novelist, film director, scenarist, actor	Called himself "assimilated Kurd"; Film "Yol" (1982)
Kılıçdaroğlu, Kemal (Nickname: Gandi Kemal; 1948; born in Ballıca Zazaki: Bolciye / Nazımiye /Tunceli – Dersim; 3.1.1.5)	Parents: Zaza Turkish	Politician,	Alevi; leader of Republican People's Party (Turkish: Cumhuriyet Halk Partisi, CHP)
Kırmızıtoprak, Dr. Sait (Dr. Şivan; 1935-1972; Civarik)	Parents: Zaza Turkish, Kurdish	Politician;	Leader of the KDP (Kurd Democratic Party); active in Northern Iraq and Turkey with Barzani and Faik Bucak (see above)
Mehmet Dersimi, Nuri (1893-1974; born in Axzonike; 2.1.1.4; 2.1.2.3)	Parents: Zaza Turkish, Kurdish, Zaza	Veterinarian, Politician	Planned Koçgiri rebellion of 1920 and advised Sayid Rıza
Pamukcu, Ebubekır (1946-1993; born in Budran / Budaran in Çermik)	Parents: Zaza Turkish; Zaza	Author and Publisher in Zazaki	Hanafi Sunni; founder of Zazaki magazine Piya (1976) and AYRE (1985)
Sheikh Said (Zazaki: Şêx Saido Piranıj, Kurdish: Şêx Seîdê Pîran; 1865 –	Parents: Zaza Ottoman; Turkish; Kur-	Religious rebellion leader	Called his rebellion a Kurdish uprising; gathered many

1925; born in Piran / Hınıs; 2.3.1.3.2)	dish		Sunni Zaza tribal small scale societies under his authority
Saıt Rıza (Seyit Rıza in Turkish; Sey Rıza or Pir Sey Rıza in Zazaki; 1863 – 1937; born in Lirtik; 2.3.1.3.2)	Parents: Zaza Ottoman; Turkish; Kurdish	Rebellion and religious leader	Gathered Alevi tribal small scale societies under his rule; until today his grave is unknown

The biographies of these prominent Zaza people show that they all claim to be "Kurdish" and that Zazaki is a "Kurdish dialect", as they are most active in the Kurdish nationalism movement. This prominence in advocating the "Kurdish" issue makes it difficult for those Zaza that do not promote a "Kurdish" relationship (2.1.2: 2.2.3: 2.3.1.3.1; 3.1.1.4.4; 3.5).

2.3.4.6.8 Racism and Anti-foreignism or Xenophobia

The Zaza people are recognized as "Turks" in their European host countries. Their Turkish citizenship is proved by their passport. Yet the identification with "the Turks" generates a perception that arose in the past.

The history of the Ottoman Empire in Europe is still present in the consciousness of the Europeans (3.1.2). This is the reason why a European will not differentiate between any groups in Turkey. Even Armenians that have been in Europe for many generations fall under this suspicion. This will not mainly become obvious in daily routine but in the mingling with officials, especially concerning bureaucratic issues like asylum application (foreigners department), financial issues (finance department), religious acts (local officials; e.g. Muslim identity card) or questions on education (education department). Also the level of unemployment and welfare recipients is higher for the Zaza people compared to the host countries population. The job departments and the social welfare institutions notice this conflict. The whole situation is an intrinsically political act and the public opinion in the European countries is sensitive to the topic.

The spiritual encounter of Islam and Christianity, the cultural clash of East-Mediterranean and Northern Europe people groups and the conflict of different levels of education come together. Such circumstances carry a lot of potential for xenophobia and nationalism. A good example is given by the so called "head scarf conflict". The European countries as well as Turkey struggle with the wearing of the head scarf or the closed cover in public. Whereas Turkey, due to a revitalization of Islamic traditions allows them to be worn nowadays, the opposite is happening in Europe started by France, and followed by Belgium. Most often, governments build their policies on tolerance and hope that the problem will not turn up. In few cases the local officials prohibited the head scarf in public positions with the argument of the religious freedom of the others. In this case the head scarf is recognized as a religious symbol.

Contrary to a rejection of the host countries' population by some Zaza, a huge number of emigrants praise those countries for the freedom of speech and daily routine, the medical care and the social insurance/care (RH, MT, MP and others).

In the 1980s and 1990s the PKK developed a programme to force Zaza and Kurds in the Diaspora to give financial support to their struggle in the homeland. Also they were expected to promote the PKK activities in Europe and the United States (Brauns 2006; Kreyenbroek & Sperl 2002:3, 102). Those forceful attempts of intimidation are still recognized by the Zaza people. They were able to repel such forceful pressure. With the imprisonment of *Abdullah Öcalan* in 1999 and the unilateral ceasefire announced in the same year the activities decreased. Since 2007 the forceful political activities restarted after the end of the ceasefire agreement with Turkey.

2.3.4.6.9 Summary

Migration movements make migrants into emigrants and immigrants. The European Union as a stable and well-off economic and political solid institution attracts foreigners. Sweden and Germany became the favourite countries for the Zaza people to migrate. First they were invited as guest labourers in the 1960s, and then they came as asylum seekers in the eighties and nineties and recently to reunite families. As a result the EU and Turkey became close partners in trade and are now working towards the full membership of Turkey in the EU. One of the requirements towards an EU membership is mother tongue based multilingual education for all language groups in Turkey. Recently huge progress in this direction is being made and the Zaza people profit from such development.

As migrants in foreign countries such as Germany, xenophobia, anti-foreign feeling and racism become daily fields of experience for the Zaza people. On the other hand these countries guarantee freedom and strong laws punish those who violently disturb those social spheres. As such, both areas are observed by government institutions that are always on the alert due to international recognition of the democratic standards in Germany or the European Union.

2.3.4.7 Summary of the Social Structure

The social structure of the Zaza people follows a feudal and hierarchical system. Kinship by descent represents the basic institutional setting. A person is classified not by his job or deeds but by his kinship relation within the wider community.

The nuclear together with the extended family (*kuflet*; *aile*) forms the central core element of the Zaza culture. The linking of such closely related social units in a small scale society is carried out on the level of the "tribe" (*ezbet*; *aşiret*; *kuflet*). Such microcultures are organized by social institutions,
- a spiritual leadership (*mıllah*; mullaharchy),
- a religious-political leadership (*şeik*) and
- a local political leadership (*ağa*; *agha*).

The families of this leading group are arranged in a feudalistic way. All three social positions are handed on by descent or in some cases entered by extraordinary courage against threats from outside or inside the Zaza community. The *mıllah* can also be appointed by the cem (constitutional gathering). Education and theological training are prerequisites for an appointment. Often the theological training is passed on within a family.

Confederations of small scale Zaza unities are based on military needs against threats from outside the people group. These confederations were either agitating against anti-Islamic tendencies or supporting the national politics. They led into religious upheavals or a total political realignment (2.1.4.6; 2.3.1.3.1; 2.3.1.3.2). One could also say that the "Kurdish question" led to the resumption of those confederations. In consequence these political alliances generated political parties or the PKK to stand together against the national oppression.

The endangerment of Zazaki as a result of an enveloping social change led to a revitalization movement which is observable nowadays. The education of children in their language and culture plays an enormous role. Bi- and Multilingualism are not only threats but obviously are a good path to a better economic job portfolio and cognitive abilities to communicate and adapt well in different cultural settings. The Diaspora reflects those opportunities and signals the economic potential that the trade business between Turkey and the European Union includes.

Besides these positive effects one should not forget about the difficulties and obstacles that a life as an emigrant in a foreign country brings with it. Besides an idealizing of the homeland, emigrants often experience xenophobia, racism or discrimination in their host countries. Vice versa the same goes for foreigners in the Zaza homeland (e.g. Arabs, Turks). The question of nationalism comes into

2.3.5 The Zaza – Traditionally Peasants

Small scale societies that are built on tribal diversity are either following a structure as nomads or peasants. In contrast to the widespread Kurds who were originally nomadic, the Zaza people claim to be settlers. The lack of any tradition and social rudiment relevant to a nomadic lifestyle supports such statements (Hayıg 2007). In close cooperation with their Armenian neighbours who were also settled they worked as craftsmen, peasants and merchants, and the reciprocal labour division hints at an originally peasantry lifestyle by the Zaza people (see Richter 2006:25).

Strict labour diffusion is not reasonable since the old traditions describe upholsterers, bakers, blacksmiths and carpet and tapestry makers out of the Zaza society. After the ethnocide of the Armenians the Zaza people took over such crafts responsibilities (Hayıg 2007). Nonetheless the construction and repairment of the Armenian irrigation systems and their specialisations in agriculture, like wheat and corn or other breeding, were never taken up.

2.3.5.1 House Construction

Another indication of sedentarism in the Zaza ethnicity is demonstrated by the way houses are constructed and shaped. Typically their houses are divided on two levels, an upper floor and a basement. People live in the former and livestock with fodder storages in the latter. A strict physical division of both spheres of life (men and animal) is obligatory. Due to economic reasons and the climate conditions ranging from +40 C in summer to -30 degrees C in winter times, animal feed is stored close to livestock. In winter times cow dung and wood is used for heating. In summer the cow dung is mixed with litter or dry grass and pressed in buckets. The dried product is stored in piles up to 2m high that are protected against wind, rain and snow by leather or other sheltering covers. The dry cowpats are taken through a hole from the inside to the outside. Sometimes the whole pile has to be held up so that it doesn't collapse.

A big challenge for the villagers in former times was the maintenance of the wooden roof. The wood was protected by a layer of dry brick clay. Every autumn and every spring season it had to be prepared for either the cold winter or the hot summer by fixing crafts with additional clay. For this activity every household owned a *loğê* which was established on the roof. It was a wooden handle with a stone cylinder about 50 cm broad. The whole tool functioned as roller.

Diagram 17 Standard Layout Plan of a House and Drawings

ver ra (Front view)

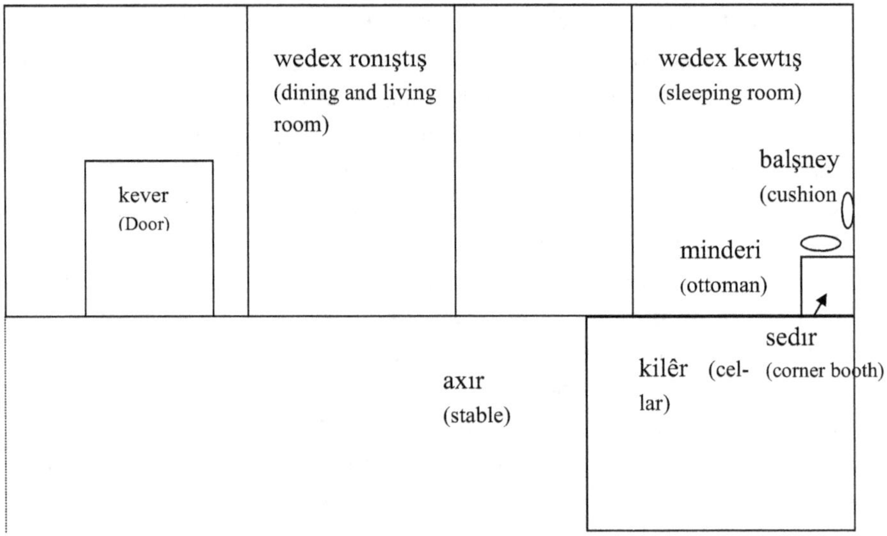

	wedex ronıştış (dining and living room)		wedex kewtış (sleeping room)
kever (Door)			balşney (cushion) minderi (ottoman)
	axır (stable)	kilêr (cellar)	sedır (corner booth)

juinê kat cor ra (Upper floor top view)

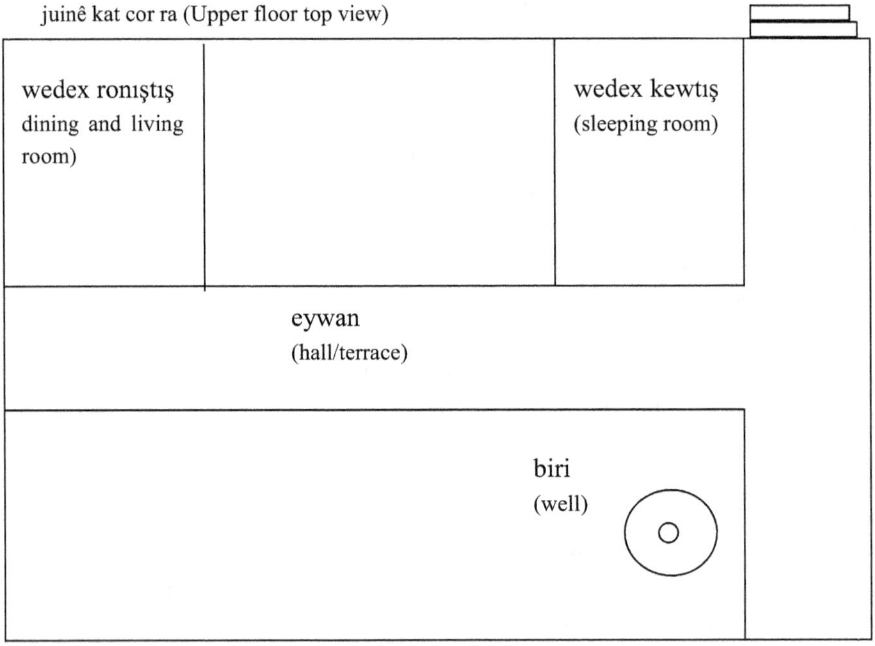

wedex ronıştış dining and living room)		wedex kewtış (sleeping room)
	eywan (hall/terrace)	
	biri (well)	

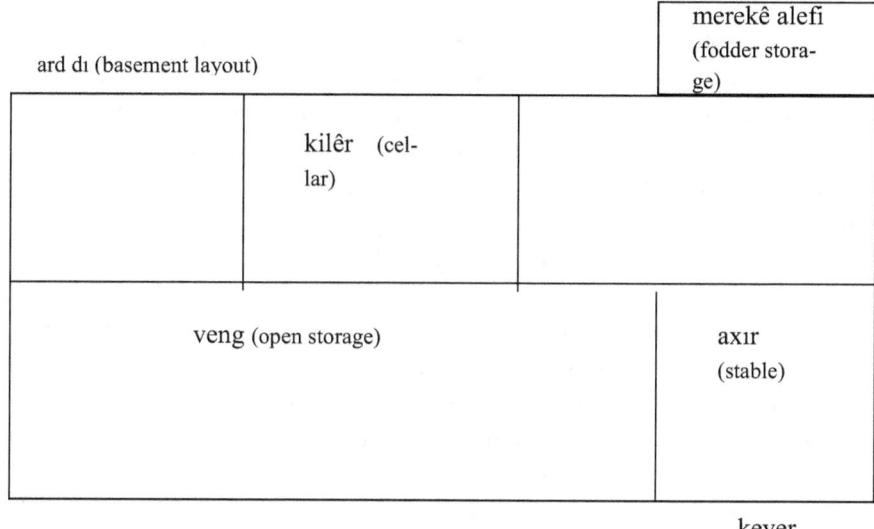

ard dı (basement layout)		merekê alefi (fodder storage)
	kilêr (cellar)	
veng (open storage)		axır (stable)
		kever (entry)

With modern house building the houses got a concrete roof with a layer of bitumen on it or in many areas metal corrugated roofs against the snow. Nowadays maybe 30% of the houses in villages still hold the traditional construction style. Only the living area that functions simultaneously as kitchen, dining and living room is heated in winter. The inhabitants sleep in the living room during extremely cold times owing to the heating of the kitchen and the underground livestock.

2.3.5.2 Clothing and Outward Appearance

In everyday life women wear coloured headscarves and casual wear. This includes bloomers, a wide outer garment, similar to men. Traditionally the festive costumes are decorated by dags with conspicuous pieces of money or gold worked in. Red is the predominant colour. Men wear baggy trousers as all over the Middle East. A broad belt with a central golden emblem reflects his social status. Moustache and thick hair are a status symbol. The latter is reflected in the fact that the "beardless" (*kose*) is considered to be without honour or prestige (Hayıg 2007: *Lajê Axay*).

Another obvious area of outward appearance is reflected in the decoration of the homes. Rugs, carpets, pillow cases, scarf patterns and other decorated items are predominantly based on black, red and beige or white. A pattern of prongs like a "Z" or "S" is sometimes thought to be typical. This could not be proved during my visits to the Zaza ethnicity; however the Zaza people refer to specific symbols on decorated items as typical. In general the patterns are simpler and do not show a higher development of decoration style, like e.g. Persian arts do. It has to be added at this point that arts are in general not developed into specific works of art but are mainly woven into daily life items. No real works of art are known; that is not to say that painting, carving or sculpturing did not evolve, but these arts play a secondary role. This possibly has to do with the work division between Armenians and Zaza in former times in which Armenians covered the development of the arts. With their disappearance their knowledge went too. More research would be necessary on this item.

The colour red is dominant in Zaza culture. Carpets, the flag waved during weddings and even the adornment of the grooms house is with red clothes or the colour red, made by Henna (loan from Arabic: حِنَّاء a red granulate made from the plant *Lawsonia inermis*, also called henna tree). The Zazaki term for red is *sur*, the flag is called *sûrok* "the red one" and the adornment on the grooms house *sûrsûrok* the "red-red one" (a flag, cloth, or symbols in red; Werner, Brigitte 2012). Ruby red is often used for honouring someone, this could be table cloths, handkerchiefs, adornment on clothing, etc. Red, one can say has a special status in the Zaza world. Referring to my informants this perception does not trace back to Turkish influence and contrasts the vivid use of green in Islam.

2.3.5.3 Ethnomusicology – Observations in the Zaza Culture

Music performs a mystery that exceeds logical apprehension and reaches into the religious sphere of a culture (Steiner 1990:283). From an ethnomusicological[76] view the religious frame of the Zaza comes into play regarding the aesthetic forms of expression. Furthermore music performs distinct and specific communicational representations, which are expressed by a culture (Nida 1990:39).

The Zaza music is characterized by a Persian and Zoroastrian influence which is very obvious in the practice of Sufi'i Dervish orders and the religions of Alevism and Sufi'i Islam (*tasavvuf* in Houston 2001:39-40) which has some influence on Sunnism as well. It is within the area of music that the Muslim Zaza and their non-Islamic neighbours do vary a lot. The difference in musical expression between the Christian-Armenian, Christian-Syrian, Jewish, Alevi and Sunni community was demonstrated recently in the EBRU exhibition which offers musical and written testimony of most of the people groups that live in Turkey, e.g. Durak 2006 exhibition catalogue with accompanied CD.

The music of the Zaza, who were sometimes addressed as *Dımılı*, became a widely recognized style of arts in the 13th and again in the 18th century. This went so far that even in the 20th century some acknowledged it as Turkish folk music (Houston 2007:40). Houston expounds the Turkish state and claims that it rejected any influence from previous Byzantine influence, specifically during its foundational state. The western influence from classical music soon decreased and functioned as an object of prestige for the upper class. Folk music became the popular vehicle for fulfilling the function of identifying with Turkish nationalism. However this Turkish folk music was often of "Kurdish" in a wider sense (Houston 2007:40) or Zaza origin (Gündüzkanat 1997:74). This development becomes obvious at the beginning of the 21st century, when, immediately after the softening of the Kurdish and Zaza language ban in 2008, five radio stations and one TV channel opened. Music and arts play an essential part in their programs (Andrews 2002d:317).

In the Southern Group the *Sheikh* sometimes took the role of a leading bard. The basic promoters of Zaza music in their homeland were travelling musicians

---

[76] Leibniz looks on music as the "secret arithmetics of our souls" (cit. in Steiner 1990:283). Ethnomusicology increased in popularity in Christian development aid due to an expanding interest in oral materials and paths of passing on the Biblical Message (*Chronological Bible Storying* CBS; Hz. Jesus-Film). Also anthropology and social sciences are increasingly interested in research on oral traditioning and the religious expression in arts.

that offered music for festivities and as a vehicle to transport traditions on an oral-aural basis. They were welcomed to play dance music and to entertain the guests at festivities (:74). Although the class of *pir mıllah* and *sheikh* mainly passed on their function by heritage, it was sometimes possible to become such a person by being taught or getting an education far away (Sunni). The Islamic centres were led by prominent spiritual teachers and based in capitals of the former empires (Bagdad, Damascus, Cairo etc.). This offered the possibility of entering different social levels.

In her work about space and subjectivity, Neyzi (2002) observes two brothers from Berlin (Germany). Both of them are musicians from the Northern Dialect area and both perform their music as a proclamation to their audience of the Zaza people's identity and struggles. In the same way Metin and Kemal Kahraman use music to motivate their people to read and write their language. Coming from this approach ethnomusicology also bears an element of language development in it (see below). Interestingly Neyzi claims that by their music the brothers bridge the gap between the Diaspora and the homeland. In music and arts space is proclaimed to be a global and holistic promotion of a cultures language and culture (:91). The Kahraman brothers themselves symbolize authority in their songs. They present their language and culture to the outside in lieu of the people group. Neyzi calls this "embodying the elders". In other words they replace the authorities from the homeland by bearing their function into the Diaspora. Maybe one does not want to go as far as Neyzi, but music and arts play an important role in the Zaza tradition and as a style of communication.

Beside vocals and chanting the following musical instruments play an important role in the Zaza society: The three-stringed guitar (*saz, tembore*), the flute (*zurna*) and the drum (*neqera*). Melodies and harmonies are fixed but the combination of them is flexible so the occasion determines the outcome. The range goes from a fast ecstatic encouragement for dance, for joyous or religious events, to a slow melancholic stance, in case for mourning, recollection or longing. Also oral traditions imply accompaniment of music as an expression of emotions or to emphasise the point of a story.

Main topics in the Zaza music are represented by the
- longing for the homeland,
- death and eternity,
- stories of misfortune,
- poverty and prosperity,

2 The Zaza

- mental return to traditional virtues and historical cultural settings,
- interpersonal love (husband-wife, sisters, parents-children,
- war and peace with a desire for peace (Questionnaire 2005).

Research in oral societies revealed that they use "music, rhyme, stories, drama and anecdotes to process stored knowledge" (Hiebert & Hiebert 1995:111). The performers use literary rhyme or poetry as style. They follow

- a chiastic (cruciform) pattern which sometimes goes across several layers (A, B, C, C', B', A'),
- similar ending in the strophic form (A, A, A, A) or
- parallelism (A, A', B, B': e.g. Dewran w/o year *Hazar Reng – Hazar Veng*, w/o author 1992. *Dersim Türküleri: Tayê Lawıkê Dersımi*).

As mentioned above in former times the melodies were imparted by travelling bards or dervishes (*pir*; 2.3.3.3; see Laut 1996:31-32; Kehl-Bodrogi 1989:177). They travelled from village to village and functioned in the social gatherings called *cemat* as spiritual, judicial and political leaders. In the Northern Group *Memo Bom* (20th century AD) became a famous *pir*. He is well known for many anecdotes, stories, songs and nuggets of wisdom. These musicians sometimes called *aşık* are central figures at weddings, circumcisions or religious or social gatherings like the *eid* festival (breaking the fast), annual meetings like *rojê gağan*, new year etc.

Although ethnomusicology covers a manifold variety of functions these musicians and music in the Zaza group covered some specific functions. The following list describes not only recent but also historical purposes:

- passing on cultural and linguistic tradition on an oral-aural foundation,
- support of the central social element of the *cemat* as a social, political and judicial event by promoting music and arts as means of people group identity,
- giving prestige to an individual or a group of people without owning a social rank or belonging to a higher class,
- expression of the people group's self identity to the outside through performances,
- sharing intertribal resources during festivities and social gatherings, thus encouraging social networks.

2.3.5.4 Ethnomusicology – Dance and Performance

Ethnomusicology is closely related to folk and square dance. Dancing plays an important role in many festivities and social activities. Traditionally the music played at weddings, folk festivals or during family or small scale celebrations is stimulated by professionals called *aşık*. They are often hired and either (sometimes) Kurmanji speaking "Kurds" from a tribe that is well known for their musical specification, or, as mentioned above spiritual leaders that act like travelling bards. Their repertoire covers around ten basic melodies which are varied in pace and rhythm. Guitar (*saz, guitar*), drum (*davul, neqara*) and flute (*zırrna / zurrna;* compact form *zuli*) are the main instruments. The categories of dance compare with other Mediterranean or even Persian people groups. Typical ways of performance are called *ğovend*. During special celebrations a dance called *kirr* is performed (2.5.3).

Whereas in the Kurmanji speaking society gender segregation leads to the formation of separated gender in dancing, the Zaza people favour mixed dancing groups. On a professional level as in dance performances no gender specific segregation was observed. Those professional performances focus on themes like love, war, circumcision, peace, reconciliation, engagement and courtship (Questionnaire on Worldview 2005).

Dancers each hold the little fingers of their neighbouring dance partners. They form a row which moves in a three-step glide around an imaginary centre. Sometimes the wedding couple, the musicians or honoured persons are dancing in this centre. A second or third row can be formed which is further away from the centre. As mentioned above the rows are often mixed and it is only in very religiously Sunni oriented environments that the gender segregation is strictly expected. All rows move in the same direction but with different pace. The first and last person of the row holds a coloured handkerchief in the hand which is waved following the rhythm. The musicians move sometimes from the centre to the outside and back. If a person is dancing very enthusiastically the musicians are free to go along with him and stimulate his dancing by playing close to him. Those motivational acts are highly appreciated by the dancers.

Mother tongue musicians started to go public since 1980 in Europe and since 2001 in the homeland. Nowadays modern music and instruments (electric guitar; synthesizer, electric drum etc.) replace the traditional style. A growing number of musicians try to combine modern and traditional music with each other. Popular Zaza performers are:

Mikail Aslan (NZ),
Servan Barıhaş (NZ),
Hasan Dewran (NZ),
Metin and Kemal Kahraman (NZ),
Zelemele (NZ),
Sait Altun (EZ),
Sait Kiliç (EZ),
Avni Polat (EZ),
Cem Astare (SZ),
ZazaVaj (SZ),
Nilüfer (Turk.).

Around 30% of their music is in Turkish and the rest in Zazaki. However, they are recognized as Zaza musicians from within the Zaza and by outsiders. Most of these musicians present the full text of their songs on the inner cover of their music media. Interested parties can thus follow up the content and learn to read the language. This is a huge contribution towards language development and standardization.

2.3.5.5 The Snake - Symbol of Peasantry

A feature of peasantry societies is demonstrated by the exceptional position of the *snake*. This is pointed out by Käser, given the positive appearance in myths of peasants. This applies for the Zaza people also. The "cult of the snake" is most distinctive and symbolizes it as a holy or sacred creature. This happens by

> a stick called çuwê haqı (God's stick), the top of which is carved in the form of a snake's head. It is preserved in a green cloth bag suspended from a wooden pillar (êrkyan) in the sanctuary of the village of Kiştim near Dersim. The stick is believed to be a piece of the rod of Moses and the bag a copy of the one carried by St. John the Baptist (Halajian cit. in Asatrian 1995a: *Dımli*) in cult ceremonies on the feast of Xızır İlyas, which is celebrated after a three-day fast, during which, according to some reports, even cattle and other livestock are not fed. On this day thousands of pilgrims gather in the village to gaze upon the holy staff (Asatrian 1995a: *Dımli*).

Geiger traces the snake-cult back to Old-Iranian devotional practices of the "dragon" or "cloud-snake", which was derived from the demon of thunder and lightning called *dahāka*. He stood in antagonism to the goddess of water and spoilt the essential water. As time went on the demon moved into a picture of a man with snake heads out of his shoulder (1882:162, 209).

The feast of *Xızır İlyas* coincides with the Armenian celebration of *Surp Sargis / Surp Sarkis* (Asatrian & Arakelova 2004:240). In the village of *Kishtim* is a sanctuary for the snake cult. During *Xızır İlyas*, Zaza pilgrims gather in the village to see the Holy Staff (*Evliya Kishtimi*, the saint of kishtim, or *Cuye Haqi* "the staff of the truth"). The great stone building is used by the representatives of the priesthood who sit around the *Holy Hearth* and begin the *Sima* (hearing) accompanied by musical instruments. To the right of the hearth on the wood-pillar (*erkyan*) hangs a green cloth bag in which is a staff. The top of this staff is carved in the form of a snake's head; this is the *Cuye Haqi*. Dersimi and Halajian report that because of the great number of people crowded here, the heart-rending spiritual songs, and the mourning and lamentation, those gathered enter into a trance and see the staff become a snake, leave the bag, and after some miraculous acts, returns into the bag and changes back into the staff. A resemblance with Hz. Moses' staff that he was called to use by godly command during the Exodus of Israel out of Egypt is obvious (Exodus chapters 7-14; Numeri 20:11).

Important to this observation is that even the Southern Group, although following the Sunni school of Islam, takes the same positive attitude towards the snake (Arakelova 1999-2000:398-399). This contrasts to the general negative stance towards the snake in Islam and Christianity.

In the myths and stories of the Zaza people (e.g. Mahmeşa by Hayıg 2007) the snake is presented as a clever and helpful animal. Humans have to fear the snake due to its capability of killing a person, but its appearance is often felt to function as a revelation or pronouncement. Sometimes the snake offers protection and is seen as a human-like creature (Asatrian & Arakelova 2004:266). Often only children can see the snake-man. In Yezidism *Xudānē mālē* - The Spirit of the Household resembles the house-snake mythology, or as Comerd points out in the Zaza belief that this is *Wāyirō čei* – "Master of the house" (1996:69-74). The "Master of the house" is often referred to as a home-dwelling snake. He lives by the fire-place or *ocax*. As Asatrian and Arakelova point out, "the Zaza *Wāyir* and the Yezidi *Xudān* are virtually different phonetic reflections of OIr. 'xwatāwan-. The Zaza *čē* "house, home" comes from OIr. 'kata-" (2004:267). Thereby a

- white snake (*maro sıpiya*) protects a well as the tutelary spirit over the sacred area. The snake lives somewhere around the well and it can transform into a human form namely a man. For this very reason the snake is reverenced by everybody who enters the sacred area.
- black snake (*maro siya*) holds magic powers and is eschewed. If an encounter is inevitable one should kill it otherwise it will take revenge. A prayer of protection by calling the name of *Allah* preserves from harm (personal conversation with RH; Questionnaire 2005).

If by chance someone comes across the love act of snakes and he manages to throw over them a shirt or a piece of cloth he is considered to have an open wish-fulfilment (MK personal conversation 2005). In contrast, observing the love act without any attempt to leave the scene brings harm (curse; taboo). A lunar eclipse is described by the expression "the snake eats the moon", which demonstrates the powers that are assigned to the snake (Questionnaire 2005-2006).

2.3.5.5.1 Agriculture and Farming

In the 18th century AD smallholders formed the most abundant societal system before industrialization (Dye 1979:33-34). The Zaza people followed a distinctive agriculture approach with many farming products. In consequence they reflect a small scale society of smallholders without a political state territory, but fixed territorial areas that they claim as their homeland (Dye 1979:33). Concerning the riches of agricultural products the unpublished lexicon of Hayıg lists fruits, vegetables, products of wheat and corn, as well as sweets made out of natural ingredients (announced 2012).[77]

In the past, due to the expectations of a peasant society any culture change was desperately rejected (Nida 1990:173). Not until the Modern era and the repressions of the last forty years did culture change accelerate and it traces back to "exterior influences" (Hesselgrave 2002:321). Besides political repression there was the rumour that military commandos disguised as "guerrilla-Kurds" take out sorties against village people. The fact that young soldiers out of the East were forced to dress like Kurds and have to fight in the front lines of up-

---

[77] Nida differentiates between societies of smallholders and small scale societies (1990:172). Hiebert & Hiebert disagree, because a clear cut distinction is not possible (1995:186). Nida does not refer to mixed models but defines the foundation of such societies as pure systems. The Zaza society represents a good example of such a mixed form.

heavals in the East against their own fellow countryman adds to these rumours. Another alarming factor is given by local government representatives in the homeland area of the Zaza who are ready to use violence by harassing the populace under their rule (Kreyenbroek & Sperl 2002:104). Zaza people report administrative distress, as well as military and police annoyance. Military activities found their climax lately in the 1990s and are recently only undertaken as a reaction to activities against the government (e.g. riots, PKK activities).

As smallholders and part of a hierarchically articulated society, the Zaza people are exposed to their own small scale societal (tribal) system and the national political system. The latter is represented by a centralistic multiparty democracy with a strong police- and military organization which is embedded in a national and international active produce and trading market based on its own Asian rules (Hiebert & Hiebert 1995:185-186). The whole setting contributes to the tensions mentioned above. The *agha* and the *sheikh* perform a stable and mediating instance as far as their surrounding system allows them to deal. The Three-Class society of the Zaza people is embodied in a commonly recognized structure as a mixed culture (:193).

2.3.5.5.2   Image of limited Good

Foster based his observations of social-economic peculiarities in societies on the perception of the *Image of limited Good* (1965:296-297). The term "Good" stands for those goods that a people group has access to. This approach is very helpful to understand the hierarchical structures of the Zaza people. A study by Malina from the New Testament reflects the settings in the Jewish society during the days of Hz. Jesus the prophet. Malina describes the relationship of the individual person as part of a patron / client setting (surrounding structure) on the vertical and as part of kindred spirit people on the horizontal level (inner structure) (2001:106; Werner 2006:32). The access to the outlying goods, those which are not immediately reached, leads to a societal imbalance and tension. In this way closed systems like the Zaza culture generate a strain on the individuum to keep balance.[78]

---

[78] *Goods* describe both physical things (high-price merchandise, food, property etc.) as well as intangible values (honour, fame, hate etc.). Smallholders and small scale societies form closed societal systems. In these the expansion of one member at the expense of others. In consequence an ongoing struggle to keep balance moves the people (Foster 1965:296-297; see above the term "culture change").

Sustained isolation of the eastern minority groups, caused by political repression, developed a vacuum on maintenance and admittance for their population. The former principle of self generation and supply was disturbed by destruction, oppression and persecution. The subsequent migration was directed towards the West, especially the large cities and tourisms centres, due to expected employment prospects. Another migration wave led into Europe, the States and Australia. Caused by the repression of non-Turkish speaking people groups their hierarchical societal system broke down. The lack of resistance and the ongoing pressure caused an inner and still ongoing process of disintegration. For this very reason the Zaza people until today demonstrate a high resistance to moving back into their homeland area.

2.3.5.5.3 Traditions related to the concept "Snake"

Tradition holds it that Adam and Eve were both tempted by a snake using wheat. The snake offered a full meal based on wheat meal to Eve and Adam being with her. Both took the meal.[79] Many stories of the genesis of people are based on Gnostic interpretations of the Jewish genesis in Genesis (1Mose) chapter 1 to 3. Often the goal is to keep the origin to a forefather or a foremother. A good example is represented by *Pirā-Fāt* - The Foremother of the Yezidis which is the patroness of women-in labour, as well as of the newborn She functions as a protecting power against the evil demon *Al* (Asatrian & Arakelova 2004:244-246, Asatrian 2001).

This belief follows the Jewish tradition in Old Hebrew content as passed on in the Hebrew Bible. Both report a temptation through a snake but they differ on the subject of temptation. The Jewish tradition has instead of wheat a fruit, traditionally accepted as an apple (1Mose 3:1-6). Following the hermeneutical and communicational principle of traditions, to shorten originals and make them easier to understand, the longer description of the Hebrew Bible should be viewed

---

[79] A interesting story of origin is given by Asatrian and Arakelova about the Yezidi people: Once, the Yezidi legend tells us, Eve claimed that childen were produced by her alone and that Adam had no part in creating them. In order to test her claim they put their seeds in separate jars and closed them. When, nine months later, they opened Eve's jar, they found serpents, scorpions and poisonous insects, while in Adam's jar there was a beautiful moon-faced child. They called the boy *Šahid bin jarr* (i. e. in Arabic "Šahid, the son of the pot"); he later married a *hūri* [paradise virgin. EW.] and became the Forefather of the Yezidis (see in detail Spät 2002:27-56). This account of the origin of the Yezidis is also confirmed in one of the Yezidis' so-called Holy Books, the "Black Book" (*Mash'afē řaš*; 2004:244).

as original. Also the proof of written testimonies by the Hebrew tradition before the 3rd century BC demonstrates its preliminary role.

As part of this description a topic is presented which is part of culture and language. The term "man" not only reflects the linguistic and different influences about its origin but also the cultural and cognitive issues of perception of the world, conscience and thought.

In addition to the concept of the snake the swallow (*hachacik*), pigeon (*bewran*) and stork (*legleg*) are considered holy animals, which achieve special adoration (Questionnaire 2005).

2.3.5.6 Summary

The Zaza people represent a peasantry and animal husbandry practicing society. They did not follow any nomadic lifestyle. All their traditions prove a history as peasants and a settled way of life. This is reflected in the construction of their houses. The basement functions as cellar, domestic stable, barn and food storage. The upper floor functions as living area with kitchen, living room and terrace. A strict division of both areas is reaching right through daily life. The clothing and outward appearance of the Zaza people follow the general needs of peasants but differ essentially in colour and decoration from the surrounding people groups. The traditional women's scarf is decorated with pieces of money in gold and represents the clan's colours. Men wear broad belts with golden belt buckles also showing the clans symbol.

The Zaza music had such an influence in the past that recent Turkish music contains many of its ethnomusicological features. The music reflects the topics of homesickness, patriotism, sexual and romantic love as well as brotherhood. In general a more melancholic and depressive attitude compared to western music is obvious. Herein the Zaza music reflects a general Mediterranean concept of music. Music is essentially used to pass on tradition. Profession in music is passed on by the spiritual leaders and reflects the basic principles of this social community. In gatherings like the *cemat* music plays an important role. Main themes in music are related to war and peace, interpersonal love, poverty and prosperity, longing for the homeland and stories of misfortune.

Compared to the western perception of the world the snake is emphasized as good and even helpful in some situations. The snake plays into the perception of the sacred and taboo. It is sometimes combined with religious concepts such as observing and guarding sacred areas.

As farmers the Zaza society depends on the limitation of natural goods. The main limitation is represented by seasonal fruits and harvests which perform the annually cyclical course of time. The *Image of limited Good* represents those social restrictions that lead to community stratification and classes. Three classes dominate the Zaza culture. Following the hierarchical structure a small upper and feudal class of *Sheikh* and *Agha* with their extended families rules the small scale society. A broad middle class of peasants forms the main body. A very poor lower class of widows, handicapped or foreigners without family or relatives is dependent on grants and the mercy of the main social body. The society in itself represents a conglomerate of many small scale societies with their spiritual and political leaders.

2.4 Linguistic and Cultural Liaison - *Merdım*

In this segment we will look at one area of overlap in a linguistic-cultural documentation of the term *merdım* "man" and its semantic context. This phrase concerns an essential section of a human society inasmuch as *humans* build up a society. The hyponym *merdım* "man" has two main meanings; it stands synonymous for "humans" as well as for the masculine counterpart to a woman. Both connotations are describing the basis of humanity. In English this is reflected by the manifold combinations that are possible with the term as for instance wo*man*, hu*man*, wolf*man*, and many others.

2.4.1 An exemplary Study - the Term "man" (*merdım*)

For this section I want to refer back to the previously described anthropological phenomenon called LEIC (*Location of Emotion, Intellect and Character*) which plays an important role in the description of a perception of the world (1.1.3.3; 2.3.2.1.3; 2.3.2.2). LEIC and conscience are closely related: The latter represents an immaterial and omnipresent organ that leads men in thought and deed. As a matter of fact a nation can also reflect core values which are expressed in the *Folk Conscience* (Germ. "Volksgewissen") that is, the "conscience of a nation".

Every "man" or human possesses a conscience which is formed by enculturation and the genetic material. A perception of the worlds reflects the conscience of a man and his society. To understand the concept "man" or *merdım* in Zazaki it is necessary to look at their perception of the world. In it, the social function, the duty and the relationship to other individuals is reflected.

2.4.2 Etymology of *merdım*

The Zaza term for "man" is *merdım* / *merdum* (human, pl. people). Derived terms are *camêrd* (brave), *mêrd* (man, masculine), *mêrdek* (man, husband; for all words see Grûba Xebate ya Vatê 2009:315).[80] The phrase originates from the Pahlavi *mertum* 'person, individual, baby' and the root *mert-tōhm 'mankind, semen of man', Farsi *merdom* 'people' (Akkoç, Keskin & Zazaoğlu 2010:52). Kurmanji uses *meriv* / *meriv, însan* / *insan, peya, zulam, merov* or *meriv* for those terms (Kocadag 2010:262). In Turkish the expression *merik*[81] occurs, although *erkek, bey* and *adam* represent the main realizations. Etymologically the Zaza word originated from Persian *mard* (man), from Iranian *martia and Indo-European *mortio* (mortal).[82] Looking at those terms it becomes obvious that the semantical environment is related to the concepts of "death" and "to perish". During my research almost all who were polled stated a semantical closeness to the expression "death" as a connotation to *merdım* (Questionnaire *on Worldview* 2005). This parallels English where "mortal" or "withering" is also connected ideologically to the phrase "man". Note that this research was based on the *ideal* and mental-semantic word environment. In reality or *real* life the interviewee did not sense this closeness (ideal vs. real).

Morality as part of religious perceptions is only connected to the physical body not to the immaterial soul. The immortality of the soul *gan* (Persian loan word) *nefes* and *rı'h* (Arabic loan words) was never questioned. Islamic and former Christian dogmatics bring about those beliefs.

2.4.2.1 Profane and Sacred

Religious studies hold "death" and "dying" to the sphere of the sacred and holy that is often evidenced with *taboo* (1.1.3.3; 2.3.2.1.4; 2.3.3.2.5). In cultural or

---

[80] Against Hadank, who does not observe a difference in use of *merdım* and *mêrdek*. He states that the terms merge and do mean "human" or "man" (1936: 62). In my research based on different texts *merdım* is sometimes ambivalent, not so *mêrdek*. The interpretation as a "human" is generally very seldom used. Definitely *merdım* can mean "human / man" or in the plural "humans / men", *mêrdek* does refer to "man / husband" but never to "human(s)" (Hayıg, Rosan 2007: "Elicanek u warda xoya" and "Gormahmed", *Mahmeşa*, Abs. I and II).
[81] Bläsing, U. 1995. "Kurdische und Zaza-Elemente im Türkeitürkischen". *Dutch Studies* 1 / 2. Leiden: Near Eastern Languages and Literatures (NELL). Online: http:www.zazaki.de/-deutsch [accessed 2017-08-20]. [Engl.: Kurdish and Zaza Elements in the Turkish of Turkey].
[82] Phonologial changes from *t to –d are proven in the Iranian languages (Windfuhr, 1989:253-255). Similiarily Hadank does so in his thesis about the Diminutive Suffix (1932:62).

2 The Zaza

social anthropology the research of funeral, death, and the handling of the decedent's property are essential elements. As demonstrated by Nida the societal customs which are brought for caused by the death of a societies member reflect the core values fundamentally (1986:117). The standard procedure is to divide the social spheres into the *sacred* and the *profane* to find out about the dealings with death and the after-world. The sacred is,

> that which is set apart to or for some person. It includes persons, places, things, and times that are symbolic or filled with some sort of set-apartness that we and others recognize. The sacred is what is mine as opposed to what is yours or theirs, what is ours as opposed to what is yours or theirs. (Malina 2001:163).

After a human died, his physical body is left behind and the soul concept (*anima*) leaves the mortal remains and enters the sphere of God. The transcendence or afterworld is perceived as either paradise or hot water (2.3.2.3). The *nefes* "soul" exists on in the afterworld sphere.

Here the perception of "the sacred" as a spiritual concept comes into focus. The area of sacredness sits closely with the concept of *taboo* and *mana* (1.1.3.3; 2.3.2.1.4; 2.3.3.2.5 Diagram 9 Model of Envy, Mana and Taboo). Benveniste relates "the sacred" in the Slavic and Baltic area to Christian ideas, whereas in the area of Iran it is seen as an Avestan and Mazdaean concept. Having this in mind he affiliates the term to Baltic / Lithuanian *šventas* as a group with OPr. *swints*, Lettish *svēts*, in Iranian *spənta-* as a verbal adjective with many derivations would conclude the semantic field of "sacred". Together with the adjective *amərəta* (> *aməša*) 'immortal', it constitutes the title *aməša-spənta* which refers to seven divinities that protect the material and moral life of man. Their supreme being is *Ahura Mazda* (Ohrmazd, Ahuramazda) the well known name for a divinity of the Old Iranian religion who was proclaimed the uncreated God by Zoroaster. These powers are incarnated to seven natural elements such as water, earth, plants metal ... (1973:446). In this concept the basic Alevi relation of nature and man is reflected (above). The concept of "holy" is also related to this topic. It is expressed in Greek *hágios* 'holy' and traces back to the Old Slavic term *svętū*. In Latin the term *sacerdos* is tracing back to *sakro-dhōt-s, the second component is derived from the Indo-European Iranian root *dhē- 'make, put', whence 'to make effective, accomplish' (:453, 468). The immortal soul *daēnā* transcends back and forth the borders of the sacred to the profane (Gignoux 2001:12, 13). Like the concept of "sacred" the *daēnā* reflects the area of purity. This area is not to be spiritually polluted. Thus both concepts are closely related to the purity / impurity manipulation or the Islamic concept of *halal* and *haram* (2.3.3.2.5; Arab.: pure / impure).

2.4.2.2 Funeral Proceedings

Looking at the funeral ritual of the Zaza people, a propinquity to Jewish people's funeral practices is obvious. There the closest next relatives or the Jewish people's community is committed to deal with the dead body. This includes the ritualized washing, the clothing with a clean and white robe without pockets and the dignified burying in a cemetery of their own spiritual orientation in the direction of the main holy sanctuary (purity aspect; e.g. Mecca for Moslems, Jerusalem for Jewish people). The body has to be laid inside a basket but in case of a vault without any coffin and gravestone. The corpse is placed on top of the plot or before the vault (Kraus, Altner & Schwarz 1999:23).

These features are in general terms also foundational to Zaza funerals. In the following the basic steps of a funeral process is described. First the concept of dying is related to whether the dying person had his eyes closed or not. In the former case the expectation is that the dead could not say goodbye to his relatives whereas in the latter his peace was settled with all relatives. As a second step a messenger starts a network of information about the death. The closest relatives are responsible for the funeral proceedings. The corpse is placed on top of stones to be shaved and cleansed. In Sunni funerals a *mıllah* or *hoca* is engaged and *pir* in case of an Alevi funeral. These professional Islamic or Alevi teachers, ritually cleans the corpse, organize and escort the funeral procession and read the mourning prayers. Men are cleansed by the spiritual leader and women by close relatives. The white robe that covers the corpse consists of three pieces of cloth. The head cloth fixes the chin, so that the mouth is closed. The torso is clothed fully. The feet are loosely swaddled in case the feet may move. The corpse is placed in a coffin and the *hoca* and whoever wants to say something is asked to do that. This can either be at home or in a mosque. As many men of the village as possible are asked to carry the coffin to the grave. The more men who are willing to carry the coffin the more honour and respect is given to a person. The grave is 1.80 m for a man and 1.40 m deep for a woman. The head of the dead and the grave is directed towards Mecca. This tradition follows the preceding Jewish tradition which orients the cemetery and every grave towards Jerusalem. Three prayers are held to commit the dead to paradise. The village mourns for three days as an act of remembrance.

Close relatives hold a forty day's lamentation during which the women mourn and lament one full week (*çeniyê jew hefta bermenê*) and long lamentation prayers are prayed (*fati'ha wanenê*). Friends and relatives are under an obligation to visit the mourning family within three days and to mourn with them. The closer the relation the more time and effort in help and support is expected. Besides the mourning part, these visitors are asked to help in the daily routine such as carrying garbage, cooking, serving other visitors, housekeeping, etc. In these days of mourning drop in visitors will always bring a gift to the closest relatives of the dead person to support the family e.g. flowers, tea, fruits, etc. It is only those gifts that will be shared with visitors like drinking tea and eating fruits. This means that there is a food restriction or partial fasting going on with the mourning.

Around the 1.80 to 1.40 m deep grave, stones are placed as a protection against wild animals. The inner walls of the grave are covered by these stones. A stone plate or heavy wood cover is put on top of the grave. Since 1980 a gravestone with reference to the dead became popular. Before that there was no reference to the dead. The relatives took out the bones and put them in a funeral urn. This could be laid together with other dead relatives in the same grave. For poor people such was the norm. Rich people always had their own grave although it was possible to be buried in a family tomb.

To ballast the lid of the coffin sometimes big stones are placed on top of the cover because the corpse is said to leave the coffin. Maybe this belief comes from superstition or because in former times people could not prove one's death in absolute terms. A mystical tradition of mischief accompanies such practices.

Parallel to Armenian tradition bread is passed on to the very poor after someone died. The deeper concept is to remember the dead as a merciful person who passes on this attitude. Nowadays in Armenia full meals are served and the graves of family members are visited during this meal (personal communication with RS 2007).

Traditionally an expression of sympathy refers to Allah and asks for his mercy and inner peace expressed as *'Elah rehmet kero; Serray şıma weş bo*. Compared to this tradition the *telqim* (prayer for the dead) asks for a blessing from Allah on the mourning. For example *'helaley wastış* means *health be demanded / wish for health*. So one can bless the mourning family members by "Ez haqê to kena helal!" or "Haqê xo mırê 'helal ki!" which both mean "Your right be my blessing". Another phrase of sympathy refers to an expression of forgiveness or sorrow for the suffering such as "Ez torê 'ef kena".

A gift for the poor (*fitre*) can be made. The poor are then expected to pray for the dead. If the death of a person falls in a Ramazan or another holy day the men are expected to bring sugar to the grave and the women to recite the Qur'an.

In the Diaspora the issue of transportation to the homeland raises questions of expense, logistics, location and funeral arrangements. The corpse needs to be prepared in a certain way, so as not to explode during the transporting. The process of decay gives rise to gas which leads to the danger of gas explosion. The transportation regulations by ship and plane are strict and cause additional costs. The funeral procedures are only in some detail different for the Northern Group following Alevism and the Sunni Southern and Eastern / Central Group.

Interestingly one will find a lot of parallels in the funeral proceedings of the Zaza and the ones described in the Hebrew Bible or the New Testament (see above; e.g. preparing the corpse with oil; stone graves etc.). This gives reason to assume an old and historical background and proximity of such traditions within the Mediterranean cultures.

2.4.2.3 Status of Widow(er)

A young widow is expected to stay six months alone to prove that she is not pregnant. The ideal for a widow in the Zaza culture is to stay alone and live together with one of their children's family or the family of the husband. In contrast a widower is expected to marry again. In general it is possible to marry again for a widow and a widower. Due to the polygamistist structure of the Islamic Zaza society a widow or a widower has good chances of finding another family. It is a question of prestige and honour how a widow or a widower behaves. In some cases the Levirate is aimed at. The brother of the dead has an obligation to marry or sorrow for his brother's widow and family. A widow that stays alone and moves into the house of one of her children will earn high prestige. If she marries again her reputation is with the new husband's family. Many traditions deal with the issues of orphanage, widow(er) or stepfather resp. stepmother. Mainly the situation for either social circle is very individually solved. The functioning Zaza society in general offers also a slot for community activities to care for the concerned persons. The integration of outsiders is easier and the societal boundaries are more dynamic than in Western society with its focus on the extended family. In other words internal principles of maintenance for widows, widowers and their family are first covered by the extended family; secondarily the wider community takes responsibility. In the case of foreigners the latter institution is responsible for care.

2.4.3 Real versus Ideal Usage of *merdım*

The term *merdım* occupies a *real* and an *ideal* meaning. Semantically the *real* and the *ideal* functions are connected to each other by thought. Whereas the *real* purpose emphasizes the more specific content of the term the *ideal* conception comes from etymology and philosophy.

2.4.3.1 Real Use of *merdım*

Going one step further in the semantical terminology relating to *merdım* one finds an indefinite usage. This function parallels to the English concepts of "someone, anybody" or "one, they". Gormahmed, section IV:

Na 'eba kes   dano xora, kes beno vını,   kes merdımandê
This cape whoever puts it on, he   will make invisible, any   man
bina   ra nêaseno.
other   to not appear.

"Whoever puts on this cape, will disappear and be invisible to other people."

In the same way *merdım* in combination with a personal pronoun functions as a placeholder for a member of a group (family or clan), *Lazê Axay*, section III (Hayıg 2007),

Merdım şımayê kı   biyê vını,   ê   pêro, ...
Men   they   which (were) disappeared they all ...

"All the men that disappeared, they all were ..."

The following table sums up the findings about the term *merdım* how it is represented in its real form:

Table 28 The real usage of *merdım*

merdım, merdımi	human, men
merden, merd	died, dead
merg	death
merdış, mıren-	die, dying
mezel[83], *mezeli*[84]	grave, cemetry
mêrde, mêrdek	husband

From a translational and linguistic point of view the term *merdım* includes,

---

[83] Following Turk. *mezar*.
[84] Originally *gorestan* (cemetry). This word is lost in daily language but orally traditioned in stories.

Table 29 Grammatical Functions of *merdım*

Grammatical function	Translation
nomen, sg. and pl.	human, people, individual
nomen, sg. and pl. in ezafe constructions[85]	man, men your men, soldiers, family and clan relatives
abstract noun	one, someone, anyone

Of interest is the derivation of the masculine noun *camêrd* (man). When asked during the research the sources considered it a contraction of *ca* (place) and *merdım* (human). One source regarded as behind the term the concept of a man, who "sticks to his word". The phrase also is used as an adjective for "brave, male, or generous".

Kesi destê camêrdi nêtepıştê. (proverb)
Nobody hand brave catches.[86]
"Nobody is able to catch the strong."

Such a usage hints at the understanding of the source. Etymologically the Pers. *jumard* is used for a "liberal, generous human" (Steingass cit. in Bläsing 1995:179) and definitely closely related to the Zazaki term. The development from *jumard* to *comerd* or *camêrd* follows current phonetical processes of incorporation of foreign expressions.

Another derivation is presented in *mêrdek* (husband) or *mêrde, mêrdê mı* (my man / husband). Both terms are interchangeable. Hadank differentiates between the diminutive form *–ek* and the determination *–eke* (1936:62, 65). The sources emphasized that the suffix *–ek*, as also used in the expression for wife (see below), points to far finiteness. This means that the basic form is represented *without* the particle *-ek*, when the addressed person or circle of persons is well known to the husband or wife. Hadank calls this form a determination (1936; 65). Givón describes its textual grammatical function as finiteness. I relate it in my work to the approach of the *functional grammar* and follow therein Givón. The marker *-ek* signales to the reader / hearer that an introduced person is referred to. (Givón, 1995; 50).

---

[85] *Nomen regens* in the *casus regens* with other nouns in *casus obliqus*, personal pronouns or adjectives as attributes (Paul 1998:30).
[86] The "hand" functions often as placeholder for an active person.

2 The Zaza

a.) *Mêrdê mı şi suk.* (husband is known to audience)
   Man my went city.
   "My husband went to town."

b.) *Mêrdekê mı şi suk.* (husbn is unknown to audience)
   Man   my went town.
   "My husband went to town." (e.g. official letters)

Both examples demonstrate that the terms are interchangeable. However *mêrdek* offers an additional function. As a derivation of a diminutive form of *mêrde* its original meaning was "manikin". This function is not recently immediately understood. Todd goes just the other way around, when he suggests the forms, but he did not research their different usages. Following Todd (2002:82), the diminutive phrase is stated only by this suffix, yet *lajêk* means "little boy". Paul (1998:198) and Selcan (1998:299) list the suffix but do not explain it. Interestingly Paul found in the neighbouring Eastern dialect of the Palu-Bingöl-area the suffix *–ek* as a marker for infiniteness (1998:198). The suffix *-ek* corresponds in the Cermik dialect to *–ê(n)*. As a result we can speak of a reciprocal influence. This is the reason why the sources from Cermik refer to indefiniteness. Although a closer study on this subject is necessary, a preliminary concordant research reveals an affinity towards unmarked personal pronouns. In consequence this points to a known person and therefore to finiteness for this usage of *–e(n)*.

The derivations *mert, merdane, merdum, cömert* made their way into the Osmanlı Turkish (Old Turkish). Also another word for human is given by *insane ma* (our people) derived from Arabic *insan* انسان The term describes the abstract noun meaning "people". The originally Arabic expression passed through the Osmanic-Turkish into Zazaki (Doğan 1996). As a loanword borrowed from Arabic it refers to a group of persons, e.g. *insanê Cermigi*, the people of Cermik.

The term *merdım* and its full concept would not be completely understood if not for its counterpart woman or *ceni. Ceni* and *cenêk (cenyêk, ceniyek)* describe a woman or a wife. Both terms are interchangeable. Due to lack of a standard or reference dialect (2.2.6) the spelling varies. The one chosen here is from the unpublished lexicon of Roşan Hayıg and Brigitte Werner (2012). The unmarked form, without the particle *–ek*, is grammatically "finite". To what extent the particle *–ek* expresses topic and focus is not investigated yet. In the folktales gathered by Rosan Hayıg these forms are seldom presented. Etymologically the term refers to Kurmanji *zin, jin, pîrek, jinik, afret* (woman, wife; Schönfeld 2004:20;

Koçadag 2010:59) as well as Persian *zan* (Bläsing 1995: 178). All these forms hint at typically Northwest Iranian occurrences.

Although some sources were not sure if the verb *ceniyayış* is really derived from the noun *ceni*, they suspected a relation. This term doesn't occurs in the mother tongue dictionaries of *Koçadag* or *Grûba xebate ya Vateyî* for whatever reasons. The verb stands also for "to have sex with". Due to the shame orientation further investigation was not possible. Nowadays *ceni* became an expression on its own and sexual connotations are still a given. A proximity to Greek *gynä* γυνὴ (woman) is possible. In the same way the terms *keyna* and *keynek* both stand for daughter and girl and are interchangeable as well as *laj* and *lajek* which stands for either son or boy.

2.4.3.2 Ideal Use of *merdım*

The ideal function of a term adds philosophic-linguistical to etymological considerations. Thus the question, which peculiarities tag *merdım*, is answered on a mental level. In anthropology and ethnography the best point to start at is by evaluating the *negative* or *rejected* and the *positive* or *laudable* areas of life. The wide spectrum of ideological and perception of the world related attributes was unveiled. Those attributes were:

Table 30 Positive Features of *merdım*

positive, laudable

	Translation	Content	Implication
zerri dayeno	give heart; generous	generous, magnanimous, candid, good-natured	centrifugal effect of *merdım*
hewl	positive, right, true, veritable, worthy	true person which does not feign but is transparent	centripetal orientation of a person
gıran	big; magnanimous; generous; heavy	generous, well known, holds prestige, honoured	attribute given by society
meyman dayış	hospitable	hospitable and open hearted to foreigners	society oriented behaviour

For *hewl* see following proverb:
'Emelo hewl, raya rınd fineno kesi ver.
"Positive or true faith leads people on the right path" (Hayıg & Werner 2012:).

2 The Zaza

Table 31 Negative Features of *merdım*

negative, rejected and poor
- includes all negations of the above mentioned characteristics
- negative, untrue, phony and incredulous person, selfish about hospitality, does not look out for prestige (infamous; 2.3.2.1.4; 2.5.4.3; 3.6.4; 3.6.5; 0),
- centrifugal society destroying features,

	Translation	**Content**	**Implication**
şewleq	chatty, dubious	someone that is not taken seriously	importance of utterances raise
qesmer, xıncik, xınçekin	Prankster without seriousness; smug	Meddler who pads out his talk	Talk and behaviour are repugnant to others; inwardly evil
pexil	jealous, envious	evil eye, greedy about prosperity, prestige without regard to others	animistic and religious concept; outwardly evil
çıkos, nêkes	envious	selfish; self-concentrated	not generous

Resuming the core values of the Zaza society the factors hospitality based on reciprocity, reciprocity in loan and sharing, generosity, greatheartedness and honour / prestige stick out (2.3.2.1.4; 2.5.4.3; 3.6.4; 3.6.5; 0). Especially in relation to one's public manner his behaviour and his talking people pigeonhole somebody. The concept of honour and prestige in small scale societies is summed up by Hiebert,

> *Prestige associations* [italics as in Orig. EW.] Many are exclusive and admit members only on the basis of wealth, heredity, status, individual achievement, or selection by members of the association. ... Prestige associations are common in tribal societies and contradict the widely held notion that primitive societies are egalitarian and democratic. (1976:252)

Prestige is gained by men and women through the accomplishment of positive peculiarities, in contrast to this honour is lost if negative specifics prevail. As mentioned above a class transition is not possible either up or down (2.3.4.4.1; 2.3.4.4.3).

2.4.3.3 Real versus Ideal - Concepts of *merdım* (Table)

In this section an overview about the concept of *merdım* in relation to real versus ideal conceptions is presented. Some features are added for reasons of clarity and comprehensibility.

Table 32 Real - Concepts of *merdım*

Zazaki	Etymology	Grammar function	Translation	Semantics
*merd	derivation			
Merdım	pers.	nomen masc.	human	Human as mortal being; person, man, woman; human in contrast to animal; individuum; generic term
Camêrd	pers. *ju-mard*	nomen. masc.	man	Man who is entrenched; man in contrast to woman; masculine in contrast to feminine
camêrd		adjective masc.	brave, strong	Entrenched and affronting death and social menace
mêrde, mêrdek		nomen, masc.	husband, manikin	Man in society as father, husband or head of the family specialized use
insan	arab.	nomen plural, abstract	humans, people	People as a group in contrast to the individual
ceni, cenêk	kurm.	nomen fem.	woman, wife	Woman in society contrasting men; wife as social role

Table 33 Ideal - Concepts of *merdım*

merdım (human)
1. Contrasting the animal world
2. Umbrella term for created descendants of Adam (man and woman)
3. Individuum before Allah in contrast to other created beings (angels, demons, Satan)
4. Real Individuum in contrast to fiction (dragons, giants, kobold etc.)
5. Physical mortal being, owning an eternal soul / anima concept

For Nr. 4 in Gormahmed (Hayıg 2007:8-14):

Dêwi	*Gorma'hmedi ra*	*na nêpostê*	*kı*	*odo*	keynera cı
Giant	Gormahmed to	her not believed	that	he will	daughter his
bışo	*biyaro.*				
can	bring.				

"The giant did not believe that Gormahmed will bring back his daughter."

2.4.3.4 Other Connotations of *merdım*

Other areas of research reveal different aspects of *merdım* and perception of the world related issues:

- *merdım* contrasts the animal world. The latter represents all other physical (created) beings (Turk. *hayvan*),
- *merdım* as direct descendant from *'Ela / Ella* (Allah) is a created being,
- *merdım* as part of creation and a physical and pure earthly generic concept contrasts to spiritual beings (angels, demons, evil spirits, Satan),
- *merdım* stand for a real being in contrast to fictional perceptions such as giants, dragons, witches etc.,
- *merdım* is both physically mortal as well as mentally immortal. As such *merdım* is existentially bound to this earth and the creator – either with or against his will,
- *merdım* describes an individuum. Sometimes the term is used as a placeholder for person or physical-psychical being,
- mortality as mentioned above leads to the following observation (2.4.2.2; 2.4.2.1):
  - the dead is ritually cleansed (same gender). The corpse is put in the grave sometimes in a coffin. The wooden lid is laid on top of the digging hole. Earth is thrown above. At the moment the

mourners leave the cemetery the dead will join them. He hits his head and recognizes that he is dead. This is the moment that his soul leaves his body. Sometimes the closing of the eyes is taken as the point of leaving the body (Questionnaire 2005). This tradition leaves the mourners with solace. However it also reveals a suppression process. The tragedy of death is ousted to the grave. Nobody would open a grave to confirm the death. This *taboo* is more and more observable in Western cultures too, due to anonymous funeral proceedings.
- o The period of mourning is forty days. During the mourning men do not shave or cut any hair and women lament with the closest relatives.

2.4.4 Summary

In this paragraph we researched the liaison of linguistics and culture to evaluate the perception of the world of the Zaza in an empirical study of the Zazaki term *merdım*. After introducing the term and its general and specialized meaning, its etymology and historical development also came into focus. Persian and Kurmanji influence led to the recent semantical linguistical environment. Its relation to the profane and sacred or mortality and immortality attracted our attention. Funeral proceedings and the dealing with dead, the corpse and the time of mourning demonstrate the social interaction during phases of challenge and change.

The specific situation of widow(er)s was used to signal the difference between a *real* and an *ideal* concept of a key term like *merdım*. These notions were discussed in detail. The *real* idea of *merdım* describes a perception of an individuum or a generic term in relation and as part of the physical world. In contrast the *ideal* perception relates to the mental and spiritual acuity of *merdım*. The empirical tool to evaluate the conceptions of real versus ideal was a questionnaire. The questions helped to inquire into the negative attitudes and the damage of prestige / honour in society. As antipole the positive properties of humans were also asked for. Gain of prestige / honour is motivating the individual towards positive attitudes. However a class transition is not possible.

Connotations of *merdım* in a religious setting like the Alevi and Sunni background of the Zaza people declare the human as part of creation and in a relation to creation and / or the creator. Western naturalistic thinking is best reflected in the Zoroastrian concept of the Alevi Northern Group. Yet the mystic relationship to creation is unique in Alevism.

After these remarks about their societal system and their religion which is the reason for the divide in a Northern and Southern dialect group we are now looking at the perception of the world of those groups. The Zaza perception of the world comes into play when their decision making process is investigated.

2.5 The Perception of the World – "Zazaness"

This paragraph is partially a summary of the previous discussion. A perception of the world always reflects the cultural foundation of a culture *and* language. Nonetheless the focus of the following paragraph is a cultural anthropological one based on ethnographic study. As such it describes the concept of the world in a wider setting and as part of "comparative anthropology" puts it in relation to the Western perceptions of the world. Such a comparative undertaking is an outcome of ethnography with the aim of avoiding ethnocentrism (1.1.2.2).

Conception of the world reflect the way the world is perceived by a people group. Ideological systems serve to explain and rationalise thoughts, deeds as well as the universe and the earth as part of it (Lingenfelter 1996:220; Spradley & McCurdy 1989:280). In the framework of a perception of the world the essential questions of life, the cognitive associations of things and the social aspects of life are resolved and brought in relation to each other. In short perceptions of the world can be outlined as "strategies to explain the world" (Käser 2004:60). The core values and needs are reflected in such a perception of the world (2.3.4.2.).

The concept of the world of the Zaza people is based on an *emic* (inner) and an *etic* stance (outward). Observations by the ethnographer are revealing *emic* aspects of the people group. A diary with quotes from the Zaza people group as representation of an etic stance is used to balance the data (1.1.2.3.2). Within these poles the mediating aspects are represented in a combination of both.

2.5.1 Cosmology and the Zaza-Pantheon

One of the features that a people group reflects in their perception of the world is the conception of the universe called their *cosmology*. Kraft researched the deep lying thought structures and came up with a diagram as shown below. It excellently represents the cosmology of the Zaza people in broad outline (1979:61ff, Fig. 7.1). Typically for a small scale society built on tribal structures the Zaza people follow a *holistic* and *integral* episteme (:113). It links the

- real and unreal,
- visible and invisible,
- natural and supernatural,
- cultural and supracultural,
- absolute and relative (Hiebert & Hiebert 1995:113),
- world and afterworld,
- physical and transcendental,
- physical and metaphysical or
- material and spiritual,
- endospheric and exospheric world,

with each other.

Diagram 18 Cosmology of the Zaza people

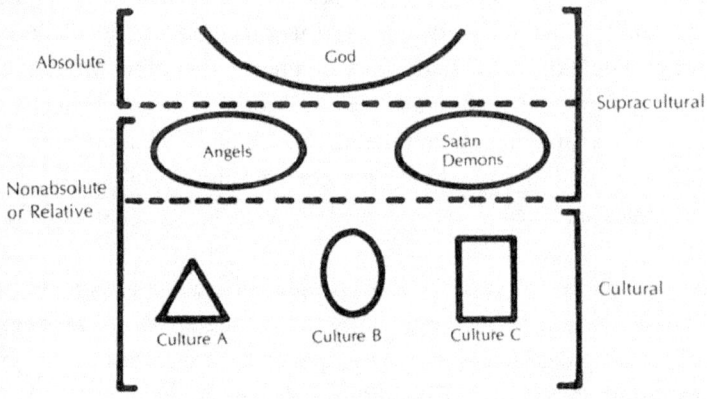

Here Zoroastrian, Animistic, Gnostic, Christian, and Islamic elements are all present (2.3.3.8). One disadvantage of the overlap of all these religious influence is that the original concepts of origin and creation are hidden. That is why we differ between a *historical view* and the *recent awareness* of people.

Another related depiction comes from Lingenfelter who refers to the linking of individuals in a social system. In his structure the Zaza community fits best as a system with "group oriented and highly interlinked hierarchy" (1996:188). The cosmology of such societies is grounded on the opposition of the adept and the marginalized or the insider and outsider concept. This antagonism refers to the preservation of religious rituals and symbols (:194; Geertz 1993:107-108, 112, 126). One has to distinguish an inner *endospheric* area of the people group from an *exospheric*. The latter are not reflected in the Zaza cosmology (Kohl 1993:31; RH 2008 *Zaza and Zazaki*). The foundation of the cosmology is represented by Jewish, Christian and Islamic ideologies of creation and origin, because the recent dominant religion Islam is based on these religions.

All three ideological foundations represent the tension between the theories of creation and evolution. Despite the fact that the research about the "origin of all being" follows contradictory opinions, creation is a concept to all three religions. The biblical narrative from Genesis, which was revised in the Qur'an, represents the story of the origin of humankind (Bouman 1977:1-6). The Northern Group tends toward a Zoroastrian and dualistic cosmology, whereas the Southern and Eastern Zaza relate to a creationist perception. Modern school education introduced the western, evolutionary approach to the Zaza (e.g. principles of mutation and selection, survival of the fittest; Darwin 1859). This perception is overlaid and mixed up with traditional narratives.

A part of cosmology is revealed in the appreciation of stellar constellations either with an attitude towards astrology or astronomy. For instance the Zaza people perceive a shooting star as a bad omen, since it signals that a person died. A wish to the spectator(s) is granted if observing a constellation of two bright stars. Stars also function to show the way in the dark or to demonstrate specific constellations that lead through the year, following western zodiac signs. The rainbow is understood as a sign from Allah. Nonetheless one changes his gender if he walks underneath it. Summing this up, the forces behind the stars are considered to generate – evil or good – effects in this world, although they are of a spiritual nature (parallel spiritual world concept).

Another area of cosmology is presented by the pantheon of gods and goddesses that an ethnicity adores. The excellent study by Asatrian and Arakelova about the Yezidi Pantheon performs a good foundation of looking at the Zaza people (2004). The closeness of Kurmanji-speaking Yezidism and the underlying Alevistic belief system of the Zaza ethnos is well presented in common religious practices (2.3.3.2.1; 2.3.3.3). Although many of the divine protecting powers like *Pirā-Fāt* ("old fat woman"; derivation from Fatima the Prophet Muhammed's daughter; see Mewlid appendix 5), or *Xatūnā-farxā* in Yezidism are not known to the Zaza people, the system of protection by supernatural powers is well developed (Asatrian 1995b:31). The snake plays an important role in this. The protective power of the snake is well reflected in its function as guardian of paths, wells and creeks. We discussed the practice of Zaza peasants, mentioning the cattle-protecting powers *Sarikō-šuān* and *Mamō-gāvān* ("Lord of the Herdsmen", "Memed of the working animals") at the same time defaming *Wāyirō xirāv* ("Lord of the Evil"; 1996; 2.3.3.2.1; 2.3.3.3; Comerd 1996:4-9; see further Asatrian 1995b). The dualistic concept of both opposing powers is reflected by the attitude to balance both by a strong emphasis on living in harmony with nature and men (:8-9). Comerd stresses the perception of animals as "waka lüye" (sister fox), "bıra verg" (brother wolf); "apo hes" (uncle bear). He notes that if children are educated with such an attitude towards animals and nature they will never kill or harm their "relatives" (:ibid.).

Parallels are also found especially in the concept of a *Holy Triad* (Asatrian & Arakelova 2004:231; *Ali-Xızır-Cemaat*), the devotion of mountains and natural formations (:238-242; e.g. the mountain *Duzgın Baba* in Dedekurban 1994: 12, 15; rocks in Molyneux-Seel 1914: 58), the formation of a sacred clergy (:232-233; pir, seyyid, baba, sheikh, mursid;), the scarification of the seven not closer defined spiritual powers (in Yezidism seven avatars of *Malak-Tāwūs*; :232). Another Shi'a element is reflected by the Yezidi Thunder-God *Māma-řašān* and his epithet "lion" (*Šēr Mahmadē řašān*, or *Šēr Mahmad řašān*; :234). Like in the Yezidi Pantheon the lion plays an important role in the Zaza religion too. The heroic folktale Ma'hmeşa (Hayıg 2007:37) describes the lion as a protecting power also performing supernatural activities. Many Zaza idioms refer to the lion as a god-like spiritual force.

Additional to these divine reflections, the symbol of the pearl plays a role in Islamic Mysticism. The pearl signals the eternal being of the soul (e. g. in Gnosticism), the core of the universe as the source of the material world (e. g. Alevism) or the pearl reflects feminity, the moon, the sun or stars (e. g. Zoroastrianism). The enclosure and eternal dynamic of the symbolism that accompanies the pearl is spread all over the Mesopotamic-Indian area. The Gnostic Hymn of the Pearl that was found at Nag Hamadi and which is part of the apocryphal Acts of Thomas reflects the eternal principles of a circular time perception about the soul. The Hymn is also perceived in Zoroastrianism. A phallic deity like *Milyāk'atē-qanǰ* in Yezidism as a Holy Angel is not known to the Zaza people, although the conceptions of angels is far wider than the Biblical or Christian one (Arakelova 2007:329-333).

In some way, the perception of the world behind the divine powers mentioned leaves space for a pre-Islamic Zaza pantheon that dealt with many gods, which had and still have an effect (e.g. in Folk Islamic traditions) from the supernatural into the physical realm. Gnostic concepts are reflected by the Shi'a rite that the Zaza people follow.

2.5.2 Islam – Recent Foundation

The Zaza people moved through different religious phases. Animistic, Zoroastrian, Christian and at lastly Islamic religious influence left their traces. The relation of the "supernatural" to the "absolute and relative natural" follows the traditional perceptions of small scale societies that are structured in a tribal way. This includes the relation of a concept of God and supernatural powers within a culture as well as its impact on the surrounding cultures (centrifugal and centripetal influence; Kraft 1979:61ff, Fig. 7.1).

The concept of the universe and the earth is nowadays mainly taken from Islamic understanding, not withstanding the multi-religious influence on the Zaza people. The Qur'anic teachings about the origin of creation and mankind are enriched by Folk Islam.

The monotheistic dogma of the "oneness" of God (Arab. توحيد *tauhid*) dominates Zoroastrian conceptions. The former notion views *Allah* as creator of the world and every individual person (Sure 55:1-78; Schirrmacher 1994a:221; humans, animals, plants). The latter, viewing creation as exposed to a "good" Creator-God and his evil antagonist which together define the course of the world (Brockhaus multimedial 2007: Parsiism). In Folk Islamic approaches the dualistic conception of the rule of the world is revitalised. As such Folk Islam plays an important role in the Zaza community. Particularly the capability of the *Sheikh* to soothe supernatural powers reflects such beliefs. Another consequence leads to power concentration on one person or her individual role or status as a medium between the worlds and the powers.

2.5.3 Feasts and Celebrations

Ethnomusicology and dance reveals the expressing of emotions and thoughts. Both also enrich the culture and its gatherings (2.3.5.3; 2.3.5.4). Another cultural expression is reflected by their annual and individual schedule of celebrations

and feasts. The annual or lifelong repetition of ceremonies and celebrations represent the circle of life which an individual is linked to in his society. They determine the lapse of time and offer a framework to combine
- work and recreation,
- the profane and sacred (family, devotion etc.),
- seasonal and yearly aspects (harvest, full moon, new year etc.)

with each other. The following celebrations could be identified:

Table 34 Feasts and Celebrations

Name	Time	Content	Where / Who (source)
Kormışkan; parallels *Newroj*	Last week in March	4-7 days celebration with dance called *kirr* close to *ğovend*; spring season	SZ (MA)
Newroj	21st March	Fire and gathering; spring season	All (Kehl-Bodrogi 1989); also Kurmanji speakers
Hewt Mala	21st March; last week	4-days celebration with dance *ğovend*	NZ (HC 2012)
pukê pıra	15th January	Children ask for sweets; (pleasant) anticipation towards spring	SZ (MT)
roşanê qurbana	Ramazan (following lunar calendar)	One full month traditional fasting; no food during daylight	All
roşanê roji	Last day of Ramazan (1-2 days)	Turk. *Şeker Bayramı*; breaking the fasting / Ramazan	All (MT)
Khalê Gağani	December	Close to St. Niklas; children are given sweets for their behaviour during the year; Armenian New Year	NZ (Hawar Tornecengi 2009 *Khalê Gağani*; Sweetnam 2004:231-232)

2 The Zaza

Name	Time	Content	Where / Who (source)
Kormışkan; parallels *Newroj*	Last week in March	4-7 days celebration with dance called *kirr* close to *ğovend*; spring season	SZ (MA)
Newroj	21st March	Fire and gathering; spring season	All (Kehl-Bodrogi 1989); also Kurmanji speakers
Hewt Mala	21st March; last week	4-days celebration with dance *ğovend*	NZ (HC 2012)
pukê pıra	15th January	Children ask for sweets; (pleasant) anticipation towards spring	SZ (MT)
roşanê qurbana	Ramazan (following lunar calendar)	One full month traditional fasting; no food during daylight	All
roşanê roji	Last day of Ramazan (1-2 days)	Turk. *Şeker Bayramı*; breaking the fasting / Ramazan	All (MT)
Khalê Gağani	December	Close to St. Niklas; children are given sweets for their behaviour during the year; Armenian New Year	NZ (Hawar Tornecengi 2009 *Khalê Gağani*; Sweetnam 2004:231-232)
Roze Xızıri Xıdırê Les Xızır İlyas Hz. *'Ali-bayrami (the feast of 'Alī), also known as Ağa-bayrami (God's feast)*	*Asma Xızıri* 'Month of Xizir', or the *Asma Xilaşi* 'Month of Xilas'; Between January and February; close to	a three-day fast followed by a time of visiting friends and neighbours and of distributing holy bread along with portions of meat of the slaughtered qırvan; incarnation of	NZ and SZ (RH; Sweetnam 2004:231-232; Asatrian 1995a:197-198)

Name	Time	Content	Where / Who (source)
Kormışkan; parallels *Newroj*	Last week in March	4-7 days celebration with dance called *kirr* close to *ğovend*; spring season	SZ (MA)
Newroj	21st March	Fire and gathering; spring season	All (Kehl-Bodrogi 1989); also Kurmanji speakers
Hewt Mala	21st March; last week	4-days celebration with dance *ğovend*	NZ (HC 2012)
pukê pıra	15th January	Children ask for sweets; (pleasant) anticipation towards spring	SZ (MT)
roşanê qurbana	Ramazan (following lunar calendar)	One full month traditional fasting; no food during daylight	All
roşanê roji	Last day of Ramazan (1-2 days)	Turk. *Şeker Bayramı*; breaking the fasting / Ramazan	All (MT)
Khalê Gağani	December	Close to St. Niklas; children are given sweets for their behaviour during the year; Armenian New Year	NZ (Hawar Tornecengi 2009 *Khalê Gağani*; Sweetnam 2004:231-232)
	Armenian feast of Surb Sargis (Saint Sergius)	Hz. Ali	
Flexible Fasting from 1 to 12 days	Random	Religiously motivated limitation	NZ (Kehl-Bodrogi 1989)
12 days fasting	Month of Muharrem	Remembrance of the Twelve Imams and the martyrdom of	NZ (Sweetnam 2004:231-232; Shankland

2 The Zaza

Name	Time	Content	Where / Who (source)
Kormışkan; parallels Newroj	Last week in March	4-7 days celebration with dance called *kirr* close to *ğovend*; spring season	SZ (MA)
Newroj	21st March	Fire and gathering; spring season	All (Kehl-Bodrogi 1989); also Kurmanji speakers
Hewt Mala	21st March; last week	4-days celebration with dance *ğovend*	NZ (HC 2012)
pukê pıra	15th January	Children ask for sweets; (pleasant) anticipation towards spring	SZ (MT)
roşanê qurbana	Ramazan (following lunar calendar)	One full month traditional fasting; no food during daylight	All
roşanê roji	Last day of Ramazan (1-2 days)	Turk. *Şeker Bayramı*; breaking the fasting / Ramazan	All (MT)
Khalê Gağani	December	Close to St. Niklas; children are given sweets for their behaviour during the year; Armenian New Year	NZ (Hawar Tornecengi 2009 *Khalê Gağani*; Sweetnam 2004:231-232) Hussein 2002:199-2005)

These feasts and celebrations show the closeness between spiritual and daily life. *Ramazan* as the longest feast in the Southern and Eastern Sunni group is reflected in a twelve day fast of the Northern Alevi people. Influence from Christianity is reflected by the *Khalê Gağani, Xızır İlyas* or *Xıdırê Les* celebration. New Year is connected to the first day of spring. Most of the people groups in the Northern part of the Fertile Crescent area celebrate this event due to the budding of nature in spring and to expel winter.

Besides those annual and regular feasts circumcision, godparenthood (*kerwa*), wedding and the birth of boys are celebrated. Circumcision is part of the initiation procedure of boys into the Zaza community often in the 12th to 13th year of age. The *kerwa* (godfather) provides the boy with wealthy presents according to his own wealth. As a result he gains prestige through responsibility. A wealthy *kerwa* is obviously preferred but at the same time circumcision becomes an institution to form economic or social alliances. The interests need to be balanced. This balance differentiates circumcision in the Zaza ethnicity from a religious ritual as in other Islamic ethnicities, as it is also considered to be a social event.

2.5.4 The Family – Centre of Society

In the first place, the concepts of prestige and honour depend on the function and position one holds within the family (Ember 1993:183). Small scale societies following tribal structures in general and Mediterranean cultures specifically are prestige oriented. The essential questions of life are relating to honour and prestige and contrast to the less considered question of guilt or sin (Malina 2001; Müller 2004b). In this the Zaza people follow the superior majority of the world's population, which shows shame-orientation in conscience and behaviour (Wiher 2003:106-107 and 2007 for Islamic coined cultures; 1.1.3.3).

Out of this results the communal position of a member of the Zaza culture within the whole community. In this societal framework the outstanding importance of the core and extended family is very well demonstrated by following social particularities as common practices:
- Honour killing,
- blood feud,
- social role of women (gender role),
- the handling of envy,
- exchange of girls (avoiding poverty) and
- the rituals of honouring others (Werner 2006:69).

2.5.4.1 Honour Killing and Blood Feud

The aforementioned social mechanisms characterize the Zaza culture until today even though blood feud and honour killing are strictly sanctioned by national laws. These mechanisms are triggered on the level of the family or even the individual (rape, abduction, adultery etc.) but punished by the collective on the extended family or clan / tribe level. This is the reason why intertribal contro-

2 The Zaza

versies avert larger covenants of small scale societies. In other words the focus towards inner conflicts restricted the Zaza people to their tribal structure. Thus conflicts from outside gave rise to larger alliances. One event in the year 2002 demonstrated impressively the group dynamic processes. Pope John Paul II. honoured an agha of a tribe from Palu publicly for the establishment of peace between two extended families that took revenge in blood feud for many generations (TG 2005 *Newsletter*). These methods show the basic social differences between the societies of the West based more on individualism and the collectivistic Eastern people groups. Instead the Turkish society is not structured in small scale societies but does develop a post-feudalistic elite system which is split into political and economic classes (about the Turkish history see 3.1.2).

2.5.4.2 Code of Honour – (Sexual) Purity and Impurity

The Turkish society uses specific terminology related to the code of honour and - like the Zaza people - institutional organizations to guarantee the preservation of honour in the sexual area. Women are mainly affected by these honour related social institutions (Schirrmacher 2007a:164). Islamic laws exemplified by the *Sharia* (Turk.: *şeriat*) are another reason for the sociocultural orientation towards sexual purity versus impurity. UNESCO speaks of 5.000 honour killings of women per year in predominantly Islamic countries (ibid.). The main argument goes that those women dishonoured their families (World and Press 2006 Killings of Honour *1st March 2006*). Another example comes from the New Testament which, based on the Hebrew Bible (Numeri 35; Deut 19; Josua 20; 22 times) indicates blood feud as a negative (sinful) way to protect honour (e.g. Lukas 11:51). In the New Testament honour is a basic attitude of Hebrew culture (Malina 2001:41-43). In the Islamic context small scale societies, based on tribal structures, developed the institution of honour killings for two reasons. On one side to protect the society against transgressions and on the other to suppress women. An Islamic legal basis is not given (Schirrmacher 2007a:164, 171; s. a. Kehl-Bodrogi 1997 for Turkey). In general the practice of polygamy leads to both, the protection of women in cases of poverty *and* to their discrimination (Ahmed 1988:521; Schirrmacher 1994a:302-349).

2.5.4.3 Exchange of Girls

To avoid poverty the Zaza and the Kurmanji speaking Kurds practice the exchange of girls. The idea is that one family exchanges their daughter for the other family daughters to marry the sons of wealthier families. In this way they bypass the practice of bridewealth by gaining honour and prestige since they performed an alliance with the other family. One explanation could be that prescriptive marriages and the institution of bridewealth are overcome. This is mainly true because this practice follows the concept of reciprocity in loan and sharing which includes hospitality which is fundamental to the honour and prestige orientation of the Zaza people (2.3.2.1.4; 2.4.3.2; 3.6.4; 3.6.5; 0). In the worst case if a new wife is treated badly the other family will treat the exchanged girl in the same way. The balance of honour is at risk in such cases and revenge, envy and enmity seems at hand.

2.5.4.4 Greeting Rituals - Honour, Respect and Proximity

Behaviour patterns which relate to the conservation of honour and respect are demonstrated in gestures and rituals of daily life. Reverence to the elderly or highly respected during the greeting ritual is expressed by first a kiss on the hand and then the forehead. The receiver conceives his pleasure with a nod or a smile. People of the same social level greet each other with a (token) kiss first on the right, then on the left cheek. Same sex, specifically men shake hands, women hug each other. Proximity in communication is expressed by going hand in hand or walking close (by same sex). Spouses do not walk close together and men mostly walk in front of women. In public the demonstration of sexual attraction either from spouses, relatives or foreigners will never be shown. Therefore public life goes on with a loose gender segregation which is punctuated during dance, public gatherings (*cem, cemat*) or in the case of pulling the work force together for harvest or larger projects (e.g. ploughing, threshing etc.). People of the same social position within one class normally stand very close and therefore speak quietly. For respected persons a distance of fifty centimetres is normal. Compared to Western attitudes this is closer and therefore often considered by Westerners as impolite, since the expected zone of neutrality is broken. On the other hand Zaza people think of Western behaviour as impolite as distance is taken to emphasize aloofness and arrogance, implying that the Western person automatically takes up a higher position. This reciprocal misunderstanding shows the importance of privacy related to the sphere of intimacy.

2.5.4.5 Summary

The core and extended family constitutes the central organisational institution in all societies. Its protection is therefore a basic obligation of the responsible people in charge. Within the Zaza community the patriarch and the small scale society's leadership (*sheikh*, *mıllah*, *agha*) undertake this duty. The options to punish any violation of the taboos and rules of society are given by honour killing and blood feud. Sexual harassment or infringement is received as a direct insult on the family's 'name' that is its honour and prestige. The individual as well as the collective is always asked to balance purity and impurity issues in such a way that one is proclaimed as being in the state of the "pure". This task is a challenge since reality shows that people have to struggle with impurity to reach the status of purity. The 'fear of God' becomes thus a strong motive to balance out one's condition.

The practice of exchanging girls in prescriptive marriages is one way to avoid poverty and to bypass bridewealth and fulfil the responsibility of maintaining a family by not losing manpower.

Greeting rituals reflect the principles of the honour system in the Zaza society. Older people are highly respected and hold high esteem whereas people of the same status are treated equal. Younger people are not addressed at all but it is expected that they show respect and reverence to the older person.

2.5.5 Envy

Envy was mentioned above as part of the cultural setting and the shame orientation of the Zaza people. Since it is such a driving force for human behaviour, it takes here its own section of discussion in relation to the concept of *merdım* (2.3.2.1.3; 2.3.2.1.4; 2.3.2.2). Envy goes with the notion of vanity. In general envy does not take up much attention in research. Hesselgrave researched more about envy in psychological, social and anthropological writings and comes to the conclusion, "the anthropological literature revealed that it is extremely widespread across the world and is often an important factor affecting behaviour" (2002; 211). Envy is thus another tool to describe the perception of the world in plausible ways. As Malina points out, the gap between our Western guilt oriented conscience in societies that are based on individualism and the shame oriented collective societies of the East is enormous (2001:109; 2.3.2.1.3; 2.3.2.1.4).

Looking back in history Aristotle as a member of a Mediterranean culture describes the subject of envy as, "this 'love of honour' produces envy. Since the ancients were intensely desirous of fame and honour and thought that all things existed in limited supply, envy naturally follows love of honour"(2001:112). Referring to what Aristotle said honour / prestige and envy go hand in hand. The organ where the longing for prestige is anchored is in the conscience (2.3.2.1.4).

The balancing or gain of prestige is one driving force in shame oriented societies. Social rituals, symbols and activities of daily life reveal the importance of the individual's striving for honour and prestige by either avoiding any conflict that brings with it imbalance of social harmony or to proactively gain prestige (Werner 2006:14-16, 25-26, 69; see also Malina 2001:109-110).

Reciprocal resentment is based on fundamental mistrust or lack of trust in the other (2.3.2.1.3). The Zaza people experienced political oppression from the outside and inner pressure through fierce culture change leading to the instability of cultural norms and settings. The dynamic drives of envy take especially effect in such milieus as they suggest benefits for the operator. At the same time envy leads to active responses like cultural adjustments to balance the social harmony. In the Zaza culture envy forms an antithesis to honour. Envy protects the society against violations of their social set of laws; also envy is an indicator for the individual's conscience to stay in social balance (Werner 2006:67-69). Regulations to maintain the state of honour in daily life situations of the Zaza people and other collectivistic cultures are complex and are underpinned by envy-structures (Malina 2001:109; Kehl-Bodrogi & Pfluger 1997; 2.3.2.1.4).

The spiritual aspect of envy, as it is developed in Zaza society, is one of prevention and mediation between the physical and metaphysical world. The former is definitely demonstrated in the appearance and the handling of power-balance in relation to the "evil eye" or the *chamzah* as magical or esoteric ideas (2.3.2.1.4).

In the Zaza culture envy is related to the metaphysical sphere and the antipoles of prestige and shame follow the principles of shame-oriented cultures (1.1.3.3; see evil eye 2.3.2.1.4).

2.5.6 Envy and the Concept of *merdım*

We described the location of the conscience as LEIC following Käser (1998 and 2004; 1.1.3.3; 2.3.2.1.3; 2.3.2.1.4). Envy in the Zaza society is thus enculturated by education and environment as an antipole to the positive peculiarities of the community (Diagram 9 Model of Envy, Mana and Taboo). In other words, members who follow the social ideal of gaining honour / prestige are generating envy. In strongly hierarchically structured cultures this happens only within the same class and / or social layer, due to the impossibility of class transition. Plutarch stated that envy is not a driving force towards socially higher levelled members (Käser 1998:114). In consequence the drive of envy structures is mainly oriented towards the members of the same or lower class(es). Or at least the effects towards higher classes are not meaningful.

Family and *blood feud* as described above are good examples of balancing social rites (2.5.4.1). Damage of honour is punished by tribal controversy, with the aim of gaining back prestige by enforcement. In former times no national government took the initiative to rule such controversies. This is the reason why the menace of a long-term social conflict asked for extreme brutal reaction to take revenge and to prevent further aggression (1998:119). Although the Hebrew culture in the times of the prophet Hz. Jesus was structured aristocratically it becomes obvious that the New Testament often refers to envy. Most objections against the prophet Hz. Jesus came from prejudice of the higher-level, questioning his authority. The prophet Hz. Jesus asked them and his disciples to "pray for your enemies" (Mk. 11,28; Lk. 6,27). Thus the principle of reconciliation was based on forgiveness and not any more on revenge as it was expressed in the Hebrew Bible or afterwards in the Qur'an (Sure 4,16; 16,126 etc. most of the references point to Muslims as executors of the Islamic law – Sharia Turk.: *şeriat*).

2.5.7 Envy and Hospitality

Hospitality is a reciprocal practice following the principle of "give and take". As Benveniste notes, hospitality is founded on the idea "that a man is bound to another (Latin *hostis* always involves the notion of reciprocity) by the obligation to compensate a gift or service from which he has benefited" (1973:76). He traces the origin back to the concept of Sanskrit *pátiḥ* 'master' / husband' and in Greek *pósis* πόσις 'husband', or in composition as in *despótes*. Hospitality is a practice which needs one person to offer it and one to make use of. Such a notion is echoed in Sanskrit *dam pátiḥ* (master of the house), *viś* (master of the clan), *jās* (master of the 'lineage') and Gothic *gasts* and Old Slawic *gosti* is 'guest', whereas that of Latin *hostis* is 'enemy'.

The Latin term can be traced back to the concept of foreigner or stranger which resonates in the whole semantic field of "foreigner / stranger". Thus the "favourable stranger" becomes the "guest" and the "hostile stranger" the enemy (1973:72, 75). The proximity of both extremes in their origin is also reflected in the stories which deal with hospitality. The "guest" who enters the house of the "beardless" [the evil person. EW.], soon becomes the enemy to the hospitable master of the house when he tried to rob him (Hayıg 2007:26-28 *Lazê Axay* [Son of the Agha]).

The one who gives hospitality possesses status and earns prestige. Nonetheless different levels of attention are given to receivers of hospitality to protect a society and its norms and settings. First, absolute priority is given to close relatives, secondary courtesy goes to members of the same small scale society, who will be welcomed as a part of the extended family. Zaza people from other tribes, Non-Zaza and travellers without reference are respected but need approval from the authorities in charge (upper class members) before they are given lodging. Nowadays, due to the lack of functioning structures, oftentimes national institutions (major, military, and police) acquire the function to evaluate foreigners without any internal reference to the upper class. Everybody who comes in with valued references is welcomed by the Zaza community and passed on to those who would accommodate them.

All of the highly valued societal ideals can also produce envy. In the case of hospitality this leads to mistrust about how the leaders (Agha, Sheikh) spend the community property. For example the expense for housekeeping for hosting guests in relation to their social rank would come under close scrutiny. In this case envy functions as a limiting force which demarcates the levels of attention to a guest expressed in hospitality.

With this change, the core values and the cultural adjustments are shifting. This brings us to culture change within the Zaza ethnicity. Culture change and language shifting go hand in hand.

2.5.8 Culture Change in Zaza Community

Change has always to do with the perception of time. Time comprehension can be distinguished in a *general* awareness and a *specific* apprehension.

The former general awareness is expressed in linguistical features such as the tempora system of verbs or the temporal relations in text discourse, e.g. markers for points of departure on the sentence and text level. In Zazaki such markers are e.g. *wextdê / wext dê veri zi* ("in former times", Hayıg 2007:83 Axa beno), *rozê* ("one day", Hayıg 2007:83 Axa beno), *a wıni* ("thus", Hayıg 2007:84 Axa beno). These markers imply the temporal relation of sentences and texts within oral stories or written books. Having a look at the tempora system of Zazaki (2.2.9.1.8; 2.2.9.2.7) one finds a time framing, based on the past and the present. Future expressions are either put in the present (NZ) or marked by a small particle (*do*; SZ). The time setting shows a *linear* perception centered on the present. English and German are also following a linear time perception but they focus much more on the relation of the event in regard to the near, far or very far (*Questionnaire* 2005).

The specific notion of time is related to the perception of the world expressed in the perception of the world. Coming from a religious angle the core values of the Zaza people allow for a circular insight of time. For instance the contrast of the world and the afterlife in a mystical sense admits the thought that life is circular. This means that even reincarnation is part of the Zaza perception of the world. In my research I did not get a direct hint of a belief in reincarnation. Besides a dogmatic Islamic view of the afterworld as a place for men to recreate, there is also the conception that a person or the soul is part of an eternal cycle. Within that cycle, different levels or worlds can be climbed.

Cultural and linguistic change is caused by industrialization, approximation to the West and urbanization. The breakup of peasantry and the feudalistic structures, as well as of the organization of the tribal and the extended family leads to a change of perception of the world, core values and needs (Gündüzkanat 1997). Research on ethnomusicology within the Zaza community reveals an adaption to western life style, including the traditional celebrations. Adding to this development the assimilation process towards the national and dominant government of the country of migrations educational system endangers Zazaki (2.2.6; 2.2.10).

2.5.9 Summary

The perception of the world of the Zaza people reflects a *holistic* and *integral* episteme (:113). It links the real and unreal, visible and invisible a well as natural and supernatural world with each other. The cosmology of the Zaza people is based on the different religious influences that follow them. Islam as the last and dominant religion holds the whole people group together. However there is no homogeneity in the three different linguistically and religiously split Northern, Southern and Eastern Groups. It is within this gap that the whole Zaza society faces challenges. Alevism approximated Islam in the 20th century on account of the oppression that the political changes of the newly found Republic of Turkey brought with it. In the cause of secularization, religious groups emerged and the devotees of Alevism tend towards socialistic parties. Again this political move brought with it that Alevism became an outlet for the rage of conservative Islamic groups.

The core family, as part of the important extended family, forms the central institutional feature of the Zaza society. The extended family is that sphere of education in which the core values are passed on to the children. The perception of the world is shaped in the realm of this smallest societal grouping by enculturation, acculturation and education. For this very reason a special protection is given to this institution and its members. Most of the ethical and moral norms and settings relate to the protection of the extended or core family and its members. In collectivistic and small scale societies like the Zaza people very harsh restrictions – taken from a Western view – are in place to secure inner and outer peace and balance. As such repudiation / expulsion, public punishment or other methods of societal regulations are in place.

The shame orientation of the Zaza culture in relation to the principles and the attraction of the opposite subjects of *envy* and *prestige* give rise to blood feud, honour killings and a specific code of honour. Striving for prestige is accompanied, or even based on concepts of honour. Honour is demonstrated against higher class members, older members of the society and religiously or political active members.

Envy rules the conscience and reflects the societal regulations on an individual's level. In an overall scheme the people group demonstrates common regulations by expressing a folk conscience. For instance the individual would punish adultery within his family based on his conscience, but the extended family would punish such trespassing based on their folk conscience. For instance the motivation to prevent adultery by the individual would be by

- revenge against a rival,
- defence of his / her children or
- To get rid of his aggressions caused by the trespassing.

Folk conscience instead would protect every individual and the core families. The latter, guarantees stable families in which the women and the children – as the weakest social members – are given the highest priority to protect their sphere against intrusion motivated by sexual or base motives. From a Western point of view it is important to look at the Islamic and Mediterranean perception of the worlds from this angle. The dynamics of the *Sharia* (Turk.: *şeriat)* that is the combination of the Islamic law taken from the *Qur'an* and brought to life by the *Hadith* (traditional commentary and interpretation of the Qur'an) build up *and* reflect the foundation for such a protection.

Culture change in the Zaza community is caused by globalization, urbanization, increasing mobility, migration processes and life in the *Diaspora*. The main factors that were processed by the people in the Diaspora were the chance of economic support for the homeland based Zaza, a well educated bi- and multilingualism (Zazaki, host language, English, Kurmanji, Turkish), the development of educational and language material. The big challenge for the Zaza people would be to find the right partners during the process to revive their cultural and linguistical heritage. Thus their future orientation needs to be closely related to the economic and political processes that drive the Republic of Turkey (3.2).

2.6 Mother Tongue Issues - Projects

This section deals with mother tongue issues. The importance of the mother tongue in questions of identity is basic to the recent development of mother tongue education to revive Zazaki and the Zaza culture. The global rediscovery of mother tongue as an important tool to fight language extinction or language death started with an initiative in 2007 led by UNESCO and its implementation by UNICEF (UNESCO / SIL International Bangkok 2007. *Promoting Mother Tongue-based Multilingual Education (MLE)*.). The conception of this programme is to foster bi- or multilingualism by starting the first two years with education in their mother tongue and then switching smoothly during the second year into the national language. Research proved that cognition and language capabilities develop much better if education is started in the mother tongue. It is a win-win situation for nation states because the national or language of wider communication still covers higher education and the standard in education increases. Questions of national prestige and the saving of money due to a higher rate of higher educated people in the national language are covered as well as the opportunity for smaller or non-national language groups to develop their language and culture. Obstacles to MLE are

- the need for a reference or standard dialect. This can cause internal tensions for a smaller language group such as the Zaza people, since no social institution can take up the responsibility for the whole group. The question will still be, which language will function as reference or standard dialect?

- to the national language group if the non-national groups will not give in by using the national higher education system but develop their own and independent education system.

The *mother tongue* is the language of first acquisition. Unknown to us is whether the brain starts from scratch, being a blank sheet or if existing neurological networks are adjusted to the sounds that the unborn recognizes. Either way the mother tongue is learned automatically and not by reading and writing. The latter comes at an age when the brain has fully developed the mother tongue. The first three years are essential to organize the memory. The retrieval and deposition structure for common and syntactical knowledge are performed and connected.

The mother tongue is a unique gift of humankind. Every child starts life under the effect of being closely bound to the mother in her womb. In general every language is learnable. The child experiences the mother tongue close to the mother's heartbeat not just by sounds but also by the vibrant movement of her womb, her lungs, her inner organs and her organs of speech. The mother tongue becomes the inner rhythm of the unborn's communication system. During the first years it is mainly the mother that communicates to the baby. Without doubt the essential inheritance or development of the linguistical and communicational capability of the human race is one of the global wonders.

In the case of Zazaki the mother tongue was used to hand down traditions and to acculturate children to the society. Zazaki never developed as a language of wider education or as an economic tool. This is even more astonishing as in the 19th century AD Christian development aid attempts led to the education of Zaza in public schools. Unfortunately English and Turkish were forced. The only remainder is one religious poem called *Mewlid Nebi*. It includes stories about the Birth of the Prophet from around 1920 AD (Appendix 5) and some rudiments of a translation of the New Testament from 1903. Recently the importance of the mother tongue came more into focus for the Zaza people. Now the question will be how to mobilize the whole people group to revive the language and pass it on to the children.

2.6.1 The Mother Tongue Speaker

The mother tongue speaker represents to the ethnographer an, if not *the* important resource (1.1.2.4). The ethnographer looks through him into a culture as if with a microscope. He is the medium to approach a culture and its linguistic background. Working with the mother tongue speaker is the only way to partici-

2 The Zaza

pate in a foreign culture and at the same time to contextualize the cultural background belonging to the subject of research (Sánchez-Cetina 2007:398, 408).

The backdrop of working with mother tongue speakers is their bias towards their dialect and their extended family (ethno- and egocentrism), lack of education, economical reasons (wages, claims) and the possible delays caused by the teamwork. Often the motivation to work with outsiders is only on the financial level. Offers about linguistic education are not much welcomed because the mother tongue speaker thinks he knows all about his language. The problem here is that the linguistic research and understanding of the mother tongue asks for tools of description (grammar, phonology, morphology etc.). It is one of the big challenges to a researcher from outsider to motivate mother tongue speakers in those areas.

2.6.2 Lingua Franca and National Language

Looking back in history language issues were used quite often as a tool to oppress people. Colonialism by political or religious invasion was construed to implement the language of the invaders as the language of wider communication. Only very few exceptions are known in history, like the Hittites that carried over the regional languages after the invasions. Normally the occupying forces compel the defeated to translate everything so that the invaders language becomes the *lingua franca*. The idea comes from racialist or hegemonial (ἡγεμονία hēgemonía, military leadership) ambitions which demonstrate the superiority of the invading culture. The same happened to the Zaza people. Zazaki is implemented into a language of wider communication that in itself functions as mother tongue to a huge group of people. The enduring forced contest led to a stable bilingualism by men in general and women under forty. An alternate would be if the invading party would allow mother tongue education with a transition to a standardized training in the language of wider communication for higher education.

The global use of English found a climax in the $19^{th} - 20^{th}$ century due to Christian development Aid attempts (2.1.4.5; Walls 2005:62). In Turkey hospitals, schools, translation agencies and universities remind us of those days. Redhouse for instance worked on an English-Turkish lexicon which still represents the standard (2002 see under Computer Tools). Besides translations of the Bible (Werner 2012), some universities introduced English as a language of higher education (e.g. Boğaziçi Üniversitesi).

2.6.3 Mother Tongue – Entering a People's Heart

Beside the above mentioned cultural development of the mother tongue as a worldwide phenomenon, the subject also raises many questions to neurolinguistic and cognitive sciences. The human ability to incorporate every language system and to manage or even acquire in theory every language represents still a huge area of questions (Fabbro 1999). In cultural anthropology, linguistics, social, cognitive and communication sciences the research with brain damaged patients opened insights to the acquisition, development and management of the mother tongue. All findings confirmed that language as a communicational factor is central to the active participation in a community. Social networks and the "belonging to" factor are not imaginable without language (1.1.3.2.1). Out of this fact the demand for global mother tongue education evolved.

The Zaza people did not think of any mother tongue education due to the strong emphasis of the national government on the *lingua franca* for the last eighty years. With the revival of Zazaki as a language of education the desire to pass on the cultural heritage in their language arose. Since the turn of the millennium the slowly increasing opportunities for such an education supported this view. Kurmanji and Zazaki speaking people groups now started with small language classes. The aim is to educate small children in Zazaki and Kurmanji so that they enculturate in their mother tongue.

2.6.4 Mother Tongue Education – A global Basic Right

UNESCO in general and specifically UNICEF recommended to the world's governments to carry on elementary education in the mother tongue. Education and school projects will be supported. The goal is to have at least for a minimum of 2 year's mother tongue education for all children worldwide by the year 2040. The transfer from the mother tongue to the national or in some cases the language of wider communication is basic to this conception (UNESCO Bangkok 2007: *MLE*).

Experiences from Africa and Asia since the 1980s support the approach. In general the children raised their educational standards by knowing how to read and write more than one language. Bilingualism leads to a better occupational outlook because the whole area of translation and intercultural communication adds to all the other job opportunities (UNESCO Education for ALL (EFA) News 2006. *Governments encouraged to adopt multilingual education for ethnic minorities*; UNESCO 2007: *Register of Good Practices*; UNESCO Bangkok 2007: *MLE*).

The beginning of such demands goes back to initiatives in 1953 when the UNESCO proclaimed such approaches. It was not until 1968 that they were publicly advertised:

> It is axiomatic that the best medium for teaching a child is his mother tongue. Psychologically, it is the system of meaningful signs that in his mind works automatically for expression and understanding. Sociologically, it is a means of identification among the members of the community to which he belongs. Educationally, he learns more quickly through it than through an unfamiliar linguistic medium. (UNESCO 1953 cit. in Fasold 1993:293).

Programmes like that ask for freedom of speech and the public recognition of the mother tongue language as a medium of education, an important tool to understand and communicate well to the authorities and the public use. A full participation in a political-social system is only possible if reciprocal communication between the administration and the citizens is given. This is only possible if governmental institutions support those means (Tsunoda 2006:144-145). The goal of UNESCO's approach is to describe and preserve dwindling or endangered languages and cultures. Often the cognitive and socializing advantages of bi- or multilingual education are not known by governments. Therefore the campaign offers help to set up primary education schedules which aid minority groups to start with their mother tongue and then to transfer to the national language of wider or higher education. Educational material for children and transfer schedules, as well as teachers training material, are necessary to start the programmes.

In the case of the Zaza people the lack of dialect standardization within the whole community presents a great obstacle to establish a proper programme. As a forerunner to the public school mother tongue oriented adaptation language classes for children are given at the main community centres in the cities. The government is still not convinced whom and with which material to teach (2.2.4; 2.2.6; Human Rights Education Associates 2006. *Turkey: A Minority Policy*, 67). The lack of a reference or standard dialect in Zazaki, the religiously motivated segregation of boys and girls (sometimes the refusal of girls education) and the lack of educational centres in the villages and bad public transport form obstacles to starting programmes. This is a globally observed phenomenon which is addressed to the Kurmanji speaking people group also.

2.6.5 The Homogenous Unit Principle (HUP)

Out of Christian Development Aid the *Homogenous Unit Principle* (HUP) arose. The idea is to address larger homogenous units within a society by development aid. Such units can share labour and bear the charges more easily than an individual or small group.

In relation to mother tongue education a homogenous unit could be a local dialect group with a close common lexicon and pronunciation. The alphabet would fit easily and educational material is produced in teamwork. For the Zaza people the former upper class structure would be a good starter to provide support and to lead and arrange such programmes. Hopefully an alliance of small scale tribal societies would take over the responsibility of enlarging the project to a dialectical border whose speakers would not accept the proposed alphabet. The pronunciation or phonological limitations do not prevent further advances which start with adapting the already developed material to other dialects of Zazaki as a template. Such an approach would lead to a wider acceptance by the national government. For the Kurmanji speaking Kurds such an attempt is under way.

2.6.6 Summary

In this paragraph we looked at mother tongue issues that affect the Zaza people. The importance of the mother tongue can be traced back to the newborn. The uniqueness of the unborn is that it not only hears but feels the mother tongue while being close to the mother's glottis. After birth it is the mother who educates the child with her voice. Every human has this experience.

For an outsider, the mother tongue speaker is the only emic resource for any research on the language or culture. The researcher needs to balance between the emic and the etic aspects of study (ethnographer) to guarantee a successful outcome in linguistic and cultural anthropology.

The *lingua franca* and / or the national language plays a main factor as it provides higher education and employment prospects. The mother tongue is the basic tool to communicate within the same group and to express thoughts and to develop ideas with a people group that shares the same social pretension (self-identity, nationality, sense of belonging etc.). For this very reason any approach to mother tongue education has to be realistic and needs to transfer to that language which provides the best entrance into a wider economy and society. Nonetheless the cognitive potential of a child is best addressed if it is first educated in reading and writing its mother tongue. UNESCO started such approaches in 1953 but gained experience and worldwide recognition mainly within the last 10 years. Acronyms like EFA (Education For All) or MLE (MultiLingual mother tongue Education) stand for such attempts.

Educational material for children and transfer schedules as well as teachers training material are necessary to start the programmes. The best fit within those approaches would be to address homogenous smaller units. This includes tribes or alliances of extended families which are easy to mobilize to run such a programme. Their leadership from the upper class could provide support and function as the patron over the project. Hopefully alliances of the Zaza community build on this assessment by adapting the material to their dialect. This would also support the standardization process.

2.7 Summary

In this whole chapter we discussed the Zaza society, looking at the Zaza from the angle of
- the *people*, questions about their origin and identity,
- the *language*, linguistical considerations about Zazaki, and
- the *culture*, history, religions, social structure, peasantry, culture change, Diaspora and migration status,
- an example of a cultural and linguistic liaison based on the understanding of the term *merdım* (man, human, being etc.)
- the *worldview*, cosmology, Islam, celebrations, family and kinship, envy and again culture change, and
- *mother tongue* issues, specifically Zazaki mother tongue education.

Concerning the origin of the Zaza people I promote two basic approaches, either the Daylam-Thesis or the early settlement in the recent homeland. Concerning the former, it is assumed that the Zaza people originated together with the Hewram / Goran people from the southern shore of Caspian Sea, particularly a province called Daylam (2.1.3.1.1; 2.1.3.2).

Going into depth, the peculiarities of the Zaza *people* (3-4 Mill.) circle around their struggle of identity in relation to the larger Kurmanji speaking society (~16 Mill.). Since the question of identity never arose in the past, the challenge is to decide which factors constitute a people group to be separate. A differentiation between linguistic and cultural factors is essential to avoid mixing up realities. Linguistically Zazaki and Kurmanji are considered two languages. Ethnically the term "Kurds" was used in the past for all nomadic or peasantry practising collectivistic people groups which lived in Eastern Anatolia. They were considered to be mountaineers in the Tauros and Zagros mountains following Islam. Nowadays with much more knowledge about the population of this area a differentiation is necessary. There is a large Zaza group which emphasizes that they are Kurds with another dialect. These are mainly those in the Eastern and Southern parts of the Zaza homeland with direct contact to the larger Kurmanji group. Others are not concerned or undecided about the issue and a growing number is focusing on independence from the Kurmanji group. The latter group accentuates linguistical and cultural facts. Looking at the religions, ethnomusicology, feasts and celebrations, labour divide and trade one will notice that in practice the Zaza people are much more separated from the Kurmanji group than considered on the surface. Partially different religious settings (Hanafi, Shafi'i, Yezidism), different themes of music, different annual celebration schedules and different conceptions of labour division within gender are just some of those observations.

The Indo-European and North-western Iranian language Zazaki belongs to a language belt which covers the mountainous regions of Eastern Anatolia, West Iran and the eastern parts of Northern Iraq. Most of the languages in this area do show common features. Zazaki offers a very complex verb system with few roots, three tempora, two genera and modi known to Western languages. Active and passive as well as transitive and intransitive forms are given. A split ergative in the past goes together with intransitivity. Irregular verbs are few. Besides the *casus rectus* (nominative) Zazaki shows a *casus obliquus*. The three main dialects differ grammatically in expressing the genera on nouns and verbs (e.g. 2nd fem. in the Southern Group) and in tempora (e.g. future particle *do* in Southern Group). Also the pronunciation and the lexicon show diversity.

The culture of the Zaza people shows long intervals of freedom and peace as well as times of upheaval and unrest. A time of total self administration or independence is not known. In the Ottoman Empire the Zaza people lived relatively independently and under self rule. Special tax collectors communicated with the landlords (*agha*) and lived only in the big cities not in the homeland area of the Zaza people. In history three main upheavals led by the Zaza people became popular. Interestingly they are commonly counted as "Kurdish" rebellions. However there was little interaction between the initiating Zaza people and the Kurmanji speaking people group:

2 The Zaza

- the 1920 *Koçgiri* revolt (proclamation of a state "Kurdistan"),
- the 1925 *Sheikh Said* riot (Southern and Eastern Zaza) and
- the 1937-1938 so called *Tertelê Dersimi* (Northern Group).

With the 20th century AD they experienced oppression, caused by the two World Wars, the disintegration of the Ottoman Empire, the foundation of the new Republic of Turkey, the new policies of anti-feudalism and a strict centralism. Zaza small scale societies formed alliances with each other and became the main forces for the proclamation of the "Kurdish Question" as it is known today in Turkey. In consequence the use of their language became a political issue. After ninety years the language got endangered and the culture assimilates increasingly to the socialistic and capitalistic agenda that the national government is following. Although culture is constantly changing and language is shifting, Zazaki demonstrates resistance to change. Unfortunately this change can also be a sign for its ineffectiveness in interactions with modern educational media. Since it is not practised as a language of education the Zaza people do not use their language in dealing with modern media (slowly changing).

As one part of a culture but with a special focus in this work, the *religions* of the Zaza people were investigated. They originated historically from Animism, Parsiism / Zoroastrianism, Manichaeism, Dualism, Christianity, Gnosticism and Islam. Islam entered the area in the 7-8th century AD, thereby it developed into a Sunnism following Hanafi school among the Southern Group, a Shafi'i practice of the Eastern Group and a Shi'a following mystical orientation as part of Sufi'ism namely Alevism of the Northern Group. Neighbouring people groups religiously influenced the Zaza people and in the same way were influenced by their religions. For instance due to their close contact with the Kurmanji speaking people the Eastern Group follow the school of Shafi'i. The Southern Group was much more influenced by the Silk Roads and the main Islamic school of Hanafi. Islamic orders and groups play an important role in history and the recent spiritual life of the Zaza ethnos. Those are the *Naqshebendi*, the *Nurcu* (including its offshoot the *Işıkçılar*), the *Süleymanlı*, the *Ticani*, the *Bektaşi*, the Mevlana. Islamic sects and parties coming from outside are not commonly recognized (e.g. Hisb Allah, Hamas, Aciz Mend etc.). Up until today it is not definitely researched or known who influenced whom, when and how.

Looking at the *worldview* of the Zaza people, the centralistic perspective of the LEIC (Location of the Emotions, the Intellect and the Character; 1.1.3.3) sticks out. Thus the *zerre* (inner parts, heart) as a metaphysical organ above the stomach and the intestines is representing the location of the conscience and the sentiments. It is here that the LEIC as the driving non-physical human organ is placed. The centralistic view leads to the perception of the same distanced extremities in relation to the nonphysical centre. The awareness of the human and bodily sphere of an individual is recognized by equal distance. Daily life activities like travelling, running and working with the hands are considered to come out of the inner centre where the motivation is seated. The inner composure carries a high value and has to be balanced. Craft, eating, social gathering etc. are often done in a sitting position due to this centralistic perception of the world. The Zaza perception of the world contrasts thereby to the Western head perception. The latter perceives the hand-activity as much more valuable than the feet-motion, due to dissimilar distance of the head to the extremities.

The mother tongue became the last issue of this chapter. Mother tongue education is essential for the survival of a culture. It is within mother tongue that traditions, perception of the worlds, core values and norms are passed on. Extreme culture changes and language shifts in on the long term only be overcome when children have access to a good part of the cultural and linguistic repertoire of their community. With this knowledge they start performing their own way of life and adapt this knowledge to modern day life by using their mother tongue. Multilingual mother tongue education is an approach that was initiated by UNESCO, and involves focusing for at least 2 years on mother tongue education including a smooth transfer to the national language during the second class. It is within this approach that Zazaki and Kurmanji speakers could form alliances and share human and material resources. At the moment the Kurmanji group is further ahead in this approach than the Zaza.

To understand a people group well enough, the wider environment comes into focus. Looking at historical and economic developments in this area new perspectives are opened up. We will now take a look at this wider environment of the Zaza people. The focus will be on the homeland area and its specific situation as well as the circumstances and the relation of the migration countries to the Republic of Turkey.

3 Turkey – A Socio-Historical Overview

The necessity to describe the socio-historical and socio-cultural background of a people group in an anthropological study comes out of the manifold influences that the Zaza people face from the outside. The neighbouring people groups in the present *and* the past manipulated the development of their culture and worldview as well as in reverse. The reciprocal influence by neighbouring cultures is a stimulation either to take over or to refuse cultural aspects of the neighbour.

This chapter is thus to be seen as information concerning the wider foundational socio-cultural background of this anthropological study. The following chapter presents the development and recent *co-* and *con*text of the Zaza people in Turkey. Some preliminary remarks about general developments will give a meaningful framework.

The Republic of Turkey is an ethnically diverse country which developed out of the Sublime *Ottoman State* or the *Ottoman Empire*. The absolute break with the aristocratic *Sultanate* (political Supreme Head since 14th century) and the *Caliphate* (religious Supreme Head in personal union) did destroy inner structures of administration and power sovereignty. However ideologies implemented by the Ottoman rulers survived and sometimes break through. One of those ideologies is *Pan-Turanism*, also called *Pan-Turkism* (2.1.3.1.4; 3.1.1.2.2); another one is *Pan-Islamism*. It would be fair to say that the Republic of Turkey still struggles to balance those two ideologies. In the same way the effort is to find a positive way to integrate these in a functioning democracy. It is necessary to say that all modern democracies fight with related issues. Often the leftist and rightist ideologies support either nationalism or religious-like attempts.

In the past the Zaza people demonstrated strong religious beliefs. Some rebellions of the Zaza people started as religious upheavals (2.3.1.3.2). For this reason conservative and religious Islamic parties are welcomed by the Southern and Eastern Group whereas the Northern Group tends toward leftist and socialistic parties. However since the disenchantment with the *Cumhuriyet Halk Partisi* (CHP), founded by Mustafa Kemal Paşa Atatürk, the whole Zaza community tend to lean in general to the leftist parties. This tendency made them even more unreliable or suspect to the larger Turkish society. These is aggravated by the fact that most Turkish people count the Zaza to the ethnically 'Kurdish' population and therefore address them to the highly disliked 'Kurdish Question' (2.2.3.6). The Zaza people did never show a tendency to overcome such charges, but they also never got a voice in the public due to an oppressive constitution.

Turkey is the homeland of the Zaza people and only very few voices ask for an independent state. The campaign aims at more political and self-ruling freedom in a federalist construction in the homeland area of the Zaza that is the Euphrates / Tigris headwaters. Having a say in Turkish politics in relation to the concerns of the Zaza group and the area they inhabit and not just to adapting to national politics is important for the populations in Eastern Anatolia. The two unsolved interior challenges for the Republic of Turkey are the ongoing 'Kurdish Question' as well as the strong antipathy against 'Alevism' by the Islamic majority of Sunnis. Unfortunately both hit the Zaza people internally due to a rejection of Kurdish nationalism and the inner religious split in an Alevism and Sunnism following group. Thus the main problem is the close involvement of Zaza groups - by far not the whole group - in the 'Kurdish movement'.

3.1 Turkey and the Diverse Ethnicities

The area of what is today Turkey is part of the *Fertile Crescent* which is considered to be the cradle of humankind. It includes the Eastern part of Turkey down to the Egyptian Nile delta in the south, the Western planes of Iran and the Arabian Peninsula.

Inhabitation of Turkey stretches a long way back. The first documentation starts with the high civilization of the Hittite (extensively in Seufert & Kubaseck 2004:47-48; 14th-11th century BC). The Hittites are mentioned in the Hebrew Bible (Gen 15:20). For a long time this was ignored and the Hebrew Bible accused of fabrication. Their Indo-European language belonged to the extinct Anatolian branch. The investigations of William Wright in 1884 AD brought forth the decoding of the hieroglyphic inscriptions of Hittite. With this the Hebrew description of the 'Hatti' חתי became known as the Hittite Empire of those days. The brutal Assyrian Empire replaced the reign of the Hittites from the 9th to the 6th century AD (2King 17). The short lasting empires of the Babylonians (6th-5th century BC) and the Persian / Medes Empire (4th century BC) replaced the Assyrians, and operated a moderate style of self ruling provinces by paying tribute to the central government. This is very well documented in the Hebrew Bible. The very short rule of *Alexander the Great* and his Empire (reigned from 334-

323 BC) led to a split of his rival generals, family and friends called the *Diadochi*. It was *Perdiccas* who started off and soon the area of Turkey became a war zone. With the breakdown of the last Diadoch *Antioch the Great* and the emergence of the Roman Empire in 168 BC the area became part of the larger *Asia Minor* and the Roman province of *Syria* (Seufert & Kubaseck 2004:55).

The Ottoman Empire started with the demise of the Seljuk Sultanate of Rum around 1300 AD. The dynasty of *Osman I.* quickly expanded out to the Balkans, Greece, Italy, the East and the South. The vision for its spread was Oman's dream of an Empire throughout the four rivers: Euphrates, Tigris, the Danube and the Nile. Although constantly growing, the capture of Constantinople in 1453 by *Mehmet II.* and the thereby consequent fall of the Byzantine Empire became the central symbol of power. Sulta*n Suleiman the Magnificent* (1520–1566) undertook the task of strengthening and even overtaking the enormous expansions of his predecessor Sultan *Selim I.* Sultan *Selim* became the symbol of supremacy which is why his name is passed on from generation to generation until today. Sultan *Suleyman* represented the ideal of an Ottoman Emperor. The 16th and 17th century became the heyday of the Ottoman Empire. Its decline started in the 19th century and ended in 1922 AD with the proclamation of the Republic of Turkey on the 29th October 1923.

During the *Tanzimat* reforms (1808-1876), which were introduced by Sultan *Mahmud II.* (1808-1839) and Sultan *Abdülmecid I.* (1839-1861) an ongoing reorganisation of the Ottoman state began. The basic ideological foundation grounded in *Pan-Turanism / Pan Turkism* and *Pan-Islamism*. The ones to suffer became the non-Islamic and non-Turkish people groups within the Ottoman Empire since they would not accept the ideology of either Pan-Islamism or Pan-Turkism. The more influential ethnicities with an ability to show strong resistance and a history of independence, liberty and even their own state (e.g. Armenia, Greek, Persia, etc.) were not supportive of the conception of Pan-Turkism. The intervention of Western colonial powers in the central parts of the Ottoman State brought about the concentration of Ottoman politics in the central area of today's Turkey. Their realm of activity comprised the Balkans, Eastern Anatolia, Egypt and the Near and Middle East. Official *millets* (nation-status) like the Greek, Armenian and Syriac Churches as well as the Jewish community operated under a second class citizenship (*dhimmi*-status). In periods of political instability they became the target of nationalistic aggression. *Millets* had to pay tribute, were often not allowed to work in the Turkish administrative or security system (police, military, secret service etc.), were sometimes resettled or restricted to geographical settlement and had to follow public rules of submission to the Islamic population (e.g. leave the street or bow before Muslims). The *tanzimat* reforms ended in 1872 / 1876 by the successor of Sultan Abdulmecid and the establishment of the first Ottoman Constitution.

Apart from those ethnicities that held the status of *millet*, the non-Turkish people groups without any official recognition were treated as feudal vassals. It was expected by the rulers that they hold a military and political allegiance. They paid tribute by taxes to the Sultanate but were independent and self ruling. During the reorganisation periods of the Tanzimat their feudalistic and tribal social structure were disrupted by the ruling power. It is important to emphasize that such attitudes are still obvious. The larger non-Turkish ethnicities within the core heartland of Turkey were the Kurmanji speaking people group, the Zaza, the Laz, the Romanes and Arabic speaking people groups. The non-Turkish and non-Islamic people groups were the Jewish people, the Armenians, the Greeks, the (As-) Syrian people, the Aramaeans. Other objects of aggression were the Alevis and the Yezidis.

3.1.1 Historical Sketch of the Turkish People

The Turkish people started with a group called 'Gök Türks' (Sky Turks) in the 5th century AD / 1st century BH with *Bumin Qaghan* (d. 552). He and his sons succeeded other nomadic confederations in the area of Inner Asia. They are documented since 522 AD and gave their followers the naming *Türks / Turks*. Their obligation to the trade on the Silk Roads made them wealthy and well known. They moved out to the Middle East and Africa until the 9th century. In that way they adopted Buddhism, and often Persian mystic religions. The spread of Islam conquered them fully and they and the Arabic Bedouins became the main propagators of Islam in the Middle and Near East.

3.1.1.1 Seljuk Empire (11th -12th Century AD)

In the 11th century (1060-1080 AD / 5th century AH) the Central-Asiatic Seljuk invaded from Bagdad to *Anatolia*. Their empire stretched from the area of the Persian plains and reached into the heartland of the Byzantine Empire to what is today the area of Cappadocia. With them the Ural-Altaic Language family and within it the Altaic branch of Turkic languages became the youngest in the area of the Near East. Their Empire was founded and expanded by *Tughril Beg* in

1037 AD, following the efforts by the founder of the Seljuq dynasty, *Seljuq Beg*, later named Seljuk. Starting from their homeland area around the Aral Sea they spread out over Khorasan, Persia, Eastern Anatolia and the Near East. *Alp Arslan* became the leading light of this Empire on account of his victory at the *Battle of Manzikert* (in 1071 AD) in which he effectively neutralized the Byzantine threat. The Seljuk Empire filled a political vacuum left by the power play of the Byzantine and Persian empires. Any attempt at more liberal views of Islam like the *Mu'tazilites* (9th century AD) were banned by their conservative and strict understanding of the Islamic *Sharia* (Turk.: *şeriat*). This traditionalist approach continued with the Mongol invasions during the 11th – 13th century AD / 5th – 7th century AH (2.1.3.1.1; 2.1.3.1.4; 2.1.3.1.5; 2.3.1.1; 2.3.3.4;- 3.1.1; 3.3; 0). Seljuk Turkish was put into writing using the Arabic alphabet and became the standard for the later Ottoman Empire (Ostler 1006:101; Franz 1988b:33-34, 38; Werner 2012).

3.1.1.2 Ottoman Empire (13th-20th Century AD)

Much is written about the Ottoman Empire its rise (13th century AD) by the *Osman* dynasty, its heyday with *Suleiman the Magnificient* (15th to 17th centuries AD / 10th to 12th century AH) and its steady decline punctuated by the *Tanzimat* reforms (19th century AD / 14th century AH). Its *lingua franca* became known as the *Osmanlı Turkish* and was built on the Seljuk Arabic alphabet and their language.

In relation to the Zaza people and the Kurmanji speaking Kurds the Ottoman Empire constituted a form of government which functioned as a patronage system against exterior enemies like the Persian, Russian or other powers. Interior politics focused on a tribute based tax system and general subordination but allowed for self ruling. The Zaza people were independent and self reliant as they ruled their small scale societies. It was in these days that the Ottoman Empire became popular as an interreligious, cross-cultural and liberal regime. This naive and blue-eyed picture of the Ottoman Empire does not reflect reality. Second class citizenship of the non-Islamic population comprised

- rude discrimination such as
    - the ban on being in public administrative bodies (e.g. military, security institutions, police, politics),
    - the privilege of Muslims in all areas of public life (education, economy),

- meeting a Muslim in public meant offering him free passage in all cases
- non-Islamic groups sometimes were stigmatised by clothing, proper names or living conditions (ghettoization).
- military occupation, forced observation by the security apparatus, resettlement or settlement dispositions or edicts.
- strong refusal and antipathy by the larger conservative Muslim population which led to the perpetual fear of aggressive encroachment and mobilization of the mob.

Many attacks against non-Islamic people groups are reported from those days. From an anthropological point of view it was envy driven by jealousy and irrational xenophobia that determined the relation of the ruling system to the *millets*. Beneath the fear of loss of welfare and wellbeing by the non-Islamic groups the fact is that it was just easy to plunder these often unarmed people because they were second class citizens and criminal prosecution was not to be expected.

3.1.1.2.1 Politics on Minor Ethnicities – Tanzimat-Reforms

The Sultan *Mahmud II.* (1808-1839) became a reformer due to pressure by outward political powers. His innovations led to some relief for the non-Islamic and non-Turkic ethnic groups in the realm of the Caliphate (Zürcher 2004:67-69). His *tanzimat* reforms started in 1839 and ended in 1876 with the proclamation of an Ottoman Constitution. To begin with changes in social law came into action. The social changes included (Seufert & Kubaseck 2004:71, 80):

> His subjects of arbitrary state would get inviolability of the person, the property and their religion, the abolition of the tax lease and the uniform regulation of the taxation, the public of court proceedings, and the legalization of the levying of recruits and the reduction of the armed forces office hours.

It is during this important epoch that the French influence became central, first on the military, later also on the linguistic-cultural area. Mustafa Kemal Paşa Atatürk who had a background of military education implemented the French etiquette on the administrative as well as on the social level (Zürcher 2004:15, 21-22).

The mechanics, of the oppression of minorities included child abduction, military occupation, military court, mass evacuation, mass deportation, resettlement and concentration camps. The following systematic, political undertakings follow a main timeline:

- The child abduction, persecution, deportation and resettlement of Christian minorities in the Balkans during the 18th century.
- The persecution, resettlement and deportation of Armenians to the Syrian desert and concentration camps from 1896 to 1915/1922, the military occupation, evacuation and deportation of non-Turkish people groups from their homeland area.
- The shattering of the *tertele / Tertelê Dêrsimi* (2.3.1.1; 2.3.1.3.2; 2.3.3.3) in 1937/1938. In consequence the Turkish government started to evacuate the province of Dersim, deported families, destroyed villages and announced a 10-year ban of any resettlement in the area (Çağlayan 1998:178-180).

3.1.1.2.2 Ideologies of Pan-Turkism and Pan-Islamism

The reforms introduced by Sultan *Mahmut II.* (1785-1839) led to a new epoch which affects politics towards smaller ethnicities until today. Another era was promoted by Sultan *Abdul Hamid* II. (1842-1918). His reform movement was based on the so called three *Tanzimat* (renewal-reforms; (2.1.4.3; 2.1.4.4; 2.1.3.1.4; 3.1.1.2.2; 3.4.1):

1.) Changes in the *administrative body* following the example of European countries. The Sultan ordered his military system with the help and under the instructions of the Prussian army. The administration system was formed by and after the French model (Berkes 1959:67).
2.) Introduction of the ideology of *Pan-Islamism* on the national level but with international impact towards the Arabic and Christian countries (:73).
3.) Introduction of the ideology of *Pan-Turanism / Pan-Turkism*. Foundational to this ideology is the concept of Turanism that aims to cover all Turkic people groups under one roof or union (:78; extensively in Zürcher 2004:56-70; Franz 1988b:38; Richter 2006:10; Laut 1996:26; Seufert & Kubaseck 2004:80; comparable with the concept of *Pan-Arabism* introduced in 1930 see Müller 2001:144).

Although the *Tanzimat*-reforms officially came to an end with the Ottoman Constitution (1876), they still formed influential and helpful conceptions to the exercise of power (Zürcher 2004:67-69, 127, 131). Both, the Young Ottomans who fought for the renewal of the Sultanate as well as the Young Turks and Mustafa Kemal Paşa Atatürk used the foundations of these ideologies to substantiate their authority (:ibid.; 3.4.1.1).

To understand why the scope of arts, and the areas of public life and politics were influenced by these ideologies, particularly Pan-Turkism, it is interesting to take a view on the promoters or representatives of them (Steinbach 1988:155-156):

- Literate *Ömer Seyfeddin* (1884 - 1920),
- Poet *Emin Yurdakul* (1869 - 1944),
- Literate *Halide Edip* (1884 - 1964),
- Turkologist *Mehmet Fuad Köprülü* (1890 – 1966; Jaeschke 1951:64-70),
- *Namik Kemal* as pioneer of the reform movement (1840 – 1888;:18; Zürcher 2004:69),
- he influenced *Ziya Gökalp* (* 23rd March 1876 in Diyarbakır, † 25. October 1924 in Constantinople).

The opinion of those ideologists was differed referring to the question whether all or only one of the ideologies should be predominant. Some refused e.g. Pan-Islamism since they claimed Islamism in general not to be Turkish; others refused Pan-Turkism in favour of local authority (e.g. Kurdish nationalism). Some emphasized the need for social reforms based on socialism. Either way, as general lines of development the ideological concepts expressed in the *Tanzimat* reforms (1839-1876) are still active today.

Ideologies combined with reform movements often shift into realities. Some of their negative outcomes were pogroms (1896, 1905, 1915), resettlement operation agendas (1915, 1925, 1938), and educational "Turkishization" activities, e.g. Turkish teachers were sent to the East; propaganda material was used that denies non-Turkish presence etc. (Steinvorth & Elger 2008:36; 3.6). The non-Islamic and non-Turkish people groups or microcultures within the Ottoman Empire experienced the worst oppression during its last century, due to a lack of competent authority structures (3.4.1).

3.1.1.2.3 Ziya Gökalp – A Turkish Nationalist and Zaza

Ziya Gökalp is an interesting character. He is from a Zaza background and therefore epitomizes in a peculiar form the self-abnegation of the Zaza people on the political level for the benefit of Turkish nationalism. He established modern Turanism as part of a national Pan-Turkism approach by driving 'Turkisation' forward ideologically. He is called "Father of Turkish Nationalism" Steinbach 1988:155; Ramsauer 1965; Heyd 1950; Berkes 1959; Zürcher 2004:131). *Mustafa Kemal Paşa Atatürk* based his whole political agenda on the conceptions of

Ziya Gökalp, although Gökalp was never directly mentioned or addressed in Mustafa Kemal Paşa Atatürks affairs and although Gökalp never held public office (Steinbach 1988:159). Ziya Gökalp was consequently following his thoughts. As a follower of Durkheim he assumed that neither genetical code nor birth were responsible for the socialisation of man, but only the environment. It is within enculturation and education that a person and his LEIC is formed and coined. From this perspective it was natural for him to find himself being a Turk in a Turkish environment (Berkes 1959:22; 3.1.1.4.5).

For this very reason the ideology of Pan-Turkism became an essential ideological impetus for the political powers in Turkey. The "National Workers Party" (MHP) reflects such attitudes impressively (:156). Its main promoter *Alparslan Türkeş* died in 1997, however the radical forces of Pan-Turkism also use Pan-Islamism as a foundation and are therefore against Mustafa Kemal Paşa Atatürk's conceptions of Laicism and gender equality (Bruinessen 1989a:13, 15).

3.1.1.2.4 An Extra View on Pan-Islamism

So far, the impression was given that Pan-Islamism as an ideology somehow accompanied other ideologies like Pan-Turkism just to support it and possessed no value in itself. Sometimes both ideologies add to each other, but sometimes they even exclude each other. If Pan-Islamism became the predominant ideology of an individual or a group they often followed predecessors in this approach. Looking at the religious reform era of Islam in the 19th century AD / 13th century AH three main reformers stick out. These are *Jamaluddin Afghani* (1838-1897), *Hz. Mohammed Abduh* (1849-1905) and *Rashid Rida* (1865-1935; see biographies in Gibb 1947; Keddie 1972; Kedourie 1966; Kerr 1966). Bruinessen suggests their influence was as reformers who wanted to go back to the origin of the meaning of Islam. They requested the renewal of interpretation of the Holy Book the Qur'an and the Hadith by newly educated religious teachers who overcome the solidified practices and dogmas since the existence of Islam. A renewed and modern civilization build on Islam should be able to stand the Western trend into Modernity (*Dogma of Pan-Turkism*). Whereas the former two did not apply for a split of religion and politics the latter *Rashid Rida* proclaimed a reformed Caliphate which was democratically controlled. Although born and settled in Syria and İstanbul their ideologies did not became a reality in the Ottoman Empire but in other parts of the Islamic World (Bruinessen 1989a: 18-19).

Following Bruinessen's argument, it becomes obvious that those thoughts influenced the Young Ottomans as well as the *Young Turks* immensely. The implementation of the revolutionary powers within the Ottoman Empire started in the 1870s / 13th century AH, a date that is closely related to the public debut of these three reformers.

During the regime of Mustafa Kemal Paşa Atatürk, Islam became a means of addressing Turkish nationalism for the common people. Within this approach Mustafa Kemal Paşa Atatürk on the one side damned Islam for being the reason of any ancientness, but at the same time he praised it for being superior to all other religions (Laut 2000:65-66). Although his personal faith never became obvious Mustafa Kemal Paşa Atatürk employed chief ideologists to formulate theories of nationalism based on Islamic beliefs (3.1.1.4.5).

3.1.1.3   Young Turks (20th Century AD)

The Ottoman Empire ended with the interventions of the *Young Turks* who arranged their military coups (1908 and 1913) in such a way that the Caliphate became secondary and the Sultanate obsolete. The period of the Young Turks is nowadays idealized as a movement of progress and prominence of power. It is indisputable that the Young Turks formed an effective and productive conglomerate of different political parties. Their success in founding the *Committee of Union and Progress* (CUP) as an organizational umbrella supporting their goal of establishing a secular and strong government was built on the ideologies of materialism and positivism, *Pan-Turanism / Pan-Turkism* as well as the less targeted *Pan-Islamism*. They established the basis for the succeeding Republic of Turkey. Their hierarchy and orientation was influenced by the military. The period of the Young Turks was overshadowed by ethnical cleansings directed at the non-Islamic people groups in the Ottoman Empire of their times and WWI. (Turk.: *soykırım*). It was as a result of their German ally and its defeat that the Young Turks struggled in their politics to progress further in the restructuring of the Sultanate. In consequence the colonial powers Great Britain, France, Greek and Italy took advantage to apply their influence on the Bosporus and the Near East. The dissection of the central parts of the former Ottoman Empire was at hand.

3.1.1.4   The Republic of Turkey (1923 AD – today)

It was only the clever military and political tactical manoeuvring of *Mustafa Kemal Pascha* (1881-1938) that hindered this. He became the dominant father figure of the Republic of Turkey and earned the title *Atatürk* (father of the Turks) since 1934. His vision was built on the ideologies of the Young Turks and their propagandists in full agreement with their vision. It is thus understandable that the fundamental principles of the *Tanzimat* reforms generally shine through in the newly found Nation of Mustafa Kemal Paşa Atatürk.

3.1.1.4.1 Young Turks in the new Republic of Turkey

The main pioneering strategist and promoters of the Young Turk ideology which often survived the transformation into the new Republic of Turkey were the following persons. It has to be noted that at the same time these persons became dubious characters to the new rulers because of their influence:

- *Osman Hamdi Bey* (1842–1910), a painter,
- *Emmanuel Carasso Efendi*, a lawyer and a member of the prominent Sephardic Jewish Carasso family,
- *Mehmet Cavit Bey* (1875–1926) a Dönmeh (convert) from Thessalonica, Jewish by ancestry but Muslim by religion since the 17th century, who was Minister of Finance, hanged for treason in 1926,
- *Marcel Samuel Raphael Cohen* (aka Tekin Alp: 1883–1961), born to a Jewish family in Salonica under Ottoman control (now Thessaloniki, Greece), became one of the founding fathers of Turkish nationalism and an ideologue of Pan-Turkism,
- *Agha Efendi* (1832–1885) established the first Turkish newspaper and, as postmaster, brought the postage stamp to the Ottoman Empire.
- *Ziya Gökalp* (1875–1924), a Turkish nationalist and Zaza from Diyarbakır, publicist and pioneer sociologist,
- *Talaat Pasha*, whose role before the revolution is not clear,
- *Ahmed Riza* (1859–1930), worked to improve the condition of the Ottoman peasantry
- *Enver Pasha*, a military officer.

3.1.1.4.2 Atatürk – The Father

The Republic of Turkey cannot be understood without understanding the "father of all Turks" that is Mustafa Kemal Paşa Atatürk so called since the 1930s (Traub 2008:22; Zürcher 2004:188). In 1881 in Saloniki (today's Thessaloniki / Greece) a minuscule customs officer *Ali Riza* and his wife *Zübeyde*, a farmer's daughter, had a boy whom they named *Mustafa*. Family names or surnames were not used in those days. One of Mustafa's teachers with the same name called him Mustafa *Kemal* (Arab. "completion"; Zürcher 2004:86). He was an excellent student who completed the whole military track, following the French example. His model was the French Enlightenment with its radical anti-Clericalism. He banned the traditional Arabic call to prayer from the minaret as well as the *Dervish* orders. At the beginning of his reign he held to his anti-Islamic clergy and traditionalistic attitude. Later on he balanced this approach in favour of political advance. After he became de facto an autocrat in 1923 he started what we can call a "dictate of education". In 1926 after an assassination attempt on him he used his revenge as a warning to his environment and executed political enemies as well as critical companions. Although he adopted 13 children, he never overcame his solitariness which was ended by cirrhosis of the liver initiated by his alcohol consumption in November 1938 (:23).

The influence and importance of Mustafa Kemal Paşa Atatürk is demonstrated by the celebration of the two holidays of the *founding of the state* (Turk.: Cumhuriyet Bayramı) on the 29th of October initiated and closely connected to his person and the celebration of his death on the 10th November at 09.05 o'clock (*Atatürk remembrance day*). Steinbach concludes Mustafa Kemal Paşa Atatürk's life-work was the establishment of a "dictatorship of education" by the "first man" (*tek adam*) to transfer the illiterate middle and lower class system into an educated middle class. His emphasis on the "people" and the "nation" (the *millet*) at first led him to massive counterinsurgency in the East (1923-1930) and later on into his role as the educator of his people (Steinbach 1996:161 and 1988:136-138; Heine 1988:115; Berkes 1959:77).

His politics on *non-Islamic* and *non-Turkish* people groups was based on the treaty of Lausanne in which only the non-Islamic ethnicities or microcultures, so called *millet,* were guaranteed equality. However this is window dressing since the Islamic Revelation per se believe in a second class citizenship (*dhimmi*-status) for non-Islamic subjects (Jenkins 2006:40-41; Zürcher 2004:9-11). In reality Mustafa Kemal Paşa Atatürk stylized the ideal of the total identification with the nation under the name of "Turkishness" (Seufert & Kubaseck 2004:151; Steinbach 1988:155-156; Höhlig 1997:121).

3.1.1.4.3 A new Constitution

The Turkish Constitution, first written down on the 29th October 1924, was influenced by European legislation (mainly Switzerland). The Turkish Constitution tends to emphasize Turkish nationalism by overemphasizing the function of the Turkish language as an indicator of citizenship. This tendency leads to a postponement of the remaining *millets* (*Turkey: a Minority Policy of Systematic Negation*). That is why the so called minorities or microcultures (Neuliep 2006:95-96; Myers-Scotton 2006:46) which are gathered under the roof of the Turkish state, suffer from denial or oppression. Modern approaches like the exhibition "Ebru" point out the oppression of this consciousness among Turks (Durak 2006). The Zaza people suffered by the resolute Kemalist policy of *"Tek Millet, Tek Vatan, Tek Dil, Tek Bayrak, Tek Devlet"* (one nation, one homeland, one language, one flag, one state) emphasizing the part of *"Tek dil, tek millet"* (one language, one nation). This propagandist motto declared them to be outsiders in the best case and traitors in the worst, the latter being the case if they start to intervene proactively against the 'Turkish-Only' language issue.

With the new Constitution the six fundamentals (*altı ok*) of the New Republic were introduced (3.1.1.5):

- Nationalism,
- Laicism,
- Republicanism,
- Etatism,
- Populism and
- Reformism

The Constitution very clearly stated that Turkish nationalism in the form of *Pan-Turkism* was a given (e.g. Turkish language issue in article 3 renewed in 1982), while *Pan-Islamism* was not promoted by Mustafa Kemal Paşa Atatürk and his cadre as the main topic or even at all. . Literally the Turkish Constitution from 1987, which was last changed in 2007, still states in article 3: "The Turkish state, with its territory and nation, is an indivisible entity. Its language is Turkish".

Officially many attempts were made to reduce Islamic presence or authority in public, but still Islam remained a tie at the individual level. Sanctions such as the ban on the Dervish orders or the confiscation of the Caliphate and all its property by the government (1923-1924 and 1928) were put in place. However Turkey did not became an Atheistic state. Around 1950 the public presence of Islamic institutions such as the faculty of theology in Ankara (1949) and the implementation of the very successful *Imam-Hatip*-grammar schools (1951) became obvious. By this development an Islamic clergy arose which still plays an important role in Turkish politics. Turkey as a democracy developed a very unique Islamic theological and political stance in the Islamic world. In the midst of Iran's Shafi'ism and the Arabian Sunnism (Wahhabism) Turkey performs its own quite interesting theological orientation (Hanafism and Alevism).

3.1.1.4.4 Anti-Zaza and Anti-Kurmanji Resentments

The politics of *Mustafa Kemal Paşa Atatürk* during the times of establishing the new Republic were also accompanied by circumstances that made the Zaza people and the Kurmanji speaking Kurds suspicious about the new political structure. The double-crossed advantages led to a fundamental distrust until today. At first Mustafa Kemal Paşa Atatürk liaised closely with the people groups in Eastern Anatolia against the colonial powers Italy, Great Britain and France and the further East waiting the Russian giant waiting further East. Later he abandoned them in their attempt to honour the political commitment. The changes of balance of power in the Eastern Anatolian Area during the years of 1922 and 1923 was showing such a promising basis when Mustafa Kemal Paşa Atatürk, chose to build only on his loyal military forces, that he ventured to take the risk of upheaval, which shortly afterwards occurred (Sheikh Said 1925; 2.3.1.3.2). The Turkish movement proved to be strong and steadfast during the Constitutional Era of the Republic of Turkey (1923 – 1938). With the death of Kemal Mustafa Atatürk his party (CHP) became the main player in the politics of Turkey. Attempts to educate the populations in the East by a huge army of quickly trained teachers for the underdeveloped provinces of the Republic failed. After this attempt had proved a failure, every village was asked to look for people who could teach and educate others in modern ways of life. After WWII those village institutes became a liability to the government, being accused of promoting the communist agenda (Zürcher 2004:194-195).

The Zaza of the Northern Group experienced strong oppression during the Constitutional Era. The Southern and Eastern Group were less oppressed but fell in a state of phlegmatics. Forgotten by the European powers and the centralistic Turkish power which focused mainly on its Western provinces the Zaza people and the Kurmanji speaking Kurds carved out their existence under the beady eye of the Turkish authorities. Any political attempt or the smallest favouring of autonomy or self organization were hunted suspiciously and severely punished by individual and mass penalisation.

3.1.1.4.5 Thesis about the Origin of Turks and Sun Language

The search for common ground and identity within the new Republic of Turkey led to different approaches. Attempts based on *nationalism* were welcomed by Mustafa Kemal Paşa Atatürk. He developed and promoted some of these ideas. His political career was accompanied by endeavours to buttress "Turkishness" with historical and linguistic-cultural theories (Zürcher 2004:190-191). In the nationalistic enthusiasm of the 1930s, the *Türk Tarıh Tezi* (Turkish Historical Thesis) and the *Güneş Dil Teorisi* (Sun Language Theory) were developed. The former was introduced in 1931 by the "Company for Turkish History" (*Türk Tarıhı Tetkik Cemiyeti* later *Türk Tarıh Kurumu*) and posited that Turkish speaking people migrated from Central Asia and brought into being civilizations in Mesopotamia, Egypt, Anatolia (Turkey), China, Crete, India, the Aegean Regions, and Rome. The latter was initiated by the "Company for Turkish / the Turkish Language" (*Türk Dili Tetkik Cemiyeti* later *Türk Dil Kurumu*) and it was argued that the Turkish language is the source of all the languages in the world. In the same way a Proto-language from Central Asia was imagined that was close to today's Turkey's-Turkish. Written by members of mainstream Turkish society and the intelligentsia, it was soon discredited in the Turkish academic world. However, in popular society, the theories remain, even in modern school textbooks (Hirschler 2001:147-48). Both theories are highly controversial and in general rejected by the academic body outside of Turkey.

Both theories left their marks on the Zaza people and their language Zazaki. In inner-Turkish research Kurmanji as well as Zazaki were both considered to be Altaic Turkic languages which developed in Eastern Anatolia. Such approaches were never taken seriously outside Turkey because they are not scientifically based (Gülensoy 1994; Gülensoy & Kalafat 1990). It is an irony of history that the Turkish-nationalistic motivated politicians from their or the Kurmanji speaking ranks became influential and thus became responsible for oppression of their own people. Gökalp for instance published his ideologically influenced linguistic "research" against his own judgement. It turned out to be not just an often cited and welcomed tool to oppress the Zaza people but also to dominate non-Turkish or non-Islamic people groups (Berkes 1959:20, 44; Zürcher 2004:132; 3.1.1.2.3). Besides *Gökalp* also *Ismet Inönü* another Turkish nationalist attracted negative attention. As Mustafa Kemal Paşa Atatürk's Premier he organized the bloody suppression of the Dersim upheaval called *Tertelê Dêrsimi* (turmoil; Zürcher 2004:229-234; Hirschler 2001:146; 2.3.1.3.2). General *Enver*

Kenan (7th President of Turkey, 1982-1987) acted in the same way. By a coup he implemented a military government in 1980 and consciously caused a wave of aggression against non-Turkish and non-Islamic people groups. His politics of distraction was welcomed by the next Premier *Turgut Özal*, former Premier, whose mother was a Kurmanji speaker. He caused waves of refugees into mainly Europe (Germany) in the years 1980-1992 from Kurmanji speakers and the Zaza people (Izady 1992:110; Steinbach 1996:394).

Besides the above mentioned theories the epoch from 1930 to 1938 was the most productive period ever in the Republic of Turkey for the Islamic-Nationalistic thesis ever. From the Islamic side the Institute for Turkish History claimed the origin of Islam by Turkish sources. Abraham as well as the Prophet were of Turkish origin and the Holy Book the Qur'an is full of Turkish terminology (Laut 2000:70-73). Mustafa Kemal Ataturk was well aware that for political reasons the piety of his people needed to be addressed and so he welcomed such pseudo-scientific declarations. With this move he opened the door for a public return of Islam during the 1950s.

3.1.1.4.6 Summary

The Republic of Turkey emerged from a weak, declining, and instable political world empire in the 1920s. The transition period initiated by the Young Ottomans and the Young Turks was accompanied by an adoption of the ideologies introduced as the *Tanzimat* reforms and the persecution and resettlement of a large number of non-Turkish and non Islamic ethnicities. It was Mustafa Kemal Paşa Atatürk - the father of the Turks - who implemented the Republic of Turkey on an educational autocratic basis. He is inseparably linked to Turkey. His former positive attitudes which combined all people groups to defend the area against the colonial powers gave way to his latter dictatorial politics based on Turkish nationalism. To support Turkish nationalism not just on a military or political level he welcomed theories about the Turkish superiority over all people, including the Turkish culture and Turkish as a language. The *Türk Tarıh Tezi* (Turkish Historical Thesis) and the *Güneş Dil Teorisi* (Sun Language Theory) thus became "scientific" propaganda tools that drown out any objective research in Turkey. The close network between the military, police and executive with public institutions led to a surveillance apparatus which is contrary to democratic human right issues.

3.1.1.5 The (recent) Political Situation - Political Constellation

The landscape of political parties in Turkey reflects an erratic back and forth to exercise of power within the government. The four main parties that are represented in the recent AKP led administration are (the last two hold no seats but got votes higher than 2%)

Table 35 Political Parties in Turkey

Adalet ve Kalkınma Partisi	AKP
Justice and Development Party	Recep Tayyip Erdoğan
Cumhuriyet Halk Partisi Republican People's Party	CHP
	Kemal Kılıçdaroğlu
	(2.3.4.6.6)
Milliyetçi Hareket Partisi	MHP
Nationalist Movement Party	Devlet Bahçeli
Barış ve Demokrasi Partisi	BDP
Peace and Democracy Party	Selahattin Demirtaş
	(2.3.1.3.1; 2.3.4.6.6)
Genç Parti	GP
Young Party	Cem Uzan
Saadet Partisi	SP
Felicity Party (replacement of *Refah partisi*)	

Other parties in Turkey contribute also in a more oppositional way to the party scene:

Türkiye Komünist Partisi	TKP
Communist Party of Turkey	
Demokrat Parti	DP
Democratic Party	
Demokratik Sol Partisi	DSP
Democratic Left Party	
Demokratik Sol Halk Partisi	DSHP
Democratic Left People's Party	
Eşitlik ve Demokrasi Partisi	EDP
Equality and Democracy Party	
Saadet Partisi	SP
Felicity Party	
Özgürlük ve Dayanışma Partisi	ÖDP

Freedom and Solidarity Party
Büyük Birlik Partisi, BBP
Great Union Party
Yeşiller Partisi
Greens of Turkey
Yurt Partisi YP
Homeland Party
Anavatan Partisi ANAP
Motherland Party
Millet Partisi MP
Nation Party
Toplumcu Demokratik Parti TDP
Socialist Democratic Party
Hak ve Özgürlükler Partisi HAKPAR
Rights and Liberties Party

Besides these parties there is another pool of such political institutions which are more or less successful and sustainable:
- Independent Republic Party (*Bağımsız Cumhuriyet Partisi*, BCP),
- Independent Turkey Party (*Bağımsız Türkiye Partisi*, BTP),
- Labour Party (*Emek Partisi*, EMEP, Liberal Democratic Party (*Liberal Demokrat Parti*, LDP),
- Marxist-Leninist Communist Party (Turkey: *Marksist-Leninist Komünist Partisi*),
- National Party (*Ulusal Parti*),
- New Party (*Yeni Parti*), Peace and Democracy Party (BDP),
- People's Ascent Party (*Halkın Yükselişi Partisi*, HYP),
- People's Voice Party (*Halkın Sesi Partisi*, HAS PARTİ),
- Revolutionary Socialist Workers' Party (*Devrimci Sosyalist İşçi Partisi*, DSİP),
- Rights and Equality Party (*Hak ve Eşitlik Partisi*, HEPAR),
- Social Democratic People's Party (*Sosyaldemokrat Halk Partisi*, SHP),
- Socialist Democracy Party (*Sosyalist Demokrasi Partisi*, SDP),
- Turkey's Change Movement (*Türkiye Değişim Hareketi*, TDH),
- Turkey Party (*Türkiye Partisi*, TP),
- Workers' Party (*İşçi Partisi*, İP).

In the past the main political players stayed the same (e.g. *Erbakan* d. 2011, *Erdoğan, Gül,* etc.) but their political influence and expression changed from one period of governance to the other. The recent party of *Recep Tayyip Erdoğan* (AKP) holds a record with ten year's in power and being voted for another 5 year period. The politics moved between either a secular and non-religious or a religious pro-Islamic approach. The CHP of *Mustafa Kemal Paşa Atatürk* still holds high prestige and strong influence.

The main ideologies or fundamentals (*ok*) that drive politics in Turkey today are based on the six essentials from Mustafa Kemal Paşa Atatürk (*altı ok*) and other modern influences:

- Kemalism,
- Laicism,
- Reformism and Modernization,
- Neo-liberalism,
- Pan-Islamism,
- Nationalism, Pan-Turkism or Pan-Turanism and
- Socialism.
- Republicanism,
- Etatism, and
- Populism.

Neoliberalism is accompanied by Capitalism in a socialistic form and threatens Kemalism which works towards more governmentally controlled processes.

Only very few parties address the politically central questions of the "Kurds / Kurdish Question" or "Alevism / Alevism question" (e.g. BDP very clearly states its Pro-Kurdish stance). Most parties that dealt with these issues were closed down by the government (e.g. HADEP 1995-2003). However more and more individuals claim their "non-Turkishness" as a way of requesting liberty of language in the parliament or multi-lingual approaches in public (e.g. officials, politics, and national gatherings). The formation of political parties for the people groups of Eastern Anatolia is difficult, if not to say impossible, due to the vague definition of what will be considered a political offender. People are therefore used to staying in the larger parties which serve different purposes but not their interests of freedom of language etc. The disillusion goes as deep as the recent attempt to start mother tongue language classes at universities (e.g. Tunceli University, Mardin Artuluk University, etc.), which were not welcomed by students as expected. The enrolment dropped to Zero in 2011. One can question the framework of such education classes (e.g. ideology of teachers, anonymity of student, etc.). The agreement of the inner restrictions, in failing to find any worth in the Zazaki language and culture, *and* the outer complication of starting educational mother tongue proposals are the great obstacles for the Zaza ethnos.

3.1.1.6 Positive Effects of the Past and the National State

The Ottoman Empire was strong on the relative liberty and self-government of the people groups that lived under their surveillance. The system of *millet,* the close military activities with the Kurmanji and Sorani speaking Kurds in East Anatolia and Northern Mesopotamia (North Iraq) during different historical epochs are validate this attitude.

The Turkish State is built on a strong "educational dictatorship". The ideal of education is driving the Turkish national sentiment. In this Turkey represents a unique structure. In consequence the centralisation, the setting of priorities and the way to earn prestige and status is by education. This contrasts with the feudalistic and relational focus of the Zaza ethnicity and the Kurmanji speaking Kurds. As a positive outcome, even those people groups, that do not have Turkish as their mother tongue, can enter the qualified world of employment, and the higher ranks of the officials and administration. However, the security apparatus, the military and the area of ambassadors is reserved for educated Turkish mother tongue speakers, exceptions provided.

Through this emphasis on education Turkish became an important factor in the Near and Middle East. After the dissolution of the USSR the Turkish speaking nations developed and are now among the global players in politics and economy. The people groups that live within this market and political influence all profit from this development. Compared to other areas of the globe, the political situation is relatively stable and the economy not too bad. Access to luxury, good health care and social security is given, far above basic human needs.

3.1.1.7 Summary

The History of the Turkish people reveals some important aspects to understand the present as well as the origins of the Republic of Turkey. As the main players in the area of what is called "Turkey" everything depends on these people groups. Their nation state is built around their language and their culture. The dominant political topics are thus "Pan-Turkism" or "Pan-Turanism", as well as

"Pan-Islamism" as the linking component of the Turkish people groups. Having said this the term "Turks" does not refer to a single people group but to a heterogeneous conglomerate of different Turkish speaking ethnicities. In total it is astonishing how comprehensively the whole Turkish speaking people groups as a Turkic language branch of close to 180 Million people are able to communicate to each other.

The Altaic speaking Turkish people from today's area of Mongolia came to official recognition in the 6th century AD. They moved into the recent homeland area by migration around the 9th century AD. Their spread over Central Asia to the south led them to Persia and the area of the Fertile Crescent. The foundation of the Seljuk Empire during the 11th-12th century AD over the recent area was marked by an expansion phase. Their spread was fast and overwhelmingly successful. The same goes for their decline which gave place to former rulers. During the whole phase the Byzantine Empire was in decline, but still in power. The Armenians, the Syriac churches including the Maronites, the Orthodox and Catholic branches as well as the Assyrian and the Chaldean church together with the Byzantines formed a Christian block within and against the expanding Islamic Seljuk.

The clash of the main monotheistic religions Islam, Christianity and Judaism in the area of the Golden Horde runs through all the ages. With the nascence of the *Ottoman Empire* during the 14th century AD, started by the clan of *Osman*, one of the largest Empires arose. It is difficult to determine the linking components of an Empire which lasted over six centuries (14th – 20th century AD). In retrospect the main mechanisms of cohesion were Islam and a centralistic Sultanate expressing the religious and political heart of the Empire. Non-Islamic groups were given independent and self ruling authority expressed in the term *millet*. Non-Turkish ethnicities like the Kurmanji speaking Kurds and the Zaza people clashed from time to time with the Ottoman rulers due to religious differences like *Alevism* or *Shafi'ism* in contrast to Turkish Hanafi Sunnism.

During the time of a declining Sultanate and the military Young Turks revolution the Christian and Jewish citizens, although already restricted to a second class existence (*dhimmi*-status) within Islam rulership, were removed. The non-Turkish residents were either utilised or offered to help in those undertakings. The years of 1896, 1905 and lastly 1915 represented the climax and extinction of these non-Islamic ethnicities. The non-Turkish populace started to intervene in Turkish politics in those years by expressing their independence and individualism. Conflicts, such as uprisings became the standard intervention method. In general those groups were self ruling in the framework of their own territories.

As the Ottoman Empire started to decline, the colonialist powers Italy, Great Britain, France and Greece occupied the Eastern territories. The remaining Turkish heartland was the centre from which *Kemal Mustafa Atatürk* started his counteroffensive. His impressive ability to gather the scattered resistance groups and rule them under poor circumstances, as well as his military foresight is well illustrated by his adoration by the Turkish nation even today. His political cornerstones are best expressed by the ideologies Kemalism, Centralism, military led Socialism, and Islam led Laicism. Whereas in the beginning of the struggle for freedom Mustafa Kemal Paşa Atatürk included the people groups of the East, he suddenly changed politics after the establishment of the Republic of Turkey. He fought them because of their resistance and adherence to the Sultanate and feudalism. Their rejection of innovation and the danger of Russian influence from the East led him to strict military occupation, resettlement arrangements and other drastic measures in the Eastern territories.

During the military coup turbulences of 1960, 1971, 1980, 1997 (military memorandum) the political situation in Turkey was unstable and democracy was limited to military surveillance. The non-Turkish people groups were limited to adaptation and adjustment under the Turkish majority government. Consequences such as torture, arrest, relocation or the ban of settlement in some areas, as well as continuing military presence and ongoing monitoring of travel became part of the daily life of those people. The military educated and trained the Eastern Anatolian youngsters in the West and sent them back for military service to the East to fight their own people. Since 2002 the situation is changing dramatically and mother tongue use and even training for adults is possible. The guerrilla fighting became less, during the one sided ceasefire of the Kurdish resistance group. Since 2010 tensions are growing and fights in the East increasing. Recently the people groups do not suffer any more and a feeling of hope and progress drives the East of Turkey.

3.1.2 Outside Turkey – Europe and the World

The history of the European relationship with the Ottoman Empire and the Republic of Turkey has roots back to the Middle Ages and is closely related to the encounter of Christianity and Islam. This paragraph reflects the historical developments in relation to the topic "how non-Turkish and / or non-Islamic people groups relate to the Turkish powers". Turkey as a part of Europe and a crossing to Asia always played an important role, either as an area of the Eastern Churches or later as the influential Ottoman Empire

In medieval times the Franconian emperor *Charlemagne* met with the governor of *Saragossa* (777 AD), *Sulaiman al Arabi*, who was sent away by the Emir of Cordoba at the Reichstag in Paderborn (Germany). The meeting ended in a pact of mutual assistance. This led to interrelations between *Charlemagne* and the Abbasidian Caliph *Harun al Rashid* from Baghdad, the sovereign from the novel *The Thousand Nights and one Nights* (Faruk 1999 *Zwischen Preussenadler und Hakenkreuz* [Engl. Between the Prussian Eagle and the Hakenkreuz (swastika]).

The Arabian conquests during the 7th and 8th century AD / 1st century AH led to an Islamic wave across the Iberian Peninsula and Aquitaine, the latter being today's south-western France. Also Sicily and Southern Italy were threatened. "Under their leader, Tariq bin Ziyad, they had crossed the Strait of Gibraltar (Jibl al-Tariq, 'the mountain of T'ariq) in 711, and after defeating the Visigothic king Roderik found themselves masters of the country (Ostler 2006:99-100; s. a. Busse 1988:86)." The Christian principalities in the Western Gothic Empire were too weak to organize themselves into an effective resistance movement. But after the reorganisation, beginning in the 8th century, the *Reconquista* started from the North (Busse 1988:86). Islamic principalities (Arab. *taifas*) replaced the ecclesiastical and politically Christian influenced area (Kemnitz 2002:7-8). The penetration of the Arab forces into Aquitaine was stopped by *Karl Martell* in 732 AD in the well-known battles at Tours and Poitiers. Later on the intruders were forced back beyond the *Pyrenees* (Busse 1988:86). Finally in 1492 AD the last remnants of Arabian reign was forced out, when the *Nasride of Granada* were dispersed.

The legacy of seven hundred and fifty years of Arabian influence forced *King Charles V.* to use only Castilian Spanish and to prohibit the use of Arabic for contracts and in public in the year 1526 AD (Ostler 2006:100), more than thirty years after the ban on Arabic books (1492). Still today the notable art of the Arabian times can be seen in architecture or mural paintings throughout the whole Iberian Peninsula. Sicily was recaptured in the 11th century by the Normans. Italy resisted the penetration of Arab troops.

Encounters between Turkish people and European powers during the early Middle Ages were mainly through globetrotters (e.g. *Marco Polo* 13th century)

or ecclesiastical-representatives (e.g. *Francis of Assisi* in 1182-1226 AD) and therefore on a personal level. As the Ottoman Empire expanded over the Balkan Peninsula, conflicts in the Christian-Islam encounter increased. The climax was the capture of the Balkan and the siege of Vienna in 1529. The second siege in 1683 initiated another period of menace for Europe and shows the long period of Ottoman and Islamic expansion into Europe.

Beginning with humanism, the renaissance of Christian thinking in the 15th century generated political and spiritual movements against the expansion of the Ottoman Empire. The reaction to the Islamic threat got increasingly harsher, as e.g. Papal polemics demonstrate (Güvenç 2010 *Das Bild des "Türken" in Europa* [The conception of the "Turk" in Europe]). During the period of the Reformation the Christian world in Europe was confused. The political confrontation with the Ottoman Empire and Islam initiated another front. The tension is best expressed in Martin Luther's polemic pamphlet *Vom Krieg wider die Türken* and *Heerpredigt wider die Türken* [Engl. About the struggle against the Turks and the military sermon against the Turks] (Luther 1909 30/II:81-148 and 30/II:149-197) published in the year 1529.

In the 16th century a catholic movement of Christian development aid focused on the Middle East and Asia. The historic Christian churches there, were all integrated between the 3rd and the 8th century AD. This comprised mainly the Nestorians, the Armenian Apostolic Church, the Byzantine Church, the Albanian, the Turkic, the Syrian-Jacobite Churches, the Syriac Churches and the Maronites (Antes 1988:49-51; Busse 1988:90; Hage 1978:362-364; Jenkins 2006:45, 47; Miller 2002:31, 39; Ostler 2006:90; Reifler 2005:158-159; Schmitt 1981:26-27; Ter-Mikelian [1892] 2009). After the expansion of Islam in the 7th and 8th century AD / 1st century AH and the Ottoman Empire in the 13th century / 7th century AH these churches either fought against the Islamic imperators (e.g. Poland, Albania, Serbia) or existed as so called *millet* (see Zaza neighbours; 2.1; 2.3.3.4) under the Islamic government. Here their status due to the *Sharia* (Islamic law; Turk.: *şeriat*) made them a minority or second-class citizen (Baumann 2005:13; Islaminstitut 2007:23-24; Schirrmacher 2008a:108-109).

Summarizing the encounter between Arabian and Turkic forces in the Middle Ages, the clash of religions is blatant. The fight against the Islamic penetration was based on the *Reconquista* and also the crusades (Busse 1988:86-87). All resistance movements by Christians in those days had the goal of recapturing political control over the lost areas. During these times the close cooperation of secular and ecclesiastical authority is best seen in the power play of the Vatican, then called "Rome".

The politics and culture of the Ottoman Empire did partially go over into the newly found Republic of Turkey. Thus the long lasting tradition of picking up the French culture and German military technology from Europe continued politically, economically and culturally in the new Republic (Heine 1988:106-107; Olson 1989:119-120).

From an anthropological point of view the encounter of the Asian Turkish people with the European Westerners led to a mix of genetical, religious, cultural and linguistic information. The Turkish Diaspora developed a Euro-Islamic weave. This adaptation of Islam seeks to conform with the European national constitutions but at the same time to introduce their own Islamic juridical institutions which implement the *Sharia* in national contexts. The new convergence of religion in Europe does also changes the attitudes and perception of the world of the European citizens. Only a few take a European stance by looking at the EU as a united and homogenous people, quite the contrary. Recently the trend is to more nationalism and focus on people's origin. Having said this, Christianity gains more attraction on the national level as a factor of identification. Since Christianity is basic to all European countries it thereby serves as an identity marker for Europeans on the national as well as the international level. Now that Christianity has become this indicator the Turkish and European sides are confronted by a religious split which essentially tells the difference between the perception of the worlds of the two populations.

3.1.3 Germany and Turkey

European wars led to many Ottoman and Turkic prisoners in the 17th century. Mainly from 1689-1698 there are records from thousands of captured Muslims. Most prisoners stayed faithfully to their Islamic faith and returned to their native countries. But we know hardly anything or only very little about it. In 1968 the German Orientalist Otto Spieß published an essay on this topic in which it is said that there were some conversions to Christianity among the prisoners. These Turks were completely wrapped up in the German national traditions of their chosen settlement area (Spies & Pritsch 1964:9 and 1968; Olbrich 1996:9).

The German relationship with the Ottoman Empire started in 1739 AD when twenty Turkish "long fellows" from the 6th infantry regiment (Germ. "Lange Kerle" [Tall Guys]; Infanterieregiment No. 6) were provided by the Herzog of

Kurland to the Prussian King *Friedrich Wilhelm* I. This event began the story of Islam in Germany (Faruk 1999 *Between Preussenadler and Swastika* [Engl. Between the Prussian Eagle and the Hakenkreuz (swastika]). The Prussian King welcomed "his Mohammadans" and opened up a mosque by persuading them to practice their daily spiritual duties. Hence an Ottoman presence accompanied the Prussian period till the end of the Weimar period.

The Prussian King *Frederik II.* - later called "the Great" - separated Muslim units of military troops (1740 AD). In 1745 a squadron of Bosniacs, Albanians and Tartars joined the Prussian military. This happened because the King of Prussia wanted to recruit a popular Tartarian squadron, but his Saxonian chamberlain lost all the recruitment money in a casino in Warsaw. While the Tartars, a "Bosnia corps" could not be recruited, an Albanian jewellery dealer who lost all his investment, offered "Frederic the Great" a squadron of light lancers instead. Frederic the Great had sufficient humour and let himself in for the trade. The newly formed "Bosniac corps" was made up of Bosnians, Albanians and Tartars.

Another incident happened in 1760 AD. It led to an increase in Ottoman and Muslim presence within the Prussian ranks. It was triggered by a rumour stating that the Sultan Caliph in Constantinople had declared the "holy war" against Russia, due to his friendship with Prussia. Subsequently numerous Muslim soldiers, serving in the Russian army changed sides and went over to the Prussians. In 1762 an Imam was ordained as preacher of the "Prussian Mohammedans" and the regulations (Germ. "Matrikel") of the "Bosniac corps" included freedom of religious practice for the Muslim soldiers.

As the Regiment was re-established in 1762 the Muslim riders earned "the full approval of the king". Ten years later when the Western (1772) and Polish parts of Prussia (1793/1795) were unified, the few noble descendants living there, mainly the Tatars[87] of the "Golden Horde"[88] affiliated with the Prussian

---

[87] The term "Tatars" is not clearly defined. Within the context of this documentation "Tatars" are the Muslim descendant of the Crim-Tartars. They are settled in the former Polish-Lithuanian Commonwealth, which nowadays became the states of Poland and Lithunia. Besides this definition the term also covers a medieval people group settled south of the Lake Baikal; a people group settled in Eastern Siberia – North Eastern China; Turco-Tatars settled in the Eurasia part of Russia; the Crim-Tatars.

lancers with pleasure. On August 23rd 1795 the king granted the Tartars in "New Eastern Prussia" (Germ. "Neu-Ostpreussen") not only the free practising of religion and a free residential district but also a corps of light cavalry. From 14th October 1799 the Bosnian regiment became the Muslim "little noble people" (Oghlanis; Germ. "Kleine Edelleute") of New Eastern Prussia called the "Towarczy" (*comrades*) by a royal ordinance of *Frederic William* III. In 1807 it changed into the regiment "Uhlans" (of Oghlani = *noble boy/squire*). A document from this time states:

> As dissident in the Polish nobility republic merely and simply just tolerated, the supporters of the prophet helped in the catastrophe of 1806/1807 with the dedication of a king, who respected and also protected every religion.

In the Prussian - French war on February 7th and 8th, 1807 AD Napoleon's army suffered its only defeat at Prussian *Eylau*. Parts of the troops were Muslim units. The bravery of these participating Muslims was motivated, according to the reports from that time, by the demand "to thank the king for the safeguarding of their traditional life-forms and religion and the religious freedom that was granted to them" (cit. in Faruk 1999 *Between Preussenadler and Swastika* [Engl. Between the Prussian Eagle and the Hakenkreuz (swastika)]). The regiment was divided in 1808. Although the era of Muslim units within the Prussia military ended at this time, the tradition in both regiments the "Bosniac" and the "Towarczy", lived on as is made obvious by the use of the "Tszhapka", a stylized Tatari prayer cap on their leather helmets.

The remains of these long lasting historical relationships are not so many, due to the fact that the religious factor was always a hindrance between both parties to dealing with each other trustfully and equally. Nonetheless one can find places like the Islamic cemetery at Blucherstraße in Berlin since 1798 (nowadays allocated to Columbiadamm), the so-called "Red Mosque" in the park of the château of Schwetzingen as the centre of the "Turkish garden" (built from 1780 to 1785 by the Palatine Elector Carl-Theodor), which was gratefully used from by *Zuaven* and *Tuerkos* as a place of prayer, when they were prisoners after the German / French war in 1870/1871. Another reminder was the establishment by Emperor *Wilhelm* II. of a Mosque in Wunsdorf at Zossen with a minaret for the

---

[88] "Golden Horde" describes a turco-mongolian Empire from the 13.-14th Century AD / 7th Century AH centered in East-Europe and West-Sibiria. One of *Genghis Khan's* grandchildren named *Batu Khan* (reigned from 1236–1255) established it in 1236 AD / 6th Century AH (Bauer *Goldene Horde* [Golden Horde]).

"Mohammedan prison camp" in 1914 and a military cemetery in Zehrendorf (one hour drive from Zossen) for the fallen Muslim soldiers. *Wilhelm* II. promised the Sultan that he could "be assured that the Kaiser will be its friend at all times" (Müller & Siegert 2010 *Wilhelm II. Deutschlands letzter Kaiser* [Engl. Wilhelm II. Germanys last Emperor]; Baumann 2005:15).

During the 1940s German intellectuals, be they Jewish or non-nationalistic, who were forced to leave the Third Reich established and improved the university system of the Turkish republic. Unfortunately there are no remainders of a relationship between German and Turkish universities these days.

In the beginning of WWII. Turkey preserved its neutrality but sympathized with the ideologies of the national-socialistic regime. Mustafa Kemal Paşa Atatürk's death in 1938 brought so many domestic political questions with it that Turkey was unable to take any position. Neutrality was a safe haven. During WWII. the Drittes Reich and Turkey signed a non-aggression pact in 1941 to guarantee Turkey a sort of neutrality and Germany a buffer zone against Russian interventions in the Bosporus. At the end of WWII. in 1944 Turkey ended its diplomatic relations with the Third Reich to declare war and fulfil the terms of the UN Charter against Germany.

The Federal Republic of Germany started relationships as soon as 1955 when the economy started to boom and the acquisition of foreign labourers became necessary (2.3.1.4). In 1960 those migrations began, and since then an increasing number of Turkish citizens are a solid part of the population in Germany. With them Islam became a fixed factor in Germany. Tensions between Germans and either Muslim or Turkish citizens arise from time to time, such as the capture of the PKK leader *Abdullah Öcalan* in 1999, when "Kurdish" uprisings occurred all over Germany, or the visit of the AK leader and Minister-President of Turkey *Recep Tayyip Erdoğan* to Germany in 2011, when he demanded Turkish speaking education in Germany. Recently a nationalsocialistic right-winged conspiracy by a radical group revealed at least 9 killings of non-German citizens in the years 2000-2010. This sort of xenophobia is closely observed by Turkey and other nations. Another case was the imprisonment of an English teenager in Turkey who was accused of rape. Such incidents lead to reciprocal accusations.

However politically and economically German-Turkish relations are stable and generally positive.

3.1.4 The European Union and Turkey – A Rapprochement

The Turkish rapprochement towards the European Union (EU) reaches back to the Ottoman Empire. Since Sultan *Abdul Hamid* II. (3.1.1.2.1) and his reform movements, the European Nations were the focus of the Ottoman Rulers. The clash of Western modernisation and Ottoman ancientness led to an ongoing competition and envy or jealousy from the Turkish side (Elwan 1988:221; Kruse 1988:213; Steinbach 1988:155-156; 3.1.1.2.1; 3.1.1.2.2). Totally different is the perception of the other cardinal national powers and their threat. For instance the North (Russia) which is feared for his military power, the East (Iran) or the South (Syria / Arabic Nations) which are perceived as even more backward.

The brotherhood in arms with the German Kaiserreich during WWI. and later with the Nationalsocialistic Third Reich Germany during WWII. led the Republic of Turkey to alienation from the European powers. However her strategically important location between the Near East and Europe and the importance of the Bosporus as a port of military surveillance soon generated interests. Her membership of the *North Atlantic Treaty Organization* (NATO) in 1952 and exploratory talks with the predecessor of the *European Union* the *European Union of Economy* (Europäischen Wirtschaftsvereinigung EWG) brought Turkey closer to the West. The expectations from the West were based on the assumption that she would flourish economically and were thus mainly of economic interest (Steinbach 1996).

Another strategical consideration came out of the *Cold War*. One of the main concerns of the West regarding Turkey was her approximation towards the former USSR. The West was afraid and put much effort into the relationship with Turkey to avoid any agreement between Turkey and the USSR. As a matter of fact the membership of the EU was always delayed. The reason for that was the unstable political situation with five coups d'état (1960, 1971, 1980, 1997, 2007) and the overwhelming influence of the military council. In 1995 the negotiations became more concrete and proceedings regarding full membership started with the German Federal Chancellor *Gerhard Schröder* (Socialist Party) in 1999 – 2002. With the start of membership application interviews from 2003 (Seufert & Kubaseck 2004) to 2005, Turkey came under the spotlight of different European institutions which investigated the framework and conditions that need to be fulfilled before full membership. In 2005 those investigations ended positively and Turkey has to work on its acceptance of all minorities or microcultures, the admission of all languages for mother tongue education in the school system and the abolition of the military council. Progress in those areas is controlled by a European institution. The political framework for the conditions was set in 2006, yet its practical implementation will be a tedious process. In 2006 the EU granted Turkey the status of a potential candidate country. Regular observation is made public in Turkish and EU publications as well as in some special Newsletters (e.g. Türkei-Information 2008. EU-Fortschrittsbericht 2008. FES Newsletter 13/2008:1 [Turkey-Information 2008. EU Progress Report 2008. FES Newsletter 13/2008:1]).

Turkey's progress towards the EU was marked in 2007 by a so called "electronic coup d'état". The military council did not allow the AKP presidential candidate *Abdulallah Gül* to get in power. After three approaches he was voted in by a simple majority. The military threatened Premier *Erdoğan* with an intervention if he pushed further for his candidate. In 2010 the military council got its comeuppance which led to the resignation of the whole military council and its displacement. Another area of progress was to be seen in the approach towards education for non-Turkish mother tongue speaking and non-Islamic people groups in their mother tongue. The education was officially allowed in 2008 but only for adults. Private schools that addressed the need of such mother tongue education still face a lot of harassment, either because of structural issues with the buildings where they meet, questions of the right of assembly or other issues (personal communication with parties concerned; KHRP 49-50: Article 2, 5, 6-9, 11). For instance the KHRP Draft Report 2007 called *Education Rights in Turkey*. (Kurdish Human Rights Project) is complaining about the control of the "Ministry of National Education" (Turkish: *Milli Eğitim Bakanlığı*) that hinders mother tongue speakers who are educated abroad as teachers to work in Turkey (article 7).

The EU is still evaluating the progress of political and social developments in Turkey. The USA in contrast is putting much pressure on the EU to proceed with the membership of Turkey. Within this power-play the question is not *if* but *when* the Turkish state will be part of the EU. Recent politics towards an economic trade union with the surrounding nations and the destabilisation with Israel are more or less a reaction by Turkey against the interests and demands of the EU. Neutral observers claim that Turkey will become a full or restricted member of the EU within the next ten years but only on condition that the recent political path will proceed in the same way.

One of the outcomes of the EU membership approach of Turkey is the public appearance of the people groups of Turkey that are living in the Diaspora. These people groups use the opportunity to proclaim their origin before the institutions of the EU and at the same time that their homeland is Turkey. As an example the Zaza people claim "Turks" as their nationality but "Zaza" as their ethnicity and Zazaki as their language. The EU parliament in Strasbourg is regularly addressed by delegations and petitions about the public recognition of their diverse ethnicity within the Turkish nation state. Other people groups use this opportunity also: Kurmanji speaking people groups, Laz, Adyghe, Circassian et al. Besides the question of gender equality in the secular and spiritual area the human rights question about diverse ethnicity is a deprived area within the ongoing talks between the EU institutions and the government of Turkey.

3.1.5 Summary

The historical flashback of the Turkish people starts with the Gök Turks in the 5th century AD / 1st century BH. The invading people groups of the Mongolian-Altaic area settled all over Central Asia, the Middle and Near East. Their Altaic branch of language came out of the Ural-Altaic language family. They came as far as Egypt and the area of the Fertile Crescent. Although influenced by Buddhism, Shamanism and smaller local belief systems they soon implemented Islam as a tool for their invasion. The first larger empire that was run by Turkic people was the Seljuk Empire (11th-13th century AD / 5th-6th century AH). It started with *Tughril Beg* and spread under *Seljuq Beg* in the area of the Persian plains. It reached into the heartland of the Byzantine Empire which is today the area of Cappadocia.

The Ottoman Empire (14th-20th century AD / 7th-13th century AH) that started with the dynasty of Osman removed the remainders of the Seljuk and Byzantine Empires. It reached its military and political apogee under *Suleyman the Magnificent* (1520-1566) and was one of the largest empires ever. The heartland of the Ottoman Empire was settled after the fall of Constantinople through the Ottoman Sultan *Mehmet II*. With the decline of the Ottoman rulers the Sultans *Mahmut II.* (1785-1839) and *Abdul Hamid* II. (1842-1918) started reform which still affects the politics of smaller ethnicities (2.1.4.3; 2.1.4.4; 2.1.4.3; 2.2.8.2; 2.3.1.3.1; 2.2.8.2; 3.1.1.2; 3.5; HC 2011). The three *tanzimat* reforms (1838-1876) introduced by the former Sultan claimed,

1) a renewal of the *administration body* mainly the military and social affairs,

2) *Pan-Islamism* as a tool to use religion as the linking element between the various ethnicities under Ottoman rule,
3) *Pan-Turkism* as a strategy to combine the Turkic people groups under one roof as a ruling class.

The latter Sultan put the reforms into operation. As a very negative outcome of these ideologies pogroms against the non-Islamic people groups in the Ottoman heartland – what is today's Turkey – started in 1896, 1905 and worst in 1915 when the ethnocidal resettlement undertakings towards the Syrian desert finding its climax in the extinguishing of the Armenian, Jewish and Syrian presence in the East. Under the jurisdiction of the Turkish official Kurdish troops called *Hamidiye*, named after their founder Sultan Abdul Hamid II., consisting of Kurmanji speakers and Zaza people started these pogroms in the East.

The latter two ideologies became both a model for other modern Islamic countries (Pan-Arabism, Pan-Brotherhood) and foundational to the new Republic of Turkey. The Young Ottomans as well as the Young Turks used them for their goals. Ziya Gökalp became the "father of Turkish nationalism" which he derived from the *tanzimat*-reform of Pan-Turkism. He, as a Zaza, exemplifies the either-or pattern of the new constitution (from 1982 / 2007 article 3) and the politics within the Turkish Republic. Be either a "Turk" using Turkish or stay an outsider to the society. Pan-Islamism as an independent ideology was more or less used to consolidate the Turkish state in phases of political instability and mainly after 1950 when Islam went public.

The Republic of Turkey came into place in 1923 after an immense military and political performance by the "father of all Turks" *Mustafa Kemal Paşa Atatürk*. His strategies didn't just thwart all the active powers and interests but guaranteed the heartland of the Ottoman Empire to become a self sustainable nation. Unfortunately his attitude towards the Kurmanji speaking people groups in the East and all other *non-Turkish* and *non-Islamic* groups changed dramatically within his 15 years of "educational dictatorship". A former alliance of all people in the East was soon replaced by a military apparatus that served only Mustafa Kemal Paşa Atatürk and his interests.

Germany played an extraordinary role during the Ottoman Empire and later during WWI. and WWII. The German Kaiserreich as well as the nationalsocialistic Regime were companions in arms with Turkey. At the end of WWII. in 1944 Turkey ended its diplomatic relations with the Third Reich to declare war and fulfil the terms of the UN Charter against Germany.

3 Turkey – A Socio-Historical Overview 389

The European Union has offered Turkey membership options since 1960 but more concrete in 1999 when the socialistic government of Germany encouraged Turkey to apply for full membership. Recently the status of a potential member has been given and Turkey needs to improve in its areas of human rights on the level of gender equality in the public religious area as well as its attitudes towards mother tongue education for the various ethnicities that are settled in its national territory.

3.2 Inside Turkey – Linguistic Considerations

To understand the diversity and varieties of language families, branches and small language groups in the Republic of Turkey an overview will be given. In general the languages which somehow impact the Zaza community belong to the language families of
- Turkic languages,
- Indo-European languages,
- Caucasian languages / Kartvelian languages,
- Semitic languages,
- Slavic languages.

Within each of these families the separate language branches are represented in Turkey. The following overview demonstrates the heterogeneous and various language groups in the Republic of Turkey (references are with the author). The ethnical influences from Europe and Asia split the area in such a way that it was necessary to split both parts from each other. The language groups of Asian Turkey are presented first, since they form the majority and the less researched.

3.2.1 Turkey (Asia)

Table 36 Language Groups in Turkey - Asia

Language Name	ISO	Inv.	Language Family
Abaza	abq	1995	NW Caucasian
Abkhaz	abk	1980	NW Caucasian
Adyghe / West Circassian	ady	2000	NW Caucasian
Arabic, Mesopotamian Spoken	acm		Semitic
Arabic, North Levantine Spoken	apc		Semitic
Arabic, North Mesopotamian Spoken	ayp	1992	Semitic
Assyrian Neo-Aramaic	aii	1990	Semitic
Avar	ava		NE Caucasian

Azerbaijani, South	azb		Turkic
Chaldean Neo-Aramaic	cld		NE Semitic
Chechen	che	1996	NE Caucasian
Crimean Tatar	crh		Turkic
Dargwa	dar		NE Caucasian (Dagwa L.)
Dimli (Southern Zaza)	diq	1999	Indo-European
Georgian	kat	1980	Caucasian / Georgian
Hértevin (Eastern Aramaic / Syriac)	hrt	1999	Semitic
Kabardian / East Circassian	kbd	2005	NW Caucasian
Kazakh	kaz	1982	Western Turkic
Kirmanjki (Northern Zaza)	kiu		Indo-European / NW Iranian
Kumyk	kum		Turkic (Dagestan)
Kurdish, Northern (Kurmanji)	kmr	1980	Indo-European
Kyrgyz	kir	1982	Turkic
Lak	lbe	1996	NE Caucasian
Laz	lzz	1980	Caucasian / Georgian
Lezgi	lez	1996	NE Caucasian (Lezgin L.)
Osetin / Ossete	oss		Indo-European / East Iranian
Persian, Iranian	pes		Indo-European
Syriac	syc		Semitic
Turkish	tur	1987	Turkic
Turkish Sign Language	tsm		Turkic
Turkmen	tuk	1982	Turkic
Turoyo / Surayt (Neo Aramaic)	tru	1994	Semitic
Uyghur	uig	1981	Eastern Turkic
Uzbek, Northern	uzn		Turkic
Uzbek, Southern	uzs	1982	Turkic

As one goes from the West to the East and from the North to the South of Turkey one will find the various influences from the language families. The Indo-European language family shows its sway from the West (Hellenistic) and from the East (Iranian). In the south-west the Semitic group is mainly represented and the Caucasian languages have a large impact in the north-east.

Looking on the European side some differences are obvious. It is mainly the Indo-European language family which dominates this part of Turkey.

3.2.2 Turkey (Europe)

Table 37 Language Groups in Turkey - Europe

Language Name	ISO	Inv.	Language Family
Albanian, Tosk	als	1980	Indo-European / Albanian
Armenian	hye	1980	Indo-European / Armenian
Balkan Gagauz Turkish / Balkan Turkic	bgx	1993	Turkic
Bulgarian	bul	2001	Indo-European / Balto-Slavic
Domari	rmt	2000	Indo-European / Aryan
Greek	ell	1993	Indo-European / Hellenic
Ladino	lad	1976	Indo-European / Italic
Pontic	pnt	2009	Indo-European / Hellenic
Romani, Balkan	rmn		Indo-European / Aryan
Serbian (Serbo-Croatian)	srp	1980	South Slavic
Tatar	tat		Turkic
Ubykh	uby		NW Caucasian

The overwhelming dominance of Indo-European languages in the European part of Turkey as well as in the surroundings by Greece and Bulgaria attracts linguists. The linguistic influences on the people groups, anthropological developments and social studies on the language and culture of the populations in this area are the subject of many studies.

As mentioned above Zazaki is mainly influenced by (2.2; 2.2.1; 2.2.2):
- Kurmanji (Indo-European / NW Iranian),
- Persian (Indo-European / SW Iranian)
- Armenian (Indo-European / Armenian),
- Syriac and Neo Aramaic (Semitic), and the
- historical influence from Parthian / Arsacid Pahlavi / Pahlavanik (Indo-European / NW Iranian) and Old Persian (Indo-European / Old Persian).

3.3 Anthropological-Linguistic Perspective

From an anthropological point of view the multi ethnical situation in Turkey and the encounter with the diverse linguistic groups perform a wide field of research. There are huge differences in the anthropological background of the Zaza people and the Turks.

- Peasantry versus nomadism. Although many of the Turkish people settled as early as the 11th century AD / 5th century AH they still have a tradition referring to nomadic practices. Even those who blame nomadic groups of ancientness consider nomadic lifestyle as part of their culture by history. In contrast the Zaza never expressed or referred to nomadism but on settlement in the peasant tradition.
- The Turkish perception of the world is based on different religious beliefs such as Shamanism and Buddhism, which were foundational to the new religion of Islam (2.3.3.4; 2.3.5.3). Yet some practices still remain like transformation processes during frenzy, e.g. humans becoming non-human.
- The Zaza people do not have an imperialistic attitude like the Turkic people. The latter show since their Mongol invasions (11th – 13th century AD / 5th – 7th century AH) of Europe, the Middle East and Egypt that Turkic people inherit a sense of invasion (invader-atttude; 2.1.3.1.1; 2.1.3.1.4; 2.1.3.1.5; 2.3.1.1; 2.3.3.4; 3.1.1; 3.3; 0). In contrary the Zaza people take a guarding stance by protecting their inhabited property (protector-attitude). Both behaviours have their origin in either a nomadic (Turk) or a peasantry (Zaza) background. In contrast with the Kurmanji speaking Kurds the Zaza people didn't even develop a *Mir*-Princedom (royalty structure) but formed a more socialistic structure (feudalistic-socialism; 2.3.4.1; e. g. *cem / cemat* gatherings).
- The tribal and feudalistic system of the Turks was based on nationalism and covered larger groups than the Zaza tribal social structure. The cohesive links of the Turkish people is based on heroism and power play. Successful warriors were able to easily set up invading troops by alliance. This means that in contrast to the Zaza people consanguinity is secondary for the Turkic people.
- The Turkish Alevitic as well as the Kurmanji speaking Kurdish movement is totally different than the Zaza Alevism. The former relate to the

Dervish orders by following the *Haçi Bektaş tarikat* and the latter follows its own custom (2.3.3.3).

There are also other distinctions, but for now and because others worked on this too (e. g. Andrews 2002a and b; Bruinessen w/d *The debate* ..., 1989b) we leave it at that.

Looking at an anthropological perspective from the angle of social stratification within the people groups of the Turkish ethnicity and the Zaza ethnos it is obvious that the Turkish people are nowadays better educated and more Westernized. The structure of the Turkish societies follows industrialism in a more or less socialistic form. Thus the political and capitalistic establishment (upper class) dictates to the middle class on a democratic basis. The more one is educated the more one follows capitalism. This level forms an upper middle class. The lower middle class follows traditional craft or is farmer. The lower class includes marginalized people like orphans, handicapped / widows / people without family, etc. Thus, a three layer stratification as in the Zaza people group is obvious. However the important Turkish middle class is built on different foundations from the feudalistic Zaza (capitalism vs. peasantry).

3.4 Christianity and Religious Orientation in Turkey

The rapprochement of Islam and Christianity had its climax in the 11th and 12th century AD / 5th and 6th century AH when the Arabic literature became a source of the original Greek philosophers. The Islamic conquests offered access to the huge libraries of Egypt and the Near East. The Greek mythologies were translated into Arabic and stored for future generations. Thus happened before Scholasticism when Western scholars became interested in the original writings of the Greek authors. They learned Arabic to access these sources. With the decline of Islamic influence in the Western parts of Europe in the Middle Ages the relationship came to an end.

One of the areas which is less covered by Turkish authors as well as Western enlightened researchers is the presentation of Christianity in the 20th century AD and its presence in East Anatolia. The reason for that lies first in the Turkish conception of Pan-Islamism which allows discussion about non-Islamic ethnicities only in a very limited frame. Second the historical interrelations between the Islamic people groups in Turkey against non-Islamic people bring about an underlying sense of silence. This is sad, because it is conducive to a general silence about all tragedies in the past. Outside of Turkey the issues are discussed intensively, as the publications from Dadrian (1997a and b), Hofmann (1986), Lepsius (1986) and many others demonstrate (2.3.1.3.2; 2.1.4.4; 3.1.3). In a position of being one of the most powerful nations in the area of the Near East Turkey does not allow for any historical reprocessing. In contrast the parties concerned demand such a development.

Another area of spiritual orientation is outlined by the inner-Islamic orders of Turkey which carry out an influential political and religious momentum in the nation state structure. Both areas are now in focus. In both cases we reduce the focal point to its relevance for the Zaza people, their homeland, their history and their recent being. This subject is also not in public discussion; the Islamic orders have always taken political a position which made them suspicious. Their low profile in public is thus not reflecting their real reputation and influence.

3.4.1 Christians in Turkey

When speaking of Christianity in Turkey or the Ottoman Empire, first the Byzantine Empire comes into the centre of attention. The Byzantine Church is known as the 'Eastern Church' in contrast to the Roman Catholic 'Western Church'. However the Syriac Churches, the Kopts, the Greek Orthodox and the Armenian Apostolic Church have shared the fate and development of the Ottomans. Remains of the Eastern Church are still found in Turkey and all over the Near East (ruins of churches, Hagia Sophia, etc.). With the fall of Constantinople (1453; today İstanbul) the Byzantines and with them the influential Eastern Church came to an end. The Western Church enhanced its influence and the fronts between West and East became the dividing line between Christendom and Islam. The remaining Christians of other denominations in Turkey gained their status as second class citizens (*dhimmi*-status) under the Islamic law (2.3.3.2.4; 2.3.3.7.2). The other churches, mentioned above, lived in the shadow of the Byzantine Church which was not by far the only presence of Christendom in the East. Today one will find following churches in Turkey:
- Armenian Orthodox,
- Syriac Orthodox,
- Chaldean Catholic,
- Greek Orthodox and smaller numbers of
- Bulgarians, Georgians, and Protestants.

The Armenian Apostolic Church, the Syrian and the Greek Orthodox Church used their own script in the Ottoman Empire. This difference separated them and at the same time gave them an ethnic identity in the midst of the Muslim Seljuks or later the Turkish rulers. Their Bible translations were considered to be state of the art for expressing high education (Gundert 1977; Riggs 1940:245, 247). These Churches work on Bible Translation with the Turkish Bible Society (TBS) even today (w/o A. *Türkische Bibelgesellschaft: „Christentum kein Import aus dem Westen"* [Engl. The Turkic Bible Society: "Christianity is not an import from the West"]). The religious language of the Ottomans was Arabic. The Islamic liturgy, the Qur'an and the Islamic clergy used Arabic as the holy and sacred language. Although Arabic has its niche it did not become the language of daily life but stayed an artificial *lingua franca* with little widespread use.

3.4.1.1 Armenia - The Armenian Apostolic Church

The *Armenian Apostolic Church*, or *Armenian Apostolic Church*, is the oldest national church (301 AD). The homeland of the Armenians called *Armenia*. This is an exonym given by Old Persian inscriptions (515 BC). The endonym is *Hayk'*, which became in the Middle Ages *Hayastan*, by addition of the Iranian suffix *-stan* (Land). The province of the Church was at the same time the state demarcation and known as the land around the *Ararat* which is still the Armenians national coat of arms documented since 2492 BC. Times of independence and times under the rule of other powers alternated in the history of Armenia. Such powers were: Assyrians, Greeks, Romans, Byzantines, Arabs, Mongols, Persians, Ottoman Turks and Russians. Before Christianity, Armenia was following the religion and philosophy of *Ahura Mazda* called *Mazdean Zoroastrianism*, its worship focused on *Mihr* (Avestan Mithra; 2.1.1.5.2; 2.3.3.2.2; 2.3.3.3; 2.3.3.7.3). Christianity spread into the country as early as AD 40. It came through two of Hz. Jesus' twelve apostles, namely *Thaddaeus* and *Bartholomew,* according to tradition. It was King *Tiridates* III. (238–314 AD) who made Christianity the state religion (301 AD). The foundational beliefs of the Zaza people and the Armenians are both performed by Zoroastrianism / Parsiism (East Asia area).

An essential tradition based on historical evidence is presented by the devotion of the *Holy Surp Sarkis*. The importance of this cult lies in the sending attitude of the Holy Man. This attitude still drives the Armenian Apostolic Church today, although the Great Experiment revealed that in contact with Islam pace and intensity were close to nil (2.1.4.5). *Surp Sarkis* was a Christian Roman general in the 4th century AD. Around 313 AD, right after the tolerance edict of Milano given by the Imperator *Constantin* I. (306-337 AD), he started proactively to promote Christianity to his troops. Large numbers of soldiers followed Christianity as a result. With the Imperator *Julian* (361-363 AD) a time of Anti-Christian and pro Gentile propaganda started in which *Surp Sarkis* left for Armenia with his son *Mardiros*. The Armenian King *Diran* recommended that *Surp Sarkis* should leave for Persia since *Julian's* troops followed him. The Persian King *Schapur* II. (310-379) gave him refuge and took him into his army. After getting knowledge about the promotion of Christianity by *Sarkis* and the conversion of huge parts of the King's troops he urged *Sarkis* to follow the Persian gods. In 363 AD *Sarkis* died by decapitation. A few days before his son died in a scuffle with Persian soldiers who wanted to arrest him and his father. The Armenian Apostolic Church made *Surp Sarkis* its national Saint and Matyr. Many Armenian Apostolic churches bear his name (e.g. Saint Sarkis Church, Nor Nork, Yerevan).

3.4.1.1.1   1860 – 1920 – Struggles, Wars and Persecution

The combination of political and spiritual power, like in the other later nation churches, e. g. Roman Catholic Church, Byzantine Church, Aramaic Church, etc. always led to disputes, wars and conflicts. The confrontation between the newer Islamic powers and these traditional and long established churches always involved conflict. In the case of the Armenian Apostolic Church its zenith was reached by the ethnocide in 1915 AD (1915-1923) which was preceded by local and less tragic but nonetheless cruel exterminations in 1895-1896 and 1905 (2.1.3.1.4; 3.1.1.2.2). The history of this oldest worldwide State Church reveals the struggle of the Ottoman with the Russian Empire. The former united nation became split into a "Western Armenia" which after the Turkish-Persian wars (1602-1639) fell under the jurisdiction of the Ottoman Empire, while the "Eastern Armenia" parts were partially independent but after the Russo-Turkish War (1828-1829) were ceded to the Russian Empire. This split caused serious hardship because both Empires considered "the Armenians" to be scheming elements. During the centuries the division into a "Western" and "Eastern" part led to a linguistic and social division.

3.4.1.1.2 Dispersion of Armenian People in Eastern Anatolia

The areas of Western Armenia in the Ottoman territory that were mainly inhabited (more than 50%) by Armenians are located around Lake Van in the East and a huge area north of Adana. The Zaza homeland area had an Armenian population of 25-50%. The Northern Group following Alevism was mainly influenced by the high Armenian population in their area (2.3.3.3.4). It is this relationship which is recently of high interest in Armenian science and research. The Armenians were also present in a few cities of the Southern Group but in large areas there one finds no traces of Armenians. Looking at the dispersion of the Armenian people in the 19th century over the Eastern Anatolian area following main centres (higher than 50% population) are (names in brackets are from an transcripted Armenian map; Cuinet, Selenoy & Seydlitz 1896):

- North of Adana (formerly Kozak sanjak);
- the whole area around Lake Van (area: Bulauyk, Torlu, Tauros; cities: Wan / Van; Musch / Muş; Chiyskala; Bitlis; Adilat);
- today's Ağrı and Kars (area: Achalkuk, Alexandropol, Medschingert, Alaschkert, Bayaset, Chuyskala);

An Armenian population of 20-40% is mainly found in:

- the rest of Eastern Anatolia north-west of the line Urfa (Şanlıurfa) – Adijaman (Adiyaman) – Malatia (Malatya) – Sivas (Siwas) – Amasya (Amasia) – Samson (Samsun);
- around the city of Adana (district Adana, and today's Nigde);
- the district of Kayser (Kaisarie)
- the northern districts of Northern Iraq Mosul and Arbil.

To sum this up a general presence of up to 10% of Armenian population is given over the whole Eastern Anatolian area, the centres are north of Adana, around Lake Van and north to today's Georgia and Armenia.

3.4.1.1.3 History meets the Present

The history of the Armenians in the Ottoman Empire and the Republic of Turkey represents a controversial topic in Islamic countries mainly in Turkey. Every historian or author who tries to claim accuracy on the issue faces resistance. *Orhan Pamuk* (author) or *Hrant Dink* (Armenian reporter; shot in 2007) are publicly known victims of this dilemma. The blind spot of the massacres on the Armenians even occupies the European Union which demands a process of coming to terms with the past by the Turkish government. Interestingly it is not just Turkey but also Germany that is accused of having an active part in the massacres, at least that of 1915 (Dadrian 1997a and b; 2.3.1.3.2; 2.1.4.4; 3.1.3; 3.4). Dadrian accuses Germany of active cooperation in the planning and logistical preparation of the deportations and targeted killings. The fact that high ranking officials of the German army seized the *St. Giragos Armenian Apostolic Church* in Diyarbakır and used it as a military base and their local headquarters from 1913 to 1918 is evidence for such accusations. He states:

> ... the close cooperation at the Ottoman General Headquarters between Turkish officers, especially War Minister Enver on the one hand and high-ranking German officers on the other; and the evidence that the deportation of the victim population was the result of the pressures and initiatives of these military leaders. ... They favor the acceptance of the view that German authorities cannot entirely be seen as divorced from a degree of involvement in the decision-making processes relating to the deportations and massacres. (1997b:182-183; 2.3.1.3.2; 2.1.4.4; 3.1.3; 3.4).

Dadrian wants to give evidence to an overall planned ethnocide with such intensity that he sometimes loses the focus by looking at the local level (Kieser 2000:32). Also Lepsius who was close to the areas of conflict and who gathered and evaluated all the diplomatic correspondence between German and Turkish diplomats during the years 1914-1918 comes to another conclusion (Lepsius 1986 cit. in Baumann 2007:117). As Hofmann noticed in the preface to the diplomatic files compiled by Lepsius,

> ... the fact of the annihilation of the Armenians by the documents in the archives of the Germans are putting strain on Turkey and speaks the German foreign policy free of the reproach of a responsibility for the Turkish genocide. (Hofmann cit. in Baumann 2007:117; Schäfer 1932:122).

Lepsius claims the background to the Armenian ethnocide in the activities of the Young Turks "Committee for Unity and Progress", which also set up branches all over the provincial towns (Lepsius 1986; also Richter in 1930, s. 2006:76-77; extensively Zürcher 2004:114-115). But it would not only be the upheaval during the establishment of the Republic and the propaganda of Pan-Islamic supporters but also the menace of a Russian invasion that shaped politics in the first two decades of the 20th century. Since the 18th century Russia played the part of a protecting power to the Armenians, the military counterpart to the Ottomans. *Peter the Great* and his successor *Katharina* II. granted Armenia autonomy and self-administration (1768). With the peace treaty of *Küçük Kaynarçı* (1774) Russia emerged as the protective power of all Christians in Eastern Anatolia. Nonetheless Russian politics became oppressive and the Armenians were caught

3 Turkey – A Socio-Historical Overview   399

in the middle of two oppressors (Renz 1985:95-97). The Russian-Turco wars (1877-1878) increased the need of the Ottoman rulers to find European partners. Unfortunately the Armenian citizens were considered to be taking a stance for the Russians, due to the split into an Eastern-Russian Armenia and a Western-Ottoman Armenia (Zürcher 2004:114-115; see above).

The strongest Armenian powers were the resistance troops *Henchak*, *Armenakan*, *Dashnaktsutiun* during the Armenian persecutions under Sultan *Abdul Hamid* II. and the *Young Turks*. The Armenian Apostolic Church played an active and important role too. However they could not hinder or stop the mass deportations and persecutions in Western Armenia. Until today, based on the demand of reunification, some politically active followers of these resistance organizations ask for the demarcation border from President *Woodrow Wilson* in the *Treaty of Sèvres* (10 August 1920) which would include the northeastern part of Turkey and a corridor to the Black Sea. The main parties recognise that the Treaty of Sèvres was never ratified by either the United States of America or the Ottoman Empire. Yet the range of opinions stretches from those who only want an apology and acceptance of the ethnocide, to others who demand the whole Mount Ararat region, and still others who ask for the demarcation line of Wilsonian Armenia.

3.4.1.1.4   Armenia Today – Influence on the Zaza people

Today in Armenia a large *Yezidi* Kurmanji Kurdish (also Yezidi or Kur.: Êzidî), a smaller *Sunnism* practicing Kurmanji Kurdish (northwestern part) and a very small Jewish community are enriching the religious setup of the nation.

In 2009 Turkey and Armenia signed protocols to normalize their relationships. One cross-border station was opened for trade and public transit, also a regular flight between İstanbul and Yerewan was set in place. However this policy of rapprochement does not reflect the low official profile which is expected from Armenian Christianity in Turkey.

As mentioned above the Zaza people share the Zoroastrian belief system with the Armenians (2.3.3.2.2; 2.3.3.2.4). Also there are some communalities with the religion practiced by the Yezidis called *Yezidism* founded by Sheikh *Adi ibn Musafir* (12th century AD). In Yezidism God placed the world under seven holy beings, sometimes angels, whose chief is *Melek Taus* (Peacock Angel). The Turkish Yezidis immigrated to Europe due to the rejection and discrimination of their syncretistic Sufi'i religion by the Hanafi Sunni Turks. They settled all over Europe but mainly with the highest proportion in Germany. The conception of *metempsychosis* as a transmigration of the soul also reflects a belief which reaches back to Zoroastrianism (2.3.3.3.4). In general the perception of dualism as the struggle between good and evil reaches through the perception of the worlds of all belief systems influenced by Zoroastrianism.

Armenian institutions (e.g. the State University in Yerewan) have a strong interest in researching the history of the Armenian population in Eastern Anatolia. Besides the Church and Nations history, the other people groups that inhabit the area are also of interest. Much research is done from such institutions about the Zaza and Kurmanji people groups, as well as on linguistical grounds on all language groups who are related such as Talysh, Southern Tati, Gilaki, Gorani, Semnani and other Southern Caspian languages (2.1.2.2; 2.2.2).

3.4.1.1.5 Summary

The Armenian Apostolic Church, as the oldest State Church (301 AD), inhabited the region of today's Zaza homeland, and for this reason there is reciprocal influence. Less is known about the relationship of the Zaza people with the Armenian Apostolic Church in times before the Ottoman Empire. Much belongs to the thesis about the origin of the Zaza one holds (2.1.3.1). During Ottoman times, in the years ahead of anti-Christian enterprises the Armenian Apostolic Church got, beside 17 other, the status of a *millet*. Self rule and relative political freedom was only restricted by a second class citizenship under Islamic Law *Sharia* (Turk.: *şeriat*) and the tax obligation to the Sultanate. The basic horror came with anti-Christian and anti-Jewish actions which led into the Armenian ethnocide. A German participation, by military logistics and weaponry, marks one of the dark spots of German history. The events of those days harm the relationship between Turkey and Armenia until today and just recently, since 2009, timid attempts are undertaken to open up borders and start economical relations. The Russian guardianship of Armenia will always be a point of mistrust in the relationships, as well as Turkey's political Pan-Islamic and Pan-Turkism stances. Armenia cramped by Turkey and Azerbaijan, two nations with a historical relationship, has lot of reasons to build on the Russian guardianship.

3.4.1.2 Syriac Orthodox Church

The Syriac Orthodox Churches claim their origin in the Apostle St. Peter in Antioch. *Syriac*, a dialect of Aramaic, functions as liturgical language. Different views about the nature of Christ, the position of Mary and some concepts about God are separate these churches from the Western Church. Prayers nine time daily and distinct liturgical practices constitute the peculiarity of the Eastern Rite. The *Syriac Orthodox Church* reflects the theological *Oriental Orthodox Churches* and their doctrine follows the refusal of *Pope Dioscorus*, Patriarch of Alexandria and the other 13 Egyptian Bishops, to accept the Christological dogma which held that Hz. Jesus is in two natures: one divine and one human (Council of Chalcedon). They would accept only Christ as "of or from two natures" but never "in two natures." The whole debate of these days was also about political, ecclesiastical and economic issues. The denominations of the worldwide Church started to form their foundations. Important for the future of the Eastern Church was the (un-conscious) decision to be a part of the superior powers. With the rise of Islam the Church could easily survive in the shadow of the mosque since it did not claim to be the superior power per se. So to say, a political clash which would have led to a direct struggle with other political systems (e.g. Islam) was not a given.

Christians were given second class citizenship (*dhimmi*-status) within Islam. They often could hold high political positions, and like the Jewish populations were responsible for various professions and exploited fields of activity (Griffith 2010:17). The Arabic and Aramaic speaking Christian Church within the realm of Islam developed a high degree of contextualization to the surrounding environment which astonishes people from the West.

The Syrian Church was spread all over the Zaza homeland area but mainly in the larger cities (e. g. Mardin, Cizre, Diyarbakır etc.). In general it played a secondary role compared to the Armenian Apostolic Church in the living area of the Zaza. In some areas Christian Zaza are until today connected to the Syrian Orthodox rite called "Assuri", but this term does not reflect so much a theological or denominational position as a differentiation from Muslims.

From an anthropological point of view it is interesting that the religious affiliations of people groups in the Near and Middle East play a central role in their perception of the world. Compared to the Western separation of religion and daily life activities, is the demarcation line in the Zaza society is fluid and porous. Religion and "normal life" are intermingled. The perception of the "Other", that is the identification of oneself in relation and separation from the "Other" goes through an appreciation of religious and social values. A person is identified by his being and belonging to a religious or social group (collectivism). This is closely related to the question of the *Image of limited good* (2.3.5.5.2). Having said this, the question of accessibility to goods does not just define the social position of an individual within a populace, but in a wider sense on the level of relations within people groups, also reveals the relations to each other group.

The ongoing oppression caused manifold peculiarities by ethnicities, be they subjugated for religious, racist, political or ethnical reasons. Christians and other religiously repositioned second class people groups developed a state of *low public profile*. This means they stay within their realm that is the Church, the synagogue or kindred spirit and proclaim their faith or ideology only vaguely to outsiders. They would never go public with any claims or accusations about the "Other". The "Other" and "We" conception is identical with an "outsider" and "insider" perception. The "outsider" is emphasized as "foreigner, enemy or taboo". It is demonstrated by history that such a state led to the establishment of intelligentsia, while higher education and academic activity became an outlet for official appreciation (e.g. the Jewish intelligentsia in Germany during the Weimarer Republic, Armenian intelligentsia during the USSR).

3.4.1.3 Protestant Church

The protestant Church was the last denomination in the Ottoman Empire that was given the status of *millet* (19th century). Before WWI seventeen *millets* are reported in the Ottoman Empire: e.g. Orthodox Christian churches - Catholics, Samaritans, Karaites, the Greek, Syrian, Aramaic, Armenian and Assyrian peoples groups, and the Jewish people (2.1). From early on the protestant movement was closely connected by Muslims to the principles of *misyonerlik* (Mission works), the *haçlı seferi* (the Crusades 1095-1291), Western imperialism and colonialism (Schirrmacher 1992:61-63).

3.4.1.3.1 Historical Background – Turkish Church History

The "Great Experiment" (1820-1915) initiated a protestant interest in the heartland of the Ottoman Empire (2.1.4.5). Soon after its beginnings in the 1820s this provoked harsh anti-Christian resentments. The movement developed under increasing persecution. Polemics against the prophet Hz. Mohammed or the Qur'an were strictly forbidden (Schirrmacher 1992:61). Although the converts kept a low public profile the measurements against them became tougher. In the 1860s the government arrested Turks that converted to Christianity (20-75 persons), 40 were sent into exile and others to the galleys. After an incident at the end of 1864, with a Christian development aid worker, called Pfander the foreign development aid came to an end or standstill (:63). This is a restricted view, because it was in these years that other Christian development aid workers saw the climax of interest in Christianity (Blincoe 2000:24). The protestant movement concentrated on the Eastern Anatolian area and was successful under the Armenians, Syrians and partially the Alevis (2.1.4.3; 2.1.4.4; 2.1.4.3; 2.2.8.2; 2.3.1.3.1; 2.2.8.2; 3.1.1.2; 3.5; HC 2011). It goes without saying that "success" under such circumstance meant martyrdom and suffering for those who either converted or became more active and outgoing with their Christian faith. The protestant movement was always in contrast loyal to the state- and when Sultan *Abdul Hamid* II. officially allowed Roman Catholic Christian activities, this was never extended to protestants. This contrast generated animosities on both sides. Even in religion the motto, "competition is good for business" works out. The traditional churches revived their manner of outreach. However at the end – although one cannot speak of an end at all – Christianity as a whole came under suspicion. A jealous attitude against the foreign interventions and the settled traditional churches generated envy in the Muslim population.

The suspicion against Christians in general, including the Protestants increased. At the beginning of the 20th century, in 1910, the military Mufti of Edirne made the following statement about the protestants, "being Turkish (Turkdom) and Islam are one; if Islam ceases one cannot speak of nationality any more. Missionaries are the cholera bacillus which poisons our nation" (Fahreddin cited in Kieser 2000:302). Obviously he was arguing on a Turkish-Islamic nationalism base. The xenophobia and jealousy against all non-Turkish and non-Islamic social elements moved towards a climax. The Pan-Turkism and Pan-Islamic concepts of the 19th century merged during the disintegration of the Ottoman Empire and formed a national movement built on Islam. The decline of the Caliphate as the central religious institution led to a Turkish nationalistic – Islamic ideology. This philosophy constitutes the Turkish Republic since Mustafa Kemal Paşa Atatürks death in the midst of the 20th century until today.

After its cessation a new interest started in the 1960s when Turkey was opening its borders anew and many guest labourers moved to Europe and Overseas. This migration movement was observed by the Allies (Great Britain, USA and France) and national organization started to work in Turkey. Besides economical, international security policy related and political reasons the interreligious encounter generated a relationship with Western countries. With them came Christianity as a new denomination beside the traditional *millet* that were represented by the national Churches. One of the outcomes of these developments is an increase in Turkish Bible Translations to recently 5 official versions covering all translational and linguistic styles. Also the *non-Turkish* as well as the *non-Islamic* people groups are addressed by the activities of such initiatives. The national protestant Church is growing slowly, but is more and more going public. The use of former Church buildings or the growth of Turkish Christian reading material to understand the Christian Holy Scripture better, as well as the establishment of their own theological thinking are proof of these developments. The encounter between Islam and Christianity still leads to persecution and official discrimination of Christians. However Christianity in Turkey is becoming a public area, paralleling the evolvement of Euro-Islam in Europe.

3.4.1.3.2 The Church – Status Indicator of Turkey

The protestant movement is thereby both, an index of Islamisation as well as the victim of the Turkish nationalist movement.

Recently Pikkert summarized his long-term observations and experiences in Turkey. He claims that since 1997 a rise of outgoing and brutal Islamic activities against Christians can be observed (2008:162). He counts the deadly assassinations in,

- the beginning of 2006 in Trabzon against the Italian Priest *Ajadrea Sarro*, by a 16 year old boy shouting "God is Great" (Allah-u-akbar),
- July 2006 in Samsun the French Catholic Priest *Pierre Bruinessen* who was stabbed and
- on 18th April 2007 an attack on the 46-year old German *Tilmann Geske* and his two Turkish friends who had converted to Christianity *Necati Aydin*, *Uğur Yüksel* in Malatya (the latter in Keyser 2008:3).

Additional to that the year 2006 also saw seemingly random attacks against Christians emerging,:

- On 8 January *Kamil Kiroğlu* (Protestant church leader in Adana), was beaten by five young men.
- In February a Catholic friar was attacked in Izmir by a group of young men who had threatened to kill him.
- On 12th March *Henri Leylek*, a Capuchin priest, was attacked in the Mediterranean city of Mersin.
- In December the priest of the Tepebasi church in Eskisehir was attacked (European Stability Initiative 2011: *Murder in Anatolia* …).

In 2008 the "Protestant Churches of Turkey" formed an alliance to document and publish all threats against the Turkish Churches. Their annual reports (2008-

2011) present many violations of human rights and even of Turkish Law (see Online: URL: www.protestankiliseler.org [accessed 2017-02-02] [Engl. Protestant Churches]). Additional to public discrimination, Islamic groups provoke the Christians by denunciation, threatening letters and encroachment. The suspected nationalist movement of Ergenekon used religious reasons to stir up the anger against Christians (3.6). The many different oppressive and disturbing influences on the Christian communities by so many different groups intimidate those people that are interested in drawing their own conclusion about Christianity.

3.4.1.3.3   Anthropological Considerations

From an anthropological point of view the Protestant movement brings with it some challenges to the establishment and realignment of people's enculturated knowledge. The challenge of ethnography and anthropological research to deal with a spiritual clash between two monotheistic religions that claim exclusivity is enormous. Christianity as well as Islam strain to permeate the individual and society. Coming from this perspective the perception of the world, thought, conscience and daily life accomplishment is so closely related to religion, that it is difficult to find out about the deeper core values. In the Eastern Anatolian area and people groups the process of religious conversion is experienced through all the ages. Emerging powers and ongoing struggles in the homeland area of the Zaza people led to a religious to and fro within the Zaza people group (2.3.3.1; 2.3.3.2). The protestant teachings of a loving God, who sent his messenger for reconciliation in the person of Hz. Jesus of Nazareth and the individual support of every believer by the Holy Spirit brought in a totally new concept to the Islamic (Southern and Eastern Group) and Alevism (Northern Group) practicing people. The restoration and assessment of a relationship with the Creator was totally contrasting to the deistic consideration of Islamic theology. Converts were either asked to leave their community, or their whole families or small scale people groups converted together to avoid discrimination. The main criterion for belonging to a specific religious orientation was to gather either in the mosque, the Church or the synagogue. Most Zaza people were illiterate, thus Bible Translations did not emerge. The few Turkish Bible translations were only rarely used for the reason that books were expensive and not a culturally accepted tool. The very few approaches to translate the Bible into Kurmanji or Zazaki failed because the initiating people were forced to leave the country due to accusations of conspiracy (e.g. Blincoe 1998:71-72; Kieser 2000:129-130). Instead oral-aural traditions with Christian content started to increase but got lost in the turbulences of the wider anti-Christian pogroms (1998:75-79).

The confusion brought about through the to and fro of conversion, is best shown in the perception of many *Kızılbaş / Qızılbaş* people as *Prote* (protestants), although no Christian development work was done in their environment. The reason can be traced back to their identification with their surrounding Armenian neighbours (Kieser 2000:74). It is mainly within the Alevi perception of the world that the protestant conception was easily included. In contrast, the Sunnism practicing Southern and Eastern Group was more resistant to protestant Christians. This has to do with the general attitude of Islam against Christianity as second class citizenship of non-Muslims (*dhimmi*-status) in the realm of the *dar al-Islam* (دار الإسلام; the house of Islam). The church represents the *dar al-harb* (دار الحرب dār al-harb; House of War) which in itself is always expected to be the "Other". This Otherness cannot be overcome by any attempt from the Christian side but is arbitrarily dependent on the Islamic attitude, be it supportive or hostile. Envy, jealousy and xenophobia are easy to generate, develop and used as a tool for manipulation. As such the society is split in a superior and a subordinating societal class, one that manipulates and persecutes and the other class that has to allow the hostilities.

3.4.1.3.4 Summary

The History of the Protestant Church in the Ottoman Empire, as well as its successor the Republic of Turkey indicates the status on non-Islamic and non-Turkish elements. Even the Turkish citizens that take part in a Church experience the drawbacks of a second class citizenship. The democratic system managed to deal with religious freedom in such a way that religiously ambitioned encroachment is generally persecuted. However the general anti-Christian outlook is still based on envy. This causes guilt to be given to *misyonerlik* (mission and mission advocates), proselyting and evangelization (proclamation of the gospel). These activities are declared as aggressive, anti-Islamic and anti-Turkish. Conversion is declared a work of the West and becomes thereby a political topic.

Small congregations of Turkish protestant churches are found all over Turkey. Besides old Church buildings they meet in private places and celebrate their faith in such a way as to not arouse Islamic envy. Their way of *da'awa* and *jihad* following the Islamic terminology by invitation and proclamation is without any aggression or political motivation (2.3.3.4; 3.6.1; 3.6.5; 0). This is done by book exhibitions, Bible distribution or the offering of Bible teaching courses. People who are interested refer to and visit these groups freely.

The annual documentation of anti-Christian provocations is made public since 2008 by the alliance of the Protestant Churches. So far the government reacted positively and even helped pastors or people under threat through special guardianship by the police. However discrimination by the officials is obvious when it comes to construction approval procedures or the authorization of public gatherings.

3.4.2 Jewish Presence and Judaism

Judaism as a monotheistic revelation, is based on a view of a God who revealed himself to Hz. Moses (Hz. Musa) as *Jahwe* יְהוָה (YWHW; e.g. Gen 2:18), derived from the verbal expression "I am" אֶהְיֶה (Exodus 3:14). Also the written revelation of the Hebrew Bible refers back to the Israelite forefather, Abraham, Isaac and Jacob, referring to this God (Exodus 3:6). The names given in this revelation to the people of Israel and mankind, ahead of Israelite existence, are *Elohim* אֱלֹהִים e.g. Genesis 1:1, *El* אֵל or different derivations out of the latter. The Arabic name for God *Allah* الله refers to the same word stem. The Islamic tradition has a close relationship to the Jewish revelation because both are
- based on Semitic influence and language,
- monotheistic in focus,
- relating to each other by the Hebrew Biblical Hagar – Ishmael concept (Genesis 16 and 21 as well as 25:12) and the Qur'anic "People of the book" أهل الكتاب ('Ahl al-Kitāb) concept (Qur'an 29:46 etc.).

However a different line of choosing and descent (Isaac – Israel vs. Ishmael – Islam) and different points of emphasis in the revelation and salvation history of the two religions are counterproductive to a reciprocal affinity. It has to be noted here that the same applies also for Christianity. However, concepts of the *evil eye* and magical influences, the *predestination* into the chosen people, the direction and the way of *prayer* and the *eschatological* (towards future) perspective are similar.

3.4.2.1 History – Jewish Diaspora in the Eastern Anatolia

In times (9th – 5th century BC) when the nation of Israel was split into a Northern (Israel) and Southern kingdom (Judea) the Jewish people underwent troublesome times of exile. In 722 BC the people of Israel were sent into exile to Assur by the Assyrian King *Puls* that is *Tiglat-Pileser* and started then their presence in the eastern parts of the Middle East (Hebrew Bible 2Kings 5-27 and 17:23; 2Chronicles 5:26 and chapter 32-33). The exile ended in a diasporaic Jewish presence and the so called time of the "rebuilding of the Solomonic Temple" in Jerusalem. Jewish presence all over the Mediterranean area began with the Jewish Diaspora since the 5th century BC. The resettlement of the Jewish population of Judea in Babylon (Babel) by the Babylonian King *Nebukadnezzar* (2Ch 36:20) went through 3 phases. The last phase was in 587 BC, and it led to a huge trauma for the Jewish deportees (Psalm 137:1).

After the resettlement of the main parts of the Jewish people in their homeland *Israel*, the period of the "second temple" started with *Zerubbabel*. He rebuilt it between 520 and 515 AD on the same site (Dockery 1992:522). *Herod the Great* started to build in the years 20-19 BC the so called "Herodian Temple" which was an impressive building, sometimes called a wonder of the world. It was finished in the times of *Lucceius Albinus*, the Roman Procurator of Judea from AD 62 until 64 AD (John 2:20 and Mark 13:1; prophesied by Hz. Jesus of Nazareth in Matthew 14:15). This one lasted until 66-70 AD, when it was demolished during the end of the Romeo-Jewish wars together with large parts of of Jerusalem. Resistance to the Romans directed by *Titus*, Caeasar Vespasian's son, was on the one side given by the aristocratic priests under the direction of *Ananus* II., a former high priest, and *Jeshua* IV. Their leader was *Simon bar Giora* an Idumaean captain of a guerilla band, who became a kind of military dictator. Secondly, there was the Zealot group (fanatic)**,** under the leadership of *John of Gischala*. In July-August of the year 70 AD, *Titus*, captured Fort Antonia in the temple area and then the temple itself, which was sacked and burned.

The Jewish people settled all over the Near and Middle East. Spain became a cultural centre of the *Sephardic* Jewish culture with a language mix of Spanish, Ladino, Hebrew and Yiddish. The Jewish Diaspora in the East moved into the direction of the *Ashkenasim* with a language mixed of mainly Yiddish, Hebrew, Russian and Polish. Most popular became the Schtetl as a ghetto like area in cities where the Jewish Ashkenasim population settled. The Sephardic group was forced to resettle from Spain (Alhambra Decree, 31 March 1492) and Portugal (1497) during the last decade of the 15th century AD when anti-Judaistic pogroms (Russian: riot) introduced by the Roman Catholic Monarchs occurred all over the Iberian Peninsula. The Jewish refugees sought for refuge in Europe and the Near East, the Maghreb States, the heartland of the Ottoman Empire and

Eastern Europe countries. These places became the central locations of immigration. Constantinople, today's İstanbul, was one of those centres. Synagogues and Jewish population are still found in the Western parts of Turkey, whereas ruins of synagogues demonstrate the Jewish presence in the East of Turkey during all times (see Galatian-theory, 2.3.3.2.4; 2.3.3.7.1).

3.4.2.2 Israel and Turkey

In modern times the state of Israel and the Republic of Turkey turned out to be trade and military partners with a close national relationship. Starting in 1949, when Turkey turned into the first Muslim country to recognize the state of Israel, until 2008 Israel was the main supplier of arms to the Turkish military and police. With a free-Trade agreement in 2000 the relationships between Turkey and Israel came to a summit. Since 2008 the AKparty under the leadership of Recep *Tayyip Erdoğan* started to move towards a Muslim alliance with Iran and the Arabic countries to form a block against the West, Israel and the Russian led *Commonwealth of Independent States* (CIS). The Gaza flotilla raid on 31st May 2010 functioned as a pretext for the Turkish side to declare officially that the Turco-Israeli relations are put on ice. This policy of rapprochement towards the alleged partners of the Middle East astonished the EU as well as Israel and the United States of America. The following list shows further (negative) developments:

- 1987 Turkey supports the pro-Palestinian right to self-determination,
- 2004 Turkey denounces the Israeli assassination of a leading Palestinian terrorist as a "terrorist act" and as "state-sponsored terrorism",
- 2009 Prime Minister Erdoğan criticized Israel for the conduct in Gaza at an economic forum in Davos (Switzerland), later he blamed President Peres and left the podium upset,
- 2009 Turkey barred Israel from the joint military training exercise Anatolian Eagle (USA, NATO here Italy,)
- 2009-2011 Turkish serials and films started with a very provocative anti-Israel and anti-Judaism posture, e. g. *Ayrılık* (Farewell), *Kurtlar Vadisi* (Valley of the Wolves).

The position of Israel since 2009 is mainly to address Turkey openly. Offensive to Turkey are Israel's demand

- to close down a *Hamas* headquarter on its territory and
- to stop supporting Iran which finances the *Hezbollah*, or Party of God, (also HizbAllah or Hizbullah).

Also the French and Israeli bill to recognize the Armenian question as a genocide (2011) brings with it new tensions.

Since 2008 the remaining Jewish population of Turkey is expected to show *low public profile* in Turkey. Like the Christian and Alevitic, the Jewish presence, as non-Islamic groups, are very quickly under suspicion by the public and openly addressed as reason for trouble (Gessler 2010:6). The mob is mobilized quickly as the "enemy" stereotype is addressed constantly by press and public media.

Judaism as the preceding religion of Islam is accused of being corrupted by the Jewish clergy. The same applies to Christianity and the holy books of both religions. Judaism left its marks on the Islamic perception of the world. The prophets of the Hebrew Bible are considered holy men in the Islamic perception of the world. The Jewish and Islamic afterlife shows similarities in the concepts of justification, eschatology and justice. Though only similarities, the big differences are coming from the perception of God and the relation of mankind to God. The doctrine of election for the nation of Israel in the Hebrew Bible was never accepted by Islam theology. This gap divides both belief systems.

3.4.2.3 Anthropological Considerations

From an anthropological point of view the Arabic peninsula that influenced so much of the Islamic world, forms a world in itself. Very closed and only scarcely researchable, the conceptions of life are so strongly connected to Islamic theology that the underlying strategies of coping are hardly approachable. Folk Islamic belief systems as well as traditions from their former nomadic lifestyle perform the framework of the perception of the world. The heterogeneous richness of the manifold tribes and people groups cannot be covered by general assumptions. The recent increase in anthropological research of the Berber tribes and the Arabic nomads in the Middle East will reveal a lot of knowledge about these people groups. Their influence on the Turkish intruders to Eastern Anatolia, and the Arabs being both foreigners to this area, will be found mainly in the field of religion some rudiments. The Turkish people developed their own form of Islam, although as the foundational phase of the Republic of Turkey shows, the overlaying shape of Islamic practice is predefined by the Arabic format.

Interestingly the Zaza people do not express an affinity to Jewish people in the sphere of religion. On the contrary it seems that even anti-Jewish resentments are part of Islamic thinking. The mobilization against the Jewish and

Christian ethnicities during the Young Turk period bears a lot of evidence that such a deeper antipathy is part of the Zaza perception of the world and is caused by envy which generates jealousy.

3.4.2.4 Summary

Although the Jewish people settled a long time ago in Eastern Anatolia they are nowadays not found there anymore. The history between the Zaza people and their Jewish neighbours was always accompanied by reciprocal respect and at the same time suspicion or cautiousness. With Islam and its spread the "People of the Book" became second class citizens and the Zaza people predominant, although both were under the rule of the Turkish rulers. Theological differences and the Diasporic origin of the Jewish people also maintained mistrust.

The Islamic practice of circumcision, the day of recovering (Shabath), the principle of gathering (synagogue – mosque), the constitution of a service with sermon and the Food restrictions are all related to Judaism. Differences are mainly in aspects of salvation, the eschatological (things to come) perspective, the way of being chosen by God and the reproduction of the Jewish and Christian revelation in the Islamic revelation (Qur'an; e.g. stories of Abraham, Noah and Jonah, Hz. Jesus of Nazareth etc.).

The political and economical relations between Israel and Turkey were based on military support from Israel to Turkey and trade in both directions. Since 2009 the relationship is declining, due to a pro-Palestinian and pro-Islamic political course of the Turkish government combining with Iran and other Islamic powers in the region. Jewish people in Turkey are under threat and avoid any public activity so as not to get the attention of the officials (*low public profile*).

3.4.3 The Crescent, the Star and the Coat of Arms

One will find many rudiments about the Christian past of the area of Turkey. Also there are discernible things that can be found to be reminders of the former Christian influence.

One area concerns the naming of places, locations or cities. E.g. in Constantinople Κωνσταντινούπολις became *İstanbul* in 1930 by the Turkish Postal Law. The naming was based on a phonetic adaptation to the Turkish alphabet. By the same procedure and Law Smyrna became *İzmir*. Casarea became *Kayseri*. Anatolia became *Anadolu*, with the interesting yet etymologically wrong connotation of Turk. *anna dolu*, which means "filled mother".

Another area concerns the rebuilding and often just the conversion of churches as mosques. The best example is represented by the Hagia Sophia (Turk.: *Ayasofya*). This happened all over the country, while only a few church building remain unused. Interestingly some are again in use nowadays but as protestant churches (e.g. Bursa / İzmir / İstanbul).

The devotion of the celestial bodies, sun, moon and stars is found all over the Fertile Crescent. The triad of the symbols Crescent (sun, moon), lying crescent (sun) and star is reflected in gods or goddesses that are attached to the symbols (e.g. Ishtar, Innanu, Utu etc.). The sun crescent often took the form of a plate for something valuable to hold (e.g. pharaohs', kings, later even Maria etc.). The empires and people groups in this region practiced different forms of devotion. They created those symbols that made it to their coat of arms, arts or daily life decoration. The Crescent goes back to the Sumerians and the Accadians (2300 BC) and even further. The Moabites used the Crescent and the star as symbols of dedication (14th or early 13th – 6th century BC). The Babylonian kings considered themselves to be representatives of the powers of the sun and the moon. In these days Zoroastrianism had its origin which adopted the Crescent and the star. The Persian empires used the symbols also for their flags. The Sassanid Empire (224-651 AD) and the Parthians used the Crescent and the star as coat of arms. To trace back why the Crescent and the star became so popular in Islam is not unanimously discussed, but the Pre-Islamic Empire of the Sassanid had an effect on the Islamic conquerors to adopt the symbols. The Byzantine Empire took over the symbols of a cross for their coat of arms. Only seldom did they adopt the Sassanid symbols. In 330 AD *Constantine the Great* dedicated Constantinople to the *Virgin Maria*. The symbol of *Maria*, going back to the Egyptian and Babylonian goddesses *Nut* and *Ishtar*, was added to the Crescent. It represented the moon which stood for Artemis, the goddess of hunting. When the Ottoman troops conquered Constantinople they used the symbol of the Crescent to demonstrate their victory over the Christian Byzantine Empire. The flag below is from the 15th century AD and is coloured green. Since the 17th century the colour red is also found. The calligraphy shows the star stating *Basmallah* بسملة (bismi 'llāhi 'r-raḥmāni 'r-raḥīmi - "In the Name of Allah the Merciful") and the Crescent presenting the Islamic Creed *Shahadah* الشهادة لا اله الا الله☐محمد رسول الله (*lâ ilâha illallâh, Muḥammadur rasûlullâh* - "There is no God but Allah, and Hz. Mohammed is his messenger."). The calligraphy is normally white, but is sometimes also presented in yellow. It is a forerunner to the recent Turkish flag.

3 Turkey – A Socio-Historical Overview

It is interesting that the origin cannot absolutely be traced back. Yet the symbol of a star had also a function in the Hebrew Bible. In Numbers 24:17 the prophet Balaam reveals the divine words to the nations, "A star shall come forth from Jacob, and a sceptre shall rise from Israel, and shall crush through the forehead of Moab". This picture is often referred to King David's kingdom. It is taken up in the New Testament in the incident of the Birth of Hz. Jesus of Nazareth, which was accompanied by a mysterious star that led three Babylonian scholars to his birthplace in Bethlehem. It says in Mathew 2:9:

> When they had heard the king [Herod. EW.], they departed; and, lo, the star, which they saw in the east, went before them, till it came and stood over where the young child was.

Diagram 19 Crescent and Star - Coat of Arms

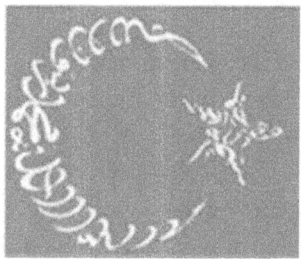

The Bible reveals in its last book an incident with a star, which is also often linked to the star of King David. The book of Revelation finishes with a picture of this star falling to earth and opening the gates of hell (Revelation 9:1): "And the fifth angel sounded, and I saw a star from heaven which had fallen to the earth; and the key of the bottomless pit was given to him". Either way, the star thus found entrance into the Christian revelation and symbolizes a messenger or a divine being which has the power to act (showing the way).

In Judaism the star symbol became popular in the 12th century AD and is known as the *Shield of David* or *Magen David* (Hebrew מָגֵן דָּוִד; Biblical Hebrew Māḡēn Dāwīḏ). The flag of Israel reflects this symbol, representing the triangle of Judah and Benjamin linked to each other. The term is a paraphrase for the God of Israel in the *Siddur*. As mentioned above Christianity used it in relation to the Old Testament a long time ago.

Having all the facts here in mind the Crescent and star symbols reveals a connotation to celestial bodies. Through the centuries the symbols were connected to gods and goddesses. Hereby the Islamic nations, as the last powers, adapted them to victory, blood (colour red) and the triumph of Islam over everything.

3.4.4 Summary

This paragraph was meant to illustrate the socio-cultural Christian environment which influences and reflects the specific situation of the Zaza people. It is within this setting that the Zaza people are best understood on historical, social and cultural factors.

The Cradle of Christianity reaches back to the area of Eastern Anatolia. This is why the struggle of religions is fought there intensely, as a clash of the origin and the centre of many philosophies. Beneath the three monotheistic Abrahamitic religions Judaism, Christianity, and Islam, the Fertile Crescent became the birthplace of Zoroastrianism, the Gnosis, Manichaeism, just to mention those religions that influenced the Zaza people and their neighbours. Christianity did not stay unaffected by those ideologies. Therefore it is interesting to follow up how the state and ethnical churches in this area evolved. The Armenian Apostolic Church forms the oldest state church, reaching back to the third century. The Armenian Apostolic Churches' history is the more interesting, since she went through and survived all the political and religious developments of the area of today's Zaza homeland. For this very reason she is closely interconnected to the history and development of the Zaza people and their neighbours. Little is known about the relationship of both people groups before the Ottoman Empire. Assumptions are dependent on the theory of origin of the Zaza people that one prefers (2.1.3.1). The highly likely - nonetheless not uncontested - *Daylam Thesis* (2.1.3.1.1) forms the state of affairs; concerning the question how far the Zaza people invaded the Christian Armenian realm. If they entered their homeland area after the 11th century AD / 6th century AH, then it would be interesting when and how the Kurmanji speaking population entered the scene or made space for the Zaza people. As with the Syriac Orthodox Churches the Armenian Apostolic Church formed a religious counterpart to the Islamic ethnicities of Eastern Anatolia. Introduced by the Ottoman Empire the Christian and Jewish communities gathered the status of *millets*. The latest *millet* became the Protestant Church movement starting in the 19th century. As a very vague and small interest group it inflamed passions of the Ottoman rulers through its success under the traditional churches and the people groups in the East, namely the Zaza ethnicity and the Kurmanji speaking Kurdish population. This was even worse as those groups never gained the status of *millet*. Envy generated jealousy and besides that the fear of pro-Russian, anti-Turkish conspiracy drove the Sultan to adopt drastic measures such as the deportations and nihilation of Jewish and Christian presence in the East. Jewish presence in Eastern Anatolia reaches back for 2.800 years, when with the Assyrian exile Jewish people entered into the East of Anatolia (Hebrew Bible 2Kings 5-27; 2Chronicles 32-33). The Jewish existence caused Christian apostles to visit the synagogues and to tell about their faith and the events in Jerusalem around Hz. Jesus of Nazareth, whom they called in Hebrew "the Messiah" (Greek: *Christ*). When Islam entered the scene in the 7th century AD / 1st century AH the Christians became second class citizens (*dhimmi*-status). With the Turkish invasions and the establishment of the Ottoman Empire the status of those *millets* made them and the people groups of Eastern Anatolia self ruling. They were asked to pay taxes and accept Ottoman military intervention and observation. This brought with it a high degree of uncertainty of political power. During the dissolution of the Ottoman Empire the Christian and Jewish people lost their independence and were forced to leave the area. Under Russian protection the Armenian Apostolic Church survived and very few members of the Syriac Orthodox Churches managed to make their way through the troublesome years of 1896 to 1927.

Looking at the rudiments of Christianity and Judaism in the Republic of Turkey we found that names of locations, cities and areas still reflect the former Christian presence. Also the rebuilding or conversion of churches as mosques is hinting at this fact. Lastly the Crescent and the star as a coat of arms in former and recent flags give evidence of some historical takeover.

3.5 Kurmanji Kurds, Zaza and the Turkish State

Much is said about the relationship of the Zaza people and the Kurmanji speaking "Kurds" (see the excellent study of Asatrian 2009; Arakelova 2000; Bläsing 1995; Leezenberg 1993). This study cannot add or keep up with all the research. But - as said in the introduction to this chapter - it will focus on the relevant influences that hint to the *co-* and *con*text of the Zaza people with their Kurmanji speaking neighbours (0).

3.5.1 History and Terminology – "Kurds", "Kurdish"

The term "Kurd" here is understood as a social or anthropological term which describes the people in Eastern Anatolia. They are split linguistically in a Northern (Kurmanji) and Southern Group (Sorani, Bahdeni) and Zazaki. For political reasons the term "Kurd" does not describe a clear cut ethnicity with a defined homeland, a homogenous language and a common history (Asatrian justifiably argues against such an unscientific approach 2009:4). A *language belt* covering the Eastern Anatolian, the Western Iranian and the Northern Iraqi area of the Fertile Crescent hints at a linguistic relationship. A common but ancient-ancestor can be traced back to *Old Persian* (2.2). During the processes of diversion the "Kurdish and related language belt" shaped the languages and dialects that we find today.

Yet the term "Kurds" as an ethnological term was first mentioned in historical records in cuneiform Sumerian writings around 3.000 BC (Wixman 1984), which talk about the "land of the Karda". In the 5th to the 11th century immigration movements of people groups to the area of the recent Kurmanji and related languages homeland areas increased. The doubtful research of Izady reports that as early as the 6th century, Jewish Talmudic scripture, particularly the *Targum*, consistently interprets *Ararat*, the traditional heartland of Armenia, to mean *Kurdistan* (Targums of Genesis 8:4, Isaiah 37:38, and Jeremiah in Izady 1992:96). The Talmud reports the settlement of Jewish deportees in Kurdistan under the Assyrian King *Shalmaneser III.* (858-824 BC). *King Saladin, Ṣalāḥ ad-Dīn Yūsuf ibn Ayyūb* (Arabic: صلاح الدين يوسف بن أيوب, Ṣalāḥ ad-Dīn Yūsuf ibn Ayyūb, Sorani: سەلاحەدین ئەیوبی, Selah'edînê Eyubî; 1138 – 1193) a hero in Islamic history was of Kurdish origin. He defeated the Crusaders and liberated Jerusalem from the invading Franks in 1187 AD. There is no evidence that Saladin or his fellow warriors ever thought of a Kurdish political identity. Quite to the contrary he gave the "fertile Shahrizur plain in the heart of Kurdistan as a fiefdom to one of his Turkish mamluks" (Loizides 2010:513). Saladin was born in Tigrit (Northern Iraq) and died in Damascus (Syria). During the period of the Ottoman Empire the Kurds participated in the administration and were given great autonomy as Muslims by *Mir* Princedoms. However the majority of the Kurmanji speaking Kurds living in Turkey follow the Islamic school of Shafi'i, in contrast to the Hanafi following Ottoman Turks and Southern Zaza. Their split into a larger Alevi group and small groups of Yezidi and Christians shows some parallels to the Zaza and the Gorani people, which both have also roots back to Zoroastrianism, Christianity and Islamic Shi'ism. A few Kurds belong to Sufi'i orders and others to Shi'a Islam.

The black spot of the *Hamidiye* troops (2.1.4.3; 2.1.4.4; 2.3.1.3.1; HC 2011), the "Kurdish" rebellions (2.3.1.3.2) and the modern military fight (e.g. PKK; 2.2.7.2) describes the Zaza people's brotherhood in arms within Kurdish history.

A fair and reasonable view accepts that there is more than pure neighbourhood but also less than ethnic accordance.

3.5.2 Kurdish Population – Inside the Fertile Crescent

The "Kurdish" people are spread out over (East) Syria, Northern Iraq, Northwestern Iran, and Eastern Turkey (Eastern Anatolia). Small groups and the Diaspora are settled mainly in Europe (Germany), Russia, Kazakhstan, the USA and very small groups in other parts of the world (e.g. Australia). There are many suggestions about the population of the "Kurds".

Table 38 Estimations of Kurds (overview)

Who	Number
Asatrian 2009:2-3	20-22 Millions: p. 3 Turkey 7-8 million; Northern Iraq 4-5 million, western parts of Iran 5-6 million; north and north-eastern parts of Syria 3-4 million
Franz 1988:32	13 Millions
Heper 2007:1[89]	11,5 Millions in Turkey (15.5 per cent)
Houston 2001:101	8-15 Millions
Loizides 2010:514; *Kurd* (2009), in Encyclopædia Britannica Online	20-25 Millions
McCarus 2009:	28 Millions: Northern Kurdisch ~20 million; Central Kurdish 5 millions; Southern Kurdish 3 millions
McDowall 2004:3	24-27 Millions
Wikipedia *Kurdish People*	28-35 Millions: Turkey 14-19 million; Northern Iraq 4,5-7 million, western parts of Iran 5,4-7,5 million; north and north-eastern parts of Syria 1,3-2 million

The numbers show clearly that the range of speculations about the (Kurmanji speaking) "Kurdish" population in Turkey starts around 8 Millions and can go up to 19 Million, due to lack of a census or in relation to political conviction.

---

[89] He refers to two surveys: Çarkoğlu, Ali & Toprak, Binnaz 1006. *Değişen Türkiye'de Din, Toplum ve Siyaset*, 29. Istanbul: TESEV. Milliyet (Istanbul daily), 22 March 2007.

3.5.3 Genetics, Space and Subjectivity

In some interesting research on the genetic relationship of the Zaza people with the "Kurds" (assuming they are Kurmanji speakers) it is claimed that a hypothesized northern Iranian origin for the Zazaki speaking people could not be proved, but instead, that they are genetically closely related to the Kurmanji speaking Kurds (Nasidze 2005:412). The argument goes on one side against the Daylam-Thesis (2.1.3.1.1) on the other it does not say where those "Kurds" are originally coming from or how this relationship could be explained. A genetic proximity should not be overemphasized, because it does not say too much about the origin but more about the development of the genetic pool. For this reason it is possible that the genetic material approximated because for a long time these people groups have shared the same geographical area, agriculture, etc. Also intermarriage and forced assimilation could play a role. Such socio-historical developments are not explained by such a study, although maybe considered. However the findings make clear that there are more than social or cultural relations.

The question is why the "Kurdish movement" never gained independence for their people. The long list of "Kurdish" rebellions against the Turks is noticeable. Seventeen upheavals between 1920 and 1938 (Heper 2007:1) are noted during the Ottoman Empire and the Republic of Turkey. The fact is that Turkish politics aimed to keep its Eastern provinces economically weak and underdeveloped to maintain political power, in the worst case by military invention. The Turkish language issue and its foundational Turkish nationalist movement hindered any basic Kurdish movement and encouraged Kurdish powers to military formation. This caused the founding of the PKK in 1978 (2.2.7.2; 2.3.1.3.1). The question above and the development of military and / or political resistance points the way to the topic of space, subjectivity and relatedness.

The relationship between Kurmanji speaking Kurds, Turks and the Zaza ethnicity in their mutual relatedness is focused on from a Zaza perspective (see 2.1.2.5). The focus was on space and subjectivity. Now the focal point is from a Kurmanji speaking angle. The question is, whether the struggle of "Kurdishness" versus "Zazaness" (chapter 0), "Turkishness" (3.1), "Alevismness / Alevism" or "Sunnismness / Sunnism" was successfully delayed to a Third Space which could be called "Kurdish / Zaza Nationalism" (2.1.2.5; 3.6).

3 Turkey – A Socio-Historical Overview

Table 39 Overview – Struggle in Space and Subjectivity (Kurmanji focus)

	Zaza	Turks	Alevis	Sunnism	Third Space
Kurmanji Speaker	√	√		√	Kurdish / Zaza Nationalism

Table 39 reveals the areas of contingence which also bring forth a lot of pressure. It is within this Third Space of a combined nationalism that most of the Zaza and Kurmanji people reach out for common ground. The linguistical approach of the "Vate" group (2.2.3.2), the radical move of the PKK, the politics way of the different parties and other attempts towards recognition are all addressed to achieve that interrelated space of joint nationalism. In this Sunnism and the dominance of Kurmanji are taken for granted.

Looking at the deadlock in the struggle for identity by the Zaza people within the wider framework of its surrounding neighbours, one is drawn to the conclusion that another space - the Third Space - could fill the search for recognition. Third Space concepts could be found in

1. socio-cultural frameworks,
2. ethnomusicological approaches built on arts,
3. Islamic movements,
4. Christian movements.

Hopeful first beginnings are obvious in what I would call *socio-cultural frameworks* (1). Within those, cross-cultural interrelatedness is intended strongly. Mainly individuals and small associations take the initiative to teach non-Turkish linguistical and cultural knowledge and traditions. A sort of enlightenment movement shines through such initiatives. Nonetheless financial shortcome, lack of support by individuals and pressure from Turkish and Kurmanji speakers afflict such approaches. Another approach (2) can be found in the *ethnomusicological* realm of arts and music. This area was mentioned above (2.1.2.5). It should be added that the European Union supports initiatives built on cross-cultural research or interchange (scholarships, etc.) like exhibitions, painting, Mediaworks, etc. Few initiatives in that direction are found in Turkey. A third way (3), to deal with the struggle of identity within the relationship of the Zaza, the Turks and the Kurmanji speakers is found in the movement of Islamic orders. *Nurcu* (including its offshoot the *Işıkçılar*), *Süleymanlı*, *Ticani*, *Dervish*, *Bektaşi* and the *Naqshebendi* form a podium for the three mentioned people groups to gather under the umbrella of Islam (see low; 2.3.1.3.2; 2.3.4.3.1;

2.3.4.4.3). A fourth way (4) is displayed in the protestant movement. Here either a new religion, for converts of non-Christian ideologies, or a return to Christian basics for members of Christian communities, contributes to a society, built on the revelation of Hz. Jesus of Nazareth. The problem for this community will be the development of linguistical and culturally contextualized groups of devotees, because the Turkish officials are eagerly observing this movement. However it is within such awakenings that freedom for pluralisation is offered and identities can be newly established. The goal is not to deny cultural or linguistic concepts but to adapt the message to it.

3.5.4 Summary

In the course of this research it became obvious that the question "Kurdishness" expressed in the terms "Kurdish", "Kurds" or "Kurdistan" cannot be answered by linguistic reasoning alone. Historically, science has to take into account also anthropological, sociological and political arguments. The geographical area of what was historically termed "Kurdistan" included areas of non-Turkish people groups in Eastern Anatolia in contrast to the Turkish populated areas in the West of the Ottoman heartland. Travellers, Turkish officials and people from that area referred to the area in non-political ways such as "my homeland" (Zazaki *welatê ma*) or "the East".

The marginalized "Kurdish" people are a conglomerate of many ethnicities that trace back to Old or Middle Persian and that share common religious background. Through the centuries, they went from polytheistic deism through Christianity to Islam. This commonly shared religious history, although it is directed nowadays to differently practiced religions, generated traditions that are widely shared. In folk tales (e.g. giant stories, etc.), initiation rites (e.g. circumcision), feasts (e.g. *Newroz* – New Year = Zazaki *Newroj / Kormışkan* etc.) and musical themes (e.g. love, desire, etc.) the overlap is obvious. "Kurdishness" is expressed in attitudes such as hospitality based on reciprocity, reciprocity in loan and sharing, brotherhood, loyalty to kinship and small scale society (2.3.2.1.4; 2.4.3.2; 2.5.4.3; 3.6.4; 3.6.5; 0). Different emphases on either of these social values mark the social stratification of the "Kurdish people". Yet the Zaza people are much stronger on the loyalty principle towards their kin than for example the Bahdeni people are (2.3.2.1.4).

To add another component to the discussion I approached the issue from a Space, Subjectivity and Third Space aspect. Here four developments came into focus. They can be split in the *socio-cultural framework* concept, the *ethnomusicological* approximation built on arts, and lastly the *Islamic* and *Christian* movements. They all have in common that they get input from outside. In other words *external impetus*, but afterwards they begin to develop an *internal impulse* based on internal efforts. The mother tongue based and socio-cultural weave has its roots in cross-cultural and intercultural communication endeavours that point to the multiethnic diversity of Turkey. The same is valid for the *ethnomusicological* space which overlaps with the former. Ethnomusicology offers research tools to develop cross-cultural concepts. The religious based advances of an Islamic Third Space come from the Pan-Islamic movement, which is often combined with nationalistic tendencies (Turkish Islamic nationalism). The Christian movement goes back to the protestant *millet* (around 1870 AD). Nowadays it is a self reproducible and self sustainable movement. All of these Third Space processes contain the chance to overcome the struggle of identity, but yet none can hold steady to have overcome it.

3.6 Islam and Turkey

In this paragraph particular developments in Islam that effect the situation of the Zaza people are discussed. The goal is to thrash out those that were not mentioned above and which reflect the actual circumstances in the East. Looking at the people groups of Turkey and their allegiance to Islam, it is obvious that this is the driving religion. The Turkish, the Kurmanji speaking and the Zaza people - at least the Southern Group - incorporated and acculturated Islam. It can be said that the practiced form of Islam in the Southern and Eastern Group of the Zaza people is fundamental and bigoted (2.3.3.2.5; 2.3.3.4). Yet *Hanafi* (Southern and Eastern Zaza) and *Shafi'i* (Eastern Kurmanji Kurds and Zaza) Islam is considered to be an essential part of daily life. This means the confession and preservation of Islamic traditions and status is important. This could be one reason why the demarcation to Alevis, Yezidis and Christians within their own ethnicity is absolute.

Although the demarcation line between the various religious groups is strictly respected, the social interaction of those groups was enormous in the past. During the rise of Islam in the 7th to the 8th century AD / 1st to the 3rd century AH the conquerors (Arab Bedouins) were mainly not forcing the ethnicities to change their way of life, but tried to support the public life (economy, trade, social life) by taking taxes only (Hoyland 1997:11, 15).

3.6.1 Propagation Strategies

The strategies of promoting Islam are summarized in the concepts of *da'awa* دعوة (invitation) and *jihad* جهاد (struggle). Both concepts add to each other (Troeger 2005a and b; Ellul 2009; Mordecai 1999; Schirrmacher 2008b; Ye'or 2009:39-41). Methods of *da'awa* are found in

- sermon,
- apologetic and informative teaching,
- open proclamation and
- outgoing activities to invite outsiders.

The direction or Islamic mission is from within the *umma* (Muslim community) to the non-Muslim world by *ingathering*, whereby the gathered people are free to decide. Within *jihad* the *dar al-Islam* or *dar as-Salam* (house of Islam / Peace) takes active steps to expand the abode of Islamic influence. The non-Islamic world is considered as *dar al-harb* (House of War). The expressions reveal that the area of the "Other" or "foreign" is viewed as a hostile counterpart. The principles of "Otherness" and "Foreignness" are essential conditions to drive the Islamic movement (2.3.3.4; 3.4.1.3.4; 3.6.5; 0). Without a visualization of an enemy the whole Islamic power play does not function well. Islamic missionary strategies are found in

- political activity (e.g. treaty, federations etc.),
- military actions (e.g. uprising, war etc.),
- development aid movements (e.g. Red Cross in contextualized form: Arab. *al-Hilâl al-Ahmar*, Turk. *Türkiye Kızılay Derneği*), and
- financial and administrative takeover of former non-Islamic organizations and institutions.

The direction is from within the Islamic *umma* (community) to the outside world by *incorporation* and *absorption*, whereby the absorbed people have little influence on the process and seldom any real choice.

3.6.2 The Islamic orders – Workforces of da'awa and jihad

Islamic institutions that work on invitation and struggle, as well as on the inner power strengthening level are the Islamic orders in which the Zaza people often have a presence, sometimes even a leading role. The aspect of strengthening the Islamic fortitude is central to all religious orders. Nonetheless, as exemplified in the *Naqshebendi* order, the most popular one in Turkey, the decentralized structure of the order connects its members through a brotherhood which is comparable to Freemasonry. The *Milli Selamet Partisi* (MSP; National Salvation Party) whose founder was *Necmettin Erbakan* in 1972, is a direct outcome of the orders activities. With the succeeding *Refah Partisi* (RP; Welfare Party) the movement went on (Bruinessen 1989:3). One branch of the *Naqshebendi* order, the *Süleymanlıs* are often negatively referred to in the press. The founder *Süleyman Hilmi Tunahan*, called *Süleyman Efendi* (1888-1959), was a Naqshebendi Sheikh who started his own conservative Qur'anic teaching courses. After his death the network of these courses grew immensely and the chiliastic orientation of the movement attracted lots of devotees. *Süleyman Efendi* is considered to be the last of the 33 great teachers (*murshid / mürşıd / murşid*) and following him means "real Islam" and thus a direct entry to paradise. The fanatic expression of the Süleymanlıs and the refusal to pray behind other Imams that do not belong to their movement, irritates other Muslims and leads to open rejection of the sect (positive: Kısakürek 1977:269-272; Albayrak 1979: 165-168; critical report from an insider Akyildiz 1978). The *Süleymanlıs* are found more in the South of Turkey and parts of West Europe.

Another increasing religious group, since the 1950s, is the *Nurcu* movement (including its offshoot the *Işıkçılar*). *Said Nursi* (1873-1960) wrote *Risale-i Nur* (essays on the divine light). This compilation is seen as a religious bridge between tradition and the Modern. He was a member of the *Naqshebendi* order, but left it due to the institutional mysticism that he denounced. In his opinion the Islamic Reformist movement of the Young Turks was not taking the *Sharia* (Turk.: *şeriat*) seriously enough. So he started the movement of "Islamic unity". The Sufi'ism following course of the Nurcu movement forms something new, by combining Folk Islam, magic, and mystical and spiritual practices.

The *Ticani* order became a militant work force against the nation state. This led to revenge by the officials, which led to the decimation of this movement. It was predominantly in the 1950s that they experienced a rough time by pubic trials and accusations after they went public by demolishing statues of Mustafa Kemal Paşa Atatürk.

3.6.3 Principles of Invitation

The principle of *da'awa* is addressed by these Islamic orders though the invitation to share their mystical experiences and to be in unity with God or the Divine. On the front of *jihad*, the Islamic orders are highly political and they penetrate all levels of politicians, administration and the officials (2.3.3.4; 3.4.1.3; 3.4.1.3.4; 3.6.1; 4). The Zaza people are taking part in these orders. These orders could be seen as a Third Space (see above). *Pan-Islamism* as one of the underlying principles of Turkish identity, the other being *Pan-Turkism*, is well addressed in these orders and as such they are natural promoters to gather Islamic elements under their roof (3.1.1.2.2). The ideology of Pan-Islamism came in and still comes in to the political sphere in waves. Recently such a wave is on the ascent. The Zaza people experience thereby both the freedom to be more outgoing with their ethnical identity and at the same time the need to conform to the political restrictions set by the Turkish majority. This walk on a tightrope provokes and forces the Zaza community to political and military action (legal and illegal resistance). It is interesting that the Islamic brotherhood concept (unity, equality, security) does not overcome the desire for self rule or the implementation of mother tongue education. It seems that even the Islamic orders are not open to branches of mother tongue using members within their structure. This would be a breakthrough to consolidate Islamic and nationalistic needs.

3.6.4 Anthropological Considerations

The following paragraph deals with the active propagation of Islam from an anthropological point of view. There is on the one hand the function and effect on society that this Islamic movement takes and on the other hand the dynamics that conversion in the area of Eastern Anatolia takes up.

3.6.4.1 Islamic Missions – Ingathering and Incorporation

Two tendencies drive the Turkish Islamic sphere. First there is the above mentioned outgoing Islamic mission by *ingathering* and *incorporation*. Second one will find efforts to strengthen the inner cohesion of the existing Islamic institutions and people groups. The *madrasa* and theological training centres in Eastern Anatolia (e.g. Muş, Diyarbakır, Şanlıurfa etc.) and Saudi Arabia (Medina, Mecca, etc.) were or are highly respected places for people in Turkey to get education in Islamic theology. The *mılah* (mullah; spiritual teacher; Turk.: *hoca*) as part of the Islamic clergy and a trained theologian is responsible for either people or a geographical area. He is mainly focusing on either his kinship, a small scale society or a geographical area. His responsibility is about Islamic spirituality (e.g. circumcision, weddings, funerals, Islamic teachings). Within the outer and inner mission of Islam a tendency for superiority hinders the overcoming of the inner failure to accept other ways of living. Everything that is not considered "Islam" or the *dar al-Islam / dar as-Salam* (house of Islam; 2.3.1.3; 2.3.3.2.3) is refused or taken as secondary, if not oppressed.

The deeper values of following the Islamic Law, the *Sharia*, and at the same time to taking part in a society and culture with its culture-specific orientation are flowing into the perception of the world. The core values of hospitality in reciprocity (reward is expected), reciprocity in loan and sharing, loyalty to kinship and small scale society, and the traditions of Animistic origin based Shamanism drive the concept of "Turkishness (2.3.2.1.4; 2.4.3.2; 2.5.4.3; 3.6.5; 0). These underlying values are overlaid by the Islamic practices of faith, both together forming the Turkish conscience.

3.6.4.2 Conversion – The Individual versus Microcultures

One of the most outstanding features of Islam is the jealous or better said the vitriolic handling of conversion. A Muslim who changes his thinking and decides to take up another religious ideology is called *murtad* (apostate). He is dealing with apostasy, which is perceived as treason. This is considered the worst a person can do and is cursed and punished by the death penalty. The person loses face in a way that there is no turn back into the *umma*, the Islamic community (Schirrmacher 2008c: 109-111). Although some Islamic sects (e.g. the Ahmadiya movement, et.) do not ask for the death penalty they consider it a sin. The social pressure that this handling brings with it, is even increased by the fact that in Islamic countries non-Islamic microcultures or people groups are directly (*jihad*) or indirectly (*da'awa*) forced to convert to Islam. In cultures following shame-orientation losing face is the worst thing to happen. With that in mind, an individual can only convert from the low prestige to the more prestigious religion, thus from a non-Islamic religion to Islam. Going the other way round would cause repudiation in the best and death in the worst case. The best alternative to the risky individual conversion is mass conversion. In this way the critical mass of kin, relatives or the small scale society needs to overcome the point of revenge which hurts individuals physically. This happened back and forth in the past, when Christian people converted to Islam by pressure of being annihilated (Griffith 2010:34, 102). The other way round is rare, and if it occurs the individual is forced to leave his environment. The only refuge would be the West or the big cities in the West of Turkey, where anonymity is ensured. Mass conversions from Animism or Islam to Christianity by small scale societies are reported in the 19th century AD in the Northern Group (2.3.3.2.4). Foregoing persecution of these people displayed the seriousness of the peril. Larger groups are much more survivable.

The complexity of conversion in the territory of Eastern Anatolia goes along with political changes. People groups referred to the dominant powers or their leadership when it came to decide which religion to follow. The ruling class had either to subordinate to the invaders (e.g. Arab Bedouins, Seljuks, Mongols, etc.) or to be loyal to their people (e.g. Armenian Apostolic Church, Alevis, etc.). For the people under political-religious pressure the normal way to survive is to avoid any suspicion, and not awaken any envy or jealousy that could cause reaction. This is a difficult situation because there is no protection against arbitrary sanctions. The Zaza people developed a strategy by looking after their own business and adapting to the ruling powers and their religions only as far as absolutely necessary. Some Zaza groups started with military resistance, others went into politics and still others left the school system as soon as possible and started their own business or stuck to their family duties. The community in itself found a way to deal with the menace of cultural adaptation or lost language, although after eighty years of oppression the situation is difficulty now. The religious conversion of Zaza people who had a different background is still known to the others and is sometimes a stigma. I mentioned a group of villages around Gerger who are known as "Christian" although not all citizens are or had such a background (2.1.4). Armenians that survived the atrocities of the Young Turks and the Caliphate in the second decade of the last century converted or were converted to Islam to survive any new threat. Thereby they lost their identity and today only a few refer back to their origin or even know of it. This loss of identity and the total dependence on their new environment left a trauma, which is obvious in the denial of any Christian background at all. The Armenian Apostolic Church can seldom refer to survivors who passed on their history. However recent attempts have tried to trace back family roots to the area of the well populated Eastern Anatolian soil formerly occupied by Armenians. Similarly in the Northern Group following Alevism converts are not outgoing at all. The reason is best found in the elaboration of their history (2.3.3.3.

3.6.5 Summary

Islam in Turkey has a history of close to a thousand years. The encounter between Judaism, Christianity and Islam is one of the foundational and characteristic features of this geographical area. The Islamic promotion and propaganda expressed in *da'awa* دعوة (invitation) and *jihad* جهاد (struggle) directed and directs the expansion of Islam into the realm of formerly non-Islamic and Christian ethnicities (2.3.3.4; 3.4.1.3.4; 3.6.1; 3.6.5). Inside Islam the most powerful movements are the Islamic orders of *Naqshebendi*, the *Nurcu* (including its offshoot the *Işıkçılar*), the *Ticani* and the *Süleymanlı* (2.3.1.3.2; 2.3.4.3.1;2.3.4.4.3). In Turkey one is expected to be a Muslim because Turks or Turkish citizenship is linked to Islam. Pan-Islamism and Pan-Turkism are interrelated in Turkish nationalistic-Islam. Every non-Muslim is therefore seen as a non-Turk and thus an outsider. "Turkishness" is achieved by a belonging to the *umma* (Islamic community), accepting the history and superiority of the Turkish race and subordination under the ruling political and Islamic powers. Besides these overall values, hospitality based on reciprocal expectations, reciprocity in share and loan, affiliation and the unity and solidarity of the kinship are also core values and basic to the Turkish perception of the world (2.3.2.1.4; 2.4.3.2; 2.5.4.3; 3.6.4; 0).

Islam as a Third Space in which the people groups of Turkey could overcome their struggle for identity does not function in this way at the moment. The assumed dominance, historical development and blunt oppression of the Turkish rulers, as followers of the Hanafi habit, scares off not just all non-Islamic ethnicities (e.g. Jewish people, Christians, Atheists, etc.), but also the Shafi'i-, Yezidi and Alevi practicing Islamic people. The self-centeredness of Islamic teaching in general and the Islamic groups in particular does not attract those groups to cooperate or ally with each other. In consequence every Islamic group is separate. However, some fundamentalist Islamic parties (e.g. AKP, etc.) and organizations (e.g. Hisb Allah; Hamas etc.) are growing in numbers and influence. Conversions to Islam are mainly built on military or oppressive initiatives covered by the strategy of *jihad*. Conversion in general is a devotion to another religion. Since Islam is strict on converts from Islam (*murtad*) and punishes apostasy seriously, individual conversion is rare. Alternatives are microcultures or people group conversions, which guarantee a social environment. In history such mass conversions of tribes in the Northern Group are reported. Individual converts are often traumatized since they were either forced or they had no chance to express their decision to their kin.

3.7 Summary

In the third chapter the wider environment of the River People came in focus. The history of the Turks and its manifold ethnicities was taken into account to show how the Zaza people were and are influenced. The Seljuk Empire as the first historically Turkish Empire represented the platform for the kingdom of the *Osman* dynasty to disperse over the whole Mediterranean, the Balkans and the Arabian Peninsula. The Ottoman Empire and its conception of the *millet* (taxed groups "protected" by the Islamic superiors) guided them to relative self dependence and self rule under tax obligation and subordination to the Ottoman authorities. The *tanzimat* reforms meant to overcome the inner crisis of the Ottoman Empire in the 19th century AD / 13th century AH. Sultan *Abdul Hamid* II. took over the principles of *Pan-Islamism* and *Pan-Turkism* introduced thereby and started to get rid of any suspicious people groups in his empire. Non-Islamic and non-Turkish ethnicities were oppressed first with the help of loyal Islamic and non-Turkish subjects such as the Kurmanji speaking and the Zaza people. They were given authority and called *Hamidiye* troops. Soon their deeds became widely known as the most cruel and brutal procedure because they were rewarded to take over the property of the killed or deported. This dark period of the Zaza and Kurmanji people turned against them when they came under the suspicion of the new Republic of Turkey (1923). The Turkish ideology turned down any attempt for independence, self rulement or even recognition of these people down and thus the "Kurdish Question" was born. The "Kurdish Question" itself became a European issue with the spread of the "Kurdish" people (including Kurmanji, Sorani and Zaza speaking ethnicities) as guest labourers since 1960. Germany as the main centre of Diaspora developed into an ideological and financial centre for military and political activity. This was obvious with the foundation of the PKK in 1978. Their activists went into hiding all over Europe. Their training centres in Lebanon, the Gaza strip and West Jordan Palestine recruited Europeans from left-winged terrorist cells like the *Red Army Faction* (Germ. "Rote Armee Fraktion" – RAF in Germany).

Although there is a high rate of bilingualism, the manifold people groups of Turkey (close to 40 ethnicities and languages), would demand a cultural and linguistical pluralistic and federal governmental structure with a nation-wide *lingua franca* (Turkish). The relationship and application status for full membership of the European Union moves politics into this direction. The changes cause interior political tensions. At the same time the increase of power by the military PKK and the appeasement politics of the recent AKP government are processing a lot of initiatives to mother tongue education and self ruling non-Turkish institutions.

Christianity in history developed out of the Ottoman heartland introduced by the apostles, mainly St. Paul. The expansion of the Christian message showed the way to nation Churches. Those Churches are the Roman Catholic (380 AD), the Armenian Apostolic (301 AD), Georgian (350 AD), Russian or Orthodox Churches. However beside the nation churches widespread Christian congregations developed and covered North Africa, the Near and Middle East, Europe and Asia. The fast, unexpected and unrestrained Islamic extension during the 6th century caused fundamental changes of politic powers and authority. Christianity was made a religion based on a second class citizenship. Nonetheless it was enduring. Conversions back and forth were related to political circumstances, but mainly in the direction from Christianity to Islam, due to oppression, military pressure or increasing Islamic influence. In the 19th century AD Christian development aid run by protestant organisations made the traditional Churches rethink their Christian Creed. The challenge also influenced the Eastern Anatolian people groups and stirred up suspicion, envy and jealousy of the Ottoman authorities. Although installed as the youngest of the 17 *millet* the protestant movement caused the vast deportation and almost obliteration of the Christian and Jewish presence in Eastern Anatolia. Fortunately the Russian Empire as a counterpart to Western colonial powers and the emerging Republic of Turkey offered the Armenian Apostolic Church and the Armenian people the opportunity to establish their own state (1918) in the former "Eastern Armenia" area. Western Armenia became part of Turkey with a very small Armenian population left.

Jewish people and Judaism were present in today's area of Turkey since their dispersion, caused by the Assyrian exile (8th century BC). 2.800 years ago the Jewish people of the Northern Kingdom called Israel were forced to resettle in Eastern Anatolia. Synagogues and a vivid Diasporic life evolved. Later on around 50 AD the apostle Paul visited those synagogues and confronted the Jewish people with the message of the arisen Messiah (the letter to the Galatians in the New Testament). Judaism left it marks mainly through Christianity in the culture of the Zaza people, as well as the Kurmanji speaking ethnicity. Be it circumcision, the concept of a holy day (Shabath), restrictions of food or the direction to pray, such concepts were coming from Judaism and encorporated in the Islamic revelation or tradition. Judaism in itself is not the origin of such practices since the Jewish Law has its roots in even older practices which by revelation of the Hebrew Bible were centralised on the worship and adoration to the Hebrew God who called and revealed himself as *Jahweh* (YHWH). He was called *Elohim, El* or many other derivations from *El* which forms the same root as the Arabic *Allah*.

The terminology and conceptions around the "Kurds" are historically overlaid by travel descriptions and ethnographical studies of the past. While often all non-Turkish people in the Eastern Anatolian area (Turkey; Northern Iraq; Western Iran) are packed into this substratum sometimes only the Kurmanji and related speaking language groups are addressed by this term. The resulting struggle for identity of the Zaza people (notice that other people groups experience the same struggle), demands solutions. I presented the Third Space approaches that are recently under way. Within the Zaza people and in different areas there is the attempt to overcome the oppression of Kurmanji Kurdish nationalism in Turkey. However the affinity and high acceptance of Kurmanji speaking dominance within the Zaza people is in contrast to a movement of self dependence and self rule.

To expand its realm, Islam evolved the strategies of *da'awa* (invitation) and *jihad* (struggle). The Islamic orders are the main contributors to promote the inner strengthening of Islam; as well as its propagation through political and economical channels. The Pan-Islamic stance of the Turkish government contributes also to the increase in the defamation of non-Islamic people groups and their religion. One has to keep in mind that Turkish Islam is in competition with the Islam of the Arabian countries who promote their form as the "real Islam". The Turkish version is often considered to be artificial or secular. In general "Turkishness" is so closely related to Islam that the deeper core values of hospitality based on reciprocal expectation, reciprocity in loan and share, loyalty to kinship and small scale society and nationalism (Pan-Turkism) are often intermingled (2.3.2.1.4; 2.4.3.2; 2.5.4.3; 3.6.4; 3.6.5; 0).

4 Comprising Epilogue

This reflection gives an overview about the assumptions and conclusions that were drawn during the research. Anthropology as a scientific discipline offers helpful tools for understanding people groups. The researcher gathers by ethnography, personal diary and qualitative questionnaires the emic and etic stances of the people group, based on his observation (participant observation) and the people's descriptions or their utterances (e.g. speech, idiom etc.). Applied anthropology goes even a step further as it combines social sciences, philosophy, psychology and cognitive sciences in research. In the first place cognitive anthropology serves this study with an approach to enter concepts like

- the *LEIC* (Location of Emotions, the Intellect and the Character),
- the *Uncertainty Reduction Theory*,
- the *envy* mechanisms in society,
- the shame and guilt orientation of *conscience*,
- the *Image of limited Good*(s),
- the space and subjectivity conception built on *Third Space* theory,
- the *ethnomusicological* psychology of arts, music and performance / dance.

The research, which is based on these tools, offers a platform to compare cultures and societies based on their perception of the world, expressed in their core values. On this deeper level the society's religious ethics, their moral standards and the foregoing cognitive interplay are revealed by the research tasks mentioned. The perception of the world of the Zaza people and their specific context, especially their relationship to the Kurmanji speaking Kurds, offer an excellent example of how e.g. "Zazaness" (Zaza perception of the world) can be compared to "Kurdishness" (Kurdish perception of the world) or "Turkishness" (Turkish perception of the world). Since enough research is done on the Turkish population of Turkey concerning "Turkishness", and also on the Kurmanji speaking Kurds of Turkey expressed in "Kurdishness", it was the task of this thesis to add "Zazaness" to the discussion.

We started our tour of the River People with an introduction to *applied anthropology*. In this comprehensive study the task of the thesis included the historical, anthropological and linguistical description of the River People. This people group lives in close relation to the Kurmanji speaking ethnicity under the rule of the Turkish government and its institutions. The main question for the River people is about their struggle for identity on linguistical, anthropological, religious and social grounds. The very complex topic of identity was broken up by a description of (chapter 2),

- the people group as people, resp. name, origin, identity (2.1),
- their language (2.2),
- their culture (0),
- their religion (2.3.3),
- their social structure (2.3.4),
- their background as peasant (2.3.5),
- an example of the use of the term *merdım* (man, person, human; 2.4.3),
- their perception of the world ("Zazaness"; 2.5) and
- mother tongue issues (2.6).

The question of *identity* is closely related to the naming of people groups. In the case of the Zaza people endonyms like *zonê ma* (our language) or *Dimıli* did not resist against exonyms such as *Zaza* or *Zazaki*. The origin is not unequivocal and could be either a geographical reference or a defamatory word. The distinction from the Kurmanji speaking ethnicity is not arguable on linguistic arguments alone, although this area offers the plainest proof. A differentiation in a *wider language belt* (Germ. "Sprachbund"), which includes "Kurmanji and related languages", would contain Zazaki also. A closer language belt on the Southern Caspian languages and dialects would enclose Gorani, Hewrami / Hawrami, Talysh, Southern Tati, Gilaki, Semnani, Laki, Bakhtiari, Luri, Mazandarani, Sangsari, but not Kurmanji and its close relatives. Another distinction is found in the origin of Zazaki in Old Persian and the Parthian language, whereas Kurmanji traces back to Middle Persian and is thus closer to Farsi than Zazaki.

The many theories about the *origin* of the Zaza could be supported by the theory of Celtic immigration through big mass migration movements around 2000 BC along the Danube River. Such a theory would prefer the early settlement of the Zaza people or their predecessor in the recent homeland. Another theory is following mass migration from the Southern shores of the Caspian Sea. We have a lot of evidence that the Zaza ethnicity originated from there. In this theory they moved to the West at around 1.000 AD together with other ethnic groups such as the Gorani. The area of settlement in the headwaters of the Euphrates / Tigris rivers presents a mountainous area which is inhabited by the Northern Group, an area of open plains with deep valleys (Southern Group) and a mix of middle height mountains and valleys (Eastern Group). Their status as a non-Turkish ethnicity forced them to be part of the "Kurdish Question", which besides Alevism is one of the two obstacles of the Republic of Turkey.

Zazaki as an Indo-European language is part of the Northwestern Iranian branch. It is traced back to Parthian, evolving from Old Persian. Together with other Southern Caspian languages it forms a close language belt (Germ. "Sprachbund"). On linguistic grounds Kurmanji and Zazaki are counted as individual own languages, however the discussion reveals an affinity on cultural and social grounds. The three main dialects of the Northern, the Southern / Central and the Eastern group are split up into various local idiolects. The huge challenge for the Zaza people will be to develop a standard or reference dialect as a mediating language. Experience shows that forced standardization as well as natural development are globally observed. Recently, the basic principles of standardization attempts are looking for common etymological roots, observing which one survived and then distributing dictionaries or lexicons as tools for education, authors or as standards for publications. On Zazaki, the Vate group (pro-Kurmanji), some individuals and some magazines are working in that direction. The danger is to introduce e.g. Kurmanji terminology for ideological reasons.

Zazaki grammar demonstrates some peculiar features, such as a split ergative system, a future marker (*do*), a three way ezafe system, few verb roots with an extended pre- and suffix system and many compound roots and particles.

Looking at the Zaza culture some interesting facts are outstanding. First, although a small people group, they are highly political and advancing their spiritual tasks proactively. For this reason they are main players when it comes to political expressions, be they military rebellions, the founding of political parties or other initiatives. Those undertakings are closely related to an attitude that they consider themselves to be part of the "Kurdish" movement. The tension is with those groups of the Zaza people that consider themselves as "Zaza", speaking the language of Zazaki with no social-anthropological link to the Kurmanji speaking Kurds. Those Zaza are recently under pressure from the pro-Kurdish and pro-Kurmanji and Zazaki speaking groups. They are forced to take an extremist or isolated position without any hope of being heard by the officials.

Looking at the religions of the Zaza ethnicity, most Southern and Eastern speaking Zaza groups follow the Hanafi Islamic school rite, whereas a few are of the Shafi'i school. Training in Islam is given at theological training centres called *madrassa*. Alevism with its long tradition since Zoroaster (6th century

BC), is built on a dualistic view of the natural and divine powers. *Ahura Mazda* as the main principle of power drives those forces. Modern spiritual life in the Northern Alevi group has little or no active input from spiritual leaders, since these structures are lost due to emigration. The *cemaat* (religious, cultural and political gathering), the *baba, rayber, mürşid* and *pir* structure or other Alevitic forms of religious life lost their function and members to maintain them.

The *Zaza society* is based on small scale societies following close kinship ties. Loyalty to the tribe and to kinship, based on the paternal bloodline has highest priority. Marriage is within the own kin, with the aim of minimizing any tension with other small scale societies. The principles of girl abduction, rape to blackmail cross-tribal or cross-religious marriage – mainly Muslims with non-Islamic girls –, honour killing and blood feud are very strongly based on the loyalty principles. The level to cause any conflict is extremely low, while social sanctions are carried out rapidly. The goal is to keep society balanced and determine the demarcation of the sphere of *taboo* and *mana*. Thus one will avoid any reason to cause such social mechanisms. Hospitality based on reciprocity, reciprocity in share and loan based on the expectation of return, brotherhood, gender equality within a clear cut gender separation (2.3.2.1.4; 2.4.3.2; 2.5.4.3; 3.6.4; 3.6.5)are essentials within the social expectations and stratification.

The three level structure of the *Zaza society* includes a strong but small upper class. To it belongs the Islamic clergy such as the religious body of *baba, rayber, mürşid* and *pir* for the Northern Alevism following group. And the *sheikh, mıllah* and sometimes *hoca* (Turkish loan) institution for the Southern and Eastern Group based on *mullaharchy*. The broad middle class consists of peasant, traders, and craftsmen. The lower class covers widows, handicapped and people without kin and foreigners. These structures are dissolving and replaced by economic structures based on the former structures. The change goes from peasantry to industrialization. The European and mainly German Diaspora demonstrates an enormous financial and ideological factor. Many craftsmen received education and training in Germany and are now taking that knowledge to the homeland. Peasantry is still an important factor for self supply. Huge monocultural agricultural companies are playing an increasing role. In tradition and religion the *snake* is a symbol of formerly Animistic and peasant cultures. It reflects Old Iranian mystical conceptions of the cloud, thunder and lightning and dragon gods.

4 Comprising Epilogue

Ethnomusicology provides us with information about the huge influence that Zaza music has in the area. Even modern "Turkish" music is to some degree based on Zaza music style. However, only a few Zaza musicians are popular in Turkey and the surrounding countries.

Following the thesis of this study anthropology and linguistics are interlinked. One without the other will not maintain scientific data about a people group to describe it extensively. A case study about this thesis is given by a semantic field examination. To demonstrate the close link between a cultural and linguistic liaison we looked at the semantic field of the term *merdım*. The terminology related to the designation of *merdım* (human, pl. people), includes derived forms thereof such as *camêrd* (brave), *mêrd* (man, masculine) and *mêrdek* (man, husband). Semantics are revealing *merdım* as a generic term that covers a *real* versus an *ideal* meaning. The *ideal* meaning contents the core values and expectations towards a member of the society. The real meaning instead expresses the outer level of the Zaza culture and the practices that contribute to prestige and honour.

The *worldview* of the Zaza people or "Zazaness", as it could be also called, is based on their cosmology, their spiritual and their social conceptions. The view of the physical and metaphysical world is based on a deeper Animistic concept which is overlaid by Zoroastrian or dualistic notions. Christian impressions deliver monotheistic and thoughts which are then oriented towards Islamic principles. This is obvious in concepts like blood feud, honour killing, the (sexual) purity versus impurity values, and gender relations. In these areas the Zaza people practice inhuman activities that are coming from Folk or traditional Islamic religious activities following the principle of direct revenge. The preceding Jewish and Christian revelations consider such practices also, although in the New Testament it is replaced by love of the neighbour and God. Envy is thus considered to be the main driving force and the easiest research area. The motivation, process and regulation of the production principles of envy related course, reveals deeper inner values and their linking to outwardly directed actions. The Zaza people follow in the area of purity and impurity concepts of Islamic principles out of the *Sharia* (Turk.: *şeriat*), however they don't take the five pillars very seriously and tend towards a realistic form of Islam. There is no general rule or description that would fit all Zaza people, but there is the tendency to claim being "Islamic" or "Moslem" and at the same time to emphasize the inner attitude and not the outward practices. The Alevism following Northern Zaza would not even go to mosque or follow any of the religious deeds. And although the Southern and Eastern Group focuses more on those activities they are not forcing themselves to keep all the Islamic Laws.

Recently the *mother tongue* became an important factor to demonstrate identity. Mother tongue based education, authors and writers courses, training in traditional arts and music and even the public organization of cultural, social and political meetings in Zazaki or related to Zazaki are increasing. The proclamation and request for international acceptance of Zazaki as a distinct language and the Zaza as an ethnicity is on the agenda of many Diasporic and Turkish Zaza led institutions.

To encompass the perception of the Zaza people the environment and context of this people group is taken into account. In chapter 3 the wider context includes,

- the research of the "Turks" from an inner and outer perspective,
- the different people groups in Turkey that were or are related to the Zaza people,
  - such as Christianity and the
  - Jewish people,
- the "Kurds" and
- Islam.

These areas are researched under the premise *how* and *in which way* they have linguistically and culturally influenced the Zaza ethnicity in history and presence.

The "Turks" are originally from the Mongolian area and entered the area of the *Fertile Crescent* in multiple waves. The origin of the Turkic people is found in the area of Altai (Mongolia). As nomads they spread out over all the area. The presence of Turkic speaking people in today's Turkey goes back to the Seljuk dynasty which established the *Seljuk Empire* (11th to 14th century). After that Osman established the Ottoman Empire, one of the most widespread and long-lasting in world history (14th to 20th century AD / 8th to 15th century AH). Before the Seljuk times the people groups of Eastern Anatolia formed self-contained nation state or small scale societies. The *Armenian Apostolic* Church (301 AD) and the Georgian *Apostolic Autocephalous Orthodox* Church (starting in 326 established in 523 AD) give examples of those nation states based on kingdom. Following the Daylam-Thesis, since we do not know of Zaza presence then, it is assumed that they entered from the Caspian Sea pushed by the invading Seljuks, Mongols or Turks. There is little or no evidence that they had settled in their recent homeland area before the Seljuk invasions. Under Ottoman rule the Zaza people experienced relative independence. Beside the tax obligation and partial supervision by Ottoman authorities we find self-rule by *princedom* in the Kurmanji speaking ethnicity, the ruler being called *Mir* (17th-19th century AD / 12th-14th century AH) and *sheikhdom* in the Zaza society. The Islamic clergy formed a small scale society related *mullaharchy* and as a political instance in the villages operated the *aghadom* run by village and tribal *aghas*. Although political and religious power was often intermingled every societal institution had its emphasis. The *agha* in a position as a landlord functioned as a mediator and representative of his small scale society or village to outsiders. He also ruled internal conflicts. His few religious obligations were to supervise the religious meetings. The *Sheikh* dominates the political and religious area with an emphasis on the latter. The *mullah* holds a religious position which through his influence is sometimes political according to his ambitions (e.g. by sermon, networking, through his Islamic order, etc.).

The traditionally Christian people in the area of Eastern Anatolia experienced their own rule up to the 7th century. With the Islamic expansions and later the Mongol and Turkish invasion (2.1.3.1.1; 2.1.3.1.4; 2.1.3.1.5; 2.3.1.1; 2.3.3.4;- 3.1.1; 3.3) the political and religious situation made them second class citizens (*dhimmi-status*) under Islamic rule. Tax obligation, restriction of work (e.g. some political positions and the security apparatus), supervision by the Ottoman / Turkish authorities, oppression on property and expansion and other highhandedness encumbered them in daily life. The Zaza people also used their superiority over these people groups as a reason to plunder rape and abduct them. Victims were mainly girls for marriage or boys as cheap labour. The other way round was seldom or nil because the normal social mechanisms of honour killing, blood feud and abolition were foreign and thus a deterrent to the Christian people. With the powers of the *Hamidiye* troops (Kurmanji and Zazaki speaking peoples) the Christian minorities were defencelessly victims to their Islamic neighbours. The extinction and deportation of them maintained a vacuum on craft and productive – trade oriented – peasantry. This, together with the dissatisfaction about the orientation of the new republic of Turkey led to uprisings run by Zaza leaders and mainly supported by Zaza small scale societies in 1920, 1921, 1925, 1930, 1937/1938 and smaller ones in between. The consequences were strict oppression of the new Turkish government and a denial of any non-Turkish or non-Islamic attitude. Alevism, Christianity, the Jewish people, the Zaza, Laz, Kurmanji, Arabians, Adyghe, Circassians and other small groups were threatened under suspicion. The "Alevi-" and "Kurdish Questions" are still the two big challenges for the Turkish Republic.

The terminology around the "Kurds" is increasingly politicized. Whereas on linguistical grounds a clear cut distinction between Zazaki and Kurmanji is proved, an affinity on societal and anthropological foundations is given. However I tried to present tools and data which demonstrate further evidence, that also in the following areas the two ethnicities differ:

- perception of the world,
- conscience,
- LEIC (Location of Emotions, Intellect and Character),
- ethnomusicology and arts,
- the social stratification,
- the historical setting as peasants (Zaza) and nomads (Kurmanji speaking Kurds),
- the manipulation of
  - the Limited Goods,
  - envy,
  - purity and impurity and
- the *Uncertainty Reduction Theory*.

The Third Space theory asks for areas which overcome other areas of struggle. I came up with four areas that would perform social realms of common tasks to find identity different from Zaza / Turkish or Kurmanji nationalism, which causes so much trouble. The areas are:

1. socio-cultural frameworks,
2. ethnomusicological approaches built on arts,
3. Islamic movements,
4. Christian movements.

The most promising area seems to be the socio-cultural framework, although xenophobia often destroys such good approaches. How far religious - Islamic or Christian - methods are helpful seems not to work in the case of the former and the latter does not give enough evidence for proof.

The principles of Islam like *da'awa* (invitation) and *jihad* (struggle) are working strategies to expand the *dar al-Islam* / *dar as-Salam* (house of Islam / Peace) and to convert the *dar al-harb* (House of War as non-Islamic world; 2.3.3.4; 3.4.1.3.4; 3.6.1; 3.6.5; 0). Conversion in the Islamic sense is meant to be a political and religious change into the *umma* (Islamic brotherhood) and the principles of the Islamic Law *Sharia* (Turk.: *şeriat*). The range of methods goes from public promotion (e.g. advertisements, video, talk shows, etc.) to political and military intervention (e.g. Islamic invasions, claim to transference non-Islamic area etc.). In the case of the Zaza people the conversion to Islam overlaid the deeper core values. Animistic, Alevitic and Christian concepts are still active but no longer distinguishable. However the cultural basics are nowadays performed on Islamic education and practice. The religious differences between the Northern Group, practising Alevism and the Southern / Central Group as well as the Eastern Group, practising Islam are enormous. The latter by following the Hanafi school and partially following Shafi'ism. If an orientation towards cultural concepts helps to overcome this gap it is not obvious recently. Such approaches are mainly on the level of authorship, research and mother tongue education in Kindergarden or pre-schools.

Appendices

Appendix 1 Homeland Area of the Zaza

Settlement area of the Northern Group (Northern Zaza) = Tunceli (Dersim)
Settlement area of the Southern Group (Southern Zaza) = Elazığ and south
Settlement area of the Eastern Group (Eastern Zaza) = Bingöl, Mutki, Kulp

(source: I am thankful to http://www.d-maps.com/carte.php?num_car=4146&-lang=de; copyright-free maps).

Appendices 441

Appendix 2a Branch of Indo-European Languages

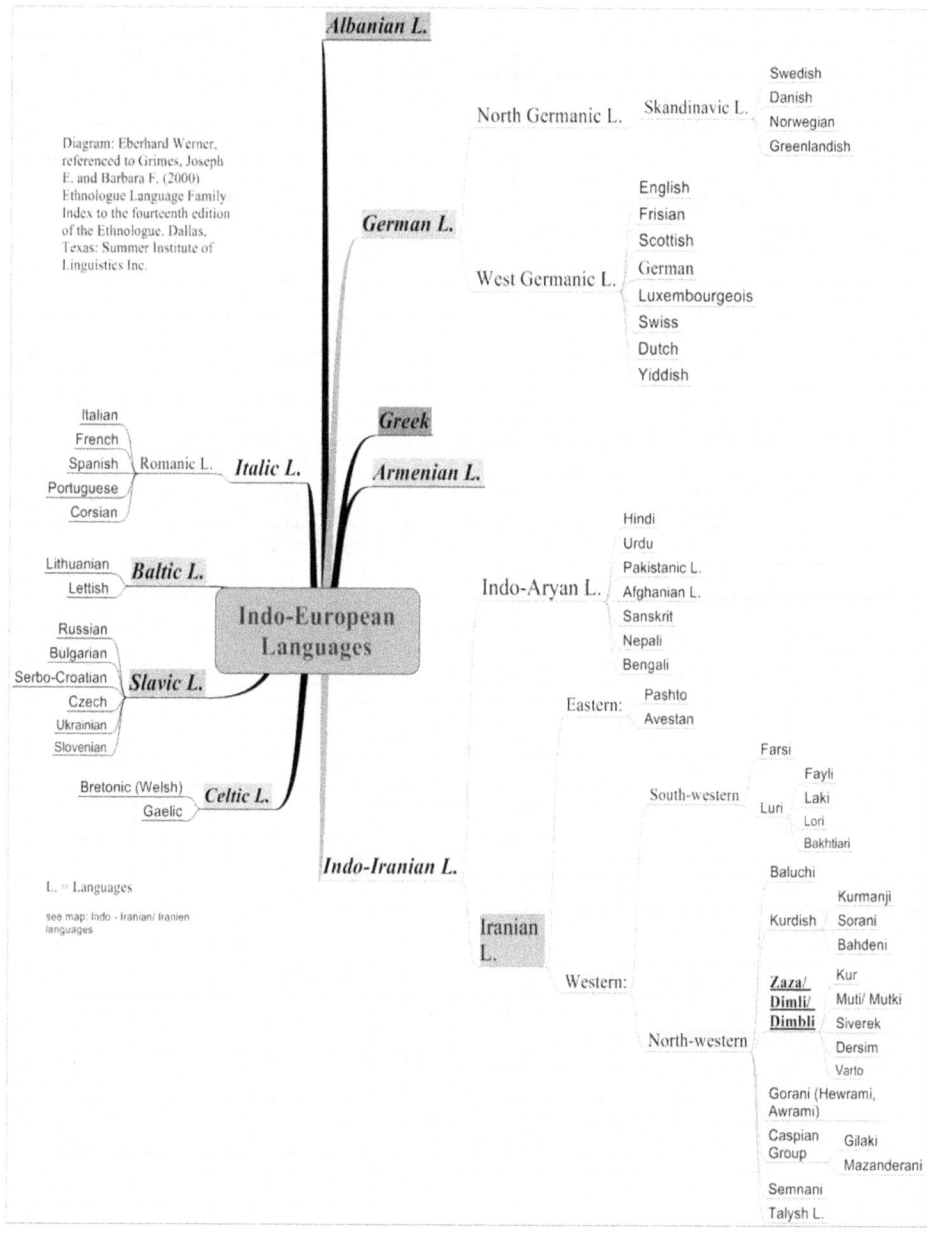

Appendix 2b Branch of Iranian Languages

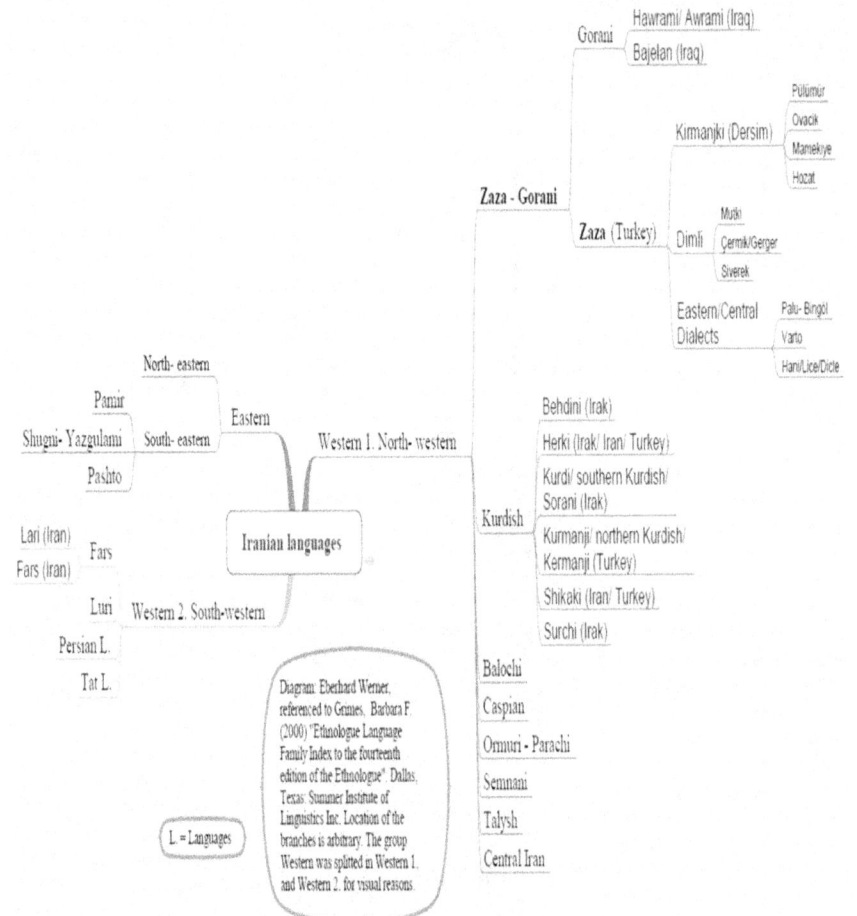

Appendix 3 Extended family-structure - Çermug Area

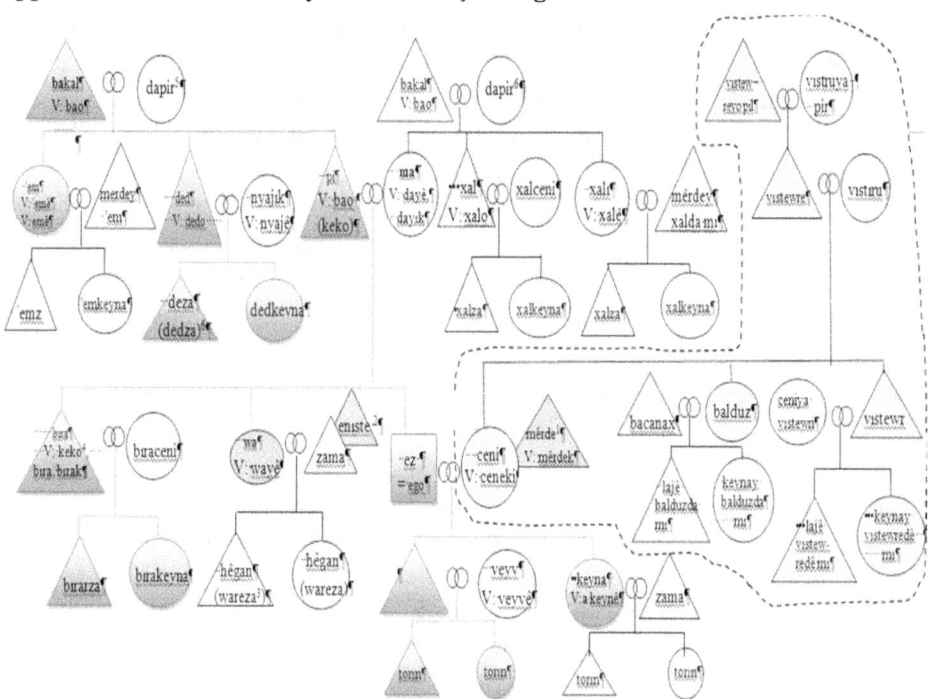

- ⋯ez⋯ → „I" (EGO); masculine
- ◯ feminine
- △ masculine
- ⓐ married
- → paternal bloodline (Zazaki: *çulqle*)
- → of brother-in-law (Zazaki: *kuta waxewra*)
- V: → Vocative, in case it deflects from Nominative

Footnotes:

[1] mèrde → „Husband"; *mèrdey mı* = my husband (if EGO is feminine)
[2] eniste → If EGO is feminine the husband oft he sister ist not called *zama*, but *eniste*.
[3] wareza → Old Zazaki form (in brackets) seldomly used today; *hêgan* is of Turkish origin.
[4] keko → Possible to adress the bigger brother or even the father with.
[5] dapir → The grandma can also be adressed by *dapir* or *dayık, dayê* (see „mother").
[6] deza → The shortcut *deza*, following mother tongue speakers is derived from *ded-za*.

Appendix 4 Chronology of Turkey and her Minority Policy

This text is a translation from Kieser, Hans-Lukas 2000. *Der verpasste Frieden* [Engl. The missed Peace.], 583-588. Zurich: Chronos. (by permission of author).

11th century	*Turkish-Seljuk* penetration into Asia Minor. 1071 victory over Byzantines at Malazgirt, east of Lake Van.
14/15th century	Advancement of the Ottoman dynasty under whose leadership the Turks conquer Asia Minor and the Balkans.
1453	Constantinople becomes the capital of the Ottoman Empire. In *1461* the sultan establishes the *Armenian patriarchy of Constantinople* which, operating under his authority, presides over the *Ottoman Armenian* community (*millet*) from this time on.
16th century	The most important *Kurdish* princes ally themselves with the Ottoman Sultan Selim I. against Shi'ite Persia. The Ottoman state adopts a clearly *Sunni* character. The sultan accepts the autonomy of the Kurdish emirates under his sovereignty. The Ottoman Persian bordering areas remain a topic of discussion between the two powers.
1828	Russia conquers Persian Armenia as well as a tip of the Ottoman South Caucasus.
1830-1831	H. G. O. Dwight and Eli Smith undertake an expedition into Kurdistan and Armenia under the auspices of the *American Board of Commissioners for Foreign Missions* (ABCFM). Their report published in 1833 provides the informational basis for the missionary penetration of that region.
1831	Foundation of the *Roman Catholic Millet* under French backing.
1831-1833	Mehmed Ali of Egypt conquers Ottoman Syria and threatens Asia Minor.
1838	The Ottoman market is opened for British goods.
1839	Ottoman defeat of the Egyptians near Nizip. The European powers intervene in this "Oriental crisis" which touches their Middle Eastern interests. The edict of Sultan Abdulmecid called *Hatt-ı Şerif* of Gülhane goes into effect.
1839-1876	The so-called Ottoman reform era (*Tanzimat*) is heralded which attaches to the previous renewal programme of Sultan Mahmud II. and to certain liberal postulates, for example religious freedom and

the principle of equal rights of the subjects (*Hatt-ı Şerif* und *Hatt-ı Hümayun*).

During the 1830s and 1840s the Ottoman government destroys the Kurdish emirates and employs governors (*Valis*). The Bedir Khans emirate falls in 1847. The Ottoman aim is the modernization and centralization of the empire, particularly the largely autonomous eastern parts of the empire following the French example.

In the second half of the century Sunni sheikhs replace the Emirs and begin ruling over entire tribes, taking on an integrated role in the Kurdish society.

In the newly established eastern provinces, outside of the provincial centres, neither the new administration nor the liberal principles are put into effect. Conditions become chaotic and double taxes are collected from the people (both central state taxes and previous taxes of the Armenian and Kurdish small farmers - *raya* - to local rulers).

In spite of all this, the liberal framework permits a blossoming of the *Millet*-school system. The oriental, particularly Armenian, Christians are promoted by the missionaries. During the 1840s the *ABCFM* and the *Capuchin Monks* start with stations based in the eastern provinces.

1850   The *Protestant Millet*, supported by British diplomacy, splinters off of the *Armenian-Gregorian* and *Greek-Orthodox Church* in 1847 and is confirmed by *ferman* ("order") of the Sultan. In 1854 the ABCFM people formulate a broadly circulating civilian "constitution" of this *Millet* that uses a democratic model.

1856   Shortly before the peace treaty of Paris which put a final stroke under the Crimean War (1853-1856), Sultan Abdulmecid releases *Hatt-ı Hümayun*. This confirms the liberal principles that were announced in *Hatt-ı Şerif* and contributes to the dynamisation of the Protestant movement in the Asia Minor provinces.

1863   The sultan recognizes the new "constitution" of the Armenian Millet which, like the Protestant one, stipulates a chosen representative assembly.

1876   Abdulhamid II. becomes sultan.
Balkanise: Anti-Ottoman rebellions and war with Serbia; the Sub-

	lime Porte gains militarily acceptance. The sultan enacts a constitution which provides parliamentary elections on 23.12.1876.
1877/78	The defeat by Russia in the Balkans and the Muslim streams of refugees traumatize the young sultan. He suspends the constitution and dissolves the parliament. The Russian-Turkish War leads to an interregnum in major parts of the Kurdish-Armenian area of settlement. The reorganization of that region becomes a topic of the Berlin meeting in 1878 under the term "Armenian question". This obliges Turkey to make administrative reforms and to inner protective measures against Kurdish and Circassians acts of violence (article 61 of the *Berlin declaration*). Abdulhamid *and* the by the Tanzimat reforms uncertain Kurds fear for their position of power in the Eastern provinces. Both oppose the demands for international reform because they understand that it will lead to Armenian autonomy and strengthen the Non-Muslims.
1880-1882	Rebellion of the Kurdish Sheikh *Ubeydullah* who refers to national Kurdish rights and requests support of Europe. He fails militarily against the Persians and the Ottomans.
1880s	Out of disappointment over the lack of effective reforms an Armenian revolutionary movement arises: Foundation of the *Hunjak*-Party, 1887 in Geneva and the Dashnak-Party, 1890 in Tbilis.
1881/83	*Dette publique ottoman* and *Régie of the Tabacs*: International committees organize the foreign debt administration by the collection of a part of the Ottoman state revenue (e.g. national bankruptcy in 1875).
1889	Foundation of the *secret committee* of *the Ottoman unity,* the predecessor of the young Turkish Comité Union et Progrès (CUP), inspired patriotically and republican. Muslim students of the military Medical school in Constantinople become members.
1891	Abdulhamid convinces the Kurds to form a central state by creating a privileged position for Sunni tribes. These tribes, called *Hamidiye* regiments, enjoy tax exemption and are not subject to the civilian courts. As a result of Abdulhamid's politics of Islamic Unity together with the Islamic school of Hanafi state loyalty, the nightmare of a general Armenian conspiracy spreads to the villages.

1894	Heavy military oppression of a peasants' revolt that was attempted by a group of *Hunjak* revolutionaries in Sasun. As a result of the brutal repression the reform question is reintroduced into international diplomacy.
Oct.-December 1895	Extensive Anti-Armenian massacre with Kurdish participation (about 100,000 dead in few weeks). Reports from the American Christian developmental aid stations and diplomatic eyewitnesses find their way to the European and North American press. A broad wave of indignation in 1896 spreads far beyond the church, particularly in Switzerland and provides the impetus for the foundation of Armenian relief organizations.
August 1896	After the seizure of the Ottoman Bank in İstanbul by *Daschnak* activists an elaborate massacre takes place at the Armenian Municipality in front of numerous foreign observers.
15.9.1896	A massacre in *Egin* (Kemaliye) at *Harput*, costs the lives of 1,000 Armenians within one day. One man involved in taking over the Ottoman Bank was from Egin, a small town with prosperous Armenian dealers and clothing manufacturers.
1881/83	*Dette publique ottoman* and *Régie of the Tabacs*: International committees organize the foreign debt administration by the collection of a part of the Ottoman state revenue (e.g. national bankruptcy in 1875).
1889	Foundation of the *secret committee* of *the Ottoman unity*, the predecessor of the young Turkish Comité Union et Progrès (CUP), inspired patriotically and republican. Muslim students of the military Medical school in Constantinople become members.
1891	Abdulhamid convinces the Kurds to form a central state by creating a privileged position for Sunni tribes. These tribes, called *Hamidiye* regiments, enjoy tax exemption and are not subject to the civilian courts. As a result of Abdulhamid's politics of Islamic Unity together with the Islamic school of Hanafi state loyalty, the nightmare of a general Armenian conspiracy spreads to the villages.
1894	Heavy military oppression of a peasants' revolt that was attempted by a group of *Hunjak* revolutionaries in Sasun. As a

	result of the brutal repression the reform question is reintroduced into international diplomacy.
Oct.-December 1895	Extensive Anti-Armenian massacre with Kurdish participation (about 100,000 dead in few weeks). Reports from the American Christian developmental aid stations and diplomatic eyewitnesses find their way to the European and North American press. A broad wave of indignation in 1896 spreads far beyond the church, particularly in Switzerland and provides the impetus for the foundation of Armenian relief organizations.
August 1896	After the seizure of the Ottoman Bank in İstanbul by *Daschnak* activists an elaborate massacre takes place at the Armenian Municipality in front of numerous foreign observers.
15.9.1896	A massacre in *Egin* (Kemaliye) at *Harput*, costs the lives of 1,000 Armenians within one day. One man involved in taking over the Ottoman Bank was from Egin, a small town with prosperous Armenian dealers and clothing manufacturers.
1896-1908	Young Turkish, Kurdish and Armenian rebels cooperate in the exile. They condemn the massacre and the Hamitic autocracy and plead for Muslim-Christian solidarity in an article printed in the magazine *Kurdistan* (published in Geneva, 1898).
1905	Local disturbances in the eastern provinces due to the Russian and Iranian revolution. The army was hesitant to help because of pay delays.
1906/7	Foundation of the secret *Ottoman Liberty Committee* in Saloniki which later merges with young Turkish exile organizations to form the *Union et Progrès* in 1907. Most unionists are recruited from young Muslim officers and employees. Mustafa Kemal (Atatürk) is also part of them.
23.7.1908	Reinstatement of the constitution of 1876, thanks to the Young Turkish take-over. This provides hope for a renewal of the Ottoman Empire's glory and for an improvement in its relationship with the minorities. In this the ABCFM sees a central task of contributing to the construction of a democratic and pluralistic multi-national state. The Alevis publicly assert their independent identity again after staying on the sidelines for centuries. The Armenian

	Daschnak forms an alliance with the unionists for the parliamentary elections. Many organizations, motivated by ethics and Kurdish nationalism, are founded. Most Kurdish chieftains, however, remain obliged to the sultan and the common Islamic banner and brace themselves against the new dictators.
	The publicly prior-ranking Unionist aim does not consist of political liberalism but the "restoration of the Ottoman sovereignty." After 1908 the Islamic cohesion of the previous Sunni power carriers is increasingly surmounted by organized *Turkish nationalism*.
Autumn 1908	Bulgaria proclaims its independence (5 October), Austria annexes Bosnia and Herzegovina (6 October), Crete proclaims its annexation with Greece (6 October).
April 1909	An attempted coup by both Islamist and liberal forces against the CUP is suppressed militarily, *Abdulhamid* is removed. As a rescuer "of the revolution" the army strengthens its position.
	Massacres in the *region* of Adana demand numerous mainly Armenian victims. In the eastern provinces brewing *anti-Christian* massacres do not come to violence. Trust between the communities and the new regime is destroyed. The Unionists tighten their power personally and legally and start a policy of *Turkish-Cultural Unification*.
1911-1913	Tripolis War and Balkan Wars.
23.1.1913	A coup d'état leads unionist hardliners (Enver, Cemal, Talat) to dictatorship.
8.2.1914	Adoption of an international plan for the reform of the six eastern provinces ("Armenian reforms"): Official recognition of the regional languages, disarming of the *Hamidiye*, international control.
2.8.1914	Secret *German-Turkish* alliance five days after WWI started: As a price for participating in the war the regime gets the opportunity to claim full sovereignty and therefore to annul the Armenian reforms. The army surrenders and faults the economy (*Dette Publique*). The mobilization of troops and requisitions hit the eastern provinces hard.

14.11.1914	Declaration of Jihad after the beginning of the war of aggression against Russia.
January 1915	The major Caucasus offensive of *Enver Pasha* becomes a military and human catastrophe at *Sarıkamış* (nearly 90,000 fall, primarily Kurdish) and contributes to the spreading of epidemics in the eastern provinces. The Russian army penetrates into the northeastern tip of the country.
After Feb. 1915	The war regime organizes a sweeping propaganda disparaging the Armenians as traitors and conspirators. Armenian soldiers in the Ottoman army are disarmed. At the end of April the Armenian elites are protracted and murdered in the whole of Asia Minor.
As of June 1915	Systematic "deportations" of the Armenians from the whole of Anatolia are organized using telegraph communication: Separation and systematic murder of the men; Destruction of the majority of the women and children on death marches to the Syrian desert; systematic assignment of Armenian property to the state and to the Muslim population. Dersim Kurds grant thousands of victims of the persecution asylum while many other Sunni Kurds are actively participating in decimating the Armenians. The deportations are part of a gigantic plan of ethnic redesign of Asia Minor to lay the base for an ethnic Turkish nation-state.
Autumn 1915	Foundation of predecessor organizations of the *Near East Relief* in the USA. These improvise a cross-denominational emergency assistance effort in cooperation with the remaining missionaries and diplomats in the Asia Minor provinces.
From 1916	Hundreds of thousands of Kurds are also affected by the evacuation measures of the regime. They shall be wrapped up "in Turkism" scattered throughout Anatolia (see Jakob Künzler). Bad organization leads many to die from hunger, cold or epidemics.
As of November 1917	The Bolshevists order the retreat from the northeast of Turkey (Erzincan, Erzurum). Yet the Armenians settled under Russian protection do not persevere in Turkey. Armenian gangs are responsible for repulsive atrocities.

28.5.1918	Foundation of the independent republic of Armenia with its centre at Yerevan. The unpopular Unionist war regime again manages to instigate the Kurds to mobilize for themselves, by stirring up the fear of a possible extensive Armenian state which would contain a part of the Kurdish area. Exiled Armenians actually cherish such ideas while the allied representatives do not take a clear position.
30.10.1918	Truce agreement of Mudros between Ottomans and Allies.
Spring/summer 1919	Return of the missionaries to parts of the eastern provinces. The *Barton Relief Commission, King Crane Commision* and *Harbord Mission* as investigating committees with missionary connections request that the USA commit itself to the long-term development of Asia Minor and particularly its eastern parts. Clarence D. Ussher's plan for a repatriation of Armenian and Kurdish refugees into the major parts of eastern provinces finds no audience at the Parisian peace talks.
15.5.1919	Greek occupation of Izmir. The indignation about it contributes to the construction of a Muslim defensive front under the leadership of *Mustafa Kemal Pasha* (Atatürk). It traces back to local Unionist organizational units and constitutes itself first in the administratively intact eastern provinces as an Anti-Armenian front. It wins the support of most Sunni Kurdish leaders, mainly because of their participation in the genocide, thinking it best to keep their interests in a federation with the Unionist Kemalists. Cf. conventions of Erzurum (23.7. - 6.8.1919) and Sivas (4.-13. 9. 19919).
1.6.1919	The American senate rejects the political mandate over Armenia.
9.4.1920	The Kemalists defeat the French troops in Urfa.
23.4.1920	Disclosure of the *Great National Assembly* in Ankara as a counter parliament to the Sublime Porte.
10.8.1920	Treaty of Sèvres between the Sublime Porte and the Allies. It prescribes parts of the Ottoman eastern provinces as an independent Armenia and an independent Kurdistan. Moreover, the region of Izmir is awarded to Greece and a stripe of Northern Mesopotamia to France.

	In opposition to such "imperialistic wheelings and dealings" in Paris, the Kemalists and Bolshevists agree to a friendship pact in Moscow on 24. 8. 1920.
23.9.1920	The first Kemalist lead offensive against Armenia: Until December the offensive focuses on conquest of the western part of former Russian Armenia. Later the Eastern Part is invaded by the Red Army (6. 12. 1920). The Kemalist-Bolshevist friendship pact from 16.3.1921 respects the Turkish annexations.
Jan.-June 1921	A further Kemalist offensive is lead against the Alevi Kurds in the *Koçgiri*-Dersim region. These groups fight as one because of the Kurdish independence fixed in Sèvres.
1921/22	Definite expulsion of missionaries from the eastern provinces by the Unionist-Kemalist authorities.
1.11.1922	Abolition of the Sultanate.
24.7.1923	In the *treaty of Lausanne* between the Allies and the Kemalists, the Allies accept the status quo of the Turkey that Muslim nationalists have created in Asia Minor in the interest of a normalization of their relations. The document hides the Kurdish and Armenian question. The Armenian homestead and Kurdish autonomy disappear as a topic of international diplomacy - not least because Turkey is already one factor *avant la lettre* in the discrepancies between Russia and the West that is the later Cold War.
29.10.1923	Proclamation of the *Republic of Turkey*. The Kemalists' promise to establish Kurdish autonomy is broken in favour of a centralist united state.
3.3.1924	Abolition of the Caliphate.
Febr. 1925	The Kurdish Naqshebendi Sheikh *Said* from Palu leads a rebellion against the young republic in the name of Islam and the Kurdish nation. The Alevi Kurds do not participate. With great effort and logistical support (iron rail transport) from the French mandatory power in Syria the government manages to suppress the rebellion in early summer. From this time on it is the main task of the Turkish army to keep the Kurds quiet, maintaining a long-term state of emergency. Economic and

	cultural development of major parts of the Eastern region is not taking place. The state continues with the Unionist policy of coercive resettlements.
March-Nov. 1925	Parallel to the Anti-Kurdish repression, the regime meets antidemocratic and antireligious arrangements: Special authorities, Special courts, Press curb, Ban of opposition parties and Ban on religious orders, facilities and clothes. Only the remarks of Sunnism steered by the state are allowed in the public domain. An ideological base of the republic becomes the "Turkish ideal", which is a secular and ethnocentric *Turkish nationalism*. The words "Kurd" and "Kurdistan" start to be ostracized.
1926-1930	The leader state with a united party passes drastic, progressive reforms from above, such as the adoption of the western calendar (26.12.1925), the Swiss code of civil law (17.2.1926), the Latin script (1.11.1928) and women's suffrage (3. 4. 1930).
1927-1930	The organization *Hoybûn* (Hoyboon), founded in Lebanon, rallies the Kurdish nationalistic strength and cooperates with the Armenian *Daschnak*. It participates in the Ararat rebellion which is suppressed in 1930 by the Turkish army under Iranian help.
1937-1938	Ethnocide in the Kurdish Alevi Dersim: Massacre and coercive resettlement of many thousands who fought against the military penetration and Turkishization of Dersim under the leader *Seyit Rıza*. The leaders of Dersim appeal in vain to the League of Nations and to western diplomacy.
10.11.1938	Death of Mustafa Kemal Atatürk.
1940s and 50s	Time of the "Kurdish silence" in Turkey. The self-censorship of Kurdish families who move to the towns from the country is the reason that numerous children no longer learn their mother tongue correctly.
1947	The Truman doctrine of *anticommunist containment* makes Turkey an important ally of the USA and strengthens the position of the Turkish armed forces (a NATO member since 1952). This constellation of support makes it possible for the Turkish diplomacy to perpetuate the denial of the genocide of the Armenians. The political corset, being supported from out-

side, prevents the internal developments of civilian companies, democracy and pluralism. At that time a formulated belief in the progress of modern Turkey by orientalists like Bernard Lewis delivers the historiographical background of this policy vis-à-vis the allies.

For the 1960s years	The Armenian question "rises from the dead as a Kurdish question" (Hasan Reşid Tankut, Türk Tarih Kurumu, 1961).

Appendix 5 Mewlid Nebi – Birthday Poem of the Prophet

Ellay dayena Pêxemberi	The Birthday of the Prophet
(Biyayena Pêxemberi)	(The Being of the Prophet)
(Mewlidê Nebi)	(*Mewlid*[90] of the Prophet)
Osman Efendi	Osman Efendi

Bı namey wahêrê no erd u azmin,	In the name of the Lord of Heaven and Earth,
Kı ma dest kerd bı no gırwedo rengin.	We have created a powerful (colorful) masterpiece.
Şıma hemdê xo Ellay rê biyarin,	You all give thanks to the Lord,
Şew u roj qaydey ey dı bıqarin.	Day and Night he brought to conclusion certainly.
Pêxemberi rê selawati biyarin,	Take to the Prophet the Confession of faith,
Tım u tım derdê cey ver dı bınalin.	Moaning all the time because of all his pain.
Misalê nayıni zanê tı merdım!	This example is well known to you mankind!
Tı cıtêrı nê gırwey toxım,	You farmer who sows the seed,
Kı to zana kı, duniya senino,	You have known how the world is,
Bızanê a dıni cayê cıwêniyo.	You know the other World; it is a place full of riches.[91]
Wedaro ey cıtêr, çıçiy bıkarro!	The farmer reaps what he has sowed!
Kı cıtêr çıçiy karrıt, ey wedaro.	For what the farmer sows, so shall be his harvest!
Beso tewbe biyarên, hey xedarin!	Better for you to repent, oh cruel ones!
Dıni dı toxımê hewli bıkarrin!	Sow everlasting seed for the other World!
Gunadê xo rê rayi bın bınalin!	Let the sins be cast off (underfoot)!
Bırışyin hersi çıman ra bık abın.	Let the teardrops fall.
Bıbo 'ef u gunay mayo kı vêrdo,	May forgiveness be granted for our sin, for she is gone,
Gunakaro kı hersê xori gırêdo.	The sinner discards the rage of his youth.
Selawat bıwanên rınd u bolli,	Read the prayer of the Prophet often and accurately,
Bırasnê pêdıma qandê Resuli.	Following the *Resul* (the Prophet).
Kam kı adıri ra xelas xo rê wast,	*He, who wants to escape from the fire (of Hell),*
Wa bıwanin Ehmedi rê esselat.	*Read Ehmed's (the Prophet) confession of faith.*[92]
Zew hikayet qal keran to rê, bıra,	Brother, let me tell you a story,
Qedrê Mewlıdi bızanı tı cı ra.	Value the worth of the birthday poem.

---

[90] Poem by Süleyman Celebi on the Birthday of the Prophet – hereby referred to as Birthday-Poem (2.3.3.5.2).

[91] Literally the "threshing floor" as an allegory of the rich farmer's prosperity.

[92] The proper name *Ahmed/Ehmed* here and later forms a synonym to *Resul* (envoy) or *Pêxember* (the prophet), which stands for Hz. Muhammad. The term *esselat* equals *selawat* (also a rhyme format).

Bexdadi miyan dı bi ceniyin,	There once was a woman from Bagdad,
Zeydê cay nêdi bi kes erbabê din.	The likes of whom was not to be found anywhere.
A ceni rê da bı, *Resul Alemin*,	The woman was given, the Messenger of all mankind,
Lajekêndo salih u ehli yeqin.	A son of prosperity open to all mankind.
Çaxo may merd, mend altunêdê cey,	One day when the mother died, only Gold remained,
Lajeki altun gırot, bı warısey.	Taking the Gold, the son, however, remained an orphan.
Labayê vatên, bı ney çıçiy bêro.	He then said: "What shall I buy with it?"
Ez bı riyê inan şaş biyan, ya Rebbena!	I wonder what shall I do, oh Lord!
Tım bı no fıkıra ez şiya aşt u naşt,	Because of this dilemma I went back and forth,
Waneyayên cayên dı Mewlıd ame raşt.	Somewhere, somehow the Prophet's Birthday Poem would be read properly.
Dine kerd Mewlidê, o roj ey temam,	On that day he heard the Mewlid, properly, for the first time
Hewnê di, a şew qılayaya qeyam.	He dreamt, on this night that the world perished.[93]
Zew zi vatên e'hli Mewlidê, sela,	There is a saying regarding the Prophet's Birthday Poem, *sela*,
Rew şıma bêrên bı cennet ca bı ca.	Soon, from all corners of the world, you will enter paradise.
Ez zi kewtan zerre, va ê lajeki,	I also entered it, says the boy,
Hım uja koşkêndo berzo rınd mı di.	I also saw a huge palace there.
Va mı zerri kerd şıran koşki miyan,	I wanted to enter the palace,
İta cayê to niyo, va bekçiyan.	This place is not for you, the guardians answered.
Kami kı Mewlidê Nebi da wendenı,	Whoever reads the Prophet's Birthday Poem,
Wa bıbo no qesro 'Ali cayê cı.	The highly exalted palace shall be his place.
Çaxo kı aya bi, arina bı ey peran,	Thereafter, waking up, he used his gold (money),
Qandê Mewlidê Nebi boll goşt u nan.	For the sake of the Mewlid, much meat and bread.[94]
Hadıre kerd zad u veynda çend peyan,	He prepared the person[95] and sent for many protectors,
Wend inan Mewlid, va nêvıst berey.	They read the Mewlid, but not too late.
Hurgı serr no tarza va ê serweri,	Every year in this fashion, says the Leader,
Wendı mewlidı, kerdi sa pêxemberi.	They read the Mewlid, they were pleased with the Prophet!

---

[93] This is a comparison with the development of the Bible or the handover of the Qur'an. Literally: "In this night humankind heard it" (türk. duydu insanlik).

[94] In an idiomatic sense: "The Mewlid is only a small contribution of Islam in comparison to the Qur'an or the Tesfil (Commentary to Qur'an)."

[95] *Zad*: a (religious) person.

Çaxo 'ecel ame, di ê hadıran,	When the hour of death drew near, the attendees saw it,
O bı kêf u bı huwate da bı gan.	He laughing and rejoicing as he gave his soul.[96]
Kesi ferq nêkerd kı merdo, va o ciwan,	Nobody recognized that the boy was dead,
Jew va rışto, va hekimên ard inan.	One they sent for a doctor.
Çön hekiman di kı, merdo va, şıma,	The doctor saw that he was dead, saying,
Pey nêzanın merdo no merdım, bıra.	"Does not any of you recognize that this person is dead, my brothers?!"
Va no razi kerdo Rebbul Alemin,	"This one satisfied him, Lord of all Humans!"
Aferin no haldê ney rê aferin!	"Bravo, for this behavior praise be to him!"
Çımi akerdi lajeki, va ey di ma,	The boy opened his eyes: He saw us,
Meskenê xo dı mı cennet di neka.	From my spot I now saw paradise.
Çunki hurgı serrı mın Mewlıdê cey	Every year that the Prophet's Birthday Poem,
Wend, biyan cennet dı enbıryanê ey	I read, and became his neighbor in Paradise.
Wenden dı, hem bıwanın va şıma,	Let it be read and then you will read,
Hurgı Mewlıdi bıyarın rınd bı ca.	Everything which was in the Prophet's Birthday Poem, implement it the right way.
Ey hına va u terıkna na dıni,	Thus sayeth He, leaving world,
Ganê xo resna cennet di bı, ê Nebi.	His body entering Paradise, he is the Prophet.
Çunkı Mewlidi rê hurmet kerd bı ey,	The Prophet's Birthday Poem is praised,
Bıbı cennet mesken u hem cayê cey.	Paradise became his residence and place to stay.
Ey cema'etin şıma zi serr bı serr,	Hey, you people, every year,
Qedrê Mewlıdi bızanên serr bı serr.	You shall value the Prophet's Birthday Poem.
Sa kerê nê sultanê hurna dıni,	Rejoice over the Sultan of the Worlds,
Tabi bı cennet dı enbazê Nebi.	Surely in Paradise everyone will be a friend of the Prophet.
Ya Xuda, noyo receyê ma rusiyan,	O God, it is he who pronounces our pleas as guilty,[97]
'Ef kerê ma u bırasnên tı inan.	Forgive us and draw us near to you.
A dıni u na dıni dı di necat,	*In this and the next world face forgiveness,[98]*
Kam kı wend pêxemberi rê esselat.	*He who reads it, focuses the ritual prayer on the Prophet.*

---

[96] This refers to the Islamic Angel of Death called *'azrail*. Following tradition, this Angel of Death *'azrail*, was asked by Hz. Mohammed during his call to paradise not to be too cruel to him. Instead he asked him (the Angel of Death) to cover his appearance and take people undetected. The men of Hz. Mohammed would therefore not be scared and discouraged about his death (tradition in the *Tesfil*, a well recognized historical commentary to the Qur'an).
[97] *Riyê to rusyo vo*, "You blamed yourself".
[98] *Necatê mı vo*. 'Forgive me.'

Goşê xo sernên cema'etê, Rebbê ma,
Kerdi xezney xo miyani eşkera.

Kaf u nuni ardi pêhet, emrê kerd,
Bıbı icat erd u azmin, germ u serd.

Nurdê xo ra kerd nurê Ehmedi,
Ê nuri ra xelq kero Muhammedi.

Be'edê (bahdê) cey Adem xelıqna herrı ra
Ame o nur, çaredê ey dı ruwa.

Be'edo Hewa bibi peyda, ame rew,
Çare dı vınderdı, zeydê menga new.

Be'edo ame pê dıma o nur resa,
Kalıkê Ehmedi dı, bi eşkera.

Kalıkê ey va kı Ebdulmutalib!
Bı semedê des laji, ya Reb, ya 'Hebib!

Rayda to dı ez zewi qurban keran,
Ta mı rê verdê illahi ê newan.

Ey kerem di, xo ra Ellay da bı ey,
Pê dıma va bi, cı rê des lajê cey.

Ke'be dı ronışt u venda çend peyan,
Va kı ez do wahdê xo rê ca bıdan.

Qure bıerzê va cema'etê xo rê,
Taa kı nê gırwi, bı qure sax kerê.

Qure eşt u kewt bı Ebdullahi ser,
Razi nêbi ney rê, cem'ato bêxeyr.

Va senin razi bê ney rê serweri,
O do bıbo piyê nê Pêxemberi.

Open up the ears of the people, Oh our Lord,
He reveals the treasurer to us.

The letters "Kaf" and "Nun" he brought together, and he commanded,
He created Heaven and Earth, heat and cold.

His light flowed over to the light of *Ehmedi* (the Prophet),
Of this light *Mohammed* was to be created.

After that he created *Adam* out of earth,
From his forehead the light shone, taking root and sprouting there.[99]

After that *Eva* followed, coming with great speed,
On the forehead the light perched, waiting for ninth months.

After that the light came which enveloped him,
The grandfather of *Ehmed* (the Prophet), understood it.

His grandfather said: "*Abdulmutalib!*"[100]
For the sake of ten sons, oh Lord, oh God![101]

To follow in your way, I will sacrifice one,
But please, for the love of God spare me the other nine.

He saw the wonder, granted to him from God,
One after another, he granted him ten sons.

He sat in the *Ka'aba* (in Mecca) and called some of his protectors,
He said I will accomplish my prayer wishes.[102]

Draw lots for your people,
Until such a time as this subject is determined properly by lots.

He drew lots and it pointed to Abdullah (the Prophet; Servant of God),
But they were not satisfied, this gathering of evil.

In what way should the leaders be content with the outcome?,
He will be the father of the Prophet.

---

[99] The symbol of a sprouting branch characterizes spiritual vital energy.
[100] Name of Hz. Muhammads uncle.
[101] Arabic *Hebib* describes a friend / confidant or God (only in religious context).
[102] Arabic *wahi* means „Words" (*qısey*).

Appendices

Va peyanê hadıran, dest bıdê ey,	You attendees, pass him your hand,
Cadê ey dı ronım ma des devey.	We will lay down ten camels instead of him.
Des fini no tarza qure erziya,	Ten times the lot were drawn with the same way result,
Hurgı des, namedê ey dı vıjiya.	All the ten times, his name was drawn.
Fına zondesi kı eşt qure inan,	Finally, at the eleventh time they drew the lots,
Qure nofin kewt bı namey ê devan.	The lot at this time fell on the names of the camels.
Çend devey va duz bi, şırê qurbani rê,	Some camels (all) in one row, went to the sacrifice,
Kerd bı qurban ey devan, vanê cı rê.	The camels were sacrificed, for him.
Çaxo kı devey bi qurban, Ellay resa,	At this moment when the camels were sacrificed, God appeared,
Pêro vıjan (vıjiyay) va kı no gırwe reya.	All those whom he appeared thought that it is now accomplished (salvation).
Kam kı adıri ra xelas xo rê wast,	*He who wants to be saved from the fire (of Hell),*
Wa bıwanin Ehmedi rê esselat.	*Oh he should read the prayer to* Ehmed[103] *(the Prophet).*
Ta kı Abdullah resa bı, wastê kın,	When Abdullah entered into adulthood, he requested
Ardı ey rê cayêndo boll rınd ra keynekên.	A beautiful girl from a prosperous region brought to him.[104]
Name Emina bi, xo boll rınd bi,	The name was *Emina*, she was very kind,
Nêresayê nengudê ay keynekên zi.	Not even the nail of a finger of the other girls could touch her.[105]
Da bı pêr malêndo boll u veyve kerd,	His father having a large estate property and held the wedding,
Gırd u werdi werd, keyandê xo rê berd.	The big and the small had eaten; enough remained to bring home leftovers.
Pêhet amey ê, şewênda xeyrı dı	They met in the Holy Night,
Va, mırazê xo gırot, zew bı dıdı.	His wish came to be, one has become two.
Emina va, a şew ame vengı mı rê,	*Emina* said: During this night a voice came to me,
Va kı, ganê to bı dı'ha (duwa) Ehmedi rê.	The voice said that your body is a prayer to *Ehmed* (the Prophet).
Nê serri ra verdê wextın, ey bıra!	Before those years, anytime, o brother!
Dı şewin hewni di, Xeyri Ebdullah.	Two nights he had dreams, *Xeyri Abdullah*[106].
Di kı darên paştida ey ra vıjiya,	He saw, how a tree growing out of his back,
Gılê ey, zeft (zept) kerdo no dınya, bıra.	His branch ruled over the whole earth, brother.

---

[103] Hz. Muhammad (Hz. Muhammed).
[104] For marrying her.
[105] The other girls were unable to hold a candle to Emina.
[106] Worthy – *xeyr* - Servant of God – *Abd Allah*.

Çunki şewra bı, şı Ebdullah jewi,
Va cırê, mın emşo hewnê xeyri di.

Hewnê xo qal kerd ey merdımi rê,
Hewnê cey tebir kerd merdımi cı rê.

Paştida to ra va beno lajên teber,
O do bıbo dınya dı raşt pêxember

O Resulo, ê gılê ze şerʻe cey,
Perrê dari ze heme ommeta cey.

Va Emina, hurgı serr dı se kera?
Ame vengên, to dı esto Mustafa.

Adem ame, va mı rê menga verên,
Va, Emina to nıka di dewletên.
Ame menga dıdını dı Şit, bıra,
Pizedê mı rê sılamên ard bi ca.

Ame menga hırını İdris, deza,
Va, werrekê mın bı tiya Emina!

Ame Nuh, menga çıʻhari bêguman,
Va kı, pizey to yo waʻhêrê Qurʼan.

Ame menga panci Hud va Emina,
Pizeyê to yo ʻHebibê Rebbê ma.

Ame menga şeşi İbrahim Xelil,
Va, lajê to bıbo ma rê delil.

Ame menga hewti İsmail bı zemin,
Va kı, Lajê to Muhammed neslê mın.

Ame menga heşti Musa va bızan,
Lajê to pêxemberê axır zeman.

Ame menga newi İsa ba (bı) ʻedeb,
Va kı, Lajê to bıbo mirul ʻEreb.

Kam kı wazeno gunay cı ʼef bıbo,
Wa bıwano Ehmedi rê esselat.

Va Emina çen (çend) new mengi bi temam,
Ame xayıb ra melekê da selam.

It was morning, when Abdullah went,
I had good dreams last night.

He told another man about the dream,
The man interpreted his dream to him.

Out of your back will come a son (as help),
He will be a true prophet.

He is the Messenger, this branch is like his people,
The leaves of the tree are like his brothers in faith.

Emina said: In all these years, what shall I do?
A voice came out: You are pregnant with *Mustafa* (the Prophet).

Adam came, and he told me last month,
He said: "*Emina*, now you found your refuge."
It came during the second month of *Schit* [107], oh brother,
My womb was greeted.

During the third month *Idris*, cousin,
"My example, you are mine, *Emina*!"

In the fourth month *Nuh*, without doubt.
"Your womb is the Master of Qurʼan".

In the fifth month *Hud*, said *Emina*,
Your womb (inner parts) is from the root of our Lord.

It came the sixth month *Abraham Xelil*,
He said: "Your son will serve as proof to us."

In the seventh month *Ismael*, as the surface of earth,
He said: "Your son Mohammed is my descendant/breath."

It came the eight month *Moses*, you should know,
Your son is the last prophet for all.

It came the ninth month Jesus with admiration,
He said: "Your son will be the ruler of the Arabs."

Whoever wants forgiveness of his sins,
Go on, he shall read the Prophet's prayer.

Emina thought that nine months were enough,
An angel came as a miracle and greeted her.

---

[107] All the following names of Months are proper names.

Appendices

Va, werrekê mın bı tiya Emina!
Hay bı to bo, dewletên emşo deya.

Emşo beno to ra menga çarêsi,
Zeydê cey dunya dı nêdi qet kesi.

Name da cı Heq Te'ala Emina,
Ehmed u Mehmud u Muhammed Mustafa.

Va, mı di hirê meleki eşkera,
Hurgı jewi dest dı bayraq bıra.

Jewi berd mexrib u jewi zi rojhılat,
Jewi Ke'ebi ser dı daçıkna (denışkna) bı raşt.
Boll meleki zi inandır (inan dı) bi bızan,
Keyey ma zey ke'ebi tewaf kerdên inan.

Ez bı no hal dı biyan, amey mı di,
Qapi (kêveri) ra kewti zerre hirê ceni.

Ju cı ra Hewa, ceniya Adem Nebi,
Ju zi Asiya, ceniya Fir'ewni bi.

Ju zi maya İsay bi, Meryem namey ay,
Ez seni vazan bı to rındeya cay.

Hurgı jew ronıştı kıştêda mın,
Qarşu dı vınderdı jew xızmetê mın.

Perdeyê çımandê mın wedariya,
Boll 'ecêbi di mın, o çax eşkera.

Huriyê cenneti ameyê şiyên,
Tayın temaşa, tayın xızmet diyên.

Ez biyan teyşan u pizeyê mın veşa,
Aw inan ra wast u mın, inan zi dê.

Zeydê vewra sıpe serd u tam şeker,
Mın şımıt, kewtan zi bıxo hem bêxeber.

He said: "You are my example *Emina*!"
This news goes to you, in this night a world was born[108].
In this night for you there is the fourteenth month,
Like him nobody ever was seen on earth.

Lord-God gave them the name, *Emina*,
Ehmed and *Mehmud* and *Muhammed Mustafa*.

He said: "I have revealed three angels,
Each of them had a flag in his hand, oh brother."

One carried it to the North, another to the South,
Another ran it up on top of the *Ka'aba* [109] (in Mecca).
Also many angels were with them, you should know,
They made our home like the Ka'aba, a place for lamentation.

In this state I froze, as I saw their coming,
Through the door three women entered.

One of them was *Eve*, the spouse of the prophet *Adam*,
The other was *Ayshe*, the spouse of the Pharao.

Another one was the mother of *Jesus*, named *Mary*,
How can I express her beauty to you?

For every individual person who sat beside me,
It was one who stood opposition to me, that being my servant.

The curtain before my eyes fell, [110]
In public I saw strange things.

The virgins of Paradise came and went,
Some observed, while others served.

I was thirsty and my stomach burnt,
I longed for water and they handed it to me.

Like white snow, cold and sugar-sweetened flavor,
I drank, and slept without any disturbance.

---

[108] Meant is the Prophet.
[109] Kaaba (or Qaaba; Arabic: الكعبة al-Ka'bah; English: The Cube).
[110] The concept behind is that a human is not able to see God, because his countenance is covered by a curtain permanently. This is the same concept as in the Hebrew Bible.

Be'edo (bah'do) teyrên amê, dest eşt paştiya mın,
Va vıleyna paşt u aşt u naştê mın.
Ame dınya, a se'at sultanê din,
Nurê dı xerq bı (gum bı) va no 'erd u azmin.
'Hemme mexluqê dıni venda u va:
Merheba to rê Muhammed Mustafa!
Merheba ey melhemê pizey kulan!
Merheba ey serwerê pêxemberan!
Merheba kani şefa'et, merheba!
Tı bı xeyr amey, to rê se merheba!

Merheba ey tı recaciyê ma rusiyan!
Merheba dermanê qelbê nêweşan!

Merheba ey mexzenê şer'ı Rebbi!
Merheba ey serwerê hurna dıni!

Merheba ey nurê çımê Hommetan!
Merheba pêxemberê axır zeman!

Merheba ey tı imamê Enbiyan!
Merheba ey tı delilê Ewliyan!

A şew kı Ehmed ame na dıni,
'Erd u azmin mujde (mıjdiyani) dê, va jewbini.
Va, inan kêf kerd u vatên hurgı jew,
Hemdullillah ame ma rê menga new.

Ke'ebe va, a şew kêfan ra reqıs kerd,
Kerdı kêf Ellay rê wextên secde kerd.

Ame azmin ra melekê bêguman,
Va, inan ard jew ibrıq, ju legan.

After that a bird came, he laid his hand on my back,
He massaged my back hither and yon.

At that moment came the Sultan in the world,
Immersed into (divine) light were the heaven and earth.
The whole creation shouted and said:
"Welcome *Mohammed Mustafa* (the Prophet)!"
Welcome oh curer of stomach ulcer,
Welcome to the leader of the prophets!
Welcome, *kani şefa'et*, welcome.
You are gratefully welcomed, be greeted a thousand times.

Welcome, he who advocates the ashamed before God,
Welcome, to the one who is our medicine for the broken hearted.[111]

Welcome, originator of the *şeriat* of God, (religious law),
Welcome leader of this world and the afterlife.

Welcome, light to the eyes of the congregation of Hz. Mohamed,
Welcome Prophet to the whole earth.

Welcome, teacher (Imam) of all prophets!
Welcome, you proof to the Saints!

In this night, the Prophet was born to the world,
Heaven and Earth gave each other the Good News, told it to each other.
"They rejoiced and each one said:
The Prophet came to us after nine months."

The Ka'aba sagte: "In this night they danced for joy,
They rejoiced before God and fell on their knees".

From heaven a real angel came,
"They carried a pitcher of water and a bowl (for ritual cleansing)."

---

[111] Merhaba functions here as an invocation on the Prophet or "God; Help!"

Zewi gırot bı, destê dı dısmalên herir,
Barek Ellah fike ya Bedr el Munir!

Ê meleki va bı awda kewseri,
Pak şıt ganê ê Pêxemberi.

Va İnan ard morê Pexemberi,
Na miyaneya, qolunca dı vıst berey.

Ta inan mor kerd, cayê mori ra,
Lailaillellah va neqışna.

Bı çınayê cenneti pışt qundaxê cey,
Eştı dısmalên bı serdê rıdê ey.

Cayên dı rona, ew bı izet, ey bıra!
'Heyretên boll di bı ma gırwey hına.

Çaxo akerdi hurna çımi Emina,
Nêdi dorkoşeydê xo dı ay, Nebi.
Zerre amê geyrê, nêdi lajê xo.
'Hersi rışnay va: "No gırwe do se bo?

Naştı, aştı çımi çarnay di Nebi,
Cayêndo tenha dı kerdo secdeyê Rebbi.

Va ruyê xo hetê Ke'ebi kerdı bı ey,
Rebbi ra kerdên reca ommeta xo.

Hey xedarın, ya şıma vanê kı ma
Ommeta Pêxemberan bi, zuri ra.

Hey xedarın ya senin, zuri niyo ê bêheya!
Çewresın, ma reca kerdi Rebbi ra.

Umrê ma resa bı çewres, zalimın!
Nêşınê ma rayda raştı ra va mın.

One took it, in one hand a wonderful fine cloth,
Upion which was written: *"Barek Ellah fike ya Bedr el Munir!"*[112]

This angel, he said, with heavenly (holy) water,
Washed the body of the prophet.

"They brought the seal of the Prophet,
They stroked the back smoothly (taking their time)."

They sealed the site of the seal, there they
Tinkered *"lailallella"*.

They clothed him with a Heavenly dress,
They covered his countenance with a cloth.

They laid him somewhere and he was honored, oh brother!
The surprise was immense, oh such deeds!

At the moment when the eyes of *Emina* opened,
She did not see him at her side, the Prophet.
She entered and walked around, but she could not find her son.
Her eyes watered (she cried): "Just, what is happening?"

Her eyes wandered hither and yon, she saw the Prophet,
But he had been praying (doing penance) in a quiet place.

He oriented his face towards the Ka'aba,
Asking God for help on behalf of the religious community.

Oh Cruel ones, you say that we are,
The Prophets congregation of faith, but this is a true lie.

Oh you Cruel ones, what is this? It is not just a lie, it is shameless!
As long as the Forty (days), we pleaded forgiveness from the Lord.

Our lives continue up until forty (years), oh Cruel,
I say, we are not following the right path.

---

[112] Literally: Blessing of God and *Bedr* to *Munir*!

Arêbên pêser, bınalın, ey bıra! Hım bıyarên tewbe, ta 'ef bê şıma.	Come together, bend down, oh brother! Repent and forgive each other.
Ey dıma boll nêşi, va kı pêrê cey, 'Ecel ame, merdo, Pêxember bı sey.	Many haven't followed him, said his father, His time (and end) has come, he died and the Prophet has became an orphan.
Be'edo may zi merd, bıra va ey dıma, Yetım verday, ta kı bı çewres, resa.	After that his mother died, after him, brother, He remained parentless, until he turned forty.[113]
Ta bı çewres serrı, Ellay da bı ey, Kerd bi in'am va cı rê Pêxemberey.	Up until his 40th year, that God gave to him, He elevated him to the Prophethood of the *Inam*.[114]
Ayet Ayet ame Qur'an bı temam, Kılm kerım ma zi qısey bes, wesselam.	The divine commissions became the Qur'an, Our debates should be short, *wesselam* (peace).
Kam kı wendo pê dıma resna selat, *A dıni dı adıri ra di necat.*	*He who continually recites the ritual prayer[115],* *He will be saved in the other world from the fire (necat).*
Çunki ita bı temam Mewlıdê cey, Mu'ecizatê ey bıwanım çend qısey.	Now the Prophet's Birthday Poem is complete, It's continual recitation is a matter of but few words.[116]
Ganê ey va nur bı nêdi kes, Serseya ey mu'ecizat no to rê bes.	His soul was the divine light, hidden from view, His shadow, a recitation, is enough for you.
Hurgı wext parçeyêndê hewri ey sera, Kerdê sersey, çunkı geyrain (geyrayên) dıma.	The trails of a clouds cover him, giving him shade, following his footsteps.
Vereko (kavıreko) pewte bı axu va cı rê, Axu tewrê mın biyo, mewı mı ra!	The lamb was boiled, it was poison to him, Poison is in me (I am poisoned), never eat from it!
Çaxo kı dara xurma ronê ê Nebi, Dest dı xurma dê u herkesi meywe di.	As soon as the *Nebi* (the Prophet) planted the date-tree, It bore fruit which every saw.
Va kı, engıştan ra ê Pêxemberi, Aw ard u werd (şımıt), cı ra boll eskeri.	He said that from the fingers of the Prophet, He had water brought and many soldiers drank from it.
Hım bı engıştan işaret aşmi ra, Kerdo aşmi bi dı felqey tew bıra.	He also pointed with the fingers a sign upon the moon, And the moon split in two, oh brother.
Eger bıbose serrê umrê mın temam, Ez bıamoran bê to niyo temam.	When my years come to an end, I will count them, but without you (the story) I will not finish.

---

[113] Literally: He stayed back as an orphan until he was grown up.
[114] Literally: *Inam* in Persian is „problem".
[115] *Selat*: Prayer in which God is asked for the blessing of the Prophet Mohammed.
[116] Literally: To recite it all the times takes not much effort.

Appendices

Çunkı ita kerd temam ma mu'ecizat.
Arêbên pêser buwanên esselat.

Çön temam bı mu'ecizatê ê Nebi,
Qal keran mi'eracê cey to rê senini.

Ganê ey, va çunkı nur bı nêdi kes,
Serseya ey, mu'ecizat da to rê bes.

Va şewa duşenbi dı o Ressul,
Ame keyedê Ummehanı kerd qebul.

Va bı Cebraili, Ellay a se'at,
Şo bı cennet, tı biya çendên xelat.
Biya estorên u tacên jew kemer,
Hım biya qatên çına, rew şo bı ser.
Nê hediyan (xelatan) tı berı pêxemberi rê!
Rew bêro mı rê, ê serweri rê.

Şı bı Cennet, Cebrail di kı wuja,
Xeylê estori çerenê ca bı ca.
Jewi zi çımi kerdê sıpe bermı ra,
Nêçereno boll zayif (gıdi) kewto bıra.
Va kı, heywani, bı to çıçiy resa,
Ya seni hına biyo, no dest u pa?

'Hesretên anto Boraqi va cı rê,
Se hezar serriyo bı mın no 'hal resa.
Ame vengên, ya Muhammed! Va jewi,
Ez biyan sersem (tewş) bı eşqdê wahêri.

Hım mı rê o wext ra werdenı bi 'heram,
Mın rı'hatey nêdi o çax ra temam.
Çendı kı Cennet biyo mı rê mekan,
Labelê adırdê eşqi dı veşan.

Because the recitation ends at this point,
Gather around and let the Confession of Faith be read.

Because the Recitation of the Prophet ends here,
I will tell you all about his ascension.

His soul was the divine light, therefore hidden from sight,
His shadow brought forth the recitation, this is enough for you.

He said: On the night of Tuesday, he *Resul* (the Prophet),
Comes to the house of Ummhan and he takes him in.

It was said to Gabriel by God in this hour:
Go to Paradise, bring some gifts.
Bring a horse, a crown and a belt,
Beside that bring also an outfit, and hurry on up.
This gift is to be brought to the Prophet,
He shall hurredly come to me, and to the leader (the Prophet).

He entered Paradise, where Gabriel saw him,
Many horses grazed all around him.
His eyes turned white from weeping at this sight,
It was not grazing and looked lean, oh brother.
He said (to the animal), animal, what happened to you,
How did this happen, alas your hands and your feet (the body)?

Homesickness had reached *Boraq*, he said to him,
I have been in this condition for one thousand years.
A voice appeared: "Oh, Mohammed!" One said,
"I was irritated be the love of the owner (of the voice)."

Moreover, in those days food was impure to me,[117]
Since then I have found no peace.
The more Paradise became my dwelling,
The more (but) the fire of love burned (within) me.

---

[117] Religious Impurity: "I couldn't eat any more."

Vajı zanê kamo Muhammed, tı bıra?	Say brother, "do you know who Mohammed is?"
Beso no adır dı ganê mın veşa.	It is enough that my body burned with this fire.
Cebrail va Boraqi rê Boraq,	Gabriel said to Boraq, Boraq,
Bı mırazê to deya, mekı meraq!	Worry not, for your demand is now fulfilled!
Muhammedo kı tı vana Pêxembero,	Mohammed, whom you call Prophet,
A dıni u na dıni dı serwero.	Is the leader of this and that world.
Qandê cey Ellay xelıqna herrı ra na dıni,	Therefore out of earth Allah created this world,
Oyo hım sultanê nê hurna dıni.	He is the absolute king over both worlds.
Kerdo de'ewet Xalıqi emşo bı ey,	This evening the *Xalıq* invited him,
Bê, bıresnan to beran nıngandê cey.	Come, let me bring you to his feet.
Va gırot estor u rew ame bı ser,	He said: He took the horse and it came to him,
Da selam u va kı, Ya Xeyrul Beşer!	He greeted it aying: "O *Xeyrul Besher!*"
Va bı to kerdo selam ya Mustafa!	He said: You greeted him, oh *Mustafa!*
Xalıqê nê 'erd u azmin bıra.	*Xaliqe* (Creator) of heaven and earth, brother.
Va kı: Wa bêro, mın kerdo de'ewet bı ey,	He said: "He shall come, I invited him,
Çendı wexto ez biyan aşıqê cey.	So long have I loved him."
Wa bıvino Cennet u hem adıri,	Oh, he shall see both Paradise as well as the fire of Hell,
'Erş u kursiyo u qelem, lewhê seri.	*Ersh*, chair (teacher's desk) and pencil, and the sign above.
Nê 'hemme wazenê hurgı zew mı ra,	All of them want something from me,
Tozê nıngan bıancê çıman zey kıla.	Therefore he will grind the dust of his feet, in his eyes.
Mın zi ardo to rê Cennet ra Boraq,	I have brought you *Boraq* from Paradise, as well as
Emşo şewa Qedri u ni'emet telaq.	The worth and the wealth of all things, this evening.
Cadê xo ra rew werışto Pêxember,	Up from his dwelling the Prophet rises,
Tac na serredı, gırêda hım kemer.	The Crown on his head, and his belt fastened on.
Nışt bı estor u Cebrail kewt bı ver,	He mounts the horse and *Gabriel* goes before him,
Va kı şi bi ta resay ê Qudsi ser.	They take off and reach the holy place.
Ame ruhê Enbiyan qarşu temam,	The soul of the prophet alighted on them,
Ey cema'eti rê, o serwer bı imam.	He is the leader and *Imam* to the congregation of faith.
Mescidê Qutsi dı, dı rıkati nemaz,	At the place of prayer, the holy place, he performed,
Kerd bı inan, ard bı Ellay boll niyaz.	the *rıkat* [118] (prayer) two times, bowed down deeply and prayed to God.

---

[118] A series of ritual movements which form a part of the *namaz* (ritual prayer).

Appendices

Nışt bı estor u ame cado verên,	He mounted his horse and returned to where he had come from,
Nerdibanên (merdiwanê) di, va uja ta bı azmin.	He saw the stairs, which wound their way up to heaven.
Nerdiban ra kewt bı ray o şı Nebi,	Up he climbed and went to the Prophet,
O resa cayên kı name sıdre bı.	He arrived at a place named *Sidre*.
Çun resa sıdre, Va, Ya Mustafa!	Cun reached *Sidre* and says: "O *Mustafa*!"
Cebrail nêşı dıma, o mend cı ra.	*Gabriel* didn't follow him, he stayed behind.
Va kı Cebraili rê bı ta xerib,	He said to *Gabriel*, here it was disconcerting,
Qandê çıçiy ez terıknan ya 'Hebib!	Why did you leave me, oh *Habib* (Prophet)?
Va kı Cebraili, ya Xeyrul Beşer!	He said to Gabriel, oh *Xeyrul Besher*!
No hına ray to yo Sahib Kerem.	In this way is your way, *Sahib Kerem* (Lord).
Ez veşena ya Nebi ul muxterem!	I burn, oh *Nebi ul muxterem* (highly honored Prophet)!
No hına bêran eger ez to dıma.	Coming in this way after you.
Kam kı adıri ra xelas xo rê wast,	*He, who wants to be saved from the fire,*
Wa Resuli rê buwanên esselat.	*He shall read the esselat (Prayer) on the Prophet.*
Çaxo Cebraili dır kerdên kelam,	When *Gabriel* was angry (*kelem*),
Ame Refref Ehmedi rê da selam.	The *Refref* (heavenly animal) came and greeted *Ehmed* (the Prophet).
Va uja ra rew gırot ê Refrefi,	He said, "This being took him quickly from there,
Berdı 'erşi serdı rona ey Nebi.	And laid the *Nebi* (Prophet) on the *ersh* (holy place) and placed him down."
Nofın vengên ame va: Mustafa!	This time the voice came and said: "*Mustafa*!"
Ya 'Hebib el mucteba, Xeyrel (Xeyrul) wera!	Oh *Hebib el mucteba, Xeyrel wera.*
Bı bı to, rewnayo ez aşıq biyan,	I have loved you for a long time,
Kerdo koleyê to mın hemme ins u can.	I made all the beings and the inanimate world your servants (laid them down before you).
Şi bi nezdı çun va Refref ca dı mend,	They went there, for the *Refref* (heavenly animal) remained at his place,
Ehmedi ra Mim werışt u mend E'hed.	Mim departed from *Ehmed* (the Prophet) and what remained was *E'hed*.
Bı hes u bı herf, a şew new hezar,	It was the voice and the scripture, in this night of nine thousand,
Mustefay dı kerdi qısey gırdi kar.	Debating long hours with *Mustafa*.
Çı mırazê bı to yo hurna dıni	Whatever your wishes are for both worlds
Esto, vazı, ez bı to dan, ya Nebi!	If they exist, tell me, and I will give them to you, oh Prophet!
Va, mırazê mın ilahi her zeman	He thought that his demand would be in his presence forevermore,
'Ef kerê tı ommeta mın rusiyan.	

Da bı to mın ommeta va ya Resul! \
Mın inan 'ef kerdo, mın kerdo qebul.

Labelê, va hurgı roj panc weqti nemaz, \
Wa bıkerê, mı rê biyarê niyaz.

Ta bı o me'ena (mahne) ez inan şa keran, \
Cennetê xo ez ina rê ca keran.

Va bı emrê xalıqi ê serweri, \
Ame keydê Ummehanı zey veri.

Çunkı şewra bı, çıçiy di bı Nebi, \
Kerd Sehaban rê hikayet, zekı di.

Va inan, ey tı şefi'ê ma rusiyan! \
Wa mubarek (embarık) bo, bı to mi'erac inan. \
Va kı, mi'eracê şıma zi bı niyaz, \
Da şıma u bıkerên panc weqti nemaz.

Kam kı nê panc weqtan biyaro rınd bı ca, \
Me'hşerê Kubra dı ancax o bı şa.

Ya eger jewi terıkna (terıq) ey bıra! \
'Ar bıbo şari miyan dı rusiya.

Kam kı wendo pê dıma resna seleat, \
Adırê Cahnımi ra o bı necat.

Ya ilahi hurmetê Pêxemberi, \
Ey cenabi Mustefa tacê serri!

Hurmetê 'hersandê çımê sadıqan, \
Adırê kulandê pizey aşıqan.

Forgive those believers which are guilty[119].

(God said), I gave you the community of believers, oh Prophet! \
I forgave them, and I accepted them anew. \
However, recite every day for five times the ritual prayer, \
You shall do that; and such recite to me your desires. \
So I will favor them in this way, \
My paradise I will prepare for them. \
He said under the command of the leader of God, \
As before he came to the house of (the woman) *Umhan*. \
When morning arrive, what did the Prophet see? \
He was made the closest confidant of Mohammed, like seeing it as if in a folktale. \
They said: "Oh *Shefi* we are the guilty ones!" \
Blessed by the Prophet, it happened as the ascension. \
He said that your ascension became like a prayer of petition, \
He gave it to you and five times you should pray the ritual prayer. \
He who fulfills it five times, has acted in the right way, \
In the Last Judgment in *Kubra*, where he will be able to enjoy himself. \
If one where to give him up, o brother! \
He shall be considered evil by the people, he who is guilty. \
He who read this and has confessed the Salat (prayer), \
He will not see the fire necat. \
Oh the presence of God, generating respect for the Prophet, \
He dressed Mustafa with a crown on his head. \
The respect brings tears to good friends eyes, \
Fire is like an ulcer in the intestines of lovers.

---

[119] Zazaki: *ri siya* = black face. In a transferred sense the "stigmatized" or "guilty".

Hurmetê ey yarê xarê Ehmedi,	His respect is like the love for *Ehmed*,
Hım 'Umer Faruq u Şahê Sermedi.	As well as to *Umer Faruk* and the *Shah of Semed*.
Hurmetê Tewrat u İncil, Zebur,	The respect for the Hebrew Bible and the New Testament, the Palms[120],
Nurê Furqan, Cennet, Xılman u Hur.	The divine light of *Furqan*[121], the paradise, *Xilman* and *Hur*.
Qedrê Osman Xelilê Muhemedi,	The importance of *Osman Xelile* of Mohammed,
Hım 'Eliyyul Murtaza lajê dedi.	Also of *Eliyyul Murtaza* the son of the uncle.
Padişahê dinê İslami bı ma,	He was our king of the Islamic belief,
Verdê ya Rebbi bı may u lajiya.	Before the Lord are the mother and the son.
Ey di textê Ehmedi dı ya Xuda!	He saw on the throne *Ehmed*, oh God!
Tı bı se serri kerê ya Rebbena!	Yes God fulfill the hundred years!
Roj bı roj keskun kerê şemşêrê cey,	Day by day you shall sharpen his sword,
Yoxkerê (kor kerê) duşmenandê dindê cey.	Destroy the enemies of his religion.
Ey dıma tı ommeta Pêxemberi	Thereafter the community of believers they should,
Şa kerê, ya Rebbi roja me'hşeri.	Rejoice! Oh Lord on the day of the Last Judgment.
Pir u pirbaban, peyanê hazıran,	The ancestors[122], the protectors prepared in advance,
Tı bı enbazê Resuli kı inan.	You shall gain them as friends of the envoy.
Hım peyanê hazıran, ya Rebbena!	Also the protectors prepared in advance, oh Lord!
Tı bı Cennet dı şa kı inan, Ya Xuda!	You shall bring them pleasure in Paradise, oh God!
Wa'hêrê nê zadi Rebbel 'alemin,	The owner of the good man is the almighty God of all,
'umr u maldê ey bereket tı defin!	Life and property will accumulate the blessing!
Hım vıraştoxê kıtabdê xaseki	Also the creator of the wonderful book,
Lajê muftidê kamandê Sewregi.	Is the son of the Mufti of Siverek.
Yanê Osman Eshedo lajê qıji,	Again the *Osman Eshedo* is the youngest son,
Lajê Haci Eyyub Efendidê Babıji.	The son of *Haci Hiob Efendi* from Bab.
Ey u laji pir u pirbabê veri,	He and the son of the former ancestors,
'Ef kerê, ew şa kerê tı ê beri.	Forgive, and give pleasure to this great family.

---

[120] The terms are *not* congruent with the Biblical Canon of Christianity. The *tewrat* corresponds to the Jewish *Torah* that are the five books of Moses. The *Zebur* is identical with the Psalms, and the *Injil* conforms with the four gospels of the New Testament.
[121] The horse of Mohammed during his ascension.
[122] Literally: father and grandfather.

O yo kı yazu kerdo (nusto) no mewlıdê ma,
Cennet dê 'edni miyan dı bıdı ca.
Kam kı wend u pêdıma resna selat,
Adırê Ca'hnımi ra o bı necat.
Duwa:
Rebena atina fil dunya 'heseneten we fil axireti 'heseneten we qina 'ezabennar.
Amin
Çulçi Mustafa yazmış, dı'adên wano tı mabın.
Osman Efendi (1853-1929)

Heci Eyyub Efendizade Osman Efendi serrda 1853 dı Sukda Soreg dı ameyo dıniya.
Piyê cı Heci Eyyub Efendi, maya cı Emina Xanıma.
Piyê cı Heci Eyyub Efendi, sukda Suleymani dı Qadiyin kerda ew uja dı şiyo heqeyda xo. Osman Efendi Baxdad dı Universite wanano, qedineno u ageyreno Soregı. Demeyê Soreg dı maneno, dıma dano pıro şıno Mısır. Uja dı Fakultedê Ezheriye dı waneno, qedineno u peyser ageyreno Soregı ew uja dı Muftiyey, azayina umumiya meclisdê ili (il genel meclis üyeliği) ew ma'hkemandê Soreg dı azayin keno.
Osman Efendi, çorşmedê Soreg dı xeylê sılasneyeno u sineyeno. Merdımêndo zaf zerritenık, zerrinerm u merdımsinayox beno. Qelbê kesi nêşıkneno ew meymanan rê kêverê cı tım akerde beno. Mılet qandê mısayenda dıni şiyê cı hetek u cı ra heqdê İslamiyetin dı persi pers kerdê. Wexta şarê ma 'hendı Tırki nêzanayê ew Mufti Efendi rê vatê, "mayê 'Erebi zi, Tırki zi fahm nêkemı, to ra recay ma, Xutbe u Wahzana Zazakiya bıdı, ew Mewlıdi zi Zazakiya bıwan kı ma cı ra çiyê fahm bıkemı".
Osman Efendi, qısanê nina qal gêno u

It is he, who wrote for us this poem of the prophet's birthday,
Offer him his place in Paradise.
He, who read this and recites the selat (Prayer),
The fire necat will not touch him.
Prayer (Arabic):
Rebena atina fil dunya 'heseneten we fil axireti 'heseneten we qina 'ezabennar.
Amen
The saddle of Mustafa wrote:
"dı'adên wano tı mabın".
Osman Efendi (1853-1992)

Haci Hiob's son Osman Efendi was born in 1853 in the city of Siverek.
His father was Haci Hiob Efendi, his mother Emina Xanıma.
The father Haci Hiob Efendi was a judge in the town of Suleymaniye and he died there. Osman Efendi studied in Bagdad at the University, after finishing his studied he came back to Siverek.
He stayed there some time, after which he moved to Egypt. There he studied at the faculty in Ezheriye.
After completing his work he once again returned to Siverek, working as Mufti and later became a member of the city council and hold a seat at the court of Siverek.
Osman Efendi's popularity grew and he was warmly welcomed in the area of Siverek. He was gentle, humble and a friend of the people.
He never hurt anyone and his door was always open to guests. People came to him to learn about religion and questions of the Islamic Law. In these days our people knew less Turkish and they asked the Mufti, "we don't know Arabic and Turkish, we ask you to preach and teach in Zazaki, and recite us the Prophet's Birthday Poem (Mewlid) in Zazaki, so that we understand the things about him."
Osman Efendi took their request serious and supported them in understanding things better, by

qandê fahm kerdenı, Xutbe u wahzana Zazakiya dano.

Ew qandê Zazayan zi 1886 dı Mewlıdê Nebi nusneno u bı Zazakiya waneno. Namey dewda Osman Efendi Babo, coy ra cı rê vanê Osman Efendiyo Babıj. Osman Efendi 24-03-1929 dı şıno 'heqeyda xo.

Mı no ma'hlimat kıtabdê (Koyo Berz) *Namdarê Soreg* ra gıroto. (Berz, Koyo 1995. Namdarê Sêwregı 1. Stockholm: Iremet Förlag. [Engl. Famous People of Siverek].

Elifbayê Zazaki: R. H.

preaching and teaching in Zazaki.

In the year 1886 he published the Prophet's Birthday Poem in Zazaki and read it aloud. The village that Osman Efendi was from was called Bab which is why he is also called *Osman Efendi the Baban*. *Osman* Efendi died on the 24th March 1929.

This information has been collected from the book *Namdare Soreg* written by *Koyo Berz*. (Berz, Koyo 1995. Namdarê Sêwregı 1. Stockholm: Iremet Förlag. [Engl. Famous People of Siverek].

Zazaki alphabet: R. H

Index

abduction 247, 276, 338, 434
Abdul Hamid II. 107, 109, 152, 191, 286, 363, 385, 387, 399, 403, 428
Abdulallah Gül 386
Abdullah Öcalan 144, 299
Abraham 226, 248, 372, 407, 411, 414
acculturation 52, 267, 289, 346
adept 192, 331
Adıyaman 103, 104, 397
Adyghe 199, 387, 389, 437
agha 187, 244, 245, 253, 271, 274, 280, 284, 288, 300, 312, 315, 339, 341, 354, 437
aghadom 274, 287, 437
agriculture 311, 434
Ahl-e Haqq 93, 224
Ahura Mazda 217, 222, 317, 395, 434
Alevism 52, 59, 62, 64, 65, 66, 67, 71, 82, 102, 114, 134, 188, 194, 201, 216, 220, 224, 232, 235, 240, 248, 255, 258, 260, 261, 305, 318, 320, 329, 345, 355, 358, 370, 375, 377, 392, 403, 421, 426, 427, 434
Alexander the Great 358
Allah 150, 157, 203, 220, 233, 242, 272, 311, 319, 327, 333, 404, 430
allative 164
Alp Arslan 361
alphabet 139, 352, 361
Altaic 360, 371
Anatolia 11, 99, 100, 102, 148, 360
animal husbandry 275, 288, 314
animal world 327
Animism 65, 149, 205, 216, 218, 221, 227, 232, 236, 238, 239, 258, 262, 263, 279, 325, 330, 355, 425, 434, 435, 439
anthropology 11, 17, 20, 21, 23, 26, 28, 30, 33, 34, 44, 49, 50, 52, 85, 204, 213, 233, 235, 267, 277, 293, 305, 324, 350, 352, 357, 381, 391, 405, 410, 431, 438
anti-Christian 113, 400, 402
anti-Islamic 368
anti-Jewish 400, 410
Arab 189, 232, 428
Arabic 46, 59, 64, 67, 100, 102, 129, 148, 151, 168, 192, 196, 231, 248, 249, 253, 266, 271, 277, 289, 294, 296, 304, 323, 360, 361, 363, 368, 370, 379, 385, 393, 395, 407, 409, 410, 430
Arabic peninsula 410

Arabization 246, 257
Aramaeans 59, 100, 256, 360
Aramaic 391
Ararat 395, 399
archaeology 293
Ardalani 84, 85, 111
Aristotle 213, 221, 341
arithmetics 305
Armenia 56, 228, 298, 319, 395, 399, 452
Armenian 63, 64, 74, 80, 96, 100, 107, 108, 109, 116, 228, 247, 301, 391, 414, 450
Armenian Apostolic Church 52, 83, 102, 109, 110, 112, 113, 115, 148, 152, 190, 201, 228, 229, 231, 237, 256, 257, 264, 301, 304, 305, 359, 360, 377, 380, 388, 394, 395, 396, 397, 398, 399, 401, 415, 426, 429, 436, 447, 448, 450, 453
arts 226, 294, 304, 305, 306, 307, 364, 412, 419, 431, 436, 438
Asia 100, 188, 236, 350, 360, 379, 387, 389, 395, 429, 445
Asia Minor 227, 237, 359, 451, 452
aşık 307, 308
aşiret 61, 277
assimilation 12, 67, 99, 110, 118, 153, 186, 195, 418
Assyrian 201, 228, 377
Assyrians 204, 395
asylum 12, 75, 144, 294, 298, 299, 450
Australia 143, 313, 417
authority 38, 204, 267, 271, 306
Avesta 116, 223, *See* Zoroastrianism
Baba Duzgın 235, 238, 244, 261
Bahdeni 72, 84, 85, 111, 116, 167
Bajalan 127, 129
Bakhtiari 73, 84, 85, 111, 223, 432
Balkans 89, 101, 118, 224, 359, 428, 444
baptism 48, 260
bard 306, 307
beardless 304, 343
behaviour 204, 214, 324
Bektaşi 65, 66, 67, 224, 235, 239, 241, 276, 419
Bıçax 277, 281, 285
bigotry 232, 237, 247, 421
bilingualism 123, 147, 152, 155, 160, 231, 288, 289, 291, 300, 347, 349, 350, 428
Bingöl 13, 52, 60, 103, 131, 132, 150, 187, 232, 243, 258, 290

Index

birth 74, 168, 219, 233, 249, 251, 260, 264, 266, 338, 352, 365
blood feud 203, 206, 338, 339, 341, 343, 434, 435, 437
blood relationship 36, 270
brain 39, 41, 124, 151, 348, 350
bridewealth 288, 340, 341
brotherhood 314, 420, 424, 434
brotherhood in arms 385
Buddhism 218, 222, 246, 262, 360, 387, 392
Bulgaria 391, 394, 449
Byzantine Church 394, 396
Byzantine Empire 97, 228, 229, 257, 359, 361, 377, 380, 387, 394, 412
Caliphate 193, 248, 253, 366, 426
capitalism 186, 245, 288, 355, 375, 393
Caspian Sea 63, 82, 86, 88, 92, 100, 101
Caucasian 389, 390
Celts 89, 101, 432
cemat 239, 242, 244, 253, 264, 307, 340, 392
cemetery 318, 328, 383
ceni 324
Central Asia 88, 371, 377
centralism 212, 355, 370
centrifugal 324, 325, 333
centripetal 324, 333
Çermik 52, 103, 131, 132, 138, 185, 253, 281, 297
Chaldean 229, 377, 390, 394
chamzah 219, 342
children 13, 22, 39, 65, 117, 147, 202, 230, 269, 334, 346, 353, 450
CHP 370
Christian development aid 305
Christian Development Aid 257, 259, 352
Christianity 43, 48, 65, 83, 101, 146, 191, 194, 208, 216, 222, 227, 230, 232, 237, 246, 257, 260, 262, 264, 270, 286, 291, 298, 330, 331, 355, 377, 378, 393, 394, 395, 396, 403, 406, 410, 414, 415, 420, 421, 426, 427, 429, 438, 439
cin 233
Circassian 199, 282, 387, 389, 437, 446
circumcision 48, 226, 249, 308, 338
clan 43, 102, 268, 269, 275, 277, 314, 321, 338, 343, 377
class society 266
class transition 288, 328, 342
climate 301
coffin 318, 327
cognition 30, 35, 38, 41, 230, 300, 314, 350, 431
collectivism 202, 214, 215, 265, 267, 280, 338, 339

colonialism 36, 112, 294, 349, 402
communication 30, 38, 42, 52, 54, 75, 117, 153, 204, 209, 230, 253, 274, 287, 289, 290, 292, 306, 319, 340, 348, 350, 421, 450
concept of time 166
conscience 11, 37, 38, 39, 44, 45, 46, 48, 50, 202, 204, 206, 210, 212, 214, 233, 276, 314, 315, 338, 341, 346, 356, 405, 425, 431, 438
Constantinople 364, 394
contextualization 19, 34, 46, 420
continental climate 105, 106, 107, 114
conversion 48, 82, 108, 229, 237, 257, 258, 381, 396, 405, 412, 424, 425, 427, 428, 429, 438
copula 167, 181
core value 35, 37, 50, 167, 205, 207, 214, 268, 271, 280, 286, 291, 317, 329, 344, 346, 405, 425, 427, 430, 435, 439
corpse 233, 318, 327
cosmology 17, 23, 28, 54, 329, 331, 345, 353, 435
craft 226, 257, 301, 356, 393, 434
creation 248, 327, 328, 329, 331, 333, 405
Crescent 412, 413
cross-cultural 13, 18, 28, 46, 53, 54, 190, 212
cultural transformation 187
culture 11, 12, 15, 17, 18, 20, 21, 22, 23, 24, 26, 29, 30, 31, 34, 35, 36, 38, 39, 41, 42, 43, 44, 45, 46, 49, 51, 52, 54, 55, 57, 59, 70, 71, 73, 74, 75, 79, 85, 92, 95, 96, 103, 117, 118, 124, 132, 145, 147, 150, 160, 353, 435
culture change 35, 311, 342, 353
da'awa 188, 406, 422, 423, 425, 430, 438
dance 306, 308, 340
Danube 101, 359, 432
dar al-harb 231, 256, 406, 438
dar al-Islam 195, 231, 246, 256, 406, 422, 425, 438
Daylam 69, 100, 101, 189, 223
Daylam-Thesis 63, 82, 84, 88, 92, 97, 100, 101, 128, 189, 216, 228, 414, 418, 436
death 20, 39, 197, 219, 231, 246, 263, 306, 316, 328, 347, 370, 450
dede 244
defilement 46, 233
democracy 127, 357
democratization 288
demon 157, 206, 218, 233
deportation 109, 112, 129, 226, 257, 398, 414, 428, 450
Dersim 103, 194, 195, 261, 262, 281, 283
Dervish 262, 307
descent 265, 270, 300

dhimmi-status 109, 229, 231, 246, 258, 359, 368, 377, 394, 401, 406, 415
Diadochi 359
dialect 50, 97, 351
Diaspora 12, 13, 58, 65, 74, 80, 117, 135, 142, 144, 147, 154, 160, 186, 187, 199, 201, 225, 238, 256, 260, 265, 271, 287, 289, 292, 300, 306, 320, 347, 353, 381, 387, 417, 428, 434
Dicle 11, 52, 60, 92, 106, 135, 193, 269, 296
diminutive 323
dining room 303
discrimination 36, 113, 196, 258, 291, 300, 339, 361, 399
Diyarbakır 56, 61, 67, 74, 94, 99, 104, 109, 114, 117, 127, 128, 138, 191, 194, 256, 364, 367, 398, 401
dragon 327
drum 306
dualism 217, 221, 222, 225, 263, 355, 434
Dunbeli 68, 69
Duzgın Baba 103
dyadic-dynamic model 18, 26, 27, 54
Eastern Anatolia 11, 50, 51, 52, 56, 64, 65, 74, 82, 83, 86, 93, 94, 100, 101, 102, 111, 120, 122, 124, 191, 198, 226, 241, 256, 257, 294, 354, 361, 370, 375, 398, 403, 405, 410, 414, 415, 417, 420, 424, 429, 430, 436, 437
Eastern Group 59, 79, 102, 103, 106, 186, 188, 235, 245, 264, 282, 320, 323, 345, 355, 370, 405, 406, 421, 433, 434, 436
economy 21, 111, 115, 117, 138, 160, 230, 245, 266, 276, 287, 294, 299, 312, 339
Edessa 256
education 13, 21, 29, 69, 112, 117, 133, 146, 185, 230, 232, 253, 271, 280, 294, 346, 355, 361, 395
educational dictatorship 368, 376, 388
Egypt 226, 246, 249, 251, 285, 296, 310, 358, 359, 371, 387, 392, 401, 444
Elazığ 114, 117, 159
elenctics 37, 279
elite 266, 284
emic 12, 13, 28, 36, 56, 69, 72, 84, 265, 292, 329, 352, 431
enculturation 12, 30, 42, 45, 124, 206, 215, 242, 271, 346, 365, 421
endogamy 36, 239, 270, 277, 288
endonym 60, 68, 395, 432
England 109, 136, 366, 370, 378
English 15, 17, 46, 131, 162, 163, 250, 262, 316, 344, 347, 348, 384
Enlightenment 205, 368, 419

Enver Kenan 372
Enver Pasha 367, 450
envy 46, 50, 201, 204, 205, 206, 207, 209, 220, 338, 340, 341, 344, 346, 353, 362, 406, 411, 426, 435, 438
ergative 162, 166, 177, 185, 186
Eropean Union 68, 409
Erzurum 56, 60, 99, 450, 451
ethics 11, 31, 34, 44, 48, 241, 280, 431, 448
ethnocentrism 26, 27, 29, 214, 329
ethnocide 57, 66, 80, 107, 152, 194, 288, 366, 396
ethnographer 54, 228
ethnography 11, 17, 22, 24, 26, 28, 30, 33, 50, 54, 55, 69, 75, 186, 204, 207, 324, 329, 405, 431
ethnomusicology 186, 305, 306, 307, 308, 314, 345, 419, 421, 431, 435, 438
etic 13, 28, 36, 56, 69, 84, 265, 267, 292, 329, 352, 431
etymology 322, 323, 328
Euphrates 11, 51, 56, 63, 92, 97, 99, 102, 105, 106, 127, 152, 188, 278, 358, 359, 432
Euro-Islam 199, 381
Europe 89, 101, 119, 188, 210, 294, 313, 370, 378, 389, 392, 423
European Union 147, 200, 292, 294, 295, 299, 300, 381, 385, 386, 397, 429
Evil 45, 201, 205, 215, 217, 219, 220, 222, 240, 255, 260, 325, 331, 400
evil eye 205, 207, 208, 214, 219, 223, 264, 325, 342, 407
evolution 235, 331
exogamy 239
exonym 60, 64, 68, 395, 432
export of goods 294
expulsion 94, 109, 193, 275, 278, 346, 452
extended family 96, 203, 214, 261, 266, 267, 269, 270, 280, 284, 293, 300, 320, 338, 340, 346, 538
ezafe 165, 173
ezbet 214, 261
Farsi 68, 86, 117, 118, 120, 122, 129, 148, 158, 164, 432
federalism 200, 358
Female Genital Mutilation 226
Fertile Crescent 86, 89, 101, 216, 224, 235, 294, 337, 358, 377, 387, 412, 414, 416, 436
feudalism 110, 145, 186, 187, 195, 265, 266, 271, 273, 274, 275, 277, 287, 300, 339, 345, 355, 360, 376, 393
finiteness 323
fire 223, 261
flute 306

Index

folk conscience 207, 346
Folk Islam 66, 208, 215, 218, 220, 221, 239, 262, 264, 288, 333, 410, 423, 435
folk music 305
foreignness 25, 29, 69, 147, 153, 164, 199, 203, 259, 292, 298, 315, 340, 410, 434
forgiveness 343
France 143, 145, 194, 293, 299, 366, 370, 378, 379, 403, 451
Freemasonry 286, 423
funeral procession 249, 318, 320, 328
Galatia 227, 256
Galatians 208, 226, 237, 256
gender segregation 308, 338, 340, 365, 434
generation gap 293
generosity 325
Gerger 98, 103, 132, 145, 281
German 13, 20, 21, 32, 46, 71, 113, 131, 135, 162, 163, 194, 199, 216, 250, 291, 294, 299, 366, 381, 385, 388, 398, 404, 434
Germany 12, 28, 136, 192, 216, 291, 294, 299, 372, 384, 385, 388, 398, 400, 417, 428
giant 327
Gilaki 84, 85, 223, 400
girl exchange 339, 341
globalization 18, 29, 287, 347
Gnosticism 65, 217, 222, 235, 239, 330, 355, 414
God 47, 66, 150, 157, 168, 193, 203, 208, 222, 223, 241, 244, 249, 251, 260, 262, 317, 333, 341, 399, 404, 407, 410, 412, 413, 423
godparenthood 83, 258, 338
gods 22, 205, 216, 220, 255, 262, 331, 333, 396, 412, 413, 434
Gökalp 59, 249, 364
Golden Horde 377, 382
Good 45, 201, 205, 215, 217, 219, 220, 222, 255, 331, 400
Gorani 51, 63, 65, 72, 84, 85, 93, 99, 103, 116, 127, 130, 165, 185, 216, 223, 224, 400, 432
grammar 162, 322
grandparents 269
grave 298, 318, 320, 321, 327
Great Experiment 107, 112, 256, 260, 402
great-grandparents 269
greatheartedness 325
Greece 359
Greek 59, 98, 102, 107, 221, 324, 360, 391
guilt orientation 17, 46, 50, 55, 201, 204, 341, 431
guitar 306
Güneş Dil Teorisi 371, 372
Guran 51

Haci Bektaş Veli 65, 223
Hadith 66, 209, 227, 248, 346, 365
Hamidiye troops 107, 109, 191, 388, 416, 428, 437, 446, 447, 449
Hanafi 60, 93, 108, 135, 148, 216, 221, 225, 232, 235, 248, 249, 355, 370, 377, 399, 416, 421, 427, 433, 439
Hanbali 249
Hani 52, 103, 232, 253, 273, 282
Harput 74
Hawrami 51, 72, 127, 432
Hazan 250
headscarf 298, 304, 314
heaven 251, 263, 413
Hebrew 210
Hebrew Bible 203, 210, 218, 222, 225, 313, 320, 343, 358, 407, 408, 410
hedonism 291
Helika Gızıkıne 255
hell 250, 254, 263, 413
Hinduism 218, 246
history 26, 36, 53, 101, 107, 187, 265, 353
Hittites 95, 96, 189, 201, 204, 349, 358
hoca 318, 424, 434
holistic 212, 215, 241, 330, 345
home decoration 304
homeland 300, 306, 311, 313
homogenous 21, 216, 267
honour 38, 46, 203, 206, 271, 279, 280, 320, 325, 328, 338, 339, 340, 342, 346, 435
honour killing 234, 276, 338, 339, 341, 346, 434, 435, 437
hospitality 208, 325, 340, 343, 420, 425, 427, 430, 434
host country 298
Hozat 74
human rights 301, 372, 387, 389, 405
humanism 26, 205, 215, 380
Hz. Ali 66, 241, 244, 249, 335
Hz. Jesus of Nazareth 83, 157, 208, 312, 343, 395, 401, 405, 413, 420
Hz. Mohammed 66, 74, 192, 208, 231, 241, 242, 246, 248, 249, 259, 402, 412
Hz. Moses 310
ideology 99, 187, 241, 331, 357, 365, 366, 371, 414
illiteracy 53, 146, 151, 160, 230
Image of limited Good 17, 50, 312, 315, 431
Imam 252, 423
immortality 327, 328
imperialism 34, 192, 392, 402

impurity 258, 339, 341, 435, 438
Incarnation 244
incest taboo 269
indefiniteness 171, 321, 323
individualism 202, 277, 339, 341
individuum 61, 312, 326, 327
Indo-European 12, 56, 98, 116, 119, 389, 391
Indo-European language family 116, 118, 119, 185, 390
industrialization 275, 288, 311, 345, 393, 434
infiniteness 323
initiation 226, 267, 270, 338, 420
institution 187, 215
interdisciplinary 28, 37, 44
intermarriage 70, 108, 117, 258, 277, 289, 418
Intersubjectivity 27
intuition 28, 30, 39
Iran 56, 63, 65, 66, 73, 84, 85, 86, 88, 99, 101, 103, 110, 129, 216, 217, 222, 235, 354, 385, 409, 411, 417
Iranian 56, 116, 166, 390
Iranian language 50, 120, 354
Iranian language family 120, 130
Islam 46, 59, 108, 148, 168, 188, 195, 199, 203, 207, 208, 209, 216, 222, 226, 235, 242, 249, 256, 258, 262, 264, 267, 272, 287, 296, 298, 299, 300, 305, 318, 320, 330, 331, 333, 338, 343, 345, 353, 354, 366, 372, 375, 378, 381, 384, 393, 401, 406, 410, 413, 414, 420, 421, 425, 426, 427, 429, 438
Islamic clergy 248, 252, 271, 276, 368, 369, 395, 424, 434, 437
Islamic order 66, 192, 197, 276, 284, 286, 355, 394, 419, 422, 423, 424, 427, 430, 437
Islamisation 82, 199, 245, 246, 257, 258, 404
Ismet İnönü 371
isolation 162, 278, 313
Israel 110, 207, 225, 310, 409, 413, 429
Italy 136, 194, 359, 366, 370, 378, 379, 409
Jewish deportation 408
Jewish Diaspora 227, 266, 408
Jewish people 59, 89, 108, 109, 110, 113, 115, 148, 152, 191, 207, 210, 225, 226, 229, 231, 246, 252, 256, 266, 270, 305, 318, 331, 359, 377, 388, 402, 407, 414, 429, 436
jihad 246, 264, 406, 422, 423, 425, 427, 430, 438
Johannes Lepsius 258
Judaism 43, 48, 203, 226, 228, 235, 239, 377, 407, 410, 413, 414, 416, 427, 429
justice orientation 46
Kaiser Wilhelm II 259
Kakai 129

Karen Jeppe 259
Kemalism 375, 378
Kermanshahi 84, 85, 111
Khalê Gağani 260, 307
kingdom 246, 257
kinship 61, 69, 164, 172, 253, 265, 268, 269, 270, 277, 285, 300, 353, 420, 425, 430, 434
kiss 340
kitchen 303
Kızılbaş 62, 66, 77, 224, 239, 406
Koçgiri rebellion 74, 194, 198
Koçuşagı 196, 198
Kordi 111
Kori 223
kuflet 214
Kurdish nationalism 81, 82, 195, 248, 430
Kurdish Question 82, 355, 358, 375, 428, 433, 438
Kurdish rebellions 66, 354, 418
Kurdishness 78, 80, 101, 107, 193, 200, 295, 418, 420, 431
Kurds 12, 50, 56, 60, 62, 65, 72, 77, 107, 109, 125, 126, 132, 153, 190, 191, 193, 199, 216, 232, 246, 249, 257, 272, 279, 289, 290, 308, 311, 352, 354, 415
Kurmanji 12, 51, 56, 68, 77, 83, 84, 85, 86, 98, 111, 120, 122, 125, 128, 132, 133, 146, 148, 150, 153, 158, 165, 167, 185, 194, 224, 227, 232, 235, 239, 245, 256, 275, 289, 290, 316, 323, 328, 350, 352, 353, 360, 361, 371, 372, 388, 391, 400, 405, 414, 415, 416, 418, 428, 431, 433, 437, 438
Laicism 195, 290, 365, 375, 378
Laki 73, 84, 85, 111, 223, 432
lamentation 319
language 37, 38, 50, 115, 433
language belt 73, 84, 86, 103, 111, 122, 354
language endangerment 288
language family 119, 122, 165, 387
language learning 30, 54, 123, 135, 211
Laz 59, 275, 360, 387, 437
LEIC 44, 45, 167, 186, 202, 205, 206, 210, 212, 315, 342, 355, 431, 438
lexical borrowing 154
lexicon 311, 352
lingua franca 118, 349, 350, 361, 395, 429
linguistics 17, 18, 56, 115, 125, 188, 190, 213, 314, 328, 350, 435
Lithunia 382
livestock 301
living room 303
loaning 63, 126, 149, 154, 316, 323, 340, 420, 434
locative 164

Index

loğê 301
losing face 203, 206, 207, 209, 211, 254, 279, 425
love 216, 241, 307, 311, 314, 341, 420
loyalty 11, 32, 148, 201, 203, 247, 268, 286, 420, 425, 430, 434, 446, 447, 538
lunar eclipse 311
Luri 73, 84, 85, 111, 223, 432
madrassa 103, 201, 232, 249, 252, 264, 273, 433
magic power 311
Mahmut II 363, 387
Maliki 249
mana 233
Manichaeism 217, 222, 235, 355, 414
marble trade 294
marriage 22, 83, 266, 268, 269, 277
martyrdom 241
Marxism 261
mass movement 86, 199
materialism 366
matrifilitatio 270
Mazandarani 84, 432
Mazdaism 222, 246
Medes 189, 201
media 355
mediating 28
mediator 205, 285
Mediterranean 188, 202, 204, 208, 226, 228, 260, 308, 314, 320, 341, 346, 428
Mehmet II 387
mental 316
mental lexicon 39
merdım 321, 324, 328, 353, 435
mesnevi 249
metalanguage 33, 37
metaphysics 26, 47, 82, 204, 206, 215, 222, 244, 342, 435
metempsychosis 244, 400
Mewlid Nebi 74, 220, 249, 250, 348
microculture 33, 34, 36, 43, 190, 266, 280, 290, 300, 369
Middle Ages 66, 93, 99, 189, 285, 378, 379, 393, 395
middle class 266
Middle East 50, 118, 205, 230, 246, 271, 284, 304, 359, 360, 380, 387, 392, 401, 408, 409, 410, 429, 444
Middle Persian 117, 120, 122, 185, 420
migration 36, 63, 69, 73, 86, 91, 97, 104, 154, 187, 199, 235, 260, 287, 291, 313, 345, 353, 377, 409
migration movement 100, 101, 199, 287, 288, 291, 293, 294, 403, 416, 432

military 105, 108, 110, 160, 229, 274, 284, 300, 311, 361, 372, 408, 409, 416, 418
mıllah 59, 233, 273, 288, 341, 437
millet 59, 108, 115, 226, 229, 231, 247, 259, 360, 362, 368, 376, 377, 380, 402, 414, 421, 428, 429, 444
minaret 383
minority 188, 190, 199, 200, 201
MLE 292
mobility 55, 266, 287, 347
Modernization 375
Mongol invasions 89, 98, 100, 101, 102, 189, 232, 246, 361, 392, 437
Mongolia 98, 377, 436
monolingualism 287
monotheism 414
moon 65, 261, 311, 332
morality 316
mortality 327, 328
mosque 114, 232, 253, 264, 318, 382, 383, 401, 405, 411, 415, 435
mother 271
mother tongue 27, 42, 53, 54, 91, 118, 135, 150, 151, 153, 160, 185, 187, 230, 231, 275, 278, 287, 289, 292, 294, 308, 324, 347, 348, 350, 353, 356, 376, 378, 386, 421, 424, 432, 436
mother tongue education 114, 127, 230, 292, 347, 349, 350, 356, 386, 389, 424, 429, 436, 439
mourning 249, 306, 310
Mukri 84, 85, 111
mullaharchy 252, 273, 276, 287, 434, 437
multilingualism 148, 160, 291, 300, 347
Munzur mountains 106
Munzur River 12, 56, 103, 106, 145, 262
murder 203
Muş 103, 253
music 187, 305, 306, 307, 314
musician 306, 307, 309
Muslim 60, 232, 258, 259, 267, 343, 381, 383
Mustafa Kemal Paşa Atatürk 194, 195, 196, 197, 286, 290, 357, 362, 363, 364, 367, 370, 371, 375, 388, 403, 423, 448, 453
mysticism 52, 59, 64, 198, 235, 241, 262, 272, 276, 284, 288, 329, 423
myths 42, 54, 86, 309, 310
namas 232, 243
Naqshebendi 192, 194, 195, 196, 198, 271, 276, 284, 285, 286, 422, 423, 427, 452
nationalism 81, 114, 127, 246, 298, 300, 357, 358, 368, 372, 418, 421, 427, 430, 438
nationlism 314

NATO 385
nature 245, 261
nazar 207
Near East 230, 246, 271, 284, 359, 360, 366, 387, 394, 401, 408, 429
Nemrut 98
neqera 306
Nestorians 67, 107, 115, 146, 152, 228, 380
New Testament 260, 266, 312, 343
newspaper 156, 187, 367
nomadism 68, 94, 96, 99, 109, 121, 301, 392, 410, 438
non-Christian 64
non-Islamic 59, 64, 65, 216, 224, 227, 276, 277, 289, 359, 361, 364, 366, 368, 371, 377, 388, 393, 404, 406, 410, 422, 425, 427, 428, 437, 438
non-Turkish 59, 275, 313, 360, 362, 364, 368, 371, 377, 386, 388, 404, 420, 428, 429, 433, 437
Northern Group 59, 79, 82, 102, 103, 105, 114, 153, 186, 188, 194, 195, 197, 201, 217, 224, 235, 238, 248, 258, 260, 261, 282, 283, 306, 320, 329, 331, 345, 355, 357, 370, 397, 405, 426, 427, 432, 434, 440
Northern Iraq 56, 67, 84, 85, 86, 99, 103, 110, 116, 129, 249, 297, 354, 417
nuclear family 203, 261, 266, 269, 300, 346, 353
Nurcu 419, 423, 427
objectivity 26, 33
Old Persian 116, 157, 223, 391, 395, 416, 432, 433
oneness 333
ontology 215
oral tradition 13, 62, 68, 73, 92, 94, 99, 100, 117, 187, 190, 211, 218, 228, 262, 283, 306, 307, 344
oral-aural 32, 187, 190, 306, 307, 406
Orthodox 228, 377
Osmanlı 277, 323
Ottoman Empire 59, 66, 107, 108, 109, 112, 113, 145, 188, 189, 190, 191, 193, 199, 200, 201, 217, 226, 231, 247, 253, 257, 274, 276, 284, 286, 294, 298, 354, 355, 357, 359, 361, 377, 379, 380, 381, 394, 395, 396, 399, 400, 402, 403, 418, 420, 429, 444
paganism 258
Pahlavi 391
Palestine 110, 225, 428
Palu 51, 52, 103, 131, 132, 191, 232, 250, 253, 271, 272, 276, 285, 339, 452
Pan-Arabism 363, 388
Pan-Islamism 247, 248, 357, 359, 363, 365, 366, 375, 377, 388, 393, 398, 403, 421, 424, 427, 428, 430

pantheon 220, 237, 331, 333
Pan-Turanism 357, 363, 366, 375
Pan-Turkism 98, 146, 247, 248, 357, 359, 363, 365, 366, 375, 376, 388, 403, 424, 427, 428, 430
paradigm 165, 167
parallelism 307
Parsiism 65, 217, 235, 236, 355, 395
Parthian-Thesis 86, 88, 95, 97, 100, 107, 116, 120, 122, 223, 391, 432, 433
participant observation 23, 29, 50, 52
passive 166
paternalism 82, 252, 268, 271, 288
patrilineal 277
patrilocal 288
peace 307, 308, 314
peasantry 15, 88, 186, 188, 245, 265, 275, 287, 288, 301, 309, 311, 314, 345, 353, 392, 432, 434, 438
perfect stem 166
Persia 51, 63, 66, 86, 97, 116, 117, 120, 122, 129, 160, 189, 191, 201, 221, 236, 304, 305, 324, 328, 358, 360, 361, 377, 391, 396, 444
personal pronoun 321
Pertek 103
philosophy 24, 37, 214, 216, 221, 240, 321, 431
phlegmatics 370
phonology 352
pir 187, 240, 243, 244, 288, 306, 307, 318, 434
Plutarch 342
pogrom 388
Poland 382
politics 15, 93, 125, 187, 188, 190, 195, 197, 258, 272, 276, 284, 287, 295, 339, 370, 402, 437
polygamy 339
polylingualism 291
polytheism 217, 222
poverty 307, 314, 338, 339, 341
power balance 46, 206
power distance 204
prayer 318
pre-arranged marriage 269, 288
Pre-Islamic 226
Premier 371
prescriptive marriage 269, 288, 340
present tense 166, 181
prestige 38, 46, 201, 206, 244, 266, 271, 280, 287, 320, 325, 328, 338, 340, 342, 343, 346, 435
princedom 246, 247, 437
profane 317, 328
pronoun 164
propaganda 427

Index

prophet 242, 249
Protestantism 112, 231, 394, 402, 404, 406, 412, 414, 420, 421, 429, 445
Proto-Indo-European 101, 118, 119, 122
Proto-Iranian 119
prototype theory 213
Proto-Westiranian 119, 120, 122
proverbs 322
Prussia 200, 363, 382
psychology 21, 35, 44, 431
purity 46, 233, 339, 435
Qadr 249
Qur'an 26, 28, 203, 208, 209, 218, 220, 227, 233, 248, 249, 320, 331, 333, 343, 346, 365, 395, 402, 423
rabbit 256, 262
racism 187, 299, 300, 402
rainbow 331
Ramazan 337
rape 276, 338, 434
rayber 244
rebellions 77, 78, 98, 107, 240, 357, 416, 433, 445
reciprocity 209, 325, 340, 420, 425, 427, 430, 434
reconciliation 308, 343
Reconquista 379, 380
reflexive pronoun 165
Reformation 380
reincarnation 345
re-islamisation 148, 188, 232, 237, 247, 248
Relevance Theory 39
religion 11, 42, 44, 45, 49, 56, 64, 130, 188, 190, 195, 197, 199, 203, 205, 212, 215, 216, 218, 221, 235, 272, 276, 285, 314, 325, 345, 353, 357, 402, 414, 420, 426, 433
religious brotherhood 271
religious institution 272
Republic of Turkey 32, 274, 355, 357, 367, 376, 378, 389
repudiation 234, 346, 425
resettlement 106
respect 340
revelation 26, 48, 208, 218, 227, 407, 413, 420, 430
rhyme 307
ritual 331, 340, 342
Rojbeyani 130
Roman Catholic Church 59, 228, 231, 260, 377, 381, 394, 396, 408, 429, 444
Roman Empire 222
Romans 107, 201, 408
Roshkakai 130

Russia 110, 191, 192, 267, 294, 361, 382, 385, 395, 396, 399, 409, 415, 417, 429, 450
Russian 200, 370
sacred 217, 309, 310, 314, 317, 328
Said Nursi 194
Sangsari 84, 432
Şanlıurfa 227, 250, 256
Sanskrit 116
Sapir-Whorf hypothesis 41
Sarlî 130
Sassanid Empire 88, 97, 412
Sassanid-Thesis 88
Satan 210, 223, 327
saz 306
Scandinavia 291
school system 13, 106, 111, 117, 144, 188, 200, 230, 248, 279, 289, 331, 369, 386, 426, 444
second class citizen 109, 229, 231, 232, 246, 258, 264, 359, 361, 362, 368, 377, 394, 400, 401, 406, 411, 415, 429, 437
second generation 293
sedentarism 301
segregation 36, 233, 239
SEIC 44, 167, 202, 210
Seleucids 98
Seljuk Empire 190, 201, 237, 359, 360, 377, 387
Seljuks 87, 100, 148, 189, 229, 232, 257, 395, 426
semantics 33, 166, 214, 316, 321, 435
semiotics 33, 214
Semitic 118, 252, 389, 390
Semnani 72, 432
sexual defilement 234
sexuality 233, 340, 346
Seyit Rıza 81, 192, 195, 196, 198, 201, 238
Shabak 65, 127, 130
Shafi'ism 60, 79, 93, 108, 148, 216, 221, 225, 232, 235, 249, 264, 355, 370, 377, 416, 421, 427, 433, 439
Shamanism 240, 246, 387, 392, 425
shame orientation 17, 46, 50, 55, 201, 202, 204, 206, 271, 279, 324, 338, 341, 342, 346, 425, 431
Sharia 192, 267, 339, 343, 346, 361, 380, 400, 423, 435, 439
Sheikh 187, 197, 245, 253, 271, 272, 279, 284, 285, 288, 306, 312, 315, 333, 341, 437
Sheikh Ali 271
Sheikh Said 70, 77, 81, 98, 107, 192, 193, 195, 197, 198, 201, 277, 285, 355, 370, 452
sheikhdom 108, 252, 271, 276, 287, 437
Shi'ism 65, 129, 216, 235, 248, 355, 416
shooting star 331

Silk Road 85, 89, 107, 152, 160, 188, 190, 228, 235, 236, 248, 281, 355, 360
sin 203, 249
SINUS scale 291
Siverek 52, 74, 102, 103, 114, 131, 132, 145, 232, 250, 277, 281, 296
Slavic 389
small scale social unit 68, 98, 100, 102, 145, 187, 194
small scale society 43, 50, 60, 62, 67, 98, 130, 188, 195, 203, 215, 235, 244, 245, 266, 269, 271, 277, 280, 283, 287, 300, 311, 333, 339, 352, 420, 425, 430, 434
smallholders 311, 312
snake 240, 309, 310, 311, 313, 314, 332, 434
social science 21, 28, 34, 43, 80, 305, 431
social structure 342, 353
socialism 287, 355, 364, 375, 378, 393
society 36, 45, 267, 435, 438
sociolinguistics 23, 38
solidarity 242, 268, 286, 427, 448
Sorani 72, 84, 85, 93, 94, 111, 116, 122, 167, 416, 428
soul 206, 316, 327, 328
Southern Caspian 72, 84, 85, 89, 400, 433
Southern Group 59, 79, 102, 103, 114, 135, 137, 145, 153, 186, 188, 194, 197, 235, 245, 248, 264, 306, 310, 320, 329, 345, 354, 355, 370, 397, 405, 406, 421, 432, 434, 440
spiritual counterpart 205
spiritual world 214, 219, 220, 222, 233, 240, 262, 263, 327
split ergative 354, 433
Sprachbund 84, 85, 86, 111, 432, 433
standardization 80, 351, 353
stars 223, 261, 331, 412
stratification 253, 265, 315, 393, 434
structuralism 30
subjectivism 418, 431
subjectivity 26, 33, 50, 80
subjunctive stem 166
Sufi'ism 65, 235, 239, 286, 305, 355, 399, 416, 423
suicide 203, 206, 234
Suleiman the Magnificient 361
Süleymanlı 427
Sultanate 59, 196, 357, 360, 363, 377, 378, 384
sun 65, 261, 332
Sunni 188, 190, 195, 223, 245, 248, 305, 328

Sunnism 65, 66, 71, 80, 134, 195, 216, 221, 224, 225, 237, 248, 252, 272, 279, 355, 358, 370, 377, 399, 418, 419, 444, 450
supernatural 205, 215, 330, 333, 345
superstition 263
Surchi 116
Surp Sargis 310
Sweden 291, 293
symbolism 36, 215, 304, 331, 413
synagogue 107, 225, 402, 405, 409
syncretism 258, 262
syntax 164
Syria 56, 59, 67, 86, 103, 110, 138, 152, 189, 231, 246, 253, 305, 359, 360, 363, 365, 385, 403, 416, 417, 444
Syriac 391
Syriac Church 359, 388
Syriac Churches 229, 256, 380, 394, 400
taboo 45, 209, 233, 248, 261, 263, 287, 311, 314, 316, 328, 341
takiye 65
Talaat Pasha 367
Talysh 72, 84, 85, 158, 400, 432
tanzimat 359, 361, 362, 363, 364, 372, 387, 428
tarikat 235
Tartars 382, 383
Tauros 86, 94, 96, 104, 354, 397
tax obligation 247, 264, 400, 428, 437
telqim 319
Tertelê Dêrsimi 75, 192, 196, 197, 198, 238, 240, 245, 363, 371
theology 17, 37, 44, 83, 214, 252, 296, 369, 405, 410, 424
Third Space 80, 419, 420, 424, 427, 430, 431, 438
thought 11, 37, 38, 48, 50, 214, 314, 315, 405
Tigris 11, 97, 99, 102, 152, 278, 358, 359, 432
time perception 213
totalitarianism 108
tourism industry 293
tradition 107, 187, 242, 261, 306, 328
transcendence 26, 205, 215, 240
Treaty of Sèvres 399
tribe 43, 60, 96, 102, 110, 121, 152, 198, 214, 215, 225, 244, 246, 266, 269, 272, 277, 282, 283, 285, 290, 344, 360, 410, 444
Turgut Özal 372
Türk Tarıh Tezi 371, 372
Turkey 57, 86, 98, 102, 103, 154, 188, 200, 284, 287, 294, 300, 410
Turkic 118, 360, 377, 389

Index

Turkish 12, 32, 53, 59, 63, 68, 70, 72, 85, 100, 101, 103, 108, 137, 148, 151, 152, 187, 190, 196, 289, 290, 292, 305, 309, 347, 348, 361, 370, 372, 376, 377, 381, 385, 387, 395, 409, 419, 425, 432, 438, 446, 447
Turkish Constitution 70, 72, 146, 147, 287, 358, 368, 369, 388, 445
Turkish nationalism 418, 450
Turkishness 80, 238, 368, 371, 375, 418, 425, 427, 430, 431
Turks 72, 109, 190, 279, 289, 298, 395
ümmet 59
Uncertainty Reduction Theory 438
unemployment 298
UNESCO 68, 104, 114, 144, 150, 200, 230, 292, 339, 347, 350, 351, 356
unilineal 270
universe 212, 333
university 105, 295, 375, 384
upheaval 106, 248, 277, 355, 357
upper class 266, 352
urbanization 287, 345, 347
valence 166
vanity 341
Varto 52, 102, 105, 132, 135, 136, 258, 281
verb 165
village 106, 110, 114, 130, 146, 159, 209, 228, 250, 258, 269, 290, 301, 311, 370, 426, 437, 446, 447
vocative 164, 243
Wahhabism 232, 237, 246, 247, 370
war 197, 200, 231, 294, 307, 314, 359, 382, 383, 422, 445, 450
wedding 308, 338
Western 31, 64, 69, 101, 107, 168, 205, 211, 215, 230, 253, 286, 329, 365, 393, 429
widow 269, 315, 320
witchcraft 215
worldview 11, 15, 17, 23, 34, 38, 50, 54, 85, 166, 207, 208, 209, 212, 214, 215, 216, 218, 220, 222, 224, 238, 240, 242, 245, 261, 286, 288, 314, 315, 324, 328, 329, 345, 346, 353, 355, 357, 381, 392, 400, 401, 405, 406, 410, 411, 427, 431, 432, 435, 438
xenophobia 298, 299, 300, 362, 406, 438
Xızır 235, 238, 244, 335
Xızır İlyas 310
Yezidism 216, 217, 223, 224, 275, 313, 331, 332, 360, 399, 416, 421, 427
Young Ottomans 363, 366, 372
Young Turks 113, 152, 286, 363, 366, 367, 372, 377, 398, 399, 411, 426
Zagros 94, 354
zakat 232
Zaza 12, 102, 109, 249, 279, 304, 388, 400, 414, 428
Zaza society 57, 83, 186, 203, 209, 233, 236, 242, 253, 265, 268, 272, 287, 315, 325, 341, 434
Zazaki 12, 15, 56, 61, 85, 118, 120, 122, 125, 130, 131, 135, 146, 150, 151, 152, 154, 162, 163, 164, 165, 166, 211, 230, 249, 253, 256, 261, 271, 278, 289, 290, 292, 304, 323, 331, 344, 345, 347, 350, 352, 353, 371, 376, 387, 391, 405, 415, 418, 432, 433, 438,440
Zazaness 80, 203, 295, 418, 431, 432, 435
Zengana 130
zerri 212
Ziya Gökalp 365, 367, 371
Zoroaster *See* Zoroastrianism
Zoroastrianism 65, 149, 201, 216, 217, 222, 228, 232, 235, 239, 256, 261, 263, 264, 270, 305, 329, 331, 332, 355, 395, 400, 414, 416, 433
zurna 306

Bibliography

Overview

Bibliography	482
Websites	524
Personal Communication	527
Exegetical Tools	528
Material about the Zaza and Zazaki	529
Linguistics	529
Zazaki – Linguistics – Magazine	529
Linguistics	529
Glossaries	531
Language Learning and Literacy	532
Culture and History	532
Cultural Websites	534
Magazines	534

Ahmed, Akbar S. 2004. *Postmodernism and Islam - Predicament and Promise*. London: Routledge.

Ahmed, Munir D. 1988. Frauenfrage und Islam, in Steinbach, Udo & Robert, Rüdiger (eds.): *Der Nahe und Mittlere Osten: Politik, Gesellschaft, Wirtschaft, Geschichte, Kultur*, 521-532. Opladen: Leske + Budrich. [Engl.: Question of Women and Islam, in Steinbach, Udo & Robert, Rüdiger (eds.): The Near and Middle East: Politics, Society, Economy, History, Culture.].

Akkoç, Umut, Keskin, Mesut & Zazaoğlu, Mirzali 2010. *Vatebendo Etimolocik: Zazaca kelimlerin kökeni hakkında – Türkçe açıklamali küçük etimolojik sözlük*. 1. Capê Cerrebi. Frankfurt: Enstituyê Zazaki. [Engl.: Etymological Dictionary: On Zazaki Wordroots – A small Etymological Turkish Dictionary in Turkish. 1st trial ed.].

Aksoy, Hasan. 2004. Mevlid (Türk Edebiyatı). *İslâm Ansiklopedisi* XXIX (TDV), 482–484. Ankara. [Engl.: Turkish Islam Encyclopedia.].

Akyıldız, Mustafa 1978. *Ben bir süleymanci idim*. Adana: Kozan. [Engl.: I am a Süleymanci.].

Aland, Kurt, et.al. (eds.) 2004. *The Greek New Testament - GNT*. 4th ed. Holzgerlingen: Deutsche Bibelgesellschaft. [German Bible Society].

Aland, Kurt, Aland, Barbara & Reichmann, Viktor und frühere englische Ausgaben von Arndt, W.F., Gingrich, F.W. & Danker, F.W. (eds.) 2000. *Greek-English Lexicon of the New Testament and Other Early Christian Literature*. BDAG. 3rd ed. Chicago: The University of Chicago. [Deutsche Ausgabe: Walter Bauer's Griechisch-deutsches Wörterbuch zu den Schriften des Neuen Testaments und der frühchristlichen Literatur, 6th ed. Amsterdam: de Gruyter].

Albayrak, Sadık 1979. *Şeriat yolunda yürüyenler ve sürünenler*. İstanbul: Araştırma Yayınları. [Engl.: The Way of the Islamic Law of Walkers and Crawlers.].

Al-Khayyat, Sana 1991. *Ehre und Schande: Frauen in Irak*. Aus dem Englischen von Elfi Hartenstein. Munich: Antje Kunstmann. [Engl: Honor and Shame: Women in Iraq. Translated from Englisch by Elfi Hartenstein.].

Allen, William Edward David & Muratoff, Paul Pavlovich 1953. *Caucasian Battlefields*. Cambridge: Cambridge University Press. [Turkish edition: Allen, William Edward David & Muratoff, Paul Pavlovich 1966. *Kafkas Harekâti*. Ankara: Genelkurmay Basımevi.].

Allouche, Adel 1983. *The Origins and Development of the Ottoman-Safavid Conflict 906-962/1500-1555*. Berlin: Klaus Schwarz.

Amoretti, Biancamaria Sciarcia. 1993. Pre-Safavid Religious Topography. *The Cambridge History of Iran* 6, 632-637. Cambridge.

Andranik 1900. *Tersim* (Dersim). Tblisi.

Andreas, Friedrich Carl 1916. *Festschrift für Friedrich Carl Andreas: Zur Vollendung des siebzigsten Lebensjahres am 14. April 1916*. Leipzig: Harrassowitz. [Engl.: Festschrift to Friedrich Carl Andreas: Getting seventy on the 14th April 1916.].

Andrews, Peter Alford [1989] 2002a. A Reaapraisal, in Andrews, Peter Alford & Benninghaus, Rüdiger (eds.): Ethnic Groups in the Republic of Turkey: Supplement and Index. Beihefte zum Tübinger Atlas des Vorderen Orients Nr. 60.2, 9-25. Wiesbaden: Ludwig Reichert.

Andrews, Peter Alford [1989] 2002b. Catalogue of Ethnic Groups, in Andrews, Peter Alford & Benninghaus, Rüdiger (eds.): *Ethnic Groups in the Republic of Turkey*. Beihefte zum Tübinger Atlas des Vorderen Orients Nr. 60.2, 53-178. Wiesbaden: Ludwig Reichert.

Andrews, Peter Alford [1989] 2002c. Introduction, in Andrews, Peter Alford & Benninghaus, Rüdiger (Eds.): *Ethnic Groups in the Republic of Turkey*. Beihefte zum Tübinger Atlas des Vorderen Orients Nr. 60.2, 17-52. Wiesbaden: Ludwig Reichert.

Andrews, Peter Alford [1989] 2002d. Postscript, in Andrews, Peter Alford & Benninghaus, Rüdiger (eds.): *Ethnic Groups in the Republic of Turkey: Supplement and Index*. Beihefte zum Tübinger Atlas des Vorderen Orients Nr. 60.2, 316-322. Wiesbaden: Ludwig Reichert.

Andrews, Peter Alford & Benninghaus, Rüdiger (eds.) [1989] 2002. *Ethnic Groups in the Republic of Turkey*. Beihefte zum Tübinger Atlas des Vorderen Orients Nr. 60.2, 17-52. Wiesbaden: Ludwig Reichert.

Antes, Peter 1988. Die Religionen des Nahen und Mittleren Ostens, in Steinbach, Udo & Robert, Rüdiger (eds.): *Der Nahe und Mittlere Osten: Politik, Gesellschaft, Wirtschaft, Geschichte, Kultur*, 49-66. Opladen: Leske + Budrich. [Engl.: Religions of the Middle and Far East, in The Middle and Far East: Politics, Society, Economy, Hostory, Culture].

Arakelova, Victoria A. 1999-2000. The Zaza people as a new Ethno-Political Factor in the Region. *Iran and the Caucasus*, Vol. 3/4, 397-408. Leiden: Brill. And Online: URL: http://www.jstor.org/stable/4030804 [accessed 2017-06-14].

Arakelova, Victoria A. 2001. Sufi Saints in the Yezidi Tradition: Qawlē Husaynī Halāj. *Iran and the Caucasus* 5, 183-192. Brill: Leiden.

Arakelova, Victoria A. 2002. Three Figures from the Yezidi Folk Pantheon. *Iran and the Caucasus* 7/1-2, 57-74. Brill: Leiden.

Arakelova, Victoria A. 2004. Notes on the Yezidi Religious Syncretism. *Iran and the Caucasus* 8/1, 19-28. Leiden: Brill.

Arakelova, Victoria A. 2007. Milyāk'atē-qanj - The Phallic Deity of the Yezīdīs, Vahman, Fereydun & Pedersen, Claus V. (eds.): *Religious Texts in Iranian Languages*, 329-333. Copenhagen: Det Kongelige Danske Videnskabernes Selskab.

Arens, Edmund 2011. Religion as Communication, in Hook, Derek, Franks, Bradley & Baur, Martin W. (eds.): *The Social Psychology of Communication*, 249-265. New York: Palgrave Macmillan.

Armstrong, D.M. 1993. Bedeutung und Kommunikation, in Meggle, Georg (ed.): *Handlung, Kommunikation, Bedeutung*, 112-136. Frankfurt: Suhrkamp. [Engl.: Meaning and Communication.].

Arnaiz-Villena, A., Karin, M. & Bendikuze, N. et al. (2001). HLA alleles and haplotypes in the Turkish population: Relatedness to Kurds, Armenians and other Mediterraneans. *Tissue Antigens* 57/4, 308–317.

Asatrian, Garnik Serobi 1995a. Dımlī. *Encyclopedia Iranica*. Online: URL: http://www.iranica.com/articles/v7/v7f4/v7f447.html [accessed 2017-06-18]. [also in Asatrian, Garnik Serobi 1998. Dımıli. Ware 12, 182-187. Baiersbronn.].

Asatrian, Garnik Serobi 1995b. Divakank: A Demonological Miscellany - Iran-Nameh -. *Armenian Journal of Oriental Studies* 14, 21-35. Leiden: Brill.

Asatrian, Garnik Serobi 1998. Armenian Xoy-t'olowt'iwn (Tracing Back an Old Animal-Breeding Custom in Ancient Armenia). *Iran and the Caucasus: Research Papers from the Caucasian Centre for Iranian Studies* 2, 63-67. Yerevan: Yerevan State University.

Asatrian, Garnik Serobi 1999-2000. The Holy Brotherhood: The Yezidi Religious Institution of the "Brother and Sister of the Next World". *Iran and the Caucasus* 3-4, 209-211. Brill: Leiden.

Asatrian, Garnik Serobi 2001. Al Reconsidered. *Iran and the Caucasus* 5, 149-157. Brill: Leiden.

Asatrian, Garnik Serobi 2002. The Lord of Cattle. *Iran and the Caucasus* 6/1-2, 1-2. Brill: Leiden.

Asatrian, Garnik Serobi 2007. The Foremother of the Yezīdīs, Vahman, Fereydun & Pedersen, Claus V. (eds.): *Religious Texts in Iranian Languages*, 323-328. Copenhagen: Det Kongelige Danske Videnskabernes Selskab.

Asatrian, Garnik Serobi 2009. Prolegomena to the Study of the Kurds. *Iran and the Caucasus* 13, 1-58. Leiden: Brill.

Asatrian, Garnik Serobi 2009. Dānešnāme-ye gūyeshā-ye Kāšān [A Comparative Dictionary of Kashan Dialects], Tehran (Kashanica Foundation). [unpublished].

Asatrian, Garnik Serobi & Arakelova, Victoria A. 2003. Malak-Tawus: The Peacock Angel of the Yezidis. *Iran and the Caucasus* 7/1-2, 7-8. Leiden: Brill.

Bibliography

Asatrian, Garnik Serobi & Arakelova, Victoria 2004. The Yezidi Pantheon. *Iran and the Caucasus* 8/2, 231-279. Leiden: Brill.

Asatrian, Garnik Serobi & Gevorgian, N. KH. 1988. Zaza Miscellany: Notes on some religious customs and Institutions, in *Acta Iranica, Encyclopédie Permanente des Études Iraniennes*. Publiée par le Centre International d'Études Indo-Iraniennes. Hommages et Opera Minora. Volume XII. A Green Leaf. Papers in Honour of Professor Jes P. Asmussen. Extrait. Diffusion, 500-508. Leiden: Brill.

Asatrian, Garnik Serobi & Livshits, Vladimir 1994. Origine du système consonantique de la langue kurde. *Acta Kurdica* (The International Journal of Kurdish and Iranian Studies) I, 81-108. London: RoutledgeCurzon.

Asher, Ronald 1994. *The Encyclopedia of Language and Linguistics*. Oxford: Pergamon.

Aslan, Mikail 2003. *Kilıtê Kou - The Key of the Mountains - Dağların Anahtarı*. İstanbul: Kalan. [CD-ROM].

Ateş, Ahmed 1979. Mesnevî. *İslâm Ansiklopedisi* VIII, 127–133. İstanbul: Millî Eğitim Basımevi.

Auernheimer, Georg 1984. Kultur, Identität und interkulturelle Erziehung. *Demokratische Erziehung* 12, 23-26. Köln: Pahl-Rugenstein. [Engl.: Culture, Identity an intercultural Education. Democratic Education.].

Avestis, Aharonyan (Awetis, Aharoneau) 1911. *Armenische Erzählungen*. (Transl. by Agnes Finck-Gjandschezian). Leipzig: Reclam. [Engl: Armenian Folktales].

Aygen, Gülşat 2010. *Zazaki/Kirmanckî Kurdish*. Munich: Lincom.

Badenberg, Robert 2003. *Sickness and Healing: A Case Study on the Dialectic of Culture and Personality*. edition afem. Nuremberg: VTR.

Badenberg, Robert 2007. *Das Menschenbild in fremden Kulturen: Ein Leitfaden für eigene Erkundungen. Handbuch zu Lothar Käsers Lehrbuch Animismus*. Nuremberg: VTR. [Engl.: Conception of Man in foreign Cultures: A Guide to own Investigations. Handbook accompanying the Textbook of Lothar Käser *Animism*.].

Bailey, Denise 2003. An overview of the classification of Iranian languages. Working Paper. Göttingen: Universität Göttingen. (unpublished).

Bailey, Denise 2010. Gorani summary. Working paper. SIL International. (unpublished).

Balz, Horst & Schneider, Gehard 1980. *Exegetisches Wörterbuch zum Neuen Testament*. ExWBNT. 3 Vol. Stuttgart: Kohlhammer. [Engl. Exegetical Dicionary to the New Testament].

Banton, Michael (ed.) 1966. *Anthropological Approaches to the Study of Religion*. London: Tavistock.

Barihas, Şervan 2003. *Şervan: Ra u Rêçe*. Ethno Müzik Yapım. [CD-ROM]. [Engl.: Servan: Way and Demand.].

Barker, Kenneth L. 2003. Bible Translation Philosophies with special Reference to The New International Version, in Scorgie, Glen G., Strauss, Mark L. & Voth, Steven M. (eds.): *The Challenge of Bible Translation: Communicating God's Word to the World*, 51-63. Grand Rapids: Zondervan.

Barnard, Alan & Spencer, Jonathan 2004. *Encyclopedia of Social and Culural Anthropology*. Reprint. London: Routledge.

Barnwell, Katharine [1987] 1992. *Teacher's Manual to accompany Bible Translation: An Introductory Course in Translation Principles*. Reprint. Dallas: SIL International.

Barnwell, Katharine [1975] 1999. *Bible Translation: An Introductory Course in Translation Principles*. 3rd ed. Reprint. Dallas: SIL International.

Baroja, Julio Caro 1966. *Honour and Shame: A Historical Account of Several Conflicts*. (Translated from Spanish.).

Baron-Cohen, Simon 2004. *Vom ersten Tag an anders: Das weibliche und das männliche Gehirn*. Düsseldorf: Walter. [Engl.: From the Beginning on different: The female and male Brain].

Barrett, Karen Caplovitz 1995. A Functionalist Approach to Shame and Guilt, in Tangney, Price June & Fischer, Kurt W. (eds.): *Self-conscious Emotions: The Psychology of Shame, Guilt, Embarrassment, and Pride*. New York: Guilford, 25-63.

Bartholomew, Doris A. & Schoenhals, Louse C. 1983. *Bilingual Dictionaries for Indigenous Languages*. Hidalgo: SIL International.

Bascom, Robert 2003. The Role of Culture in Translation, in Wilt, Timothy (ed.): *Bibletranslation: Frames of Reference*, 81-111. Manchester: St. Jerome.

Bauer, Brigitte 2000. *Archaic Syntax in Indo-European: The Spread of Transitivity in Latin and Fench*. Trends in Linguistics 125. Berlin: Walter de Gruyter.

Bauer, Laurie, Holmes, Janet & Warren, Paul 2006. *Language Matters*. London: Palgrave.

Baumann, Andreas 2005. Die Begegnung von Evangelium und Islam - Die Notwendigkeit ihrer Erforschung, in Baumann, Andreas, Sauer, Christof & Troeger, Eberhard (eds.): *Christliches Zeugnis und islamische Da'wa*, 11-18. Nuremberg: VTR. [Engl.: Encounter of Gospel and Islam – The Necessarity of their Research].

Baumann, Andreas 2007. *Der Orient für Christus: Johannes Lepsius - Biographie und Missiologie*. Gießen: Brunnen. [Engl.: The Orient for Christ: Johan Lepsius - Biography and Missiology].

Beer, Bettina & Fischer, Hans 2003. *Wissenschaftliche Arbeitstechniken in der Ethnologie*. 2. rev. ed. Berlin: Dietrich Reimer. [Engl.: Scientific Methods in Cultural Anthropology].

Behagel, Otto 1909. Beziehungen zwischen Umfang und Reihenfolge von Satzgliedern. *Indogermanische Forschungen* 25, 110-142. Berlin: Walter de Gruyter. [Engl.: Relations in Scope and Order of Sentence Constituents. Indo-Germanic Research.].

Bell, Roger T. 1991. *Translation and Translating: Theory and Practice*. New York: Longman.

Benedict, Ruth. 1946. *The Chrysanthenum and the Sword: Patterns of Japanese Culture*. Boston: Houghton and Mifflin Co.

Benedictsen / Christensen, Andreas 1921. *Les dialectes d'Awroman et de Pawâ*. Copenhagen.

Benninghaus, Rüdiger [1989] 2002. Hemşinli – Islamisierung, in Andrews, Peter Alford (ed.): *Ethnic Groups in the Republic of Turkey*, 483-484. Wiesbaden: Ludwig Reichert. [Engl.: Hemşinli – Islamisation.].

Benveniste, Emilé 1973. *Indo-European Language and Society*. Coral Gables: University of Miami Press.

Berkes, Niyazi 1959. *Turkish Nationalism and Western Civilization*. New York: Columbia University Press.

Berz, Koyo 1993. *Sîyamed û Xeca*. Stockholm-Spanga: Apec. [Engl.: Siyamed and Xeja.].

Berz, Koyo 1995a. *Kole Nêba: Şeher ê Dimlî*. Stockholm: Weşanxaney Îremetî (Iremet Förlag). [Engl. I am not a Slave: Prophet of Dimli].

Berz, Koyo 1995b. *Namdarê Sêwregı 1*. Stockholm: Iremet Förlag. [Engl. Famous People of Siverek].

Bhabha, Homi 1994. *The Location of Culture*. London: Routledge.

Bischof-Köhler, Doris 2004. *Von Natur aus anders: Die Psychologie der Geschlechtsunterschiede*. 2nd ed. Stuttgart: Kohlhammer. [Engl.: Different by Nature: Psychology of Gender-Differentiation].

Bläsing, Uwe 1995. Kurdische und Zaza-Elemente im türkeitürkischen Dialektlexicon. *Near Eastern Languages and Literatures* (NELL) 1/2, 173 – 218. Leiden. Also Online: URL: http://home.arcor.de/fidemes/Blaesing-1995-Kurdisch-Zaza.pdf [PDF-File]. [Engl. Elements of Kurdish and Zaza in the Turkey-Turkish Dialectlexicon].

Blass, Regina 1990. *Relevance Relations in Discourse: A Study with Special Reference to Sissala*. Cambridge: Cambridge Univesity Press.

Blau, Joyce 1989. Gurani et Zaza, in Schmitt, Rüdiger (ed.): *Compendium linguarum Iranicarum*, 336-340. Wiesbaden: Ludwig Reichert.

Bligh, John 1969. *Galatians: A Discussion of St Paul's Epistle*. London: St Paul Publications.

Blincoe, Robert 1998. *Ethnic realities and the church - lessons from Kurdistan - a history of mission work, 1668 - 1990*. Pasadena: Presbyterian centre for mission studies.

Boeschoten, Hendrik & Verhoeven, Ludo (eds.) 1991. *Turkish Linguistics Today*. Leiden: Brill.

Bollig, Michael 2006. *Risk Management in a Hazardous Environment: A Comparative Study of two Pastoral Societies*. Studies in Human Ecology and Adaptation, Vol. 2. New York: Springer.

Bosch, David J. 1991. *Transforming Mission: Paradigm Shifts in Theology of Mission*. Maryknoll: Orbis.

Botterweck, G. Johannes & Ringgren, Helmer (eds.) 1973. *Theologisches Wörterbuch zum Alten Testament (ThWBAT)*. Stuttgart: Kohlhammer. [Engl: Theological Dicionary tot he Old Testament.].

Bourne, Phil 2009. Summary of the Contextualization Debate. *St Francis Magazine* 5/5, 58-80. Loretto: Saint Francis University. Online on the Web: URL: http://stfrancismagazine.info/ja/images/pdf/6PhilBoureSFM5-5.pdf [PDF-File] [accessed 2010-06-09].

Brandes, Sabine 2008. Schützende Hand: Die Chamsa soll den bösen Blick abwehren. Der Aberglaube erfreut sich in Israel großer Beliebtheit. *Jüdische Allgemeine* 39-40, Rosch Haschana, 25. September 2008. Berlin. Jüdische Presse GmbH. [Engl.: Guarding hand: The Chamsa shall prevent against the evil eye. Superstition becomes popular in Israel. Jewish Common. Jewish Press.].

Brentjes, Burchard 1996. Araber, in Cancik, Hubert & Schneider, Helmuth (eds.): *Der Neue Pauly: Enzyklopädie der Antike*, Bd. 1: A-Ari, 944-945. Suttgart: J.B. Metzler. [Engl.: The Arabs.].

Brockhaus 2009. *Sozialwissenschaften*. Brockhaus premium multimedia. Gütersloh: Bibliographisches Institut & F. A. Brockhaus AG. [Engl.: Social Sciences.].

Brown, Rick u. a. 2000. Some Key Concepts and Terms Which Are Often Misunderstood in the Arab World. Horsleys Green. (unpublished).

Brown, Rick 2005. Translating the Biblical Term „Son(s) of God" in Muslim Contexts. *International Journal of Frontier Missions* 22/4, 135-145.

Bruinessen, Martin M. van w/d. "The debate on the ethnic identity of the Kurdish Alevis", Working paper together with Malvern, Victoria (Australia). Centre for the Study of Asia & the Middle East. Deakin: Deakin University.

Bruinessen, Martin M. van 1989a. Die Türkische Republik, ein säkularisierter Staat? in Blaschke, Jochen & Bruinessen, Martin M. van (eds.): *Islam und Politik in der Türkei*, 13-52. Berlin: Edition Parabolis. [Engl.: The Turkish Republic, a secularized State? in Blaschke, Jochen & Bruinessen, Martin van (eds.): Islam and Politics in Turkey, 13-52].

Bruinessen, Martin M. van 1989b. Vom Osmanismus zum Separatismus: Religiöse und ethnische Hintergründe der Rebellion des Scheich Said, in Blaschke, Jochen & Bruinessen, Martin M. van (eds.): *Islam und Politik in der Türkei*, 109-166. Berlin: Edition Parabolis. [Engl.: From Osmanism to Separism: Religious and ethnical Background of the Sheikh Said Uprise, in Blaschke, Jochen & Bruinessen, Martin M. van (eds.): *Islam and Politics in Turkey*, 109-166].

Bruinessen, Martin M. van [1989] 1992. *Agha, Sheikh and State - On the Social and Political Structures of Kurdistan*. London: Zed.

Bruinessen, Martin M. van 1994. Genocide in Kurdistan? The Suppression of the Dersim Rebellion in Turkey (1937-38) and the Chemical War Against the Iraqi Kurds (1988), in Andreopoulos, George J. (ed.): *Conceptual and historical dimensions of genocide*, 141-70. Philadelphia: University of Pennsylvania Press.

Bruinessen, Martin M. van [1989] 2002. The Ethnic Identity of the Kurds, in Andrews, Peter Alford & Benninghaus, Rüdiger (eds.): *Ethnic Groups in the Republic of Turkey*. Beihefte zum Tübinger Atlas des Vorderen Orients Nr. 60.2, 613-621. Wiesbaden: Ludwig Reichert.

Buckingham, Marcus & Clifton, Donald O. 2001. *Now Discover your Strengths*. New York: The Free Press.

Buda, Richard & Elsayed-Elkhouly, Sayed M. 1998. Cultural Differences between Arabs and Americans: Individualism-Collectivism Revisited. *Journal of Cross-Cultural Psychology* 29, Nr. 3: 487-492.

Büyükkaya, Necmetin 1992. Zazaca – Türkçe sözlük listesi/ Qısebendê Zazaki – Tırki. [Zazaki – Turkish wordlist]. *Kalemimden Sayfalar*, 419-468. Spanga-Stockholm: APEC.

Bumke, Peter J. [1989] 2002. Kurdish Alevis - Bounderies and Perception, in Andrews, Peter Alford & Benninghaus, Rüdiger (Eds.): *Ethnic Groups in the Republic of Turkey*. Beihefte zum Tübinger Atlas des Vorderen Orients Nr. 60.2, 510-518. Wiesbaden: Ludwig Reichert.

Bunge, Mario & Ardila, Ruben [1987] 1990. *Philosophie der Psychologie*. Tübingen: Mohr Siebeck.

Burton, Laurel Arthur 1988. Original Sin or Original Shame. *Quarterly Review 8*, Nr. 4:31-41.

Buss, Arnold 1980. *Self-consciousness and Social Anxiety*. San Francisco: W. H. Freeman.

Busse, Heribert 1988. Das arabisch-islamische Weltreich und seine Nachfolgestaaten, in Steinbach, Udo & Robert, Rüdiger (eds.): *Der Nahe und Mittlere Osten: Politik, Gesellschaft, Wirtschaft, Geschichte, Kultur*, 81-96. Opladen: Leske + Budrich. [Engl.: The Arabic-Islamic Empire and its Succeeding Countries].

Bußmann, Hadumod 2002. *Lexikon der Sprachwissenschaft*. 3rd ed. Stuttgart: Kröner.

Caglar, Ayse S. 1998. McDöner: Dönerkebab und der Kampf der Deutsch-Türken um soziale Stellung. *Soziologus* 48/2, 111-135. Berlin.

Çağlayan, Ercan 2011. Osmanlı Belgelerinde Zazalar ve Zazaca Üzerine Notlar. T.C. Bingöl Üniversitesi: *Uluslararisi Zaza Dili Sempozyumu*, 13-14th Mayis. Bingöl. [Engl.: References about the Zaza people and the Zaza Language out from Ottoman Documents. T.C. Bingöl Üniversitesi: *International Conference about the Zaza Language*, 13-14th May. Bingöl.].

Çağlayan, Hüseyin 2003. *38 ra Jü Pelge*. İstanbul: Vêjiyayışê Tiji.

Çağlayan, Hüseyin 1998. Dersim, eine alevitische Oase im Islam. *Ware* 12, 176-181. Baiersbronn. [Engl.: Dersim, an Alevitic Haven in Islam.].

Callow, Kathleen 1998. *Man and Message: A Guide to Meaning-based Text Analysis*. Oxford: University Press of America.

Campbell, Barth L. 1998. *Honor Shame, and the Rhetoric of 1 Peter*. SBL Dissertation Series 160. Atlanta: Scholars Press.

Carekiz, C. 1999. *Bava Gul*. İstanbul (Beyoglu): Vejiyayise Tij/Tij Yayinlari. [Engl.: Father Gul.].

Çar, Gagan 1997. *Zarathuş ra: Vendidad*. Stockholm: Zaza Förlag.

Çarkoğlu, Ali & Toprak, Binnaz 1006. *Değişen Türkiye'de Din, Toplum ve Siyaset*, 29. İstanbul: TESEV. [Engl.: Religion, Society and Politics in a Changing Turkey.].

Carnie, Andrew 2002. *Syntax: A Generative Introduction*. Oxford: Blackwell.

Carrithers, Michael 1992. *Why Humans have Cultures: Explaining Anthropology and Social Diversity*. Oxford: Opus.

Carson, D. A. 2003. The Limits of Functional Equivalence in Bible Translation and other Limits, too, in Scorgie, Glen G., Strauss, Mark L. & Voth, Steven M. (eds.): *The Challenge of Bible Translation: Communicating God's Word to the World*, 65-113. Grand Rapids: Zondervan.

Cavalli-Sforza, Luigi Luca 1994. *The History and Geography of Human Genes*. Princeton: Princeton University Press.

Çelebi, Evliya 1896. *Seyahatname*. First print. İstanbul.

Çelker, Xal 1993. Ma, Welatê Ma, Zon u Dinê Ma. Halkımız, Yurdumuz, Dilimiz ve Din Sorunu. Isim konusu ve kısa bir tarihçemiz. *Ware: Zeitschrift für Zaza-Sprache und Kultur* 5, 41-51. [We, our homeland, and our Language and Religion. Ware: Magazine for the Zaza-Language and Culture.].

Cengiz, Daimi 2001. *Dersim Fablları-I*. Ankara: Kalan Yayınları. [Engl. Folkstories of Dersim.].

Cengiz, Seyfi 1993. *Dersim ve Dersimli*. London: Desmala Sure Yayınları.

Charmoy, François Bernard 1868-1875. *Chèref-Nâmeh, ou fastes de la nation kourde*. 2 Vols. St. Petersburg.

Chater Melville 1928. The Kizilbash Clans of Kurdistan. *National Geographic Journal* 54/4. London.

Chesterman, Andrew 1997. *Memes of Translation: The Spread of Ideas in Translation Theory.* Amsterdam: John Benjamins.

Chesterman, Andrew 2001. Proposal for a Hieronymic Oath, in Pym, Anthony (ed.): *The Translator: Studies in Intercultural Communication. Return to ethics* Vol. 7/2, 139-154. Manchester: St. Jerome.

Chouraqui, André N. 1994. *Reflexionen über Problematik und Methode der Übersetzung von Bibel und Koran.* Tübingen: Mohr Siebeck. [Engl.: Reflections on the Problem and Method of Translating the Bible and the Quran].

Çiçek, Nazmi 2011. The Effect of Turkish as Official Language on Bilingualism in the Village of Êxê (Bulgurcuk). Power Point Presentation. Yerevan: Mardin Artuluk Universitesi. [unpublished].

Clark, Herbert H. & Clark, Eve V. 1978. Universals, Relativity, and Language Processing, in Greenberg, Joseph H. (ed.): *Universals of Human Language*, 225-299. Stanford: Stanford University Press.

Clicqué, Guy M. 2001. *Differenz und Parallelität: Zum Verständnis des Zusammenhangs von Theologie und Naturwissenschaft am Beispiel der Überlegungen Günter Howes.* Frankfurt/M.: Peter Lang. [Engl.: Difference and Prallelism: To the Understanding of the Connection of Theology and Natural Science at the example of the Considerations Günter Howes].

Coenen, Lothar, Beyreuther, Erich & Bietenhard, Hans 1986. *Theologisches Begriffslexikon zum Neuen Testament.* 7th ed. Wuppertal: Brunnen.

Comas, D., Calafell F., Bendukidze, N., Fañanás, L. & Bertranpetit, J. (2000). Georgian and Kurd mtDNA sequence analysis shows a lack of correlation between languages and female genetic lineages. *American Journal of Physical Anthropology* 112/1, 5–16.

Comerd, Munzır 1996. Yitiqatê Dersımi de Wayırê Çêi (Asparê astorê kimenti): Sarê Çêi xıravunu ra 'be neweşiye ra sevekneno, karê dine raşt beno rızqê çêi dano, malê çêi 'be qısmetê çêi keno jêde, nasivê çêi sevekneno. [Turkish S. 69-74: Dersim İnancı'nda Ev ve Aile Tanrısı (Wayırê Çêi): Ev halkını her tür kötülükten, kötü melklerden ve hastalıklardan koruyor, İşlerinin İye gitmesini sağlıyor, evin rızkını veriyor, malını ve kısmetini artırıyor, nasibini koruyour.]. *Ware* 9, 10-14. Baiersbronn. [Engl.: Dersim Belief about the Master of the House.].

Comerd, Munzır 1996. Yitiqatê Dersımi de Wayırê Mali: Sarık Şüan xêro, Memık Gavan Xıravıno. Wayırê Malê Yavani ki sultan Duzgıno. Serva Duzgıni Dersımıci Malê yavani nekisenê, dersim de "Avci" çino! [Turkish S. 128-140: Dersim İnancı'nda Hayanlar Tanrısı (koyun, keçi, inek vb. küçük - ve büyükbaş hayvanlar): Sarık Şüan iyi, Memık Gavan kötü Tanrıdır. Sultan Duzgın da Dağkeçisi, geyik vb. Haynaların Tanrısıdır. Dersimli'ler Duzgın'dan Dolayı Bunları Avlamazlar, Dersim'de Avcı Yoktur!]. *Ware* 10, 4-16. Baiersbronn. [Engl.: Dersim Belief about the Master of the Cattle: The Good shepherd, the bad Memık Gavan.].

Comerd, Munzır 1997. Yitiqatī Dêrsımi de Duzgın (Asparê astorê kimenti): Wayır u sıtarê dina u darewo! Sultan u Qumandanê Dêrsimi 'be pilê jiar u diarunê Dêrsimi Duzgıno.

Duzgın roştiya, evdıl Musa tariyo!. Vervê Eskerê Evdıl Musay de eskerê Duzgıni vındeno [Turkish S. 84-103: Dersim İnancı'nda Duzgın (Doruat'in süvarisi): Can ile Cihann Tanrısı, Rehberi ve Himayesidir! Dersim'in Sultanı ve Kumandanı Duzgın'dır. Ayrıca Dersim'deki Kutsal Yer ve Yatırların da Başıdır. Duzgın Aydınlığı Simgeliyor, Evdıl Musa'ysa Karanlığı! Evdıl Musa'nin Askerleri'ne Karşı, Duzgın'ın Askerleri'ne Duruyor.]. *Ware* 11, 15-31. Baiersbronn.[Engl.: Dersim Belief about Duzgın.].

Comerd, Munzır 1997. Yitiqatī Dersımi de Helıka Gızıkıne. *Tija Sodırı* 5/2, 32-37. Baiersbronn. [Engl.: Dersim Belief about Helıka Gızıkıne.].

Comerd, Munzır 1998. İtiqatī Dêsımi de mori 'be ewliya ra, [Turkish: Dersim İnancı'dan Yılan ve Tarikat Değneği, 121-129. *Ware* 12, 58-69, [Turkish: 113-126]. Baiersbronn. [Engl.: Dersim Belief about the Serpent and the Wand-Orders.].

Comerd, Munzur 1998. Yitiqatī Dersimi de Xizir. *Ware* 12, 83-100, [Turkish: 113-126]. Baiersbronn. [Engl.: Dersim Belief about Xızır.].

Comrie, Bernard [1981] 1989. *Language Universals and Linguistic Typology - Syntax and Morphology*. 2nd ed. Chicago: The University of Chicago Press.

Corwin, Gary 2008. Issues of Identity in a Muslim Context: Common Ground? *emq* 44/1, 8-9. Wheaton.

Coseriu, Eugenio [1988] 2007. *Sprachkompetenz: Grundzüge der Theorie des Sprechens*. 2nd revised ed. Tübingen: Gunter Narr.

Croft, Williams 1990. *Typology and universals*. Cambridge: Cambridge University Press.

Csirmaz, Aniko & Ceplová, Markéta 2004. Other Options without Optionality, in Kenstowicz, Michael (ed.): Studies in Zazaki Grammar. Working Papers on Endangered and Less Familiar Languages 6, 11-30. Cambridge: MIT.

Cuinet, Vitar, Selenoy, G. L. & Seydlitz N. von 1896. *Verteilung der Armenischen Bevölkerung: Türkisch Armenien, Kurdistan, und Transkaukasien nach Alexander Supa*. Gotha: Justus Press. [Engl.: Dispersion of the Armenian Population: Turkish Armenia, Kurdistan, and Transcaucasia.].

Cyert, Richard M. & March, James G. 1963. *A Behavioral Theory of the Firm*. Englewood Cliffs: Prentice-Hall.

Dadrian, Vahakn N. 1997a. *German Responsibility in the Armenian Genocide - A Review of the Historical Evidence of German Complicity*. Cambridge: Blue Crane.

Dadrian, Vahakn N. 1997b. *The History of the Armenian Genocide – Ethnic Conflict from the Balkans to Anatolia to the Caucasus*. Oxford: Berghahn.

Danks, Joseph H. (ed.) 1997. *Cognitive Processes in Translation and Interpreting*. Thousand Oaks: SAGE.

Darwin, Charles, 1859. *On the Origin of Species by means of Natural Selection, or the Preservation of favoured Races in the Struggle for Life*. London: John Murray. And Online: URL: http://caliban.mpiz-koeln.mpg.de/~stueber/darwin/origin/origin.html [accessed 2017-04-19].

Dedekurban, Ali Haydar 1994. *Zaza halk inançlarında 'kült'ler*. Ankara: Zaza Kültürü Yayinlari.

Delamont, Sara 2004. Ethnography and participant observation, in Seale, Clive, Gobo, Giampietro & Gubrium, Jaber F. (eds): *Qualitative Research Practices*, 217–229. London: SAGE.

Dersim Türküleri - Tayê Lawıkê Dêrsımi w/o Author. 1992. Ankara: Berhem Yayınları. [Engl.: Songs from Dersim.].

Dersimi, Nuri Mehmet [1952] 1988. *Kürdistan Tarıhınde Dersim.* Halep (Aleppo), Syria: Anı Matbaası. (reprint: Cologne 1988). [Dersim in the History of Kurdistan.].

Dersimi, Mehmet Nuri 1986. *Hatiratim.* [My Memoirs]. 2nd ed. Stockholm: Roja Nû Yayinlari.

Deutscher, Guy 2010. *Through the Language Glass: How Words Colour Your World.* London: William Heinemann.

Dewran, Hasan w/o Date. *Hazar Reng – Hazar Veng: Lyrik & Musik in der Zaza Sprache.* Frankfurt: Brandes Apsel. [CD-ROM].

Dewran, Hasan 2007. *Almanya de ju şênroza Khalê Gağani - Khalo Sıpe.* Mannheim: Selbstverlag. [CD-ROM]. [Self Published].

Dewran, Hasan 2008-2009. *Khalê Gağani.* Self Published. [CD ROM].

Diedrich, Hans-Christian 2004. *Potsdam ehrt „Schutzengel der Armenier".* Glaube in der 2. Welt, 25-26. Also Online: URL: http://www.kirchen.ch/g2w/Archiv/0401.htm [accessed 2017-03-11]. [Potsdam honors "Guardian Angel of the Armenians". Faith in the 2. World.].

Dil, Anwar S. 1975. *Language Structure and Translation: Essays by Eugene A. Nida.* California: Stanford University Press.

Dockery, D. S. et al. 1992. The Temple, in Nashville, T. (ed.): *Holman Bible Handbook,* 522. Nashville: Holman Bible Publishers.

Doğan, Mehmet 1996. *Büyük Türkçe Sözlük.* İstanbul: Bahar Yayınları. [Engl.: Large Turkish Dictionary.].

Dozier, Edward P. 1955. The concepts of 'primitive' and 'native' in Anthropology. *Yearbook of Anthropology,* 187-202. Thomas, W. L. jr. (ed.). New York.

du Toit, A. 1998. History of Palestinian Judaism in the period 539 BC to AD 135, in du Toit, A. (ed.): *The New Testament Milieu, Vol. 2.* Guide to the New Testament. Halfway House: Orion Publishers.

Duden 1963. *Herkunftswörterbuch.* Mannheim: Dudenverlag. [Engl.: Etymological Lexicon.].

Dunmore, George 1857. Dersim. *Missionary Herald,* 220. Boston: Crocker & Brewster.

Durak, Attila 2006. *Ebru: Reflections of Cultural Diversity in Turkey.* İstanbul: Metis. (inkluding music CD (Kalan) with traditional songs).

Dye, Wayne T. 1979. *The Bible Translation Strategy: An Analysis of its Spiritual Impact.* Ukarumpa: Summer Institute of Linguistics.

Eberhard, Elke 1970. *Osmanische Polemik gegen die Safaviden im 16. Jahrhundert nach arabischen Handschriften.* Freiburg: Schwarz. [Engl.: Ottoman Polemics against the Safavids in the 16th century following arabic Writings.].

Eggan, Fred 1971. Social Anthropology and the Method of Controlled Comparison, in Graburn, Nelson (ed.): *Readings in Kinship and Social Structure,* 173-187. New York: Harper & Row.

Eisenstadt, Samuel N. 1961. Anthropological Studies of Complex Societies. *Current Anthropology* 2, 201- 222.
Eliade, Mircea 1991. *Geschichte der religiösen Ideen.* 5 Bde. Freiburg: Herder Spektrum. [Engl.: History of the religious Idea].
Ellul, Jacques [1996] 2009. Foreword, in Ye'or, Bat: The Decline of Eastern Christianity under Islam: *From Jihad to Dhimmitude. Seventh-Twentieth Century, 17-21.* Seventh printing. Madison: Fairleigh Dickinson University Press. (Transl. by Kochan, Miriam and Littman, David).
Elwan, Omaia 1988. Gesetzgebung und Rechtsprechung, in Steinbach, Udo & Robert, Rüdiger (eds.): *Der Nahe und Mittlere Osten: Politik, Gesellschaft, Wirtschaft, Geschichte, Kultur*, 221-254. Opladen: Leske + Budrich. [Engl.: Elwan, Omaia 1988. Legislation and Jurisdiction, in Steinbach, Udo & Robert, Rüdiger (eds.): The Near and Middle East: Politics, Society, Economy, History, Culture, 221-254. Opladen: Leske + Budrich.].
Ember, Carol R. & Ember, Melvin 1993. *Cultural Anthropology.* 7th edition. New Jersey: Prentice Hall.
Erlmann, Veit 2004. But what of the ethnographic ear? Anthropology, sound and the senses, in Erlmann, Veit (ed.): *Hearing Cultures: Essays on Sound, Listening and Modernity*, 1– 20. Oxford: Berg.
Evans-Pritchard, Edward E. 1937. *Witchcraft, Oracles and Magic among the Azande.* Oxford: Clarendon.
Evans-Pritchard, Edward E. 1971. The Failure of the Comparative Method, in Graburn, Nelson (ed.): *Readings in Kinship and Social Structure*, 187-190. New York: Harper & Row.
Extra, Durk & Gorter, Guus 2001. *The Other Languages of Europe: Demographic, Sociolinguistic and Educational Perspectives.* Multilingual Matters 118. Bristol: Multilingual Matters.
Eymann, Dorothea 1996. Frausein in Japan: Das Rollenverständnis der Japanerin seit dem 2. Weltkrieg bis zur Gegenwart, dessen Wurzeln und biblische Bewertung im Kontext christlicher Gemeinden. Historisch beschreibende und biblisch-exegetische Untersuchung in der japanischen Gesellschaft. MA Thesis. Korntal: Columbia Biblical Seminary and Graduate School of Missions - externes Studienzentrum Korntal. (unpublished). [Engl.: Being a Woman in Japan: The Understanding of Japanes women since WW II. up to the Present, origins and Biblical Rating in the Context of Christian Communities.].].
Fabbro, Franco 1999. *The Neurolinguistics of Bilingualism: An Introduction.* Hove: Taylor and Francis.
Fasold, Ralph W. [1984] 1993. *The Sociolinguistics of Society.* Oxford: Blackwell.
Feldtkeller, Andreas 1997. Die Zeit zur Mohammedanermission im Oriente ist noch nicht gekomen - Motive eines Zögerns in der Mission des American Board und bei Gustav Warneck, in Becker, Dieter & Feldtkeller, Andreas (eds.): *Es begann in Halle... Missionswissenschaft von Gustav Warneck bis heute*, 87-105. Erlangen: Evangelisch-lutherische Mission.
Felix, Wolfgang 1995. Deylamites: i. In the Pre-Islamic period. *Encyclopedia Iranica* 7/4, 342-343.

Feuerherdt, Alex 2008. Wir wollen euch in Köln nicht. Jüdische Welt. *Jüdische Allgemeine* 39-40, 2. September 2008. Berlin: Jüdische Presse GmbH. [Engl.: We don't want you in Colon. Jewish Common.].

Firth, John Rupert 1957. *Papers in Linguistics 1934-1951*. London: Oxford University Press.

Fischer, Hans [1983] 2003. Ethnologie als wissenschaftliche Disziplin, in Beer, Bettina & Fischer, Hans (eds.): *Ethnologie - Einführung und Überblick*, 13-31. 4th ed. Berlin: Dietrich Reimer. [Engl.: Ethnology as Scientific Discipline].

Fischer, Hans & Beer, Bettina [1983] 2003. *Ethnologie – Einführung und Überblick*. 4th ed. Berlin: Dietrich Reimer. [Engl.: Anthropology – Introduction and Overview.].

Fischer, Kurt W. & Tangney, June P. 1995. Self-conscious Emotions and the Affect Revolution: Framework and Overview, in Tangney, Price June & Fischer, Kurt W. (eds.): *Selfconscious Emotions: The Psychology of Shame, Guilt, Embarrassment, and Pride*, 3-22. New York: Guilford Press.

Fishman, Joshua 1972. *Language and Nationalism: Two Integrative Essays*. Rowley: Newbury House.

Fluck, Hans-Rüdiger 1996. *Fachsprachen. Einführung und Bibliographie*. 5. ed. Nachdruck der 2. durchges. u. erw. ed. von 1976. Tübingen: Francke.

Forced Evictions and Destruction of Villages in Turkish Kurdistan w/o Author. 1996. *Middle East Report* 199. Turkey: Insolvent Ideologies, Fractured State, 8-9. Also Online: URL: http://www.jstor.org/pss/3012884 [accessed 2008-09-29].

Foster, George M. 1965. Peasant Society and the Image of the Limited Good. *American Anthropologist* 67, 293-315.

Franz, Erhard 1988a. Familie, Klan und Stammeswesen, in Steinbach, Udo & Robert, Rüdiger (eds.): *Der Nahe und Mittlere Osten: Politik, Gesellschaft, Wirtschaft, Geschichte, Kultur*, 511-520. Opladen: Leske + Budrich. [Engl.: Family, Clan and Tribal System, in The Middele and Far East: Politics, Society, Economy, History, Culture].

Franz, Erhard 1988b. Sprachen und Völker, in Steinbach, Udo & Robert, Rüdiger (eds.): *Der Nahe und Mittlere Osten: Politik, Gesellschaft, Wirtschaft, Geschichte, Kultur*, 29-48. Opladen: Leske + Budrich.

Freeman, Derek 1983. *Margaret Mead and Samoa: The Making and Unmaking of an Anthropological Myth*. Cambridge: Harvard University Press.

Freeman, Derek 1998. *The Fateful Hoaxing of Margaret Mead: A Historical Analysis of Her Samoan Research*. Boulder: Westview Press.

Fröhlich, Anne-Sophie 2008. Tanzende Verbindung: Religiöse Bruderschaften sind in der Türkei offiziell verboten, üben aber großen Einfluss aus. *Spiegel Special: Land im Aufbruch - Türkei*, 28-29. Hamburg. [Engl.: Dancing Alliance: Religious Brotherhoods are publically forbidden in Turkey, but wield wide influence. *Spiegel Special: Awakening Country – Turkey*.].

Frost, Michael & Hirsch, Alan 2004. *The Shaping of Things to come. Innovation and Mission for the 21st-Century Church*. 4th ed. Peabody: Hendrickson.

Fuchs, Ottmar 1984. Für wen übersetzen wir? in Gnilka, Joachim & Rüger, Hans Peter (eds.): *Die Übersetzung der Bibel: Aufgabe der Theologie*, 84-124. Bielefeld: Luther-Verlag. [For whom do we translate? In Gnilka, Joachim & Rüger, Hans Peter (eds.): *The Translation of the Bible: The Task of Theology.*].

Gabelentz, Georg von der [1891] 1972. *Die Sprachwissenschaft: Ihre Aufgaben, Methoden und bisherigen Ergebnisse.* Reprint of 2nd ed. From 1901. Tübingen: Narr. [Engl.: *Linguistics: Its Tasks, Methodology and Previous Results.*].

Gadamer, H. G. 1972. *Wahrheit und Methode.* Tübingen: Mohr Siebeck. [Engl.: *Truth and Method*].

Galtung, Johan 1985. Struktur, Kultur und intellektueller Stil. Ein vergleichender Essay über sachsonische, teutonische, gallische und nipponische Wissenschaft, in Wierlacher, Alois (ed.): Das Fremde und das Eigene: Prolegome interkulturellen Germanistik, 151-193. Munich: Judicium. [Engl.: Structure, Culture and intellectual stile. A comparative Essay about saxonian, teutonian, gallic and nipponian Science, in Wierlacher, alois (ed.): The foreign and the Own: Prolegome of intercultural Germanistics.].

Gass, Susan & Ard, Josh 1987. Second language acquisition and the ontology of language universals, in Rutherford, William (ed.): *Language Universals and Second Language Acquisition*, 33-68. 2nd ed. Amsterdam: John Benjamins.

Geertz, Clifford 1966. Religion as a Cultural System, in Banton, Michael (ed.): *Anthropological Approaches to the Study of Religion*, 1-46. London: Tavistock.

Geertz, Clifford [1973] 1993. *The Interpretation of Cultures: Selected Essays.* London: Fontana.

Geiger, Wilhelm 1882. *Ostiranische Kultur im Altertum.* Erlangen: Andreas Deichert. [Engl.: East Iranian Culture in ancient times.].

Geiger, Wilhelm, Kuhn, Ernst & Bartholomae, Christian 1899. Kurdische Dialekte. *Grundriss der iranischen Philologie*, Bd. I. Leipzig. [Engl.: Kurdish Dialects. Layout of Iranian Philology.].

Gessler, Philipp 2010. Kopf einziehen: Türkei - Die jüdische Gemeinde ist wohlgelitten - wenn sie still bleibt. Jüdische Welt. *Jüdische Allgemeine* 6, 6. Februar 2010. Berlin: Jüdische Presse GmbH. [Engl.: Keep the Head down: Turkey - The Jewish Community is well-liked - as far as they remain silent. Jewish World. Jewish Common 6, 2010-02-06. Berlin: Jewish Press.].

Gibb, Hamilton Alexander R. 1947. *Modern Trends in Islam.* Chicago: University of Chicago.

Gibran, Khalil 2003. *Der Prophet.* Munich: dtv. [Engl.: The Prophet.].

Gignoux, Philippe 2001. *Man and Cosmos in Ancient Iran.* Roma: Istituto Italiano Per L'Africa E L'Oriente.

Gilbert, Lela 2008. Eine „Abtrünnige" in Israel. Lela Gilbert interviewte die ehemalige Muslimin Nonie Darwish. *Wort aus Jerusalem* 1, 28-30. ICEJ. [An "Apostate" in Israel. Lela Gilbert interviews the former Muslima Nonie Darwish. Word from Jerusalem.].

Gilchrist, John 2002. *Facing the Muslim Challenge: A Handbook of Christian - Muslim Apologetics.* Second ed. Cape Town: Life Challenge Africa.

Gilmore, David D. (ed.) 1987. *Honour and Shame and the Unity of the Mediterranean.* AAA Special Publication 22. Washington: American Anthropological Association.

Gilsenan, Michael 1982. *Recognizing Islam: Religion and Society in the Modern Arab World.* New York: Pantheon Books.

Gilsenan, Michael 1993. Lying, Honor, and Contradiction, in Bowen, Donna Lee & Early, Evelyn A. (eds.): *Everyday Life in Muslim Middle East,* 23-33. Bloomington: Indiana University Press.

Gleason, Henry A. jr. 1974. Linguistics and Philology, in Black, Matthew & Smalley, William A. (eds.): *On Language, Culture, and Religion: In Honor of Eugene A. Nida*, 199-212. Paris: Mouton.

Gnoli, Gherardo 2007. Old Persian xssaca-, Middle Persian ssahr, Greek ethnos, in Macuch, Maria, Maggi, Mauro & Sundermann, Werner (eds.): *Iranian Languages from Iran and Turan: Ronald E. Emmerick Memorial Volume,* 109-118. Wiesbaden: Harrassowitz.

Goerling, Fritz 2007. Translation of 'Grace' in Jula of Cote d'Ivoire, in Müller, Klaus W. (ed.): *Mission als Kommunikation: Die christliche Botschaft verstehen.* Festschrift für Ursula Wiesemann zu ihrem 75. Geburtstag, 183-207. Nuremberg: VTR.

Goodenough, Ward Hunt 1957. Cultural Anthropology and Linguistics, in Garvin, Paul C. (ed.): *Report of the Seventh Annual Round Table Meeting on Linguistics and Language Study. Georgetown University Monograph Series on Language and Linguistics* 9, 167-173. Washington: Georgetown University.

Gordon, Raymond G. Jr. (ed.) 2005. *Ethnologue: Languages of the World.* 15th ed. Dallas: SIL International. Online: URL: http://www.ethnologue.com [accessed 2017-01-10].

Greenberg, Joseph 1963. Some universals of grammar with particular reference to the order of meaningful elements, in Greenberg, Joseph (ed.): *Universals of Language*, 73-113. Cambridge: M.I.T.

Greenberg, Joseph H. 1968. *Anthropological Linguistics: An Introduction.* New York: Random House.

Greenberg, Joseph H. 1978. Diachrony, Synchrony, and Language Universals, in Greenberg, Joseph H. (ed.): *Universals of Human Language*, 62-91. Stanford: Stanford University Press.

Griffith, Sidney H. 2010. *The Church in the Shadow of the Mosque: Christians and Muslims in the World of Islam.* Oxford: Princeton University Press.

Grimes, Joseph E. 1995. *Language Survey Reference Guide.* Dallas: SIL International.

Grimes, Joseph E. & Grimes Barbara F. 2000. *Ethnologue.* 14th ed. Dallas: Summer Institute of Linguistics. Online: URL: http://www.ethnologue.com [accessed 2017-01-10].

Grûba Xebate ya Vateyî [2001] 2009. *Ferhengê Kirmanckî (Zazakî) – Tirkî, Tirkî – Kirmanckî.* Üçuncü Baskı. İstanbul: Vate Publishing House. [Engl.: Vate Çalışma Grubu 2009. 3rd ed. Kirmancki (Zazaki) – Turkish, Turkish – Kirmancki Dictionary.].

Grûba Xebate ya Vateyî [2001] 2009. *Türkçe – Kırmancca (Zazaca) Sözlük, Ferhengê Tirkî – Kirmanckî (Zazakî).* Üçuncü Baskı. İstanbul: Vate Publishing House. [Engl. Vate Çalışma Grubu 2009. Kirmancki (Zazaki) – Turkish, Turkish – Kirmancki Dictionary. 3rd ed.].

Gülensoy, Tuncer 1994. *Kürtçenin etimolojik sözlügü.* Ankara: Türk Tarih Kurumu Basimevi. [Engl.: Kurdish etymological dictionary.].

Gülensoy, Tuncer & Kalafat, Yasar Kaya 1990. Dogu Anadolu dil arastirmalari. *Erciyes Üniversitesi Sosyal Bilimler Enstitüsü* 4/34, 4ff. Kayseri: Erciyes Üniversitesi. [Engl.: Research about the East Anatolian Language.]

Gündüz, Deniz 2006. *Kırmancca / Zazaca Dil Dersleri: Türkçe Açıklamalı Kürtçe.* İstanbul: Vate Yayınevi. [Engl.: Kirmanca / Zaza Language Lessons: Kudish explained in Turkish].

Gündüzkanat, Kahraman 1997. *Die Rolle des Bildungswesens beim Demokratisierungsprozess in der Türkei unter besonderer Berücksichtigung der Dimli (Kirmanc-, Zaza-) Ethnizität.* Münster: LIT. [Engl.: The Role of the educational system during the Process of Democratization in Turkey under the special Consideration of the Dimli (Kirmanc-, Zaza-) Ethnicity].

Gundert, Wilhelm 1977. Bibelübersetzungen V: Übersetzungen ins Türkische, in Krause, Gerhard & Müller, Gerhard (eds.): *Theologische Realenzyklopädie (TRE),* 299-310. Berlin: Walter de Gruyter. Also Online: URL: http://books.google.com/books?id=iEEsRpX_-MaUC&pg=RA1-PA299&lpg=RA1PA299&dq=Turkish+Bibles+Ali+Bey&source=web-&ots=7Zyl7hzg_3&sig=I1aCDgG3dDzPYdIEX_uJhPH02wk&hl=de&sa=X&oi=book-_result&resnum=2&ct=result [accessed 2017-11-04). [Engl.: Bible Translations V: Translations into Turkish.].

Gutt, Eeva 1999. Preparing a Dictionary. Workpaper. Lörrach. (unpublished).

Gutt, Ernst-August 1992. *Relevance Theory: A Guide to Successful Communication in Translation.* Dallas: SIL International/UBS.

Gutt, Ernst-August [1991] 2000. *Translation and Relevance: Cognition and Context.* Manchester: St. Jerome.

Hadank, Karl 1930. *Mundarten der Guran, besonders das Kandulai, Aurami und Badschalani.* Berlin: Verlag der preussischen Akademie der Wissenschaften. [Engl.: Dialects of the Guran].

Hadank, Karl 1932. *Mundarten der Zaza, hauptsächlich aus Siwerek und Kor.* Berlin: Verlag der preußischen Akademie der Wissenschaften in Kommission bei Walter de Gruyter & Co. (Reihe: Kurdisch-Persische Forschungen, Abt. III, Band IV, hg. durch Mann, Oskar). [Engl.: Dialects of the Zaza].

Hage, Wolfgang 1978. Der Weg nach Asien: Die ostsyrische Missionskirche, in Schäferdiek, Knut (ed.): *Die Kirche des frühen Mittelalters. Kirchengeschichte als Missionsgeschichte,* 1. Halbband, 360-393. Munich: Kaiser. [Engl.: The Way to Asia: The East-Syrian mission-Church].

Haig, Geoffrey 2001. Book Review: Grammatik der Zaza-Sprache. Nord-Dialekt. *Linguistics* 39/1, 181-197. Berlin: Walter de Gruyter.

Haig, Geoffrey 2004. Alignment in Kurdish: A diachronic perspective. Kiel: Universität Kiel. (unpublished Habitilation Thesis). Also Online: URL: http://www.linguistik.uni-kiel.-de/KurdAlignment.pdf [PDF-File] [accessed 2017-01-25].

Haig, Geoffrey & Paul, Ludwig 2001. Kurmanjî Kurdish, in Garry, Jane & Rubino, Carl (eds.): *Facts about the World's Languages,* 398-403. New York: The H.W. Wilson Co.

Halajyan, Gevorg. 1973. *Dersimi hayeri azgagrutyun.* Yerevan.

Halliday, Michael A. K. 1984. Language as code and language behaviour: a systemic-functional interpretation of the nature of ontogenesis of dialogue, in Fawcett, R. P., Halliday, Michael A. K. Lamb & Makkai, A.: *The semiotics of culture and language*, Vol. I, London and Dover: Frances Pinter.

Hayıg, Rosan & Werner, Brigitte 2012. *Zazaca - Türkçe Sözlük: Türkçe – Zazaca Sözcük Listesi*. İstanbul: Tij Yayıncılık. [Engl.: Zaza – Turkish Lexicon: Turkish – Zaza Wordlist. Tij Publishing House.].

Hayıg, Rosan 2007. *Mahmeşa: Vızêr ra Ewro Istanıkê Zazayan – Mahmescha: Zaza Volksmärchen von Damals und Heute – Mahmesha: Zaza Folktales: Then and Now*. İstanbul: Vêjiyaişê Tiji/Tij Yayınları.

Healey, Alan [1975] 1989. *Language Learner's Field Guide*. Ukarumpa: Summer Institute of Linguistics.

Heine, Peter 1988. Die Herausbildung der modernen Staatenwelt, in Steinbach, Udo & Robert, Rüdiger (eds.): *Der Nahe und Mittlere Osten: Politik, Gesellschaft, Wirtschaft, Geschichte, Kultur*, 115-134. Opladen: Leske + Budrich. [Engl.: The forming of the modern States, in Steinbach, Udo & Robert, Rüdiger (eds.): The Near and Middle East: Politics, society, economy, history.].

Heinrichs, Wolfhart (ed.) 1990. *Studies in Neo-Aramaic*. Atlanta: Scholars Press.

Hendry, Joy 1999. *An Introduction to Social Anthropology: Other People's Worlds*. New York: Palgrave.

Hengirmen, Mehmet 1996. *Türkce Dilbilgisi*. Ankara: Engin. [Engl.: Turkish grammar (Standard Work on Turkish; Ankara University)].

Hennerbichler, Ferdinand 2004. *Die Kurden*. Mosonmagyarovar: Edition fhe. Also Online: URL: http://www.fhe.cc/html/DieKurden-fhe-Sprache.pdf [PDF-File] [accessed 2017-01-16]. [Engl.: The Kurds.].

Heper, Metin 2007. *The State and Kurds in Turkey. The Question of Assimilation*. New York: Palgrave Macmillan.

Hesselgrave, David J. 1983. Missionary Elenctics and Guilt and Shame. *Missiology: An International Review* 11, Nr. 4: 461-483.

Hesselgrave, David J. [1984] 2002. *Counseling Cross-Culturally: An Introduction to Theory & Practice for Christians*. Reprint. Eugene: Wipf and Stock.

Heyd, Uriel 1950. *Foundation of Turkish Nationalism*. London: Luzac.

Hiebert, Paul G. 1976. *Cultural Anthropology*. Philadelphia: J. B. Lippincott.

Hiebert, Paul G. 1985. *Anthropological Insights for Missionaries*. Grand Rapids: Baker.

Hiebert, Paul G. [1994] 1998. *Anthropological Reflections on Missiological Issues*. Reprint. Grand Rapids: Baker.

Hiebert, Paul G. & Hiebert Meneses, Eloise 1995. *Incarnational Ministry: Planting Churches in Band, Tribal, Peasant, and Urban Societies*. Grand Rapids: Baker.

Hines, Melissa 2004. *Brain Gender*. Oxford: Oxford University Press.

Hirschler, Konrad 2001. Defining the Nation: Kurdish Historiography in Turkey in the 1990s. *Middle Eastern Studies* 37/3, July, 145-166. Frank Cass: London.

Höhlig, Monika 1997. *Kontaktbedingter Sprachwandel in der adygeischen Umgangssprache im Kaukasus und in der Türkei: Vergleichende Analyse des russischen und türkischen Einflusses in mündlichen adygeischen Texten*. Munchen: Lincom Europa. [Engl.: Caused by contact – Language change of the aygaean Language in Caucasus and in Turkey: Comparative analyses of the Russian and Turkish Influence in oral adygeam Texts.]

Hofmann, Tessa 1986. Vorwort zur Neuausgabe, in Lepsius, Johannes [1919]: *Deutschland und Armenien 1914-1918*, 7-12. Reprint. Bremen: Donat und Temmen. [Engl.: Preface to Reprint, in Lepsius, Johannes [1919]: Germany and Armenia 1914-1918.].

Hofstede, Geert 1984. *Culture's Consequences: International Differences in Work-related Values*. Beverly Hills: Sage.

Hofstede, Geert H. 1991. *Cultures and Organizations: Software of the Mind. Intercultural Cooperation and its Importance for Survival*. London: McGraw-Hill.

Hofstede, Geert 1993. *Interkulturelle Zusammenarbeit: Kulturen, Organisationen, Management*. Wiesbaden: Gabler. [Engl.: Intercultural Teamwork: Cultures, Organisations, Management.].

Hofstede, Geert 1997. *Lokales Denken, globales Handeln: Kulturen, Zusammenarbeit und Management*. Actualised Version of German edition. Munich: Beck. [Engl.: Local Thinking, global handling: Cultures, Teamwork and Management.].

Holland, Dorothy & Quinn, Naomi 1987. Culture and Cognition, in Holland, Dorothy & Quinn, Naomi (eds.): *Cultural Models in Language and Thought*, 3-40. Cambridge: Cambridge University Press.

Honeyboon 1995. *The Case of Kurdistan against Turkey*. 2nd ed. Stockholm: Sara publishing and distribution.

Horn, Paul 1988. *Grundriß der neupersischen Etymologie*. Hildesheim: Georg Olms. [Engl.: Outline of the New-Persian Etymology.].

Houston, Christopher 2001. *Islam, Kurds and the Turkish Nation State*. Oxford: Berg.

Hoyland, Robert G. 1997. *Seeing Islam as Others saw it: A Survey and Evaluation of Christian, Jewish and Zoroastrian Writings on Early Islam*. New Yersey: The Darwin Press.

Hudson, Richard Anthony [1980] 1987. *Sociolinguistics*. Cambridge: Cambridge University Press.

Hübschmann, Heinrich 1904. Die altarmenischen Ortsnamen. *Indogermanische Forschungen, Zeitschrift für Indogermanische Sprach- und Altertumskunde* (Strassburg) Band XVI/Heft 3-5, 197-490. [Engl.: The old-Armenian name of villages. Indogermanic Studies, Magazine for the study of Indogermanic Language and History.].

Hübschmann, Heinrich 1962. *Armenische Grammatik - Armenische Etymologie*. Hildesheim: Georg Olms. [Engl.: Armenian Grammar – Armenian Etymology].

Hug, Theo 2001. Erhebung und Auswertung empirischer Daten: Eine Skizze für AnfängerInnen und leicht Fortgeschrittene, in Hug, Theo (ed.): *Wie kommt Wissenschaft zu Wissen? Einführung in die Methodologie der Sozial- und Kulturwissenschaften*, Bd. 2, 11-29. Baltmannsweiler: Schneider Verlag Hohengehren. [Engl.: Elevation and evaluation of empirical data: An outline for beginners and easily advanced, in Hug, Theo (ed.): How does science come to knowledge? *Introduction to the methodology of the social and studies of civilization*].

Icken, Angela 2010. Die Entwicklung von Sinus-Migrantenmilieus. Ein neuer Diskussions- und Forschungsansatz zum Thema Integration, in Prömper, Hans et.al. (eds): *Was macht Migration mit Männlichkeit? Kontexte und Erfahrungen zur Bildung und Sozia-*

len Arbeit mit Migranten, 37-49. Opladen: Babara Budrich. [Engl.: The Development of Sinus-Migration Milieus. A New Approach on the Theme Integration in Discussion and Research, in Pömper, hans et.al. (eds.): What does Migration to Masculinity? Contexts and Experiences for Education an*d Social Work with Migrants.*].

Islaminstitut 2007. Fatwa zu der Frage: Wie müssen Muslime mit Christen umgehen? *Orientierung* 5. Wiesbaden: Orientdienst. Online: URL: http://www.islaminstitut.de [accessed 2007-12-26). [Engl.: Fatwa on the Question: How should Muslims relate to Christians?].

Itô, J. & Mester, A. 1999. The Phonological Lexicon, in Tsujimura, N. (ed.): *Handbook of Japanese Linguistics*, 62-100. Maiden: Blackwell.

Izady, Mehrdad R. 1992. *The Kurds: A Concise Handbook.* Washington: Taylor & Francis.

Jabbour, Nabeel T. 2008. *The Crescent Through the Eyes of the Cross*. Colorado Springs: Navpress.

Jacobson, C. M. 1993. *Rastnustena Zonê Ma, Handbuch für die Rechtschreibung der Zaza-Sprache*. Bonn: Verlag für Kultur und Wissenschaft. (Zazaki and German). [Engl.: *Handbook to the Spelling of the Zaza-Language.*].

Jacobson, C. M. 1999. *Zazaca Okuma-Yazma El Kitabı*. 2nd ed. İstanbul: Vêjiyaişê Tiji/Tij Yayınları. [Engl.: *Handbook for Writing- and Reading in Zazaki*].

Jacobson, C. M. 2001. *Rastnustena Zonê Ma (Dımılki – Kırmancki – Zazaki) eve Fekê Gola Dêsimi/Zazaca Yazım Kılavuzu*. 2nd ed. İstanbul: Vêjiyaişê Tiji/Tij Yayınları. (Zazaki and Türkisch.) [Engl.: *Orthography „Our Language" (Dimli – Kirmanc – Zazaki) with special reference to the area of Dersim.*].

Jaeckel, Ralph & Erciyeş, Gülnur Doğanates 1996. *A Dictionary of Turkish Verbs in Context and by Theme - Örnekli ve Temjatik Türkçe Fiiler Sözlüğü*. Washington: Georgetown University Press.

Jaeschke, Gotthard 1951. *Der Islam in der neuen Türkei. Eine rechtsgeschichtliche Untersuchung*. Leiden: Brill. [Engl.: Islam in the new Republic of Turkey: A juridical-historic Study.].

Jenkins, Philip 2006. *Die Zukunft des Christentums: Eine Analyse zur weltweiten Entwicklung im 21. Jahrhundert*. Giessen: Brunnen. (Engl. Original 2002: The next Christendom. The Coming of Global Christianity. New York: Oxford University Press).

Johnson-Laird, Philip N. 1983. *Mental Models*. Cambridge: Harvard University Press.

Justi, Ferdinand [1880] 2006. *Kurdische Grammatik*. Reproduktion. Sankt Petersburg: Kaiserliche Akademie der Wissenschaften.

Käser, Lothar 1977. Der Begriff „Seele" bei den Insulanern von Truk. Freiburg: Albert.Ludwigs-University. [unpublished Doctoral Thesis]. [Engl.: The term „soul" with the islander of Truk.].

Käser, Lothar 1998. *Fremde Kulturen: Eine Einführung in die Ethnologie für Entwicklungshelfer und kirchliche Mitarbeiter in Übersee*. 2nd ed. Lahr: Liebenzeller Mission. [Engl. Foreign Cultures: An Introduction into Cultural Anthropology for Development Workers and Christian Staff Overseas. 2nd ed.].

Käser, Lothar 2004. *Animismus: Eine Einführung in die begrifflichen Grundlagen des Welt- und Menschenbildes traditionaler (ethnischer) Gesellschaften für Entwicklungshelfer und*

Bibliography

kirchliche Mitarbeiter in Übersee. Bad Liebenzell: Liebenzeller Mission. [Engl.: Animism: An Introduction in the terminological Foundation oft he conception of man and world in traditional (ethnical) societies for Chrristian development workers and Churchal workers in Oversea.].

Kağitçibaşi, Cigdem 1997. Individualism and Collectivism, in Berry, J.W, Segall, Marshall H. & Kağitçibaşi, Cigdem (eds.): *Handbook of Cross-Cultural Psychology,* Vol. *3, Social Behavior and Applications.* 2nd ed. Needham Heights (Mass.): Allyn & Bacon.

Kahn, M. 1976. Borrowing and Variation in a Phonological Description of Kurdish. Ph.D. Diss. Michigan: University of Michigan. [umpublished].

Karan, Mark E. w/o Date. A Simple Introduction to Qualitative Data and its Qualitative or Quantitative Analysis. SIL International/University of North Dakota. (unpublished).

Kaschuba, Wolfgang 2003. *Einführung in die Europäische Ethnologie,* 2nd ed. Munich: Beck. [Engl. Introduction to European Cultural Anthropology. 2nd ed.].

Kasdorf, Hans 1976. *Gemeindewachstum als missionarisches Ziel – ein Konzept für Gemeinde- und Missionsarbeit.* Bad Liebenzell: Liebenzeller Mission. [Engl.: Church Growth as Goal of Missions – a Concept for Church and Missionary Work].

Kassühlke, Rudolf 1978. Übersetzen - das Unmögliche möglich machen, in Meurer, Siegfried (ed.): *Eine Bibel - viele Übersetzungen: Not oder Notwendigkeit?* 19-62. Stuttgart: Ev. Bibelwerk. [Engl.: Translation – Making real the unreal, in Meurer, Siegfried (ed.): One Bibel – many translations: Destitute or Need.].

Kaya, Ali [1999] 2010. *Başlangıcından Günümüzde Dersim Tarihi.* 1st ed. İstanbul: Demos Yayınları. [Engl.: Modern History of Dersim. 3 editions from 1999-2009 with Can Yayınları].

Kaya, Mehmed S. 2011. *The Zaza Kurd of Turkey: A Middle Eastern Minority in a Globalised Society.* London: I.B.Tauris.

Keddie, Nikki 1972. *Sayyid Jamal ad-Din "al-Afghani". A political Biography.* Berkeley: University of California.

Kedourie, Elle 1966. *Afghani and 'Abduh: An Essay on religious Unbelief and political Activism in modern Islam.* London: Frank Cass and Co.

Kehl-Bodrogi, Krisztina 1989. *Die Kizilbaş Aleviten - Untersuchungen über eine esoterische Glaubensgemeinschaft in Anatolien.* Reihe: Islamkundliche Untersuchungen 126. Berlin: Edition Parabolis. [Engl.: The Kizilbaş Alevis – Investigations about an Esoteric Religious Community in Anatolia.].

Kehl-Bodrogi, Krisztina 1998. Wir sind ein Volk! Identitätspolitiken unter den Zaza (Türkei) in der europäischen Diaspora. *Sociologus* 48/2, 111-135. [Engl.: We are one People Group! Politics of Identity in the Zaza Community (Turkey) in the Diaspora.].

Kehl-Bodrogi, Krisztina [1989] 2002. Das Alevitum in der Türkei: Zur Genese und gegenwärtigen Lage einer Glaubensgemeinschaft, in Andrews, Peter Alford & Benninghaus, Rüdiger (Eds.): *Ethnic Groups in the Republic of Turkey.* Beihefte zum Tübinger Atlas des Vorderen Orients Nr. 60.2, 503-510. Wiesbaden: Ludwig Reichert. [Engl. Alevism in Turkey: On the Origin and Temporary Situation of a Denomination].

Kehl-Bodrogi, Krisztina & Pfluger, Ingrid [1991] 1997. *Die Ehre in der türkischen Kultur: Ein Wertesystem im Wandel.* 7. ergänzte ed. Berlin: Die Ausländerbeauftragte des Senats von Berlin in Zusammenarbeit mit dem Paritätischen Bildungswerk e.V. [Engl.: Honour in the Turkish Culture: A System of Values in Change.].

Kemali, Ali 1992. *Erzincan Tarihi, Coğrafi, Toplumsal, Etnoğrafi, İdari, İhsai inceleme Araştırma Tecrübesi*. İstanbul: Resimli Ay Matbaası. [Engl.: History of Erzincan, Geography, Population, Ethnographie, Verwaltung, Economy and Trade research].

Kemnitz, Eva-Maria von 2002. Muslims as Seen by the Portuguese Press 1974-1999: Changes in the Perception of Islam, in Shadid, Wasif A. R. & Van Koningsveld, Sjoerd (eds.): *Intercultural relations and religious authorities: Muslims in the European Union*, 7-26. Leuven: Peeters.

Kenstowicz, Michael (ed.) 2004. *Studies in Zazaki Grammar*. Working Papers on Endangered and Less Familiar Languages 6. Cambridge: MIT.

Kerr, Malcolm H. 1966. *Islamic Reform: The political and legal Theories of Muhammad 'Abduh and Rashid Rida*. Berkeley: University of Chicago.

Keskin, Mesut 2008. Zur dialektalen Gliederung des Zazaki. Masterarbeit. Frankfurt: Johann Wolfgang von Goethe Universität. [unpublished]. [Engl.: On the Dialectical Outline of Zazaki.].

Keskin, Mesut 2011. Notes on Zaza-Armenian Language Contact. Frankurt: Goethe University. Power Point Presentation. [unpublished].

Keskin, Mesut 2012. *Zonê Ma Zanena? Zazaki für Anfängerinnen und Anfänger – Nord-Zazaki*. İstanbul: Geoaktif Yayınları. [Engl.: Zonê Ma Zanena? Zazaki for Beginners – Nord-Zazaki.].

Kess, Joseph F. [1992] 1993. *Psycholinguistics: Psychology, Linguistics, and the Study of Natural Language*. Reprinted with corrections. Amsterdam: John Benjamins.

Keyser, Fritz 2008. Mörder mit gutem Draht zur Polizei. *Vaihinger Zeitung* 12, 3. [Engl.: Murderers with a Good Conection to the Police.].

Khan, Emir Djeladet & Lescot, Roger 1986. *Kurdische Grammatik - Kurmanci Dialekt*. Bonn: Verlag für Kultur und Wissenschaft. [Engl.: Kurdish Grammar – Kurmanji Dialect.].

Kielhöfer, Bernd & Jonekeit, Sylvie [1983] 1998. *Zweisprachige Kindererziehung*. Zehnte Auflage. Tübingen: Stauffenburg. [Engl.: Bilingual Childrens Education].

Kieser, Hans-Lukas 1997. Mehmet Nuri Dersimi, ein asylsuchender Kurde, in Kieser, Hans-Lukas (ed.): *Kurdistan und Europa. Beiträge zur kurdischen Geschichte des 19. und 20. Jahrhunderts / Regards sur l'histoire kurde* (19-20e siecles), 187-216. Zürich: Chronos. Also Online: URL: http://www.hist.net/kieser/mak7/NuriDersimi.pdf [PDF-File] [accessed 2010-06-25]. [Engl.: Mehmet Nuri Dersimi, an Asylum Seeking Kurd].

Kieser, Hans-Lukas 2000. *Der verpasste Frieden: Mission, Ethnie und Staat in den Ostprovinzen der Türkei 1839-1938*. Zürich: Chronos. (also in Turkish: Kieser, Hans-Lukas [2005] 2010. *Iskalanmış barış: Doğu vilayetleri'nde misyonerlik, etnik kimlik ve devlet 1839-1938*. 3 Baskı. İstanbul: İletisim.). [Engl.: The missed Chance for Peace: Missions, Ethnos and State in the Eastern Provinces of Turkey 1893-1938.].

Kipling, Rudyard [1894] 2000. *The Jungle Books*. Harlow: Penguin.

Kısakürek, Necip Fazıl 1977. *Son devrin din mazlumları*. İstanbul: Büyük Doğu Yayınları. [Engl.: Modest Religious People of The Last Age.].

Kittel, Gerhard [1933] 1978. *Theologisches Wörterbuch zum Neuen Testament.* ThWBNT. Vols. 1-10/2. Stuttgart: Kohlhammer. [Engl.: Theological Dictionary to the New Testament].

Kloss, Heinz 1968. Notes concerning a language-nation typology, in Fishman, Joshua, Ferguson, Charles & Das Gupta, Jyotirindra (eds.): *Language Problems of Developing Nations*, 69-86. New York: John Wiley and Sons.

Kocadağ, Burhan 1992. *Lolan Oymağı ve Yakin Çevre Tarihi.* İstanbul: Taş Matbaası.

Kocadag, Çeko 2010. *Ferheng: Kimanckî (ZaZakî) – Kurmancî Kurmancî – Kirmanckî (Zazakî).* Berlin: Weşanen Komkar. [Engl.: Dictionary: Zazaki-Kurmanji Kurmnaji Zazaki.].

Koehler, Ludwig & Baumgartner, Walter (eds.) 2000. *The Hebrew and Aramaic Lexicon of the Old Testament.* HALOT. Leiden: Koninklijke Brill. [CD-ROM].

Krämer, Walter [1992] 2008. *Statistik verstehen: Eine Gebrauchsanweisung.* 7. ed. Munich: Piper. [Engl.: Kraemer, Walter 2008. Understanding Statistics: A Manual. 7th ed.].

Kraft, Charles H. [1979] 1980. *Christianity in Culture: A Study in Dynamic Biblical Theologizing in Cross-Cultural Perspective.* Vorwort von Bernard Ramm. Maryknoll: Orbis Books.

Krahl, Günther, Reuschel, Wolfgang & Schulz, Eckehard 1999. *Lehrbuch des modernen Arabisch.* 5. ed. Berlin: Langenscheidt.

Kraus, Wolfgang, Altner, Günter & Schwarz, Meier 1999. *Bioethik und Menschenbild bei Juden und Christen - Bewährunsgfeld Anthropologie.* Neukirchen-Vlyn: Neukirchener Verlag. [Engl: Bioethics and Conception of Man by Jewish people and Chistians.].

Kreyenbroek, Philip G. & Sperl, Stefan [1992] 2002. *The Kurds: Contemporary Overview.* Reprint. London: Routledge.

Kreyenbroek, Philip G. & Rashow, Khalil Jindy 2005. *God and Sheikh Adi are Perfect: Sacred Poems and Religious Narratives from the Yezidi Tradition.* Wiesbaden: Harrassowitz.

Kroeber, Alfred Louis 1953. Concluding Review, in Tax, Sol et.al. (eds.): *An Appraisal of Anthropology today*, 357-382. Chicago.

Kruse, Hans 1988. Öffentliche Verwaltung, in Steinbach, Udo & Robert, Rüdiger (eds.): *Der Nahe und Mittlere Osten: Politik, Gesellschaft, Wirtschaft, Geschichte, Kultur*, 211-220. Opladen: Leske + Budrich. [Engl.: Kruse, Hans 1988. Public Administration, in Steinbach, Udo & Robert, Rüdiger (eds.): The Near and Middle East: *Politics, Society, Economy, History, Culture*, 211-220. Opladen: Leske + Budrich.].

Küçük, Yalçın 1990. *Kürtlerin üzerine Tezler.* İstanbul. [Engl.: Informations/Theses about the Kurds.].

Kuhn, Thomas S. 1970. *The Structure of Scientific Revolution.* 2nd revised ed. Chicago: University of Chicago Press.

Kusch, Andreas 2003. Sozialwissenschaften und Missiologie - Versuch einer Verhältnisbestimmung, in Müller, Klaus W. (ed.): *Mission in fremden Kulturen*, 340-351. Edition afem. Mission academics 15. Nuremberg: VTR. [Engl.: Social Sciences and Missiology, Test of Determination, in Müller, Klaus W. (ed.): Mission in Foreign Cultures, 340-351st edition afem. Mission academics 15. Nuremberg: VTR].

Kußmaul, Paul 2007. *Verstehen und Übersetzen: Ein Lehr- und Arbeitsbuch.* Tübingen: Gunter Narr. [Engl.: Understanding and Translating: A Text- and Workingbook].

Langenscheidt Taschenwörterbuch 1995. *Türkisch: Türkisch - Deutsch; Deutsch - Türkisch.* Berlin: Langenscheidt. [Engl.: Langenscheidt Pocket Dictionary 1995. Turkish. Turkish – German; German – Turkish].

Langer, Robert 2008. Alevitische Rituale, in Sökefeld, Martin (ed.): *Aleviten in Deutschland: Identitätsprozesse einer Religionsgemeinschaft in der Diaspora*, 65-108. Bielefeld: Transcript. [Engl.: Langer, Robert 2008. Alevitic Rituals, in Sökefeld, Martin (ed.): *Alevis in Germany: Processes of Identification in a Religious Community in the Diaspora*, 65-108. Bielefeld: Transcript.].

Larson, Mildred 1984. *Meaning-Based Translation: A Guide to Cross-language Equivalence.* New York: University Press of America.

Latourette, Kenneth Scott 1953. *A History of the Expansion of Christianity: The First Five Centuries*, Vol. 1. London: Eyre and Spottiswoode.

Laut, Jens Peter 1996. Vielfalt türkischer Religionen. *Spirita: Zeitschrift für Religionswissenschaft* 10/1, 24-36. Marburg: Diagonal. [Engl.: Variation of Turkish Religions. Spirita: Magazine for Science of Religion.]

Laut, Jens Peter 2000. Zur Sicht des Islam in der Türkischen Republik bis zum Tode Atatürks, in Wolfgang Schluchter (Hrsg.): *Kolloquien des Max Weber Kollegs VI-XIV (1999/2000)*, 59-75. Erfurt: Max Weber-Kolleg. [Engl.: On the Perspective of Islam in the Turkish Republic until the Death of Ataturk, in Wolfgang Schluchter (eds.): *Colloquia of the Max Weber Kolleg VI-XIV (1999/2000)*, 59-75. Erfurt: Max Weber-Kolleg.

Le Coq, Albert von 1912. *Choros Zaturpanskij: Reisewege und Ergebnisse der deutschen Turfanexpeditionen.* Orientalisches Archiv. Leipzig: Hiersemann, Bd. 3, 116-127. [Engl.: Choros Zaturpanskij: Ways of Travel and Results of the German Turfanexpedition. Orientalistic Archive.].

Le Coq, Albert von 1926. *Auf Hellas Spuren in Ostturkistan: Berichte und Abhandlungen der II. und III. Deutschen Turfan-Expedition.* Leipzig: Hinrichs. Also Online: URL: http://dsr.nii.ac.jp/toyobunko/VIII-1-B-31/V-1/page/0005.html.en [accessed 2017-06-10]. [Engl.: On Hellas Ways in Eastern Turcistan: Essays and Documents from the II. and III. German Turfanexpedition.]

Le Coq, Albert von 1928. *Von Land und Leuten in Ostturkestan. Berichte und Abenteuer der 4. Deutschen Turfanexpedition.* Leipzig: Hinrichs. Also Online: URL: http://dsr.nii.ac.jp/toyobunko/VIII-5-B2-14/V-1/page/0005.html.en [accessed 2017-03-10]. [Engl.: About Country and Men in Eastern Turcistan. Essays and adventures of 4th German Turfanexpeditin.].

Leezenberg, Michiel 1993a. Gorani Influence on Central Kurdish: Substratum or Prestige Borrowing? Amsterdam: University of Amsterdam. (unpublished). Also Online in the Internet: URL: http://home.hum.uva.nl/oz/leezenberg/GInflCK.pdf [PDF-File] [accessed 2010-01-27].

Leezenberg, Michiel 1993b. The Shabak and the Kakais: Dynamics of Ethnicity in Iraqi Kurdistan. Kurdish Academy of Language. Amsterdam: University of Amsterdam. (unpublished). Also Online: URL: http://www.kurdishacademy.org/?q=node/133 [accessed 2017-03-05].

Lentz, Wolfgang 1926. Die nordiranischen Elemente in der neupersischen Literatursprache bei Firdosi. *Zeitschrift für Indologie und Iranistik*, Bd. IV, 271, 281 und 284. Leipzig: Deutsche Morgenländische Gesellschaft. [Engl.: The Northiranic Elements in the New Persian Literary Language by Fidosi].

Lepsius, Johannes 1897. Bericht über die Mission im Orient, in *Bericht über die Erste allgemeine Studenten-Konferenz des „Studentenbundes für Mission" abgehalten in Halle a.S. vom 24.-26. April 1897*, 141-144. Studentenbund für Mission (ed.). Halle: Verlag des Studentenbundes für Mission. [Engl.: Bulletin about the Mission in the Orient, in Report about the First General Students-Conference of the "Federation of Students for Mission" at Halle a.s. from the 24th-26th April 1897, 141-144. Federation of Students for Mission (ed.). Halle: Publisher of the Federation of Students for Mission.].

Lepsius, Johannes 1925. 30 Jahre Deutscher Orient Mission. *OLDOM*, 109-111/129-134. [Engl.: 30 years of German Orient Mission.].

Lepsius, Johannes [1919] 1986. *Deutschland und Armenien 1914-18: Sammlung diplomatischer Aktenstücke*. Nachdruck. Potsdam: Tempelverlag. [Engl.: Germany and Armenia. Collection of documents from the archives].

Lerch, Peter J. A. (1857-58). *Forschungen über die Kurden und die iranischen Nordchaldäer* (2 volumes). St. Petersburg. Reprint (1979). Amsterdam: Academic Publishers Associated. (Translation of the revised Russian Version under the pseudonym Petr Ivanovich Lerkh [1856-1858]. *Isledovanija ob Iranskix Kurdax i ix predkax severnyx Xaldejax*. (3 vol.). St. Petersburg: I. Glazlinov.). Online: URL: http://books.google.de/books/download/-Forschungen___ber_die_Kurden_und_die_ira.pdf?id=NXsLAQAAIAAJ&output=pdf&sig=ACfU3U3Zb1xsggsrvpcGbK6nwkfxYfNLvQ [accessed 2010-06-30]. [Engl.: Investigations on the Kurds and the Iranian Northern Chaldeans.].

Levtzion, Nehemia 1997. Eighteenth century Sufi Brotherhoods: Structural, Organisational and Ritual Changes, in Riddell, Peter G. & Street, Tony (eds.): *Islam: Essays on Scripture, Thought and Society. A Festschrift in Honour of Anthony H. Johns*, 147-160. New York: Brill.

Liebi Roger 2003. *Herkunft und Entwicklung der Sprachen*. Holzgerlingen: Hänssler. [Engl.: Origin and Development of Languages].

Liem, Ramsay 1997. Shame and Guilt among first- and second-generation Asian Americans and European Americans. *Journal of Cross-Cultural Psychology* 28/4, 365-392.

Lingenfelter, Sherwood G. & Mayers, Marvin K. 1986. *Ministering Cross-Culturally: An Incarnational Model for Personal Relationships*. Grand Rapids: Baker.

Lingenfelter, Sherwood G. 1996. *Agents of Transformation: A Guide for Effective Cross-Cultural Ministry*. Grand Rapids: Baker.

Livingstone, Greg 1993. *Planting Churches in Muslim Cities: A Team Approach*. Grand Rapids. Baker. (dt. Livingstone, Greg 1996. *Gemeindegründung in der Islamischen Welt: Dynamik der Teamarbeit*. Gießen: Brunnen.).

Lockwood, William B. 1972. Gorani and Zaza, in *A Panorama of Indo-European Languages*, 243-244. London: Hutchinson.

Lockwood, William B. 1972. *A Panorama of Indo-European Languages*. London: Hutchinson University Library. [Germ. Lockwood, William B. 1979. *Überblick über die indogermanischen Sprachen*. Tübingen: Gunter Narr].

Löffler, Roland 2005. Kritik am Armenier-Völkermord und Sicherung der eigenen Institutionen. Zur Arbeit der „Orient- und Islamkommission" des Deutschen Evangelischen Missionsausschusses während des Ersten Weltkrieges. *ZMiss* 31/4, 332-353. Frankfurt: Lembeck. [Engl.: Critics on the Armenian Genocide and Protection of the own Institutions. On the Work of the "Commissions of the Orient and Islam" during WWI as part of the German Protestant Missionary Commission].

Loewen, Jacob A. 1975. *Culture and Human Values: Christian Intervention in Anthropological Perspective*. Pasadena: William Carey.

Loizides, Neophytos G. 2010. *State Ideology and the Kurds in Turkey*. Middle Eastern Studies 46/4, 513–527, July 2010. London: Routledge. And Online: URL: http://works.bepress.com/cgi/viewcontent.cgi?article=1015&context=neophytos_loizides [accessed 2017-02-08].

Lomen, Martin 2003. *Sünde und Scham im biblischen und islamischen Kontext. Ein ethnohermeneutischer Beitrag zum christlich-islamischen Dialog*. Edition afem, mission scripts 21. Nuremberg: VTR. [Engl.: Sin and Shame in the Biblical and Muslim Context. A Ethnohermeneutical Study Contributing to the Christian-Islamic Dialogue].

Long, Lynne (ed.) 2005. *Translation and religion: Holy untranslatable?* Clevedon: Multilingual Matters.

Longenecker, Richard N. 2002. *Vol. 41*: *Word Biblical Commentary: Galatians*. Word Biblical Commentary. Dallas: Word, Incorporated.

Lukens-Bull, Ronald 2005. *A Peaceful Jihad. Negotiating Identity and Modernity in Muslim Java*. New York: Palgrave Macmillan.

Luzbetak, Louis [1988] 1993. *The Church and Cultures: New Perspectives in Missiological Anthropology*. Maryknoll: Orbis.

Lynd, Helen Merell 1958. *On Shame and the Search of Identity*. London: Routledge and Kegan Paul.

Lynd, Helen Merell 1961. *On Shame and the Search of Identity*. New York: Science Editions.

Maccoby, Eleanor Emmons 1999. The Two Sexes. Growing up Apart - Coming Together, in Fustenberg, Frank F. jr. & Cherlin, Andrew J. (eds.): *The Family and Public Policy*. Cambridge: The Belknap Press of Havard University Press.

MacKenzie, David Neil 1961. The Origins of Kurdish. *TPhS*, 68-86.

MacKenzie, David Neil 1961-1962. *Kurdish Dialect Studies*. 2 Vols. London: Oxford University Press. [Engl.: Northern and Central Kurdish Dialects].

MacKenzie, David Neil 1963. Kurmandji, kurdi, gurani. Narody Azii i Afriki 1, 162-170.

MacKenzie, David Neil 1981. Kurds and Kurdistan, V. Language. *Encyclopaedia of Islam*. New Ed. 5, 479-480.

MacKenzie, David Neil [1989] 2002. The role of Kurdish language in ethnicity, in Andrews, Peter Alford & Benninghaus, Rüdiger (eds.): *Ethnic Groups in the Republic of Turkey*. Beihefte zum Tübinger Atlas des Vorderen Orients Nr. 60.2, 541-542. Wiesbaden: Ludwig Reichert.

MacKenzie, David Neil 2003. *Gûrânî*. Encyclopedia Iranica 11/4, 401-403. New York: Columbia University.

Malina, Bruce J. 1986. *Christian Origins and Cultural Anthropology: Practical Models for Biblical Interpretation*. Atlanta: John Knox.

Malina, Bruce J. 2001. *The New Testament World - Insights from Cultural Anthropology*. Louisville: Westminster John Knox Press.

Malina, Bruce J. & Rohrbaugh, R. L. 1992. *Social Science Commentary and the Synoptic Gospels*. Minneapolis: Fortress.

Mallory, James P. & Adams, Douglas D. 2009. *The Oxford Introduction to Proto-Indo-European and the Proto-Indo-European World*. Oxford: Oxford University Press.

Malmisanıj 1992. *Zazaca – Türkçe Sözlük: Ferhengê Dımılki – Tırki*. İstanbul: Deng Yayınları.

Malmîsanij [1991] 2000. *Folklorê ma ra çend numûney*. İstanbul: Berdan.

Malottke, Tanja 2006. *Lehnwortadaption im Zazaki*. Studienarbeit. Norderstedt: GRIN. (Engl.: Loan word Adaptation in Zazaki).

Mardin, Şerif 1989. „Bediüzzaman" Said Nursi und die Mechanik der Natur, in Blaschke, Jochen & Bruinessen, Martin M. van (eds.): *Islam und Politik in der Türkei*, 197-232. Berlin: Edition Parabolis. [Engl.: "Bediuzzaman" Said Nursi and the Mechanics of Nature, in Blaschke, Jochen & Bruinessen, Martin M. van (eds.): *Islam and Politics in Turkey*, 197-232].

May, Karl 1951. *Durchs wilde Kurdistan*. Veränderte ed. Bamberg: Karl May Verlag. [Engl.: Through wild Kurdistan.].

Mayring, Philipp 1994. *Qualitative Inhaltsanalyse. Grundlagen und Techniken*. 5. ed. Weinheim: Deutscher Studien Verlag. [Engl.: *Qualitative contents analysis. Bases and techniques.*).

McCarus, Ernest N. 2009. Kurdish, in Windfuhr, Gernot (ed.): *The Iranian Languages*, 587-633. New York: Routledge.

McDowall, David 2004. *A Modern History of the Kurds*. Reprint. London: I. B. Tauris.

McGavran, Donald A. [1955] 1968. *The Bridges of God: A Study in the Strategy of Missions*. 2nd printing. New York: Friendship Press.

McGavran, Donald A. 1975. The Biblical Base from Which Adjustments Are Made, in Yamamori, Tetsunao & Taber, Charles R. (eds.): *Christopaganism or Indigenous Christianity*, 35-55. Pasadena: William Carey. (ursprünglich: London: Lutterworth Press).

McGee, R. Jon & Warms, Richard L. 2004. *Anthropological Theory: An Introductory History*. 3rd ed. Boston: McGraw-Hill.

Mead, Margaret 1937. Interpretive Statement, in Mead, Margaret (ed.): *Cooperation and Competition Among Primitive Peoples*, 493-505. New York: McGraw-Hill Bock.

Mead, Margaret 1964. *Anthropology: A Human Science*. Princeton: Van Nostrand.

Merdımin, W. K. 2005. *Mewlıd: Mela Ahmedê Xası*. İstanbul: Hivda İletişim. [Engl.: The Poem of the Prophets Birthday: Mullah ahmed Xasi.].

Minorsky, Vladimir Fedorovich 1920. Notes sur la secte des Ahle Haq. *Revue du monde Musulman* 40-41, 19-97. [Engl.: Notes about the sect of Ahle Haq.].

Minorsky, Vladimir Fedorovich 1921. Notes sur la secte des Ahle Haq II. *Revue du monde Musulman* 44-45, 205-302.
Minorsky, Vladimir Fedorovich 1928. Etudes sur les Ahl-i Haqq, i, 'Toumari'- Ahl-i Haqq. *Revue de L'historie des Religiones*, 90-105.
Minorsky, Vladimir Fedorovich 1943. The Guran. *Bulletin of School of Oriental and African Studies*, 75-103.
Minorsky, Vladimir Fedorovich 1960. Ahl-i Hakk. *The Encyclopedia of Islam* 1, 260-263.
Minorsky, Vladimir Fedorovich [1928] 1965. Daylam. *Encyclopedia of Islam*, Vol. 2, 189-194. (or [1926] Supplement E, 240-248).
Minorsky, Vladimir Fedorovich 1932. La domination des Daylamites. *Société des Études Iraniennes* (Paris) no. III, 1-26.
Mordecai, Victor 1999. *Der Islam - eine globale Bedrohung?* Holzgerlingen: Hänssler. (engl. Orig.: Modercai, Victor 1997. *Is Fanatic Islam a Global Threat?* Talmidim Publishing.).
Morris, Brian 1987. *Anthropological Studies of Religion: An Introductory Text*. Cambridge: Cambridge University Press.
Müller, Ernst Wilhelm 2001. *Kultur, Gesellschaft und Ethnologie: Aufsätze 1956-2000*. Mainzer Beiträge zur Afrika-Forschung. Hamburg: LIT.
Müller, Friedrich 1864. Beiträge zur Kenntnisse der neupersischen Dialekte. III. Zaza-Dialekt der Kurdensprache. *Sitzungsberichte der Kaiserlichen Akademie der Wissenschaften* (Wien) 48: 227-245.
Müller, Gerhard 2001. Taufe III. *TRE*, Bd. 32, 674-696. Berlin: Walter de Gruyter. [engl.: Baptism].
Müller, Harald 2001. *Das Zusammenleben der Kulturen - ein Gegenentwurf zu Huntington*. 5. ed. Frankfurt: Fischer. [Engl.: Mueller, Harald 2001. *The living together* of *the cultures - an alternative plan to Huntington*. 5th ed.).
Müller, Klaus W. (ed.) 2003. *Mission in fremden Kulturen*. Edition afem, mission academics 15, Nuremberg: VTR.
Müller, Klaus W. 2004b. Elenktik. Vorlesungsskript. Gießen: Akademie für Mission und Gemeindebau. [unpublished]. [Engl.: Elenctics. Working Paper.].
Müller, Klaus W. 2009. *Das Gewissen in Kultur und Religion: Scham- und Schuldorientierung als empirisches Phänomen des Über-Ich /Ich-Ideal. Lehrbuch Elenktik*. Nuremberg: VTR.
Muller, Roland 2001. *Honor and Shame: Unlocking the Door*. Philadelphia: Xlibris Corporation.
Mutlu, Servet 1996. Ethnic Kurds in Turkey: A Demographic Study. *International Journal of Middle East Studies* 28/4, 517-541.
Myers-Scotton, Carol 2006. *Multiple Voices: An Introduction to Bilingualism*. Oxford: Blackwell.
Nasidze, Ivan (et.al.) 2005. MtDNA and Y-chromosome Variation in Kurdish Groups. *Annals of Human Genetics* 69, 401-412. (Quinque, Dominique, Ozturk, Murat, Bendukidze, Nina, Stoneking, Mark). Also Online: URL: http://www.middleeastinfo.org/forum/index.php?s=29ad9a8c9995f1f80d32a866da3dd007&showtopic=5373 [accessed 2010-07-01].

Nebel, A., Filon, D., Brinkmann, B., Majumder, P. P., Faerman, M. & Oppenheim, A. (2001). The Y chromosome pool of Jews as part of the genetic landscape of the Middle East. *American Journal of Human Genetics* 69/5, 1095–112.

Neill, Stephen [1964] 1990. *Geschichte der christlichen Missionen*. Herausgegeben und ergänzt von Niehls-Peter Moritzen. 2. ergänzte Auflage. Erlangen: Verlag der evangelisch-lutherischen Mission. (Englisches Original: *Christian Missions*. Harmandsworth: Penguin.).

Neill, Stephen [1964] 1974. *Geschichte der christlichen Mission*. Herausgegeben und ergänzt von Moritzen, Niehls-Peter. Erlangen: Verlag der evangelisch-lutherischen Mission.

Nestmann, Liesa [1989] 2002. Ethnicity in Eastern Turkey, in Andrews, Peter Alford (ed.): *Ethnic Groups in the Republic of Turkey*, 543-580. Wiesbaden: Ludwig Reichert.

Neuliep, James William, [1957] 2006. *Intercultural Communication: A Contextual Approach*. 3rd edition. London: Sage.

Neyzi, Leyla 2002. Embodied Elders: Space and subjectivity in the Music of Metin-Kemal Kahraman. *Middle Eastern Studies* 38/1, Jan., 89-109. London: Frank Cass.

Nichols, Johana 1992. *Linguistic Diversity in Space and Time*. Chicago: University of Chicago Press.

Nida, Eugene A. [1947] 1961. *Bible Translating: An Analysis of Principles and Procedures, with Special Reference to Aboriginal Languages*. London: United Bible Societies.

Nida, Eugene A. [1954] 1975. *Customs and Cultures: Anthropology for Christian Missions*. Reprint. Pasadena: William Carey.

Nida, Eugene A. 1957. *Learning a Foreign Language: A Handbook Prepared especially for Missionaries*. Ann Arbor: Friendship Press.

Nida, Eugene A. [1960] 1990. *Message and Mission: The Communication of the Christian Faith*. Rev. Ausgabe mit einem Vorwort von Charles Kraft. Pasadena: William Carey.

Nida, Eugene A. 1964. *Toward a Science of Translating - with Special Reference to Principles and Procedures Involved in Bible Translating*. Leiden: E.J. Brill.

Nida, Eugene A. 1975. *Exploring Semantic Structures*. Munich: Wilhelm Fink.

Nida, Eugene A. [1975] 1979. *Componential Analysis of Meaning: An Introduction to Semantic Structures*. The Hague: Mouton.

Nida, Eugene A. & Taber, Charles R. 1969. *The Theory and Practice of Translation*. Leiden: E.J. Brill. (German Version: Nida, Eugene A. & Taber, Charles R. 1969. *Theorie und Praxis des Übersetzens unter besonderer Berücksichtigung der Bibelübersetzung*. New York: Weltbund der Bibelgesellschaften. Transl. by Kassühlke, Rudolf & Loewen, Jacob A.).

Niebuhr, Carsten [1778] 1792. *Travels through Arabia and other Countries in the East*. Transl. by Heron, Robert. Edinburgh: R. Morison and Son. (German: Niebuhr, Carsten [1778] 1997. *Reisebeschreibung nach Arabien und andern umliegenden Ländern*. (Orig: Kopenhagen: Möller). Nachdruck. Zürich: Manesse).

Niebuhr, Carsten 1774-1778 und 1837. *Reisebeschreibung nach Arabien und anderen umliegenden Ländern*. 2 Bände [1774-1778]. Kopenhagen 1774-1778; Band 3 [1837]: *Reisen durch Syrien und Palästina*. Hamburg.

Nord, Christiane [1997] 2001. *Translating as a Purposeful Activity: Functionalist Approaches Explained*. Reprint. Manchester: St. Jerome.

Nord, Christiane 2003. *Textanalyse und Übersetzen: Theoretische Grundlagen, Methode und didaktische Anwendung einer übersetzungsrelevanten Textanalyse.* 3rd ed. Tübingen: Julius Groos. [Engl.: Textual Analysis and Translation: Theoretical Foundations, method and didactic application of a translation relevant Analysis of Text].

Nord, Christiane 2004. Loyalität als ethisches Verhalten im Translationsprozess, in Müller, Ina (ed.): *Und sie bewegt sich doch ... Tanslationswissenschaft in Ost und in West, Festschrift für Heidemarie Salevsky zum 60. Geburtstag,* 234-245. Frankfurt/M.: Peter Lang. [Engl.: Nord, Christiane 2004. Loyality as ethical Behaviour in the Translational Process, in Müller, Ina (ed.): And she is still moving ... *Tanslation Science in East and into the West, Celebration Document for Heidemarie Salevsky for the 60th Birthday,* 234-245. Frankfurt: Peter Lang.).

North, Eric M. 1974. Eugene A. Nida: An appreciation, in Black, Matthew & Smalley, William A. (eds.): *On Language, Culture, and Religion: In Honor of Eugene A. Nida,* vii-xx. Paris: Mouton.

Oehring, Otmar 1983. Die Verfassung der Dritten Türkischen Republik. Eine kritische Einführung und deutsche Übersetzung. *Orient: Zeitschrift des deutschen Orient-Instituts* 2, 301-357. Opladen: Leske + Budrich. And Online: *Die Verfassung der Republik Türkei vom 7. November 1982.* URL: http://www.verfassungen.de/tr/tuerkei82.htm [2008-07-03].

Olbrich, Berthold 1996. Der Islam in Deutschland. Hausarbeit. Kirchberg: Bibelschule Kirchberg. (unpublished).

Olson, Robert 1989. *The Emergence of Kurdish Nationalism and the Sheikh Said Rebellion, 1880-1925.* Austin: University of Texas Press.

Ong, Walter J. 2002. *Orality and Literacy: The Technologizing of the Word.* London: Routledge.

Oranskij, Iosif 1979. *Iranskie yazyki v istoriceskom osvescenii.* Moskva. [Iranian languages and their historic documentation].

Ostler, Nicholas [2005] 2006. *Empires of the Word: A Language History of the World.* New York: Harper.

Oxbrow, Mark 2005. Emerging Mission in Oxbrow, Mark & Garow, Emma (eds.): *Emerging Mission: Reporting on a Consultation. Bangalore/India (November),* 1-8. London: Indian Society for Promoting Christian Knowledge.

Pamukçu, Ebubekir (ed.) 1984-1986. *Ayre: Pêserokê Ziwanî.* [The Mill: Language Magazine.]. Stockholm.

Pamukçu, Fahri 2001. *Gıramerê Zazaki - Zuwanrêznayi.* [Zazaki Grammar.] İstanbul: Vêjiyaişê Tiji / Tij Yayınları.

Parkin, Robert 1997. *Kinship: An Introduction to Basic Concepts.* Oxford: Blackwell.

Paul, Ludwig, 1992. Ein neues Volk? Die Zaza in Südostanatolien. *Pogrom: Zeitschrift für bedrohte Völker* 165/23, 73. Göttingen: Gesellschaft für bedrohte Völker. [Engl.: A new people group? The Zaza of Southern East Anatolia].

Paul, Ludwig 1994. *Kurdisch: Wort für Wort.* Kauderwelsch Band 94. Bielefeld: Reise Know-How.

Paul, Ludwig 1998. *Zazaki: Grammatik und Versuch einer Dialektologie.* Wiesbaden: Ludwig Reichert. [Engl.: Grammar and Attempt of a Dialectology].

Paul, Ludwig [1989] 2002. Zaza(ki) - Dialekt, Sprache, Nation?, in Andrews, Peter Alford & Benninghaus, Rüdiger (eds.): *Ethnic Groups in the Republic of Turkey: Supplement and Index*. Beihefte zum Tübinger Atlas des Vorderen Orients Nr. 60.2, 190-198. Wiesbaden: Ludwig Reichert. [Engl.: Dialect, Language, Nation?].

Paul, Ludwig 2007. Zur Lage der Gorani-Dialekte im Iran und ihrer Erforschung, in Macuch, Maria, Maggi, Mauro & Sundermann, Werner (eds.): *Iranian Languages from Iran and Turan: Ronald E. Emmerick Memorial Volume*, 285-296. Wiesbaden: Harrassowitz. [Engl.: On the situation and investigation of the Gorani dialects in Iran].

Paul, Ludwig 2009. Zazaki, in Windfuhr, Gernot (ed.): *The Iranian Languages*, 545-586. New York: Routledge.

Paul, Ludwig 2012. Die Herkunft und Stellung des Zazaki und das Verhältnis von Sprache zu Ethnie [Turkish translation: Zazac'nın Kökeni ve Konumu ve Etnik Kökeni ile Dilin İlişkisi, in Varol, Murat & Elaltuntaş, Ömer Faruk (eds.): *1. Bingöl Symposium on the Zaza Language (13th-14th May 2011) [1. Uluslararası Zaza Dili Sempozyumu (13-14 Mayıs 2011)*.], 13-18 [Turkish translation: 19-29]. Bingöl: Bingöl Üniversitesi Yayınları. [Bingöl University Publications]. [Engl.: Origin and Status of Zazaki and the Relation of Language an Ethnicity.].

Paul, Ludwig & Gippert, Jost 2009. Konferenz „Zazaki". Notices. Berlin: Dersim Gemeinde Berlin 15.11.2009. (unpublished).

Paul, Ludwig & Haig, Geoffrey 2001. Kurmanjî Kurdish, in Garry, Jane & Rubino, Carl R.G. (eds.): *Facts about the World's Languages: An Encyclopedia of the World's Major Languages, Past and Present*, 398-403. New York: New England.

Payne, Thomas E. 1997. *Describing Morphosyntax: A Guide for Field Linguists*. Cambridge: Cambridge University Press.

Pericliev, Vladimir 2009. Kaingang and Austronesian – Similarities between Geographically Distant Languages. *Current Issues in Unity & Diversity of Language. Papers selected from 18th Intl. Congress of Linguists*. Seoul.

Peters, Ken 1989. Touching the Mystical Heart of Islam. *emq* 25/4, 364-369. Wheaton: evangelical press association.

Petrov, E. [1863] 1998. Tschapachdshur und Dersim. Schreiben von Trapzunta, "Die Dersimer". spb. Wendomostjax. Lauf der militärischen Ereignisse an der Kaukasusfront. Band IV. *Ware* 12, 148-150. Baiersbronn. [Engl.: Tschapachdshur and Dersim. Letter of Trapzunta, "The Dersimers". spb. Wendomostjax. Events on the Caucasus-Front. Vol. IV.].

Pickett, W. [1933] 1953. *Christian Mass Movements in India*. Nashville: Abingdon.

Pikkert, Peter 2008. *Protestant Missionaries to the Middle East: Ambassadors of Christ or Culture?* Scotts Valley: Create Space.

Pinker, Steven 1999. *How the Mind Works*. London: Penguin.

Pöhlmann, Horst Georg [1977] 1991. *Der Atheismus oder der Streit um Gott*. 6. Auflage. Gütersloh: Gütersloher Verlagshaus Mohn.

Principe, Walter H. 1991. The Unity of the Church and the Multitude of Nations, in Felmy, Karl Christian & Kretschmar, Georg u. a. (eds.): *Kirchen im Kontext unterschiedlicher Kulturen: Auf dem Weg in das dritte Jahrtausend*, 69-90. Göttingen: Vandenhoeck & Ruprecht.

Quintana-Murci, L., Chaix, R., Wells, R. S. et al. (2004). Where west meets east: the complex mtDNA landscape of the southwest and Central Asian corridor. *American Journal of Human Genetics* 74/5, 827–845.

Racey, David 1996. Contextualization: Contextualization: how far is too far? emq, Vol. 32/3, 304-310. Wheaton: evangelical press association.

Ramsauer, Ernest E. 1965. *The Young Turks: Prelude to the Revolution of 1908*. Beirut: Khayats.

Rappaport, Roy A. 1999. *Ritual and Religion in the Making of Humanity*. Cambridge: Cambridge University Press.

Reifler, Hans Ulrich 2005. *Handbuch der Missiologie: Missionarisches Handeln aus biblischer Perspektive*. Nuremberg: VTR.

Reiß, Katharina & Vermeer, Hans J. [1984] 1991. *Grundlegung einer allgemeinen Translationstheorie*. 2nd ed. Tübingen: Niemeyer.

Renner, Egon 1980. *Die Kognitive Anthropologie: Aufbau und Grundlagen eines ethnologisch-linguistischen Paradigmas*. Berlin: Duncker und Humblot. [Engl.: *Cognitive Anthropology: Construction and Bases* of *an Ethnological Linguistic Paradigm*.).

Renz, Alfred 1985. *Land um den Ararat: Osttükei - Armenien*. Zweite durchgesehene Auflage. Munich: Prestel. [Engl.: Country around the Ararat: Eastern Turkey. Second rev.ed. Munich: Prestel].

Reuter, Christoph 2003. *Selbstmordattentäter: Warum Menschen zu lebenden Bomben werden*. Munich: Goldmann. [Original 2001: *Mein Leben ist eine Waffe. Selbstmordattentäter - Psychogramm eines Phänomens*. Munich: Bertelsmann.].

Rich, Cladius James [1836] 2007. *Narrative of a Residence in Koordistan, and on the Site of Ancient Nineveh; With Journal of a Voyage Down the Tigris to Bagdad, and an Account*. Repr. Whitefish: Kessinger.

Richards, M., Macaulay, V., Hickey, E. et al. (2000). Tracing European founder lineages in the Near Eastern mtDNA pool. *American Journal of Human Genetics* 67/5, 1251–1276.

Richter, Julius [1930] 2006. *Mission und Evangelisation im Orient*. Reprint der 2nd ed. Nuremberg: VTR.

Ricoeur, Paul 1988. *Time and Narrative*. Vol. 2. Trans. Kathleen McLaughlin and David Pellauer. Chicago: University of Chicago Press.

Riggs, Charles T. 1940. The Turkish Translations of the Bible. *The Moslem World* XXX, 236-248. London: Christian Literature Society for India.

Riggs, Henry H. 1911. The Religion of the Dersim Kurds. *Missionary Review of the World*, 734-743. London/ New York.

Roberts, John R. 1997. The Syntax of Discourse Structure. *NOT* 11/2, 15-34. Dallas: SIL International.

Roberts, John R. 2003. Features of Persian Discourse Structure. Horsleys Green: SIL International. (unpublished).

Robinson, Douglas 1997. *Translation and Empire: Postcolonial Theories Explained*. Manchester: St. Jerome.

Rommen, Edward 2003. *Namenschristentum: Theologisch-soziologische Erwägungen*. edition afem. 2nd ed. Nuremberg: VTR.

Rosch, Eleanor H. 1973. Natural Categories. *Cognitive Psychology* 4, 328-50.
Rosch, Eleanor H. 1978. Principles of Categorisation, in Rosch, Eleanor H. & Lloyd, Barbara B. (eds.): *Cognition and Categorisation*, 27-48. Hillside: Erlbaum.
Rynkiewich, Michael A. 2011. *Soul, Self, and Society: A Postmodern Anthropology for Mission in a Postcolonial World*. Eugene: Cascade.
Sachs, Lothar 1990. *Statistische Methoden 2: Planung und Auswertung*. Heidelberg: Springer. [Engl.: *Statistical methods 2: Planning and evaluation*.).
Sallisbury, Murray I. 2002. STEPS: Skills for Translating and Exegeting the Primary Scriptures. Guildford. (unpublished).
Sánchez-Cetina, Edesio 2007. Word of God, Word of the People: Translating the Bible in Post-Missionary Times, in Noss, Philip A. (ed.): *A History of Bible Translation*, 387-408. Roma: Edizioni di Storia e Letteratura.
Sanjek, Roger [1996] 2004. Ethnography, in Barnard, Alan & Spencer, Jonathan (eds.): *Encyclopedia of Social and Cultural Anthropology*, 193-198. Reprinted. London: Routledge.
Sanneh, Lamin [1989] 1992. *Translating the Message: The Missionary Impact on Culture*. 4th ed. Maryknoll: Orbis.
Sanneh, Lamin 1990. Gospel and Culture: Ramifying effects of scriptural translation, in Stine, Philip C. (ed.): *Bible Translation and the Spread of the Church: The last 200 Years*, 1-23. Leiden: Brill.
Sanneh, Lamin 2003. *Whose Religion is Christianity? The Gospel beyond the West*. Grand Rapids: Eerdmans.
Sanneh, Lamin 2007. Bible Translation and Scripture Use in Christian History. Lectures at European Training Programme (etp). 11th - 23rd June. Horsleys Green. (unveröffentlichte Mitschrift).
Sapir, Edward 1961. *Die Sprache: Eine Einführung in das Wesen der Sprache*. Munich: Max Hueber. (Deutsche Übersetzung des englischen Originals: Sapir, Edward [1921] 1949. *Language: An Introduction to the Study of Speech*. New York: Harcourt, Brace and World).
Sauer, Christof 2004. *Form bewahren: Handbuch zur Harvard-Methode*. GBFE-Studienbrief 5. Lage: Gesellschaft für Bildung und Forschung in Europa e.V.
Schäfer, Richard 1932. *Geschichte der Deutschen Orient-Mission*. Potsdam: Lepsius, Fleischmann & Grauer. [Engl.: History of the German Orient-Mission.].
Scheffczyk, Leo 2001. Grundfragen christlicher Anthropologie, in Breid, F. (ed.): *Der Mensch als Gottes Ebenbild. Christliche Anthropologie*. Referate der „Internationalen Theologischen Sommerakademie 2001" des Linzer Priesterkreises in Aigen/M., 9-28. Buttenwiesen. [Engl.: Basic Questions of Christian Anthropolgy, in Breid, F. (ed.): *Man as the Imago Dei. Christian Anthropology*. Lectures at the "International Theological Summer Acadamy 2001" of the Linzer Circle of Priests in Aigen/M.].
Schirrmacher, Christine 1992. *Mit den Waffen des Gegners: Christlich-muslimische Kontroversen im 19. und 20. Jahrhundert dargestellt am Beispiel der Auseinandersetzung um Karl Gottlieb Pfanders Mizan al-haqq' und Rahmatullah ibn Halil al-Kairanawis Izhar al-haqq' und die Diskussion um dass Barnabasevangelium*. Islamkundliche Untersuchungen, Bd. 162. Berlin: Klaus Schwarz. [Engl.: With the Armors of the Enemy: Christian-Islamic

Controversies in the 19th and 20th Century exemplified by the Dispute about Karl Gottlieb Pfanders Mizan ah-haqq' and Rahmatullah ibn Halil al-Kairanawis Izhar al-haqq and the Discussion about the Gospel of Barnabas. Research on Islam.].

Schirrmacher, Christine 1994a. *Der Islam 1: Geschichte, Lehre, Unterschiede zum Christentum.* 2 Bände. Neuhausen-Suttgart: Hänssler. [Engl.: Islam 1: History, Teaching, Differences to Christianity.].

Schirrmacher, Christine 1994b. *Der Islam 2: Geschichte, Lehre, Unterschiede zum Christentum.* 2 Bände. Neuhausen-Suttgart: Hänssler. [Engl.: Islam 2: History, Teaching, Differences to Christianity.].

Schirrmacher, Christine 2007. Der „Ehrenmord" - ein „Schandemord" - Nicht nur ein sprachlicher Unterschied: Frauen als Opfer archaischer Stammesbräuche, religiös begründeter Traditionen und Umbruchssituationen in der Migration, in Müller, Klaus W. (ed.): *Mission als Kommunikation: Die christliche Botschaft verstehen.* Festschrift für Ursula Wiesemann zu ihrem 75. Geburtstag, 162-180. Nuremberg: VTR.

Schirrmacher, Christine 2008a. *The Islamic View of Major Christian Teachings: The Role of Jesus Christ, Sin, Faith, and Forgiveness - Essays.* Bonn: Verlag für Kultur und Wissenschaft.

Schirrmacher, Christine 2008b. *Islam and Society: Sharia Law - Jihad - Women in Islam - Essays.* Bonn: Verlag für Kultur und Wissenschaft.

Schirrmacher, Christine 2008c. *The Islamic View of Major Christian Teachings: The Role of Jesus Christ, Sin, Faith, and Forgiveness - Essays.* Bonn: Verlag für Kultur und Wissenschaft.

Schmidt-Salomon, Michael 2005. *Manifest des evolutionären Humanismus: Plädoyer für eine zeitgemäße Leitkultur.* Aschaffenburg: Alibri.

Schmitt, Rüdiger 1981. *Grammatik des Klassisch-Armenischen mit sprachvergleichenden Erläuterungen.* Innsbrucker Beiträge zur Sprachwissenschaft Bd. 32. Innsbruck: Institut für Spachwissenschaft der Universität Innsbruck.

Schmitt, Rüdiger 1989. *Compendium linguarum Iranicarum.* Wiesbaden: Ludwig Reichert.

Schmitt, Rüdiger 2000. *Die iranischen Sprachen in Geschichte und Gegenwart.* Wiesbaden: Ludwig Reichert.

Schmitt, Rüdiger 2009. *Die altpersischen Inschriften der Achaimeniden.* Wiesbaden: Ludwig Reichert.

Schnelle, Udo 1991. Neutestamentliche Anthropologie – Jesus, Paulus, Johannes. Neukirchen-Vlyn: Neukirchener.

Schönfeld, Rudolf & Schönfeld, Marianne 2004. *Ferhengoka biçûk.* Gießen: Self published.

Schogt, Henry 1992. Semantic Theory and Translation Theory, in Schulte, Rainer & Biguenet, John (ed.): *Theories of Translation: An Anthology of Essays from Dryden to Derrida*, 193-203. Chicago: The University of Chicago Press.

Schulze, Wolfgang 2000. *Northern Talysh.* Munich: Lincom Europa.

Schulz-Goldstein, Esther 2012. Vom Glanz der frühen Jahre: Dêsım und seine daylamitische Vergangenheit. Vortrag gehalten am 3. November in Mannheim auf dem Kulturtag der Zaza. Arbeitspapier und PDF-file. Mannheim. [Engl.: Schulz-Goldstein, Esther 2012. The splendor of the early years: Dêsım and his Daylamitic Past. Paper presented at the Day of

Zaza Culture on the 3rd November in Mannheim. Working paper and PDF file. Mannheim.].

Scorgie, Glen G. 2003. Introduction and Overview, in Scorgie, Glen G., Strauss, Mark L. & Voth, Steven M. (eds.): *The Challenge of Bible Translation: Communicating God's Word to the World*, 19-34. Grand Rapids: Zondervan.

Selcan, Zülfü 1998a. *Die Entwicklung der Zaza-Sprache*. Ware 12, 152-163. Baiersbronn. And Online: URL: http://www. http://www.arikah.net/enzyklopadie/Zazaische_Sprache/-EntwicklungZSpr_A5Selcan.pdf [PDF-File] [accessed 2008-01-18].

Selcan, Zülfü 1998b. *Grammatik der Zaza-Sprache – Nord-Dialekt (Dersim-Dialekt)*. Berlin: Wissenschaft & Technik.

Şener, Cemal 1993. *Alevilik Olayı. Toplumsal Bir Başkaldırının Kısa Tarihcesi.* 11. Baskı. İstanbul: Ant Yayınları.

Seufert, Günter 1997. Between Religion and Ethnicity: a Kurdish-Alevi Tribe in Globalizing İstanbul, in Öncü, Ayşe & Weyland, Petra (eds.): *Space, Culture and Power*, 157-176. London: Zed Books.

Seufert, Günter & Kubaseck, Christopher 2004. *Die Türkei- Politik, Geschichte, Kultur.* Munich: Beck.

Shaked, Shaul 2007. The Iranian canon of scriptures and writings, Vahman, Fereydun & Pedersen, Claus V. (eds.): *Religious Texts in Iranian Languages*, 11-26. Copenhagen: Det Kongelige Danske Videnskabernes Selskab.

Shaw, Daniel E. & Van Engen, Charles E. 2003. *Communicating Gods Word in a Complex World: God's Truth or Hocus Pocus?* New York: Rowman & Littlefield.

Shindeldecker, John 2001. *Türkische Aleviten heute*. İstanbul/Göztepe: Sahkulu Sultan Külliyesi. (also in Engl.: Turkish Alevis today).

Sick, Ingeborg Maria 1929. *Karen Jeppe: Im Kampf um ein Volk in Not*. Stuttgart: Steinkopf. [Engl.: Karen Jeppe: Fighting for a People Group].

Singelis, Theodore M. u. a. 1999. Unpacking Culture's Influence on Self-esteem and Embarrassability: The Role of Self-construals. *Journal of Cross-Cultural Psychology 30*, Nr. 3: 315-341.

Singgih, E. G. 1995. Let Me Not be Put to Shame: Towards an Indonesian Hermeneutic. *Asia Journal of Theology* 9/1, 71-85.

Shankland, David [1989] 2002. Anthropology and Ethnicity: the Place of Ethnography in the new Alevi Movement, in Andrews, Peter Alford & Benninghaus, Rüdiger (eds.): *Ethnic Groups in the Republic of Turkey: Supplement and Index*. Beihefte zum Tübinger Atlas des Vorderen Orients Nr. 60.2, 199-205. Wiesbaden: Ludwig Reichert.

Skjœrvø, Prods Oktor 2007. The Avestan Yasna: Ritual and Myth, Vahman, Fereydun & Pedersen, Claus V. (eds.): *Religious Texts in Iranian Languages*, 57-84. Copenhagen: Det Kongelige Danske Videnskabernes Selskab.

Skjœrvø, Prods Oktor 2009. Kurdish, in Brown, Keith & Ogilvie, Sarah (eds.): *Concise Encyclopedia of Languages of the World*, 625-626. New York: Elsevier.

Soane, Ely Bannister 1912. *To Mesopotamia and Kurdistan in disguise: With Historical Notices of the Kurdish Tribes and the Chaleans of Kurdistan*. London: John Murray.

Soane, E. B. 1921. *A Short Antology of Guran Poetry. Journal of the Royal Asiatic Society.* London. [A collection of 27 poems plus a number of fragments made by Abdul Mu'min in the years 1783-1785].

Sökefeld, Martin 2008a. Einleitung: Aleviten in Deutschland - von takiye zur alevitischen Bewegung, in Sökefeld, Martin (ed.): *Aleviten in Deutschland: Identitätsprozesse einer Religionsgemeinschaft in der Diaspora*, 7-36. Bielefeld: Transcript. [Engl.: Sökefeld, Martin 2008a. Introduction: Alevis in Germany - from takiye to an Alevitiv Movement, in Sökefeld, Martin (ed.): *Alevis in Germany: Processes of Identification in a Religious Community in the Diaspora*, 7-36. Bielefeld: Transcript.].

Sökefeld, Martin 2008b. Sind Aleviten Muslime? Die alevitische Debatte über das Verhältnis von Alevitentum und Islam in Deutschland, in Sökefeld, Martin (ed.): *Aleviten in Deutschland: Identitätsprozesse einer Religionsgemeinschaft in der Diaspora*, 195-218. Bielefeld: Transcript. [Engl.: Sökefeld, Martin 2008b. Are Alevis Muslims? The Alevitic Debate about the Relationship of Alevism and Islam in Germany, in Sökefeld, Martin (ed.): *Alevis in Germany: Processes of Identification in a Religious Community in the Diaspora*, 195-218. Bielefeld: Transcript.].

Sperber, Dan 1975. *Rethinking Symbolism.* Cambridge: Cambridge University Press.

Sperber, Dan 1982. *On Anthropological Knowledge.* London: Cambridge University Press.

Sperber, Dan & Wilson, Deirdre [1986] 1995. *Relevance: Communication and Cognition.* 2nd ed. Oxford: Blackwell.

Sphar, Asa 1997. A Theology of Shame as Revealed in the Creation Story. *The Theological Educator* 55 (Frühjahr): 64-74.

Spiegel, Friedrich 1871-1873. *Eränische Altertumskunde*, 3. vols. Leipzig: Engelmann.

Spies, Otto & Pritsch, Erwin 1964. Klassisches Islamisches Recht. *Handbuch der Orientalistik.* Ergänzungsband III. Orientalisches Recht. Leiden: Brill.

Spies, Otto 1968. Schicksale türkischer Kriegsgefangener in Deutschland nach den Türkenkriegen, in Gräfe, Erwin (ed.): *Festschrift Werner Caskel: zum 70. Geburtstag, 5 März 1966, gewidmet von Freunden und Schülern*, 316-335. Leiden: Brill.

Spiro, Melford E. 1965. *Children of the Kibbutz.* New York: Schocken. [Also: Spiro, Melford E. [1958] 1975. *The Children of the Kibbutz: A Study in Child Training and Personality.* In assistance with Audrey G. Spiro. Cambridge: Harvard University Press].

Spiro, Melford E. 1966. Religion: Problems of Definition and Explanation, in Banton, Michael (ed.): *Anthropological Approaches to the Study of Religion*, 85-126. London: Tavistock.

Spiro, Melford E. 1972. Cognition in Culture and Personality, in Spradley, James P. (ed.): *Culture and Cognition: Rules, Maps, and Plans*, 100-110. New York: Chandler.

Spradley, James P. 1972. Foundations of Cultural Knowledge, in Spradley, James P. (ed.): *Culture and Cognition: Rules, Maps, and Plans*, 3-40. New York: Chandler.

Spradley, James P. 1979. *The Ethnographic Interview.* New York: Holt, Rinehart and Winston.

Spradley, James P. 1980. *Participant Observation.* New York: Holt, Rinehart and Winston.

Spradley, James P. & McCurdy, David W. [1975] 1989. *Anthropology: The Cultural Prespective.* 2nd ed. Prospect Heights: Waveland.

Steinbach, Udo 1988. Ideengeschichte im Zeichen von Kolonialismus, Unabhängigkeitsbewegung und Modernisierung, in Steinbach, Udo & Robert, Rüdiger (eds.): *Der Nahe und Mittlere Osten: Politik, Gesellschaft, Wirtschaft, Geschichte, Kultur*, 135-184. Opladen: Leske + Budrich.

Steinbach, Udo 1996. *Die Türkei im 20. Jahrhundert – schwieriger Partner Europas.* Bergisch Gladbach: Lübbe.

Steiner, George 1990. Von *realer Gegenwart: Hat unser Sprechen Inhalt?* Munich: Carl Hanser. [Engl. *Real Presences.* Chicago: University of Chicago.].

Steiner, George [1981] 2004. *Nach Babel: Aspekte der Sprache und des Übersetzens.* Frankfurt am Main: Suhrkamp. [Engl. Steiner, George [1975] 1998. *After Babel, Aspects of Language & Translation.* 3rd ed. Oxford: Oxford University Press.].

Steinvorth, Daniel & Elger, Katrin 2008. Verlorene Naivität. *Spiegel Special: Land im Aufbruch - Türkei*, 36. Hamburg. [Engl.: Lost Naiveté. Spiegel special: Nation in the Awakening – Tukey.].

Stipek, Deborah 1998. Differences between Americans and Chinese in the Circumstances evoking Pride, Shame, and Guilt. *Journal of Crosscultural Psychology* 29/5, 616-629.

Steuerwald, Karl 1974. *Türkçe – Almanca Sözlük.* Wiesbaden: Otto Harrassowitz. [Engl.: Turkish – German Dictionary.].

Stolze, Radegundis 1999. *Die Fachübersetzung: Eine Einführung.* Tübingen: Narr. [Engl.: The Technical Translation: An Introduction.].

Strohmeier, M. & Yalcin-Heckmann, L. 2000. *Die Kurden – Geschichte – Politik – Kultur.* Munich: Becksche Reihe. [Engl.: The Kurds – history – Politics – Culture.].

Sundermann, Werner 1989. Parthisch, in Schmitt, Rüdiger (ed.): *Compendium Linguarum Iranicarum*, 114-137. Wiesbaden: Ludwig Reichert. [Engl.: Parthian.]

Sweetnam, Denise L. [1994] 2004. *Kurdish Culture – A Cross-Cultural Guide.* 2nd ed. Bonn: Verlag für Kultur und Wissenschaft (Publishing House on Culture and Science). (includes an article from Jacobson, C. M. about *Alevi religion and Zaza*, 220-232).

Taft, Ronald 1981. The Role and Personality of the Mediator, in Bochner, Stephen (ed): *The Mediating Person: Bridges between Cultures*, 53-88. Cambridge: Schenkman.

Tangney, June Price & Fischer, Kurt W. (eds.) 1995. *Self-conscious Emotions: The Psychology of Shame, Guilt, Embarrassment, and Pride.* Mit einem Vorwort von Joseph Campos. New York: Guilford Press.

Tangney, June Price 1995. Shame and Guilt in Interpersonal Relationships, in Tangney, Price June & Fischer, Kurt W. (eds.): *Self-conscious Emotions: The Psychology of Shame, Guilt, Embarrassment, and Pride*, 114-139. New York: Guilford Press.

Tangney, June Price, Burggraf, Susan A. & Wagner, Patricia E. 1995. ShameProneness, Guilt-Proneness, and Psychological Symptoms, in Tangney, Price June & Fischer, Kurt W. (eds.): *Self-conscious Emotions: The Psychology of Shame, Guilt, Embarrassment, and Pride*, 343-367. New York: Guilford Press.

Tapper, Richard 1991. Anthropologists, Historians and Tribespeople. On Tribe and State Formation in the Middle East, in Khoury, Philip S. & Kostiner, Joseph (eds.): *Tribe and State Formation in the Middle East*, 48-73. London: University of California Press.

Tarlo, Emma 1996. *Clothing Matters: Dress and Identity in India*. London: Hurst & Company.

Taşçı, Hülya 2008. Die zweite Generation der Alevitinnen und Aleviten zwischen religiösen Auflösungstendenzen und sprachlichen Differenzierungsprozessen, in Sökefeld, Martin (ed.): *Aleviten in Deutschland: Identitätsprozesse einer Religionsgemeinschaft in der Diaspora*, 133-154. Bielefeld: Transcript. [Engl.: Taşçı, Hülya 2008. The second generation of Alevis between the Tendency of Breakup and processes of Linguistic Segmentation, in Sökefeld, Martin (ed.): *Alevis in Germany: Identification Processes of a Religious Community in the Diaspora*, 133-154. Bielefeld: Transcript.].

Taylor, Edward Bennett 1871. Primitive Culture. Reissue. Cambridge: Cambridge University Press.

Taylor, John G. 1868. Journal of a Tour in Armenia, Kurdistan and Upper Mesopotamia ... in 1866. *Journal of the Royal Geographical Society* 38, 281-361. London.

Ter-Mikelian, Arsak [1892] 2009. *Die Armenische Kirche in ihren Beziehungen zur Byzantinischen (vom IV. bis zum XIII. Jahrhundert)*. Charleston: Bibliolife. (original: Leipzig: Georg Fock). [Engl.: The Armenian Church in its Relationship with the Byzantine].

The American Heritage Dictionary of the English Language [2000]. *Structuralism*. 4th ed. Orlando: Houghton Mifflin. And Online: URL: http://www.thefreedictionary.com/structuralism. [accessed 2017-04-29].

The United Bible Societies and SIL International 1990. A Statement of Working Relationship on Translation Publishing and Distribution. 1990. Dallas: SIL International. (unpublished paper).

Thiel, Josef Franz 1992. *Grundbegriffe der Ethnologie: Vorlesungen zur Einführung*. 5. ed. Berlin: Dietrich Reimer.

Thilo, Martin 1939. *Was die Araber sagen*. Bonn: Ludwig Röhrscheid. [Engl.: What the Arags tell.].

Thomas, Alexander [1992] 1996. Aspekte interkulturellen Führungsverhaltens, in Bergemann, Niels & Sourisseaux, Anreas L. J. (eds.): *Interkulturelles Management*, 35-58. 2nd ed. Heidelberg: Physica.

Timpe, R. L. 1985. Shame, in Benner, David G. (ed.): *Baker's Encyclopedia of Psychology*, 1074-75. Grand Rapids: Baker.

Todd, Emmanuel 1983. *La troisième planète: Structures familiales et systèmes idéologiques*, Paris: Editions du Seuil. (English translation: Todd, Emmanuel 1985. *The Explanation of ideology: Family Structures and Social Systems*. Oxford: Basil Blackwell.).

Todd, Terry L. 1985. A Grammar of Dımılı (also known as Zaza). Ph.D. Dissertation. Michigan: University of Michigan. [unpublished].

Todd, Terry L. 2002. *A Grammar of Dımılı (also known as Zaza)*. 2nd edition. Stockholm: Iremet Förlag. Also Online: URL: http://www.forum-linguistik.de/Zaza-Dimli/page2.html [accessed 2017-08-28].

Todd, Terry L. & Werner, Eberhard 2012. The Sacredness of Minority Language and Mother Tongue Based Multi Lingual Education [Turkish translation: Azınlık Dillerinin Kutsallığı ve Anadil Temelli Çok Dilli Eğitim, in Varol, Murat & Elaltuntaş, Ömer Faruk (eds.): *1. Bingöl Symposium on the Zaza Language (13th-14th May 2011)* [*1. Uluslararası Zaza Dili*

Sempozyumu (13-14 Mayıs 2011).], 89-99 [Turkish translation: 101-109]. Bingöl: Bingöl Universitesi Yayınları. [Bingöl University Publications].

Toerne, Arnika 2011. Narratives of Violence and Suppression: Autobiographies of Zaza Alevi Dedes in Dersim. Paper presented at the 15th anniversary of the Journal Iran and the Caucasus. Yerevan: Yerevan State University. [unpublished].

Tomaschek, Wilhelm 1877. *Zentralasiatische Studien.* Wien: Sogdiana. [Engl.: Central Asian Studies.].

Toury, Gideon 1995. *Descriptive Translation Studies and Beyond.* Amsterdam: John Benjamins.

Traub, Rainer 2008. Ich bin die Türkei. *Spiegel Special: Land im Aufbruch - Türkei*, 22-23. Hamburg. [Engl.: I am Turkey. *Mirror* special: Country on the Awakening.].

Triandis, Harry C. 1994. *Culture and Social Behavior.* New York: McGraw Hill.

Triandis, Harry C. 1995. *Individualism & Collectivism.* Boulder: Westview.

Triebel, Johannes 2007. Auf dem Weg zu guter Nachbarschaft? Anmerkungen zur neuen Islam-Handreichung der EKD "Klarheit und gute Nachbarschaft". *theologische beiträge* 38/6, 353-358. Witten: Brockhaus. [Engl.: On the Way to a good neighbourhood? Notes on the Handout to Islam by the EKD (Protestant Church Germany) "Clarity and good neighbourhood".].

Tritton, Arthur S. [1947] 1990. *Muslim Theology.* Westport: Hyperion. (Originalausgabe, London: Luzac).

Troeger, Eberhard 2005a. Der Griff des Islam nach Europa. Vortrag vom 11.02.2005 Working Paper. Gießen: Freie Theologische Hochschule.[unpublished]. [Engl.: The Grab of Islam for Europe. Lecture on the 11th February 2005.].

Troeger, Eberhard 2005b. Christliches Zeugnis und islamische Da'wa, in Baumann, Andreas, Sauer, Christof & Troeger, Eberhard (eds.): *Christliches Zeugnis und islamische Da'wa*, 19-66. Nuremberg: VTR. [The Christian Testimony and Islamic Da'awa, in Baumann, Andreas, Sauer, Christof & Troeger, Eberhard (eds.): Christian Testimony and Islamic Da'wa.].

Trudgill, Peter [1974] 1983. *Sociolinguistics: An Introduction to Language and Society.* Rev. ed. London: Penguin.

Tsunoda, Tasaku 2006. *Language Endangerment and Language Revitalization.* Berlin: Walter de Gruyter.

Tucker, William F. 1989. Introduction, in Olson, Robert: *The Emergence of Kurdish Nationalism and the Sheikh Said Rebellion*, 1880-1925, xv-xix. Austin: University of Texas Press.

Türkdoğan, Orhan. 1997. *Etnik Sosyoloji.* İstanbul: Timaş Yayınları. [Engl. Ethnical Sociology].

Tunçay, Mete 1989. Der Laizismus in der Türkischen Republik, in Blaschke, Jochen & Bruinessen, Martin M. van (eds.): *Islam und Politik in der Türkei*, 53-94. Berlin: Edition Parabolis. [Engl.: The Laicism in the Republic of Turkey, in Blaschke, Jochen & Bruinessen, Martin M. van (eds.): *Islam and Politics in Turkey*, 53-94].

Turgut, Harun w/o Date. *Türkçe Açıklamalı Zazaca Dilbilgisi.* 215 pages. Robert Koch Str. 43. 28277 Bremen: Selfediting. [Engl.: Turkish Zazaki-Grammar].

Turgut, Harun 2001. *Zazaca – Türkçe Sözlük*. İstanbul: Tij Yayınları. [Engl. Zazaki – Turkish Dictionary].

Tymoczko, Maria 2003. Ideology and the Position of the Translator: In What Sense is a Translator 'In Between'?, in Calzada-Pérez, Maria (ed.): *Apropos of Ideology: Translation Studies on Ideology - Ideologies in Translation Studies*, 181-205. Manchester: St. Jerome.

Underhill, Robert 2001. Turkish, in Garry, Jane & Rubino, Carl R.G. (eds.): *Facts about the World's Languages: An Encyclopedia of the World's Major Languages, Past and Present*, 766-769. New York: New England.

UNESCO / SIL International Bangkok 2007. *Promoting Mother Tongue-based Multilingual Education (MLE)*. Bangkok: Asia-Pacific Programme of Education for All. Also Online: URL: www.unescobkk.org/education/appeal [DVD] [accessed 2017-06-16].

Vahman, Fereidun & Asatrian, Garnik Serobi 1990. Gleanings from Zâzâ vocabulary, in Duchesne-Guillemin, J. (ed.): *Iranica Varia, Papers in Honour of Ehsan Yarshater* (= Acta Iranica 30), 267-275. Leiden.

Vander Werff, Lyle L. 1977. *Christian Mission to Muslims: the Record. Anglican and Reformed Approaches in India and the Near East*. South Pasadena: William Carey.

Vannerem, Mia & Snell-Hornby, Mary 1986. Die Szene hinter dem Text: „scenes-and-frames semantics" in der Übersetzung, in Snell-Hornby, Mary (ed.): *Übersetzungswissenschaft - eine Neuorientierung: Zur Integrierung von Theorie und Praxis*, 184-205. Tübingen: Francke. [Engl.: The scene behind the "text": "Scenes and Frames semantics" in Translation).

Verroj, Seîd 2003. *Kurmancî – Dimilî – Tirkî & Tirkî – Dimilî – Kurmancî*. İstanbul: War. [Engl.: Kurmanji – Dimili – Turkish & Turkish – Dimili - Kurmanji.].

Vicedom, Georg F. [1958] 2002. Missio Dei: Einführung in eine Theologie der Mission, in Müller, Klaus W. (ed.): Missio Dei: *Einführung in eine Theologie der Mission - Actio Dei: Mission und Reich Gottes*, 27-109. New edition. Nuremberg: VTR.

Waard, Jan de 1991. Translation as Cultural Transfer, in Felmy, Karl Christian & Kretschmar, Georg u. a. (eds.): *Kirchen im Kontext unterschiedlicher Kulturen: Auf dem Weg in das dritte Jahrtausend*, 745-751. Göttingen: Vandenhoeck & Ruprecht.

Waard, Jan de & Nida, Eugene A. 1986. *From One Language to Another: Functional Equivalence in Bible Translation*. Nashville: Nelson.

Wallbott, Harald G. & Scherer, Klaus R. 1995. Cultural Determinants in Experiencing Shame and Guilt, in Tangney, Price June & Fischer, Kurt W. (eds.): *Self-conscious Emotions: The Psychology of Shame, Guilt, Embarrassment, and Pride*, 465-487. New York: Guilford.

Walls, Andrew F. 2005. *The Cross-Cultural Process in Christian History*. 3rd ed. New York: Orbis.

Walter, Mary Ann 2004a. Loan Adaptation in Zazaki, in Kenstowicz, Michael (eds.): *Studies in Zazaki Grammar* . Working Papers on Endangered and Less Familiar Languages 6, 97-106. Cambridge: MIT.

Walter, Mary Ann 2004b. Vowel Adaptation in Zazaki. Working Paper. 27th Generative Linguistics in the Old World. 18-21 April 2004. (unpublished).

Wassman, Jürg 2003. Kognitive Ethnologie, in Fischer, Hans & Beer, Bettina (eds.): *Ethnologie: Einführung und Überblick*. 4th ed. 331 ff. Berlin: Dietrich Reimer. [Engl.: Cognitive

Anthropology, in Fischer, Hans & Beer, Bettina (eds.): Anthropology: Introduction and Overview.].
Weber, Max 1972. *Wirtschaft und Gesellschaft*. 5. ed. Tübingen: Mohr. [Engl.: Economy and Society].
Wei, Li [2000] 2007. *The Bilingualism Reader*. 2nd ed. London: Routledge.
Wei, Li [2000] 2007. Dimensions in Bilingualism, in Wei, Li (ed.): *The Bilingualism Reader*, 4-22. 2nd ed. London: Routledge.
Weizsäcker, Carl Friedrich von 1960. Komplementarität und Logik, in von Weizsäcker, Carl Friedrich (ed.): *Zum Weltbild der Physik*, 281-331. Nachdruck der 8. ed. Stuttgart: S. Hirzel. [Engl.: Weizsaecker, Carl Friedrich von 1960. Complementarity and Logic, in von Weizsäcker, Carl Friedrich von (ed.): *To the Conception of the Worlview of the Physics*, 281-331. Reprint of the 8th ed. Stuttgart: P. Hirzel].
Wendland, Ernst R. 2003. A Literary Approach to Biblical Text Analysis and Translation, in Wilt, Timothy (ed.): *Bibletranslation: Frames of Reference*, 179-230. Manchester: St. Jerome.
Wendland, Ernst R. 2006a. *Translating the Literature of Scripture: A Literary-Rhetorical Approach to Bible Translation*. Dallas: SIL International.
Wendland, Ernst R. 2006b. *LiFE-Style Translating: A Workbook for Bible Translators*. Dallas: SIL International.
Wendland, Ernst R. 2008. *Contextual Frames of Reference in Translation: A Coursebook for Bible Translators and Teachers*. Manchester: St. Jerome.
Werner, Brigitte 2003a. Reflexives Pronomen (xo) und unpersönliches Personalpronomen (cı). (unpublished worksheet).
Werner, Brigitte 2003b. *Terminologie der erweiterten Familienstruktur der Zaza (Çermug)*. Zaza Press 13, 20-21. Stockholm: ZazaPress. (Originaltitel des Artikels: *Jenealoji*). Also Online: URL: http://zazaki.de/zazaki/Kinshipdiagram_deutsch.pdf [PDF-File] [accessed 2017-03-06]. [Engl.: Terminology of the extended Family Structure of the Zaza *(Çermug)*.].
Werner, Brigitte 2007. Features of Bilingualism in the Zaza Community. Working paper. Marburg: Philipps Universität. (unpublished).
Werner, Brigitte 2008a. Grammar Sketch for Zaza (Dialect of Çermık-Siverek-Gerger). Working papers. Giessen. (unpublished).
Werner, Brigitte 2008b. Anleitung zum Sprachelernen des Zazaki für Anfänger. (unpublished teaching material). [Engl.: Language Learning Introduction for Beginners in Zazaki].
Werner, Brigitte 2012. Coding of Background Information in Zazaki Narrative (SIL International) [Zaza Romanıinda Temel Bilgirlerin Kodlanışı (Uluslararası SIL)], in Varol, Murat & Elaltuntaş, Ömer Faruk (eds.): 1. Bingöl Symposium on the Zaza Language (13th-14th May 2011) [1. Uluslararası Zaza Dili Sempozyumu (13-14 Mayıs 2011).], 49-68 [Turkish translation: 69-87]. Bingöl: Bingöl Universitesi Yayınları.
Werner, Brigitte 2012. Vignette: What a color can tell. *EAA Anthropology Newsletter* 2/5, 3. Dallas: SIL International.
Werner, Eberhard 2011. *Bibelübersetzung in Theorie und Praxis: Eine Darstellung ihrer Interdisziplinarität anhand der Ausbildungspraxis*. Hamburg: Kovač. [Engl.: *Bible Transla-*

tion in Theory and Practice: An Overview about its Interdisciplinarity exemplified on the Practice of Training.].
Werner, Eberhard 2011. Worldview and Conscience: LEIC a Tool to Cognitive Anthropology. Paper presented at the Translation, Anthropology, Linguistics Conference in Horsleys Green. SIL International. [unpublished].
Werner, Eberhard 2012. Bibelübersetzung – Schnittstelle zwischen Kulturen. Untersuchungen zu den iranischen Sprachen und Kulturen. Bonn: Verlag für Kultur und Wissenschaft. [Engl.: Bible Translation – Interface between Cultures. Investigations on Iranian Languages and Cultures. Bonn: Publishing House of Culture and Science.].
Werner, Eberhard 2012. Toward an Ethical Code in Bible Translation Consulting. Journal of Translation (JOT) 8/1, 1-8. Dallas: Summer Institute of Linguistics. Dallas: Summer Institute of Linguistics. Also Online: URL: http://www.sil.org/siljot/2012/1/928474548941/-siljot2012-1-01.pdf [PDF] [accessed 2014-05-29].
Werner, Eberhard [2013]. Turkish, in Noss, Philip A. (ed.): Dictionary of Bible Translation. (announced).
Werner, Brigitte & Werner, Eberhard 2007. Outline of Narrative Discourse Features in Dimli-/Southern Zazaki. Holzhausen: etp. (unpublished worksheet).
Werner, Oswald 1996. Ethnographic Translation: Issues and Challenges. Sartoniana 7, 59-135. Gent: University of Gent.
Wheatcroft, Andrew 2005. Infidels: A History of the Conflict between Christendom and Islam. New York: Random House.
White, Paul J. 2003. The Debate on the Identity of 'Alevi Kurds', in White, Paul J. & Jongerden, Joost (eds.): Turkey's Alevi Enigma: A Comprehensive Overview, 17–32. Leiden: Brill.
Whorf, Benjamin Lee 1956. Science and Linguistics, in Carroll, J. B. (ed.): Language, Thought, and Reality: Selected Writings of Benjamin Lee Whorf, 207-19. Cambridge: M.I.T. Press.
Whorf, Benjamin Lee 1963. Sprache, Denken, Wirklichkeit: Beiträge zur Metalinguistik und Sprachphilosophie. Reinbek bei Hamburg: Rowohlt. (ed. und übers. von Krausser, Peter). [Engl.: Language – Thought – Reality: Essays on Metalinguistics and conversation philosophy.].
Wiher, Hannes 1998. Missionsdienst in Guinea: Das Evangelium für eine schamorientierte, von Animismus und Volksislam geprägte Gesellschaft. Edition Afem, Mission Scripts, Band 14. Bonn: Verlag für Kultur und Wissenschaft.
Wiher, Hannes 2003. Shame and Guilt: A Key to Cross-Cultural Ministry. Edition IWG, Mission Academics, Bd. 10. Bonn: Verlag für Kultur und Wissenschaft.
Wiher, Hannes 2007. Scham- und schuldorientierte Aspekte des Islam, in Müller, Klaus W. (ed.): Mission im Islam, 224-230. Nuremberg: VTR.
Wilson, David 2010. A Dialect Survey of Zazaki. Working Paper. Dallas: GIAL. (unpublished).
Windfuhr, Gernot 1989. New West Iranian, in Schmitt, Rüdiger (ed.): Compendium linguarum Iranicarum. Wiesbaden: Ludwig Reichert.

Windfuhr, Gernot 2009. Dialectology and Topics, in Windfuhr, Gernot (ed.): *The Iranian Languages*, 5-42. New York: Routledge.
Winter, Ralph D. 2008. Editorial Comment. *Mission Frontiers* 30/5, 4. Pasadena: US Center for World Mission.
Wippich, Werner 1984. *Lehrbuch der angewandten Gedächtnispsychologie*, Vol. 1. Stuttgart: Kohlhammer.
Wixman, Ronald 1984. *The peoples of the USSR: An Ethnographic Handbook*. London: Macmillan.
w/o Author. 2006. Killings of honour. *World and Press*, 1st March Issue. Bremen: Schülers und Schünemann.
Wolf, Lothar 1975. *Aspekte der Dialektologie: Eine Darstellung von Methoden auf französischer Grundlage*. Tübingen: Niemeyer.
Wolff, Hans Walter 1984. *Anthropologie des Alten Testaments*. 4th ed. Munich: Kaiser.
Woodberry, Dudley J. 2008. Power and Blessing: Keys for Relevance to as Religion as Lived, in Van Engen, Charles E, Whiteman, Darrell & Woodberry, Dudley J. (eds.): *Paradigm Shifts in Christian Witness: Insights from Anthropology, Communication, and Spiritual Power. Essays in Honor of Charles H. Kraft*, 98-105. New York: Orbis.
Xasî, Ehmedê 1899. *Mewludê Nebî*. Diyarbekır: Çapxaneyê Lîtografya. [Engl.: The Prophetes Poem on his Birthday.].
Ye'or, Bat [1996] 2009. *The Decline of Eastern Christianity under Islam: From Jihad to Dhimmitude. Seventh-Twentieth Century*. Seventh printing. Madison: Fairleigh Dickinson University Press. (Transl. From French by Kochan, Miriam and Littman, David).
Yonan, Gabriele 1989. *Ein vergessener Holocaust. Die Vernichtung der christlichen Assyrer in der Türkei*. Holzhausen (etp-Bibliothek): Eigenverlag. [Engl.: The annihilation of the christian assyrians in Turkey].
Yonan, Gabriele 1992. *Christliche Minderheiten in der Türkei*. Berlin. [Engl.: Christian minorieties in Turkey].
Yuzbashian, K. N. 1962. Deylamity v 'Provestvovanii' Aristakesa Lastiverttsi (Deylamites in the history of Aristakes of Lastivert). *Palestinskiĭ sbornik* 7/70, 146-151.
Zilan, Bilan 2011. Vate Çalişma Grubu ve Kirmanccayi (Zazacayi) Standartlaştirma Çalişmalari. Working Paper presented at the Zaza Conference in Yerewan from 28-30th October 2011. Mardin: Artuluk Universitesi. [unpublished]. [Engl. The "Vate" Study Group and its Efforts in Standardization of Kirmanchki (Zazaki)].
Zürcher, Erik Jan [1993] 2004. *Turkey: A Modern History*. Rev. ed. London: I. B. Taurus.

Websites

Aksoy, Serap 1995. *The GAP Project in Southeastern Turkey: The Potential for Emergence of Diseases*. Online im Internet: URL: http://www.cdc.gov/ncidod/eid/vol1no2/aksoy.htm [accessed 2017-08-18].

American Anthropological Association [1971] 1986. *Statements on Ethics: Principles of Professional Responsibility Adopted by the Council of the American Anthropological Association*. Airlington. Online: URL: http://www.aaanet.org/stmts/ethstmnt.htm [accessed 2017-04-29].

American Anthropological Association 1998. *Code of Ethics of the American Anthropological Association*. American Anthropological Association Statement on Ethnography and Institutional Review Boards. Airlington. Online: URL: http://www.aaanet.org/committees/-ethics/ethcode.htm also http://www.aaanet.org/committees/ethics/ethicscode.pdf [PDF-File] [accessed 2017-04-29].

American Anthropological Association 2004. *American Anthropological Association Statement on Ethnography and Institutional Review Boards*. Airlington. Online: URL: http://www.aaanet.org/stmts/irb.htm [accessed 2017-04-29].

Arts & Humanities Research Council 2010. *Between Kismet and Karma: South Asian Women Artists Respond to Conflict*. Online: URL: http://www.ahrc.ac.uk/News/Latest/Pages/kismetandkarma.aspx [accessed 2017-02-07].

Asatrian, Garnik Serobi 1995. Dımli. *Encyplopedia Iranica*, 197-198. Online im Internet: URL: http://www.iranica.com/articles/dimli# [accessed 2017-08-16].

Azis, Alis 2006. *The Kurdish Platform*. Online: URL: http://www.ike-europa.com/modules.php?name=News&file=article&sid=27 [accessed 2017-02-01].

Bauer, Martin 2010. *Goldene Horde*. Online: URL: http://www.uni-protokolle.de/Lexikon/Goldene_Horde.html [accessed 2017-02-20]. [Engl.: Golden Hord.].

Burghardt, Franz Josef 2006. *Ausländer nach Staatsangehörigkeiten 2006*. Stand 31.12.2006. Online: URL: http://www.auslaender-statistik.de/ [accessed 2017-02-19]. [Engl.: Foreigners following Citizenship.].

Die Verfassung der Republik Türkei vom 7. November 1982. Online: URL: http://www.verfassungen.de/tr/tuerkei82.htm [2017-03-03]. [Engl.: The Turkish Constitution from 07 November 1982.].

Dimle. Online: URL: http://www.iranica.com/articles/v7/v7f4/v7f447.html [accessed 2017-12-10].

Encyclopædia Britannica 2009. *Kurd*. Encyclopaedia Britannica Online: URL: http://www.britannica. com/EBchecked/topic/325191/Kurd. [accessed 2017-02-10).

Encyclopedia Iranica 2007. *Dimle*. Online: URL: http://www.iranica.com/articles/v7/v7f4/v7f 447.html. [accessed 2017-02-10].

Etnopedia 2010. Online: URL: http://de.etnopedia.org [accessed 2010-05-14].

EUbusiness 2006. *Turkey's Kurds yearn for official status for their language*. Online: URL: http:www.eubusiness.com/East_Europe/060312145509.l59u0zw0 [2017-02-18].

European Stability Initiative 2011. *Murder in Anatolia: Christian Misionaries and Turkish Ultranationalism*. Berlin: ESI. Also Online: URL: http://www.esiweb.org/index.php?lang=de&id=67&newsletter_ID=53. [accessed 2017-02-04].

Faruk, Muhammed 1999. Between Preussenadler and Swastika: Islam in Germany from 1739–1945. Dunia Hochschulschrift. Soest. And Online: URL: http://www.enfal.de/grund 12.htm. [accessed 2017-02-19].

Fenffe, Gregor Delvaux de 2009. *The Mao Bible*. Online: URL: http://www.planet-wissen.de/laender_leute/china/mao_zedong/china_mao_bibel.jsp [accessed 2017-02-01].

Forsey, Martin Gerard 2010. Ethnography as participant listening. *Ethnography* 11, 558-572. London: Sage. Online: http://eth.sagepub.com/content/11/4/558.full.pdf+html [PDF-File] [accessed 2014-03-12].

Gippert, Jost 2005. *Stammbaum der iranischen Sprachen*. Online: URL: http://www.zazaki.de/deutsch/gippert-stammbaum%20iraniische%20sprachen-geradlinige%20entwicklung.jpg [accessed 2017-02-18].

Government Turkiye 2006. *Cermik*. Online: URL: http://cermik.gov.tr/ [2011-12-10].

Güvenç, Bozkurt 2010. *Das Bild des "Türken" in Europa*. Yeni Vatan Gazetesi. Wien. Also Online: URL: http://www.yenivatan.com/Das-Bild-des-Tuerken.60.0.html [accessed 2010-05-03]. (english: Güvenç, Bozkurt 2010. *Europes picture of the „Turk"*. Yeni Vatan Gazetesi. Vienna. And Online in the Internet: URL: http://www.yenivatan.com/Das-Bild-des-Tuerken.60.0.html [accessed 2017-02-03]. [Engl.: The image of the "Turk" in Europe.].

Hejaro 2007. *Kurdische Dialekte/Lehceyên Kurdî*. Online: URL: http://pauker.at/VIP/Hejaro/kate_de/4495 [accessed 2017-02-28]. [Engl. The Kurdish Dialects].

Hennerbichler, Ferdinand 2004. *Die Kurden*. Mosonmagyarovar: Edition fhe. Also Online: URL: http://www.fhe.cc/html/DieKurden-fhe-Sprache.pdf [PDF-File] [accessed 2009-01-16]. [Engl.: The Kurds.].

Hürriyet Gazete Haberleri 2008. *DTP challenges PM in Kurdish*. Online: URL: http://www.hurriyet.com.tr/english/domestic/11076708.asp?scr=1 (accessed 2017-02-01).

Human Rights Education Associates 2006. *Turkey: A Minority Policy of Systematic Negation*. 11 October 2006. Online: URL: http://www.hrea.org/lists/wcar/markup/msg00276.html [accessed 2017-02-17].

IHD Bericht 2002. *Türkischer Innenminister gründet Kommission "Gefährliche Namen"*. Türkischer Menschenrechtsverein. Online: URL: http://www.nadir.org/nadir/periodika/kurdistan_report/2002/105/07.htm [accessed 2017-02-29]. [Engl.: Report of IHD 2002. Turkish Minister of Interior establishes commission "Dangerous Names". Turkish Association for Human Rights.].

Izady, Mehrdad 1992. *The Map collection of Geography section at Kurdistanica*. Online: URL: http://kurdistanica.com/?q=gallery&g2_itemId=56 [accessed 2017-02-24].

KHRP Draft Report: Education Rights in Turkey. Kurdish Human Rights Project. 18 June 2007. Online: URL: www.khrp.org/content/view/309/2/ [accessed 2017-11-18].

Kurdistan Save the Children. *What We Do* 2009. Online: URL: http://www.ksc-kcf.com/Whatwedo/tabid/61/Default.aspx [accessed 2009-01-18].

Lezgin, Roşan 2011. *Mewlidê Ehmedê Xası*. Online: URL: http://www.zazaki.net/haber/-mewlid-neb-y-ehmed-xas-57.htm. [accessed 2017-11-16].

Müller, Wolfgang & Siegert, Roland 2010. *Wilhelm II. Deutschlands letzter Kaiser: Kaiserbesuch 1898 – Besuch beim Sultan und Palästina-Reise*. Online: URL: http://www.wilhelm derzweite.de/dokumente/osman1898.php [accessed 2017-02-26]. [Engl.: Wilhelm II. Germanys last Emperor: Visits of the Emperor 1898 – Visit to the Sultan and his Travel to Palestine.].

Papke, Werner 1999. *Das Zeichen des Messias*. Online: URL: http://www.kahal.de/017-WP-ZDM.pdf [PDF-File] [accessed 2017-02-18]. [Engl.: The Sign of the Messiah].

Ruciyar, Baran 2008. Aleviten: Kizilbash – Alewiten. *Kurdica*. Auszug aus Ronahî 8/2004. Online: URL: http://www.kurdica.com/News-sid-KizilbashAlewiten-142.html [accessed 2017-02-22].

Ruciyar, Baran 2009. *Hewramî (Gorani)*. Online: URL: http://qirayis.de/Content-pa-print page-pid-95.html [accessed 2017-01-16].

Selcan, Zülfü 1997. *Die Entwicklung der Zaza-Sprache*. Ware 12/1998, 152-163. Baiersbronn. And Online: URL: http://www. http://www.arikah.net/enzyklopadie/Zazaische_-Sprache/EntwicklungZSpr_A5Selcan.pdf [PDF-File] [accessed 2017-01-18]. [Engl.: The Development of the Zaza-Language.].

Temizbas, Suvar w/o Date. *Dimli: Wir, unsere Heimat und unsere Sprache*. Online: URL: http://www.coli.uni-saarland.de/fs-coli/procs/temizbas.html [accessed 2017-05-18]. [Engl.: Dimli: We, our Home and our language.].

Tezcür, Güneş Murat 2009. *Kurdish Nationalism and Identity in Turkey: A Conceptual Reinterpretation*. European Journal of Turkish Studies (ejts): Social Sciences on Contemporary Turkey. Online: URL: http://ejts.revues.org/index4008.html [accessed 2017-01-21].

The destruction of Kurdish villages w/o Date. Online: URL: http://users.westnet.gr/~cgian/-villages.htm [accessed 2017-02-10].

The Heritage Web Site from Ismaili.net 2010. *The Fortress of Alamut*. Online: URL: http://www.ismaili.net/histoire/history06/history602.html [accessed 2017-02-23].

The Shannon-Weaver Model. w/o Date. Online: URL: http://www.cultsock.ndirect.co.uk/-MUHome/cshtml/introductory/sw.html [accessed 2017-02-01].

Todd, Terry L. 2002. *A Grammar of Dimili (also known as Zaza)*. 2nd edition. Stockholm: Iremet Förlag. Also Online: URL: http://www.forum-linguistik.de/Zaza-Dimli/page2.html [accessed 2017-01-28].

Tornecengi, Hawar, 2009. *Khalê Gağani*. Online im Internet: URL: http://www.radiozaza.de/Hawar%20Torn%EAcengi/KHALK%CAK%20(Khal%EA%20Gagani).htm [accessed 2017-12-28]. [Engl.: Father Winter / Old Gagan].

Türkei-Information 2008. *EU-Fortschrittsbericht 2008*. Newsletter Türkei der Friedrich-Ebert-Stiftung Nr. 13/November, 1. İstanbul: Friedrich-Ebert-Stiftung. Online: URL: http://library.fes.de/pdf-files/bueros/tuerkei/04293/tuerkeiinformation2008,13.pdf [PDF-File] [accessed 2017-01-20]. [Engl.: EU-Report of Progress 2008. Newsletter Zurkey oft he Friedrich-Ebert-Foundation.].

UNESCO Bangkok 2007b. *Promoting Mother Tongue-based Multilingual Education (MLE)*. Bangkok: Asia-Pacific Programme of Education for All. Also Online: URL: www.unes cobkk.org/education/appeal [CD-ROM] [accessed 2017-02-16].

Watson, Paul Joseph & Jones, Alex 2008. The *Fruits of Globalization: Rotten To The Core*. Online: URL: http://www.prisonplanet.com/articles/november2005/081105rottentothecore. htm [accessed 2017-02-11].

White, Paul (no date). *Ethnic Differentiation among the Kurds: Kurmancî, Kizilbash and Zaza*. Online: URL: http://www.members.tripod.com/~zaza_kirmanc/research/paul.htm#2 [accessed 2017-05-18].

w/o A. 2008. *Peter Pikkert on The Great Experiment*. Islam and Christianity. Online: URL:http://islamdom.blogspot.com/2008/12/peter-pikkert-on-great-experiment.html [2017-01-30].

w/o A. 2009. 15 languages endangered. Online im Internet: URL: http://www.hurriyet.com.tr/english/opinion/11068922.asp?yazarid=294&gid=260 [accessed 2017-06-27].

w/o A. 2011. *Zoroastrianism and Parsiism*. Online: URL: http://encyclopedia2.thefreedictionary.com/Zoroastrianism+and+Parsiism [adressed 2012-03-13].

w/o A. w/o Date. Online: URL: *Sufis - Die Freimaurer des Ostens*? Hamburg: internetloge.de / internetloge.org. [accessed 2017-01-20]. [Engl.: Sufis - The Freemasons of the East?].

w/o A. w/o Date Türkische Bibelgesellschaft: „Christentum kein Import aus dem Westen". APD. Katholisches Magazin für Kirche und Kultur. Online Im Internet: URL: http://www.katholisches.info/?p=1873 [accessed 2017-11-24]. [Engl.: The Turkic Bible Society: "Christianity is not an import from the West"].

Zaza: Sprache 2007. Online: URL: http://de.wikipedia.org/wiki/Kurdische_Sprache [accessed 2017-12-10]. [Engl.: Zaza: Language.].

Zaza: Volk 2007. Online: URL: http://de.wikipedia.org/wiki/Zaza [accessed 2017-12-10]. [Engl.: Zaza: People.].

Ziya Gökalp 2008. Online: URL: http://de.wikipedia.org/wiki/Ziya_Gökalp [accessed 2017-12-10].

Personal Communication

AT 2011. *Alevism, Islam, Naqshebendi and the Armenization of the Zaza people*. Personal communication on 25th November 2011. Wetzlar.

Dewran, Hasan 2011. *Alevism and religious Influence on the Zaza people*. Personal communication. Zaza Cultural Celebration Mannheim, 16th October.

HC 2011. *Alevism, Islam, Naqshebendi and the Armenization of the Zaza people*. Personal communication on 25th November 2011. Wetzlar.

HT 2010. *Kizil Baş and other Groups in Alevitism*. Personal communication on 18th January 2010. Gießen.

IS 2009. Diyarbakır. Personal communication on 03rd December 2010. Gießen

Jacobson 2009. *Anthropological Insights*. E-mail Correspondence 11th March 2009.

MA 2012. *Zazaki, Kumanji, Zaza-Kurds*. Personal communication on 26th January 2012. Gießen.

MT 2008. *Zazaki.* Personal communication on 20th December 2008. Gießen.
RH 2006. *Zaza and their neighbours.* Personal communication on 15th April 2006.
RH 2007. *Names of Zaza-Tribes and their structure.* Personal communication on 20th June 2007.
RH 2008. *Zaza and Zazaki.* Personal communication on 03rd March 2008.
RH 2010. *Origin of our people.* Personal communication on 13th February 2010. Gießen.

Exegetical Tools

BDAG 2000. *Greek-English Lexicon of the New Testament and Other Early Christian Literature.* Aland, Kurt, Aland, Barbara & Reichmann, Viktor und frühere englische Ausgaben von Arndt, W.F., Gingrich, F.W. & Danker, F.W. (eds.). 3rd ed. Chicago: The University of Chicago. [Deutsche Ausgabe: Walter Bauer's Griechisch-deutsches Wörterbuch zu den Schriften des Neuen Testaments und der frühchristlichen Literatur, 6th ed. Amsterdam: de Gruyter].
BHT 2001. *Hebrew Old Testament.* Holzgerlingen: Deutsche Bibelgesellschaft.
ELBIWIN kompakt 2002. *Neuer sprachlicher Schlüssel zum Neuen Testament.* Ingenierbüro Matthias Frey. Reutlingen. [CD-ROM]. [Engl.: New linguisticak Key to the New Testament.].
ELBIWIN kompakt 2002. *Lexikon zur Bibel.* Ingenierbüro Matthias Frey. Reutlingen. [CD-ROM]. [Engl.: Bibellexicon.].
ExWBNT 1980. *Exegetisches Wörterbuch zum Neuen Testament.* Balz, Horst & Schneider, Gehard. 3/1-3. Stuttgart: Kohlhammer. [Engl.: Exegetical Wordbook tot he New testament.].
GNT 2004. *The Greek New Testament.* Aland, Kurt, u. a. (eds.). 4th ed. Holzgerlingen: Deutsche Bibelgesellschaft.
HALOT 2000. *The Hebrew and Aramaic Lexicon of the Old Testament.* Koehler, Ludwig & Baumgartner, Walter (eds.). Leiden: Koninklijke Brill. [CD-ROM].
ThBLexNT [1971] 1986. *Theologisches Begriffslexikon zum Neuen Testament.* Coenen, Lothar, Beyreuther & Bietenhard, Hans. 2. Bände. 4th ed. Studienausgabe/7. ed. Gesamtausgabe. Wuppertal: Brockhaus. [Engl.: Theological Lexicon of Terminology tot he New testament.].
ThHWBAT 1984. Jenni, Ernst (ed.). *Theologisches Handwörterbuch zum Alten Testament.* 2. Bd. 3. durchgesehene ed. unter Mitarbeit von Claus Westermann. Munich: Chr. Kaiser. [Engl.: Theological concise Dictionary tot he Old Testament.].
ThWBAT [1970] 1973. *Theologisches Wörterbuch zum Alten Testament.* Botterweck & Ringgren. Bd. 1-10. Stuttgart: Kohlhammer. [Engl.: Theological Lexicon to the Old Testament.].
ThWBNT [1933] 1978. *Theologisches Wörterbuch zum Neuen Testament.* Kittel, Gerhard. Bd. 1-10/2. Stuttgart: Kohlhammer. [Engl.: Theological Wordbook to the New Testament.].

Material about the Zaza and Zazaki

Linguistics

Crandall, Marie 2002. Discourse Structures in Zazaki Narrative. Magisterarbeit. Johannes Gutenberg-Universität, Mainz. (unpublished).

Crystal, David [1980] 2003. *A Dictionary of Linguistics & Phonetics*. 5th edition Oxford: Blackwell.

Dooley, Robert A. & Levinsohn, Stephen H. 2000. *Analyzing Discourse: A Manual of basic Concepts*. Dallas: SIL International.

Givón, Talmy [1984] 1990. *Syntax: A functional-typological Introduction*. 2 vols. Amsterdam: John Benjamins.

Jacobson, C. M. 1993. *Zazaca, Okuma – Yazma: El Kitabi*. 1st ed. Bonn: Verlag für Kultur und Wissenschaft.

Paul, Ludwig 1998. *Zazaki: Versuch einer Dialektologie*. Wiesbaden: Ludwig Reichert.

Roberts, John R. 1997. The Syntax of Discourse Structure. *Notes On Translation*, 11/2, 15-34, Dallas: SIL International.

Roberts, John R. 2003. Features of Persian Discourse Structure. Unpublished work: SIL International.

Todd, Terry L. 2002. *A Grammar of Dimili (also known as Zaza)*. 2nd edition. Stockholm: Iremet Förlag. Online: URL: http://www.forum-linguistik.de/Zaza-Dimli/page2.html [accessed 2008-01-28].

Zazaki – Linguistics – Magazine

Linguistics

Bläsing, Uwe 1995. Kurdische und Zaza-Elemente im türkeitürkischen Dialektlexikon; Ethymologische Betrachtungen ausgehend vom Nordwestiranischen. In *Dutch Studies* 2: 173-220. (Retrieved May 2007 from the World Wide Web: http://home.arcor.de/fidemes/-Blaesing-1995-Kurdisch-Zaza.pdf) [PDF-File]. [Enl.: Kurdish and Zaza-Elements in the Turkey-turkish Dialect lexicon; Etymological Considerations starting from Northwest-Iranian.].

Blau, Joyce 1989. Gurânî et Zâzâ. In Rüdiger Schmitt (ed.), *Compendium Linguarum Iranicarum*, 336-340. Wiesbaden: Ludwig Reichert.

Crandall, Marie 2002. Discourse structures in Zazaki narrative. Magisterarbeit, Johannes Gutenberg Universität Mainz. (unpublished).

Çelker, Xal 1993. Ma, Welatê Ma, Zon u Dinê Ma. Halkımız, Yurdumuz, Dilimiz ve Din Sorunu. Isim konusu ve kısa bir tarihçemiz. *Ware: Zeitschrift für Zaza-Sprache und Kultur* 5, 41-51.

Gippert, Jost (1996). Die historische Entwicklung der Zaza-Sprache. *Ware: Pêseroka Zon u Kulturê Ma: Dımıli – Kırmanc – Zaza, Periodical of the Zaza Language and Culture*

(Baiersbronn, Germany) amor 10: 148-153. (Retrieved May 2007 from the World Wide Web: http://titus.uni-frankfurt.de/personal/jg/pdf/jg1996f.pdf) [PDF-File].

——— *Stammbaum der iranischen Sprachen.* Retrieved May 2007 from the World Wide Web: http://www.zazaki.de/deutsch/stammbaumiranischesprachen-geradlinig.htm

Lerch, Peter (1857-58). *Forschungen über die Kurden und die iranischen Nordchaldäer* (2 volumes). St. Petersburg. Reprint (1979). Amsterdam: Academic Publishers Associated.

Lockwood, William B. 1972. Gorani and Zaza. In *A Panorama of Indo-European Languages*, 243-244. London: Hutchinson.

Malmisanıj 1983. Le verbe composé dans le dialecte dumilî (Dimilkî de lêkerê hevdudanî). *Hêvî: Revue Culturelle Kurde* (Paris) 1: 67-82.

——— 1984. Variantes dialectales en dumilî (Dimilkî miyan di cîyayeya vatisan). *Hêvî: Revue Culturelle Kurde* (Paris) 2: 86-103.

Müller, Friedrich 1864. Beiträge zur Kenntnisse der neupersischen Dialekte. III. Zaza-Dialekt der Kurdensprache. *Sitzungsberichte der Kaiserlichen Akademie der Wissenschaften* (Wien) 48: 227-245.

Neyzi, Leyla (2002). Embodied Elders: Space and subjectivity in the Music of Metin-Kemal Kahraman. *Middle Eastern Studies* 38/1, Jan., 89-109. London: Frank Cass.

Pamukçu, Fahri (2001). *Gıramerê Zazaki - Zuwanrêznayi.* [Zazaki Grammar.] İstanbul: Vêjiyaişê Tiji / Tij Yayınları.

Paul, Ludwig 1998a. The position of Zazaki among the West Iranian languages. In Nicholas Sims-Williams (ed.), *Proceedings of the 3rd European Conference of Iranian Studies held in Cambridge, 11th to 15th September 1995,* Part I: Old and Middle Iranian Studies, 163-177. (Beiträge zur Iranistik, Bd. 17). Wiesbaden: Ludwig Reichert.

——— 1998b. *Zazaki: Grammatik und Versuch einer Dialektologie.* (Beiträge zur Iranistik, Bd. 18.) Wiesbaden: Ludwig Reichert.

——— 2002a. The constituent order of nominal compounds in Zazaki and other Iranian languages. *Sprachtypologie und Universalienforschung* (Berlin) 55/1: 64-79.

——— 2002b. Zaza. In C. E. Bosworth et al. (ed.), *Encyclopaedia of Islam (New Edition),* Volume 12, 491-492. Leiden: Brill.

Sandonato, M. 1994. Zazaki. In Peter Kahrel & René van den Berg (eds.), *Typological Studies in Negation,* 125-142. Amsterdam: John Benjamins.

Selcan, Zülfü 1998a. *Grammatik der Zaza-Sprache, Nord-Dialekt (Dersim-Dialekt).* Berlin: Wissenschaft und Technik Verlag.

——— 1998b. Die Entwicklung der Zaza-Sprache. *Ware: Pêseroka Zon u Kulturê Ma: Dımıli – Kırmanc – Zaza, Periodical of the Zaza Language and Culture* (Baiersbronn, Germany) amor 12: 152-163.

Todd, Terry L. 1985. A grammar of Dimili (also known as Zaza). Ph.D. dissertation, University of Michigan.

——— 2002. *A Grammar of Dimili (also known as Zaza).* 2nd edition. Stockholm: Iremet Förlag.

Glossaries

Aydar, Mehmet 2003. *Zazaca – Türkçe Sözlük*. [Zazaki – Turkish Dictionary.] Yenişehir, Ankara: Doruk Yayınları.

Büyükkaya, Necmetin 1992. *Zazaca – Türkçe sözlük listesi/ Qısebendê Zazaki – Tırki*. [Zazaki – Turkish wordlist.] In *Kalemimden Sayfalar*, 419-468. Spanga, Sweden: APEC.

Can, Mesut 1997. *Zazaca – Türkçe Sözlük*. [Zazaki – Turkish Dictionary.] İstanbul: Kaynka Yayınları.

Canpolat, Musa 2006. *Zazaca-Türkçe Sözlük*. İstanbul: Can Matbaacılık. [Engl.: Zazaki-Turkish Dictionary.].

Çem, Munzur 1994. *Ferhengê Kurdi – Tırki (Zazaki)*. [Kurdish – Turkish (Zazaki) Dictionary.] Stockholm: Published privately.

Erdem, Turan 1997. *Ferheng. Zazaki – Tırki/ Tırki – Zazaki*. [Dictionary. Zazaki – Turkish/ Turkish – Zazaki.] İstanbul: Doz Basim Yayın.

Gündüz, Deniz 2006. *Kırmancca / Zazaca Dil Dersleri: Türkçe Açıklamalı Kürtçe*. İstanbul: Vate Yayınevi. [Engl.: Kirmanca / Zaza Language Lessons: Kudish explained in Turkish].

Kocadag, Çeko 2010. *Ferheng: Kimanckî (ZaZakî) – Kurmancî Kurmancî – Kirmanckî (Zazakî)*. Berlin: Weşanen Komkar. [Engl.: Dictionary: Zazaki-Kurmnaji Kurmanji – Zazaki.].

Malmisanıj 1992. *Zazaca – Türkce Sözlük/ Ferhengê Dımılki – Tırki*. [Zazaki – Turkish Dictionary.] 2nd edition. İstanbul: Deng Yayınları.

Özcan, Mesut 1997. *Zazaca – Türkçe Sözlük*. [Zazaki – Turkish Dictionary.] İstanbul: Analiz Basım Yayın Tasarım Uygulama.

Paul, Ludwig 1998. Wörterverzeichnis Zazaki – Deutsch, Deutsch – Zazaki. In *Zazaki: Grammatik und Versuch einer Dialektologie* (Beiträge zur Iranistik, Bd. 18), 291-337. Wiesbaden: Ludwig Reichert. [Wordlist Zazaki – German, German – Zzaki. In Zazaki: Grammar and Attempt of a Dialectology (

Turgut, Harun w/o Date. *Türkçe Açıklamalı Zazaca Dilbilgisi* [Turkish Zazaki-Grammar]. 215 pages. Robert Koch Str. 43. 28277 Bremen: Selfediting.

Turgut, Harun 2001. *Zazaca – Türkçe Sözlük*. [Zazaki – Turkish Dictionary.] İstanbul: Vêjiyaişê Tiji / Tij Yayınları.

Vate Çalışma Grubu (ed.) 2004a. *Ferhengê Kirmanckî (Zazakî) – Tirkî, Tirkî – Kirmanckî*. İkinci Baskı. İstanbul: Vate Publishing House. [Grûba Xebate ya Vateyî 2004. 2nd ed. Kirmancki (Zazaki) – Turkish, Turkish – Kirmancki Dictionary.].

Vate Çalışma Grubu (ed.) 2004b. *Türkçe – Kırmancca (Zazaca) Sözlük, Ferhengê Tirkî – Kirmanckî (Zazakî)*. İkinci Baskı. İstanbul: Vate Publishing House. [Grûba Xebate ya Vateyî 2004. Kirmancki (Zazaki) – Turkish, Turkish – Kirmancki Dictionary. 2nd ed.]

Grûba Xebate ya Vateyî [2001] 2009. *Ferhengê Kirmanckî (Zazakî) – Tirkî, Tirkî – Kirmanckî*. Ücuncü Baskı. İstanbul: Vate Publishing House. [Vate Çalışma Grubu 2009. 3rd ed. Kirmancki (Zazaki) – Turkish, Turkish – Kirmancki Dictionary.].

Grûba Xebate ya Vateyî [2001] 2009. *Türkçe – Kırmancca (Zazaca) Sözlük, Ferhengê Tirkî – Kirmanckî (Zazakî)*. Ücuncü Baskı. İstanbul: Vate Publishing House. [Vate Çalışma Grubu 2009. Kirmancki (Zazaki) – Turkish, Turkish – Kirmancki Dictionary. 3rd ed.].

Verroj, Seîd 2003. *Ferheng Kurmancî – Dimilî – Tirkî & Tirkî – Dimilî – Kurmancî.* [Kurdish – Dimli – Turkish and Turkish – Dimli – Kurdish Dictionary.] İstanbul: WAR (Turgut Ersoy).

Language Learning and Literacy

Diljen, Haydar 1996. *Ziwanê Ma Alfaba.* [The Alphabet of 'Our Language'.] İstanbul: Yön Matbaası.

Jacobson, C. M. (1993). *Rastnustena Zonê Ma, Handbuch für die Rechtschreibung der Zaza-Sprache.* Bonn, Germany: Verlag für Kultur und Wissenschaft. (Written in Zazaki and German.)

——— 1999 *Zazaca Okuma-Yazma El Kitabı.* [Reading and Writing Handbook for Zazaki.] 2nd edition. İstanbul: Vêjiyaişê Tiji / Tij Yayınları.

——— 2001 *Rastnustena Zonê Ma (Dımılki – Kırmancki – Zazaki) eve Fekê Gola Dêsimi / Zazaca Yazım Kılavuzu.* [The Orthography of 'Our Language' (Dimli – Kirmanc – Zazaki) with Reference to the Dersim Area.] 2nd edition. İstanbul: Vêjiyaişê Tiji / Tij Yayınları. (Written in Zazaki and Turkish.)

Paul, Ludwig 1994. Das Zazaki. In *Kurdisch Wort für Wort,* 123-132. Kauderwelsch Band 94. Bielefeld, Germany: Reise Know-How Verlag. [Engl.: Zazaki. In Kurdish Word for Word.].

Rozşêne 1992-2000. Dersa Zonê Ma/ Zazaki für Anfänger, Lektionen I-XI. *Ware: Pêseroka Zon u Kulturê Ma: Dımıli – Kırmanc – Zaza, Periodical of the Zaza Language and Culture* (Baiersbronn, Germany) amor 1-13.

Culture and History

Agathangelos, Timuroğlu, Vecihi 1991. *Dersim Tarihi.* [History of Dersim.] Ankara: Yurt Kitap-Yayin.

Andrews, Peter Alford (ed.) 1989, 2002. *Ethnic Groups in the Republic of Turkey.* Wiesbaden: Ludwig Reichert.

Astare, Kemal 1995a. *Gulbahare: Merselei – Erzählungen: Zaza – Deutsch.* Bonn: Verlag für Kultur und Wissenschaft.

——— 1995b. *Volksmärchen aus Kurdistan: Hauptsächlich aus Dersim.* Winterthur: Ararat-Verlag.

Bruinessen van, Martin 1992. *Agha, Sheikh and State: The Social and Political Structures of Kurdistan.* London: Zed Books.

Bumke, Peter J. 1979. Kizilbaş-Kurden in Dersim (Tunceli, Türkei): Marginalität und Häresie. *Anthropos* 74: 530-548.

——— 1989. The Kurdish Alevis - Boundaries and perceptions. In Peter Alford Andrews (ed.), 510-518.

Cengiz, Daimi 2001. *Dersim Fablları – I.* [Fables from Dersim.] Kızılay, Ankara: Kalan Basım Yayın Dağıtım. (Written in Zazaki, translated into Turkish.)

Cengiz, Seyfi 1996. *Dynamics of the Kurdish Kirmanc-Zaza Problems in Anatolia*. Ed. by Paul White. Malvern, Australia: Deadkin University, Kurdish Study Group.

Comerd, Munzır 1996. Yitiqatê Dersımi de Wayırê Çêi (Asparê astorê kimenti): Sarê Çêi xıravunu ra 'be neweşiye ra sevekneno, karê dine raşt beno rızqê çêi dano, malê çêi 'be qısmetê çêi keno jêde, nasivê çêi sevekneno. [Turkish S. 69-74: Dersim İnancı'nda Ev ve Aile Tanrısı (Wayırê Çêi): Ev halkını her tür kötülükten, kötü melklerden ve hastalıklardan koruyor, İşlerinin İye gitmesini sağlıyor, evin rızkını veriyor, malını ve kısmetini artırıyor, nasibini koruyour.]. *Ware* 9, 10-14. Baiersbronn. [Engl.: Dersim Belief about the Master of the House.].

Comerd, Munzır 1996. Yitiqatê Dersımi de Wayırê Mali: Sarık Şüan xêro, Memık Gavan Xıravıno. Wayırê Malê Yavani ki sultan Duzgıno. Serva Duzgıni Dersimıci Malê yavani nekisenê, dersim de "Avci" çino! [Turkish S. 128-140: Dersim İnancı'nda Hayanlar Tanrısı (koyun, keçi, inek vb. küçük - ve büyükbaş hayvanlar): Sarık Şüan iyi, Memık Gavan kötü Tanrıdır. Sultan Duzgın da Dağkeçisi, geyik vb. Haynaların Tanrısıdır. Dersimli'ler Duzgın'dan Dolayı Bunları Avlamazlar, Dersim'de Avcı Yoktur!]. *Ware* 10, 4-16. Baiersbronn. [Engl.: Dersim Belief about the Master of the Cattle: The Good shepherd, the bad Memık Gavan.].

Comerd, Munzır 1997. Yitiqatī Dêrsımi de Duzgın (Asparê astorê kimenti): Wayır u sıtarê dina u darewo! Sultan u Qumandanê Dêrsimi 'be pilê jiar u diarunê Dêrsimi Duzgıno. Duzgın roştiya, evdıl Musa tariyo!. Vervê Eskerê Evdıl Musay de eskerê Duzgıni vındeno [Turkish S. 84-103: Dersim İnancı'nda Duzgın (Doruat'in süvarisi): Can ile Cihann Tanrısı, Rehberi ve Himayesidir! Dersim'in Sultanı ve Kumandanı Duzgın'dır. Ayrıca Dersim'deki Kutsal Yer ve Yatırların da Başıdır. Duzgın Aydınlığı Simgeliyor, Evdıl Musa'ysa Karanlığı! Evdıl Musa'nin Askerleri'ne Karşı, Duzgın'ın Askerleri'ne Duruyor.]. *Ware* 11, 15-31. Baiersbronn.[Engl.: Dersim Belief about Duzgın.].

Comerd, Munzır 1997. Yitiqatī Dersımi de Helıka Gızıkıne. *Tija Sodıri* 5/2, 32-37. Baiersbronn. [Engl.: Dersim Belief about Helıka Gızıkıne.].

Comerd, Munzır 1998. İtiqatī Dêsımi de mori 'be ewliya ra, [Turkish: Dersim İnancı'dan Yılan ve Tarikat Değneği, 121-129. *Ware* 12, 58-69, [Turkish: 113-126]. Baiersbronn. [Engl.: Dersim Belief about the Serpent and the Wand-Orders.].

Comerd, Munzur 1998. Yitiqatī Dersimi de Xizir. *Ware* 12, 83-100, [Turkish: 113-126]. Baiersbronn. [Engl.: Dersim Belief about Xızır.].

Dersimi, Nuri Mehmet 1952. *Kürdistan Tarıhında Dersim*. [Dersim in the History of Kurdistan.] Halep (Aleppo), Syria: Anı Matbaası. (reprint: Cologne 1988).

Ferber, Oda and Doris Gräßlin 1988. *Die Herrenlosen: Leben in einem kurdischen Dorf*. Bremen, Germany: Edition CON.

Fırat, Gülsün 1997. *Sozioökonomischer Wandel und ethnische Identität in der kurdischalevitischen Region Dersim*. (Bielefelder Studien zur Entwicklungssoziologie, Band 65). Saarbrücken, Germany: Verlag für Entwicklungspolitik. [Engl.: Socio-economic Change and ethnic Identity in the Kurdish-Alevi Region Dersim.].

Hübschmann, Heinrich 1904. Die altarmenischen Ortsnamen. *Indogermanische Forschungen, Zeitschrift für Indogermanische Sprach- und Altertumskunde* (Strassburg) Band XVI, Heft 3-5: 197-490.

Kaya, Ali [1999] 2010. *Başlangıcından Günümüzde Dersim Tarihi*. 1st ed. İstanbul: Demos Yayınları. [Engl.: Modern History of Dersim. 3 editions from 1999-2009 with Can Yayınları].

Kehl-Bodrogi, Krisztina 1993. Die 'Wiederfindung' des Alevitentums in der Türkei: Geschichtsmythos und kollektive Identität. *Orient* 34: 267-282.

────── 1998a. Neuere Entwicklungen unter Zaza in Europa. *Ware: Pêseroka Zon u Kulturê Ma: Dımıli – Kırmanc – Zaza, Periodical of the Zaza Language and Culture* (Baiersbronn, Germany) amor 12: 164-167.

────── 1998b. „Wir sind ein Volk!", Identitätspolitiken unter den Zaza (Türkei) in der europäischen Diaspora. *Sociologus* (Berlin), Bd. 48, 2: 111-135.

MacKenzie, David N. 1989. The role of Kurdish language in ethnicity. In Peter Alford Andrews (ed.), 541-542.

Minorsky, V. 1928. Daylam. In *Encyclopedia of Islam (1965)*, Volume 2: 189-194.

────── 1932. La domination des Daylamites. *Société des Études Iraniennes* (Paris) no. III: 1-26.

Nestmann, Liesa 2002. Ethnicity in Eastern Turkey, in Andrews, Peter Alford (ed.): *Ethnic Groups in the Republic of Turkey*, 543-580. Wiesbaden: Ludwig Reichert.

Olson, Robert 1989. *The Emergence of Kurdish Nationalism and the Sheikh Said Rebellion, 1880-1925*. Austin: University of Texas Press.

Petrov, E. [1863] 1998. Tschapachdshur und Dersim. Schreiben von Trapzunta, "Die Dersimer". spb. Wendomostjax. Lauf der militärischen Ereignisse an der Kaukasusfront. Band IV. *Ware* 12, 148-150. Baiersbronn. [Engl.: Tschapachdshur and Dersim. Letter of Trapzunta, "The Dersimers". spb. Wendomostjax. Events on the Caucasus-Front. Vol. IV.].

Sweetnam, Denise L. (2004). *Kurdish Culture: A Cross-Cultural Guide*. 2nd edition. Bonn: Verlag für Kultur und Wissenschaft.

Cultural Websites

http://mamekiye.de/08 (Dersim-Zaza)
http://www.zazaki.de (http://www.zazaki.de/englisch/index.htm)

Magazines

Ayre: Pêserokê Ziwanî. [The Mill: Language Magazine.] (1984-1986). Ebubekir Pamukçu (ed.). Stockholm.

Berhem: Sosyal ve Kültürel Araştırma Dergisi. [Written Works: Social and Cultural Research Magazine.] (1988-1991). Stockholm.

Çıme: Peserokê Zuwan u Edatê Zazayan, Journal of Zaza Language and Culture, Zaza Dili ve Kültürü Dergisi. [The Spring.] (2005-present). Augsburg, Germany.

Dersim: Tunceli Kültür ve Dayanışma Derneği Yayın Organı [Dersim: Publication of the 'Tunceli Culture and Solidarity' Association.] (1995-?). Tunceli Kültür ve Dayanışma Derneği (ed.). İstanbul.

Desmala Sure: Vengê Dêsımi. [The Red Handkerchief: Voice of Dersim.] (1991-1994). Marne, Germany.

Gımgım: İstanbul Varto Kültür Derneği (ed.). İstanbul. (4 issues).

Işkın: İki aylık Kültür, Düşün ve Sanat Dergisi. [The Işkın Plant: Bi-monthly Magazine of Culture, Philosophy and Art.] (2002-2004). Tunceli Kültür Sanat ve Dayanışma Derneği (ed.). Tunceli, Turkey.

Kormışkan: Ziwan û Kulturê Zazayan, Journal of Zaza Language and Culture. [The Kormışkan Festival.] (1995-1997). Koyo Berz (ed.). Uppsala, Sweden.

Miraz: Edebiyat u Felsefe. [The desire: Literature and Philosophy.] (2006-present). İsmail Söylemez (ed.). Malatya, Turkey.

Munzur: Halkbilimi – Etnoloji – Antropoloji – Edebiyat dergisi (2000-?) [The Munzur River: Magazine of Folk-study, Cultural Anthropology, and Literature.] Mesut Öscan (ed.). İzmir, Turkey.

Munzur: İki Haftalık Siyasi Haber Yorum Gazetesi. [The Munzur River: Bi-weekly Newspaper of Politics, News, and Commentary.] (2004-present). Tunceli, Turkey.

Pir: Hakkı Çimen (ed.). Germany: Duisburg.

Piya: Peserokê Zıwan u Kültürê Dımıli. [Together: Journal of Zaza Language and Culture.] (1987-1993). Ebubekir Pamukçu (ed.). Stockholm. (As from no. 6 (out of 16), the name of the magazine was changed to: Peserokê Zıwan u Kültürê Zaza.)

Raa Zazaistan: Politics [Way of Zazaistan]. Ardwan, Ç., Soy, Elier, Hese, Korca Mirseydan, Soşen Bıra. (1991). Ebubekir Pamukçu. Sweden. (3 issues).

Raştiye: Peseroka Zonê / Ziwanê u Kulturê Zaza. [Truth: Magazine of the Zaza Language and Culture.] (1991-1995). Paris.

Şewq: [Night] (1995). Hannover, Almanya / Germany. (8 issues). (Zaza – Kurmanji – German).

Tija Sodıri: Perloda Zon u Zagonê Kırmanc-Zazay. [Early Morning Light: Magazine of Zaza Language and Culture.] (1995-1998?). Frankfurt.

Ütopya: İstanbul.

Vate: Kovara kulturî. [The Spoken Word: Magazine on Culture.] (1997-present). Vate Çalışma Grubu (ed.), Malmîsanıj (former ed.). Beyoğlu-İstanbul, Turkey: Vate Publishing House.

Vengê Zazaistan: Zon u Kulturê. [Language and Culture], Siyasetê Zazayan / Zaza Halkın Gerçek Sesi / La voix du Zazaistan. (2000-2002). 'Association culturelle des Zaza' (ed.). Livry Gargan, France. (4 issues).

Ware: Pêseroka Zon u Kulturê Ma: Dımıli – Kırmanc – Zaza / Periodical of the Zaza Language and Culture. [The Mountain Pasture.] (1992-2003). Baiersbronń, Germany.

Wayir: [Master]. (1995-2000). İstanbul Tunceli Kültür Derneği. İstanbul.

Waxt: [Time]. (1990-1991) Almanya / Gemany / Darmstadt. (4 issues).

Zaza Press: Journal of Zaza Language and Culture. (2000-2004). Faruk Yakup (ed.). Stockholm. And Online: URL: http://www.zazapress.info.se/ [accessed 2017-03-09].

Zazaki: (2008). Yaşar Aratemur. Mehmed Duedunıc, Heseni Zerner (eds.). Germany: Augsburg. (Dialect of Bingoel, Palu, Elazığ.).

Zerqê Ewroy: Mahmut Pamukçu (1990). Germany: Wetzlar. (4 issues). (Zaza – Turkish).

Final Summary

The headwaters of the Rivers Euphrates and Tigris are important sources of life, not just to animals or plants but also to a few people groups. One of those groups are the Zaza ethnos. They inhabit the area of the rivers Murat, Kara Su, and the headwaters of the Euphrates and Tigris. In this ecological environment they developed their way of life, together with their neighbor, the Armenians and the Kurmanji speaking ethnicity. They share a common history under Roman, Byzantine, Seljuk and Ottoman rule. However each people group developed its peculiar cultural and linguistical orientation. After a strong Avestan and Zorastrian (Persian religions) influence, Christianity and at last Islam directed the religious and political fate of the Zaza homeland. The foundation of the Republic of Turkey (1923) and the newly found governments of the Near East after the decline of Colonialism delineated the last major change to East Anatolia.

The point of reference for this study is given in a short anthropological introduction (chapter 1). Anthropology as one of the driving forces to describe foreign cultures and their social and linguistic organization ist best qualified to present the Zaza ethnicity to the outside (etic posture). The introduction on Applied Cultural Anthropology is limited to those research questions that are of interest for this study.

In the second chapter the Zaza people come into focus. This includes, their naming by endo- and exoterms, the sources of historical information and their oral-aural way of passing forth traditions. Their recent struggle as a smaller ethnos under the influence of the larger Kurmanji speaking Kurds and the recent tendency towards mother tongue education in the Eastern parts of Turkey take up an important part of this study (2.1.2-2.1.4). The whole question of identity is related to the issue of origin, the self-perception of the Zaza people and their recent call for mother tongue education in their language. Starting with the question of identity the different theories on *origin*, the settling area and the migration movements in the past and recently are described. The second area of research concerns with the *language* of this people group. *Zazaki* as an Indo-European language of the North Western Iranian language branch form a smaller branch with Gorani / Hewrami (Iran / Northern Iraq). After a short description of the different Zazaki dialects, a proposal of an orthography, an overview on the recent discussion of standardization and a detailed list of verbal root forms are presented. Bilingualisms, illiteracy and the influence of the neighbouring languages leads to active code switching, loan words and borrowing, which is demonstrated on various examples. Zazaki as a North Western Iranian language belongs to a "Caspian languages" belt in which the "Kurdish and related languages belt" performs a distinct pattern. The term "Kurdish", in this study, relates to all Iranian languages of the North- and South Western paradigm. They show universal features, such as an ergative and ezafe system, as well as a complex verb system. The political and sociological issues of "Kurdishness" versus "Zazaishness" are extensively discussed.

The Zaza *culture* is viewed from its fundamental outcomes, its religious orientation, its social stratification and its perception of the world. The obvious peculiarity of the Zaza society is best demonstrated on its linguistical and religious split in a Zoroastrian or Alevism following Northern Group, a Hanafi Sunnisms following Southern Group and an Eastern Group that is split in an Alevism and Hanafi or Shafi'i Sunnism following track. The dialects vary in vocabulary as well as on the grammar level. The Zazaki dialect vacuum does not reach to the Kurmanji dialects or other "Kurdish or related languages" (see above). Yet, the anthropological and sociological split is not as strong as the linguistical. Whereas Kurmanji and Zazaki are two languages, both cultures show some similarities in the annual circle of common celebrations and the ethnomusicological and ethnoartistic performance of symbols, dancing and feasts. There is strong evidence of a common religious orientation of the Zaza people by an Animistic and Zoroastrian perception of the world. Conversion back and forth reaches out to Christianity and a very strong influence by Islam since 400 years. During the historical development of the Zaza people, influence from outside led to Christianization and at least two Re-Islamization movements (16th and 18th century). Folk Islam and a bigot submission to religious devotion are remarkable features of the Zaza religiosity, this is why religion takes up a huge section of the cultural description.

The social straticfication of the Zaza people in a three-class society based on feudalism and strong collectivism reveals high coherence and cohesion between the families, the clans and the tribes. In this paternal society the transfer of class is not possible. Patrifocal marriage, bride wealth, exchange and abduction of girls and non-Zaza boys, blood feud and honour killings, as well as a strong hierarchical leadership mark the ethnicity. Mullaharchy, Pirdom, Sheikhdom and

Aghadom are characteristic for most of the people groups of the wider area and so for the Zaza people. The strongest feature is a political aghadom (landlordship) and a religiously-political sheikhdom. The role of a sheikh as an influengtial mystical leader is well reflected in Zaza tradition.

The Zaza *worldview* is built on a mix of linear and circular time, and a narrow space perception. The low profile towards an Image of Limited Good, the high handling of Uncertainty Reduction (URT) and the strong *haram* (impure) and *helal* (pure) awareness are symbolizing a consciousness oriented on defilement and based on a shame and honour orientation. Hospitality, loyalty to the leadership and the extended family are effects thereof.

In the last chapter the wider *environment* of the Zaza people came into focus. To understand the historical, the recent and some of the future developments in the Zaza people group the influences of the nation state, Islam in general, the neighbouring ethnicities, specifically the larger Kurmanji speaking ethnos is illustrated. The eventful history of the Zaza homeland, influenced by Greek, Roman, Persian, Byzantine, Russian, Ottoman and Turkish interests left its traces on the Zaza people. However, it is astonishing how self ruled they carried out their daily life regarding the strong powers that went by. Obviously Zazaki and the Zaza ethnos influenced their environment too. The 1980s could be seen as a new orientation on self esteem and detachment of national (Turkish) and regional (Kurmanji) paternalism. Historically the interreligious more or less peaceful cohabitation of the people groups in Eastern Anatolia ended after the Armenian ethnocide. The Zaza people took part in those massacres and harmed thereby their relationship to the persecuted. The centralistic and dictatorial reorganisation of the new republic led the people groups of Eastern Anatolia into absolute dependency on the gouvernmental powers. The recent increase in political power by the Kurmanji speaking ethnicity causes on the one hand mistrust and on the other hope in the Zaza ethnos. The tendency is towards a close relationship between the Zazaki and Kurmanji speaking ethnicities to strengthen their political influence. However the danger is that the smaller Zaza ethnos will not get the attention that they are asking for. This fear is driving the Zaza people politically as well as sociologically. The Diaspora plays therein a huge role.

Although the recent turmoil of the Maghreb and Near Eastern Arabic nations did not directly effect the long going struggle of the Kurmanji and Zazaki speaking ethnicities in Turkey, they add up to indirect political advantages. Mainly the changing situation in Syria and the influential Northern Iraqi *Herêmî Kurdistan*

("Kurdistan Regional Government" KRG) represent huge challenges for the political stability in the wider context of people groups belonging to the area of "Kurdish and related languages".

The anthropological considerations that could be taken out of the wider environment of the Zaza ethnos show that inner and external impacts have a great effect on the development of the Zaza homeland as well as the Zaza people themselves. Their deep core values are slowly changing due to assimilation and migration processes. The slow re-vitalisation of Zazaki, the dissolution and replacement of the traditional three-class stratification, the loss of leadership and the tribal cohesion on the small scale society level and the economical underdevelopment of the homeland confront the Zaza society with many challenges.

Detailed Table of Content

Tables 7
Table of Diagrams 8
Abbreviations 9
Preface 11
Introduction 15
1 Anthropology and Ethnography 17
1.1 Area of Research 17
   1.1.1 Cultural Anthropology vs. Social Sciences 20
   1.1.2 Ethnography 22
      1.1.2.1 Empirical Research - Qualitative and Quantitative Methods 22
      1.1.2.2 Ethnography - Qualitative vs. Quantitative Research 23
      1.1.2.3 Perspective of Ethnography 25
         1.1.2.3.1 Definition of Ethnography 25
         1.1.2.3.2 Poles and Points of View in Ethnography 26
         1.1.2.3.3 Intuitive Enterprise 28
         1.1.2.3.4 Trends in Ethnography 28
      1.1.2.4 The Ethnographer and the Informant 30
      1.1.2.5 Ethics and Ethnography 31
      1.1.2.6 Ethnography and Translation / Linguistics 32
      1.1.2.7 Summary 33
   1.1.3 Society - Culture, Language, Thought and Conscience 34
      1.1.3.1 Culture – a Definition 34
         1.1.3.1.1 Culture Change 35
         1.1.3.1.2 Culture and Society in Social Sciences 36
      1.1.3.2 Language, Society and Thought – Cognitive Anthropology 37
         1.1.3.2.1 Language 38
         1.1.3.2.2 Thought and Language 38
         1.1.3.2.3 Sapir-Whorf-Hypothesis and Enculturation 41
         1.1.3.2.4 Homogenous Unit Principle (HUP) 43
      1.1.3.3 Conscience – LEIC, Shame and Guilt - Orientation 44
      1.1.3.4 Society and Religion – an Anthropological Stance 49
   1.1.4 Summary 49

Detailed Table of Content 541

1.2 Project-Description 50
1.2.1 Sherefname and Seyahatname 51
1.2.2 Linguistic and Anthropological Specifications 52
1.2.3 Method of Research 52
1.3 Summary 54
2 The Zaza 56
2.1 The People 57
2.1.1 Origin of the People Name 59
    2.1.1.1 Zaza and Zazaki 60
    2.1.1.2 "Stammerer" 61
    2.1.1.3 *Zone Ma* and Geographical References 61
    2.1.1.4 Nuri Dersimi - Kırmancki 62
    2.1.1.5 Other Notations (Dımili, Kızılbaş, Alevis, Nusayri or Dunbeli) .. 62
        2.1.1.5.1 Dımli / Dımılı and the Daylam-Thesis 63
        2.1.1.5.2 Kızılbaş / Qızılbaş or Alevis 64
        2.1.1.5.3 Gini and Nusayri 67
        2.1.1.5.4 Dunbeli, Dumbeli, Donbeli or Dombeli 67
    2.1.1.6 Summary 68
2.1.2 Question of Identity - Kurds and / or Zaza or Zaza-Kurds 69
    2.1.2.1 Argument by Linguistics - Anthropological Considerations 71
    2.1.2.2 Argument by Culture and Language 72
    2.1.2.3 Written Interior and Exterior Evidential 73
    2.1.2.4 Lack of Differentiation between both Ethnicities 77
    2.1.2.5 Other Perspective – Space and Nationalism 80
    2.1.2.6 Historical Perspective – Principle of Armenization 82
    2.1.2.7 Summary 83
2.1.3 Theories of Origin 85
    2.1.3.1 Place and Culture of Origin 88
        2.1.3.1.1 Daylam-Thesis (Parthian-Thesis) 88
        2.1.3.1.2 Medes-Thesis 94
        2.1.3.1.3 Sassanid- or Anatolia Thesis 96
        2.1.3.1.4 Other Theories of the Zaza-Origin 97
        2.1.3.1.5 A Framework of the Origin of the Zaza People ... 99
    2.1.3.2 Summary 101
2.1.4 Settling Area - Homeland 102
    2.1.4.1 Southern Group (SZ) 103

    2.1.4.2 Northern Group (NZ) 105
    2.1.4.3 Central / Eastern Group (EZ) 106
    2.1.4.4 Neighbouring peoples - Turks, Armenian and Kurmanji Kurds . 107
    2.1.4.5 The "Great Experiment" 111
    2.1.4.6 A Religious and Cultural Turkish Minority 113
    2.1.4.7 Summary 114
2.2   The Language – Zazaki 115
   2.2.1 Zazaki – Part of the Indo-European Language Family 118
   2.2.2 A Northwestern Iranian Language within a Language Belt 120
   2.2.3 Zazaki – General Remarks 123
    2.2.3.1 Language versus ("Kurdish") Dialect - Definitions 124
    2.2.3.2 Language vs. ("Kurdish") Dialect – Discussion (Vate Group) ... 124
    2.2.3.3 Language versus ("Kurdish") Dialect - Gorani 127
    2.2.3.4 Zazaki - Independent but Ethnically close to the "Kurds" 130
    2.2.3.5 Main Dialects of Zazaki - Classification 131
    2.2.3.6 Summary of the Zazaki – Discussion on "Kurdish" 132
   2.2.4 Dialectical Disparity and the Zaza Ethnicity 133
   2.2.5 The Southern Group in Çermik – Investigations 135
   2.2.6 Reference resp. Standard Dialect - Renaming 136
   2.2.7 Çermik 138
    2.2.7.1 Orthographic Alphabet Proposal 139
    2.2.7.2 Distribution of the Speakers – Danger of Language Death 142
    2.2.7.3 Summary on "Çermik" 145
   2.2.8 Illiteracy and bilingualism 146
    2.2.8.1 Linguistical Influences – The Mother Tongue Lexicon 148
    2.2.8.2 Ottoman-Turkish Influence 151
    2.2.8.3 Language Prestige 153
    2.2.8.4 Lexical Borrowing 154
    2.2.8.5 Examples of Lexical Borrowing 156
    2.2.8.6 Code switching 158
    2.2.8.7 Summary 160
   2.2.9 Language Description and Specific Features 160
    2.2.9.1 General Description 161
      2.2.9.1.1 Syllable Pattern 162
      2.2.9.1.2 Grammatical Characteristics 162
      2.2.9.1.3 Ergative 163

	2.2.9.1.4	Case System 163
	2.2.9.1.5	Ezafe-Structures 164
	2.2.9.1.6	System of Personal Suffixes 165
	2.2.9.1.7	Reflexive and Impersonal Pronouns 165
	2.2.9.1.8	Verbal System 165
	2.2.9.1.9	Passive and Causative 166
	2.2.9.1.10	Copula 167
	2.2.9.1.11	Emotive Language in Zazaki 167
	2.2.9.1.12	Example of Dialectical Variations – Months and Days 168
2.2.9.2		Summary - A Grammatical Scetch 170
	2.2.9.2.1	Nouns 171
	2.2.9.2.2	Case Endings 172
	2.2.9.2.3	Ezafe Morphemes 173
	2.2.9.2.4	Pronouns 174

Personal pronouns 174
Demonstrative pronouns paradigm 175
Personal pronoun *cı* 175
Reflexive Pronoun *xo* 175
Relative Pronoun *kı* 175

	2.2.9.2.5	Adjectives 176

Demonstrative Adjectives 176

	2.2.9.2.6	Numbers 177
	2.2.9.2.7	Verbs 177

Stem System 178
Endings 179
Ending chart: expl. *şiyayış*= go (unregular);*kerdış*=do (regular) 179
Verb of Existence 180
Passive Morpheme 180
Causative Morpheme 181
The Copula 181
Complex Verbs (with verbal affix) 182
Compound Verbs (two-part verbs) 182

  2.2.10 *Summary – Zazaki the Language* 185
2.3 The Society 186
  2.3.1 *Historical Background – Political Past and Present* 188
    2.3.1.1 Northern- and Southern / Eastern Group 188

2.3.1.2 Silk Road – Influence by Ruling Powers 190
2.3.1.3 Foundation of the Republic and Status as Minority 190
2.3.1.3.1 Zaza and / or Kurdish Initiatives 191
2.3.1.3.2 Sheikh Said and Seyit Rıza - Rebellions 192
2.3.1.4 Developments in the Homeland and Diaspora 198
2.3.1.5 Summary 200
2.3.2 Fundamentals 201
2.3.2.1 Shame-orientation, Collectivism and Envy 201
2.3.2.1.1 Collectivism 202
2.3.2.1.2 Uncertainty Reduction Theory 204
2.3.2.1.3 Envy, Religion, LEIC and Conscience 204
2.3.2.1.4 Envy and the "Evil Eye" in the Mediterranean Area 207
2.3.2.2 "Location of Emotions, Intellect and Character" (LEIC) 210
2.3.2.3 Centralistic and Holistic Perception 212
2.3.2.4 Prototype Theory – Connecting Language and Thought 213
2.3.2.5 Summary 214
2.3.3 Religion 214
2.3.3.1 Religions of the Zaza People 216
2.3.3.2 Origins of the Zaza Religions 216
2.3.3.2.1 Animism 218
2.3.3.2.2 Zoroastrianism / Mazdaism and Alevism 221
2.3.3.2.3 Jewish Influence - Judaism 225
2.3.3.2.4 Christianity 227
2.3.3.2.5 History of (Sunni) Islam – Purity / Impurity Manipulation 231
2.3.3.2.6 The Purity – Impurity Manipulation – *haram* and *helal* 232
2.3.3.2.7 Religious Influences - An Historical Attempt 235
2.3.3.2.8 Summary 236
2.3.3.3 Alevism – Animism in Northern Group 237
2.3.3.3.1 Alevism in Turkey - Revival 238
2.3.3.3.2 Origin and Practices 239
2.3.3.3.3 Recent Peculiarity of Alevism 240
2.3.3.3.4 Content and Implication 241
2.3.3.3.5 Leadership in Alevism - Then and Now 244
2.3.3.3.6 Summary 245
2.3.3.4 Islamisation Process 245
2.3.3.5 Sunnism (Southern and Eastern Group) 248

Detailed Table of Content 545

    2.3.3.5.1   Four Schools of Sunnism - Hanafi 248
    2.3.3.5.2   Mewlid – A Poem representing a Religious Stance 249
    2.3.3.5.3   Leadership – Islamic Clergy 252
  2.3.3.6   Different World Conception – Alevism and Sunnism (2 Ex.) 254
  2.3.3.7   Modern Religious Life 255
    2.3.3.7.1   Christian-Islamic Influence on the Religious Identity 256
    2.3.3.7.2   Christian Influence and Practices 257
    2.3.3.7.3   Zoroastrianism Influence and Practices 261
  2.3.3.8   Summary 263
2.3.4   Social Structure 265
  2.3.4.1   Structure of the Zaza Society 266
  2.3.4.2   Descent and Family Structures 267
    2.3.4.2.1   Nuclear and Extended Family 269
    2.3.4.2.2   Descent and Kindred 270
  2.3.4.3   Gentry – Sheikhdom, Aghadom and Mullaharchy 271
    2.3.4.3.1   The Sheikh - Sheikhdom 271
    2.3.4.3.2   The Millah / Mullah - Mullaharchy 273
    2.3.4.3.3   The Aghadom – Landownership and Political Leader 274
    2.3.4.3.4   Summary 275
  2.3.4.4   Small Scale Society – Tribal and Clan System 277
    2.3.4.4.1   Structures of Small Scale Societies – The Patriarchate 277
    2.3.4.4.2   Designation of Small Scale Societies 280
    2.3.4.4.3   Hierarchical Structure – The Naqshebendi 284
    2.3.4.4.4   Signs of Disintegration 287
    2.3.4.4.5   Summary 288
  2.3.4.5   Language Endangerment and Identity Loss 288
  2.3.4.6   Emigration and Immigration – Diaspora and Bilingualism 290
    2.3.4.6.1   A Microculture in the European Union 291
    2.3.4.6.2   Bi-, Multi- and Polylingualism 291
    2.3.4.6.3   Multilingual Mother Tongue Education 292
    2.3.4.6.4   Germany – A representative Stance 292
    2.3.4.6.5   The EU and Turkey – Partners of Trade 294
    2.3.4.6.6   Integration and Education – Famous Zaza People 295
    2.3.4.6.7   Famous Zaza People of the Past and Present 295
    2.3.4.6.8   Racism and Anti-foreignism or Xenophobia 298
    2.3.4.6.9   Summary 299

		2.3.4.7	Summary of the Social Structure	300
	2.3.5	*The Zaza – Traditionally Peasants*		301
		2.3.5.1	House Construction	301
		2.3.5.2	Clothing and Outward Appearance	304
		2.3.5.3	Ethnomusicology – Observations in the Zaza Culture	305
		2.3.5.4	Ethnomusicology – Dance and Performance	308
		2.3.5.5	The Snake - Symbol of Peasantry	309
			2.3.5.5.1 Agriculture and Farming	311
			2.3.5.5.2 Image of limited Good	312
			2.3.5.5.3 Traditions related to the concept "Snake"	313
		2.3.5.6	Summary	314

2.4 Linguistic and Cultural Liaison - *Merdım* 315
   2.4.1 An exemplary Study - the Term "man" (merdım) 315
   2.4.2 Etymology of merdım 316
      2.4.2.1 Profane and Sacred 316
      2.4.2.2 Funeral Proceedings 318
      2.4.2.3 Status of Widow(er) 320
   2.4.3 Real versus Ideal Usage of merdım 321
      2.4.3.1 Real Use of *merdım* 321
      2.4.3.2 Ideal Use of *merdım* 324
      2.4.3.3 Real versus Ideal - Concepts of *merdım* (Table) 326
      2.4.3.4 Other Connotations of *merdım* 327
   2.4.4 Summary 328

2.5 The Perception of the World – "Zazaness" 329
   2.5.1 Cosmology and the Zaza-Pantheon 329
   2.5.2 Islam – Recent Foundation 333
   2.5.3 Feasts and Celebrations 333
   2.5.4 The Family – Centre of Society 338
      2.5.4.1 Honour Killing and Blood Feud 338
      2.5.4.2 Code of Honour – (Sexual) Purity and Impurity 339
      2.5.4.3 Exchange of Girls 339
      2.5.4.4 Greeting Rituals - Honour, Respect and Proximity 340
      2.5.4.5 Summary 340
   2.5.5 Envy 341
   2.5.6 Envy and the Concept of merdım 342
   2.5.7 Envy and Hospitality 343

2.5.8 Culture Change in Zaza Community 344
2.5.9 Summary 345
2.6 Mother Tongue Issues - Projects 347
2.6.1 The Mother Tongue Speaker 348
2.6.2 Lingua Franca and National Language 349
2.6.3 Mother Tongue – Entering a People's Heart 350
2.6.4 Mother Tongue Education – A global Basic Right 350
2.6.5 The Homogenous Unit Principle (HUP) 352
2.6.6 Summary 352
2.7 Summary 353
3 Turkey – A Socio-Historical Overview 357
3.1 Turkey and the Diverse Ethnicities 358
3.1.1 Historical Sketch of the Turkish People 360
   3.1.1.1 Seljuk Empire (11th -12th Century AD) 360
   3.1.1.2 Ottoman Empire (13th-20th Century AD) 361
      3.1.1.2.1 Politics on Minor Ethnicities – Tanzimat-Reforms 362
      3.1.1.2.2 Ideologies of Pan-Turkism and Pan-Islamism 363
      3.1.1.2.3 Ziya Gökalp – A Turkish Nationalist and Zaza 364
      3.1.1.2.4 An Extra View on Pan-Islamism 365
   3.1.1.3 Young Turks (20th Century AD) 366
   3.1.1.4 The Republic of Turkey (1923 AD – today) 366
      3.1.1.4.1 Young Turks in the new Republic of Turkey 367
      3.1.1.4.2 Atatürk – The Father 367
      3.1.1.4.3 A new Constitution 368
      3.1.1.4.4 Anti-Zaza and Anti-Kurmanji Resentments 370
      3.1.1.4.5 Thesis about the Origin of Turks and Sun Language 371
      3.1.1.4.6 Summary 372
   3.1.1.5 The (recent) Political Situation - Political Constellation 373
   3.1.1.6 Positive Effects of the Past and the National State 376
   3.1.1.7 Summary 376
3.1.2 Outside Turkey - Europe and the World 378
3.1.3 Germany and Turkey 381
3.1.4 The European Union and Turkey – A Rapprochement 385
3.1.5 Summary 387
3.2 Inside Turkey – Linguistic Considerations 389

	3.2.1 Turkey (Asia)	389
	3.2.2 Turkey (Europe)	391
3.3	**Anthropological-Linguistic Perspective**	392
3.4	**Christianity and Religious Orientation in Turkey**	393
	3.4.1 Christians in Turkey	394
	3.4.1.1 Armenia - The Armenian Apostolic Church	395
	3.4.1.1.1 1860 – 1920 – Struggles, Wars and Persecution	396
	3.4.1.1.2 Dispersion of Armenian People in Eastern Anatolia	397
	3.4.1.1.3 History meets the Present	397
	3.4.1.1.4 Armenia Today – Influence on the Zaza people	399
	3.4.1.1.5 Summary	400
	3.4.1.2 Syriac Orthodox Church	400
	3.4.1.3 Protestant Church	402
	3.4.1.3.1 Historical Background – Turkish Church History	402
	3.4.1.3.2 The Church – Status Indicator of Turkey	404
	3.4.1.3.3 Anthropological Considerations	405
	3.4.1.3.4 Summary	406
	3.4.2 Jewish Presence and Judaism	407
	3.4.2.1 History – Jewish Diaspora in the Eastern Anatolia	407
	3.4.2.2 Israel and Turkey	409
	3.4.2.3 Anthropological Considerations	410
	3.4.2.4 Summary	411
	3.4.3 The Crescent, the Star and the Coat of Arms	411
	3.4.4 Summary	414
3.5	**Kurmanji Kurds, Zaza and the Turkish State**	415
	3.5.1 History and Terminology – "Kurds", "Kurdish"	415
	3.5.2 Kurdish Population – Inside the Fertile Crescent	417
	3.5.3 Genetics, Space and Subjectivity	418
	3.5.4 Summary	420
3.6	**Islam and Turkey**	421
	3.6.1 Propagation Strategies	422
	3.6.2 The Islamic orders – Workforces of da'awa and jihad	422
	3.6.3 Principles of Invitation	423
	3.6.4 Anthropological Considerations	424
	3.6.4.1 Islamic Missions – Ingathering and Incorporation	424
	3.6.4.2 Conversion – The Individual versus Microcultures	425

    3.6.5 Summary 427
3.7   Summary 428
4   Comprising Epilogue 431
Appendices 440
    Appendix 1 Homeland Area of the Zaza 440
    Appendix 2a Branch of Indo-European Languages 441
    Appendix 2b Branch of Iranian Languages 442
    Appendix 3 Extended family-structure - Çermug Area 443
    Appendix 4 Chronology of Turkey and her Minority Policy 444
    Appendix 5 Mewlid Nebi – Birthday Poem of the Prophet 455
Index 472
Bibliography 482
    Websites 524
    Personal Communication 527
    Exegetical Tools 528
    Material about the Zaza and Zazaki 529
    Linguistics 529
    Zazaki – Linguistics – Magazine 529
    Linguistics 529
    Glossaries 531
    Language Learning and Literacy 532
    Culture and History 532
    Cultural Websites 534
    Magazines 534
Final Summary 536
Detailed Table of Content 540

www.ingramcontent.com/pod-product-compliance
Lightning Source LLC
Chambersburg PA
CBHW070754300426
44111CB00014B/2405